Legal Research and Writing for Paralegals

Editorial Advisory Board for Paralegal Education

Legal Research and Writing for Paralegals

Third Edition

Deborah E. Bouchoux
Georgetown University
Washington, D.C.

1185 Avenue of the Americas, New York, NY 10036
www.aspenpublishers.com

Permissions
Aspen Publishers
1185 Avenue of the Americas
New York, NY 10036

Printed in the United States of America

ISBN 0-7355-2412-2

2 3 4 5 6 7 8 9 0

Library of Congress Cataloging-in-Publication Data

Bouchoux, Deborah E., 1950–
Legal research and writing for paralegals / Deborah E. Bouchoux.—3rd ed.
p. cm.
Includes index.
ISBN 0-7355-2412-2
1. Legal research—United States. 2. Legal composition. 3. Legal assistants—United States—Handbooks, manuals, etc. I. Title.
KF240.B68 2002
340'.07'2073–dc21 2001046084

About Aspen Publishers

Aspen Publishers, headquartered in New York City, is a leading information provider for attorneys, business professionals, and law students. Written by preeminent authorities, our products consist of analytical and practical information covering both U.S. and international topics. We publish in the full range of formats, including updated manuals, books, periodicals, CDs, and online products.

Our proprietary content is complemented by 2,500 legal databases, containing over 11 million documents, available through our Loislaw division. Aspen Publishers also offers a wide range of topical legal and business databases linked to Loislaw's primary material. Our mission is to provide accurate, timely, and authoritative content in easily accessible formats, supported by unmatched customer care.

To order any Aspen Publishers title, go to *www.aspenpublishers.com* or call 1-800-638-8437.

To reinstate your manual update service, call 1-800-638-8437.

For more information on Loislaw products, go to *www.loislaw.com* or call 1-800-364-2512.

For Customer Care issues, e-mail CustomerCare@aspenpublishers.com; call 1-800-234-1660; or fax 1-800-901-9075.

Aspen Publishers
A Wolters Kluwer Company

For my husband, Don, and my children Meaghan, Elizabeth, Patrick, and Robert, who have provided immeasurable support and inspiration in helping me achieve my goal of writing a legal research and writing textbook for paralegal students

Summary of Contents

Section I Legal Research: Primary Authorities 1

Section II Legal Research: Secondary Authorities and Other Research Aids 175

Section III Legal Writing 539

Appendices

Contents

Chapter 7 Miscellaneous Secondary Authorities 223

Chapter 8 Legal Citation Form 261

Chapter 9 Updating and Validating Your Research 329

Chapter 10 Special Research Issues 385

Section III Legal Writing 539

Chapter 14 Back to Basics 541

Chapter 15 Strategies for Effective Writing 567

Chapter 17 Legal Memoranda 623

Chapter 18 Legal Briefs 639

Chapter 19 Postwriting Steps 661

Appendices

Preface

You will soon discover that legal research is truly a "hands-on" subject While there are numerous books to be found that discuss methods and techniques, there is no substitute for actually performing the task of legal research. A simply analogy can be drawn to driving a car: You may find several manuals that discuss driving and provide tips on better driving, but simply reading about operating a car is not a substitute for actually driving a car yourself. Similarly, you will learn the most about legal research, about which shortcuts are invaluable, and which techniques are non-productive, only by doing legal research. To that end, library assignments are placed at the conclusion of each chapter so you can see and use the books discussed in each chapter. You should never have to use a book or set of books that have not been discussed in the chapter you have finished reading or any preceding chapter. Take the time to explore the books by reviewing the foreword, table of contents, and index found in each volume. Familiarize yourself with all of the features of the books and you will simplify your legal research.

Performing legal research can be both frustrating and gratifying. It can be frustrating because there is often no one perfect answer and because there are no established guidelines on how much research to do and when to stop. On the other hand, legal research is gratifying because you will be engaged in a task that requires you to *do* something and one in which you will be rewarded by finding the right case, statute, or other authority.

You should view legal research as an exciting treasure hunt—a search for the best authorities to answer a question or legal issue. In this sense, the task of using and exploring the law library for answers to legal issues or questions should be a welcome relief from the assignments of other classes, which may be passive in nature and involve copious amounts of reading.

I would encourage you to research with other students if you are comfortable doing so. Often you will learn a great deal by comparing notes with others who may be able to share successful strategies for effectively using various books or finding the answers to research problems. Naturally, sharing ideas and tips for research techniques should not be viewed as an excuse not to do the work yourself or a license to use answers discussed by others. In other words, you should research with other students (if you find it useful to do so) but you should never write together. Not only is this practice dishonest, but it will prevent you from effectively learning the skill of legal research. Ultimately, an employer is not interested in how many "points" you obtained on a class exercise or what grade you obtained, but in whether you can be depended upon to research an issue competently. As adult learners and professionals, you should concentrate on learning the skill of legal research rather than focusing on the number of right answers you can obtain.

While this text shows case names and book titles in italics, underlining or underscoring is also acceptable according to the *Bluebook: A Uniform System of Citation* (Columbia Law Review Ass'n et al. eds., 17th ed. 2000), which is the standard reference tool for citation form. There is variation among practitioners, so check with your firm or office to determine if there is a preference.

When you begin reading this book, most of you will be unfamiliar with cases, statutes, constitutions, or the numerous other legal authorities. As you progress in class and through the chapters and assignments in this text, you will readily be able to measure your progress. When you complete this text and your legal research class, you will have gained thorough mastery of legal research and writing techniques as well as familiarity with the numerous sets of law books that you will be required to use in your profession.

This third edition addresses some changes in legal research and developments in the publishing industry that affect research. Perhaps the biggest news relating to research itself is the increasing accessibility of legal sources on the Internet. Cases, statutes, regulations, and legislative history are available on the Internet 24 hours a day, seven days a week, at no cost. Thus, some legal research can be now done from home. Each research chapter in this third edition provides addresses for relevant sites to allow you to retrieve information from the Internet and a new chapter, Chapter 12, is devoted solely to conducting research using the Internet. Bear in mind, however, that many Internet sites are transient and often, without warning, a well-known and often used site will disappear.

The increasing availability of legal authorities on the Internet has also resulted in some changes in citation form. The *Bluebook* now permits citation to the Internet. These and many other changes in citation form addressed in the seventeenth edition of the *Bluebook,* released in late 2000, are discussed in Chapter 8.

Finally, the legal publishing world itself is changing. In the mid-1990s, West Publishing was purchased by Thomson Corp. West then acquired many of its competitors, forming a conglomerate known as West Group. Mead Data Central, the owner of LEXIS, the first computerized legal research system, sold LEXIS to Reed Elsevier, PLC, and it is now known as LEXIS-NEXIS. Additional upheavals in the publishing field are expected to occur due to the public's increasing reliance on the free materials available on the Internet.

In brief, learn to be flexible in doing research. Sometimes the materials you need are not on the shelves and you will need to switch directions. Sometimes new methods of locating materials emerge. In any event, you will find legal research an interesting hunt for the authorities you need, whether in conventional print sources, on LEXIS-NEXIS or Westlaw (the computer-assisted legal research systems), or on the Internet.

Deborah E. Bouchoux

September 2001

Acknowledgments

I would like to express my deep appreciation to the many individuals who contributed greatly to the development of this text and its third edition. First, I would like to express my gratitude to Susan M. Sullivan, the Program Director of the Lawyer's Assistant Program at the University of San Diego, who provided me with my first opportunity to teach and who suggested I write a legal research and writing text. She has been a good friend and colleague.

My current Program Director, Gloria Silvers, of the Legal Assistant Program at Georgetown University in Washington, D.C., has also been a tremendous influence and help to me, and I thank her for her continuing encouragement.

A special thank you should be extended to the following individuals who so graciously provided me with sample briefs and writing projects: David Gryce, Peter Riebing, and Scott Schwartz. Thank you to Alex Butler for his assistance in obtaining photostats for the text.

Many thanks also to the various reviewers who evaluated the manuscript on behalf of the publisher. Throughout the more than 20 years I have taught I have also received continuing evaluation from my students, who have offered their comments and insight regarding methods of teaching, productive assignments, and effective writing strategies.

Finally, my deepest appreciation to my copyeditor, Barbara Rappaport, and to the following individuals at Aspen Publishing: Curt Berkowitz, Betsy Kenny, Melody Davies, and Kathryn Porzio, all of whom offered encouragement and support throughout the development of this text. Their thoughtful comments and suggestions were welcomed and greatly contributed to this third edition.

I would like to acknowledge the following publishers who permitted me to reproduce copyrighted material for this text.

Chapter 2: The Federal and State Court Systems

Figure 2-1: Reprinted with permission from *Federal Reporter, Second Series*, copyright © 1988 by West Group.

Most of the statistical information in this chapter was obtained from http://www.uscourts.gov. and reflects 1998 data.

Chapter 3: Statutory Law

Figures 3-3, 3-4, and 3-5: Reprinted with permission from 11 U.S.C.A., copyright © 1979 by West Group.

Figure 3-6: Reprinted with the permission of LexisNexis, a division of Reed Elsevier Inc. LEXIS and Shepard's are registered trademarks of Reed Elsevier Properties Inc.

Figure 3-7: Reprinted with the permission of LexisNexis, a division of Reed Elsevier Inc. LEXIS and Shepard's are registered trademarks of Reed Elsevier Properties Inc.

Figure 3-8: Reprinted with permission of West Group.

Figure 3-10(A): Reprinted with permission from General Index to U.S.C.A., copyright © 1993 by West Group.

Figure 3-10(B): Reprinted with the permission of LexisNexis, a division of Reed Elsevier Inc. LEXIS and Shepard's are registered trademarks of Reed Elsevier Properties Inc.

Figure 3-11: Reprinted with permission from U.S.C.A. Popular Name Table, copyright © 1993 by West Group.

Figure 3-12: Reprinted with permission of West Group.

Chapter 4: Case Law and Judicial Opinion

Figure 4-1: Reprinted with permission from 565 A.2d 67, copyright © 1990 by West Group.

Figure 4-2: Reprinted with permission from 108 S. Ct. 2830, copyright © 1992 by West Group.

Figure 4-3: Reprinted with permission from *West's Law Finder*, copyright © 1988 by West Group.

Figure 4-6: Reprinted with permission from 108 S. Ct. 2611, copyright © 1992 by West Group.

Chapter 5: The Use of Digests, Annotated Law Reports, and *Words and Phrases*

Headnote [7], Gifts, Key Number 22, reprinted from 775 F. Supp. 229, 230, copyright © 1992 by West Group.

Figure 5-2: Reprinted with permission from *West's Law Finder*, copyright © 1988 by West Group.

Figure 5-3: Reprinted with permission from *Descriptive Word Index to Ninth Decennial Digest*, Part 2, copyright © 1988 by West Group.

Figure 5-4: Reprinted with permission from 29 *Ninth Decennial Digest*, Part 2, copyright © 1988 by West Group.

Figure 5-5: Reprinted with permission from 44 *Ninth Decennial Digest*, Part 2, copyright © 1988 by West Group.

Figure 5-6: Reprinted with permission from 29 *Ninth Decennial Digest*, Part 2, copyright © 1988 by West Group.

Figures 5-7, 5-8, and 5-10: Reprinted with permission of West Group.

Figure 5-11: Reprinted with permission from *Words and Phrases*, copyright © 1956 by West Group.

Chapter 6: Encyclopedias, Periodicals, Treatises, and Restatements

Figure 6-1: Reprinted with permission from *Corpus Juris Secundum*, copyright © 1954 by West Group.

Figure 6-2: Reprinted with permission of West Group.

Figure 6-3: Reprinted with permission of West Group.

Figure 6-4: Reprinted with permission of West Group.

Figure 6-5: Reprinted with permission of the publisher, Georgetown University and the *Georgetown Law Journal,* copyright © 1997.

Figure 6-6: Reprinted with permission of *California Lawyer*.

Figure 6-7: Reprinted from "Subject and Author Index" and "Table of Cases" from *Index to Legal Periodicals* with permission of H.W. Wilson Co., copyright © 1985, 1986 by H.W. Wilson Co.

Figure 6-8: Reprinted with permission of West Group, copyright © 1972 by West Group.

Figure 6-10: Copyright © 1965 by The American Law Institute. Reprinted with permission of The American Law Institute.

Chapter 7: Miscellaneous Secondary Authorities

Figure 7-1: Reprinted with permission from *Black's Law Dictionary*, Sixth Edition, copyright © 1990 by West Group.

Figure 7-2: Reprinted with permission of Martindale-Hubbell, copyright © 1992, 1993 by Martindale-Hubbell.

Figure 7-3: Reprinted with permission of Martindale-Hubbell, copyright © 1990, 1991 by Martindale-Hubbell.

Figure 7-4: Reprinted with permission of Martindale-Hubbell, copyright © 1992, 1993 by Martindale-Hubbell.

Figure 7-5(A): Reprinted with permission from volume 3 *Federal Forms*, copyright © 1989 by West Group.

Figure 7-5(B): Reprinted with permission of West Group.

Figure 7-6: Reprinted with permission from *Uniform Laws Annotated, Master Edition*, copyright © 1983 by West Group.

Figure 7-7: Reprinted with permission from *Directory of Uniform Acts and Codes*, copyright © 1993 by West Group.

Figure 7-8: Reprinted with permission of Duane Burton, copyright © 1990.

Chapter 9: Updating and Validating Your Research

Figure 9-1: Reprinted with permission from *Shepard's Michigan Citations*, copyright © 1992 by Shepard's. Reproduced by permission of Shepard's. Further reproduction of any kind is strictly prohibited.

Figure 9-4: Reprinted with permission from *Shepard's Michigan Citations*, copyright © 1990 by Shepard's. Reproduced by permission of Shepard's. Further reproduction of any kind is strictly prohibited.

Figure 9-5: Reprinted with permission from *Shepard's Northwestern Citations*, copyright © 1993 by Shepard's. Reproduced by permission of Shepard's. Further reproduction of any kind is strictly prohibited.

Figure 9-6: Reprinted with permission from *Shepard's United States Citations*, copyright © 1993 by Shepard's. Reproduced by permission of Shepard's. Further reproduction of any kind is strictly prohibited.

Figure 9-7: Reprinted with permission from *Shepard's Federal Citations*, copyright © 1990 by Shepard's. Reproduced by permission of Shepard's. Further reproduction of any kind is strictly prohibited.

Figure 9-10: Reprinted with permission from *Shepard's Alaska Citations*, copyright © 1993 by Shepard's. Reproduced by permission of Shepard's. Further reproduction of any kind is strictly prohibited.

Figures 9-11 and 9-13: Reprinted with permission from *Shepard's Federal Statute Citations,* copyright © 1992 by Shepard's. Reproduced by permission of Shepard's. Further reproduction of any kind is strictly prohibited.

Figure 9-14: Reprinted with permission from *Shepard's Alaska Citations*, copyright © 1993 by Shepard's. Reproduced by permission of Shepard's. Further reproduction of any kind is strictly prohibited.

Figure 9-15: Reprinted with permission from *Shepard's Federal Circuit Case Names Citator*, copyright © 1992 by Shepard's. Reproduced by permission of Shepard's. Further reproduction of any kind is strictly prohibited.

All Shepard's materials and Figures 9-16 and 9-17 from LEXIS reprinted with the permission of LexisNexis, a division of Reed Elsevier Inc. LEXIS and Shepard's are registered trademarks of Reed Elsevier Properties Inc.

Figure 9-18 reprinted with permission from Westlaw, copyright by West Group.

Chapter 10: Special Research Issues

Figure 10-9: Reprinted with permission from *Shepard's Federal Statute Citations*, copyright © 1992 by Shepard's. Reproduced by permission of Shepard's. Further reproduction of any kind is strictly prohibited. Reprinted with the permission of LexisNexis, a division of Reed Elsevier Inc. LEXIS and Shepard's are registered trademarks of Reed Elsevier Properties Inc.

Chapter 11: New Technology in Legal Research

All sample screens from LEXIS (Figures 11-1, 11-2, 11-3, and 11-4) reprinted with the permission of LexisNexis, a division of Reed Elsevier Inc. LEXIS and Shepard's are registered trademarks of Reed Elsevier Properties Inc.

All sample screens from Westlaw (Figures 11-6, 11-7, and 11-8) reprinted with permission from Westlaw, copyright by West Group.

Chapter 12: Legal Research Using the Internet

Figure 12-1: Reprinted with permission from FindLaw Inc.

Figure 12-2: Reprinted with permission from Georgetown University.

Figure 12-3: Reprinted with permission from Washburn University School of Law.

Legal Research and Writing for Paralegals

Legal Research: Primary Authorities

Chapter 1

Finding the Law

Chapter Overview

In this chapter we will discuss types of law libraries and their uses and introduce the sources of law in the United States. We will also examine the classification of law books as either primary or secondary sources. Finally, there is a brief introduction to the major law book publishers, who will be compared in greater detail in later chapters.

A. Law Libraries

1. Types of Law Libraries

As noted in the introduction to this text, legal research is a "hands-on" skill, requiring you to know how to use a law library. Your first task, therefore, is to locate a law library that you may use. There are approximately 3,600 law libraries in the United States. Following is a list of the most common types of law libraries with a brief description of each:

Law School Libraries All accredited law schools have their own law libraries, most of which will have tens of thousands of volumes in print and nonprint forms such as CD-ROM, microforms, electronic bulletin boards, and the World Wide Web. If you are attending a paralegal program at a four-year university that is affiliated with a law school, you will undoubtedly have access to the law library at the law school. Even if you do not attend a paralegal program affiliated with a law school, you may have access to a law school library if it has been designated as a United States Government Depository, or a partial or selective depository, meaning that certain publications of the United States government, generally statutes, and court decisions, will be sent to the law library for review and access by the general public. You can easily determine whether a law school library is a United States Government Depository by calling the reference librarian at the law library and inquiring. Some law libraries, however, while providing access to the general public to review the depository collection, will prohibit access to any other portion of the law library. The location of the approximately 1,350 depository libraries can be retrieved at the following Web site: http://www.access.gpo.gov/su_docs/locators/findlibs/index.html.

Paralegal School Libraries Some paralegal programs maintain their own law libraries, although these are typically much smaller and contain far fewer volumes than law school libraries. Generally, only students who attend these programs have access to these law libraries.

Local Law Libraries Often a county or city will maintain a law library, and these are usually open to members of the general public. These law libraries vary in size, with the largest law libraries being found in the largest counties. Often they are located near a courthouse.

Government or Agency Law Libraries Various governmental agencies, such as the Department of Justice, maintain their own law libraries. These law libraries typically serve only agency employees, and members of the general public will have no access. The Library of Congress, located in Washington, D.C., was established by the United States Congress in 1800 primarily to provide reference and research assistance to members of Congress. It has an excellent law library, which is open to any member of the general public.

Courthouse Law Libraries Many courts, both federal and state, maintain their own law libraries. State law libraries are often found in the courthouse for the county seat. Some law libraries are open to the public while others restrict access to courthouse personnel, attorneys, and their paralegals.

Bar Association and Private Group Law Libraries Often bar associations or private groups, such as insurance companies or real estate boards, will maintain law libraries. These are usually open only to members of the association or group.

Law Firm Libraries Almost every law firm will maintain a law library, some of which are nearly as extensive as a law school or courthouse law library. These law libraries are available for use only by members or employees of the firm.

You should consult a telephone book and call law schools, courthouses, and county offices in your area to determine whether members of the general public have access to those law libraries and to obtain the hours for each. Be particularly careful of law school libraries that tend to schedule their hours of operation around the law school calendar and will often close unannounced after final exams or during semester breaks.

Additionally, many public and college or university libraries are increasing their collections of law books. While these libraries typically offer only the major sets of books, such as the cases of the United States Supreme Court, federal statutes, and statutes from the state in which they are located, these public or college libraries may afford a quick answer to some legal research questions.

Finally, law libraries now exist in cyberspace with vast collections of legal materials available for free "24/7." Conducting legal research in cyberspace through the Internet is discussed in Chapter 12.

2. *Arrangement of Law Libraries*

There is no one standard arrangement for law libraries. Each law library is arranged according to the needs of its patrons or by decision of the law librarian. The best introduction to a law library is a tour given by a staff member and you should inquire whether orientation tours of the law library are given. If you cannot arrange for a tour, obtain a copy of the library handbook or guide that will describe the services offered, set forth the library's rules and regulations, and provide a floorplan of the law library. Spend an hour wandering around the law library and familiarizing yourself with its arrangement, organization, and collections. You will notice that there may be duplicate volumes of some books or even duplicate sets of books. In general, books that are widely used will have duplicates to ensure ease of use and accessibility. In many cases you can judge legal books by their titles, which usually describe their contents.

While some law libraries still use a card catalog (identical in its alphabetical organization and arrangement to the card catalogs you have used all through your schooling) to help you locate the books, treatises, and periodicals in the library, the more modern approach is the online catalog or OPAC (online public access catalog).

Most of the online catalogs are very easy to use, and you should not be intimidated. The law library staff is usually quite willing to provide instruction, and training sessions can be completed in only a few minutes. Typically, you will type in or "enter" the title, author, or subject matter you are interested in and you will then be provided with the "call number." The shelves or "stacks" in the law library are clearly marked, and locating a book is merely a matter of matching up the call number provided by the card catalog or online catalog with the appropriate stack label.

Most law school and large law firm law libraries use the Library of Congress classification system to arrange their books. The Library of Congress classification system is an alphanumeric system that arranges books on the shelves in subject order. Each book is marked with a three-line classification number, consisting of an alphanumeric combination, meaning a combination of letters, a whole number, and a decimal. For example, a book may be classified as "KF503.181." The designation "KF" is the Library of Congress identifier for American legal publications.

An unusual feature of law libraries is that, in general, they are not circulating libraries. That is, unlike other libraries that circulate their volumes by allowing one to check out books, law libraries seldom allow patrons to check out books. You can imagine your frustration if you were unable to read a case because someone had already checked out the volume containing the case. Books that are not widely used, however, may often be checked out by individuals who possess library identification cards.

3. *Law Library Staff*

Most of the larger law libraries are serviced by full-time law librarians who are not only lawyers who have been awarded a Juris Doctor degree but who also possess a Masters Degree in Library Science. Most library staff are extremely helpful and responsive to questions; however, you should diligently try to locate a book or answer before you approach library staff for help. In law school libraries, the individuals who sit at the front desk are often law students who may not be thoroughly knowledgeable about the arrangement of the library or its collections. Therefore, if you have a question, be sure to address it to one of the professional law librarians (in this regard, the reference librarians are particularly helpful) rather than a student who may be more interested in studying at the front desk than helping you locate a book. Many reference librarians are available for research consultations by appointment. While law librarians will provide useful research tips and suggestions, they will not provide legal advice.

4. *Law Library Courtesy*

You should assume that everyone who uses the law library is as busy as you and therefore you should observe standard library etiquette by reshelving properly every book you use (unless the law library you use prohibits reshelving or has a separate preshelving stack for books that are to be reshelved). Nothing is more frustrating than taking time out of a busy schedule to drive to a law library and search for the appropriate sources only to realize that a needed volume is missing. If you take books to a study carrel to read or to the photocopier to reproduce a page, you must reshelve them when you are finished. This is particularly true in school situations in which your fellow classmates will in all likelihood have the same assignments as you and will thus need to use the same books.

Do not deface the books by turning pages down or marking an answer. Finally, do not resort to unfair conduct by hiding or intentionally misplacing books. There is no excuse for such overzealous tactics that not only impede learning but reflect poorly on one who is purporting to be a member of a profession devoted to the law.

5. *Other Library Services*

Most law libraries offer a variety of other services to ensure students can conduct productive research. For example, if you are working on an extensive project, your law library may reserve a carrel for you and allow you to store books and materials there. Similarly, you may be able to reserve a group study room so you can meet with other students to brainstorm a research project. Law librarians can provide you with permits and letters of introduction to other law libraries in the area so you can retrieve materials not available at your law library. If certain materials are not maintained at your law library, the reference librarian may assist you in borrowing materials from other institutions through interlibrary loans. The ease of facsimile and online transmission results in ready access to a wealth of materials from all over the nation and the world.

B. Sources of Law in the United States

1. *Cases and Our Common Law Tradition*

While it is important to "know" the law, particularly in a field in which you may intend to specialize, it is even more important to be able to "find" the law. In this sense, proficiency in legal research is the foundation for a successful career as a paralegal. Your employer will not be interested in your final grade in any specific class as much as your ability to find accurate answers to questions relating to topics even though you may not have been exposed in school to those topics. If you cannot perform legal research tasks accurately and efficiently, you will not be a successful paralegal despite excellent grades in your coursework.

Moreover, the failure to research adequately may lead to liability for legal malpractice. In one of the earliest cases on this subject matter, *Smith v. Lewis*, 530 P.2d 589 (Cal. 1975), the California Supreme Court affirmed a lower court decision awarding $100,000 to be paid to a former client by an attorney who had failed to conduct adequate legal research. The court held that the attorney was obligated to undertake reasonable research, and stated, "[e]ven as to doubtful matters, an attorney is expected to perform sufficient research to enable him to make an informed and intelligent judgment on behalf of his client." *Id.* at 596. The ethical duty imposed on attorneys to provide competent representation to a client devolves upon those employed by attorneys as well. Thus, you will be expected to perform competent legal research not only because your employer will insist on it but because ethical standards demand it as well.

If your task is to be able to find the law, one may well ask, "What is the 'law' we are talking about?" There are numerous definitions of the word "law." On an academic or philosophical level, law is a system of rules that governs society so as to prevent chaos. On a practical level, on the other hand, United States Supreme Court Chief Justice Charles Evans Hughes suggested that the law "is what the judges say it is." This second view may give you cause for concern. If the law is what a judge says, what if the judge rules against you because of your race, or sex, or religion? What if the judge is not familiar with an area of the law? The American legal system has certain safeguards built into it to protect litigants from such scenarios.

The American legal system is part of what is referred to as the "common law" tradition. "Common law" is defined in part by *Black's Law Dictionary* 270 (7th ed. 1999) as that body of law that develops and derives through judicial decisions as distinguished from statutes or constitutions.

This common law system began in England several hundred years ago. Since at least 1300 A.D., people who may have been training to be lawyers began "taking notes" on what occurred during trials. When judges were called upon to decide cases, they then began referring to these written reports of earlier cases and following the prior cases in similar situations. The English referred to this system as the "common law" because it was applied equally all throughout England and replaced a less uniform system of law. This system of following similar previous cases was considered the most equitable way of resolving disputes: People who are involved in like situations should be treated in the same manner.

This concept of following previous cases, or precedents, is called *stare decisis*, which is a Latin phrase meaning "to stand by things decided." In its broadest sense, the doctrine of stare decisis means that once courts have announced a principle of law, they will follow it in the future in cases that are substantially similar. It is this doctrine of stare decisis that serves to protect litigants from judges who may not be familiar with an area of the law. If the judge is required to follow precedent, he or she cannot rule against you based on your race, sex, or religion. Similarly, these precedents will guide a judge who is unacquainted with a certain area of the law. In this way, stare decisis advances fairness and consistency in our legal system.

Moreover, stare decisis promotes stability in our judicial system. It would not only be chaotic but manifestly unfair if judges treated each case that came before them as being severed from our great body of legal tradition and then rendered different and inconsistent rulings on a daily basis. You can imagine the frustration of a client who seeks advice of counsel on the division of property in a dissolution of a marriage only to be informed that the division depends on which judge hears the case: that Judge Jones divides property in a marital dissolution on a 50/50 basis; Judge Smith divides the property on a 40/60 basis; and Judge Anderson divides the property differently each day depending upon his mood. The client's rights would be totally dependent upon an arbitrary assignment to a judge. Such a result is not only unjust but unpredictable. Thus, stare decisis not only encourages stability in our legal system but also aids those in the legal profession in advising clients as to the likely disposition of their cases.

Under this system or doctrine of precedent following, "the law" was thus found in the written decisions of the judges, and these decisions served as precedents that were followed in later cases involving substantially similar issues. Thus, the first source of law in the United States is judge-made case law.

2. *Constitutions and Statutes*

A second source of law in the United States is constitutions and statutes. A constitution sets forth the fundamental law for a nation or a state. It is the document that sets forth the principles relating to organization and regulation of a federal or state government. We have a United States Constitution, our supreme law of the land, and each state has its own constitution. A statute, or law, is defined by *Black's Law Dictionary* 1420 (7th ed. 1999) as "a law passed by a legislative body."

In the United States, legislatures did not become particularly active in enacting statutes until the early to mid-1800s when the United States economy began changing from a very rural base to a more urban base. This major change in American society was coupled with a tremendous population growth, due largely to immigration, and it became clear that rather than deciding disputes on a case-by-case basis, which was slow and cumbersome at best, broader laws needed to be enacted that would set forth rules to govern behavior of the public at large. For example, when people live miles apart from one another and interact on a sporadic basis, few disputes will arise. On the other hand, when people are crowded into apartment buildings and work in densely populated urban areas, the number of problems greatly increases, and there is a concomitant need for general regulation by law or statute.

3. *Administrative Regulations*

A third source of law in the United States is the vast number of administrative rules and regulations promulgated by federal agencies such as the Federal Communications Commission ("FCC"), the Food and Drug Administration ("FDA"), the Occupational Safety and Health Administration ("OSHA"), and numerous other agencies. Agencies exist in the individual states as well, and these also enact rules and regulations.

The agencies play a unique role in our legal system as they function quasi-legislatively and quasi-judicially. You may recall from basic history and civics classes that our government is divided into three branches: the legislative branch, which makes laws; the judicial branch, which interprets laws; and the executive branch, which enforces laws. Each division is to exercise its own powers, and, by a system known as "checks and balances," each functions separately from the others.

The agencies, on the other hand, perform two functions: They act as a legislature by promulgating rules and regulations that bind us; and they act as a judiciary by hearing disputes and rendering decisions.

While you may not have given a great deal of thought to the impact of the agencies in your daily life, their influence is significant and far-reaching. For example, the radio you listen to and the television you watch are regulated by the FCC; the cosmetics you use and the food or aspirin you ingest are regulated by the FDA; and the safety of your workplace is regulated by OSHA.

4. *The Executive Branch*

While the primary function of the federal executive branch is to enforce the law, it does serve as a source of law in three ways. First, treaties are entered into by the executive branch with the advice and consent of the United States Senate. These agreements between two or more nations do affect your daily life and serve as a source of law as they may relate to trade and import matters, economic cooperation, or even international boundaries and fishing rights. Second, the president, our chief executive, can issue executive orders to regulate and direct federal agencies and officials. Third, the executive branch exerts influence on the law through policies on enforcing laws.

For example, if various federal laws relating to possession of small amounts of drugs are rarely enforced, the *effect* is as if the law does not exist despite the fact that a statute clearly prohibits such acts. Nevertheless, while such an approach by the executive branch influences the law as well as societal behavior, such influence on the law is indirect and remote. In the event the government then prosecutes an individual for violation of such a previously unenforced law, the individual usually cannot raise the previous laxity as a defense. In a related example, in 1980, when the Selective Service System was reinstated to require United States males born in 1960 or later to register with the Service, several conscientious objectors refused to register. The federal government immediately prosecuted some of these individuals, who then asserted as a defense that they had been singled out for prosecution because they had been vigorous opponents of this draft registration. This defense, commonly known as "selective enforcement," is rarely successful and was not successful in the draft registration cases. To use a simple analogy, if you are cited for speeding, you cannot successfully assert that either all people who speed should be likewise cited or that none should. You would accept that you had simply been unluckier than other speeders. On the other hand, if only women are cited or only Hispanics are cited, such would appear to be the result of discrimination based on sex or ethnic origin, and a defense of selective enforcement alleging such invidious discrimination might well be successful.

C. Legal Systems of Other Countries

While every country has its own system of law, most systems are classified as either being part of the common law tradition, described above, or part of the civil law tradition. Civil law systems developed from Roman law. The Roman emperor Justinian I commissioned a comprehensive code of laws known as *Corpus Juris Civilis*, meaning "Body of Civil Law," to set forth all of the law of the Roman Empire. As a result, countries whose systems of law follow the Roman scheme of law with thoroughly comprehensive codes are said to be part of the civil law tradition. Even today many countries' codes of civil law are derived from the original Roman codes.

In general, civil law countries place much heavier reliance on their collections of statutes than on their much smaller collections of cases. These statutes are designed to address every conceivable legal issue that might arise, and it is these statutes that provide the ultimate answers to legal questions. Cases considered by judges rarely form the sole basis for any decision in civil law countries. Germany, France, Japan, Mexico, Korea, Spain, Italy, China, Austria, and the countries of Latin America are considered civil law countries.

In general, English-speaking countries or those that are prior British Commonwealth colonies are part of the common law system, which is greatly dependent on cases used as precedents, which in turn are followed in future cases that are substantially similar. Non-English-speaking countries are usually part of the civil law system, which is greatly dependent on codes or statutes intended to apply to every legal question or dispute. Because of the thoroughness of the Roman codes, statutes came to be known as the "written" law while the common law, relying as it does on judge-made case law, is often referred to as the "unwritten" law.

It is interesting to note that every state in the United States, except Louisiana, and every Canadian province, except Quebec, is part of the common law tradition. Because Quebec and Louisiana were settled by the French, their legal systems are largely patterned after the law of France, a civil law country. In fact, the Civil Code of Louisiana is closely based on the Code Napoleon, the French legal code enacted in 1804.

D. Legal System of the United States

The nature of our federalist system of government seeks to apportion power between our central or federal government and the 50 separate states and the District of Columbia. The founders of the Constitution feared that an overly strong federal government with concentrated power would ultimately engulf the separate states. Therefore, the Tenth Amendment to the Constitution was adopted. This amendment reserves to the individual states any powers not expressly granted or delegated to the federal government.

As a result, while the United States adheres to a uniform common law tradition, there is no one single legal system in this country. We have federal laws enacted by the United States Congress and federal cases decided by our federal courts, including the United States Supreme Court. Moreover, unless an area of the law has been preempted by the United States Constitution or the federal government, each state and the District of Columbia is free to enact laws as well as decide cases dealing with state or local concerns. Even within each state are smaller political subdivisions such as cities and counties, which enact local ordinances and regulations.

Thus, there is a tremendous body of legal literature on the shelves of law libraries: federal cases and federal statutes; Connecticut cases and Connecticut statutes; Florida cases and Florida statutes; Utah cases and Utah statutes, and so forth. Additionally, both the federal government and state governments promulgate administrative regulations, attorneys general issue opinions regarding legal problems, and experts publish commentary regarding the law. As early as 1821, Justice Joseph Story complained, "The mass of law is . . . accumulating with an almost incredible rapidity. . . . It is impossible not to look without some discouragement upon the ponderous volumes, which the next half century will add to the groaning shelves of our jurists." This statement was made about the time volume 19 of the *United States Reports* was published. As of 1996, the *United States Reports* covered more than 500 volumes.

All of the great mass of legal authorities can be classified as either primary authority or secondary authority. That is, every book in any law library is a primary authority or a secondary authority. See Figure 1-1.

Primary authorities are official pronouncements of the law by the executive branch (treaties and executive orders), legislative branch (constitutions, statutes, and administrative regulations and decisions), and judicial branch (cases). The key primary authorities are cases, constitutions, statutes, and administrative regulations. Thus, primary sources are those created by a governmental entity.

If a legal authority does not fall within one of the previously mentioned categories, it is a *secondary* authority. Secondary authorities may consist of legal encyclopedias, which provide summaries of many areas of the law; law review articles written about various legal topics; books or other treatises dealing with legal issues; law dictionaries; annotations, or essays about the law; and expert opinions on legal issues. In general, the secondary authorities are not the law but rather provide comment, discussion, and explanation of the primary authorities and, more important, help you locate the primary authorities.

It is critical to understand thoroughly the differences between primary and secondary authorities because only the primary authorities are *binding* upon the court, agency, or tribunal that may be deciding the legal issue you are researching. That is, if your argument relies upon or cites a case, constitution, statute, or administrative regulation that is relevant to a legal issue, it *must* be followed. All other authorities, for example, the secondary authorities, are *persuasive* only. If your argument cites *Black's Law Dictionary* for the definition of *negligence*, a court might be *persuaded* to adopt such a definition, but it is not *bound* to do so. On the other hand, if you cite a relevant case that defines *negligence*, a court must follow that definition.

Even though the secondary authorities are not binding on a court, they are often extremely effective research tools and provide excellent introductions to various legal topics. Nevertheless, you should keep in mind the purpose of the secondary authorities — to explain the primary authorities and locate the primary authorities that, if relevant, must be followed by a court.

In addition to the various authorities previously discussed, there are other books in the law library that are in the nature of practical guides or tools. These include books such as digests, which help you locate cases (see Chapter 5), form books, which provide forms for various legal documents such as wills, deeds, and contracts (see Chapter 7), and sets of books called *Shepard's Citations*, which help you update the authorities you rely upon in any legal writing (see Chapter 9). While these books are not true secondary authorities, their principal function is either to assist in locating primary sources or to serve as practical or finding guides for those in the legal profession.

Figure 1-1
Primary Authorities (binding)

Authorities	*Source*
Cases	Judiciary
Constitutions	Legislature
Statutes	Legislature
Administrative regulations	Administrative agencies
Executive orders	Executive branch
Treaties	Executive branch (federal only)

Secondary Authorities (persuasive)

Authorities
Encyclopedias
Law review articles
Periodical publications
Treatises and texts
Dictionaries
Attorneys general opinions
Restatements
Annotations
Foreign sources
Form books
Practice guides (such as jury instructions or opinions on ethics)

E. Law Book Publishing

As shown in Figure 1-1, the collection and variety of books in a law library are incredibly extensive.

Compared to the litigation explosion of the last 30 years, the early period of American history produced a fairly small number of cases. But just as the change in American society from agrarian and rural to an industrial and urban population resulted in a need for statutes to establish standards for behavior, this change also resulted in increased litigation and attendant case decisions.

For example, in the United States Courts of Appeal alone, the number of cases appealed between 1994 and 1998 increased by 5,483. In the early nineties, the total number of new cases filed in the various state courts exceeded one million — one for every 250 Americans. Add this to cases already pending and there is one court case for one of every two adults in America. The vast majority of these cases, approximately 90 percent, never come to trial. Of those state court cases that go to trial, only slightly more than 10 percent are appealed and result in a published opinion due to the fact that trial court opinions are rarely published. Nevertheless, even that number, added to the cases decided and published by the federal courts, results in approximately 50,000 cases being published each year. Additionally, Congress and the state legislatures publish thousands of pages of statutes, and thousands of pages of administrative rules and regulations are also published annually.

Thus, a tremendous amount of publication of legal authorities, both primary and secondary, occurs each year. You cannot expect to know all of the law contained in these authorities; however, you can be reasonably expected to be able to locate and use these legal authorities. That is the goal of legal research.

The actual publication of these authorities is conducted by only a handful of publishing companies. The giant in the legal publishing industry is West Group, headquartered in Eagan, Minnesota ("West").

In the mid-1990s, West was purchased for $3.4 billion by The Thomson Corporation, a Canadian publishing and information conglomerate. In the United States, the company retained its identification as "West." In 1996, West then merged with a number of other large law book publishers, namely Bancroft-Whitney, Clark Boardman Callaghan, and Lawyers Cooperative Publishing, to form West Group ("West"), which now has more than 8,000 employees, making it the preeminent provider of information to the legal market in the United States.

The merger of Lawyers Cooperative Publishing ("Lawyers Co-op") into West is of particular interest inasmuch as these two companies were for years the major publishers in the law book industry, offering competing products and services. For example, West has published federal statutes in a set known as U.S.C.A. while Lawyers Co-op published the same statutes in its set, U.S.C.S. Similarly, West has published cases from the United States Supreme Court in a set called *Supreme Court Reporter* while Lawyers Co-op published those same cases in a set called *United States Supreme Court Reports, Lawyers' Edition.* Lawyers and other legal professionals would purchase one set rather than the other based on price, convenience, habit, and ease of use, or perceived advantages of one set over the other.

Because the possibility of West acquiring a virtual monopoly on legal publication existed, West was ordered to divest itself of some of the publications it acquired through its merger. Thus, U.S.C.S. is now owned by LEXIS Publishing, a division of Reed Elsevier PLC, and will continue to compete head-on with West for readers of federal statutes.

The numerous combinations and acquisitions of publishing companies has resulted in changes in some features of some law books. For example, for years a set of books called *American Law Reports* was published by Lawyers Co-op. It therefore referred its users to other Lawyers Co-op books. In 1998, the set was acquired by West and thus it now directs readers to West-owned law books. Moreover, some of the features of the set changed slightly after West acquired it. Thus, as books are described in this text, it is possible that some of their features and layout have changed over the years with recent books in a set appearing slightly different from earlier published books in the set.

Law book publishers also face increasing competition from emerging technologies. As discussed in Chapter 11, many cases now appear in CD-ROM format at a price significantly less than print versions, or on the Internet at no cost. These inroads on print publication have caused decreases in circulation of print materials. For example, subscriptions to West's *South Western Reporter*, publishing decisions from Texas, Missouri, Arkansas, Kentucky, and Tennessee have fallen 21 percent since 1993.

Finally, the acquisition of West by Thomson comes amid increasing competition and consolidation in the legal publishing arena. In 1994, Dutch publisher Wolters Kluwer purchased legal and tax publisher Commerce Clearing House Inc. In 1994, Anglo-Dutch publishing powerhouse Reed Elsevier PLC purchased LEXIS-NEXIS, the online legal research system, from Mead Corporation for $1.5 billion. In sum, the world of legal publishing, long dominated by the giants West and Lawyers Co-op, is changing, partly due to increased competition and conglomeration and partly due to pressures brought to bear by the Internet, which allows 24-hours-a-day free access to many legal materials.

West publishes primary and secondary sources, for example, cases, statutes, and constitutions, as well as encyclopedias and other nonbinding authorities. Throughout the chapters ahead, there are frequent discussions and comparisons of West and other publishers, including analyses of similarities and distinctions between methods and organization of their publications.

In general, there are three major "families" of legal publishers, each of which incorporates other law book publishers: The Thomson Corporation (including the former West Publishing (now called West Group), Bancroft Whitney, and Clark Boardman Callaghan); Reed Elsevier PLC (including LEXIS-NEXIS, Matthew Bender, Michie Company, Shepard's, and Martindale-Hubbell); and Wolters Kluwer (including Aspen Law & Business and Commerce Clearing House). More information on legal publishers can be found at the following Internet site: Rob Richards, *A Legal Publisher's List: Corporate Affiliations of Legal Publishers*, University of Colorado Law Library, *at* http://www.colorado.edu/law/lawlib/ts/legpub.htm (last modified Nov. 17, 2000).

Additionally, some companies such as Commerce Clearing House, Clark Boardman Callaghan, and Bureau of National Affairs specialize in the publication of looseleaf services—that is, sets of books dealing with various legal topics and contained in ringed binders. The hallmark of these looseleaf volumes is that they publish information on legal topics that are subject to frequent change and that if placed in hardback volumes would quickly become out-of-date. Publication of materials in looseleaf binders allows frequent updating by replacement of individual outdated pages with current pages. The looseleaf sets are thus "evergreen."

One of the common features shared by the primary sources (cases, constitutions, statutes, and regulations) as they are initially published is that they are arranged in chronological order. That is, cases are published in the order in which the court issued the decisions. A court will not designate a month as landlord-tenant month and only hear cases dealing with landlord-tenant law before moving on to some other topic, but rather may hear a case involving burglary followed by a contract dispute followed by a probate matter. The cases appear in volumes of books, called "court reports," in chronological order.

Similarly, during any given session, a legislature will enact laws relating to motor vehicles, regulation of utilities, and licensing of real estate salespeople. The initial publication of these statutes is in the order in which they were enacted rather than according to subject matter.

This type of organization makes research difficult. If you were asked to locate cases dealing with landlord-tenant law, you would find that they have not been brought together in one specific location but rather may be scattered over several hundred volumes of cases. It is clear then that a method of obtaining access to these primary authorities is needed and, in general, the secondary authorities and digests will assist you in locating the primary authorities. For example, a secondary source such as a legal encyclopedia will describe and explain landlord-tenant law and will then direct you to cases that are primary or binding authorities relating to this area of the law. These cases, when cited in a legal argument, under the doctrine of stare decisis, must be followed by a court, while the encyclopedia discussion is persuasive only and need not be followed by a court.

F. Change in Our Legal System

While stare decisis promotes stability, fairness, and uniformity in our legal system, blind adherence to established precedents in the face of changing societal views and mores may result in injustice. For example, in 1896, the United States Supreme Court held that "separate but equal" public facilities for blacks and whites were lawful. This precedent served to justify segregation for more than 50 years. In 1954, however, in *Brown v. Board of Education*, 347 U.S. 483 (1954), the Supreme Court overruled its earlier decision and held that segregation solely according to race in public schools violated the United States Constitution. A strict adherence to stare decisis would have precluded a second look at this issue and would have resulted in continued racial segregation.

Similarly, the view of women has changed in our case law. In *Bradwell v. State*, 83 U.S. (16 Wall.) 130, 141 (1872), a concurring justice noted: "The paramount destiny and mission of woman are to fulfil the noble and benign offices of wife and mother. This is the law of the Creator." One hundred years later, Justice Brennan acknowledged, "There can be no doubt that our Nation has had a long and unfortunate history of sex discrimination. Traditionally, such discrimination was rationalized by an attitude of 'romantic paternalism' which, in practical effect, put women, not on a pedestal, but in a cage." *Frontiero v. Richardson*, 411 U.S. 677, 684 (1973).

Thus, it is clear that as society changes, the law must also change. A balance must be struck between society's need for stability in its legal system and the need for flexibility, growth, and change when precedents have outlived their usefulness or result in injustice. In discussing the fact that the United States Supreme Court can overrule its precedents to correct an injustice, Woodrow Wilson remarked that the Court sits as "a kind of constitutional convention in continuous session." It is the function of our courts to achieve both of these seemingly contradictory goals: the need for stability and the need for change.

In recent years the United States Supreme Court has shown an increased willingness to depart from its previous rulings. From 1789 to 1954 the United States Supreme Court overruled only 88 of its precedents. From 1954 to 1990, however, the Court overruled 108 of its precedents.

Nevertheless, you should not view these changes as abrupt and unsettling frequent events. Change often occurs slowly and always occurs in an ordered framework. This order is a result of the structure of our court systems into a hierarchy of lower courts, which conduct trials, and higher courts, which review the conduct of those trials by appeal.

Change in established legal precedent comes about by rulings of higher courts, which then bind lower courts in that judicial system or hierarchy. For example, a small claims court in Portland, Oregon, cannot overrule *Brown v. Board of Education*. Because *Brown v. Board of Education* was decided by the United States Supreme Court, it can only be overruled by the United States Supreme Court. Similarly, a decision by the highest court in Minnesota binds all of the lower courts in Minnesota. Nevertheless, lower courts often attempt to evade precedents by striving to show those precedents are inapplicable to the cases then before them. For example, a lower court might hold that a precedent established by a court above it dealing with the interpretation of a written contract is not binding because the lower court is interpreting an oral contract. Lower courts thus often reject precedent or refuse to follow precedent on the basis that those precedents are inapplicable to their case or can be distinguished from their case. This flexibility in reasoning results in a rich, complex, and often contradictory body of American case law.

Thus, stare decisis means more than simply following settled cases. It means following settled cases that are factually similar and legally relevant to the case or problem you are researching. Such a factually similar and legally relevant case from a court equivalent to or higher than the court that will hear your particular case is said to be "on point" or "on all fours" with your case. The goal of legal research is to be able to locate cases on point with your particular case. Such cases are binding upon and must be followed by the court hearing your case.

In the event you cannot locate cases on point in your judicial hierarchy (possibly because your case presents a novel issue not yet considered in your jurisdiction), you should expand your search for cases on point to other jurisdictions. That is, if your case presents an issue not yet decided by the Minnesota courts, often called a case "of first impression," search for on-point cases in other states. If you locate a Wisconsin case on point, it is *not* binding in Minnesota. It may, however, be *persuasive* to the Minnesota court. If the Minnesota court adopts the view espoused in the Wisconsin case, it is then a precedent in Minnesota and according to the doctrine of stare decisis is binding upon that Minnesota court and all others lower than it in Minnesota.

Among the factors that may be considered by the Minnesota court in adopting the Wisconsin view are whether the Wisconsin case is well reasoned and well written, whether Minnesota and Wisconsin have some tradition in relying upon and respecting each other's cases, whether the Wisconsin case was issued by one of the higher Wisconsin courts, and whether the Wisconsin view is shared by other jurisdictions or approved by legal scholars. See Figure 1-2.

Change in our legal system can occur not only as a result of judges expanding or overruling precedents found in cases but through repeal or

Figure 1-2
Stare Decisis and Our Judical Hierarchy

- Primary law comprises cases, constitutions, statutes, treaties, executive orders, and administrative regulations. All other legal authorities are secondary.
- Primary law from your state or jurisdiction is binding within your state or jurisdiction.
- Primary law from another state or jurisdiction is persuasive only in your state or jurisdiction.
- If your state or jurisdiction adopts the law or position of another state or jurisdiction, then that position is now binding within your judiciary hierarchy.
- Secondary law (no matter where it originates) is persuasive only.
- Higher courts in any given judicial hierarchy bind lower courts in that hierarchy.
- Higher courts can depart from a previously announced rule if there are compelling and important reasons for doing so.

amendment of a statute by a legislature or even through judicial interpretation of a statute. You may notice as you read statutes that many are broadly written, ambiguous, or vague. In such a case, judges may interpret the meaning of the statute, clarify ambiguous terms, explain the language of the statute, or declare the law invalid. For example, a statute may require a landlord to provide three days' notice to a tenant before evicting a tenant for nonpayment of rent. A question may arise as to the meaning of this provision if the third day occurs on a national holiday. If the statute does not address this issue, a court is free to determine that if the third day occurs on a Sunday or holiday, the tenant will be given an extra day's notice. While a court cannot *change* the plain meaning of a statute, it is free to *interpret* the statute. Thus, even when you locate a statute that appears directly to address your research problem, you cannot stop researching. You must read the cases that have interpreted the statute because it is judicial interpretation of a statute rather than the naked language of a statute that is binding under the doctrine of stare decisis. This research requirement brings us full circle to the practical definition of "the law" given before — that the law is what the judges say it is. In statutory construction, the law is not always what the statute says but rather what a judge says it means.

You have seen that a case from a higher court in one state or jurisdiction is binding upon lower courts in that state or jurisdiction and may be persuasive authority in other states. In contrast, a statute has no effect whatsoever anywhere other than in the jurisdiction that enacted it. When the Kansas legislature is enacting statutes relating to the licensing of real estate salespersons, it is unaffected by statutes in Nevada relating to the same topic. Any Nevada statutes on this topic lack even persuasive effect outside Nevada's jurisdictional boundaries.

G. Identifying the Holding in a Case

You can readily see that the foundation of the American legal system lies in its rich and varied body of case law. While analysis of cases will be discussed in great detail in Chapter 4, you should be aware that under the concept of stare decisis, only the actual rule of law announced in a case is binding. That is, only the holding of the case is authoritative. The holding is referred to as the *ratio decidendi* or "reason of the decision." The remainder of the language in the case is referred to as *dictum*, which is usually used as an abbreviated form of *obiter dictum*, meaning a remark "in passing." *Black's Law Dictionary* 465 (7th ed. 1999) provides that dictum is "a statement of opinion or belief considered authoritative because of the dignity of the person making it." Dictum in a case is persuasive only.

On some occasions, a court may speculate that its decision would be different if certain facts in the case were different. This type of discussion is dictum and while it may be persuasive in other cases, it is not binding authority.

In many cases, distinguishing the holding from the dictum is easily done. Often a court will set the stage for announcing its holding by using extremely specific language similar to the following: "We hold that a landlord may not commence an action to evict a tenant for nonpayment of rent without providing the tenant with a written notice to either pay rent or forfeit possession of the leased premises." On other occasions, finding the holding requires a great deal more persistence and probing.

You may notice that some cases are difficult to read and are written using archaic and outmoded language. Do not get discouraged. Reading cases takes a great deal of patience and experience. You will find, however, that the more cases you read, the more skillful you will become at locating the holding, distinguishing dicta from the holding, and understanding the relevance of the case for the future.

H. Case Citation Form

While case citation will be discussed in much more depth in Chapter 8, the sooner you begin examining the books in which our cases are published or reported and the sooner you begin reading those cases, the more confident you will become about your ability to research effectively.

All cases follow the same basic citation form: You will be given the case name, the volume number of the set in which the case is published, the name of the set in which the case appears, the page on which it begins, and the year it was decided. For example, in "reading" the citation to the United States Supreme Court case *Brown v. Board of Education*, 347 U.S. 483 (1954), you can readily see the following:

1. The case name is *Brown v. Board of Education*;
2. It is located in volume 347;
3. It is found in a set of books entitled *United States Reports*;
4. It begins on page 483 of volume 347; and
5. It was decided in 1954.

State court cases are cited much the same way. The citation *State v. Paul*, 548 N.W.2d 260 (Minn. 1996) informs you that:

1. The case name is *State v. Paul*;
2. It is located in volume 548;
3. It is found in a set of books entitled *North Western Reporter, Second Series*;
4. It begins on page 260; and
5. It is a Minnesota case decided in 1996.

While this text shows case names and book titles in italics, underlining or underscoring is also acceptable according to *The Bluebook: A Uniform System of Citation* (Columbia Law Review Ass'n et al. eds., 17th ed. 2000), which is the standard reference tool for citation form, although other citation systems exist, as discussed in Chapter 8. There is variation among practitioners, so check with your firm or office to determine if there is a preference.

Technology Tips

http://www.westpub.com	Information about West Group products and services
http://www.lectlaw.com	Inter-Law's 'Lectric Library, a variety of legal information together with links to other law-related sites
http://www.ilrg.com	Internet Legal Resource Guide, a comprehensive guide to legal resources available online
http://www.law.indiana.edu/v-lib	Web page maintained by the Indiana University School of Law called the "World Wide Web Virtual Library," providing information about publishers and vendors of law-related resources and law schools and libraries
http://www.legal.net	Legal dot Net, a site offering numerous links to law-related sources, general articles and columns, and a LegalChat room

Writing Strategies

Always support arguments with cases on point. Precedents that differ significantly from your case will not only *not* be helpful, they may actually hurt your case by causing the reader to believe that there is no authority to support the position you advocate.

Carefully scrutinize the cases you find for their weight (what level is the court that rendered the decision?), their date (when was the case decided?), their issues (are the legal issues involved in the cases you find similar or identical to ones in your case?), and the facts (are the facts involved in the cases you find similar or analogous to the ones in your case?).

Use only the "best" decisions to support your argument. Be merciless. Discard cases that provide the adversary with any ammunition. When you have selected the cases that will best advance your position, use analogy to show the reader how similar they are to your case so the reader can easily see why these cases are controlling.

Use active voice and vivid and forceful language when constructing your argument. Personalize your clients by identifying them by name ("Jean White") and depersonalize adverse parties by referring to them by a "label" (the "defendant," the "company").

Assignment for Chapter 1

1. a. Give the name of the case located at 516 U.S. 417 (1996).
   b. Give the date the case was argued.
   c. Give the date the case was decided.
2. a. Give the name of the case at 527 U.S. 471 (1999).
   b. Who delivered the opinion of the Court?
   c. Who argued the case for the Petitioners?
3. a. Give the name of the case at 465 U.S. 638 (1984).
   b. Which justice dissented?
   c. Locate a case in this volume in which the defendant's name is *Stenson* and give the name of the case.
   d. Give the citation for the case.
   e. Which justice filed a concurring opinion?

Chapter 2

The Federal and State Court Systems

Chapter Overview

As we discussed in Chapter 1, there is no one legal system in the United States. There are 52 legal systems: one system composed of cases and statutes decided and enacted by federal courts and the federal legislature, namely the United States Congress, and another system composed of cases and statutes decided and enacted by the state courts and state legislatures for each of the 50 states and the District of Columbia.

This chapter will provide an overview of the federal and state court systems. To perform research tasks, you should understand these court structures so when you are confronted with a research assignment or a case citation you will readily understand the hierarchy of cases within a given court structure, giving greater emphasis to cases from higher courts such as the United States Supreme Court and the United States Courts of Appeal than to cases from the federal trial courts, the United States district courts, or the lower state courts.

A. Federalism

As you no doubt remember from basic American history or civics classes, there are three branches in the federal government: the legislative branch, which is charged with making federal law; the executive branch, which is tasked with enforcing the law; and the judicial branch, whose function is interpreting the law.

That we have federal courts that exist separate and apart from state courts is a result of a feature of our system of government called federalism. The principle of federalism developed from the time of the drafting of the Constitution.

At the time of the Constitutional Convention in 1787, there were two conflicting ideas held by the framers of the Constitution. On the one hand, the framers recognized the need for a strong central or "federal" government to act in matters of national concern and to reduce George Washington's fear that the fledgling nation had "thirteen heads, or one head without competent powers." On the other hand, the delegates to the Convention were wary of delegating too much power to a centralized government; after all, almost all of the delegates had served as soldiers in the Revolutionary War, which had been fought against a monolithic government insensitive to the rights of the newly emerging colonies. This principle of states' rights was seen as the best protection against an encroaching central government.

The solution was a compromise: For those delegates devoted to a strong national government, the principle developed that the national government could exercise only those powers expressly delegated to it. These powers were specifically enumerated in Article I, Section 8 of the Constitution, which states that, among other things, the federal government has the power to borrow money, collect taxes, coin money, establish post offices, declare war, raise and support armies, and make any other laws "necessary and proper" for carrying out these delegated powers. This "necessary and proper" clause is often called the "elastic" clause as it makes clear that the federal government not only has the powers expressly delegated to it in Article I, Section 8 but can also take action that is not specifically mentioned so long as it is "necessary and proper" to enable it to carry out the delegated powers.

As is readily seen, these specifically enumerated powers are extremely important, and those delegates in favor of states' rights were concerned that, as a result of the compromise, the federal government was too strong and would eventually "swallow up" the states. In fact, Patrick Henry refused to attend the Convention because of his opposition to granting any additional power to the national government and expressly warned that the Constitution "squints toward monarchy. Your President may easily become King." However, the Constitution was immediately modified by the addition of ten amendments collectively known as the Bill of Rights, which were designed to protect individual liberties. The Tenth Amendment, in particular, was enacted to reassure those in favor of states' rights that the federal government would not be able to encroach on the rights of the 13 new states or their citizens. The Tenth Amendment, often referred to as the "reserve" clause, provides that any powers not expressly given to the national government are reserved to, or retained by, the individual states.

The result of the historic Constitutional Convention is our "living law"—a unique federalist system in which the states have formed a union by granting the federal government power over national affairs while the states retain their independent existence and power over local matters.

In a system based on federalism, power is shared between the national and state governments.

B. Establishment of Federal Court Structure

Article III, Section 1 of the Constitution created the federal court system. This section provides in part that "the judicial power of the United States shall be vested in one Supreme Court and in such inferior courts as Congress may from time to time ordain and establish." Thus, only the existence of the Supreme Court was ensured. It was left up to Congress to determine its composition and to create any other federal courts. In fact, the very first Congress began to work on establishing a functioning federal court system and enacted the Judiciary Act of 1789. This Act created 13 district courts in prominent cities with one judge apiece, three circuit courts to be presided over by no more than two Supreme Court justices and a district court judge, and above these, the United States Supreme Court consisting of a chief justice and five associate justices. While the Judiciary Act of 1789 has been amended several times (among other reasons, to increase the number of Supreme Court justices), the basic structure of our federal court system remains as it was in 1789: district courts, intermediate circuit courts of appeal, and one United States Supreme Court. Judges appointed to these courts are often referred to as "Article III judges."

C. Jurisdiction

The jurisdiction (or power to act) of the federal courts does not extend to every kind of case or controversy but only to certain types of matters. You will learn a great deal more about this topic in your litigation or civil procedure classes, but a brief explanation is in order here for you to understand fully why some research assignments will be researched through the exclusive use of federal law and others will be researched through the exclusive use of the law of a particular state.

There are two types of cases that are resolved by federal courts: those based on federal question jurisdiction and those based on diversity jurisdiction.

1. Federal Question Jurisdiction

The federal courts are empowered to hear cases that involve a federal question; that is, any case arising under the United States Constitution, a United States (or federal) law, or any treaty to which the United States is a party. Cases arising under the Constitution include cases alleging racial, sexual, or age discrimination; cases involving freedom of speech, freedom of the press, freedom of religion; cases involving a defendant's right to a fair trial; cases involving federal crimes such as bank robbery or kidnapping; and any other such actions pertaining to a federal law or the Constitution.

It may be easier for you to remember the scope of federal question cases if you keep in mind a simple analogy. If a *7-11* convenience store in your neighborhood were burglarized, you would expect your local law enforcement officials to investigate the crime. On the other hand, if a bank in your area were burglarized, you would expect the investigation to be handled by the FBI, our federal law enforcement officials. Similarly, *federal* questions, namely those arising under federal law or the Constitution, are resolved by *federal* courts while more local matters are typically resolved by state courts.

2. *Diversity Jurisdiction*

The other category of cases that is handled by federal courts is determined not by the issue itself (as are federal question cases) but by the status of the parties to the action.

Imagine you are a New York resident on vacation in Montana where you become involved in an automobile accident with a Montana resident. You may have some concern whether a court in Montana would treat you, an outsider, the same as it would treat its own residents, particularly in a locality in which the residents elect the judge.

To ensure that litigants are treated fairly and to eliminate any bias against an out-of-state litigant, the federal courts may resolve cases based on the diversity of the parties; that is, in general, federal courts may hear cases in civil actions between: (i) citizens of different states; and (ii) citizens of a state and citizens of a foreign nation.

Note that diversity jurisdiction is conditioned upon satisfying another key element: The amount in controversy must exceed $75,000 exclusive of interest and court costs. For example, if a resident of Oregon sues a resident of Nevada for breach of contract and alleges (in good faith) damages in the amount of $142,000, the matter may be instituted in federal court.

Over the years, the federal courts have increased the monetary amount in diversity cases in order to prevent the federal courts from becoming inundated with cases. Until 1988, the monetary amount was $10,000. When it became apparent that almost any routine "fender bender" resulted in damages in excess of $10,000, Congress increased the monetary limit to the amount of $50,000. In October, 1996, the limit was increased again to its present requirement of $75,000. There is no monetary jurisdictional limit for cases instituted in federal court based on federal questions; that is, if a plaintiff alleges she has been wrongfully discharged from her employment due to sexual discrimination, she need not allege damages in excess of $75,000.

Diversity jurisdiction has its detractors, notably Chief Justice William H. Rehnquist, who since 1987 has urged elimination of diversity jurisdiction as a basis for initiating an action in federal court. Because total elimination of diversity jurisdiction appears unlikely, Chief Justice Rehnquist has alternatively suggested that diversity jurisdiction be curtailed so as to prevent citizens of one state from suing citizens from another state in federal court. It is believed such a modification to diversity jurisdiction would eliminate "forum shopping"; that is, the selection of a particular federal court for certain perceived advantages, among them the strategy of making it difficult for individuals to defend themselves in a court not located near their residences.

Another criticism of diversity jurisdiction, especially in cases brought by a citizen of one state against a citizen of another state, is that the federal courts are becoming "clogged up" deciding non-federal questions such as routine automobile accident cases, which are better resolved by the state courts.

3. Concurrent Jurisdiction

Often one hears about cases that are being litigated in a state court when it seems clear the action involves a federal question, for instance, racial discrimination. In such cases, concurrent jurisdiction may exist, meaning the plaintiff alleged a cause of action that violated both state law and federal law. In the example mentioned above, the basis for the action, racial discrimination, violates both California law and federal law. The plaintiff in such a case then has a choice whether to proceed in state court or federal court. The decision in which court to bring an action when concurrent jurisdiction exists is often made on the basis of tactics and strategy. For example, a plaintiff may wish to proceed in a federal court because it is not as crowded with cases as the local state court, thus resulting in a more speedy trial and resolution. Moreover, any diversity jurisdiction case regardless of the amount of money involved may be brought in a state court rather than a federal court.

4. Exclusive Jurisdiction

Some matters are handled exclusively by federal courts and are never the subject of concurrent jurisdiction. For example, by federal law all bankruptcy cases are resolved by the United States Bankruptcy Courts (discussed below). Other examples of cases that are handled exclusively by federal courts are maritime, copyright, and patent cases.

D. Ground Rules for Cases

Even if a federal question is involved or even if the requirements for diversity jurisdiction are satisfied, there still remain some ground rules that must be satisfied before a federal court will hear a case. While this discussion relates primarily to federal cases, these ground rules must also be satisfied for cases brought in state courts.

In large part, these ground rules are rooted in Article III of the Constitution, which establishes the jurisdiction of federal courts and restricts federal courts to resolving "cases" and "controversies." This limitation has been construed to mean that federal courts will only resolve an actual controversy. With very few exceptions, federal courts will not consider issues that are "moot" or already resolved. In fact, it is a fraud on a court to continue with a case that is moot. An exception to this requirement is demonstrated by the well-known case *Roe v. Wade*, 410 U.S. 113 (1973), in which a pregnant plaintiff challenged a Texas law prohibiting abortion. By the time the case reached the United States Supreme Court, the plaintiff had given birth and placed the baby for adoption. The United States Supreme Court could have dismissed the case claiming it was moot—namely, that the issue had already been effectively decided upon the birth of the child and that even if the court awarded the relief the plaintiff had requested, declaring abortion lawful, the plaintiff's situation would not be affected by the ruling. However, in *Roe* the United States Supreme Court, realizing that such a case would inevitably be rendered moot by the time it would reach the Court, made an exception and heard the case.

A close corollary to this ground rule that federal courts will not consider questions that are moot is that federal courts will not render advisory opinions, even if asked by the president. The federal courts view themselves as constitutionally bound to resolve actual ongoing disputes, not to give advice. For example, President George Washington once sent the Supreme Court 29 questions on treaties and international law, asking for advice. The justices refused on the dual bases that under the Constitution, they could not share powers and duties with the executive branch and that they were forbidden to issue advisory opinions.

Finally, a plaintiff must have personally suffered some actual or threatened injury; that is, the plaintiff must be adversely affected by some conduct of the defendant and cannot base a claim on the rights or interests of some other persons. No matter how convinced you may be that a law is unconstitutional, you cannot challenge it unless *your* rights are directly affected. This requirement is referred to as "standing." For example, in *Sierra Club v. Morton*, 405 U.S. 727 (1972), the Sierra Club brought an action to prevent development of Mineral King Valley into a commercial resort. The Court concluded that the Sierra Club lacked standing as it had not alleged that it or any of its members would be affected by the defendant's activities in developing Mineral King Valley. The Court noted that standing does not exist merely because one has an interest in a controversy; one must have a personal stake in the outcome of the controversy.

In a more colorful example, in late 1999, a judge rejected a suit filed by a political opponent of Minnesota governor and former wrestler Jesse Ventura that sought to stop Governor Ventura from refereeing a wrestling match. Although the plaintiff claimed that the governor's appearance would violate a state law against using public office for personal gain, the judge stated the plaintiff had no standing because he had failed to provide evidence that he would suffer harm as a result of Governor Ventura's involvement in a Worldwide Wrestling Federation match.

E. The Federal Court Structure

1. *District Courts*

The district courts are the trial courts in our federal system. At present, there are 94 district courts scattered throughout the 50 states, the District of Columbia, and the territories and possessions of the United States. There is at least one district court in each state, and the more populous states, such as California, New York, and Texas, may have as many as four within their territorial borders. Other less populous states, such as Alaska, Idaho, and Utah, each have only one district court. There are also district courts located in Puerto Rico, Guam, the Northern Mariana Islands, and the Virgin Islands. While there may not be a federal district court located in your hometown, there is at least one in your state, thus providing you with ready access to the federal courts. See Chapter 8 for a list of all district courts.

These district courts have jurisdiction over a wide variety of cases. One day a district court judge may hear a case involving a bank robbery and the next day may resolve a civil rights question followed by a case involving a crime committed on an Indian reservation. Bankruptcy courts are considered units of our district courts with judges appointed by the courts of appeal for terms of 14 years. Each district includes a United States bankruptcy court.

The more than 600 judges who sit in federal district courts are, as are all of the judges in the federal court system, appointed by the president with the advice and consent of the United States Senate. The number of judges assigned to a particular district court will vary depending upon the number of cases the court is called upon to adjudicate. There may be as few as one district court judge assigned to a district court, or there may be nearly 30, as is the case for the increasingly busy Southern District of New York. In the event of a shift in the population that increases the caseload of a district, the United States Congress will add or approve new judgeships to enable the district court to keep pace with its increasing litigation demands. At present, there are 646 judgeships authorized in the district courts.

In early 2000, Representative Robert Andrews (Dem. N.J.) introduced legislation to split New Jersey, a single federal judicial district, into two districts, one for the northern part of the state and one for the southern part. The creation of new districts is quite rare: The last time a new district was created by splitting a district was in 1971 in Louisiana, due to geographical distance that impeded the timely administration of justice. The four criteria necessary to establish a new federal judicial district are geography, caseload, judicial administration, and community convenience. At the time of publication of this text, there was no decision regarding splitting the New Jersey district in two.

The district court judges, who are paid $145,100 per year, usually sit individually; that is, they hear cases and render decisions by themselves rather than as a panel or group as the United States Supreme Court justices sit.

The vast majority of all federal cases end at the district court level; only approximately 10 percent of these federal cases are appealed. In contrast to the new filings for the United States Courts of Appeal and the United States Supreme Court, which continue to show a marked increase each year, civil filings in the district courts are relatively stable, with an increase of 9 percent in civil filings between 1993 and 1998. This stability is generally attributed to the 1988 legislation that increased the jurisdictional amount in diversity cases from $10,000 to $50,000 and 1996 legislation that increased the jurisdictional amount from $50,000 to $75,000. Immediately after the legislation became effective, filings for diversity cases dropped sharply. Moreover, the number of trials completed in the district courts has dropped slightly, as litigants have taken advantage of various forms of alternative dispute resolution programs, including mediation and arbitration. Additionally, prisoner petitions declined after the enactment of the Prisoner Litigation Reform Act, aimed at reducing prisoner petitions.

2. *United States Courts of Appeal*

The 13 United States Courts of Appeal, sometimes called the circuit courts, are the intermediate courts in our federal system. The theory of our judicial system is that a litigant should have a trial in one court before one judge and a right to an appeal in another court before a different judge. This structure serves to satisfy the cause of justice and to ensure that a litigant who may have been denied any rights at the trial in the district court will have a second opportunity before a different judge or panel of judges in these intermediate courts of appeal. In fact, a statute directs that no judge may hear an appeal of a case originally tried by him or her.

It is critical to distinguish between the district courts, where the trial occurs, evidence is presented, witnesses testify, and a decision is rendered, and the courts of appeal, whose primary function is to review cases from these district courts. The courts of appeal do not retry a case. They merely review the record and the briefs of counsel to determine if a prejudicial error of law was made in the district court below. A second important function of the United States Courts of Appeal is to review and enforce decisions from federal administrative agencies such as the National Labor Relations Board or the Securities and Exchange Commission.

The United States is divided into 12 geographical areas called "circuits," and there is a court of appeal in each of these circuits. Additionally, there is a Court of Appeals for the Federal Circuit, as discussed below. Figure 2-1 shows the grouping of states that comprise each circuit. It is not critical to know which states or district courts fall within the boundaries of which circuits. Maps of the circuit courts are readily available in the front of each volume of West's *Federal Reporter*. You should certainly know which circuit covers the state in which you will be working and that each circuit is assigned a number and will have several states (and their district courts) within it. For example, the Ninth Circuit covers California and most of the western states.

Thus, if a trial occurs in the Northern District of California, the appeal is filed in the Ninth Circuit. Similarly, if a trial occurs in the Southern District of New York, the appeal is filed in the Second Circuit. Each of the intermediate circuit courts of appeal is free to make its own decisions independent of what other circuits have held; however, in practice, the circuit courts are often guided by decisions from other circuits. Decisions by the U.S. Supreme Court often resolve conflicts among the circuits—not only those in the lower circuit courts but in all other courts in the nation.

The Eleventh Circuit was created in 1981 to relieve some of the pressure the Fifth Circuit was facing due to an ever-increasing caseload caused by population growth. The Fifth Circuit, which had covered Texas, Louisiana, Mississippi, Alabama, Georgia, and Florida, was split, and a new Eleventh Circuit was created by the United States Congress to handle cases from Alabama, Georgia, and Florida (leaving only Texas, Louisiana, and Mississippi in the Fifth Circuit).

In the late 1990's, legislation was introduced to split the Ninth Circuit in two, creating a new Twelfth Circuit to be comprised of Alaska, Washington, Oregon, Idaho, and Montana. The bill, introduced by Senators Ted Stevens and Frank Murowski of Alaska, was a response to criticism that the Ninth Circuit was becoming glutted with cases and that the Pacific Northwest, particularly Oregon and Washington, which have seen a dramatic increase in population, should be severed from the Ninth Circuit, creating a new Twelfth Circuit. Just as new judgeships are created by the United States Congress for the district courts when the pressure of litigation so dictates, Congress may create a new circuit if the need arises. After a year-long study by a congressional commission, a panel of retired and current judges rejected the call for a breakup of the Ninth Circuit and instead recommended that it be divided into three regional sections or subcircuits, with a northern division (comprising Alaska, Washington, Oregon, Idaho, and Montana), a middle division (including Nevada, Hawaii, the Pacific islands, and the northern portion of California), and a southern division (comprising Arizona and the southern portion of California). At the time of the publication of this text, the proposal remains under study, but most of the 28 judges in the Ninth Circuit favor leaving the Ninth Circuit as it is.

In addition to the 11 "numbered" circuits (First Circuit, Second Circuit, and so forth), there is a Circuit Court of Appeals for the District of Columbia and a circuit court created in 1982 that merged the United States Court of Customs and Patent Appeals and the United States Court

Figure 2-1
The Thirteen Federal Judicial Circuits (See 28 U.S.C.A. § 41)

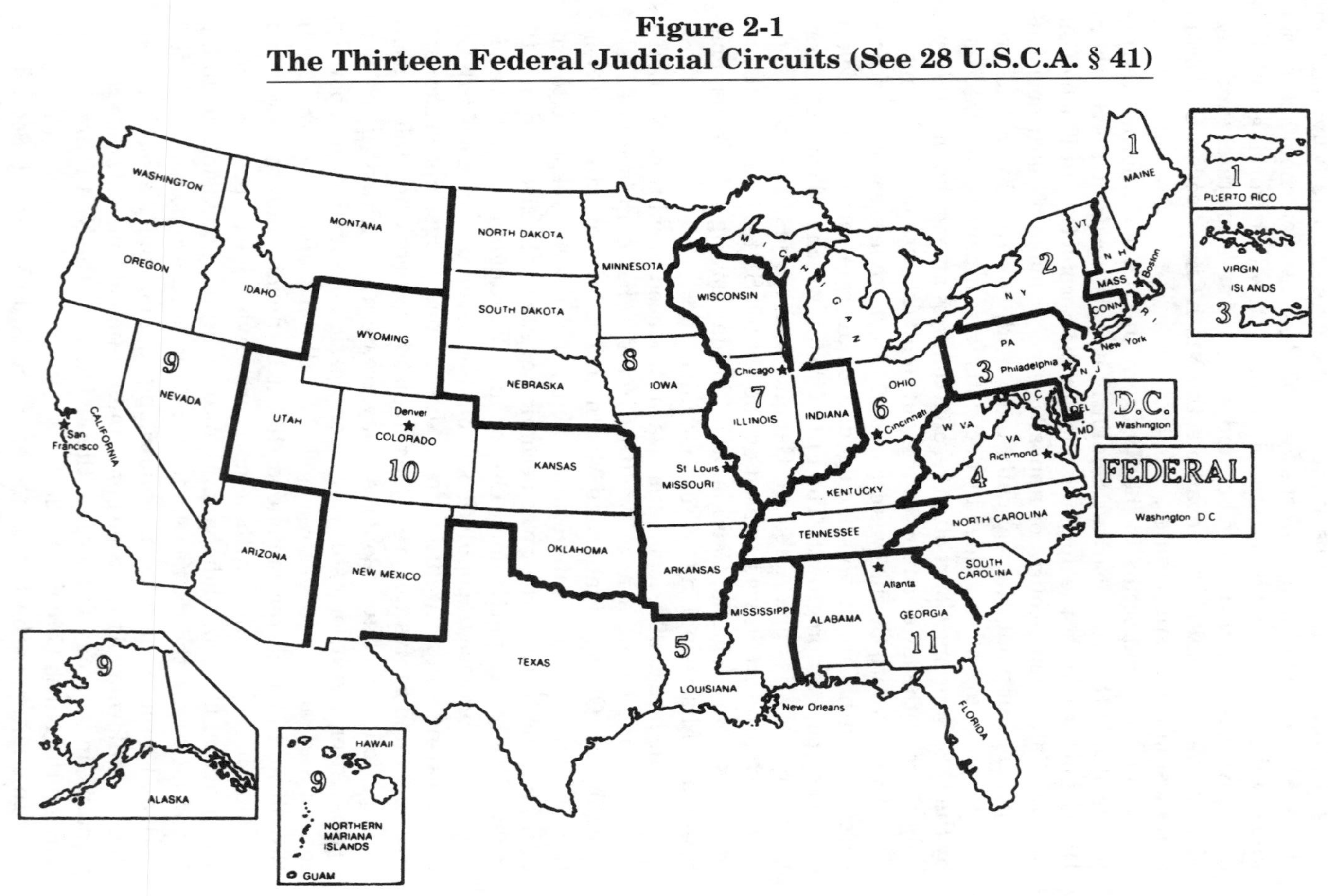

of Claims into a new court known as the Court of Appeals for the Federal Circuit, located in Washington, D.C. This court handles certain specialized appeals such as those from the United States Court of International Trade, the Trademark Trial and Appeal Board, the United States Court of Veteran Appeals, the United States Court of Federal Claims, and other specialized courts.

There are more than 170 justices who sit for the 13 United States Courts of Appeal, with each court of appeals having from six to 28 justices assigned to it, depending on the caseload for the circuit. The justices usually hear the appeals from the district courts as a panel of three justices, although they may sit *en banc* with all justices present. These federal justices are also appointed by the president and earn an annual salary of $153,900. The workload of the United States Courts of Appeal has increased substantially, primarily due to a rise in the number of criminal appeals from decisions of the United States District Courts. The United States Courts of Appeal typically issue more than 15,000 opinions each year.

For the vast majority of litigants, these intermediate courts of appeal represent the last opportunity to prevail. As you will see, the popular notion that everyone has access to the United States Supreme Court is unfounded; for most litigants the court of appeals is the last chance to win, as one who wishes to appeal a case to the United States Supreme Court is largely dependent on the Court's discretion in accepting a case for review.

3. *United States Supreme Court*

The United States Supreme Court consists of eight associate justices and one chief justice. While the chief justice is paid more than the associate justices ($186,300, to their annual salaries of $178,300), and while he has prestige and certain authority by virtue of seniority, the chief justice's vote counts equally with that of any associate justice. Nevertheless, as the presiding officer of the Supreme Court, he is responsible for administration of the Court and leadership of the federal judicial system. Upon the death or resignation of a chief justice, the president may either appoint one of the eight existing associate justices to the position of chief justice or may appoint an "outsider" as chief justice. That is, there is no seniority system whereby an associate justice works his or her way up to the chief justice position.

As are all approximately 1,700 judges in the federal system, the Supreme Court justices are appointed by the president and hold office "during good behavior." This means they are not subject to mandatory retirement and may sit as federal judges until they voluntarily resign or die. As an example of the lack of a mandatory retirement, Judge Giles Rich, of the United States Court of Appeals for the Federal Circuit, sat on the bench until his death in 1999 at age 95. While federal judges can be impeached by the Congress, this drastic remedy is seldom used, and only a handful of judges have been removed through impeachment and conviction by Congress of treason, bribery, or other high crimes and misdemeanors. To further ensure the independence of the federal judiciary, the Constitution prohibits any decrease in federal judges' salaries during their term in office. These two protections ensure that an independent judiciary decides cases free from popular passion and political influence.

The individuals who sit on the United States Supreme Court (or state supreme courts) are usually referred to as "justices" while the individuals who sit on lower courts are referred to as "judges." Occasionally, individuals who sit on intermediate appellate courts are also referred to as "justices," although in general the term "justice" is reserved for individuals on the United States Supreme Court or a state supreme court.

The Supreme Court has not always had nine justices. When the Court was established in 1790, there were only six justices. The number of justices has changed several times; at one point there were ten justices.

1998 Federal Court Caseloads

- From 1994-1998, the total number of weighted civil and criminal filings per United States district court judgeship climbed 16 percent, and bankruptcy filings per authorized judgeship soared 72 percent. Despite these increases, no new Article III judgeships have been created in eight years, and the number of bankruptcy judges authorized has not changed since 1993.
- The increase in bankruptcy cases is linked to continued high levels of consumer debt as a percentage of personal income.
- The Department of Justice (which is responsible for prosecuting federal crimes and representing the government in civil actions) is the most frequent litigator in the federal court system.
- Criminal case filings rose 28 percent in United States district courts from 1994-1998, largely due to increased filings of cases involving drug and immigration law violations.
- Drug, fraud, and immigration filings accounted for 60 percent of all criminal cases in 1998 in the United States district courts.
- Civil filings in the United States district courts rose 9 percent between 1994 and 1998, primarily due to increases in contract actions (up 35 percent), increases in cases involving defaulted student loans and civil rights filings (up 30 percent), and increases in employment actions arising under the Americans with Disabilities Act and personal injury filings, primarily in personal injury/product liability cases related to breast implant and asbestos litigation.
- Criminal cases generally make more demands on district court judges' time than civil cases and are more likely to go to trial in that 7 percent of all criminal defendants went to trial, compared to 3 percent of civil cases.
- Since 1994, the number of appeals to the United States courts of appeal has climbed 11 percent.

The present composition of nine justices has existed since 1869. The most recent attempt to alter the size of the Supreme Court occurred in 1937 when President Franklin D. Roosevelt presented a plan to the Senate for reorganization of the Court. President Roosevelt's proposal called for adding an additional justice each time any justice reached the age of 70 and did not voluntarily retire, to a maximum of 15 justices. Fierce public outcry immediately met this attempt to "pack" the Supreme Court and there has been no serious discussion of altering the number of justices since that time.

Because there is no mandatory retirement for federal judges, many have served for extremely long periods—notably Chief Justice John Marshall, widely regarded as the finest jurist produced by the United States, who served 34 years, and Associate Justice William O. Douglas, who served for 36 years. On average, Supreme Court justices have served for approximately 15 years.

In addition to their primary activities of hearing Supreme Court cases and writing opinions, each justice is assigned to one of the federal judicial circuits for the purpose of handling special and emergency matters such as stays of execution and injunctions. For example, in mid-2000, Associate Justice Anthony Kennedy, then assigned to the Eleventh Circuit, which includes Florida, rejected an emergency request to allow Elian Gonzales, a Cuban child, to remain in the United States. Similarly, Associate Justice Sandra Day O'Connor, then assigned to the Ninth Circuit, rejected a request in 2000 to delay an adoption open-records law from going into effect in Oregon. Because there are 13 federal circuits and only 9 Supreme Court justices, some justices are assigned to more than one circuit. Assignment to the circuits is made by the chief justice. A listing of the assignments is found in the front of each volume of *United States Reports*.

The United States Supreme Court is currently located in Washington, D.C. Initially, the Court met in New York City, the original capital of the United States. When the national capital was relocated to Philadelphia, the Court established its offices there. When Washington, D.C., became the permanent national capital in 1800, the Court again moved and was located in the United States Capitol. In 1929, former President William Howard Taft, who had been appointed as chief justice of the Court after his presidential term, persuaded Congress to construct a permanent building for the Court. The Supreme Court building was completed in 1935, almost 150 years after the Court was created.

By federal law the term of the United States Supreme Court commences on the first Monday in October. Typically the term ends at the end of June or early July nine months later. During the summer recess the justices continue working and reviewing the many petitions for relief the Court receives during the year. The last month of the term is often referred to as the "June crunch" as the Court struggles to finalize and release opinions before the summer recess. In the last two months of the Court's 1999 term, it produced decisions in approximately 43 percent of its cases, some of which were the most complex on its docket.

Many interesting traditions endure in the Court. The justices are seated at the bench by seniority: The chief justice occupies the center seat and the most senior associate justice sits to his right; the next most senior associate justice sits to his left and this procedure continues, with the newest member of the Court occupying the chair at the extreme right of the bench. Formal pictures of the justices also reflect this seniority arrangement.

Though seldom used, white quill pens are still placed on the tables in the Court, just as was done 200 years ago. One of the more impressive traditions is the "conference handshake," which was instituted by Chief Justice Melville W. Fuller in the late 1800s. As the justices take their seats on the bench and at the beginning of the case conferences at which they meet to review cases, each justice formally shakes hands with each of the other justices. This handshake serves as a visible reminder that while the justices may offer differing views of the law, they are united in their purpose of interpreting the United States Constitution. Because the Court has retained so many traditions, one legal historian has called it "the first Court still sitting."

Until William H. Rehnquist became chief justice, the caseload of the United States Supreme Court increased dramatically each year. In just the ten-year period between 1970 and 1980, the number of cases appealed in the federal system more than doubled. According to the Supreme Court Historical Society, over a recent 25-year period the number of appeals filed in the federal courts has grown more than six times as quickly as the country's population. While the Supreme Court justices have recognized they are overburdened and while various suggestions have been made to decrease their staggering caseload, Associate Justice Stevens has remarked that the justices are too busy to resolve the problem of being too

Figure 2-2
Jurisdiction of United States Supreme Court

I. ORIGINAL JURISDICTION
   A. Controversies between two or more states (exclusive jurisdiction)
   B. Actions in which ambassadors or other public ministers of foreign states are parties (non-exclusive jurisdiction)
   C. Controversies between the United States and a state (non-exclusive jurisdiction)
   D. Actions by a state against the citizens of another state (non-exclusive jurisdiction)

II. APPELLATE JURISDICTION
   A. Cases from federal courts
      1. United States District Courts (special statutes allow some direct appeals as well as appeals from three-judge district courts granting or denying injunctive relief to be directly appealed to United States Supreme Court)
      2. United States Courts of Appeal
         (a) Certiorari
         (b) Certification (granted only in exceptional cases)
   B. Cases from highest state courts

busy. In recent years, however, the Court has been reducing its docket and producing far fewer opinions. During the 1980s, the Court routinely decided roughly 150 cases per term. In 1999, the Court issued only 74 opinions, although the average number of pages and footnotes per opinion has increased steadily over the years.

By the authority of the Constitution, the United States Supreme Court has the jurisdiction to act not only as an appellate or reviewing court but also in very limited instances can act as a court of original jurisdiction or a trial court for cases involving controversies between two states and many cases affecting ambassadors, public ministers, and consuls. While the Supreme Court can conduct a trial in these cases, it prefers that trials be conducted in the district courts below. As might be expected, few litigants elect to have their trial conducted in this highest court as there is no avenue for an appeal if a party loses a trial before the United States Supreme Court. In cases involving controversies between two or more states, the United States Supreme Court has original and exclusive jurisdiction. For example, in 2000, Maryland initiated an action in the Supreme Court against Virginia regarding each state's rights to the Potomac River. The Supreme Court typically hears less than five original jurisdiction cases per term. See Figure 2-2 for an outline of jurisdiction of the United States Supreme Court.

The most important function of the United States Supreme Court is its appellate jurisdiction; that is, its authority to review decisions from lower courts. Cases may come to the Supreme Court from the lower federal courts or from the highest court in any state.

While a few cases, such as some cases under the Interstate Commerce Act, are directly appealable from the district courts to the United States Supreme Court, the vast majority of federal cases that the Supreme Court reviews proceed to the court in the expected "stair-step" fashion: trial in the district court, an intermediate appeal to the appropriate circuit court, and a final appeal to the United States Supreme Court.

Additionally, special statutes might allow for direct appeal to the Supreme Court. For example, you might recall that in mid 2000, the Department of Justice asked that the United States Supreme Court review the Microsoft antitrust case under a special federal statute that would have resulted in the case moving from the United States District Court directly to the Supreme Court, skipping over the intermediate court of appeals. The Supreme Court declined the case, and it was sent to the Court of Appeals for the District of Columbia. In 26 years, only two such cases have gone directly to the Supreme Court under special legislation that provides that government-initiated antitrust cases of general public importance should receive direct consideration by the Court.

The most widely used means to gain access to the United States Supreme Court from the lower circuit courts of appeal is the writ of *certiorari*. *Certiorari* is a Latin word meaning "to be informed of." A litigant who has lost an appeal in the intermediate circuit court will file a document or petition with the Supreme Court called a Petition for Writ of Certiorari. The fee for filing the Petition for Writ of Certiorari is $300. This petition will set forth the litigant's (or appellant's) basis for appeal and will enumerate the errors that were allegedly committed by the lower court(s). The Supreme Court will either grant the petition and direct the lower court to send its records and files to the Supreme Court for review (in which instance the case is often referred to as being "cert worthy") or will deny the petition, meaning that the lower court decision will stand. In the vast majority of cases, issuance of the writ, or "granting cert," is discretionary with the Supreme Court, and seldom does a litigant have an absolute right to have the Supreme Court review a case.

Approximately 7,000 petitions for certiorari are filed with the United States Supreme Court each year, and the justices typically grant cert in less than 100 of these cases. Full written opinions are issued in about 75 cases, and the remaining cases are disposed of without oral argument or formal written opinions.

Deciding which of the 7,000 petitions for certiorari to grant (which will result in the United States Supreme Court's hearing the appeal) may be as important as the actual decision ultimately reached. While some proposals for court reform have suggested a second-tier court just below the United States Supreme Court to review the petitions for certiorari and decide which of the appeals the justices should hear, the justices have steadfastly resisted such an idea, contending that their screening function in determining which appeals to hear is critical in importance. A Supreme Court historian once stated that deciding which petitions for certiorari should be granted is "arguably the most important stage in the entire Supreme Court process."

Each justice has between two and four law clerks who are usually top graduates of the nation's best law schools. Many of the justices themselves, including Chief Justice Rehnquist and Associate Justices Stevens and Breyer, have served as law clerks. These law clerks routinely work 70 to 90 hours per week (as do many of the justices) and prepare memoranda for the justices summarizing the petitions for certiorari that have been filed. All of the justices review all of the petitions or the clerks' memoranda discussing the petitions, and they meet on Wednesdays and Fridays in "conference" to discuss the petitions for certiorari. Once again, the justices sit in prescribed order by seniority at the conference table. No notes are taken, and no one other than the nine justices is ever present at these case conferences. For certiorari to be granted, only four of the nine justices need vote to accept the case for review. This process is often referred to as "the rule of four."

There are no clearly articulated or published criteria followed by the justices in determining which petitions will be deemed "cert worthy." The guideline most frequently given is that certiorari will be granted when there are "special and important" reasons for doing so. These "special and important" reasons are, of course, determined by the justices. In general, however, a review of the cases accepted by the Supreme Court reveals some common threads: If the lower courts are in conflict on a certain issue and the circuit courts of appeal are issuing contradictory opinions, the Supreme Court often grants certiorari so it can resolve such a conflict; or if a case is of general importance, the Court will grant certiorari.

Denial of the writ of certiorari is not to be viewed as a message to the petitioner from the Court that it has fully reviewed and researched all aspects of the case and it is satisfied the lower court's ruling is correct but rather that for reasons of judicial economy not every case can be heard. The Supreme Court cannot possibly review every case that litigants desire to appeal, and the appeal process must end somewhere. In most cases originating in the federal court system, the litigant had a trial conducted by a judge who was appointed by the president and confirmed by the Senate; an appeal then followed in one of the circuit courts of appeal before a panel of judges appointed by the president and confirmed by the Senate. This should be sufficient to satisfy the cause of justice. In fact, in 1925, Chief Justice William Howard Taft (formerly President Taft) stated, "[N]o litigant is entitled to more than two chances, namely, to the original trial and to a review." Denial of a writ of certiorari is the chief means the justices have of controlling their caseload and ensuring they continue to issue opinions on a timely basis.

Once the petition for certiorari has been granted, the attorneys or parties are notified and instructed to submit their written arguments, called briefs, which are then filed with the court and made available to the public.

Oral arguments are heard two weeks of every month on Mondays, Tuesdays, and Wednesdays through April. Fridays are generally reserved for discussion of cases and voting on petitions for certiorari. A typical day begins with a case at 10:00 A.M., and another at 11:00 A.M. followed by a lunch break from 12:00 noon to 1:00 P.M. The afternoon session will also be devoted to two cases, one at 1:00 P.M. and another at 2:00 P.M. In recent years, however, the Court has not heard cases in the afternoon, probably due to its decreased caseload. At least six justices must be present to hear a case. The two-week sessions when the Court hears arguments and delivers opinions are called "sittings," and the two-week sessions when the justices consider business before the Court and write opinions are called "recesses."

Usually only one-half hour is allotted to each side for oral argument. Timing is regulated by a lighting system. After 25 minutes, a white light is turned on, notifying the speaker that only five minutes remain for oral argument. A red light signals the end of the 30-minute oral argument period. During the oral argument, the justices may ask questions and often interrupt the speaker. It is rare for a case to exceed the one hour allotted for oral argument. Cameras are not authorized in the courtroom, and spectators are not permitted to take notes.

After oral argument, the justices again meet in conference and discuss the case. A preliminary vote is taken to determine the Court's disposition of the case. This is the time when the power and prestige of the chief justice are shown. If the preliminary vote is 5-4 with the majority in favor of affirming and the chief justice is in the majority, he may assign the opinion to be drafted by any of the associate justices in the majority group or may decide to author the opinion himself. When the chief justice is not in the majority, the senior associate justice in the majority group will make the assignment.

While one justice is drafting the majority opinion, others may be writing separate dissents or concurring opinions (see Chapter 4). Drafting the majority opinion may take weeks or months, and the law clerks often write the first drafts. Justice Brennan once disclosed that he circulated ten drafts of an opinion before one was approved. When the opinion is complete, it is circulated to the other justices for comments. Justices who were originally in the majority may, after reviewing the opinion, change their votes, and it is possible that what initially appeared to be a majority may vanish and the original dissenters may become the majority. While the average length of time between oral argument and issuance of the opinion is only a few months, in some instances there may be a period of more than a year before the final opinion is released. Cases that are not completed before the Court recesses in late June or early July carry over to the next term.

Finally, the last revisions are made to the opinion and it is released to the public and authorized for printing in the *United States Reports*, the official publication of the Court's work. Only the final version of the opinion is printed and only it is the law, serving as a legal precedent under the doctrine of stare decisis. At the end of the 1999 term, the Court released four decisions, comprising 18 separate writings by the justices and covering 385 pages.

While the vast majority of cases arrive at the United States Supreme Court from the various United States courts of appeal by means of the writ of certiorari, there is one other means by which cases from the United States Courts of Appeal may be reviewed by the United States Supreme Court: certification. Certification is the process by which a court of appeals refers a question to the United States Supreme Court and asks for instructions. Certification is not done for the benefit of the parties to the case. It is done at the desire of the court and typically involves questions of grave doubt. The Court itself refers to its certification jurisdiction as "exceptional." One example is a case in which conflicting decisions had been rendered by several of the courts of appeal regarding the right of the Secretary of Labor to deport Chinese citizens. Because of these conflicting decisions, one of the courts of appeal "certified" the case to the United States Supreme Court, asking for direction and instruction. The certification procedure does not play a significant role in the Court's caseload. Certification is discretionary with the Court and is granted only for exceptional cases. In addition, a party may appeal directly to the United States Supreme Court from an order granting or denying injunctive relief in any case determined by a three-judge district court.

Cases from state courts may be appealed to the United States Supreme Court from the highest court in a state if and only if a federal question is involved. Even then, the Court may, in its discretion, refuse to grant certiorari, thus rendering the state court decision final. State court cases seeking access to the United States Supreme Court have no absolute right to an appeal and are entirely dependent on the Court granting certiorari, which it does for roughly 1 percent of cases. See Figure 2-3 for a diagram of federal court structure.

4. *Specialized Courts*

In addition to the district courts, the intermediate circuit courts of appeal, and the United States Supreme Court, certain specialized courts exist in

Figure 2-3
Structure of United States Court System

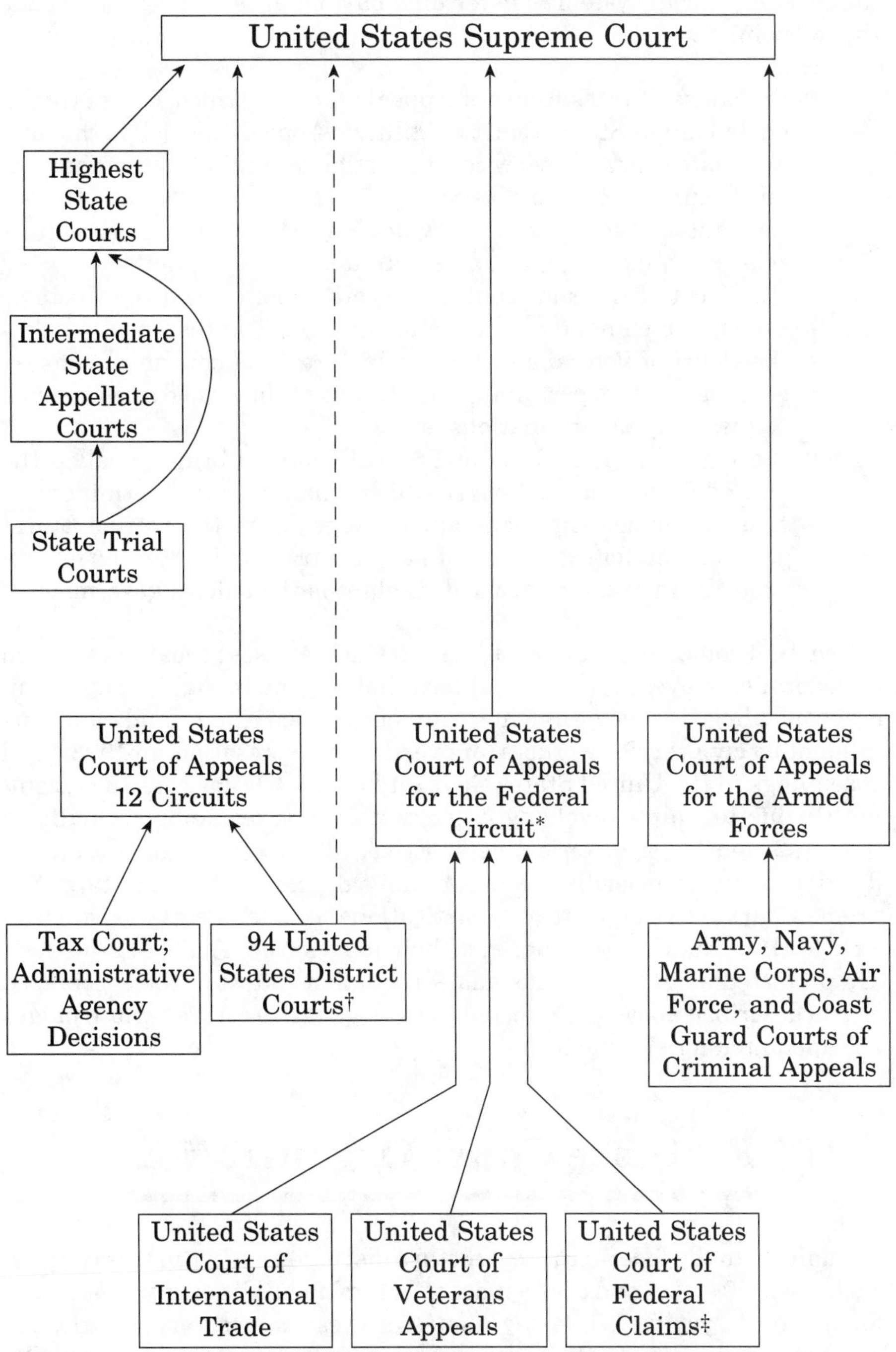

*The Court of Appeals for the Federal Circuit also receives cases from the Patent and Trademark Office, the Board of Contract Appeals, the Merit Systems Protection Board, and the International Trade Commission.

†A few cases are directly appealed from the United States District Courts to the United States Supreme Court.

‡Formerly, the United States Claims Court.

the federal judicial system to determine particular issues. These include the following:

- the United States Court of Appeals for the Armed Forces (previously United States Court of Military Appeals), which is the final appellate court to review court-martial determinations of the various branches of the military;
- the United States Tax Court, which issues decisions in tax matters relating to income, gift, and estate taxes;
- the Court of International Trade (previously called the Customs Court), which handles trade and customs disputes;
- the Court of Veterans Appeals, which reviews determinations regarding matters pertaining to veterans of the armed services such as disability determinations; and
- the United States Court of Federal Claims (formerly called the United States Claims Court), which considers and determines certain claims seeking monetary damages from the United States government, for example, claims by contractors working on federal projects. In every case, the defendant is the federal government.

A review of some recent Court of Federal Claims cases reveals a case filed by federal employees for wrongful termination, one brought by landowners who alleged a government reservoir flooded their land, and one brought by civil service workers for overtime compensation. In 1998, total case filings in the United States Court of Federal Claims rose 18 percent, mostly due to claims involving property taken, taxes, and vaccinations.

As a matter of historical perspective, it is useful to know that the district courts, intermediate courts of appeal, and the United States Supreme Court are referred to as "constitutional courts" as they exist under Article III of the Constitution, and their judges (the "Article III judges") are protected as to tenure and salary reductions. Most of the specialized courts described above are referred to as "legislative courts" whose judges are appointed for specific terms.

F. State Court Organization

In addition to the federal court structure discussed earlier in this chapter, each of the 50 states and the District of Columbia has its own arrangement for its court system. While the names of these courts vary greatly, the general organization is the same in each state and in the District of Columbia: A trial is held in one court and the losing party will have the right to at least one appeal in an appellate (or reviewing) court. Some state courts are courts of "limited" or "special" jurisdiction, meaning they can hear only certain types of cases, such as probate cases, tax cases, or cases involving certain amounts of money, while other state courts are courts of "general" jurisdiction, meaning they hear a wide variety of cases.

California's court system is typical of many states and is shown in Figure 2-4. You will note that in California, trials involving lesser amounts of money and misdemeanors are held in courts called municipal courts, while trials involving greater sums of money and felonies are held in the superior courts. Different states assign differing names to these trial courts, such as circuit court or district court. Intermediate appeals are heard by the court of appeals, with the California Supreme Court serving as the state court of last resort. You can see that this structure is extremely similar to the federal court structure in which a trial is held in the district court, an intermediate appeal follows in the United States courts of appeal, and a final appeal may occur in the United States Supreme Court.

While the majority of courts have a two-tier appellate system, in ten states (Maine, Montana, Nevada, New Hampshire, North Dakota, Rhode Island, South Dakota, Vermont, West Virginia, and Wyoming) and in the District of Columbia there is no intermediate court of appeal, and dissatisfied litigants proceed directly from the state trial court to the court of last resort in the state, usually called the supreme court. For example, in North Dakota a breach of contract case alleging damages of $50,000 would be tried in the North Dakota District Court. The party who loses would appeal directly to the North Dakota Supreme Court. (See Figure 2-5.)

In almost all states, the highest state court is called the supreme court. Maryland, however, calls its highest court the court of appeals. New

Figure 2-4
California Court Structure

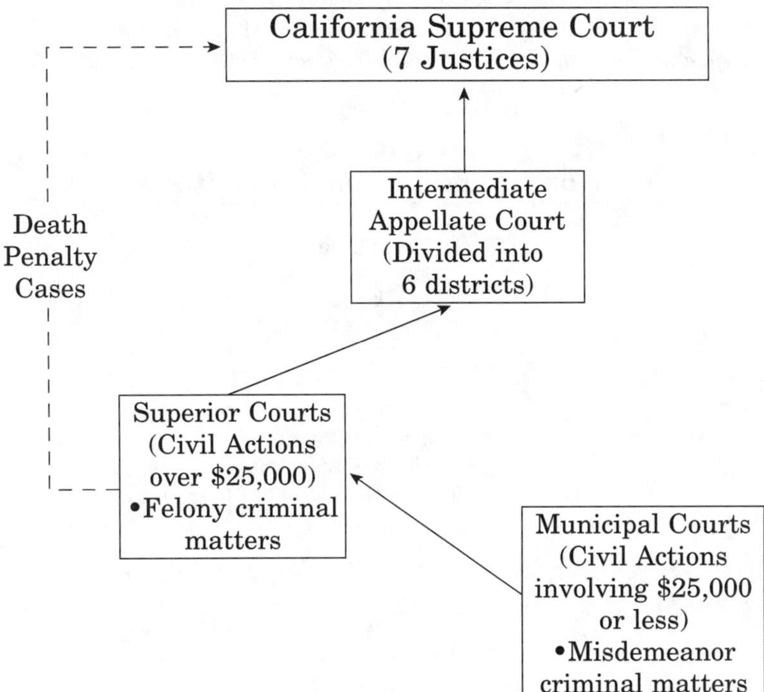

York also calls its highest court the court of appeals and calls one of the courts below it, which handles felonies and miscellaneous civil actions, the supreme court, which can cause a great deal of confusion. When reading cases from New York, therefore, exercise a great deal of caution and remember that the decisions of its highest court, the court of appeals, bind all other courts in New York, while its supreme court is not New York's highest court despite its name. Similarly, the decisions of Maryland's highest court, the court of appeals, bind all other courts in Maryland.

Decisions by the highest courts in all states are rendered by odd-numbered panels of judges (or justices) who function in a collective manner similar to the justices of the United States Supreme Court. Eighteen of the 50 states are composed of a five-member supreme court; 26 of the states are composed of a seven-member supreme court; and six of the states are composed of a nine-member supreme court.

The average salary for justices on the highest state courts is $111,706. The average salary for judges sitting on the state intermediate appellate courts is $106,395; and the average salary for state trial court judges is $96,475. Note that all of these salaries are significantly lower than the starting salaries paid to new attorneys in the nation's largest law firms, which range from $125,000 to $140,000.

While all judges in the federal system are appointed by the president and are confirmed by the United States Senate, there is great variation among the states with regard to the selection of state court judges. The majority of states use a merit selection method (somewhat similar to the federal presidential appointment method) in which the governor appoints a judge from a list of nominees provided to him or her by a judicial nominating commission. Other states elect their judges either by vote of the state legislature or the general population for specific terms.

For information about all federal and state courts, see Robert S. Want, *Want's Federal-State Court Directory* (1996), (212) 687-3774. This

Figure 2-5
North Dakota Court Structure

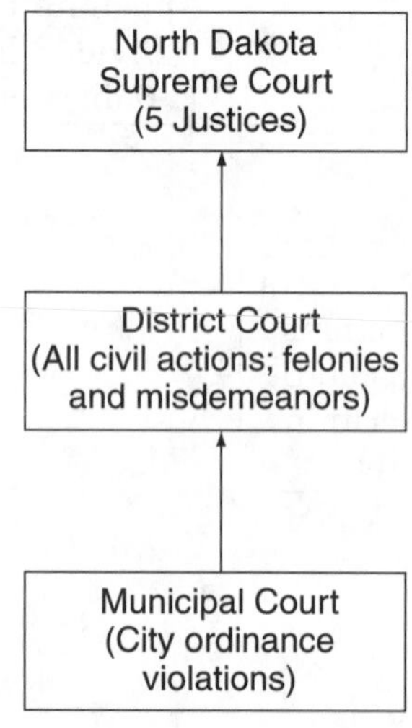

annual directory provides thorough information about federal and state courts and judges and also provides charts showing the organization of each state court system. Generally, each state's judicial Web site also includes basic information about the judicial system in that state. Table T.1 of the *Bluebook* provides a reference to each state's judicial Web site.

The state trial courts are often referred to as courts of first resort: Witnesses appear and testify, evidence is introduced, and a decision is rendered by a judge or jury. State appellate courts do not retry a case. Rather, they review the record or transcript from the trial court below, read the written briefs submitted by the attorneys for each party, listen to oral arguments in some cases, and then render a decision. No evidence is presented and no witnesses testify. It is often said that appellate courts cannot make factual determinations and are restricted to deciding issues of law. For example, if a jury convicts Defendant Smith of manslaughter, the appellate court cannot overturn or reverse this judgment on the basis that Smith seems like a fine, upstanding individual and the appellate court cannot believe Smith would have committed such an atrocious act. The trial court has already determined a fact: Smith murdered the victim. With few exceptions, it is not within the province of an appellate court to substitute its judgment for that of the jury. The appellate court may, however, reverse the judgment and order a new trial on the basis that prejudicial hearsay was incorrectly admitted at trial, that the jury instructions were improper, or that evidence used at the trial to convict Smith was obtained without a search warrant. Such issues are ones of law rather than fact. Appellate courts typically review only questions of law, not factual determinations that have already been made by a judge or jury at the trial below.

G. Citation Form

1. *Federal Cases*

a. United States Supreme Court cases:
   Vestron, Inc. v. Lowell, 347 U.S. 483 (1965).
b. United States Courts of Appeal cases:
   Bailey v. Talbert, 585 F.2d 968 (8th Cir. 1989).
c. United States District Court cases:
   Peters v. May, 697 F. Supp. 101 (S.D. Cal. 1988).

2. *State Cases*

a. In documents submitted to a state court, all citations to cases decided by courts of that state must include all parallel citations (unless court or local rules dictate otherwise):
   Janson v. Keyser, 101 Mass. 642, 415 N.E.2d 891 (1976).
b. In all other documents, cite to the regional reporter and indicate parenthetically information about the state, court, and date:
   Janson v. Keyser, 415 N.E.2d 891 (Mass. 1976).

Supreme Court Dicta

- In 1999, the Ninth Circuit was reversed in nine of ten cases; the Seventh Circuit was reversed in six of eight cases, and the Fourth Circuit was reversed in five of nine cases.
- The United States Supreme Court reverses cases from the courts of appeal approximately 80 percent of the time.
- The cost of an appeal to the Court can be as high as $500,000 with printing costs alone topping $7,000.
- After Chief Justice Rehnquist presided over President Clinton's impeachment trial, the Supreme Court law clerks gave him a T-shirt with the following slogan: "I presided over a presidential impeachment and all I got was this lousy T-shirt."
- In 1999, Justice Breyer used the pronoun "I" in a Supreme Court opinion, violating a 200-year-old tradition, begun by Chief Justice John Marshall, of speaking collectively by using the pronoun "we" in majority opinions.
- Each October before the Court begins its session, several justices attend a "Red Mass" at the Roman Catholic Cathedral of St. Matthew (where President Kennedy's funeral Mass was held), where the church blesses the forthcoming term as well as the work of other civic leaders. In 1999, six justices attended the Mass, named for the red vestments worn by its celebrants.
- Chief Justice Rehnquist, who has been on the Court since 1972, is the only one of the current justices never to have served as a trial judge.
- In 1999, the Court increased its average opinion length by 1,290 words, to 5,666 words.
- The average time on the Court's docket in 1999 was 239 days per case.
- A 1995 nationwide poll by the *Washington Post* revealed that while 59 percent of those polled could name the Three Stooges, only 17 percent could name three of the nine United States Supreme Court Justices. Justice Sandra Day O'Connor was the most frequently named justice, identified by 31 percent of those polled, while Justice John Paul Stevens was identified by only 1 percent, despite his 20-year tenure on the high Court.
- Justice Lewis F. Powell, Jr. (1971-1987) suggested the formation of the "cert pool," a group of law clerks who pool their efforts to write summaries of the thousands of petitions for *certiorari* filed in the Court each year.
- Although 47 states have allowed television coverage of at least some court proceedings, television coverage of oral arguments has been forbidden by continuous order of the Supreme Court.
- After leaving office, President John Adams stated, "My gift of John Marshall [appointed by Adams as chief justice in 1801] to the people of the United States was the proudest act of my life." One Court observer remarked that to try to describe Marshall's eloquence "would be to attempt to paint the sunbeams."

(continued)

Supreme Court Dicta (Continued)

- According to Justice Joseph Story, on rainy days the early justices would enliven case conferences with wine. On other days, even if the sun was shining, Chief Justice John Marshall would order wine anyway, saying, "Our jurisdiction is so vast that it must be raining somewhere."
- Until 1969, there was no copying machine at the Supreme Court. Justices often read blurry eighth-carbon copies of draft decisions. Justice Brennan (1956-1990) never used a word processor and hand-wrote all drafts and opinions. At present, Justice Souter is reportedly the only justice who does not use a word processor for writing his opinions.
- Injuries suffered by Chief Justice Marshall, often referred to as "the man who made the Court Supreme," in a stagecoach crash while riding circuit court were said to have hastened his death.

Technology Tips

www.supremecourtus.gov	The Web site of the United States Supreme Court provides information about the Court, its docket, a schedule of oral arguments, opinions, Court rules, visitor information, and bar admission forms.
http://oyez.nwu.edu	This site allows ordering of "The Supreme Court's Greatest Hits," a multimedia CD-ROM resource providing access to Supreme Court oral arguments, text, and images.
http://findlaw.com	FindLaw, a well-known legal site, provides easy access to federal and state cases as well as a wide variety of other law-related information and links.
http:/www.ll.georgetown.edu	This site of the Georgetown University Law Center law library provides links to federal and state court cases (select "federal" and then "judicial branch" for federal cases and links to home pages for each of the 94 district courts, or select "state, local, and territorial" and then the particular state for state court cases).
http://www.ll.georgetown.edu/Fed-Ct/	This site provides a map of the federal circuits, with links to the circuits for locating cases.
http://lcweb.loc.gov/global/judiciary.html	This site for the United States judicial branch provides access to the United States Constitution, statutes, Supreme Court opinions, opinions of the United States courts of appeal, a map of the United States circuits, and state cases.
http://www.tourolaw.edu	The site of Touro College of Law Center provides access to cases from the federal courts.
http://www.law.cornell.edu/federal/opinions.html	This site provides access to recent decisions of the United States Supreme Court, landmark decisions of the United States Supreme Court, selected United States courts of appeal cases, and selected United States district court cases.
http:/supct.law.cornell.edu/supct	This Web site provides United States Supreme Court rulings (from 1990) (opinions are posted within minutes of their issuance).
(202) 479-3360	Today's Supreme Court decisions
http://thomas.loc.gov	THOMAS (named after Thomas Jefferson) contains the full text of the United States Constitution, and other historical documents.
http://www.uscourts.gov	Federal Judiciary home page including information about the federal court system.
http://www.access.gpo.gov	GPO Access—United States Government Printing Office Site provides access to Supreme Court cases.
http://www.law.cornell.edu/	This Web site provides decisions of the Supreme Court, cases from other federal courts, and state court cases.
http://vls.law.vill.edu/Locator/fedcourt.html	Federal Court Locator, provides federal court opinions from the United States Supreme Court, circuit courts of appeal, and district courts.

Writing Strategies

When selecting cases to discuss and analyze in your writing, examine citations carefully for the signals they will give you about the level of the court that rendered the decision. When viewing a "U.S." citation, immediately think "highest court in the country"; when viewing an "F.2d" or "F.3d" citation, immediately think "intermediate federal appellate courts"; when viewing an "F. Supp." or "F. Supp. 2d" citation, immediately think "trial court — lowest court in the federal system."

While there is nothing wrong with district court cases, you should prefer cases from higher courts over lower courts, everything else being equal.

Examine opinions for clues regarding the strength and viability of a case. If the precedent you rely on was a 9-0 decision, refer to it as a "unanimous decision" or a decision by an "undivided court." Refer to cases relied upon by an adversary, if applicable, as decisions rendered by a "bare majority" or a decision by a "divided court."

If you cannot find cases as recent as you would like, try to enhance the stature of older cases by describing them as "well-established," "well-settled," or "landmark" cases. Select cases from your circuit and remind the reader of this in your writing by stating, "This circuit has held . . . ," or "Since 1967, the law in this circuit has been. . . . "

Discuss *your* argument. Do not shift the focus away from your position to your adversary's by spending all of your time refuting your adversary's contentions.

Assignment for Chapter 2

1. a. Give the name of the case located at 519 U.S. 172 (1997).
   b. Give the holding of the case.
   c. During the period of time covered by the cases in this volume, which United States Supreme Court Justice was assigned or allotted to the Fifth Circuit?
2. a. Locate a case in volume 506 of the *U.S. Reports* in which the plaintiff's name is *Herrera* and give the name of the case.
   b. Who was functioning as the solicitor general of the United States when this case was decided?
3. To which circuits are the following states assigned?
   a. North Carolina
   b. Illinois
   c. Texas
4. a. Give the name of the case located at 197 F.3d 24.
   b. Which judge issued the opinion of the court? Give both first and last name.
5. a. Give the name of the case at 77 F. Supp. 2d 859.
   b. Which of the United States district courts decided this case?
   c. Who represented Levi Mohney?

Chapter 3

Statutory Law

Chapter Overview

In this chapter we will discuss the enactment of federal and state legislation and will focus on the publication and codification of statutes. In order to conduct research efficiently and effectively, you will need a clear understanding of the procedure by which laws are passed and the sets of books in which they are found. Following this, we will focus on research techniques that will enable you to locate statutes.

A. Federal Legislation

1. *Enactment of Federal Statutes*

The chief function of the Congress of the United States is its lawmaking task. Congress is a bicameral (two-chamber) legislature. It is comprised of 100 members of the Senate and 435 members of the House of Representatives ("House").

The framers of the Constitution anticipated that most legislation would originate in the House. This expectation arose from the fact that the House is considered more representative of the country's population and its desires. Every state, without regard to its size, sends two senators to Congress. On the other hand, states that are less populous, such as Montana or Alaska, send far fewer representatives to the House than heavily populated states such as New York or California. While the Senate can introduce most types of legislation, the drafters of the Constitution correctly anticipated that most legislation would commence in the House.

Nevertheless, the Constitution provides that the House of Representatives can originate revenue-raising bills. By tradition, the House also initiates appropriation bills. Legislation can be proposed by anyone, including members of Congress, executive departments of the federal government, private individuals, or lobbyists.

There are several steps in the enactment of legislation (we will assume legislation is originating in the House):

- A bill, which is a proposed law, is introduced by its sponsor in Congress by being handed to the Clerk of the House or by being placed in a box called the "hopper."
- The bill is numbered. If the bill originated in the House, it will be labeled "H.R." Those bills introduced in the Senate are labeled "S."

Examples

(i) H.R. 41 (from the first session of the 101st Congress): "Expressing the sense of the House of Representatives that the Federal excise taxes on gasoline and diesel fuel shall not be increased to reduce the Federal deficit."

(ii) S. 324 (from the first session of the 101st Congress): "To establish a national energy policy to reduce global warming, and for other purposes."

The numbering of the bills is always sequential; that is, "H.R. 41" indicates the forty-first bill introduced in a particular congressional session.

- The bill is now printed in slip form by the Government Printing Office and sent to the appropriate committee. For example, if the bill deals with the military, it will be referred to the House (or Senate) Armed Services Committee. If it involves the judiciary, it will be referred to the House (or Senate) Judiciary Committee. The House has 19 permanent committees, and the Senate has 16. Much of the work involved in enacting federal legislation is done by these committees or by their subcommittees.
- The committee will now place the bill on its calendar. The committee's initial action is usually to request interested agencies of the government to comment upon the proposed legislation. The committee may hold hearings regarding the proposed legislation and interested parties, lobbyists, experts, and consumer advocates may testify either voluntarily or by subpoena. Cabinet officers and high-ranking civil and military officials of the government may also testify.
- After studying the legislation and holding hearings, the committee will take one of three actions: It will report (recommend) the bill without any revisions; it will report the bill with revisions and modifications; or it may "table" the bill, or fail to take any action on it, which effectively kills the bill. The committee will hold a "mark up" session and then issue a written statement, called a report, which explains the purpose of the bill, the intent of the

bill, and why the bill has been approved or modified. Generally, a section-by-section analysis is given.

- After the bill has been returned to the chamber in which it originated, it is placed on the calendar and scheduled for debate on the floor of the House (or Senate, if the bill was introduced in the Senate). While there are certain limits for the duration of debate in the House, debate in the Senate is usually not subject to any limits. The House Rules Committee may call for the bill to be voted on quickly if it is important or urgent.
- Voting occurs after debate, typically by electronic voting device.
- After a bill is passed in the chamber in which it originated, it is sent to the other chamber, which may pass the bill in its then-present form. More likely, however, the bill will be sent to the appropriate committee for analysis. This committee may also approve the measure, modify it, or table it. A report will be issued by the committee explaining the action taken by it.
- After the bill is reported out of the committee, it will be scheduled for debate and voting in the second chamber.
- If the bill is passed and the version agreed to by the second chamber is identical to the one passed by the first chamber, it will be sent to the president for signature.
- If the versions passed by the House and Senate differ, the measure is sent to "conference," the function of which is to reconcile these differing versions and produce compromise legislation acceptable to both chambers. The conference is typically comprised of senior members or "conferees" of the House and Senate committees that studied the bill, although in recent years junior members of the committee have been appointed as well as other members interested in the measure who were not on the committees. This has led to increased conference sizes, such as the 1981 conference on a budget reconciliation bill in which 250 members of Congress, divided into 58 subgroups, participated.
- The conference may continue for weeks or months as the conferees struggle to harmonize the conflicting versions of the bill. After agreement is finally reached, the conferees will prepare a report setting forth their conclusions and recommendations. This compromise measure must again be voted on by both the House and Senate.
- When the reconciled bill has been passed by both the House and Senate, it is printed by the Government Printing Office in a process called "enrollment" and is then certified as correct and signed by the Speaker of the House and then the vice president.
- The bill is now sent to the president for signature. If the president approves the bill, he will sign it, date it, and usually write the word "approved" on the bill, which has now been printed on parchment. Once the president has signed the bill, it is referred to as a "law" or a "statute" rather than a "bill." If the president fails to take action within ten days, excluding Sundays, while Congress is in session (January 3 until mid-summer), the bill will become

law without his signature. If Congress adjourns before this ten-day period and the president fails to sign the bill, it will die. This is often referred to as the "pocket veto."
- If the president vetoes, or rejects, the bill by refusing to sign it, Congress may override this veto and enact the measure if both the House and Senate vote to approve it by a two-thirds majority. Failure to secure this two-thirds vote will result in the president's veto being upheld.
- When the bill is signed, it is assigned a number in sequential order. For example, Pub. L. 106-120 would indicate the 120th public law enacted during the One Hundred Sixth Congress.
- A bill that is not enacted in a particular Congress does not carry over to the next Congress; it must be re-proposed in a following Congress if legislation is desired. For example, the Brady Bill, dealing with the sale of firearms, was introduced in several Congresses before finally being enacted into law.

See Figure 3-1 for a diagram showing how a bill becomes a law.

2. *Classification of Federal Statutes*

After the bill is enacted into law by the president signing it or by act of the United States Congress in overriding a presidential veto by a two-thirds vote of each chamber of Congress, it is sent to the Archivist of the United States, who will classify each law as public or private and will direct its publication.

Public laws are those that affect the public generally, such as tax laws, laws relating to federal lands, laws relating to bankruptcy, and the like.

Private laws are those that affect only one person or entity or a small group of persons, granting them some special benefit not afforded to the public at large. The most common private laws are those dealing with immigration or naturalization; for instance, those allowing an individual or a family to enter the United States even though the immigration quota of that country has been met. Other private laws might deal with forgiveness of a debt owed to the United States or allowance of a claim against the United States government that would ordinarily be barred due to sovereign immunity (the principle that government entities are not subject to or are "immune" from certain types of claims). See Figure 3-2 for examples of private legislation.

Laws can also be classified as permanent or temporary. *Permanent laws* remain in effect until they are expressly repealed, while *temporary laws* have limiting language in the statute itself, such as the following: "This law shall have no force or effect after January 1, 2000."

As you might expect, the vast majority of laws are permanent, as it would be extraordinarily inefficient for lawmakers to pass legislation that continually expires. Nevertheless, there are situations in which tempo-

Figure 3-1
How a Bill Becomes Law

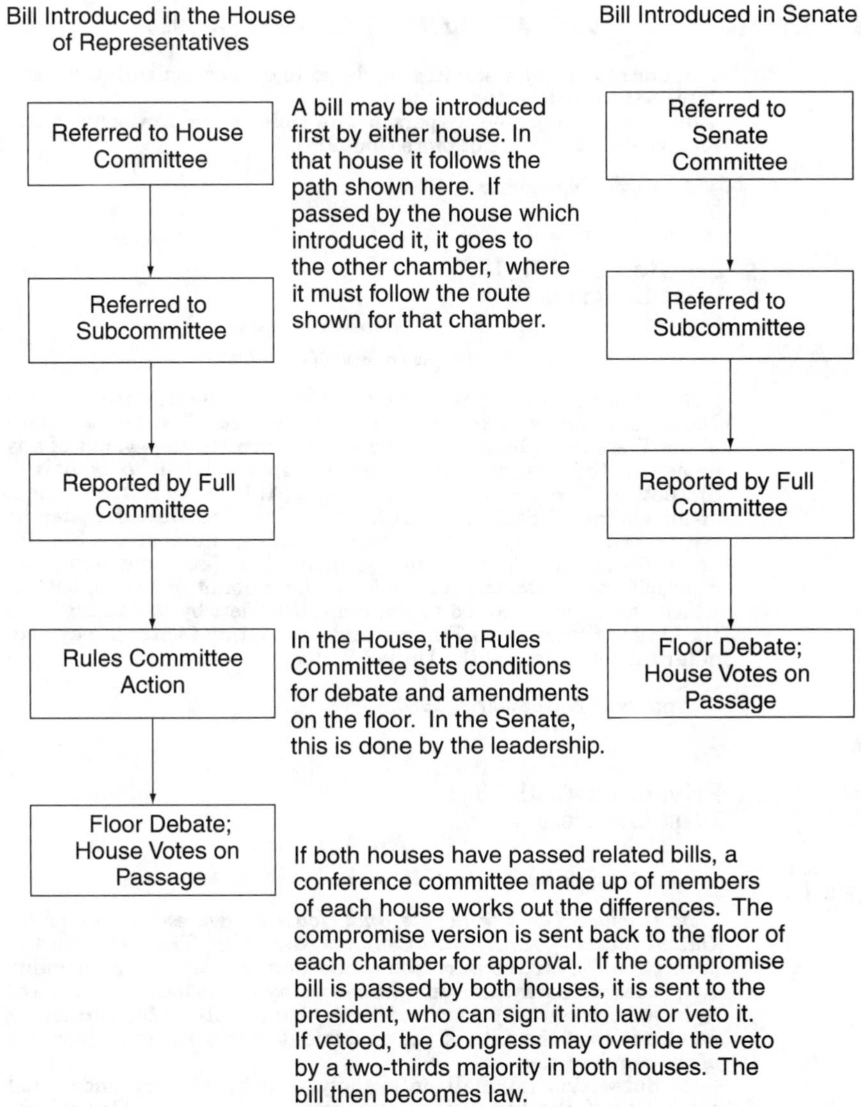

Bill Introduced in the House of Representatives

Referred to House Committee

↓

Referred to Subcommittee

↓

Reported by Full Committee

↓

Rules Committee Action

↓

Floor Debate; House Votes on Passage

A bill may be introduced first by either house. In that house it follows the path shown here. If passed by the house which introduced it, it goes to the other chamber, where it must follow the route shown for that chamber.

Bill Introduced in Senate

Referred to Senate Committee

↓

Referred to Subcommittee

↓

Reported by Full Committee

↓

Floor Debate; House Votes on Passage

In the House, the Rules Committee sets conditions for debate and amendments on the floor. In the Senate, this is done by the leadership.

If both houses have passed related bills, a conference committee made up of members of each house works out the differences. The compromise version is sent back to the floor of each chamber for approval. If the compromise bill is passed by both houses, it is sent to the president, who can sign it into law or veto it. If vetoed, the Congress may override the veto by a two-thirds majority in both houses. The bill then becomes law.

Figure 3-2
Private Laws

agent or attorney for services rendered in connection with the claim described in such section.

(b) ENFORCEMENT.—Any person who violates the provisions of this section shall be fined not more than $1,000.

Approved November 6, 1990.

Private Law 101-12
101st Congress

An Act

Nov. 8, 1990
[H.R. 3791]

For the relief of Beulah C. Shifflett.

Be it enacted by the Senate and House of Representatives of the United States of America in Congress assembled, That the Secretary of the Treasury is hereby authorized and directed to pay, out of any money in the Treasury not otherwise appropriated, to Beulah C. Shifflett of Albermarle County, Virginia, $811.20, in full settlement of all claims of Beulah C. Shifflett against the United States by reason of non-receipt of two Treasury checks numbered 5,254,109, dated September 27, 1963, in the amount of $800; and numbered 5,254,568, dated October 11, 1963, in the amount of $11.20, both of which checks were issued to Beulah C. Shifflett by the authority of the United States Army Finance and Accounting Center in payment of lawful obligations of the United States.

Approved November 8, 1990.

Private Law 101-13
101st Congress

An Act

Nov. 15, 1990
[H.R. 1230]

For the relief of Jocelyne Carayannis and Marie Carayannis.

Be it enacted by the Senate and House of Representatives of the United States of America in Congress assembled, That (a) subject to subsection (b), for the purposes of the Immigration and Nationality Act, Jocelyne Carayannis and Marie Carayannis shall be considered to have been lawfully admitted to the United States for permanent residence as of the date of the enactment of this Act upon payment of the required visa fee.

(b) Subsection (a) shall only apply to a beneficiary under that subsection if the beneficiary applies to the Attorney General for permanent residence status under that subsection within two years after the date of the enactment of this Act.

(c) Upon the granting of permanent residence to a beneficiary under subsection (a), the Secretary of State shall instruct the proper officer to deduct one number from the total number of immigrant visas which are made available to natives of the country of the beneficiary's birth under section 203(a) of the Immigration and Nationality Act or, if section 202(e) of that Act is applicable to the country, from the total number of immigrant visas which are made available to natives of such country under that section.

Approved November 15, 1990.

rary legislation is enacted. For example, in the mid-1970s, to address a critical shortage in oil and to conserve gasoline, the United States Congress enacted legislation reducing the speed limit on federal highways from 65 to 55 miles per hour. The original statute provided it would expire in one year. Near the end of that year period, after Congress heard testimony relating to decreased fuel consumption and decreased mortality rates attributed to this reduction in speed, it extended and made permanent the original temporary legislation.

3. *Publication of Federal Statutes*

a. *United States Statutes at Large*

As each law is passed, it is published by the United States Government Printing Office as a looseleaf unbound pamphlet or sheet of paper (or several sheets, depending upon the length of the law), referred to as a "slip." At the end of each congressional session, these slips are taken together and are placed in chronological order in a hardback set of volumes called *United States Statutes at Large*. Keep in mind that a session is one year and that there are two sessions for each Congress because a new Congress comes into existence every two years upon the election of the members of the House of Representatives. All of our federal laws since 1789 are contained in more than 110 volumes of *United States Statutes at Large*.

Because it can take as long as a year after the end of a congressional session for the applicable volume of *United States Statutes at Large* to arrive at a law library, you should know there are several alternate sources available that will provide you with the exact wording of a federal statute. In this regard, you should never rely on a summary or synopsis of any legislation. You must obtain and analyze the exact wording of the statute in order to ensure that your research is correct because a mere summary, in a news publication or otherwise, cannot convey the explicit nature of statutory language.

To obtain the exact wording of a federal statute without waiting as long as one year for the hardback bound volumes of *United States Statutes at Large* to become available, consult the following:

(1) Slip Laws

The slips themselves are available in certain libraries throughout the United States. More than 1,300 libraries scattered throughout the nation (including law libraries) have been designated as United States Government Depository Libraries, which will receive certain selected government materials, notably slip laws. In a large city there may be as many as four or five depository libraries. Often these depositories are large law school libraries or the libraries in courthouses in a county seat. To find out if a library is a depository library, simply call the reference librarian at a few of the libraries in your area (both law school libraries and at the largest courthouse in your region). The reference librarian will inform you if the library has been designated as a government depository. If so, any member of the public will have access to the depository materials, including the slip laws. These slips may be available as early as five to seven days after the law is enacted. Alternatively, to locate federal depository libraries, access http://www.access.gpo.gov/su_docs/locators/findlibs/index.html.

(2) United States Code Congressional and Administrative News Service *("USCCAN")*

This publication is issued monthly by West, which prints in a soft-cover or pamphlet form the complete text of all of the public laws passed during the previous month as well as newly enacted federal regulations, executive orders, and presidential proclamations. A law firm or law library subscribes to this publication in much the same way an individual might subscribe to *Time Magazine*, *Sports Illustrated*, or *Gourmet*, although the cost is substantially higher—for example, approximately $170 per year for 12 issues of USCCAN, as opposed to approximately $40 per year for 12 issues of *Gourmet*. At the end of each congressional session, the pamphlets comprising USCCAN are published in hardback volumes.

(3) United States Law Week

This weekly publication is a product of the Bureau of National Affairs, which prints the complete text of the more significant public laws enacted during the previous week (as well as summaries of recent cases decided). While *United States Law Week* will thus give you more rapid access than USCCAN (because *United States Law Week* is weekly and USCCAN is published only monthly), *United States Law Week* does not provide you with *all* of the public laws passed during the week preceding its publication but only those the publisher deems most important. Similar to USCCAN subscriptions, law firms and law libraries will subscribe to *United States Law Week* much the same way individuals arrange to receive publications they may be interested in (once again, however, the cost may be significantly higher—the current subscription rate for *United States Law Week* is approximately $600 per year).

(4) Government Printing Office

Slip laws can be purchased from the United States Government Printing Office. Call (202) 512-0000 for information or (202) 783-3238 to place an order.

(5) U.S.C.S. Advance *Pamphlets*

A monthly pamphlet issued by the publisher of U.S.C.S. and called *U.S.C.S. Advance* publishes the text of newly enacted public laws passed during the previous month. Summaries of proposed legislation are also given, together with tables that pinpoint the sections of the United States Code that have been affected by recent legislation or regulatory action.

(6) Congressional Representatives

You should also consider contacting the sponsor of the legislation or your congressional representative(s) to ask for the complete text of a recently enacted law. Most representatives have local telephone numbers, which can be found in your telephone book or local newspaper, and most of them have assistants or "staffers" who are very helpful and skillful in locating the information you need and sending it to you at no cost. All congressional representatives and their staffers have immediate access to Congressional Research Services, a division of the Library of Congress, the primary function of which is to provide research and reference assistance to the United States Congress. If your first request for information is not successful, call again. Often the information you request will be provided to you within a matter of days.

(7) The Internet

Rapid access to federal statutes can also be found on the Internet. One of the best sites for legislative information is "THOMAS—Legislation Information on the Internet," a site provided by the federal government that offers the text of proposed and enacted legislation, committee information, calendars for hearings scheduled, and House and Senate Directories. Access http://thomas.loc. gov. Research using the Internet will be fully discussed in Chapter 12.

As discussed above, at the end of each congressional session, the slip laws are compiled chronologically into the bound set of volumes called *United States Statutes at Large*. *United States Statutes at Large* contains both public and private laws, although private laws are typically found in a much smaller section near the end of each volume.

While *United States Statutes at Large* offers a wonderful historical overview of the order in which the United States Congress has enacted laws for the previous 200 years, it suffers from glaring deficiencies from a legal researcher's point of view:

- The arrangement of *United States Statutes at Large* is chronological rather than by subject or topic. Thus, if you were asked to find all of the federal laws relating to trademarks, you might find them scattered over more than 110 volumes rather than being contained in volumes devoted solely to the topic of trademarks.
- Subsequent amendments to or even a repeal of a previously passed law will not appear together with that law but will appear in the volumes relating to the session in which those amendments or repeals were enacted. That is, if a law enacted in 1970 was amended in 1980 and repealed in 1990, you would need to look at

three separate volumes of *United States Statutes at Large*—those for 1970, 1980, and 1990—to obtain the complete history and current status of this legislation.

- There is no one comprehensive index to *United States Statutes at Large*. Even though each volume of *United States Statutes at Large* contains an index and a table of contents, there is no one index to tell you which specific volumes to examine if you were charged with the responsibility of locating all of the federal laws relating to copyrights, for example. Rather, you would be forced to pick up each volume of the set and examine its index to determine if any laws relating to copyrights were contained in that volume.

b. *United States Code*

Because the organization of *United States Statutes at Large* makes research using the set so difficult, it became readily apparent that a set of books should be developed to eliminate these barriers to efficient research. The process of developing a set of books that compiles the currently valid laws on the same subject together with any amendments to those laws is referred to as "codification."

The first codification of *United States Statutes at Large* occurred in the mid-1870s. A second codification or edition followed a few years thereafter but the set or "code" in current use originates from 1925, when Congress authorized preparation of the *United States Code* (U.S.C.).

All of the statutes enacted into law and contained in *United States Statutes at Large* were analyzed and categorized by subject matter so that at the completion of this project there were 50 categories or "titles" of federal statutes. For instance, Title 7 contains statutes dealing with agriculture; Title 25 contains statutes dealing with Indians; Title 38 contains statutes dealing with veterans benefits; and Title 50 contains statutes dealing with war and national defense. The 50 titles are further divided into chapters and sections. A citation to any statute in the *United States Code* indicates the number of the title, the name of the set, the section number, and the year of the code, as follows:

42	U.S.C.	§	1396	(1983)
Title	*Set*	*Abbr. for section*	*Section no.*	*Year of code*

It is not important to know what subject each of the 50 titles refers to. It is sufficient to understand that there are, in fact, 50 groups of statutes or titles, that they are arranged alphabetically, and that these 50 titles are permanently established, meaning that any federal statute relating to agriculture will always be found in Title 7, that any federal statute dealing with Indians will always be found in Title 25, and so on. See Figure 3-3 for a listing of the 50 titles of the *United States Code*.

The *United States Code* is "official," a term whose sole meaning is that publication of the set is directed by a statute. The actual printing of the set is done either by the government itself or at its express instruction.

Figure 3-3
Titles of *United States Code* from *United States Code Annotated*

1. **General Provisions.**
2. **The Congress.**
3. **The President.**
4. **Flag and Seal, Seat of Government, and the States.**
5. **Government Organization and Employees.**
6. **Surety Bonds.**
7. **Agriculture.**
8. **Aliens and Nationality.**
9. **Arbitration.**
10. **Armed Forces.**
11. **Bankruptcy.**
12. **Banks and Banking.**
13. **Census.**
14. **Coast Guard.**
15. **Commerce and Trade.**
16. **Conservation.**
17. **Copyrights.**
18. **Crimes and Criminal Procedure.**
19. **Customs Duties.**
20. **Education.**
21. **Food and Drugs.**
22. **Foreign Relations and Intercourse.**
23. **Highways.**
24. **Hospitals and Asylums.**
25. **Indians.**
26. **Internal Revenue Code.**
27. **Intoxicating Liquors.**
28. **Judiciary and Judicial Procedure.**
29. **Labor.**
30. **Mineral Lands and Mining.**
31. **Money and Finance.**
32. **National Guard.**
33. **Navigation and Navigable Waters.**
34. **Navy *(See Title 10, Armed Forces).***
35. **Patents.**
36. **Patriotic Societies and Observances.**
37. **Pay and Allowances of the Uniformed Services.**
38. **Veterans' Benefits.**
39. **Postal Service.**
40. **Public Buildings, Property, and Works.**
41. **Public Contracts.**
42. **The Public Health and Welfare.**
43. **Public Lands.**
44. **Public Printing and Documents.**
45. **Railroads.**
46. **Shipping.**
47. **Telegraphs, Telephones, and Radiotelegraphs.**
48. **Territories and Insular Possessions.**
49. **Transportation.**
50. **War and National Defense.**

II

The *United States Code* is revised and a new edition published by the United States Government Printing Office every six years. During this six-year period, statutes may be amended or even repealed. Changes to federal statutes during the course of the six years are reflected in hardbound supplements placed on the shelf after Title 50.

c. Annotated Versions of the *United States Code*

While the *United States Code* is an efficiently organized set in that all federal statutes relating to bankruptcy have been brought together, all federal statutes relating to crimes have been brought together, and so forth, researchers typically want something more than a mere recitation of a statute. If you will remember the point made in Chapter 1, that under the concept of stare decisis, it is not the naked statutory language that controls but a court's interpretation of that statute (particularly in instances in which the statute is vague or ambiguous), you can readily see why the *United States Code*, while organized in an easy-to-understand scheme, is still unsatisfactory to researchers. That is because researchers prefer to read a statute and immediately be directed to cases that have construed or interpreted that statute.

Because the *United States Code* simply recites the exact text of a federal statute and immediately thereafter recites the exact text of the next federal statute without providing any comment regarding the law or any reference to any cases that may have interpreted that law, two private publishers, West and the former Lawyers Cooperative Publishing (now LEXIS Publishing), separately assumed the task of providing this necessary information to those in the legal profession. Because the publication of these two sets is not directed by statute, these publications are referred to as "unofficial." Both of these sets are referred to as "annotated" codes, meaning they contain "notes" referring readers to cases interpreting statutes.

(1) United States Code Annotated

West publishes an annotated version of the *United States Code* titled *United States Code Annotated*, universally referred to as "U.S.C.A." The word "annotated" means "with notes," and one of the most useful features of U.S.C.A. is the notes provided to researchers who use U.S.C.A.

U.S.C.A. is a set of approximately 200 volumes, all of which are relatively small in size for law books (approximately 5½″ × 9½″) and all of which are a deep maroon color. U.S.C.A. is divided into the very same groupings or 50 "titles" as the *United States Code* and contains the exact wording of the federal statutes contained in the *United States Code*. There is a multi-volume general index to U.S.C.A.

The front of each volume of U.S.C.A. contains a list of the 50 titles of the *United States Code*. Therefore, you need not memorize which statutes are contained within each title because you can readily determine this information.

You may have observed that there are only 50 titles to the *United States Code* (and U.S.C.A.), and yet U.S.C.A. comprises approximately 200 volumes. This arrangement arises out of the fact that some titles, such as Bankruptcy, contain numerous statutes and "spill over" into more than one volume, while other titles, such as Coast Guard, have far fewer statutes and can be contained in less than one volume. Thus, six volumes of U.S.C.A. are devoted to bankruptcy statutes while less than one volume is devoted to Coast Guard statutes.

U.S.C.A. is not valuable because it provides the exact text of federal statutes—the *United States Code* provides that as well. U.S.C.A. is valuable because of the "extra" features provided to researchers. Those are displayed in Figure 3-4 and are as follows:

(a) Historical Notes

Following the statute you will find an overview of the history of a particular statute, including the Public Law Number, the effective date of the statute, its citation to *United States Statutes at Large*, an indication of the date certain parts or subsections of the statute were added or deleted, and a basic summary of the evolution of this particular federal law.

(b) Cross References

Following the historical notes you will be sent to other federal statutes that may be of assistance in helping you understand this federal statute.

(c) Library References

In its section called "Library References," U.S.C.A. directs you to other sources in the law library, including form books, jury instructions, encyclopedias, and law review articles that also deal with the topic covered by the statute.

(d) Westlaw Electronic Research

U.S.C.A. will provide you with guidance in developing search queries so you can conduct further research relating to the statute on WESTLAW, West's computerized legal research system (see Chapter 11).

(e) *Code of Federal Regulations*

Following the library references you may be directed to sections of the *Code of Federal Regulations* (see Chapter 10) that relate to this statute.

(f) Notes of Decisions

These notes or "annotations" are the most valuable part of U.S.C.A., for it is these notes that will direct you to cases that have interpreted the statute you have just read.

If a case has discussed, interpreted, or construed the statute you are reviewing, U.S.C.A. will provide you with a citation to that case. Moreover,

Figure 3-4
Sample Pages from U.S.C.A.

Maine Corp., D.C.Mass.1970, 317 F.Supp. 1249.

On petition in reorganization proceedings for abandonment of a portion of railroad, court must not only consider financial advantages or disadvantages of abandonment to railroad debtor's estate but must also pass on question of public interest. In re Denver & R. G. W. R. Co., D.C.Colo.1940, 32 F.Supp. 244.

7. Admissibility of evidence

In proceeding on petition by trustees of bankrupt railroad in reorganization for authorization to abandon line, evidence regarding effect of proposed abandonment on public interest was relevant and thus admissible. In re Boston & Maine Corp., C.A.Mass.1972, 455 F.2d 1205.

8. Remand

Remand was required, with regard to federal district court's order authorizing trustees of bankrupt railroad in reorganization to proceed with abandonment of railroad line between two cities, in view of resumption of production at mill in one of cities and potential use of railroad by mill and in view of court's refusal to receive evidence regarding effect of proposed abandonment on public interest. In re Boston & Maine Corp., C.A. Mass.1972, 455 F.2d 1205.

§ 1171. Priority claims

(a) There shall be paid as an administrative expense any claim of an individual or of the personal representative of a deceased individual against the debtor or the estate, for personal injury to or death of such individual arising out of the operation of the debtor or the estate, whether such claim arose before or after the commencement of the case.

(b) Any unsecured claim against the debtor that would have been entitled to priority if a receiver in equity of the property of the debtor had been appointed by a Federal court on the date of the order for relief under this title shall be entitled to such priority in the case under this chapter.

Pub.L. 95–598, Nov. 6, 1978, 92 Stat. 2643.

Historical and Revision Notes

Notes of Committee on the Judiciary, House Report No. 95–595. This section is derived from current law. Subsection (a) grants an administrative expense priority to the claim of any individual (or of the personal representative of a deceased individual) against the debtor or the estate for personal injury to or death of the individual arising out of the operation of the debtor railroad or the estate, whether the claim arose before or after commencement of the case. The priority under current law, found in section 77(n) [former section 205(n) of this title], applies only to employees of the debtor. This subsection expands the protection provided.

Subsection (b) follows present section 77(b) of the Bankruptcy Act [former section 205(b) of this title] by giving priority to any unsecured claims that would be entitled to priority if a receiver in equity of the property of the debtor had been appointed by a Federal court on the date of the order for relief under the bankruptcy laws. As under current law, the courts will determine the precise contours of the priority recognized by this subsection in each case.

Legislative Statements. Section 1171 of the House amendment is derived from section 1170 of the House bill in lieu of section 1173(a)(9) of the Senate amendment.

Cross References

Allowance of administrative expenses, see section 503 of this title.
Priorities, see section 507 of this title.

Figure 3-4 (*Continued*)

Library References

Bankruptcy ⟹824. C.J.S. Bankruptcy § 1077.

Notes of Decisions

---

1. Construction

Former section 205(n) of this title which required that claims for personal injuries to railroad employees be preferred and paid out of assets as operating expenses was a "remedial statute" and should have been liberally interpreted. Powell v. Link, C.C.A.Va.1940, 114 F. 2d 550. See, also, American Surety Co. of New York v. Wabash Ry. Co., C.C.A.Mo. 1939, 107 F.2d 685.

Former section 205(n) of this title was a remedial statute and should have been construed in harmony with its purpose and the obvious intent of Congress which was to be gathered from the entire context. Bankers Trust Co. v. Florida East Coast Ry. Co., D.C.Fla.1940, 31 F.Supp. 961.

2. Purpose

The purpose of former section 205 of this title which provided that, in proceedings for reorganization of railroads engaged in interstate commerce and in equity receiverships of railroad corporations, claims of employees for personal injuries would be preferred as operating expenses, was to secure relief for injured employees of railroads which had gone into bankruptcy or receivership after injury and before satisfaction of claim therefor against railroad. Reconstruction Finance Corporation v. Missouri-Kansas-Texas R. Co., C.C.A.Ark.1941, 122 F.2d 326. See, also, American Surety Co. of New York v. Wabash Ry. Co., C.C.A.Mo. 1939, 107 F.2d 685.

3. Due process

Former section 205(n) of this title which gave preference in equity receivership of railroad to claims for injuries to railroad employees as against assets of railroad, as operating expenses, did not deny due process of mortgagees, since claim for injury was a "necessary expense of operation," and mortgagees impliedly consented to use of earnings in paying such expenses. Chase Nat. Bank of City of New York v. Mobile & O. R. Co., D.C.Ala.1939, 30 F.Supp. 565.

4. Power of Congress

Congress had power to require that claims by railroad employees for personal injuries be preferred in equity receiverships of railroad corporations in federal courts, and paid out of assets as operating expenses. Carpenter v. Wabash Ry. Co., Mo.1940, 60 S.Ct. 416, 309 U.S. 23, 84 L.Ed. 558, 42 Am.Bankr.Rep.N.S. 1, rehearing denied 60 S.Ct. 585, 309 U.S. 695, 84 L.Ed. 1035.

Congress had power to make claims of injured railway employees prior to existing lien obligations of railway company in equity receiverships of railroad companies in federal courts, including the mortgages constituting liens upon the properties of the railway company and the receivers' certificates issued under previous decrees of district court which provided that such certificates should be secured by a paramount lien upon all the fixed properties of the railway company and also upon all its surplus earnings and income not used in maintenance and operation of its properties. Powell v. Link, C.C.A.Va.1940, 114 F.2d 550.

Generally, it is for Congress to say what items of expense connected with or growing out of operation of a railroad

West has realized that a case citation standing alone might not be particularly helpful to a researcher. Therefore, you will not only be given the case citation but also a brief description of the case so you do not waste time pulling endless cases off the library shelves but instead can make an informed decision as to which cases to review based upon the quick summary or "annotation." Although West's goal is to serve as a comprehensive tool for researchers, U.S.C.A. will not send you to every case that may interpret or mention a statute. Nevertheless, you will be sent to a sufficient cross-section of cases so you can embark upon your research tasks.

Because some statutes have been interpreted in hundreds of ways on hundreds of occasions, U.S.C.A. does not merely give you a long list of annotations but organizes or indexes these annotations for you under numbered catchlines. For instance, if you have read a statute and want to read cases that interpret the statute generally, you may be directed to read the annotations listed under the catchline called "Note 1." Note 1 will then give you quick summaries of several cases that discuss this statute in a general fashion. The annotations are arranged alphabetically under numbered notes so you can readily locate court decisions on any section or portion of the statute you are researching. For example, suppose you are researching 42 U.S.C.A. § 1395(y) (West 1983), relating to exclusions from health insurance coverage. The annotations are arranged as follows:

Notes of Decisions

Generally 3
Ability of spouse to care for patient 5
Construction 1
Custodial or supportive care 6
Estoppel 13
Evidence 12
Hearing 10
Jurisdiction 9
Necessity of services 4
Notice and hearing 10
Personal comfort items 7
Pleadings 11
Purpose 2
Reasonableness and necessity of services 4
Remand 15
Review 14
Supportive care 6
Suspensions 8

Thus, if you are interested in the reasonableness and necessity of services, you would review the annotations listed under Note 4. You must then read the cases to which you are directed. While the brief digests or summaries are extremely well done, they cannot convey the subtle nuances of a case and are never a substitute for full analysis of a case. It is possible there may be no annotations following a statute, which would indicate that the statute has not been the subject of litigation and thus has not been interpreted or construed by any cases. See Figure 3-5 for a sample page of U.S.C.A. annotations.

Finally, U.S.C.A. not only contains a multi-volume general index at the end of the set, but each title is separately indexed and each volume in the set is kept current by an annual cumulative pocket part or by separate softcover supplements, the importance of which will be discussed below.

(2) United States Code Service

LEXIS Publishing also publishes an annotated version of the *United States Code* entitled *United States Code Service Lawyers Edition* and referred to as "U.S.C.S." Similar in arrangement to U.S.C.A., U.S.C.S. is a set of approximately 150 volumes, which conform in size to most law books in that they are approximately 7″ × 10″. The volumes comprising U.S.C.S. are black and have aqua-colored bands that are displayed on the spines

Figure 3-5
U.S.C.A. Annotations

Ch. 11 REORGANIZATION 11 § 1174

Library References

Bankruptcy ⚷851. C.J.S. Bankruptcy § 1085.

Notes of Decisions

Construction with other laws 1
Futility of reorganization 2
Limitations on court 3

1. Construction with other laws

Court was without jurisdiction to consider and approve equitable liquidation of estate of railroad in reorganization, since an adequate remedy at law was available through the Regional Rail Reorganization Act of 1973, section 701 et seq. of Title 45. In re Erie Lackawanna Railway Co., D.C.Ohio 1975, 393 F.Supp. 352.

Regional Rail Reorganization Act of 1973, section 701 et seq. of Title 45, does not provide a process of reorganization which is fair and equitable to the estate of a railroad undergoing reorganization pursuant to this title in that it precludes a form of liquidation under this title. In re Lehigh & H. R. Ry. Co., D.C.N.Y.1974, 377 F.Supp. 475.

2. Futility of reorganization

Liquidation of railroad undergoing reorganization should be considered only as last resort. In re Reading Co., D.C. Pa.1973, 361 F.Supp. 1351.

Liquidation of bankrupt railroad is not called for until futility of every reasonable effort to put railroad into sound financial condition becomes apparent. Id.

3. Limitations on court

In exercising its statutory power to convert capital assets of debtor to cash, railroad reorganization court must act within bounds of U.S.C.A.Const. Amend. 5 and may not by selling assets authorize unconstitutional taking of property of mortgage bondholders. In re Penn Central Transp. Co., C.A.Pa.1974, 494 F.2d 270, certiorari denied 95 S.Ct. 147, 419 U.S. 883, 42 L.Ed.2d 122.

of the book. Like U.S.C.A., this set also contains a multi-volume general index. U.S.C.S. is divided into the same 50 titles as U.S.C. and U.S.C.A. and contains the identical wording of the federal statutes published in *United States Statutes at Large.*

While U.S.C.A. contains approximately 200 volumes and U.S.C.S. contains approximately 150 volumes, you should not make the assumption that U.S.C.A. is nearly twice as valuable as U.S.C.S. or that U.S.C.A. gives you almost twice the information U.S.C.S. provides. Rather, the individual volumes in U.S.C.S. are quite large compared to the smaller size volumes used for U.S.C.A., and therefore, while the number of books in each set differs, the material contained within the books is substantially similar.

Like U.S.C.A., U.S.C.S. is "unofficial," meaning that it is published by a private publishing company without any statutory direction or mandate. Just as provided by U.S.C.A., U.S.C.S. contains the text of the federal statutes. If you are curious why these various sets (U.S.C., U.S.C.A., and U.S.C.S.) are all available, all of which provide the wording of the federal statutes, you should note a simple analogy to automobiles. All automobiles provide the same service: transportation. Yet consumers develop distinct preferences for Chevrolets, Fords, or Toyotas and may select one make of automobile over another based on habit, perceived differences, or various options available.

Similarly, all of the codifications mentioned herein (U.S.C., U.S.C.A., and U.S.C.S.) provide the same coverage: federal statutes. Yet consumers, namely law firms and law libraries, may choose to purchase one set over another based on various perceived advantages or options available.

Among the features provided by U.S.C.S. are the following:

(a) History; Ancillary Laws and Directives

Immediately following the text of the federal statute you will be provided with information relating to the effective date of the statute and amendments and revisions made to the statute. A citation to *United States Statutes at Large* is provided. This feature of U.S.C.S. is virtually identical to that feature of U.S.C.A. titled "Historical Notes," as both features show the evolution and development of the statute.

(b) *Code of Federal Regulations*

U.S.C.S. may direct you to sections of the *Code of Federal Regulations* that relate to this statute.

(c) Cross References

U.S.C.S. will direct you to other federal statutes that will assist in your interpretation of the statute in question as well as other sources, often other LEXIS Publishing sources, and the legal encyclopedia Am. Jur. 2d.

(d) Research Guide

U.S.C.S. will direct you to other sources in the library (books, encyclopedias, annotations, law review articles, for example) that may be helpful in construing and interpreting this statute. This feature of U.S.C.S. is equivalent to the feature of U.S.C.A. titled "Library References," although it is somewhat broader in scope than the Library References given by U.S.C.A. in that you are directed to numerous other sources, including a wider variety of law review articles.

(e) Interpretive Notes and Decisions

These notes or annotations are the most important of the features offered by U.S.C.S. Functioning identically to the annotations found in U.S.C.A., these notes will direct you to cases that have interpreted or discussed the statute being researched. Just as given by U.S.C.A., U.S.C.S. will provide you not only the citations to cases that have construed this statute but a short digest or summary of the cases to enable you to research more efficiently by selecting only those cases that appear promising. Just as seen in U.S.C.A., U.S.C.S. will organize the annotations for you by numbering them so that all of the cases discussing one part of the statute are brought together, all of the cases discussing another part of the statute are brought together, and so on. See Figure 3-6 for sample pages from U.S.C.S.

As you can see, the unofficial sets, U.S.C.A. and U.S.C.S., are substantially similar: Both provide the exact wording of the public federal statutes; both provide information relating to the history of the statute; both direct you to other sources in the library to enhance your understanding of the statute; and both provide you with citations and summaries or "annotations" of cases interpreting the statute.

Beyond this, both sets share additional features in common:

- The front of each volume of U.S.C.A. and U.S.C.S. contains a listing of the 50 titles of the *United States Code*;
- The citations to U.S.C.A. and U.S.C.S. are identical in form. For instance, if a statute is found at Title 42, Section 1352, it will be cited: 42 U.S.C.A. § 1352 (West 1983), 42 U.S.C.S. § 1352 (Law. Co-op. 1983), and 42 U.S.C. § 1352 (1983). Thus, once a law is categorized within one of the 50 titles of the United States Code and assigned a section number, it will retain this title and section number for U.S.C.A. and U.S.C.S.;
- Both U.S.C.A. and U.S.C.S. have conversion tables that allow you to locate a federal statute if the only information you have is the public law number or the *U.S. Statutes at Large* citation. You can convert these citations into a citation to U.S.C.A. or U.S.C.S. For example, if you know a statute is 108 Stat. 381, tables in the last volumes of U.S.C.A. and U.S.C.S. located after the volumes for Title 50 will convert this citation to 20 U.S.C. § 1085 so you can readily locate the statute; and

Figure 3-6
Sample Pages from U.S.C.S.

§ 288. Action for infringement of a patent containing an invalid claim

Whenever, without deceptive intention, a claim of a patent is invalid, an action may be maintained for the infringement of a claim of the patent which may be valid. The patentee shall recover no costs unless a disclaimer of the invalid claim has been entered at the Patent and Trademark Office before the commencement of the suit.

(July 19, 1952, ch 950, § 1, 66 Stat. 813; Jan. 2, 1975, P. L. 93-596, § 1, 88 Stat. 1949.)

HISTORY; ANCILLARY LAWS AND DIRECTIVES

Prior law and revision:

This section is based on 35 USC, 1946 ed., § 71 (R. S. § 4922).

The necessity for a disclaimer to recover on valid claims is eliminated. See 35 USCS § 253.

Language is changed.

Amendments:

1975. Act Jan. 2, 1975 (effective 1/2/75, as provided by § 4 of such Act), substituted "Patent and Trademark Office" for "Patent Office".

CROSS REFERENCES

Court of Appeals jurisdiction of appeals from judgments in civil actions for patent infringement which are final except for accounting, 28 USCS § 1292(a)(4).

Venue of civil action for patent infringement, 28 USCS § 1400(b).

Action by owner against United States in Court of Claims where invention described in and covered by patent is used or manufactured by or for United States without license of owner, 28 USCS § 1498(a).

Disclaimer, 35 USCS § 253.

RESEARCH GUIDE

Am Jur:

1 Am Jur 2d, Abatement, Survival, and Revival § 101.

20 Am Jur 2d, Costs § 63.

60 Am Jur 2d, Patents § 486.

Figure 3-6 (*Continued*)

Forms:

14 Am Jur Legal Forms 2d, Patents §§ 196:264–196:267.

Annotations:

Propriety of reference under Federal Civil Procedure Rule 53(b). 1 L Ed 2d 1796.

Right to jury trial in patent infringement action in federal court. 18 ALR Fed 690.

Modern status of federal rules of res judicata in patent litigation. 4 ALR Fed 181.

Res judicata effect of federal consent decree in patent cases. 4 ALR Fed 214.

Texts:

3 Deller, Patent Claims (2d ed) § 561.

4 Deller's Walker on Patents (2d ed) §§ 271, 278, 279, 282, 284, 287, 288.

Law Review Articles:

Zarley, Jury Trials in Patent Litigation. 20 Drake L Rev 243.

Newitt & Nelson, The Patent Lawyer and Trial by Jury. 1 John Marshall J of Practice & Procedure 59.

INTERPRETIVE NOTES AND DECISIONS

1. Generally
2. Action on valid claims
3. Deceptive intent
4. Disclaimer of invalid claims
5. Costs recovery

1. Generally

These provisions have no application where entire patent was void. Williams Calk Co. v Kemmerer (1906, CA3 Pa) 145 F 928.

These provisions apply to reissued patents. Rawson & Morrison Mfg. Co. v C. W. Hunt Co. (1906, CA2 NY) 147 F 239.

Notwithstanding fact that some of plaintiff's claims are valid and others invalid, and that plaintiff therefore has grounds to sue for damages for patent infringement, plaintiff cannot prevail where his attorney retired from patent office immediately after signing notice of allowance of plaintiff's original patent, participated in patent, acted as paid consultant in obtaining plaintiff's patent reissues and acted as attorney in prosecution of plaintiff's patent infringement suit. Kearney & Trecker Corp. v Giddings & Lewis, Inc. (1971, CA7 Wis) 452 F2d 579, 1971 CCH Trade Cases P 73735, 171 USPQ 650, cert den 405 US 1066, 31 L Ed 2d 796, 92 S Ct 1500.

Original patent claims held valid and infringed are unenforceable because of fraud involved in using retired patent examiner to prosecute reissue applications. Kearney & Trecker Corp. v Cincinnati Milacron, Inc. (1977, CA6) 562 F2d 365, 195 USPQ 402.

2. Action on valid claims

Action could have been maintained for infringement of other parts of invention although no disclaimer was filed, but in such case plaintiff could not have recovered costs. Hall v Wiles (CC NY) F Cas No 5954.

If plaintiff omitted to make a disclaimer, but brought suit for violation of patent and he was entitled to be protected in a portion of claims set up in his patent he was still entitled to damages for the valid portion of his claim, provided he was not guilty of neglect in filing disclaimer. McCormick v Seymour, (CC NY) F Cas No 8727, affd 60 US (19 How) 96, 15 L Ed 557.

Where it appeared that plaintiff was original inventor of the parts of his invention secured by alleged infringed claims, he was not required in order to entitle himself to a decree for infringement, to make disclaimer of other claims. American Bell Tel. Co. v Spencer (1881, CC Mass) 8 F 509; Whitney v Boston & A. R. Co. (1892, CC Mass) 50 F 72.

Plastic garment tag patent containing claim on prior art concept falling within general concept of inventor and not asserted against infringer does not fall within 35 USCS § 288, because

- Both U.S.C.A. and U.S.C.S. are kept current by the most typical method of updating legal research volumes: annual cumulative pocket parts. Statutes are subject to frequent repeal or amendment, and this method allows the codes to be kept current without requiring the entire set of volumes in U.S.C.A. or U.S.C.S. to be replaced. A slit or "pocket" has been created in the back cover of each volume of U.S.C.A. and U.S.C.S. Sometime during the first quarter of each year the publishers of U.S.C.A. and U.S.C.S. mail small, softcover pamphlets called "pocket parts" to law firms, agencies, and law libraries that have subscribed to U.S.C.A. and U.S.C.S. These pocket parts slip into the slits in the back of each volume of U.S.C.A. and U.S.C.S. and provide current information about the statutes in that volume, including changes or amendments to the statute and references or annotations to cases decided since the hardback volume of U.S.C.A. or U.S.C.S. was placed on the library shelf.

  Pocket parts are prepared annually. When the pocket part is received for 2001, for example, the law librarian removes and discards the old 2000 pocket part and replaces it with the new 2001 pamphlet. The pocket parts are *cumulative*, meaning that if a hardback volume was received in 1997, the 2001 pocket part found in the back of that volume will have all of the changes and updates relating to the statutes in that volume from 1998, 1999, and 2000. See Figure 3-7 for sample pages from a pocket part.

On occasion, and over a period of time, the pocket parts may become too thick to fit into the slit cut into the back of each hardbound volume of U.S.C.A. or U.S.C.S. On such occasions, the publishers will issue a softcover supplement that functions in the same way as a pocket part but sits on the library shelf next to the volume it updates.

There are few invariable or inflexible rules in legal research, but one of them is that you must always consult a pocket part (or softcover supplement) if the volume you are using is updated by a pocket part pamphlet. If you wish, you may elect to check the pocket part before reviewing the hardbound volume itself. *When* you review the pocket part is not critical; *that* you review it is critical. Oftentimes, research in a university law library can be frustrating as a volume will contain a slit or opening for a pocket part and yet no pocket part is found. If this is so, you should assume that a pocket part does exist but that it has been misplaced because the publishers of both U.S.C.A. and U.S.C.S., as a courtesy to researchers, will provide either a pocket part for each volume or a notice, which slips into the pocket and will inform you "this volume contains no pocket part." See Figure 3-8.

You can easily see the advantage of the pocket parts and supplements: rapid supplementation of the statutes and annotations at a cost much lower than replacing the nearly 200 volumes of U.S.C.A. or the approximately 150 volumes of U.S.C.S. each year. Nevertheless, the expenses associated in maintaining any law library are substantial.

Figure 3-7
Front Page of Pocket Part to U.S.C.S.

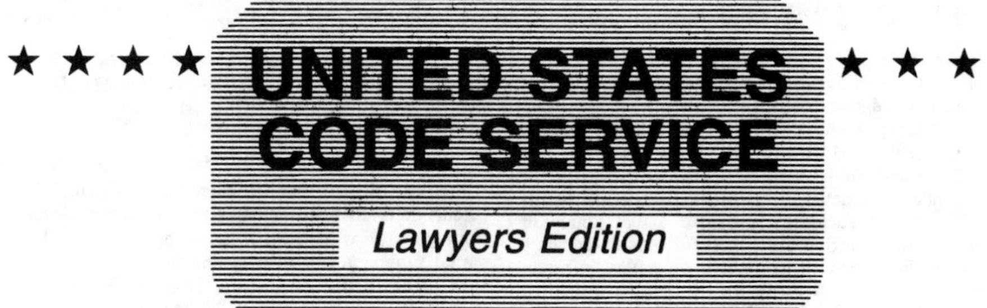

Issued in

April 2000

CUMULATIVE SUPPLEMENT

By The Publisher's Editorial Staff

35 USCS
Patents
§§ 271–End

LEXIS Publishing™

LEXIS®-NEXIS® · MARTINDALE-HUBBELL®
MATTHEW BENDER® · MICHIE™ · SHEPARD'S®

IT-132

Figure 3-7 (*Continued*)
Sample Page from Pocket Part to U.S.C.S.

fringe more recent patent than patents marked on plaintiff's cash drawers results in granting of partial summary judgment barring damages prior to 6 years before filing of suit. M-S Cash Drawer Corp. v Block & Co. (1992, CD Cal) 26 USPQ2d 1472.

Since material issue of fact exists as to whether or not plaintiff's letter to defendant contains words "U.S. Patent enclosed" provided actual notice of design patent infringement, court denies defendant's motion for summary judgement on patent infringement claim in part. Bazz, Inc. v Catalina Lighting, Inc. (1998, SD Fla) 49 USPQ2d 2009.

Settlement of previous dispute does not constitute notice of patent infringement, but later letter indicating patent number does constitute notice, so that summary judgment against collection of damages before date of letter is granted. Konstant Prods., Inc. v Frazier Indus. Co. (1992, ND Ill) 25 USPQ2d 1223, summary judgment den, in part, summary judgment gr, in part (ND Ill) 1993 US Dist LEXIS 7957.

10. Persons notified

Patent making provision of 35 USCS § 287 is not defense available to government under 28 USCS § 1498 for using patent rights. Motorola, Inc. v United States (1984, CA FC) 729 F2d 765, 221 USPQ 297.

11. Actual knowledge of infringer

Indirect evidence that defendant knew of plaintiff's patents falls short of actual notice of infringement from plaintiff who did not mark products, so that partial summary judgment against recovery of damages before notice is granted. Hoover Universal v Graham Packaging Corp. (1996, CD Cal) 44 USPQ2d 1596.

IV. PROCEDURE

13. Generally

Notice provisions are effective to limit damage amounts, but do not operate during liability determination to allow withholding of information in resistance to interrogatories because of failure of patentee to mark with patent notice. Ampex Corp. v United States (1980,US Ct Cl) 207 USPQ 440.

§ 288. Action for infringement of a patent containing an invalid claim

RESEARCH GUIDE

Federal Procedure:

Patents, Fed Proc, L Ed, § 60:1055.

Am Jur:

60 Am Jur 2d, Patents §§ 806, 928, 929, 930, 931, 938-940, 941, 943, 948, 972, 973, 1046, 1094, 1113, 1123, 1233.

Forms:

13A Fed Procedural Forms L Ed Patents §§ 52:1, 381, 461, 481.

Intellectual Property:

4 Chisum on Patents (Matthew Bender), Patent & Trademark Office Procedures § 11.07.

Texts:

Deller, Patent Claims (2d ed).

INTERPRETIVE NOTES AND DECISIONS

2. Action on valid claims

Plaintiff's disclaimer of claims 1, 2, and 11 and simultaneous retention of undistinguishable claims 3 through 6 does not preclude plaintiff's enforcement of valid and distinguishable claims 7, 8, 10, and 14 by action for infringement. Allen Archery, Inc. v Jennings Compound Bow. Inc. (1981, CD Cal) 211 USPQ 206.

4. Disclaimer of invalid claims

Maytag rule under predecessor statute that patentee who disclaimed invalid claim and failed to disclaim indistinguishable claim invalidated entire patent does not apply under USC § 253 and § 258, so that disclaimer of some claims and failure to disclaim indistinguishable claims do not invalidate entire patent. Allen Archery, Inc. v Jennings Compound Bow, Inc. (1982, CA9 Cal) 686 F2d 780, 216 USPQ 585.

Failure of patentee to disclaim invalid patent claim does not prevent patentee from enforcing any remaining claims that are otherwise valid in same patent. Allen Archery, Inc. v Browning Mfg. Co. (1987, CA FC) 819 F2d 1087, 2 USPQ2d 1490.

Withdrawing patent claims from suit without disclaimer does not invalidate patent without clear and convincing proof of bad faith. National Business Systems, Inc. v AM International, Inc. (1982, ND Ill) 546 F Supp 340, 217 USPQ 235.

Question of delay is irrelevant to filing of terminal disclaimer for claims subject to defense of obviousness-type double patenting. Bayer AG & Miles, Inc. v Barr Laboratories, Inc. (1992, SD NY) 798 F Supp 196, 24 USPQ2d 1864.

5. Costs recovery

Delay by patentee in disclaiming invalid claims affects only recovery of costs and does not invalidate otherwise valid claims. Allen Archery, Inc. v Jennings Compound Bow, Inc. (1982, CA9 Cal) 686 F2d 780, 216 USPQ 585.

Reissue of patent in suit is procedure for amending and correcting patent and accomplishes same result as disclaimer and thus preserves successful plaintiff's right to recover costs. Wycoff v Motorola, Inc. (1981, ND Ill) 217 USPQ 639.

Although patentee fraudulently concealed prior art from PTO, that event took place many years ago, and plaintiff fairly and expeditiously conducted trial so that even though patent is held invalid for fraud on PTO and for several other grounds, case is not exceptional and attorney fees to defendant are denied. Torin Corp. v Philips Industries, Inc. (1985, SD Ohio) 625 F Supp 1077, 228 USPQ 465.

Figure 3-8
Notice That No Pocket Part Exists

This Volume Contains No Pocket Part

Refer to
Separate
Soft Bound Supplement
to this Volume
for
Latest Updating Material

S1291b

To enhance the updating of U.S.C.A., West provides an additional pamphlet service. These Statutory Supplements are designed to accelerate the updating of statutes in U.S.C.A. before the publication of next year's pocket part. They include the public laws passed since the publication of the most recent pocket part and that relate to sections of the *United States Code*. Therefore, after you check the pocket part (published yearly) or supplement to determine if a statute has been amended or repealed, check the most recent Statutory Supplement (published every three to four months) to determine if even more recent changes have occurred. When new pocket parts are published at the beginning of each year, they will include all of the information previously included in the Statutory Supplements, which are then discarded.

Similarly, the publisher of U.S.C.S. publishes pamphlets called *Cumulative Later Case and Statutory Service*, which are designed to update the statutes found in U.S.C.S. Issued three times each year, these supplements contain statutory amendments and annotations to new cases. Each pamphlet is cumulative so that you need only consult the most recent issue. When the yearly pocket part for a volume of U.S.C.S. is published, the previous pamphlet will be discarded.

The publishers of U.S.C.S. also issue a monthly pamphlet to each subscriber of U.S.C.S. This is the *U.S.C.S. Advance*, and it includes newly enacted public laws, presidential proclamations and executive orders, and other presidential documents. Each monthly issue of *Advance* includes a cumulative index. A section titled "Current Awareness Commentary" includes summaries of pending legislation, and "Supreme Court Update" discusses recent United States Supreme Court cases. See Figure 3-9 for a chart showing how to update research of federal statutes.

When a statute is located under a particular title and section, for example, 42 U.S.C.A. § 1223 or 42 U.S.C.S. § 1223, any amendment or further information relating to it in the pocket parts or supplementary pamphlets will also be located under the same title and section number. Similarly, the pocket parts use the same annotation titles or catchlines as

Figure 3-9
Updating Federal Statutory Research

U.S.C.	*U.S.C.A.*	*U.S.C.S.*
Read statute in main hardbound volume.	Read statute in main hardbound volume.	Read statute in main hardbound volume.
Check hardbound supplements.	Check annual pocket part or softcover supplements.	Check annual pocket part or softcover supplements.
Check slip laws, *U.S. Law Week*, or USCCAN.	Check U.S.C.A.'s Statutory Supplements.	Check U.S.C.S.'s *Cumulative Later Case and Statutory Service*.
	Check slip laws, *U.S. Law Week*, or USCCAN.	Check slip laws, *U.S. Law Week*, or USCCAN.

the hardbound volumes so researchers can readily locate the latest decisions interpreting a statute.

When necessary, the publishers of U.S.C.A. and U.S.C.S. will issue replacement volumes for the hardback volumes in the set by simply mailing the law firm, agency, or law library a new volume together with a bill for the new volume.

d. Use of U.S.C., U.S.C.A., and U.S.C.S.

As you now know, there are three sets of codes you may use to locate and interpret federal statutes: U.S.C., U.S.C.A., and U.S.C.S. It is unlikely you will use U.S.C. very often because U.S.C.A. and U.S.C.S. provide you with the exact wording of the federal statutes found in U.S.C. together with extremely useful annotations, which refer you to cases interpreting and construing the statutes. Nevertheless, you may choose to use U.S.C. when you are primarily interested in reviewing only the statutory language itself rather than any judicial decisions interpreting the statutes.

When you are interested in researching the history of a statute, finding other sources in the law library that discuss or refer to that statute, and, most important, reviewing judicial decisions that have interpreted the statute, use U.S.C.A. or U.S.C.S. There are some differences between them. For example, U.S.C.S.'s section titled "Research Guide" refers you to far more sources in the library than does U.S.C.A.'s comparable section titled "Library References." In general, U.S.C.A. will direct you to other West publications, and U.S.C.S. will direct you to other LEXIS Publishing or Reed Elsevier publications. Additionally, the organization of the annotations within each set differs in that U.S.C.A. uses an alphabetical arrangement while U.S.C.S. uses a topic approach. Finally, U.S.C.A. and U.S.C.S. may each refer you to cases that the other set does not. In general, West's publication, U.S.C.A., attempts to be as comprehensive as possible, sending you to nearly all cases interpreting or discussing a federal statute, while the publisher of U.S.C.S. aims to provide researchers with the most significant cases, eliminating what it believes to be outmoded or repetitive cases, stating that U.S.C.S. contains "no vague or marginal cases to wade through and weigh before getting to the heart of [a] problem."

Another difference is that the language contained in U.S.C.A. is identical to the text of the *United States Code* while the language in U.S.C.S. is identical to the text of *United States Statutes at Large*. Thus, the language found in U.S.C.S. replicates the language of statutes as enacted by Congress. Only on rare occasions, however, will an error in reprinting a statute occur in the *United States Code*, and this difference may be more imagined than real.

Most experts agree that these differences are not significant for most research projects. Therefore, for the typical research project you will ordinarily use U.S.C.A. *or* U.S.C.S. but not both. Using both sets would be analogous to driving to work in a Ford and then walking home and driving to work again in a Chevrolet. In most respects, U.S.C.A. and U.S.C.S. are *competitive* sets, meaning they are equivalent. The choice of which set you ultimately use may depend on habit or convenience. If your first employer has purchased U.S.C.A. and you become familiar with the organization and arrangement of this set, you may find that you prefer to use U.S.C.A. Many people prefer U.S.C.S. due to the larger size of the books and larger and bolder typeface, which is easy to read. Some researchers prefer an integrated approach to all legal research and will consistently use all West publications when possible, thereby gaining access to all of West's books and its proprietary key number/digest system (see Chapter 5), while others prefer to use books published by the former Lawyers Co-op to obtain access to its other publications, such as A.L.R. (see Chapter 5).

In summary, if you are engaged in an extremely detailed research project, you should consult both U.S.C.A. and U.S.C.S. Ordinarily, however, one set will be sufficient for most of your research needs and most law firms, corporations, and agencies purchase only one set or the other.

The exercise placed at the end of this chapter will require you to use both U.S.C.A. and U.S.C.S., and you may find you have an immediate preference for one set over the other.

e. Research Techniques

There are three primary techniques you may use to locate federal statutes: the descriptive word approach, the title/topic approach, and the popular name approach.

(1) Descriptive Word Approach

This method of locating statutes is one that you have undoubtedly used before in other research projects. For example, if you were asked to find out how far Earth is from Mars, you would probably elect to use an encyclopedia; however, you would not simply start reading at page 1 of volume 1, hoping you would eventually stumble upon the information. You would consult the general index at the end of the encyclopedia set and look for various words that describe the problem such as "Earth," "Mars," "planets," or "solar system." The index would then direct you to the appropriate volume and page number. This is the descriptive word approach.

Both U.S.C.A. and U.S.C.S. have a multi-volume general index, which is arranged alphabetically and is usually located after Title 50, the last volume in both U.S.C.A. and U.S.C.S. When you have been assigned a legal research problem, you should try to think of key words or phrases that describe this problem. To assist in developing descriptive words or phrases, consider the following questions: *Who* is involved? *What* is the issue under consideration? *Where* did the action take place? *When* did the action occur? *Why* did the issue develop? *How* did the problem arise? You should then insert these words or phrases into the general index of U.S.C.A. or U.S.C.S., which will then direct you to the appropriate title and section of the code. See Figure 3-10.

The indices for U.S.C.A. and U.S.C.S. are both very "forgiving." For example, if you selected "landlord" and the statute is indexed under "tenant," both U.S.C.A. and U.S.C.S. will guide you to the appropriate word, as follows:

Landlord. Tenant, this index.

Figure 3-10
Sample Page from U.S.C.A. General Index

Figure 3-10 (*Continued*)
Sample Page from U.S.C.S. General Index

GENERAL INDEX

References to the Code are to Title and Section 575

U.S.C.A. and U.S.C.S. will direct you to the appropriate statute by listing the title first and then identifying the specific statute section, as follows:

Citizenship, 8 § 1409

You are thus directed to Title 8, Section 1409.

If you have difficulty thinking of an appropriate word to insert into the index, you might consider using a thesaurus to provide you with synonyms or antonyms. Generally, however, such a practice will not be necessary as the indices for both U.S.C.A. and U.S.C.S. are excellent finding tools and have indexed statutes under numerous words or topics. Thus, you need not distill your research problem into one perfect word; even phrases such as "sudden infant death syndrome" are found in the general index to U.S.C.A. and U.S.C.S., and there are typically numerous entry words in these indices for each statute.

After you have been directed to the appropriate title and section, you can readily locate the statute by scanning the library shelves. U.S.C.A. and U.S.C.S. are arranged by titles 1 through 50, and the spine of each volume that faces you is clearly marked to facilitate your research efforts.

This descriptive word approach is usually the easiest and most efficient way to locate a statute, particularly for beginning researchers. This is the technique you should use until you are extremely familiar with the organization of U.S.C.A. and U.S.C.S. and feel comfortable using the next method of statutory research: the title/topic approach.

If you cannot locate the statute you are looking for by using the general index, examine the volume of the general index to determine whether a pocket part has been inserted into the volume or a supplement has been published to assist you in locating newer statutes.

(2) Title/Topic Approach

As you know, all of the statutes in U.S.C.A. and U.S.C.S. are divided or categorized into 50 titles. It is possible that you may be so familiar with the contents and organization of U.S.C.A. and U.S.C.S. that when presented with a legal research problem, you bypass the general index and immediately proceed to remove the appropriate title from the library shelf.

Thus, if you consistently performed research in the area of bankruptcy and were asked a question relating to the filing of a petition under the United States Bankruptcy Act, you may be able to immediately recognize that this subject is covered by Title 11. You would proceed to the appropriate volume(s) relating to Title 11 and begin examining the statutes and annotations therein.

At the very beginning of Title 11 is a table of contents, which gives you an outline of the bankruptcy statutes so you can select the appropriate one. Additionally, after the very last bankruptcy statute you will be given an index to all of the bankruptcy statutes in Title 11 and you may use this to focus in on the specific statute you are seeking.

This title/topic method is best employed by researchers who are sufficiently familiar with U.S.C.A. and U.S.C.S. so they can confidently select the one particular title of the 50 titles available and review the statutes therein. Because it is possible that some statutes may be covered under more than one title and because this title/topic approach presumes a great deal of knowledge about U.S.C.A. and U.S.C.S., you should avoid using this method when you are just beginning to perform legal research.

(3) Popular Name Approach

Many of our federal statutes are known by a popular name—either that of the sponsors of the legislation (Gramm-Rudman-Hollings Act, Taft-Hartley Act, Kerr-Mills Social Security Act) or that given to the legislation by the public or media (National School Lunch Act, Pregnancy Discrimination Act, Parental Kidnapping Prevention Act of 1980). If you are asked to locate one of these statutes, you can easily do so in either U.S.C.A. or U.S.C.S.

To find such a statute in U.S.C.A., locate the last volume of the general index for U.S.C.A. In this volume there is a *Popular Name Table*, which lists in alphabetical order federal laws known by their popular names. Simply look up the law you are interested in and you will be directed to the appropriate title and section. See Figure 3-11 for a sample page from the Popular Name Table.

To locate such a statute in U.S.C.S., you should consult the Table of Acts by Popular Name found in a separate volume of U.S.C.S. (together with executive orders and presidential proclamations), which lists the federal statutes known by a popular name in alphabetical order. Just as with U.S.C.A., you will be directed to the appropriate title and section.

Finally, *Shepard's Acts and Cases by Popular Name: Federal and State* organizes federal and state statutes in alphabetical order, providing you with citations to federal as well as state laws and cases known by popular names. For federal laws, this compact set also provides a citation to *United States Statutes at Large* and gives the public law number as well as the year the statute was enacted. *Shepard's Acts and Cases* is kept current by a softcover supplement.

f. Final Research Steps

After you locate the statute you are interested in, read it carefully. Examine the historical notes and review the library references to determine whether other sources in the library provide further information on this statute or the subject matter it discusses. Then read the annotations carefully and decide which cases you will read in full based on your initial reading of the brief descriptions of these cases. Finally, check the pocket part and any of the interim pamphlets or supplements (which are arranged exactly like the numbering used in the hardback volumes) to determine if the statute has been amended or repealed and to look for annotations or references to cases that have interpreted the statute subsequent to the publication of the hardbound volume.

Figure 3-11
Sample Page from U.S.C.A. Popular Name Table

Child Protection and Obscenity Enforcement Act of 1988
Pub.L. 100–690, Title VII, Subtitle N, §§ 7501, 7511 to 7514, 7521 to 7526, Nov. 18, 1988, 102 Stat. 4485 to 4503 (Title 18, §§ 1460, 1465 to 1469, 1961, 2251, 2251 note, 2251A, 2252 to 2254, 2256, 2257, 2257 note, 2516; Title 19, § 1305; Title 47, § 223)

Child Protection and Toy Safety Act of 1969
Pub. L. 91-113, Nov. 6, 1969, 83 Stat. 187 (Title 15, §§ 401 note, 1261, 1262, 1274)

Child Protection Restoration and Penalties Enhancement Act of 1990
Pub.L. 101–647, Title III, Nov. 29, 1990, 104 Stat. 4816 (Title 18, §§ 1460, 2243, 2251 note, 2252, 2257, 2257 note; Title 28, § 994 note)

Child Sexual Abuse and Pornography Act of 1986
Pub.L. 99–628, Nov. 7, 1986, 100 Stat. 3510 (Title 18, §§ 2251, 2255, 2421, 2422, 2423, 2424)

Child Support Enforcement Act
See Federal Child Support Enforcement Act

Child Support Enforcement Amendments of 1984
Pub.L. 98–378, Aug. 16, 1984, 98 Stat. 1305 (Title 26, §§ 6103, 6402, 7213; Title 42, §§ 602, 602 note, 603, 606, 606 note, 651, 652, 652 note, 653, 654, 654 note, 655 to 657, 657 note, 658, 658 note, 664, 666, 667, 667 note, 671, 1305 note, 1315, 1396a)
Pub.L. 100–485, Title III, § 303(e), Oct. 13, 1988, 102 Stat. 2393 (Title 42, § 606 note)
Pub.L. 101–239, Title VIII, § 8003(a), Dec. 19, 1989, 103 Stat. 2453 (Title 42, § 606 note)

Child Support Recovery Act of 1992
Pub.L. 102–521, Oct. 25, 1992, 106 Stat. 3403 (Title 18, §§ 228, 228 note, 3563, Title 42, §§ 3793, 3796cc, 3796cc–1 to 3796cc–6, 3797, 12301 note)

Children With Disabilities Temporary Care Reauthorization Act of 1989
Pub.L. 101–127, Oct. 25, 1989, 103 Stat. 770 (Title 42, §§ 5117 notes, 5117a, 5117a note, 5117c, 5117d)

Children's Bureau Act
Apr. 9, 1912, ch. 73, 37 Stat. 79

Children's Justice Act
Pub.L. 99–401, Title I, Aug. 27, 1986, 100 Stat. 903 (Title 42, §§ 290dd–3, 290ee–3, 5101, 5101 notes, 5103, 5105, 10601, 10603, 10603a)

Children's Justice and Assistance Act of 1986
Pub.L. 99–401, Aug. 27, 1986, 100 Stat. 903 (Title 42, §§ 290dd–3, 290ee–3, 5101, 5101 notes, 5103, 5105, 5117, 5117 notes, 5117a to 5117d, 10601, 10603, 10603a)

Children's Nutrition Assistance Act of 1992
Pub.L. 102–512, Oct. 24, 1992, 106 Stat. 3363 (Title 42, §§ 1771 notes, 1769, 1769 note, 1776, 1786, 1786 notes)

Children's Television Act of 1990
Pub.L. 101–437, Oct. 18, 1990, 104 Stat. 996 (Title 47, §§ 303a, 303a note, 303b, 393a, prec. 394, 394, 394 note, prec. 395, prec. 396, prec. 397, 397, 609 notes)
Pub.L. 102–356, § 15, Aug. 26, 1992, 106 Stat. 954 (Title 47, § 303b)

China Aid Act
Feb. 7, 1942, ch. 47, 56 Stat. 82

China Aid Act of 1948
Apr. 3, 1948, ch. 169, title IV, 62 Stat. 158

China Appropriation Act
Feb. 12, 1942, ch. 71, 56 Stat. 89

China Area Aid Act of 1950
June 5, 1950, ch. 220, title II, 64 Stat. 202

China Trade Act (Corporations Act)
June 6, 1932, ch. 209, §§ 261–264, 47 Stat. 232

China Trade Act, 1922
Sept. 19, 1922, ch. 346, 42 Stat. 849 (Title 15, §§ 141–162)
Feb. 26, 1925, ch. 345, 43 Stat. 995–997 (Title 15, §§ 144, 146, 147, 149, 150, 160, 162)
Oct. 15, 1970, Pub. L. 91–452, title II, § 217, 84 Stat. 929 (Title 15, § 155)

g. United States Constitution

While the United States Constitution is not one of the 50 titles of the *United States Code*, nevertheless both U.S.C.A. and U.S.C.S. contain volumes for the Constitution. You will be provided with the text of the Constitution and its amendments and then, by the use of annotations, you will be referred to cases that interpret the Constitution. For example, after you read the First Amendment, you will be directed to hundreds of cases that have construed the First Amendment. You will also be provided with reference guides and cross-references to other materials to help you better understand the constitutional provision you are researching. Unannotated versions of the United States Constitution can be found in U.S.C. and in the *Am. Jur. 2d Desk Book* (see Chapter 6) and at various Internet sites, such as http://thomas.loc.gov.

Depending upon the arrangement of the law library you use, the volumes for the Constitution may precede Title 1 on your library shelves, may be located as the last volumes after Title 50, or may appear alphabetically within the set between the volumes for Conservation and those for Copyrights.

The three primary research approaches discussed above, namely, the descriptive word approach, the title/topic approach, and the popular name approach, should also be used when you are presented with a constitutional research issue. Be sure to refer to the pocket parts or softcover supplements for the applicable volumes to locate the newest cases interpreting constitutional provisions.

B. State Legislation

1. *Enactment of State Statutes*

The process of enacting and publishing legislation at the state level is substantially similar to the process described above for the federal level. Most state legislatures closely conform to the United States Congress with regard to their organization and manner of enacting law. Just as the United States Congress is divided into two chambers — the Senate and the House of Representatives — each state except for Nebraska has a legislature divided into two chambers. Such a legislature is referred to as a bicameral legislature. Nebraska has a one-house or unicameral legislature. The names given to the two chambers may vary from state to state. For example, the two houses in California are the Senate and the Assembly; the two houses in Louisiana are the Senate and the House of Representatives; and the two houses in Maryland are the Senate and the House of Delegates. Approximately four-fifths of the state legislatures meet on a yearly basis, while the remaining legislatures meet every two years.

Similar to the process of enacting federal law, much of the work in enacting state law is done by committees. When a final version of a bill is agreed upon, it will be sent to the governor of the state for signature, at which time it is referred to as a "law" or "statute" rather than a bill.

Additional information regarding the names of the lawmaking bodies for each of the states and the process of enacting legislation can be obtained from almost any general information encyclopedia.

2. *Publication and Codification of State Statutes*

Many states, particularly the most populous ones, initially publish their laws in slip form, similar in appearance to federal slip laws. At the end of the state's legislative session, these slips are taken together and compiled into books, which are generally referred to as "session laws." While some states may not use the words "session laws" and may name their compiled statutes "acts and resolves," or "statutes," or some other name, the generic title given to volumes that set forth a state's laws in chronological order is "session laws."

These session laws are analogous to *United States Statutes at Large*. That is, the volumes of session laws will contain the laws of a particular state in the order in which they were enacted. Just as researchers required *United States Statutes at Large* to be better arranged, or "codified," in order to bring together all the current laws on the same subject and eliminate laws that had been repealed, codification of the session laws of each state has also taken place.

Some states arrange their statutes by titles and chapter, such as Virginia: Va. Code Ann. § 8-102 (Michie 1996). Other states, usually the more populous ones, arrange their statutes in named titles, such as California: Cal. Evid. Code § 52 (West 1994).

Most states have annotated codes, meaning that after you are provided with the wording of the state statute, you will be directed to cases that interpret the statute. West publishes annotated codes for more than 20 states.

While the publication of each state's statutes will vary somewhat and while the publication may be official or unofficial, most state codes share the following features:

(i) The constitution of the state will be contained in the code;

(ii) The statutes will be organized by subject matter so that all of the corporation statutes are together, all of the penal statutes are together, all of the workers' compensation statutes are together, and so forth;

(iii) There will be a general index to the entire set and often each title will be separately indexed, so that after you read the last evidence statute you are given an index to all of the evidence statutes, and so forth;

Figure 3-12
Sample Page from Mass. Ann. Laws

§ 4. Uniformity Within District; Maps.

Any zoning ordinance or by-law which divides cities and towns into districts shall be uniform within the district for each class or kind of structures or uses permitted.

Districts shall be shown on a zoning map in a manner sufficient for identification. Such maps shall be part of zoning ordinances or by-laws. Assessors' or property plans may be used as the basis for zoning maps. If more than four sheets or plates are used for a zoning map, an index map showing interests in outline shall be part of the zoning map and of the zoning ordinance or by-law. (1975, 808, § 3.)

Editorial Note—

Section 7 of the inserting act provides as follows:

SECTION 7. This act shall take effect on January first, nineteen hundred and seventy-six as to zoning ordinances and by-laws and amendments, other than zoning map amendments, adopted after said date.

Total Client-Service Library® References—

82 Am Jur 2d, Zoning and Planning §§ 69–78 (Comprehensive zoning).

Law Review References—

Zoning: accessory uses and the meaning of the "customary" requirement. 56 Boston U L Rev, No. 3, p. 542, May, 1976.

Healy, Massachusetts Zoning Practice Under the Amended Zoning Enabling Act. 64 Mass L Rev 149. October, 1979.

CASE NOTES

Vote of zoning board at closed executive session was meeting held in violation of Open Meeting Law. Yaro v Board of Appeals (1980, Mass App) 1980 Adv Sheets 1839, 410 NE2d 725.

Legislative mandate of Open Meeting Law applies to zoning board of appeals. Yaro v Board of Appeals (1980, Mass App) 1980 Adv Sheets 1839, 410 NE2d 725.

§ 5. Procedure for Adoption or Change.

Zoning ordinances or by-laws may be adopted and from time to time change by amendment, addition or repeal, but only in the manner hereinafter provided. Adoption or change of zoning ordinances or by-laws may be initiated by the submission to the city council or board of selectmen of a proposed zoning ordinance or by-law by a city council, a board of selectmen, a board of appeals, by an individual owning land to be affected by change or adoption, by request of registered voters of a town pursuant of section ten of chapter thirty-nine, by ten registered voters in a city, by a planning board, by a regional planning agency or by other methods provided

(iv) The statutes are kept current by annual cumulative pocket parts, which will be placed in the back of each hardback bound volume or by supplements placed on the shelves next to the volumes being updated;

(v) Annotations will be provided to direct you to cases interpreting the statutes, typically through the use of a one-sentence summary of the case similar to the arrangement and organization of annotations provided by U.S.C.A. and U.S.C.S.;

(vi) Historical notes, which explain the history and amendments to the statute, and library references, which will direct you to other sources in the law library to assist you in interpreting the statute, will typically be provided (see Figure 3-12 for a sample page of a state statute); and

(vii) Conversion tables are provided in each volume so that if a state statute has been repealed or renumbered, you will be informed of the repealing or provided with the new section number of the statute.

3. *Research Techniques*

The same techniques used to locate federal statutes are used to locate state statutes. They are as follows:

a. Descriptive Word Approach

This method requires you to determine which words or phrases relate to the issue you are researching and then locate those words or phrases in the general index, which will then direct you to the appropriate statute.

b. Title/Topic Approach

This technique may be used when you have become so familiar with your state code that you bypass the general index and immediately locate the particular title or chapter that deals with the research problem.

c. Popular Name Approach

This method of locating statutes is used in those instances in which a state statute is known by a popular name. You can locate this statute by simply looking up the name of the act or statute in the alphabetically arranged general index.

For example, suppose you wish to determine whether the directors of a corporation may conduct a board meeting by conference call. If you elect to use the descriptive word approach, you should consider inserting some of the following words into the general index in order to be directed to the appropriate statute: "directors," "board of directors," "corporations," "meetings," or "conference calls." Researchers who are familiar with their state's code may use the topic approach and immediately locate the volumes in the state code that contain statutes dealing with corporations and review the separate index at the end of all of the corporations statutes or the table of contents, which appears at the beginning of the statutes dealing with corporations.

After locating the statute, read it carefully, examine the historical notes and library references, if any, analyze the annotations you believe appear promising, and examine the pocket part (or supplements) to ensure the statute is still in force and to locate newer cases, which may have interpreted the statute. You must then read the relevant cases in full.

You may observe that the numbering system for some state codes is unusual, with large gaps between some sections; for example, § 1815 might be followed by § 1832. Such a gap may indicate that sections 1816 through 1831 have been repealed or renumbered. Consult any conversion tables that appear in the volume to determine whether sections 1816 through 1831 have been repealed or whether they have been renumbered and subsumed within some other title or chapter in the code.

On other occasions you may notice that the numbering of state statutes is not by whole numbers but rather by decimals or subsections. For instance, § 410 may not be followed by § 411, but by § 410.10, § 410.20, § 410.30, and then by § 411. This numbering scheme typically indicates that after the state legislature enacted statutes that were numbered as § 410 and § 411, other statutes were enacted that dealt with the same general topic or subject matter and thus needed to be inserted between § 410 and § 411.

Finally, there is no one set of books that will provide you with all of the laws for all 50 states. Such a set would be unwieldy, expensive, and generally not very useful, as researchers in one state are usually not interested in the statutes of another state. There is, however, a set of books that will provide you with some of the laws of all of the states. This set is the *Martindale-Hubbell Law Directory*, which is fully discussed in Chapter 7.

4. Uniform and Model Laws

Uniform or model laws are those drafted for topics of the law in which uniformity is desirable and practical. For example, a set of laws relating to the formation, operation, and dissolution of partnerships, called the Uniform Partnership Act, has been adopted in every state but Louisiana. Once adopted in a state, a Uniform Law is then a state law like any other and can be located using any of the research techniques discussed above. Many states, however, often make changes and modifications to the Uniform Laws, resulting in laws that are highly similar from state to state but that are not perfectly uniform. Uniform and model acts are discussed in detail in Chapter 7.

C. Statutory Research Overview

When you are undecided whether to begin a project by examining federal or state statutes, keep in mind that some matters are exclusively presumed to be federal in nature. For example, establishing a uniform currency system is the province of the federal government, which eliminates the confusion that would result if each state developed its own types of coins. On the other hand, states have the power to enact laws relating to local concerns, such as establishing the death penalty in the state, residency laws for obtaining a divorce, and statutes of limitation for breach of contract matters. If you are uncertain whether an area is governed by federal or state law, examine the federal statutes first. If the topic is not covered by federal statute, proceed to examine your state statutes.

When you locate a statute, quickly review the entire scope of the statutes governing the topic. Generally, terms used in the act or statutory scheme are first defined. Definitions are usually followed by the rules announced in the statute and then by penalties for violations of the statute. Assume that each word in the statute is there for a purpose and the words are to be given their plain meaning. If the statute is vague or ambiguous, examine the cases that discuss the statute to determine how courts have interpreted the statute. You can also examine the legislative history of the statute by reviewing the documents considered by the legislature when it enacted the law, such as the transcripts of committee hearings and committee reports. Legislative history research is fully discussed in Chapter 10. Remember that it is the court's interpretation of a statute rather than the naked statutory language that is controlling under our system of law. It is the province of our courts to apply and interpret statutes and even strike down statutes as unconstitutional.

D. Citation Form

1. Federal Statutes

11 U.S.C. § 1604 (1994).
11 U.S.C.A. § 1604 (West 1996).
11 U.S.C.S. § 1604 (Law. Co-op. 1994) *or* 11 U.S.C.S. § 1604 (LEXIS Publ'g).

2. State Statutes

N.J. Stat. Ann. § 18A:35–4.4 (West 1996).
Tex. Educ. Code Ann. § 54.01 (Vernon 1995).

Technology Tips

http://lcweb.loc.gov/	Library of Congress home page
http://www.senate.gov	United States Senate home page
http://www.house.gov or http://www.access.gpo.gov/nara/cfr/cfr-table-search.html	United States House of Representatives home page (includes United States Code)
http://thomas.loc.gov	THOMAS contains full text of pending bills, key legislation, committee and congressional information, including the Congressional Record.
http://www.access.gpo.gov/su_docs	GPO Access: United States Government Printing Office site offers access to public laws, United States Code, United States Constitution, and various congressional documents and reports, and bills.
http://www.findlaw.com	FindLaw, one of the best known legal sites, provides easy access to federal and state statutes as well as a wide variety of other law-related information and links to other sites.
http://www.ll.georgetown.edu	This site of the Georgetown University Law Center law library provides links to federal and state statutes (select "federal" and then "legislative branch" to locate federal statutes or "state, local, and territorial" and then click on the desired state for state statutes).
http://www.access.gpo.gov/	This site of the United States Government Printing Office provides direct links to the United States Code and to federal public laws.
http://www4.law.Cornell.edu/uscode	The site of Cornell University provides easy access to the United States Constitution and to federal statutes, including a list of titles of the United States Code, a list of federal statutes by popular names, and a form allowing rapid access to specific sections of the Code.
http://lcweb.loc.gov/global/judiciary.html	This site, offered by the Library of Congress, provides an index to federal public laws, links to the United States Code, as well as to state statutes.
Senate Document Room, B-04 (202) 224-7860	Call for information on the status and availability of legislative documents.
House Document Room, B-18 (202) 225-3456 (phone) (202) 226-4362 (fax)	Call for information on the status and availability of House legislative documents; bills and public laws can be ordered by phone or fax.

Writing Strategies

Examine statutes as carefully as possible. Every word and phrase is meaningful. If the statute is contrary to the client's position, look to see if your issue fits within any exceptions to the statute. Review the law review articles you are directed to by the cross-references to determine if any guidance is given as to what situations the statute was designed to address or remedy.

Statutes can be long and complex. To avoid having to reproduce all of a lengthy statute in your writings, say "in pertinent part N.Y. Gen. Bus. Law § 804 (McKinney 1988) provides. . . ."

If the statute supports the client's position, say so forcefully: "Cal. Evid. Code § 601 (West 1991) [requires] or [mandates] or [imposes]. . . ."

If the statute contradicts the client's position, try to shift the focus away from the statute and toward the cases interpreting the statute that may provide you with more latitude due to vague or imprecise language: "In the seminal case interpreting Ind. Code Ann. § 14-928 (West 1992), the court. . . ."

Assignment for Chapter 3

1. What title of the United States Code relates to Crimes and Criminal Procedure?
2. Using either U.S.C.A. or U.S.C.S., cite the title and section that govern the following:
   a. Punishment for attempt to commit murder
   b. Basic pay for army and armed services band leaders
   c. Definition of "open alcoholic beverage container"
   d. Estimates for marketing allotments of sugar
3. Using the Popular Name tables for either U.S.C.A. or U.S.C.S., cite the title and section for the following:
   a. Wright Brothers Day Act
   b. Hate Crimes Statistics Act
   c. Sonny Bono Copyright Terms Extension Act
   d. ATM Fee Reform Act of 1999
4. Using either U.S.C.A. or U.S.C.S., find the term of protection for design patents.
5. Using the U.S.C.A. volumes for the Constitution, answer the following questions and cite the best case to support your answer. Give case names only.
   a. Under the First Amendment (Freedom of Religion), would a state prison's policy of allowing Jewish inmates to wear their prayer caps or yarmulkes only inside their cells deprive the inmates of their right to free exercise of religion?
   b. Under the Eighth Amendment, is use of "grue" as food unconstitutional as cruel and unusual punishment?
6. Using U.S.C.A., give an answer and cite the best case to support your answer. Give case names only.
   a. Under 35 U.S.C.A. § 101, should the "flash of genius" test be rejected in determining novelty for patent inventions?
   b. Review the statute. What is its citation in *Statutes at Large*?
   c. What American Law Reports annotation discusses the patentability of computer inventions?
7. Using U.S.C.S., answer the following questions and cite the best supporting case. Give case names only.
   a. Under 7 U.S.C.S. § 1446, are transactions authorized whereby processors of cheese sell their products to the Commodity Credit Corporation, retaining possession, and immediately repurchasing it at a lower price?
   b. Under 10 U.S.C.S. § 832, do the principles enunciated by the United States Supreme Court in the *Miranda* case apply to military interrogations of criminal suspects?
8. Using *United States Statutes at Large*, answer the following questions:
   a. What is the short title of Public Law 104-283?
   b. Give the citation for this law in *United States Statutes at Large.*
   c. What was its designation in the House?
9. Using *U.S. Statutes at Large*, find for whose relief Private Law 104-4 was enacted.

Chapter

4

Case Law and Judicial Opinions

Chapter Overview

In this chapter we will discuss judicial opinions and provide you with an understanding of the publication of cases, the elements of a typical court case, and the types of opinions written by judges. We will present the elements of analyzing and briefing cases and introduce the *National Reporter System*, a thorough and comprehensive series of case reporters, which publishes decisions from state and federal courts.

A. Selective Publication

At the conclusion of Chapter 1, you were required to locate certain published cases. This emphasis on locating cases is a cornerstone of the legal profession, primarily because of our common law tradition of reliance on case law as precedent. You will recall from Chapter 1 that the concept of stare decisis requires that a court follow a previous case from that jurisdiction if the case is materially similar to the case then before the court, although higher courts may depart from previously decided cases if a change in the law is deemed important. Due to the litigious nature of our society, each year approximately 60,000 new cases are published, and each one of these adds to the great number of cases or precedents that you may need to locate to persuade a court to rule in a client's favor. While the assignment in Chapter 1 required you to locate cases, it was easy to accomplish because the citations to the cases were given to you.

Seldom, if ever, does such a lucky event occur in the workplace. Generally, you will be provided only with an overview of the legal problem or question involved, and you will then be required to locate cases on point without the aid of a specific citation or often any direction whatsoever. In Chapters 5, 6, and 7 you will read about several publications that will help you locate relevant cases. Before you begin to locate cases, however, you will need a clear understanding of the elements of a typical court case and the process of publication of cases.

You may be surprised to learn that not all cases are published or "reported." In general, and with the exception of some trial cases from our federal courts, trial court decisions are not published. If you consider the overwhelming number of routine assault and battery cases, divorce or dissolution actions, prosecutions for driving while intoxicated, or cases relating to the possession of narcotics, you can readily see why trial court decisions are not usually published. Many of these cases add little to our body of precedents and relate only to the litigants themselves. If we were to publish the more than 100,000 cases that are decided annually in our state courts, our bookshelves would soon collapse of their own weight. As a result, usually only decisions of appellate courts are published. Because approximately 10 percent of cases are appealed, even the reporting of appellate court decisions results in a mass of publication. Therefore, in general, only appellate court cases that advance legal theory are published. Nearly 80 percent of cases disposed of by federal courts are unpublished. In fact, only the United States Supreme Court publishes all of its opinions.

In many instances, the courts themselves decide whether a case merits publication. For example, in California, California Rule of Court 967(b) specifies which appellate court cases shall be officially published:

- those that establish a new rule of law or alter or modify an existing rule;
- those that resolve an apparent conflict of authority;
- those that involve a legal issue of continuing public interest; or
- those that criticize existing law.

In most jurisdictions, including California, unpublished cases cannot be cited or used as precedents. You should not interpret the fact that many cases are not published as a conspiracy to prevent people from obtaining access to cases. Unless a case is sealed (usually for national security reasons, to maintain trade secrets, or for the protection of a minor), the case file is readily accessible at the courthouse that handled the case. If you know the name of the case, you can determine its docket number in a

Plaintiff-Defendant Index at the courthouse. You may then ask a court clerk to allow you to review the file, and you will have access to all of the pleadings filed in the case as well as the judge's decision and the final judgment. If you need a case from another jurisdiction, consult your yellow pages directory and locate an "attorneys service" company. These companies will locate and copy case files and pleadings for you for payment of a fee.

You can see, therefore, that publishing every case decided in the United States this year would not be of any great value to researchers and would simply result in needless publication. Thus, a certain amount of "weeding out" or selectivity occurs in the publication of cases. Nevertheless, the issue of selective publication of cases has sparked a great deal of controversy in recent years. In *Anastasoff v. United States,* 223 F.3d 898 (8th Cir. 2000), the court noted that allowing judges to ignore unpublished cases was unconstitutional and gave them arbitrary power. Although the decision in *Anastasoff* was later vacated on other grounds, *Anastasoff v. United States,* No. 99-3917 EM (8th Cir. 2000), the issue as to the precedential value of unpublished opinions was left unresolved, igniting fierce debate—with some experts predicting the United States Supreme Court will ultimately be called upon to resolve the issue.

The debate over the use of unpublished cases has also spread to the states, with Texas currently considering a rule that would eliminate unpublished cases and allow attorneys to cite any case (whether published or not) as authority. Similarly, legislation is pending in California—where only 7 percent of the opinions issued by the appellate courts are published and which precludes citation of unpublished cases—to allow use and citation of unpublished cases. While some individuals fear an avalanche of cases, others look forward to being able to review and cite literally hundreds of thousands of additional cases.

B. Elements of a Case

When an appellate court has reviewed the transcript of the trial below, read the written arguments (called "briefs"), which were submitted by the parties, and perhaps heard oral argument, the court will render its decision in a written opinion. It is this opinion that will be published (assuming it advances legal knowledge) and that will now serve as a precedent under the doctrine of stare decisis.

Cases that are published or reported typically contain the following elements. (See Figure 4-1 on pages 98-102):

1. *Case Name*

The name or title of a case identifies the parties involved in the action and also provides additional information about the nature of the proceeding. There are several types of case names.

Figure 4-1
Sample of a Published Case

COUGHLIN v. G. WASHINGTON U. HEALTH PLAN D.C. 67
Cite as 565 A.2d 67 (D.C.App. 1989)

Maureen F. COUGHLIN, Appellant,

v.

GEORGE WASHINGTON UNIVERSITY HEALTH PLAN, INC. and The George Washington University Health Plan and George Washington University Medical Center, Appellees. — **Case Name**

No. 87–293. — **Docket Number**

District of Columbia Court of Appeals. — **Deciding Court**

Argued Sept. 23, 1988.
Decided Oct. 18, 1989. — **Dates of Argument and Decision**

Woman brought suit against hospital and others alleging physical and emotional injury as a result of miscarriage arising from hospital's negligent mismanagement of her hypertensive condition during her pregnancy. The Superior Court, Gladys Kessler, J., granted the hospital's motion to dismiss for failure to state a claim. The Court of Appeals, Newman, J., held that: (1) the availability of a cause of action to a negligently injured viable fetus is irrelevant to whatever rights and remedies a woman may have to recover for separate injuries inflicted upon her, and (2) woman adequately alleged physical impact sufficient to form the basis for a claim of negligent infliction of emotional distress.

Reversed and remanded. — **Case Summary or Synopsis**

1. Federal Courts ⚷1066 — **Headnotes**

On appeal from a dismissal for failure to state a claim upon which relief could be granted, the Court of Appeals must construe the complaint in the light most favorable to the plaintiff and regard as true the allegations made therein, and dismissal should be upheld only when it appears beyond doubt that the plaintiff can prove no set of facts in support of her claim which

v. Silverberg Elec. Co., 402 A.2d 31, 34 (D.C. 1979). As the judge observed, PASI was simply trying to end run the motions judge's grant of summary judgment on PASI's fraudulent misrepresentation claim. *See 1901 Wyoming Ave. Co-op. Ass'n v. Lee*, 301 A.2d 70, 72 (D.C.1973).

Figure 4-1 (*Continued*)

would entitle her to relief. Civil Rule 12(b)(6).

2. Physicians and Surgeons ⟹**15(5)**

A pregnant woman, like any other patient, is owed a duty of care by her doctor throughout the duration of the patient-doctor relationship, and thus the doctor may be liable for any injury inflicted upon the woman, separate from injury to the fetus.

3. Physicians and Surgeons ⟹**15(5)**

The availability of a cause of action to a negligently injured viable fetus under the common law or statutes is irrelevant to whatever rights and remedies a pregnant woman may have to recover for separate injuries inflicted upon her, where miscarriage is alleged.

4. Damages ⟹**149**
Hospitals ⟹**8**

Woman's allegations that miscarriage resulted in physical and emotional injuries to her, caused by hospital's negligent treatment of her hypertensive condition, stated a cause of action for the mother's separate injuries.

5. Damages ⟹**50**

Woman adequately alleged physical impact sufficient to form the basis for a claim of negligent infliction of emotional distress, where woman claimed her miscarriage occurred as a result of hospital's negligent treatment of her hypertensive condition, and, as a result, she suffered preeclampsia which placed her at risk of convulsions, coma, and destruction of her placenta, she had to carry a dead fetus in utero for six days, and she was required to endure two days of painful induction procedures.

Names of Counsel

Mona Lyons, with whom William G. McLain and John W. Karr, Washington, D.C., were on brief, for appellant.

Leo A. Roth, Jr., with whom Sanford A. Friedman, Washington, D.C., were on brief, for appellees.

Before NEWMAN and FERREN, Associate Judges, and MACK,[1] Associate Judge, Retired.

Author of Opinion

NEWMAN, Associate Judge:

Maureen F. Coughlin appeals from an order of the Superior Court dismissing her action seeking recovery from George Washington University Health Plan, Inc., The George Washington University Health Plan and George Washington University Medical Center (collectively referred to as George Washington).[2] The trial court granted George Washington's motion to dismiss for failure to state a claim upon which relief can be granted. Super.Ct. Civ.R. 12(b)(6).

[1] At this juncture in the case, we are presented with a very narrow and straightforward question: whether an allegation by a woman that she sustained physical and emotional injuries arising from the negligent mismanagement of her hypertensive condition and attendant miscarriage states a cause of action for which relief can be granted. On appeal from a Rule 12(b)(6) dismissal, we must construe the complaint in the light most favorable to the plaintiff and regard as true the allegations made therein. *Vicki Bagley Realty, Inc. v. Laufer,* 482 A.2d 359, 364 (D.C.1984); *McBryde v. Amoco Oil Co.,* 404 A.2d 200, 202 (D.C.1979). Dismissal should be upheld only when it "appears beyond doubt that the plaintiff can prove no set of facts in support of his claim which would entitle him to relief." *Conley v. Gibson,* 355 U.S. 41, 45–46, 78 S.Ct. 99, 102, 2 L.Ed.2d 80 (1957) (footnote omitted); *accord Laufer, supra,* 482 A.2d 363–64 (noting this court's longstanding adherence to the rule established in *Conley*). We find that we cannot, as a matter of law, state that Coughlin herself was not injured as a consequence of

1. Judge Mack was an Associate Judge of this court at the time of argument. Her status changed to Associate Judge, Retired, on October 1, 1989.

2. Coughlin's malpractice claims against two individual defendants were subsequently dismissed by her.

Figure 4-1 (*Continued*)

George Washington's alleged conduct, or that she could not recover damages upon proof of those injuries. Accordingly, we hold that the complaint adequately sets forth a cause of action. We reverse and remand for further proceedings.

I.

Coughlin filed a complaint in Superior Court alleging that she suffered both physical and emotional injury as a result of a miscarriage arising from George Washington's negligent mismanagement of her hypertensive condition during her pregnancy. Coughlin's allegations are more fully set out in the pretrial memoranda (which the trial court treated as an opposition to a motion to dismiss), wherein she states that the tests taken during her first visit to George Washington's obstetrical clinic revealed that her blood pressure was elevated and a diagnosis of "probable chronic hypertension" was noted on her medical record. Coughlin claims that despite the well-established high risks associated with elevated blood pressure during pregnancy, George Washington did not refer her to the separate clinic for high risk obstetrical patients, but instead provided her with only perfunctory prenatal care.

Coughlin asserts that her blood pressure continued to test in the elevated range at her subsequent appointments. At her fourth and final visit, Coughlin claims that her blood pressure tested at a level high enough to warrant immediate hospitalization for monitoring and treatment or, at a minimum, strict instructions for her to refrain from going to work and remain in bed. She alleges neither action was taken.

One week later, according to Coughlin, she returned to the clinic. At this time the resident physician was unable to detect a fetal heartbeat, and fetal death *in utero* was subsequently confirmed by sonogram. Five days later Coughlin was hospitalized for induction of labor. She "delivered" the dead fetus on August 3rd, following the second day of artificial labor induction procedures, which included the administration of up to triple strength dosages of Pitocin, a drug that causes painful intensification of uterine contractions, and the rectal insertion of suppositories of Prostaglandin, a drug that also stimulates uterine contractions.

Coughlin's injuries, concomitant with George Washington's alleged negligence, were described in the pleadings as follows:

> [S]erious, permanent and painful bodily and emotional injuries, including but not limited to, unnecessary surgery and permanent injury to her body and the loss of her child; she was required to be hospitalized and to incur medical, hospital, and other expenses for the care and treatment of her injuries so sustained; she has experienced, and will in the future experience, pain and suffering, mental and emotional anguish and anxiety, humiliation, embarrassment, and distress; and has suffered and will continue to suffer the loss of her normal and recreational activities and the curtailment thereof. (Complaint, Rec. 236)
>
> [E]normous physical and emotional pain and suffering during her pregnancy, and the subsequent labor and stillbirth. Her psychological pain and suffering is continuing and permanent, inasmuch as she suffers, and will continue to suffer, from the grief and anguish associated with the unnecessary termination of a wanted pregnancy and the loss of her fetus.... Ms. Coughlin was unable to resume work for five months after the stillbirth and lost approximately $15,000 in earnings. Further, when she returned to work in January, 1983, her grief rendered her unable to function adequately and she resigned four months later on April 15, 1983. Ms. Coughlin claims lost wages at the rate of $32,955 *per annum* until she was reemployed on April 14, 1986. (Pretrial Memorandum, Rec. 261–62)

In its answer, George Washington defended on the grounds of failure to state a claim upon which relief can be granted and lack of negligence; alternatively it pleaded contributory negligence and assumption of risk. In its pretrial memoranda (which the trial court treated as a motion to dismiss for failure to state a claim), George Washington urged dismissal of the complaint on two grounds. First, George Washington argued that *if* any injury occurred, it was to the fetus and not to Coughlin, and therefore under *Greater Southeast Community Hospital v. Williams,* 482 A.2d 394 (D.C. 1984), the action should have been brought by the estate of the stillborn fetus under the District of Columbia's wrongful death and survival statutes. Second, George Washington contended, relying on *Asuncion v. Columbia Hospital for Women,* 514 A.2d 1187 (D.C.1986), that Coughlin is precluded from recovering for negligent infliction of emotional distress, because she did not incur any physical injury other than the "normal pain of delivery." The trial court dismissed for failure to state a claim.

II.

[2] A pregnant woman, like any other patient, is owed a duty of care by her doctor throughout the duration of the patient-doctor relationship, and thus the doctor may be liable for any injury negligently inflicted upon the patient. *See* W. PROSSER & P. KEETON, THE LAW OF TORTS 369 n. 30 (5th ed. 1984) ("Pregnant women have traditionally been given recovery for their own injuries caused by miscarriage."); *Bonbrest v. Kotz,* 65 F.Supp. 138, 142 (D.D. C.1946) (defendants accused of causing prenatal injury to viable fetus should be accountable for the "wrongful act, if such is proved, [for they] have invaded the right of an individual—employed as the defendants were in this case to attend, in their professional capacities, both the mother and child."); *Tebbutt v. Virostek,* 65 N.Y.2d 931, 483 N.E.2d 1142, 1146, 493 N.Y.S.2d 1010, 1014 (1985) (Jasen, J., dissenting) ("Concomitant with the view that the mother is owed a distinct duty of care, women have traditionally been given recovery for their own injuries caused by the stillbirth or miscarriage."); *Ledford v. Martin,* 87 N.C.App. 88, 359 S.E.2d 505, 507 (1987) ("When an obstetrician agrees to take on a pregnant woman as a patient, he actually acquires two patients: mother and baby."); *cf. Johnson v. Verrilli,* 134 Misc.2d 582, 511 N.Y.S.2d 1008, 1010 (N.Y.Sup.Ct.1987) ("Certainly, as their patient, the defendants owed the plaintiff a duty of care which, the complaint alleges, they breached by their omission during the last month of her pregnancy" and in light of her allegation of physical injury, dismissal of her suit was in error); *McBride v. Brookdale Hospital Center,* 130 Misc.2d 999, 498 N.Y.S.2d 256, 261–62 (N.Y.Sup.Ct.1986) ("if a mother, while giving birth is *independently physically* injured by the negligence of her attending physician who also causes the death of her fetus, then she may seek recovery for any resulting emotional upset.").

George Washington argues, however, that this jurisdiction's recognition of the separate legal personhood of a viable fetus, to whom we have ascribed a legally cognizable cause of action for injury negligently inflicted *in utero, Williams, supra,* 482 A.2d at 395 (holding that "a viable fetus negligently injured *en ventre sa mere* is a 'person' within the meaning of the District of Columbia's wrongful death and survival statutes."); *Bonbrest, supra,* 65 F.Supp. at 139 (finding that a viable fetus is a "separate, distinct, and individual entity" from its mother and thus may bring a cause of action in tort for prenatal injuries in its own right), extinguishes the mother's cause of action for her own independent injuries where a miscarriage is alleged. We find no merit in this contention.

[3] The availability of a cause of action to a negligently injured viable fetus under the common law and the statutes is simply irrelevant to whatever rights and remedies a mother may have to recover for separate injuries inflicted upon her.[3] *See Johnson*

3. It is impossible to determine from the pleadings whether the fetus in this case was in fact viable. If the fetus was *not* viable, there are authorities that would hold that injury to the nonviable fetus, in and of itself, constitutes injury to the woman. *Cf. Snow v. Allen,* 227 Ala. 615, 151 So. 468, 471 (1933) ("[s]o long as the child is within the mother's womb, it is a part of the mother, and for any injury to it, while yet unborn, damages would be recoverable by the mother in a proper case."); *Modaber v. Kelley,* 232 Va. 60, 348 S.E.2d 233, 236 (1986) ("trial court did not err by instructing the jury that 'injury to an unborn child in the womb of the mother is to be considered as physical injury to the mother' "). *Williams, supra,* 482 A.2d at

Figure 4-1 (*Continued*)

v. Ruark Obstetrics & Gynecology Associates, 89 N.C.App. 154, 365 S.E.2d 909, 917 (1988) ("recognition that the legal fiction of 'personhood' may or may not be imputed to a fetus for some purposes does not determine whether a physical injury to the Johnson fetus *in fact* caused impact or resulting injury to Mrs. Johnson"). Irrespective of the unique relationship between mother and fetus, we view the present situation as being no different from any other case where the negligent acts of a tortfeasor may yield separate and distinct claims of liability from each individual injured by his negligence.

[4] Whether the miscarriage in this case resulted in an injury to the mother is an issue of fact that must be resolved at trial through proof by competent evidence. Coughlin's complaint, while broadly drafted, confines itself to seeking recovery for the physical and emotional harm the mother sustained under the care and treatment of George Washington; we see no attempt therein to recover for any injury to the fetus.

[5] We also reject any claim that Coughlin has not adequately alleged physical impact sufficient to form the basis for a claim of negligent infliction of emotional distress. "[T]here can be no recovery for negligently caused emotional distress, mental disturbance, or any consequence thereof, where there has been no accompanying physical injury," *District of Columbia v. Smith*, 436 A.2d 1294, 1296 (D.C.1981) (citations omitted), however, "the physical injury need not be substantial to sustain" that burden. *Asuncion, supra*, 514 A.2d at 1189. Again, accepting Coughlin's allegations as true, the mother suffered multiple physical injuries as a consequence of the miscarriage and George Washington's mistreatment of her hypertension.

First, Coughlin asserts her hypertension remained untreated over the course of several months, aggravating her condition and causing pre-eclampsia, which placed her at risk of convulsions, coma, and the destruction of her placenta. Second, the fetus within Coughlin's body died as a result of George Washington's failure to treat the hypertension, and the mother had to carry the dead fetus *in utero* for six days prior to its "delivery." Finally, Coughlin avers she was required to endure two days of painful induction procedures under circumstances which did not constitute part of the "normal" birth process. *Cf. Johnson, supra*, 365 S.E.2d at 916–17 (allegations of failure to treat mother's incipient diabetes and death of fetus give rise to action for negligent infliction of emotional distress); *Ledford, supra*, 87 N.C.App. at 89, 359 S.E.2d at 507 (recovery for mental and emotional anguish permitted where mother suffered "severe abdominal pain" and surgical removal of stillborn child); *Modaber v. Kelley*, 232 Va. 60, 348 S.E.2d 233, 236 (1986) ("failure to properly treat and manage plaintiff's toxemia" constitutes physical injury to mother).

In conclusion, we note that this court long ago dispensed with the argument that problems of causation, injury and damages inherent in the peculiarly symbiotic relationship between a mother and her fetus were sufficient reason to deprive either mother or fetus of the right to recover for injuries caused by the negligence of others. *Bonbrest, supra*, 65 F.Supp. at 142–43. These problems are "not a vital basis for refusing to recognize a cause of action," *Williams, supra*, 482 A.2d at 398, but rather must be resolved at trial through the production of evidence, the ability of the parties to prove or disprove to the fact finder the various elements of their claims, and well-crafted jury instructions.

Reversed and remanded. — **Decision**

395, leaves open to question whether an independent cause of action exists for injury to a nonviable fetus; whether such an injury would be to the woman and, thus, the cause of action hers; or whether no cause of action accrues. We need not and do not decide that issue in this case, since Coughlin's complaint at least alleges injury to herself independent of any injury to the fetus, viable or not. This is sufficient to withstand the motion to dismiss. — **Dicta**

Smith v. Jones. This case name is the most common and indicates by the use of the signal "v." (for "versus") that the matter is adversarial in nature. The first listed party, Smith, is the plaintiff, who has instituted this action against Jones. Usually the case name will remain the same if the case is appealed, although some courts may reverse the order by placing the name of a defendant who lost the trial below and instituted the appeal first. For example, if Jones lost the trial and appealed the decision, the case might then be identified as *Jones v. Smith*, even though the original plaintiff was Smith. The *Bluebook* requires that only the first listed plaintiff and first listed defendant be identified in a case citation. Nevertheless, a case may involve several plaintiffs and defendants or may be a consolidation of several cases so a court can resolve cases dealing with the same legal issue at one time.

In re Smith. The phrase "in re" means "regarding" or "in the matter of." This case name designates a case that is not adversarial in nature. That is, rather than one party instituting an action against another, this case involves only one matter or party, such as a bankruptcy proceeding, a conservatorship, disbarment, or a probate matter that relates to the rights of one individual.

State v. Smith (or *United States v. Smith*). This case name generally indicates a criminal proceeding. In our legal system, when a crime is committed, the state will prosecute the action on behalf of its citizens, all of whom have been injured by the crime. Some jurisdictions identify these cases as *People v. Smith*, and four jurisdictions (Kentucky, Massachusetts, Pennsylvania, and Virginia) are known as "Commonwealths" and will identify their criminal cases as *Commonwealth v. Smith*.

In re Johnny S. Case names that indicate only a party's first name or initials (such as *In re J.B.*) are typically used to designate matters that involve minors. Often these cases relate to criminal actions involving minors, adoption proceedings, or child custody proceedings. For purposes of privacy, the minor's surname is omitted from the published opinion.

Ex rel. Smith. The phrase "ex rel." is short for "ex relatione" meaning "upon relation or information." Such a case name indicates a legal proceeding instituted by an attorney general or some other state or governmental official on behalf of a state but at the instigation of a private party who has an interest in the matter. For example, a case involving adjudication of contractor Smith's claims against the United States Postal Service might be titled *United States ex rel. Smith.*

Ex parte Smith. "Ex parte" in the title of a case indicates that the name following is that of the party upon whose behalf the case is heard.

Complaint of M/V Vulcan. A case with this type of title will involve maritime or admiralty matters or will deal with a ship or sailing vessel.

United States v. 22,152 Articles of Aircraft Parts. Such an oddly named case typically involves the forfeiture or seizure of illegal goods or contraband. For example, this case was a forfeiture action brought by the United States government, which sought title to aircraft parts that a purchaser had attempted to illegally export to Libya. *United States v. $200,000 in United States Currency* was an action brought by the government seeking forfeiture to the government of $200,000 seized by the United States Customs Department at Miami International Airport.

2. *Docket Number and Deciding Court*

Immediately beneath the case name you will be provided the docket number of the case. When the first paper or pleading in a case is filed, the clerk of the court will stamp a number on the papers. This number, referred to as a docket number, serves to identify this case as it progresses through the court. Courts do not identify cases by name, primarily due to the possibility of duplication and confusion. To request information about a case or obtain copies of the pleadings or motions submitted in a case, you must provide the docket number to the clerk, who will then retrieve the file for you. Often docket numbers provide information about a case. For instance, a docket number of "CV-99-862-CAJ" indicates the case was a civil case filed or instituted in 1999, it was the 862nd case filed that year, and it has been assigned to Judge Carolyn A. Jackson. Following the docket number, the deciding court is often identified.

3. *Date of Decision*

The date the case was decided by the court will be given. If two dates are given, one will be identified as the date the case was argued and the other will be the date the decision was issued by the court. For citation purposes, the critical date is the date of decision.

4. *Case Summary or Synopsis*

Before you are presented with the actual opinion of the court, you will be provided with a paragraph summarizing the nature and background of the case, an identification of the parties, what occurred at the court(s) below, and what this court's decision is. This introductory paragraph, often referred to as a case synopsis (or occasionally as a "syllabus"), provides a quick overview of the general nature of the case and by what procedure it arrived at this court. This summary is typically prepared not by the court that issued the opinion but rather by the editors at West, LEXIS Publishing, or some other publishing company and is intended to serve merely as a convenience to legal professionals. Thus, while it serves as a quick introduction to the case, it may never be quoted from or relied upon as authority.

5. *Headnotes*

Before the actual opinion of the court, you will be provided with short paragraphs, each of which is assigned a number and a name. These are called headnotes or digest paragraphs. (For the present time, ignore the pictorial design of the "Key" followed by another number. This Key Number System will be thoroughly described in Chapter 5.) For instance, you may be presented with the following headnote:

> **3. Criminal Law**
> To convict defendant of aiding and abetting offense against the United States, Government must prove defendant was associated with criminal venture, participated in it as something defendant wished to bring about, and sought by his or her actions to make it succeed.

Each issue of law discussed in the case is assigned a headnote. If a case discusses 20 issues of law, there will be 20 headnotes. These headnotes usually are prepared by the editors of the companies that publish the court reports and serve as a table of contents or index to the case. They allow you to determine, usually in less than one minute, whether the case is worthy of additional analysis. For example, someone in your law office may realize you are researching an assault and battery issue and may recommend that you read the case *Gingles v. Edmisten*, 590 F. Supp. 345 (E.D.N.C. 1984). When you retrieve this case, you discover the case is 40 pages long. It is possible that you could spend two hours reading this case only to realize, on the last page, that *Gingles v. Edmisten* is not at all on point and that you were steered in the wrong direction.

Headnotes help reduce the time you might spend reading a case that ultimately proves to be of no value to you and serve to give you a brief glimpse at the legal topics discussed in a case. By examining the headnotes, each of which is only a sentence in length, you can make an informed decision whether to read the case in full or whether to put the case aside.

If the issues you are researching are assault and battery, quickly scan the headnotes looking for the words "assault" or "battery." If none of the headnotes deal with these issues but rather deal solely with "licenses," "deeds," and "trusts," you can make a quick determination to set the case aside rather than spend hours reading a case that does not discuss the issues in which you are interested.

If your examination of the headnotes reveals that headnote 6 discusses battery, you should then examine the case and locate a boldface, bracketed "6." This **[6]** directs you to the portion of the case devoted to the discussion of battery. Because the headnote is only a single sentence, you should now read this section **[6]** of the case in full. If this reading looks promising, you should return to the beginning of the case and read the entire case in full.

Because the headnotes are typically prepared by publishers rather than judges, you cannot rely on the headnotes as authoritative, and you should never quote from the headnotes. You should rather use the headnotes to assist you in making an initial determination whether the case will be helpful to you and then to locate the most relevant portion of the case.

6. *Names of Counsel*

You will be provided with the names and locations of the law firms and the individual attorneys in those firms who represented the appellant and the appellee. You may wish to contact the attorneys, especially if the case presents a novel issue or represents a change in the law. While you can readily obtain copies of the briefs and papers filed in a court case from the clerk of the court, discussing the case with the attorney involved may be of particular help to you, and often the attorneys may be flattered that they are being contacted as experts in this field.

7. *Opinion*

The commencement of the opinion of the court is almost always marked by an identification of the judge or justice who authored the opinion. For example, "Petersen, C.J." would indicate Chief Judge or Chief Justice Petersen. Everything that follows the identification of the author is the court's opinion. Most opinions start with a recital of the facts in the case because without factual background, the rest of the opinion exists in a vacuum. The court will then apply the law of the jurisdiction involved to the facts in this particular case. Precedents may be cited and statutes or other authorities may be relied upon.

As you read the opinion in the case, keep in mind the key distinction between the holding in the case and *dicta*, extraneous comments made by the court that cannot serve as authority. You will notice that there are different types of opinions:

Majority opinions are those written by a member of the majority after the court has reached its decision. A majority opinion is one in which more than half of the judges or justices agree. The holding, or ratio decidendi, announced in the majority opinion is the law and serves as binding authority on lower courts in that jurisdiction.

Per curiam *opinions* are opinions by the whole court and no specific author will be identified.

Concurring opinions are opinions written by justices who agree with the actual result reached in a case, for example, that the case should be reversed, but would rely on authorities other than those depended upon by the author of the opinion. A concurring opinion often uses language such as the following: "I agree the lower court erred and its decision should be reversed; however, while my learned brethren rely on Civil Code § 52, I would rely on

Probate Code § 901." A concurring justice is essentially telling others in the majority, "You got the right answer but for the wrong reason." While some concurring justices may set forth an actual opinion giving the reasons they concur, others may simply state, "I concur," and give no opinion.

Plurality opinions are those in which a result is reached but due to the existence of numerous concurring opinions, there is no common legal ground upon which the majority has agreed. Plurality opinions are weak because they do not reflect the will of a majority.

Dissenting opinions are those written by members of the minority. Just as is seen with concurring opinions, a dissenting judge may write a full opinion giving the reasons for the dissent or may simply indicate, "I dissent." If a certain case hurts your legal position, read the dissent carefully, as it may suggest arguments against the majority opinion.

Memorandum opinions provide a holding or result but little, if any, reasoning therefor. The decisions of the United States Supreme Court that merely reflect that a writ of certiorari has been denied are examples of memorandum opinions. Other memoranda opinions may state only, "For the reasons given by the court below, we also affirm." See Figure 4-2 for examples of memorandum opinions.

Chamber opinions are written by a United States Supreme Court justice in his or her capacity as the justice assigned to a circuit rather than in the capacity of writing for the majority. For example, a decision by a Supreme Court justice to stay an execution of a convicted murderer in his or her assigned circuit is a chamber opinion.

En banc opinions are those in which all justices in a court of appeals participate. For example, if all of the justices in the Ninth Circuit sit together to decide a case (rather than the case being heard by a panel of three judges, as is the usual procedure), the decision is said to be rendered *en banc,* literally "in the bench."

Only the majority opinion is the law that is binding on lower courts. Dissenting opinions and concurring opinions are not the law and while they may be persuasive, they are not mandatory authorities that must be followed.

8. Decision

The final element in a case is the actual decision reached by the court. The final decision may be to *affirm* or uphold the determination of the lower court, to *reverse* or overturn the determination reached below, or to *remand* or return the case to the lower court for further action consistent with the court's findings. A court may also *vacate* a case or dismiss it entirely. While, strictly speaking, the word "decision" refers only to the

Figure 4-2
Sample Page from West's *Supreme Court Reporter* Showing Memorandum Decisions

1

486 U.S. 1058, 100 L.Ed.2d 930

Hugh J. SHANNON, petitioner, v. UNITED STATES. No. 87–6952.

Case below, 836 F.2d 1125.

Petition for writ of certiorari to the United States Court of Appeals for the Eighth Circuit.

June 13, 1988. Denied.

2

486 U.S. 1059, 100 L.Ed.2d 930

Frans Jacobus Smit THERON, petitioner, v. UNITED STATES MARSHAL. No. 87–6954.

Case below, 832 F.2d 492.

Petition for writ of certiorari to the United States Court of Appeals for the Ninth Circuit.

June 13, 1988. Denied.

3

486 U.S. 1059, 100 L.Ed.2d 930

ALBERTA GAS CHEMICALS LIMITED, et al., petitioners, v. E.I. du PONT de NEMOURS AND COMPANY, et al. No. 87–652.

Former decision, 484 U.S. 984, 108 S.Ct. 499.

Case below, 826 F.2d 1235.

Memorandum Opinion

June 13, 1988. The motion of petitioners to file reply brief under seal is granted. Petition for writ of certiorari to the United States Court of Appeals for the Third Circuit denied.

4

486 U.S. 1059, 100 L.Ed.2d 930

NATIONWIDE CORPORATION and Nationwide Mutual Insurance Company, petitioners, v. HOWING COMPANY, et al. No. 87–1047.

Former decision, 484 U.S. 1056, 108 S.Ct. 1008.

Case below, 625 F.Supp. 146; 826 F.2d 1470.

Petition for writ of certiorari to the United States Court of Appeals for the Sixth Circuit.

June 13, 1988. Denied.

Justice WHITE took no part in the consideration or decision of this petition.

5

486 U.S. 1059, 100 L.Ed.2d 930

N.W. ENTERPRISES, INC., petitioner, v. TEXAS. No. 87–1370.

Petition for writ of certiorari to the Court of Appeals of Texas, Fourteenth District.

June 13, 1988. Denied.

Justice BRENNAN and Justice MARSHALL would grant the petition for a writ of certiorari and reverse the judgment of conviction.

6

486 U.S. 1059, 100 L.Ed.2d 931

SECURITIES INDUSTRY ASSOCIATION, petitioner, v. BOARD OF GOVERNORS OF the FEDERAL RESERVE SYSTEM, et al. No. 87–1513.

Case below, 839 F.2d 47.

final disposition of a case, in many instances and in common usage, the words "opinion," "judgment," "decision," "case," and "holding" are used interchangeably to refer to an entire case from the name of the case to the final decision.

C. Publication of Cases

1. *Official and Unofficial Publication*

Now that you are familiar with the elements of a case, you should become familiar with the publication of cases and the features provided in the casebooks, which will assist you in your research efforts. The books in which cases are published are referred to as "reporters," and each one has a specific abbreviation. If cases are published pursuant to some statutory directive or court rule, the sets of books in which they are collected are referred to as "official" reports. Cases published without this type of governmental mandate are collected in sets of books referred to as "unofficial" reporters. Although the terms "report" and "reporter" are often used interchangeably, the term "report" usually refers to an official set of cases, such as the *U.S. Reports* or *California Reports*, while the term "reporter" usually refers to an unofficial set, such as the *Supreme Court Reporter* or *Pacific Reporter.*

Keep in mind that the terms "official" and "unofficial" have nothing to do with the quality or accuracy of the cases. Cases found in "official" sets are neither better nor more precise than those found in "unofficial" sets. The terms "official" and "unofficial" relate solely to the method of publication, not to the legal status of the cases. In the rare event of some discrepancy between two versions of a case, however, the official version will govern.

When decisions are rendered by a court, they are initially available in slip form; that is, as looseleaf sheets of paper. For example, a decision released by the highest court in Wisconsin, the Wisconsin Supreme Court, will initially be published in slip form. It may also be published on the Internet. At this stage, the opinion will consist solely of the case name, date of decision, names of attorneys, opinion, and decision. Many of the extra features discussed above, such as the headnotes and the introductory paragraph or synopsis, will not yet be present. Wisconsin publishes all of its decisions officially and therefore the case will appear next in softcover temporary volumes called *advance sheets* and thereafter in hardbound volumes known as *Wisconsin Reports* and *Wisconsin Reports, Second Series*.

Because the case itself is not copyrighted and is in the public domain, you would be free to take the case, photocopy it, perhaps add a few extra features, such as your own form of headnotes, place it in a set of volumes that you publish, and give the set your name. Such a publication would be "unofficial," as there is no statute that directs you to publish this case.

The case in your privately published volume would be word for word the same as that which appeared in the official *Wisconsin Reports*—after all, what the judge has said in issuing the opinion is "etched in stone." What may distinguish your unofficial set of case reporters from the official set would be the "extra" features such as headnotes, the case summary or syllabus, and the like.

This type of duplication of case publishing by private individuals (or companies) is exactly what has occurred, and there now exist official and unofficial sets, each of which might publish the same case and each of which might add special or extra features to the sets. This is why you cannot quote from or rely exclusively on the headnotes or case synopsis—they are not usually prepared or written by the court but by a publishing company, and therefore are not the law. Similarly, the availability of cases on the Internet (see Chapter 12) arises out of the fact that cases are not copyrightable. Thus, they can be copied and disseminated to others.

2. *Series of Cases*

You may have observed that some of the case reports on the shelves are marked *Atlantic Reporter* or *Federal Reporter,* while others indicate *Atlantic Reporter 2d Series* or *Federal Reporter 3d Series* on the spine. In some states, such as California, where there is an abundance of reported cases, some of the spines indicate *California Reports 3d Series* and even *California Reports 4th Series*.

The switch to a new series does not occur at regularly scheduled intervals, and you cannot predict when the next series will commence. It is believed that the change to a new series is done to prevent the volume numbers from getting too high. For example, volume 300 of the *South Western Reporter* is followed by volume 1 of the *South Western Reporter, Second Series,* and volume 999 of the *Federal Reporter*, Second Series is followed by volume 1 of the *Federal Reporter, Third Series*. If the volume numbers were to reach 1806, for example, the likelihood of transposing the numbers and making an error in citation form are much greater.

3. *Advance Sheets*

Publishers of official and unofficial sets usually first publish case opinions in temporary softcover books or pamphlets referred to as "advance sheets." These advance sheets are published to provide rapid access to cases and are often available within a couple of weeks after a decision is issued by a court. West publishes advance sheets for its reporters each week and sends them to law libraries, agencies, and law firms that subscribe to its services, much the same way you might subscribe to *Time Magazine* or *Sports Illustrated*.

The advance sheets are placed on the shelves next to the hardbound volumes they relate to and are meant to last only until a permanent hardbound volume is published, typically a few months. Upon receipt of the permanent volume, the advance sheets are discarded. The permanent volumes will share the identical volume number and pagination as the earlier advance sheets. Therefore, you may readily rely upon and quote from cases appearing in the advance sheets because the citation to the page a quote appears on in the advance sheet will be identical to the page a quote appears on in the later published hardbound volume. West is so exacting that if a word is hyphenated between pages 242 and 243 of an advance sheet, it will likewise be hyphenated between pages 242 and 243 of the later permanent volume. After a case is printed in a West advance sheet but before publication in hardbound form, West returns the case to the authoring judge for additional comments or corrections, which are then included in the final print version.

D. Publication of State Cases

1. *West's* National Reporter System

In 1879, West Group ("West") created and published the *North Western Reporter*. The *North Western Reporter* is unofficial; it is published by West, a private company, which is acting independently and without any direction or order from any governmental authority. In most instances, the cases "picked up" by West and published in its *North Western Reporter* were already being published officially. West, however, believed that by grouping neighboring states together from the northwest region of the United States and by adding extra features to its sets of books, it could provide better service to those in the legal profession and could create a market for its publications. The set was so successful that West followed it by creating reporters for other geographical regions of the United States. The set of books published by West that collect state and federal cases are collectively referred to as the *National Reporter System*. In these sets of books West publishes all the cases released by courts for publication as well as adding thousands of cases not released for official publication and those that were reported as memorandum decisions.

The states that comprise each unit of the *National Reporter System* can be readily seen in the map shown as Figure 4-3 and are as follows:

North Western Reporter N.W., N.W.2d	Iowa, Michigan, Minnesota, Nebraska, North Dakota, South Dakota, and Wisconsin
Pacific Reporter P., P.2d, P.3d	Alaska, Arizona, California, Colorado, Hawaii, Idaho, Kansas, Montana, Nevada, New Mexico, Oklahoma, Oregon, Utah, Washington, and Wyoming

North Eastern Reporter N.E., N.E.2d	Illinois, Indiana, Massachusetts, New York, and Ohio
Atlantic Reporter A., A.2d	Connecticut, Delaware, Maine, Maryland, New Hampshire, New Jersey, Pennsylvania, Rhode Island, Vermont, and Washington, D.C.
South Western Reporter S.W., S.W..2d, S.W.3d	Arkansas, Kentucky, Missouri, Tennessee, and Texas
Southern Reporter So., So.2d	Alabama, Florida, Louisiana, and Mississippi
South Eastern Reporter S.E., S.E.2d	Georgia, North Carolina, South Carolina, Virginia, and West Virginia

Figure 4-3
***National Reporter System* Map Showing the States Included in Each Reporter Group**

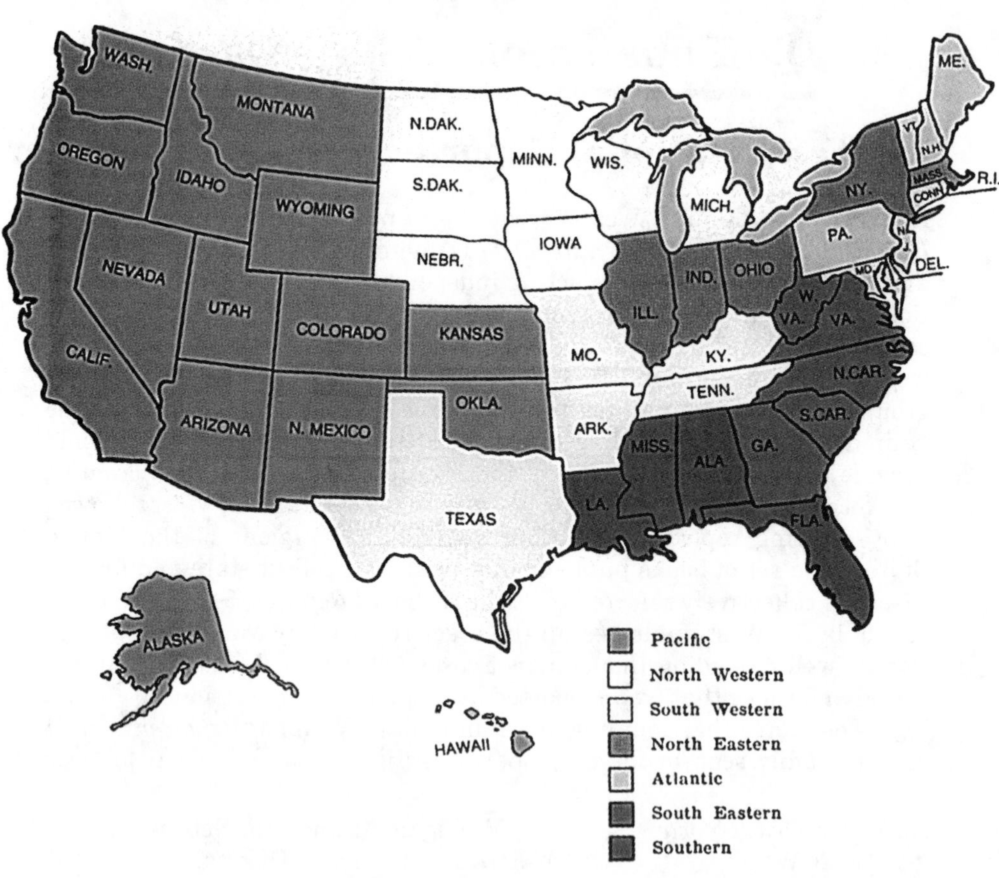

The National Reporter System also includes the Supreme Court Reporter, the Federal Reporter, the Federal Supplement, Federal Rules Decisions, West's Bankruptcy Reporter, the New York Supplement, West's California Reporter, West's Illinois Decisions, West's Military Justice Reporter and the United States Claims Court Reporter.

These geographical units were the first units created by West. It is not important to memorize or know which state is published or covered in which unit. It is sufficient if you understand the general structure of West's *National Reporter System*: It is a set of books, published unofficially, which reports many cases already published officially by many states themselves. You should know, however, which unit covers the state in which you will be working. As you can see from the map in Figure 4-3, West's grouping of the states is not a perfect geographical division. Certainly no one would view Kansas or Oklahoma as Pacific states and yet their cases have been placed in the *Pacific Reporter.* Thus, while a knowledge of geography may be helpful in considering which unit publishes decisions from a certain state, you cannot be absolutely certain unless you review the list that is found in the front of each and every volume of the books in the *National Reporter System* units.

No one state has ruled on every issue, and researchers in a state are often required to search for cases outside their home or forum jurisdiction. West's grouping of cases from neighboring states affords legal practitioners the ability to engage in such research. Although a case from one state is not binding outside its jurisdictional borders (see Chapter 1), in the absence of its own binding authority a state might adopt the position announced by another state. If it does, under our concept of stare decisis, the principle then binds the lower courts within that state.

Because West believed that New York, California, and Illinois published so many cases, it created units just for those states: the *California Reporter* (created in 1959 to publish cases from the California Supreme Court and the California Courts of Appeal); the *New York Supplement* (created in 1956, which publishes decisions of various New York courts); and *Illinois Decisions* (created in 1976 to publish cases from the Illinois Appellate Court and Supreme Court). Thus, a case citation to a California case may appear as follows:

> *Taylor v. Conrad*, 34 Cal. 3d 102, 698 P.2d 109, 206 Cal. Rptr. 911 (1983).

This citation indicates there are three sets of books in which you could locate this California case: the official *California Reports*, the unofficial *Pacific Reporter*, and the unofficial *California Reporter*. These three citations are called "parallel" citations. The publication of cases in more than one location can be a great service to a researcher: If the volume of *California Reports* that you need is missing from the shelf, you can elect to read the case in the *Pacific Reporter* or the *California Reporter*. Remember that the opinion issued by the court in *Taylor v. Conrad* will be the same no matter which of the three sets you select to locate the case. What the judge has stated in the opinion will not be revised by West's books in any manner. What will differ, however, may be the color of the set, the quality of the paper used, the typeface, and the editorial enhancements such as headnotes and the case summary or synopsis.

As is common with well-established and popular sets, all of the regional units have reached the second series (S.E.2d, A.2d, N.E.2d, N.W.2d, and So. 2d), and two reporters have reached their third series (P.3d and S.W.3d).

If you are puzzled why multiple sets of case reporters are needed, you should simply bear in mind that many different types of automobiles are also available in the United States. It is possible to buy a Ford, a Chevrolet, a Nissan, or a Toyota. Each car will provide the same function: transportation. Yet an individual may develop a preference for one manufacturer or may select one model over another based on considerations of price or available options. The same is true for law firms, corporations, and agencies. Some may elect to purchase official reports rather than unofficial reporters based upon price or some other consideration, and some may prefer the many extra features found in West's *National Reporter System*.

One of the advantages of the *National Reporter System* units lies in its grouping of states. A law firm in South Carolina that purchases the official *South Carolina Reports* will acquire a set of books that contains cases from South Carolina. If that firm purchases the *South Eastern Reporter*, however, it will acquire a set of books that contains decisions not only from South Carolina but from Georgia, North Carolina, Virginia, and West Virginia. This allows legal professionals in states without a rich or complex body of case law to review decisions from other states, which decisions might be relied upon if a case of first impression arises in South Carolina. West also markets state-specific versions of its regional reporters. For example, in Massachusetts a law firm can purchase a set called *Massachusetts Decisions* comprised of only the Massachusetts cases from the *North Eastern Reporter*.

West's *National Reporter* units often publish cases that would not otherwise be published in the official state reports. This is because West will publish cases that have been designated "not for publication" due to the fact that these cases do not advance legal theory or are duplicative of other already published cases. While West promotes its *National Reporter System* by noting that it publishes thousands of cases that are not published in the official state reports, one of the publishers of the official sets views this as a drawback. Recent marketing materials for the publisher of the official *California Reports* state, "Up to 25% of the cases in each unofficial reporter volume are depublished or otherwise superseded. Nonadmissible in court . . . the bottom line—are you paying good money for bad law?"

Additionally, the availability of unpublished opinions on the computerized legal research systems, LEXIS and Westlaw, and on the Internet has contributed to the increasing proliferation of cases. As noted earlier, some courts have attempted to reduce the mass of legal publication by enacting court rules prohibiting citation of cases in court documents unless those cases have been marked "for publication." Others require authors citing unreported cases to include a copy of the case together with any document citing the case. In any event, at present, an unreported case is not binding precedent under the doctrine of stare decisis but is rather persuasive authority only.

2. *Citation Form*

While citation form will be covered in depth in Chapter 8, at this point you should know one importance of distinguishing an official citation from an unofficial citation. The *Bluebook*, the standard guide to citation form, requires that if a state case citation is given in a document to be submitted to a court in that state, you must include a citation to the official state report (if available) as well as the citation to West's regional reporter. The official citation is to be given first. Thus, you will need to know the units in West's *National Reporter System* so that when you are confronted with a case citation such as *Neibarger v. Universal Cooperatives*, 439 Mich. 512, 486 N.W.2d 612 (1992), you will know that because the *North Western Reporter* is one of West's *National Reporter System* unofficial regional units, the citation to it should follow the official *Michigan Reports* citation.

3. *Discontinuation of Some Official Reports*

Because of the success and accuracy of West's *National Reporter System*, and because many researchers preferred using and buying the regional reporters with their convenient grouping of cases from neighboring states, many states have ceased publishing their cases officially. In fact, between 1948 and 1981, 20 states discontinued officially publishing their cases. Another reason for the discontinuation of official reports in many states is the expense of publishing cases that West will also be publishing. In the states shown below there are no longer parallel citations, and the only citation to cases from these states are to the appropriate geographical unit of West's *National Reporter System*:

State that Never Published Cases Officially	*States That Have Discontinued Official Publication and Year of Discontinuance*	*States that Continue to Publish Officially*
Alaska	Alabama (1976)	Arizona
	Colorado (1980)	Arkansas
	Delaware (1966)	California
	District of Columbia (1941)	Connecticut
	Florida (1948)	Georgia
	Indiana (1981)	Hawaii
	Iowa (1968)	Idaho
	Kentucky (1951)	Illinois
	Louisiana (1972)	Kansas
	Maine (1965)	Maryland
	Minnesota (1977)	Massachusetts

State that Never Published Cases Officially	*States That Have Discontinued Official Publication and Year of Discontinuance*	*States that Continue to Publish Officially*
	Mississippi (1966)	Michigan
	Missouri (1956)	Montana
	North Dakota (1953)	Nebraska
	Oklahoma (1953)	Nevada
	Rhode Island (1980)	New Hampshire
	South Dakota (1976)	New Jersey
	Tennessee (1971)	New Mexico
	Texas (1962)	New York
	Utah (1974)	North Carolina
	Wyoming (1959)	Ohio
		Oregon
		Pennsylvania
		South Carolina
		Vermont
		Virginia
		Washington
		West Virginia
		Wisconsin

E. Publication of Federal Cases

1. United States Supreme Court Cases

a. Publication

United States Supreme Court cases are published in the following three sets of books. Most law firms or offices will purchase only one set.

(1) United States Reports *(U.S.)*

The *United States Reports* is official. It is published by the United States Government Printing Office and comprises more than 520 volumes. Approximately 5,000 pages are published each year. Initially, cases from the United States Supreme Court were published in sets of books named after the individuals responsible for publishing the set. Thus, the initial 90 volumes of this set have names on the spines such as Dallas, Cranch, Wheaton, and Peters. In 1875, it became apparent that it was unsatisfactory to name a set after an individual who would inevitably retire or die. Therefore, in 1875, the set that reported United States Supreme Court cases was named the *United States Reports*. The older volumes were later numbered consecutively. Citations to these older cases appear as follows: *Turner v. Fendall*, 5 U.S. (1 Cranch) 117 (1801). When you observe such a citation, you should simply realize the case is very old. Cases in *United States Reports* appear initially in slip form and then in advance sheets. Some months later, the hardbound volumes are published and sent to law firms, law libraries, and other subscribers.

(2) Supreme Court Reporter *(S. Ct.)*

The *Supreme Court Reporter* is published by West and is unofficial. It is another unit of West's *National Reporter System*. This set began its coverage in 1882 and reports in full every decision rendered by the United States Supreme Court since that time. Cases initially appear in advance sheets, which are issued twice a month. The advance sheets are later discarded and replaced by semi-permanent volumes, which remain on the bookshelves for two or three years until the final permanent corrected and hardbound volumes are available.

(3) United States Supreme Court Reports, Lawyers' Edition *(L. Ed.)*

United States Supreme Court Reports, Lawyers' Edition, is published by LEXIS Publishing and is unofficial. It was created in response to a need among lawyers for less expensive books reporting Supreme Court cases than the official ones then being published. It contains all decisions issued by the Supreme Court since 1789. This set contains many useful editorial features such as quick summaries of the holdings of the cases, summaries of the briefs of counsel for the parties in the cases (given for older cases), research references, and, for some cases, annotations or essays on significant legal issues raised in the case. Be careful when reading older cases reported in *Lawyers' Edition* as it may be easy to confuse the arguments being advanced by counsel with the actual opinion of the court. Make sure you rely only on information appearing after the justice's name. Any information that precedes the majority opinion has usually been prepared by the publisher, and while it is extremely valuable and useful, it is not the law. Cases initially appear in advance sheets twice per month, and these advance sheets are discarded when the permanent volumes are received.

There are thus three parallel cites for all United States Supreme Court cases, and you can locate the 1986 case, *Batson v. Kentucky*, in three locations: 476 U.S. 79, 106 S. Ct. 1712, and 90 L. Ed. 2d 69. In the event of any conflict in versions of the cases reported in these volumes, the version of a case found in the official *U.S. Reports* governs.

Both of the unofficial sets reporting cases from the United States Supreme Court (S. Ct. and L. Ed.) include a section called "Syllabus," given before each opinion published in the set. The Syllabus is a comprehensive summary of the case to follow. While it is prepared by the Court's Reporter of Decisions, it is not the opinion of the Court itself. Therefore, it is a useful feature but cannot be quoted from. Be careful to rely only on the case itself, not on any of the editorial enhancements that accompany a case. Locate the name of the author of the opinion. This name signals the start of the opinion. Everything given after it is "fair game."

b. Rapid Access to United States Supreme Court Cases

As described above, all of the sets that publish United States Supreme Court cases issue advance sheets. Nevertheless, even the advance sheets may take four to six weeks to be received. Very rapid access to United States Supreme Court cases can be achieved through the following sources:

(1) Slip Opinions

The United States Supreme Court initially issues its opinion in slip form. These slip opinions are available at the United States Supreme Court the day a decision is announced. The slips are then immediately sent to law libraries, law book publishers, and other subscribers. The slip opinions can typically be located in law libraries within five to ten days after the date of decision. The slips will contain only the decision of the Court; they will not include any editorial features such as headnotes.

(2) Computer-assisted Research

As we will discuss more fully in Chapter 11, the computer-assisted research services LEXIS and Westlaw usually have the full text of a United States Supreme Court case within one hour after the decision is released.

(3) United States Law Week

You may recall from Chapter 3 that *United States Law Week*, a weekly publication of The Bureau of National Affairs, Inc., publishes some of the federal laws passed during the previous week. *United States Law Week* is perhaps better known, however, for publishing in looseleaf form (for example, looseleaf pamphlets, which are then maintained in ringed binders), the full text of United States Supreme Court opinions from the preceding week. Just as you may subscribe to *Architectural Digest* or *Better Homes and Gardens*, law firms and law libraries subscribe to *United States Law Week* to obtain rapid access to recent United States Supreme Court decisions. In addition to publishing the United States Supreme Court cases, *United States Law Week* also indicates which cases have been docketed or scheduled for hearing by the Court, summaries of cases recently filed with the Court, a calendar of hearings scheduled, and summaries of oral arguments made before the Court.

(4) Newspapers

Many law firms and law libraries subscribe to legal newspapers, which report news of interest to legal professionals. Often these newspapers will print United States Supreme Court cases in full as well as cases from lower federal courts or cases from the courts in the state in which the newspaper is published. These newspapers are generally available within a few days after the decision is rendered.

(5) WestFax

West has recently established a service called WestFax, which will send you the full text of cases by facsimile transmission, overnight delivery, or mail. Call 1-800-5622-FAX to order cases. The price is $7.00 per case and $1.50 per page, together with applicable taxes.

(6) Internet

As discussed in Chapter 12, Supreme Court cases are now available at no cost on the Internet. Cases appear on the Internet within a day of their release.

Until recently, the *Supreme Court Bulletin* was published weekly by Commerce Clearing House. This looseleaf service contained the full text of recent Supreme Court cases as well as useful editorial features such as a status report on cases pending before the United States Supreme Court. Unfortunately, this set ceased publication in December 1996.

2. United States Courts of Appeal Cases

The set of books that publishes cases from the intermediate courts of appeal (for example, First Circuit, Second Circuit) is the *Federal Reporter* (abbreviated "F.") and the *Federal Reporter, Second Series* and *Third Series* (abbreviated as "F.2d" and "F.3d"). The *Federal Reporter* was created by West in 1880 to publish decisions from the Circuit Courts of Appeal. While the primary function of the *Federal Reporter* is to publish decisions from these intermediate federal courts, it has published cases from various other courts as well. See Figure 4-4.

This set of reporters is unofficial and is yet another of the units in West's *National Reporter System*. In fact, the *Federal Reporter* is the *only* set that reports decisions from these intermediate courts of appeal. Although only approximately 40 percent of the cases for the Courts of Appeal are published, the *Federal Reporter* grows by about 20 to 25 hardbound volumes each year. There is no official reporter for these cases. Thus, there are no parallel cites for cases from the circuit courts. The only citation that you will encounter is to the *Federal Reporter* or *Federal Reporter, Second Series* or *Third Series*. As is typical of publication of court decisions, the cases are initially published in soft-copy advance sheets that are later replaced by hardbound permanent volumes.

While the overview of the *Federal Reporter*, as shown in Figure 4-4, is a useful historical guide, it is sufficient to know that the chief role of the *Federal Reporter* is to report decisions from the United States Courts of Appeal.

3. United States District Court Cases

You will recall from Chapter 2 that the United States District Courts are the trial courts in our federal system. You may also recall that Section A of this chapter noted that trial court decisions are not usually published. An exception to this general rule lies in the *Federal Supplement* and *Federal Supplement Second Series* (abbreviated as "F. Supp." and "F. Supp. 2d"), created in 1932 by West and which publish decisions from the United States District Courts, our trial courts. While the *Federal Supplement* and *Federal Supplement Second Series* publish decisions from other courts as well (see Figure 4-5), their key function is to report decisions from these United States District Courts, although they publish only about 15 percent of the cases heard by our federal district courts. The *Federal Supplement* and *Federal Supplement Second Series* are other unofficial West publications and are a part of West's *National Reporter System*. The *Federal Supplement* and *Federal Supplement Second Series* comprise the sole set of books that publish United States District Court cases. Thus, there are no parallel citations for United States District Court cases. Just as with other case reports, cases appear first in advance sheets and later in hardbound volumes.

Figure 4-4
Coverage of the *Federal Reporter*

1880-1912	U.S. Circuit Court Cases
1911-1913	Commerce Court of the United States
1880-1932	U.S. District Courts
1929-1932	U.S. Court of Claims
1960-1982	U.S. Court of Claims
1891-Date	U.S. Courts of Appeal
1929-1982	U.S. Court of Customs and Patent Appeals
1943-1961	U.S. Emergency Court of Appeals
1972-1993	Temporary Emergency Court of Appeals

Figure 4-5
Coverage of the *Federal Supplement*

1932-1960	U.S. Court of Claims
1932-Date	U.S. District Courts
1954-Date	U.S. Court of International Trade (formerly the United States Customs Court)
1932-Date	Judicial Panel on Multidistrict Litigation
1973-Date	Special Court, Regional Rail Reorganization Act

4. Cases Interpreting Federal Rules

Yet another unit in West's *National Reporter System*, the *Federal Rules Decisions* set, publishes cases since 1939 that interpret the Federal Rules of Civil Procedure and, since 1946, cases that interpret Federal Rules of Criminal Procedure. *Federal Rules Decisions* (abbreviated as "F.R.D.") publishes these cases in advance sheets and then in replacement hardbound volumes. They do not otherwise appear in the *Federal Supplement*. Thus, the name of this set, *Federal Rules Decisions*, is perfectly descriptive of its function: It publishes cases that construe federal rules, whether those rules relate to rules of procedure for civil cases or rules of procedure for criminal cases.

F. Star Paging

Citation form will be thoroughly discussed in Chapter 8, but for now it is sufficient if you are aware that for state court cases cited in a document submitted to a court in that state, you must give all parallel cites. Thus, if you are referring to the case *Guysinger v. K.C. Raceway, Inc.*, in a brief for a court in Ohio, the correct citation form is as follows: *Guysinger v. K.C. Raceway, Inc.*, 54 Ohio App. 3d 17, 560 N.E.2d 584 (1990).

The *Bluebook*, the uniform guide to citation form, provides, however, that there is an exception to this general rule of providing all parallel cites. That exception relates to United States Supreme Court cases for which you are to cite only to the official *United States Reports*. That is, for citation form purposes, it is as if the unofficial sets, West's *Supreme Court Reporter* (S. Ct.) and LEXIS Publishing's *Supreme Court Reports, Lawyers' Edition* (L. Ed.), do not exist (unless the citation to the *United States Reports* is unavailable).

Obviously, therefore, the publishers at West and LEXIS were in a dilemma. It would be extremely difficult for these publishers to attempt to market their sets of books because no matter how wonderful and useful the extra features contained in these unofficial sets might be, law firms and other users would be highly unlikely to purchase a set of books that could not be cited or quoted.

The publishers at West and LEXIS thus developed a technique of continually indicating throughout their sets which volume and page a reader would be on if that reader were using the official *United States Reports*. This technique of indicating page breaks in the official set is called "star paging" because the early method of indicating when a new page commenced was through the use of a star or asterisk (*).

The more common method today is to use an inverted "T." For example, if you are reading a case in West's *Supreme Court Reporter*, each page therein will provide you with the parallel citation to the official *United States Reports*. This citation is usually found in the upper corner of each page. As you are reading through the opinion, you might see language such as the following:

"We therefore hold | that the law of implied indemnity . . ."
218

Such an indication informs you that if you were reading this case in the *United States Reports*, after the word "hold" you would have turned the page to page 218. The first word on page 218 in that volume of the *United States Reports* would be "that."

Star paging is entirely self-correcting. If you have any doubt that you are converting the page numbers accurately, you can always retrieve the appropriate volume of the *United States Reports* and verify that the first word on page 218 is "that." As a result, no matter which set of unofficial books you use for United States Supreme Court cases, you can readily tell the page you would be on if you were holding the official *United States Reports*. Figure 4-6 shows a sample page illustrating star paging. Star paging is also found in some other West sets, such as in *California Reporter* and in the *New York Supplement* directing you to pagination for the official California and New York reports.

G. Specialized *National Reporter System* Sets

There are additional sets of books that are also a part of West's *National Reporter System Series*. These reporters, however, publish very specialized cases and are as follows:

1. West's Military Justice Reporter

This set publishes decisions from the United States Court of Appeals for the Armed Forces and the Military Service Courts of Criminal Appeals.

2. West's Veterans Appeals Reporter

This set publishes cases decided by the United States Court of Appeals for Veterans Claims, created in 1991.

3. West's Bankruptcy Reporter

The *Bankruptcy Reporter* publishes selected decisions that are not found in the *Federal Supplement* and that are decided by the United States Bankruptcy Courts, the Bankruptcy Appellate Panels, and the United States District Courts. Additionally, this set reprints bankruptcy appeals

Figure 4-6
Sample Page from West's *Supreme Court Reporter* Showing "Star Paging"

Reference to volume and page in official *United States Reports*

487 U.S. 677 **MORRISON v. OLSON** **2611**

Cite as 108 S.Ct. 2597 (1988)

ter the addition of "Consuls" to the list, the Committee's proposal was adopted, *id.*, at 539, and was subsequently reported to the Convention by the Committee of Style. See *id.*, at 599. It was at this point, on September 15, that Gouverneur Morris moved to add the Excepting Clause to Art. II, § 2. *Id.*, at 627. The one comment made on this motion was by Madison, who felt that the Clause did not go far enough in that it did not allow Congress to vest appointment powers in "Superior Officers below Heads of Departments." The first vote on Morris' motion ended in a tie. It was then put forward a second time, with the urging that "some such provision [was] too necessary, to be omitted." This time the proposal was adopted. *Id.*, at 627–628. As this discussion shows, there was little or no debate on the question whether the Clause empowers Congress to provide for interbranch appointments, and there is nothing to suggest that the Framers intended to prevent Congress from having that power.

Star Paging (the word "to" appears on page 675 of volume 487 of the *United States Reports*, while the word "impair" appears on page 676 of the volume)

We do not mean to say that Congress' power to provide for interbranch appointments of "inferior officers" is unlimited. In addition to separation-of-powers concerns, which would arise if such provisions for appointment had the potential to ⌊676impair the constitutional functions assigned to one of the branches, *Siebold* itself suggested that Congress' decision to vest the appointment power in the courts would be improper if there was some "incongruity" between the functions normally performed by the courts and the performance of their duty to appoint. 100 U.S. (10 Otto), at 398 ("[T]he duty to appoint inferior officers, when required thereto by law, is a constitutional duty of the courts; and in the present case there is no such incongruity in the duty required as to excuse the courts from its performance, or to render their acts void"). In this case, however, we do not think it impermissible for Congress to vest the power to appoint independent counsel in a specially created federal court. We thus disagree with the Court of Appeals' conclusion that there is an inherent incongruity about a court having the power to appoint prosecutorial officers.[13] We have recognized that courts may appoint private attorneys to act as prosecutor for judicial contempt judgments. See *Young v. United States ex rel. Vuitton et Fils S.A.*, 481 U.S. 787, 107 S.Ct. 2124, 95 L.Ed.2d 740 (1987). In *Go–Bart Importing Co. v. United States*, 282 U.S. 344, 51 S.Ct. 153, 75 L.Ed. 374 (1931), we approved court appointment of United States commissioners, who exercised certain limited prosecutorial powers. *Id.*, at 353, n. 2, 51 S.Ct., at 156, n. 2. In *Siebold*, as well, we indicated that judicial appointment of federal marshals, who are "executive officer[s]," would not be inappropriate. Lower courts have also upheld interim judicial appointments of United States Attorneys, see *United States v. Solomon*, 216 F.Supp. 835 (SDNY 1963), and Congress itself has vested the power to make these interim appointments in the district courts, see 28 ⌊677U.S.C. § 546(d) (1982 ed., Supp. V).[14] Congress, of course, was concerned when it created the office of independent counsel with the conflicts of interest that could arise in situations when the Executive Branch is called upon to investigate its own high-ranking officers. If it were to remove the appointing authority from the Executive Branch, the most logical place to put it was in the Judicial Branch. In the light of

13. Indeed, in light of judicial experience with prosecutors in criminal cases, it could be said that courts are especially well qualified to appoint prosecutors. This is not a case in which judges are given power to appoint an officer in an area in which they have no special knowledge or expertise, as in, for example, a statute authorizing the courts to appoint officials in the Department of Agriculture or the Federal Energy Regulatory Commission.

14. We note also the longstanding judicial practice of appointing defense attorneys for individuals who are unable to afford representation, see 18 U.S.C. § 3006A(b) (1982 ed., Supp. V), notwithstanding the possibility that the appointed attorney may appear in court before the judge who appointed him.

handled by the United States Courts of Appeal and the United States Supreme Court.

4. *West's* Federal Claims Court Reporter

This set (previouly called *United States Claims Court Reporter*) publishes decisions from the United States Court of Federal Claims (formerly called the United States Claims Court) from its conception in 1982 as well as Court of Federal Claims appeals handled by the United States Courts of Appeal and the United States Supreme Court.

5. *Federal Cases*

Until 1880, when West began publishing cases from the lower federal courts, there was no one comprehensive set of books that reported decisions from these courts. While several sets existed, none were adequate. Therefore, in 1880, West collected all of these lower federal court cases together and republished them in a set of books titled *Federal Cases*. *Federal Cases* is a very unusual arrangement of cases as it publishes these lower federal court cases that preceded the establishment of the *National Reporter System* in *alphabetical* order rather than *chronological* order, as is the usual format. If you examine *Federal Cases*, you will note that each case is assigned a consecutive number, with the first case referred to as No. 1, *The Aalesund*, and the last case referred to as No. 18,222, *In re Zug*.

Due to the fact it covers much older cases, *Federal Cases* is typically available at only larger law libraries. You should compare the relatively small number of volumes, 30, which cover lower federal court cases from 1789 to 1879 in *Federal Cases* with the current total of approximately 2,000 volumes covering cases from 1880 to the present in the *Federal Reporter* and *Federal Supplement*, thus demonstrating again the dramatic increase in litigation in this country.

H. Features of West's *National Reporter System*

The case reporters in West's *National Reporter System* possess a number of useful editorial features that aid in and simplify legal research. These features are found in both the advance sheets and the permanent hardbound volumes (except as noted) and are as follows:

1. *Tables of Cases Reported*

There will be at least one alphabetical table of cases in each volume of West's *National Reporter System* sets. For example, in any volume of the

Supreme Court Reporter, there will be a complete alphabetical list of all of the cases in that volume. This feature is useful if you know the approximate date of a Supreme Court case and need to examine a few volumes of the set to locate the specific case itself. Additionally, you may have inadvertently transposed the numbers in a citation and be unable to locate the case you need. The table of cases will allow you to look up the case you desire and then locate the specific page on which it appears.

Some sets of books have two tables of cases. For instance, any volume in the *Pacific Reporter* will contain one complete alphabetical list of the cases in that volume as well as an alphabetized list of the cases arranged by state so that the Alaska cases are separately alphabetized, the Arizona cases are separately alphabetized, and so on. Similarly, any volume in the *Federal Reporter* will possess one complete alphabetical list of the cases in that volume and will also separately arrange and alphabetize the First Circuit cases, then the Second Circuit cases, for example.

2. *Tables of Statutes and Rules*

The Table of Statutes will direct you to cases in a volume that have interpreted or construed any statutes or constitutional provisions. Thus, if you are interested in whether any recent cases have interpreted N.Y. Banking Law § 309 (McKinney 1982), you can consult the table of statutes in any recent volume of the *North Eastern Reporter* and you will be directed to the specific page in the volume that interprets that statute.

Similarly, there are tables listing all federal rules of civil and criminal procedure, federal rules of appellate procedure, and federal rules of evidence that are construed by any cases in a particular volume.

3. *Table of Words and Phrases*

This table alphabetically lists words or phrases that have been interpreted or defined by any cases in a volume of the *National Reporter System*. For example, you can consult the Table of Words and Phrases and determine if the words "abandonment," "negligence," or "trustee" have been defined by any cases in a volume, and you will be directed to the specific page in a volume on which such a word is judicially defined.

4. *List of Judges*

This feature is found only in the hardbound volumes of the *National Reporter System* and lists all of the judges sitting on the courts covered by that particular volume. Thus, any hardbound volume of the *Federal Reporter* will provide a list of First Circuit judges, Second Circuit judges, and so on.

5. *Key Number Digest*

While West's Key Number System will be described in full in the next chapter, for the present it is sufficient to know that in the back of each hardbound volume in West's *National Reporter System* (except the *Bankruptcy Reporter* and the *Federal Claims Court Reporter*), West will provide a brief summary of each case in the volume arranged by topic and Key Number.

I. Finding Parallel Cites

You have seen that many cases can be found in more than one place. This is because many cases are published officially and unofficially. The different citations to a case are known as *parallel cites*.

On some occasions, you may have one cite and may need the other parallel cite. This could be due to the fact that citation rules require all parallel cites or it could be for the very practical reason that the volume you need is missing from the library bookshelf and you must obtain the parallel cite to locate the case you need. There are several techniques you can use to find a parallel cite.

1. *Cross-References*

Many cases provide all parallel cites. For example, if you open a volume of *California Reports* to the case you need, at the top of each page you are given all parallel cites for this case.

2. National Reporter Blue Book

If you have an official cite for a state court case and you need the unofficial parallel cite, you can use a set published by West and titled the *National Reporter Blue Book*. This set contains complete conversion tables showing parallel cites. For example, if you look up the official cite, 321 N.C. 111, you are immediately provided with the unofficial citation, 361 S.E.2d 562.

3. Shepard's Citations

As you will learn in Chapter 9, when you Shepardize either an official or an unofficial citation, you are given the parallel cite.

4. *State Digests*

West has published sets of books called "digests" for each state except Delaware, Nevada, and Utah. These digests (discussed in detail in the next chapter) contain tables of cases, which provide parallel citations. Thus, if you look up a case by name in the *Wisconsin Digest*, you will be provided with the citation for the case in the *Wisconsin Reports* as well as in the *North Western Reporter*.

J. Summary of West's *National Reporter System*

West's *National Reporter System* is a series of sets of case reporters that publish cases from state appellate courts and from federal trial and appellate courts. All of the sets of books in the *National Reporter System* are unofficial because the books are published privately by West rather than pursuant to some statutory directive or mandate. Although West's *National Reporter System* is the largest collection of case reporters, West is not the only publisher of cases. For example, LEXIS Publishing publishes United States Supreme Court cases in its set *United States Supreme Court Reports, Lawyers' Edition.*

West publishes state court cases in various regional units, each of which contains cases from a particular geographical area. The state court units are as follows:

North Western Reporter
Pacific Reporter
North Eastern Reporter
Atlantic Reporter
South Western Reporter
Southern Reporter
South Eastern Reporter

Because the states of New York, California, and Illinois decide so many cases, West also created the following separate sets just for these states:

New York Supplement
California Reporter
Illinois Decisions

Federal cases are published in these sets of books:

Supreme Court Reporter	(cases from the United States Supreme Court)
Federal Reporter	(cases from the United States Courts of Appeal)

Federal Supplement	(cases from the United States District Courts)
Federal Rules Decisions	(cases interpreting federal rules of civil and criminal procedure)

Finally, West publishes four other sets, each of which is descriptively titled: the *Military Justice Reporter*, the *Veterans Appeals Reporter*, the *Bankruptcy Reporter*, and the *United States Claims Court Reporter*.

All of the books in West's *National Reporter System* possess a variety of useful features and all are participants in West's *Key Number System,* which is described in full in Chapter 5.

You can readily see that there are numerous sets of reporters, each identified by its own particular abbreviation. There is an excellent reference tool of abbreviations and acronyms used in legal literature, from "Ct. Cl. R." (for Court of Claims Rules) to "S.L.R.B." (for State Labor Relations Board). See Mary Miles Prince, *Bieber's Dictionary of Legal Abbreviations* (4th ed. 1993), published by William S. Hein & Co., Inc., of Buffalo, New York. A copy may be kept in the reference section of your law library. Additionally, the front of each volume of West's general encyclopedia, *Corpus Juris Secundum* (C.J.S.) includes a thorough table of legal abbreviations. See Figure 4-7 for a summary of case law publication.

Figure 4-7
Summary of Case Law Publication

	Highest Court	*Intermediate Appellate Courts*	*Trial Courts*
Federal Cases	United States Supreme Court a. *United States Reports* b. *Supreme Court Reporter* c. *United States Supreme Court Reports, Lawyers' Edition* d. *United States Law Week*	United States Courts of Appeal cases are published in *Federal Reporter* (F., F.2d, and F.3d)	United States District Court cases are published in *Federal Supplement* (F. Supp. and F. Supp. 2d)
State Cases	State Supreme Courts (examples of official sets are *California Reports* and *Georgia Reports*)	State Appellate Courts (examples of official sets are *California Appellate Reports* and *Georgia Appeals Reporters*)	Generally, trial court cases are not published

K. Briefing Cases

The importance of cases in our common law system has already been discussed. You will also recall that in our legal system it is not sufficient to merely read a statute assuming that it will provide the answer to a question or problem because it is the task of our courts to interpret and construe statutory language. Thus, reading, interpreting, and analyzing cases are of critical importance to all involved in the legal profession.

Few people find it natural to read cases. The language used by courts is often archaic, and the style of writing can make it difficult to comprehend the court's reasoning. The most common technique used to impose some order or structure on the confusing world of case law is case briefing. Do not confuse the word "brief" in this context, in which it means a summary of the key elements of a case, with the written argument an attorney presents to a court, which is also called a "brief." A case brief is a short, written summary and analysis of a case.

It is extremely common for law students to brief cases so in the event they are called upon in class to discuss a case, they will have a convenient summary to use. Moreover, practicing attorneys often desire to have cases briefed so they may save time by reading the briefs first and then, based upon the initial reading, analyze only selected cases in full. In some instances, months can go by between hearings in court, or new attorneys and paralegals may join the legal team. The case briefs for a matter handled by the team should be sufficiently readable and useful that new team members can be immediately brought "up to speed" by reviewing the briefs.

Perhaps the primary reason for briefing cases, however, is to learn how to focus on the important parts of the case in order to obtain a thorough understanding of the case and its reasoning. While you may be tempted to view case briefing as busywork and may believe you can understand a case by simply reading it through, research has shown that people tend to read quickly and see words in groupings. Briefing a case will force you to slow down and concentrate on the critical aspects of the case. After you have mastered case briefing and thus trained yourself to analyze cases properly, you likely will be able to dispense with written briefs and will be able to brief cases by merely underlining or highlighting the key portions of cases.

The first briefs you prepare may be nearly as long as the case itself. This is because it takes practice to learn to recognize the essential elements of a case. Initially, every part of the case will seem critical to you. With time, however, you will develop skill at briefing and will be able to produce a concise summary of cases. Ideally, a case brief should be no more than one typed page, although longer and more complex cases may require a longer brief.

There is no one perfect form for a case brief. Some large law firms provide suggested formats. If no form is given to you, you should use a style that best suits you and helps you understand the case and its significance as a precedent for the research problem on which you are working. Read through a case at least once before you begin to brief it so you will have a general idea as to the nature of the issues involved and how the court resolved these issues. Resist the temptation to read only the headnotes or to skim the case. A close scrutiny of the case may reveal critical analysis likely to be overlooked in a cursory reading.

It may take you several readings of a case to understand it thoroughly. You may need to take notes and prepare a diagram or flowchart showing the path the case followed in reaching this court and the relationship of the parties to each other.

Good case briefs share the following elements:

- They use complete sentences.
- They do not overquote from the opinion.
- They do not include unnecessary, distracting citations.
- They are brief, ideally one page in length.

The most common elements to be included in a case brief are the following:

1. *Name of case.*
2. *Citations.* All parallel citations should be included as well as the date of decision. These citations will enable you to retrieve the case later if you need to relocate it.
3. *Procedural history.* This is a brief summary of the holdings of any previous courts and the disposition of the case by this court. A procedural history describes how the case got to this court and how this court resolves the case. It will be significant whether the prior decision is a trial court decision or an appellate court decision. Start by briefly identifying the parties and stating the relief they were seeking or the defenses they raised. Then proceed to discuss what the court(s) below held and the final disposition by this reviewing court.
4. *Statement of facts.* A case brief should include a concise summary of the facts of the case. You need not include all facts but rather only the significant facts relied on by the court in reaching its decision. Facts that affect the outcome of a case are called "relevant facts" or "material facts." Identify the parties by name and indicate whether a party is a plaintiff, defendant, and so forth. The facts are more readable if they are presented in a narrative rather than outline or "bullet" format. Discuss facts in the past tense. A chronological presentation of the facts is usually the most helpful to a reader. If facts are disputed, note such.
5. *Issue(s).* You must formulate the question(s) or issue(s) being decided by this court. Focus on what the parties asked the court to determine. In some instances, courts will specifically state the issues being addressed. In other instances, the issues are not expressly provided and you will have to formulate the issue being

decided. Phrase the issue so that it has some relevance to the case at hand. Thus, rather than stating the issue in a broad fashion ("What is an assault?" or "Did the lower court err?"), state the issue so it incorporates some of the relevant facts of the case ("Does a conditional threat constitute an assault?"). Keep your issues or questions to one sentence in length.

There are three ways issues can be phrased: a direct question, the "whether" format, or the "under" format. A direct question might ask, "Is pointing an unloaded gun at a person an assault?" The "whether" format would phrase the same question as follows: "Whether pointing an unloaded gun at a person is an assault." The "under" format would result in the following phrasing: "Under California law, is pointing an unloaded gun at a person an assault?" Generally, any of these formats is acceptable, although some attorneys dislike the "whether" form of issue because it results in a fragment rather than a complete sentence.

6. *Answer(s)* or *Holding(s)*. Provide an answer(s) to the question(s) being resolved by this court. Rather than merely stating "yes" or "no," phrase the answer in a complete sentence and incorporate some of the reasons for the answer. For example, if the issue is "Does a conditional threat constitute an assault?," rather than merely state "no," state, "A conditional threat does not constitute an assault because a condition negates a threat so the hearer is in no danger of present or immediate harm." If you have set forth three issues, you will need three separate answers. Each answer should be no more than two sentences in length. Strive for one-sentence answers. Do not include citations.
7. *Reasoning*. The reasoning is the most important part of a brief. This is the section in which you discuss *why* the court reached the conclusions it did. Were prior cases relied upon? Did the court adopt a new rule of law? Is the decision limited to the facts of this particular case or is the decision broad enough to serve as binding precedent in similar but not identical cases? Did the court discuss any social policy that would be served by its decision? Fully discuss the reasons why the court reached its decision and the thought process by which it arrived at this decision. Re-read your issue(s) and answer(s) and then ensure that the reasoning is directly responsive to these and answers the *why* question. Citations may be included in this section but are often not necessary. Use your own words in summarizing and explaining the court's reasoning rather than overquoting from the case. This will help ensure that you understand the rationale for the court's decision.
8. *Holding*. Include the actual disposition of this case, such as "affirmed" or "reversed."

You may include an additional section in your brief summarizing concurring or dissenting opinions.

Following is a suggested format for a typical case brief:

Foley v. Connelie

435 U.S. 291, 98 S. Ct. 1067, 55 L. Ed. 2d 287 (1978)

Procedural History

Appellant, Edmund Foley, an alien, brought a class action in the United States District Court for the Southern District of New York, seeking a declaratory judgment that a statute in the State of New York that excluded aliens from the state's police force violated the Equal Protection Clause of the United States Constitution. The District Court (convening a three-judge panel) granted summary judgment in favor of the defendants (the Superintendent of the New York State Police and the Director of Personnel of the State of New York) and found the statute to be constitutional. The United States Supreme Court affirmed.

Statement of Facts

Edmund Foley, an alien eligible to become a naturalized citizen, was residing lawfully in the United States as a permanent resident. He applied to become a New York State Trooper, a position which is filled on the basis of competitive examinations. Pursuant to a New York statute which provided that no individual could be appointed to the New York State Police force unless he or she was a United States citizen, the state authorities refused to allow Foley to take the examination. Foley instituted a class action on behalf of himself and all others similarly situated, seeking a declaratory judgment that the statute was unconstitutional.

Issue

May a state statute limit appointment of members of its state police force to United States citizens?

Answer

Yes. Citizenship is a relevant qualification for state police officers.

Reasoning

The United States Supreme Court noted that while restraints upon aliens should be subjected to close scrutiny and while aliens have been extended the right to education and public welfare, along with the ability to earn a livelihood and engage in licensed professions, the right to govern and formulate and execute public policy is reserved to United States citizens. Because police officers participate directly in the execution of broad public policy in the performance of their duties, citizenship is a relevant qualification. To be constitutional, the state need only justify its classification of requiring state troopers to be citizens by a showing of some rational relationship between the interest sought to be protected and the limiting classification. In the enforcement and execution of state law, the police are required to make numerous delicate and difficult judgments, and this function is one where citizenship bears a rational relationship to the special demands of the particular position and a state is free to confine the performance of this important public responsibility to United States citizens.

Holding

The Court affirmed the decision of the court below.

The preceding brief follows a very standard format. A more thorough and comprehensive brief would include the name of the author of the majority opinion, a reference to how many justices were in the majority and how many dissented (for example, 7-2), a quick summary of any dissenting and concurring opinions, a summary of each party's contentions and legal arguments, a discussion of social policies furthered by the decision, and a final section including your comments and criticism of the case. In most instances, such a thorough brief is not needed, and the format above should suffice for most purposes. See Figure 4-8 for the form for a case brief.

Case Brief Assignment

Prepare a brief of the case *United States v. Johnson*, 32 F.3d 82 (4th Cir. 1994).

L. Citation Form

1. *Federal Cases*

a. Cases from the United States Supreme Court:
Roe v. Wade, 410 U.S. 113 (1973).
b. Cases from the United States Courts of Appeal:
Traylor v. Cohen, 597 F.2d 109 (4th Cir. 1988).
c. Cases from the United States District Courts:
Allen v. Carr, 686 F. Supp. 207 (W.D. Tex. 1980).

2. *State Cases*

a. In documents submitted to a state court, all decisions to cases decided by courts of that state must include all parallel citations:
Baker v. Dolan, 228 Cal. 901, 426 P.2d 16, 207 Cal. Rptr. 3 (1976).
b. In all other documents, cite to the regional reporter:
Baker v. Dolan, 426 P.2d 16 (Cal. 1976).

Figure 4-8
Case Brief Form

Case Name: ____________________

Case Citation: ____________________

Procedural History: ____________________

____

____

____

Statement of Facts: ____________________

____

____

____

Issues: ____________________

____

____

____

Answers: ____________________

____

____

____

Reasoning: ____________________

____

____

____

Holding: ____________________

Technology Tips

http://www.uscourts.gov	Federal Courts home page.
http://www.law.emory.edu/FEDCTS	The Courts Finder provides a map of the United States. Click links to go to specific circuits.
http://supct.law.cornell.edu/supct	This site provides United States Supreme Court rulings since 1990 and 600 important court cases prior to 1990.
http://www.access.gpo.gov/su_docs	GPO Access provides access to United States Supreme Court cases.
http://vls.law.vill.edu/locator/fedcourt.html	This site provides access to United States Supreme Court, United States Courts of Appeal, and United States District Court cases through the Villanova University School of Law.
http://www.findlaw.com	FindLaw, one of the best known legal sites, provides easy access to federal and state cases as well as providing a wide variety of other law-related information and links to other sites.
http://www.ll.georgetown.edu	This site of the Georgetown University Law Center law library provides links to federal and state cases (select "federal" and then "judicial branch" to locate federal cases and links to home pages for each of the 94 district courts or "state, local, and territorial" and then click on the desired state for state court cases).
http://www.supremecourtus.gov	The Web site of the United States Supreme Court provides information about the Court, its docket, Court rules, and its opinions.
http://www.ll.georgetown.edu/Fed-Ct/	This site provides a map of the federal circuits, with links to each circuit for locating cases.
http://lcweb.loc.gov/global/judiciary.html	This site for the United States judicial branch provides access to cases from the United States Supreme Court and the courts of appeal, a map of the United States circuits, and state cases.
http://www.tourolaw.edu	The site of Touro College Law Center provides access to cases from the federal courts.
http://www.law.cornell.edu/federal/opinions.html	This site provides access to recent decisions of the United States Supreme Court, selected cases from the United States Courts of Appeal, and selected cases from the United States District Courts.
http://www.uscourts.gov	The Federal Judiciary home page includes information about the federal court system and links to all United States Courts of Appeal.

(continued)

Technology Tips (*Continued*)

http://www.casenotes.com	This site provides information on briefing cases. Select the link for "how to brief."
http://emanuel.com/1L/briefing.html	This site provides tips and guidance on briefing cases.

Writing Strategies

In discussing cases, it is not enough to merely summarize or repeat the court's holding. You must *analyze* the case and show the reader why and how it applies to your situation.

By briefing cases, you will force yourself to concentrate on the critical elements of a case: the facts, the issues, the reasoning, and the holding. When you later discuss the case in a memo or court brief, you will be "pre-programmed" to analyze the case properly by virtue of the training you acquired by preparing case briefs.

In written projects, discuss cited cases in the past tense. Any discussion in a project in the present tense ("the Defendant argues," "a duty is owed," "the Plaintiff appeals") will be interpreted as referring to *your* case, not a cited case you are relying upon.

In discussing cases, you need not give all of the facts. Give sufficient facts, however, so a reader can see why the case is controlling. If the facts are strikingly similar to those in your case, recite them in greater detail to allow the reader immediately to grasp why the result reached in the cited case governs your case.

Confront cases that are contrary to your position head-on. Assume the adversary will locate these cases. You will minimize their impact if you discuss them yourself. Emphasize why such cases are not controlling by distinguishing them from your case. Show the reader that the facts and issues in such unfavorable cases are so different than those in your case that they cannot be relied upon.

Use "location" to minimize the impact of unfavorable cases. Discuss them briefly and only after you have set forth your strongest arguments. Discuss them in the middle of a project rather than at the beginning or end, where they will draw more attention.

Assignment for Chapter 4

1. a. Give the name of the case located at 956 P.2d 88 (Nev. 1998).
   b. Give the docket number of the case.
   c. Who delivered the opinion on rehearing?
2. a. Give the name of the case located at 606 N.W.2d 783 (Neb. 2000).
   b. Give the parallel cite for the case.
3. a. Give the name of the case located at 686 A.2d 18 (Pa. Super. 1996).
   b. What does headnote 6 discuss?
   c. Who was the chief justice of the Rhode Island Supreme Court during the period of time covered by this volume?
4. a. Locate the case in 411 S.E.2d in which the defendant's name is Klaus and give the case name and citation.
   b. Who represented the appellant in this case?
   c. Which case in this volume construes the term "net value" and on which page is it discussed?
5. a. Give the name of the case located at 36 F. Supp. 2d 1118 (1999).
   b. Which district court decided this case?
6. What is the name of the case located at 175 U.S. 677? Briefly state what topic the case discusses.
7. What is the name of the case located at 54 F.R.D. 282 (W.D. 1971)? Briefy state what topic the case discusses.
8. In which *National Reporter System* series do the decisions of the following states appear?
   a. Florida
   b. Indiana
   c. Colorado
9. Give the name of the case located at:
   a. 620 N.W.2d 362
   b. 561 A.2d 762
   c. 197 S.E. 706
10. Give the parallel citations for the case located at 118 S. Ct. 1650.
11. Locate the case at 114 S. Ct. 981. How does page 444 of the parallel *United States Reports* begin?
12. Locate the case at 131 L. Ed. 2d 465. How does page 402 of the parallel *United States Reports* begin?
13. Use the *National Reporter Blue Book* (Perm. Supp. 2000). Give the parallel citations for the following cases:
    a. 105 Or. App. 61
    b. 548 Pa. 504
    c. 6 Neb. App. 67

Chapter 5

The Use of Digests, Annotated Law Reports, and *Words and Phrases*

Chapter Overview

This chapter will complete the discussion of primary authorities (statutes, constitutions, and cases) by explaining the use of digests, which serve as comprehensive casefinders. Additionally, you will be introduced to annotated law reports, which can "speed up" the research process and provide you with an exhaustive overview of an area of the law. These annotated law reports combine elements of both primary and secondary sources and thus form a bridge between the primary sources of statutes, constitutions, and cases, which have been discussed, and the secondary authorities of encyclopedias, law reviews, treatises, and other sources, which follow. Finally, you will be provided with a discussion of *Words and Phrases*, a set of books created by West, which can be used to determine the legal meaning of certain words and phrases.

A. Using Digests to Locate Cases

1. *Introduction*

It is improbable that an individual with whom you work will simply hand you a list of citations and ask you to retrieve and photocopy the cases cited. It is far more likely that you will be presented with a description of a research problem and be tasked with determining the answer. For example, an attorney might describe a client's current problems with her landlord by posing the following scenario: The firm's client rented a house from her landlord. Two months later the client noticed the roof was leaking and notified the landlord repeatedly of this problem to no avail. A recent storm caused water to leak through the roof, causing $10,000 damage to the client's expensive furniture and rug. You may be asked to research whether the landlord is liable for the damage and whether the tenant may withhold rent from the landlord until the $10,000 damage amount is satisfied.

This common type of research assignment requires you to search for cases that are "on point," which will serve as precedents and provide an answer to the client's questions. Of course, if an area of the law is likely to be dealt with by statutes, you should remember to consult initially your annotated code to review the applicable statutes and then examine the annotations following the statutes, which will interpret the statute.

You will recall that cases are usually published in chronological order. That is, there is no one set of books called *Landlord and Tenant Law* that will contain all cases dealing with landlords and tenants. Such cases are scattered throughout the numerous sets of books. For instance, each volume in the *Nevada Reports* may contain a few cases covering this particular subject matter. You cannot simply start with Volume 1 of the *Nevada Reports* or some other set of reports hoping to eventually stumble upon the right case. Such a research technique is not only inefficient and time-consuming, it may well be ineffective, as it is possible you could examine the more than 100 volumes of the *Nevada Reports* only to discover that Nevada has not yet considered this particular issue.

Legal research requires a much more systematic approach to locating pertinent cases, and this systematic approach is aided through the use of sets of books called "digests." While there are several varieties of digests, all of them function in a similar fashion: Digests assist you by arranging cases by subject matter so that all of the assault cases are brought together, all of the bribery cases are brought together, all of the contract cases are brought together, and so on. These digests, however, do not reprint in full all of the assault cases, but rather print a brief one-sentence summary or "digest" of each assault case and then provide you with a citation so you can determine which cases you should retrieve and examine in full. In this way, digests serve as guideposts, which help direct you to the specific cases you need so you can research as efficiently and effectively as possible. Because the digests are written by publishers (primarily West) and are mere summaries of cases, the digest entries cannot be quoted from or relied upon. The cases the digests direct you to, however, will serve as binding authority.

2. *The* American Digest System

While there are different types of digests, the majority are published by West, which realized shortly after it introduced its *National Reporter System* that legal professionals needed a method of finding the cases published therein. The most comprehensive digest set published by West is the *American Digest System*, which will be described here in detail. Once you understand how to use the *American Digest System*, you will also understand how to use the other West digests because all digests are organized in substantially the same manner.

The *American Digest System* is an amazingly thorough set of books that aims at citing and digesting every reported case so you can readily locate *all* cases in a given area of law, such as corporations, trusts, negligence, or landlord-tenant law. In the *American Digest System*, West brings together all cases relating to a legal issue from *all* of the units of the *National Reporter System*. Thus, if you were researching the defenses to battery, you would be able to locate cases from the *Supreme Court Reporter, Federal Reporter, Federal Supplement, North Western Reporter, Pacific Reporter*, and others, all of which deal with defenses to battery. The *American Digest System* is therefore most useful when you have an extensive research project and you desire to know how several jurisdictions (both federal and state) have treated a specific legal topic.

West describes its combination of headnotes and topics and Key Numbers as part of the "greatest time-saving system ever invented to help [researchers] find cases worthy of further analysis."

3. *Organization of the* American Digest System

To understand how to locate cases using West's *American Digest System*, it is necessary to understand how the System is organized. You will recall from Chapter 4 that when a decision is issued by a court, it consists of a case name, a docket number, a date of decision, names of counsel, and the opinion itself. West receives a copy of the case, scans or keyboards it on Westlaw, and assigns it to its editors. These editors are attorneys who thoroughly read the case and through a 26-step process, draft the brief synopsis (which appears after the case name and which concisely summarizes the case) and the headnotes for the case. If the case discusses seven areas of law, it will have seven headnotes. If the case discusses 12 areas of the law, it will have 12 headnotes. These headnotes are the brief paragraphs that precede the opinion of the court. Each headnote is given a consecutive number, a topic name (Insurance, Covenants, Deeds, Venue, for example) based on the area of law the headnote deals with, and a "Key Number" (a pictorial design of a key and a number). Thus, a typical headnote in a case published in any West set of court reports looks like the following:

> **7. Gifts 🔑 22**
> Constructive delivery is sufficient where donor's intention to make the gift plainly appears and the articles intended to be given are not present or, if present, are incapable of manual delivery.

Such a headnote is the seventh one in the case, its topic is "Gifts," and its Key Number is 22.

The case is now complete, consisting of the original elements as provided by the court and the additional features (synopsis and headnotes) provided by West's editors. The case will be printed in an advance sheet, which is mailed to agencies, judges, law firms, law libraries, and other subscribers. The headnotes alone, however, are taken by West and published in a monthly pamphlet called the *General Digest*. Last month's *General Digest*, therefore, contains *all* of the headnotes of *all* cases published by West in its *National Reporter System* (*North Western Reporter, Pacific Reporter, California Reporter, Federal Reporter*, and so on). The headnotes are arranged alphabetically by topic name such as Abandoned and Lost Property, Abatement and Revival, Abduction, and Absentees. Within each topic name, the headnotes are arranged by Key Number, such as Absentees 1, Absentees 2, and Absentees 3.

The monthly softcover issues of the *General Digest* are later brought together ("cumulated") and published in hardcover volumes. West then began bringing together and publishing the hardcover volumes of the *General Digest* in ten-year groups called "Decennials." The word "decennial" is literally defined as a ten-year period. Thus, the *First Decennial* contains all headnotes from all of the units of the *National Reporter System* for the period 1897-1906. The *Second Decennial* contains all headnotes from all of the units of the *National Reporter System* for the ten-year period 1906-1916. For obvious reasons, the *American Digest System* is sometimes called the *Decennial Digest System*.

You should be aware that West has also created a set of books called the *Century Digest* to cover the time period 1658 to 1897 (the date coverage of the *First Decennial* commences). The *Century Digest* uses a classification scheme different from the Key Number System used in the *Decennials*. It is unlikely you will use the *Century Digest* very often, if ever, as it digests cases that are very old. West does, however, provide cross-reference tables in the *First* and *Second Decennial Digests* so you can readily locate cases in the *Century Digest* if you have a topic name and a Key Number. Figure 5-1 shows the time period covered by each of the *Decennials*.

Figure 5-1

Century Digest	1658-1897
First Decennial	1897-1906
Second Decennial	1907-1916
Third Decennial	1916-1926
Fourth Decennial	1926-1936
Fifth Decennial	1936-1946
Sixth Decennial	1946-1956
Seventh Decennial	1956-1966
Eighth Decennial	1966-1976
Ninth Decennial, Part 1	1976-1981
Ninth Decennial, Part 2	1981-1986
Tenth Decennial, Part 1	1986-1991
Tenth Decennial, Part 2	1991-1996
General Digest, 9th Series	1997-Date

As you can see, starting in 1976, West began issuing the *Decennials* in two five-year parts. This change was brought about by the explosion in case law. Thus, the *Tenth Decennial* covers a ten-year period but is issued in two parts—*Part 1*, which covers 1986-1991, and *Part 2*, which covers 1991-1996.

General Digest is the name of the set of books currently in use. As soon as the next five-year time period is completed, the name of the *General Digest, 9th Series*, will change to *Eleventh Decennial, Part 1*, and the current set will then be called the *General Digest, 10th Series.*

It is not necessary to memorize the time periods covered by each *Decennial* unit. It is sufficient to understand the general structure of the *Decennial* units: Each *Decennial* covers a ten-year period and each *Decennial* will contain all of the headnotes from all of the units of the *National Reporter System* for its particular ten-year period.

If you possess the headnote presented earlier relating to constructive delivery of gifts (**Gifts 22**), you can locate all American cases from 1658 until last month that relate to this specific subject matter. You can accomplish this task by taking the following actions:

- Locate the *Decennial* volumes for a recent time period such as the *Tenth Decennial, Part 2.*
- Find the volume covering the letter "G" (for "Gifts").
- Look up "Gifts."
- Locate Gifts 22.

You will now be presented with all United States Supreme Court cases decided between 1991-1996 relating to constructive delivery of gifts, then all United States Court of Appeals cases relating to this subject, all United States District Court cases, all Alabama cases, all Alaska cases, all Arizona cases, and so on. Each case will be described with a one-sentence summary (the "digest") and you will be provided a case citation, enabling you to locate the case and read it in full if you determine the case may be helpful.

After you have located cases in the *Tenth Decennial, Part 2*, follow the same strategy for the *Tenth Decennial, Part 1*, the *Ninth Decennial* (*Parts 2* and *1*), the *Eighth Decennial*, and so forth. In this way you will be able to find all cases decided in federal and state courts from 1658 (using the *Century Digest*) until last month (using the *General Digest, 9th Series*), which relate to constructive delivery of gifts.

4. *West's Outline of the Law*

The fact that you can locate all cases on a similar point of law from 1658 until last month arises from West's remarkable consistency in assigning topic names and Key Numbers to legal issues. In order to efficiently and systematically organize cases under topic names and Key Numbers, West developed its own outline of the law. It should be noted that this outline of the law was developed exclusively by West for its own purposes. You may or may not agree with the organization scheme developed by West. You may believe additional topic names should exist. West's outline is not an official pronouncement of the subjects discussed in cases. It has no judicial or academic authority. It is simply West's organizational blueprint for its Key Number System.

West determined that the law could be categorized into the following seven main classes; that is, that any case decided by any court would deal with one of the following issues:

Persons
Property
Contracts
Torts
Crimes
Remedies
Government

West then decided that there were 32 various subclasses within these main classes. For example, the main class "Persons" has the following subclasses within it:

Relating to Natural Persons in General
Particular Classes of Natural Persons
Personal Relations
Associated and Artificial Persons
Particular Occupations

Finally, West determined that the 32 subclasses could be further arranged into more than 400 topics. For instance, the subclass "Particular Classes of Natural Persons" has the following topics within it:

Absentees
Aliens
Chemical Dependents
Children Out-of-Wedlock
Citizens
Convicts
Indians
Infants
Mental Health
Paupers
Slaves
Spendthrifts

A complete diagram of West's outline of the law is shown in Figure 5-2. The list is also found at the beginning of any West digest volume.

A case may discuss one of these more than 400 topics in a variety of ways. For example, cases may discuss infants (one of the topics within the subclass "Particular Classes of Natural Persons" within the main class

Figure 5-2
West's Outline of the Law

Digest Topics arranged for your convenience by seven main divisions of law and their numerical designations

1. PERSONS
2. PROPERTY
3. CONTRACTS
4. TORTS
5. CRIMES
6. REMEDIES
7. GOVERNMENT

1. PERSONS

RELATING TO NATURAL PERSONS IN GENERAL

Civil Rights 78
Dead Bodies 116
Death 117
Domicile 135
Drugs and Narcotics 138
Food 178
Health and Environment 199
Holidays 201
Intoxicating Liquors 223
Names 269
Poisons 304
Seals 347
Signatures 355
Sunday 369
Time 378
Weapons 406

PARTICULAR CLASSES OF NATURAL PERSONS

Absentees 5
Aliens 24
Chemical Dependents 762
Children Out-of-Wedlock 76H
Citizens 77
Convicts 98
Indians 209
Infants 211
Mental Health 257A
Paupers 292
Slaves 356
Spendthrifts 359

PERSONAL RELATIONS

Adoption 17
Attorney and Client 45
Employers' Liability 148A
Executors and Administrators 162
Guardian and Ward 196
Husband and Wife 205
Labor Relations 232A
Marriage 253
Master and Servant 255
Parent and Child 285
Principal and Agent 308
Workers' Compensation 413

ASSOCIATED AND ARTIFICIAL PERSONS

Associations 41
Beneficial Associations 54
Building and Loan Associations 66
Clubs 80
Colleges and Universities 81
Corporations 101
Exchanges 160
Joint-Stock Companies and Business Trusts 225
Partnership 289
Religious Societies 332

PARTICULAR OCCUPATIONS

Accountants 11A
Agriculture 23
Auctions and Auctioneers 47
Aviation 48B
Banks and Banking 52
Bridges 64
Brokers 65
Canals 68
Carriers 70
Commerce 83
Consumer Credit 92B
Consumer Protection 92H
Credit Reporting Agencies 108A
Detectives 125
Electricity 145
Explosives 164
Factors 167
Ferries 172
Gas 190
Hawkers and Peddlers 198
Innkeepers 213
Insurance 217
Licenses 238
Manufactures 251
Monopolies 265
Physicians and Surgeons 299
Pilots 300
Railroads 320
Seamen 348
Shipping 354
Steam 362
Telecommunications 372
Theaters and Shows 376
Towage 380
Turnpikes and Toll Roads 391
Urban Railroads 396A
Warehousemen 403
Wharves 408

2. PROPERTY

NATURE, SUBJECTS, AND INCIDENTS OF OWNERSHIP IN GENERAL

Abandoned and Lost Property 1
Accession 7
Adjoining Landowners 15
Confusion of Goods 90
Improvements 206
Property 315

PARTICULAR SUBJECTS AND INCIDENTS OF OWNERSHIP

Animals 28
Annuities 29
Automobiles 48A
Boundaries 59
Cemeteries 71
Common Lands 84
Copyrights and Intellectual Property 99
Crops 111
Fences 171
Fish 176
Fixtures 177
Franchises 183
Game 187
Good Will 192
Logs and Logging 245
Mines and Minerals 260
Navigable Waters 270
Party Walls 290
Patents 291
Public Lands 317
Trade Regulation 382
Waters and Water Courses 405
Woods and Forests 411

PARTICULAR CLASSES OF ESTATES OR INTERESTS IN PROPERTY

Charities 75
Condominium 89A
Dower and Curtesy 136
Easements 141
Estates in Property 154
Joint Tenancy 226
Landlord and Tenant 233
Life Estates 240
Perpetuities 298
Powers 307
Remainders 333
Reversions 338
Tenancy in Common 373
Trusts 390

PARTICULAR MODES OF ACQUIRING OR TRANSFERRING PROPERTY

Abstracts of Title 6
Adverse Possession 20
Alteration of Instruments 25
Assignments 38
Chattel Mortgages 76
Conversion 97
Dedication 119
Deeds 120
Descent and Distribution 124
Escheat 152
Fraudulent Conveyances 186
Gifts 191
Lost Instruments 246
Mortgages 266
Pledges 303
Secured Transactions 349A
Wills 409

3. CONTRACTS

NATURE, REQUISITES, AND INCIDENTS OF AGREEMENTS IN GENERAL

Contracts 95
Customs and Usages 113
Frauds, Statute of 185
Interest 219
Usury 398

PARTICULAR CLASSES OF AGREEMENTS

Bailment 50
Bills and Notes 56
Bonds 58
Breach of Marriage Promise 61
Champerty and Maintenance 74
Compromise and Settlement 89
Covenants 108
Deposits and Escrows 122A
Exchange of Property 159
Gaming 188
Guaranty 195
Implied and Constructive Contracts 205H
Indemnity 208
Joint Adventures 224
Lotteries 247
Principal and Surety 309
Rewards 340
Sales 343
Subscriptions 367
Vendor and Purchaser 400

PARTICULAR CLASSES OF IMPLIED OR CONSTRUCTIVE CONTRACTS OR QUASI CONTRACTS

Account Stated 11
Contribution 96

PARTICULAR MODES OF DISCHARGING CONTRACTS

Novation 278
Payment 294
Release 331
Subrogation 366
Tender 374

4. TORTS

Assault and Battery 37
Collision 82
Conspiracy 91
False Imprisonment 168
Forcible Entry and Detainer 179

Figure 5-2 (*Continued*)

Fraud 184
Libel and Slander 237
Malicious Prosecution 249
Negligence 272
Nuisance 279
Products Liability 313A
Seduction 350
Torts 379
Trespass 386
Trover and Conversion 389
Waste 904

5. CRIMES

Abduction 3
Abortion and Birth Control 4
Adulteration 18
Adultery 19
Affray 22
Arson 36
Bigamy 55
Blasphemy 57
Breach of the Peace 62
Bribery 63
Burglary 67
Common Scold 86
Compounding Offenses 88
Counterfeiting 103
Criminal Law 110
Disorderly Conduct 129
Disorderly House 130
Disturbance of Public Assemblage 133
Dueling 140
Embezzlement 146
Embracery 147
Escape 151
Extortion and Threats 165
False Personation 169
False Pretenses 170
Fires 175
Forgery 181
Fornication 182
Homicide 203
Incest 207
Insurrection and Sedition 218
Kidnapping 232
Larceny 234
Lewdness 236
Malicious Mischief 248
Mayhem 256
Miscegenation 261
Neutrality Laws 273
Obscenity 281
Obstructing Justice 282
Perjury 297
Piracy 301
Prize Fighting 312
Prostitution 316
Rape 321
Receiving Stolen Goods 324
Rescue 337
Riot 341
Robbery 342
Sodomy 357
Suicide 368
Treason 384
Unlawful Assembly 396
Vagrancy 399

6. REMEDIES

REMEDIES BY ACT OR AGREEMENT OF PARTIES

Accord and Satisfaction 8
Arbitration 33
Submission of Controversy 365

REMEDIES BY POSSESSION OR NOTICE

Liens 239
Lis Pendens 242
Maritime Liens 252
Mechanics' Liens 257
Notice 277
Salvage 344

MEANS AND METHODS OF PROOF

Acknowledgment 12
Affidavits 21
Estoppel 156
Evidence 157
Oath 280
Records 326
Witnesses 410

CIVIL ACTIONS IN GENERAL

Action 13
Declaratory Judgment 118A
Election of Remedies 143
Limitation of Actions 241
Parties 287
Set-Off and Counterclaim 352
Venue 401

PARTICULAR PROCEEDINGS IN CIVIL ACTIONS

Abatement and Revival 2
Appearance 31
Costs 102
Damages 115
Execution 161
Exemptions 163
Homestead 202
Judgment 228
Jury 230
Motions 267
Pleading 302
Process 313
Reference 327
Stipulations 363
Trial 388

PARTICULAR REMEDIES INCIDENT TO CIVIL ACTIONS

Arrest 35
Assistance, Writ of 40
Attachment 44
Bail 49
Deposits in Court 123
Garnishment 189
Injunction 212
Judicial Sales 22A
Ne Exeat 271
Pretrial Procedure 307A
Receivers 323
Recognizances 325
Sequestration 351
Undertakings 392

PARTICULAR MODES OF REVIEW IN CIVIL ACTIONS

Appeal and Error 30
Audita Querela 48
Certiorari 73
Exceptions, Bill of 158
New Trial 275
Review 339

ACTIONS TO ESTABLISH OWNERSHIP OR RECOVER POSSESSION OF SPECIFIC PROPERTY

Detinue 126
Ejectment 142
Entry, Writ of 149
Interpleader 222
Possessory Warrant 305
Quieting Title 318
Real Actions 322
Replevin 335
Trespass to Try Title 387

FORMS OF ACTIONS FOR DEBTS OR DAMAGES

Account, Action on 10
Action on the Case 14
Assumpsit, Action of 42
Covenant, Action of 107
Debt, Action of 117G

ACTIONS FOR PARTICULAR FORMS OR SPECIAL RELIEF

Account 9
Cancellation of Instruments 69
Debtor and Creditor 117T
Divorce 134
Partition 288
Reformation of Instruments 328
Specific Performance 358

CIVIL PROCEEDINGS OTHER THAN ACTIONS

Habeas Corpus 197
Mandamus 250
Prohibition 314
Quo Warranto 319
Scire Facias 346
Supersedeas 370

SPECIAL CIVIL JURISDICTIONS AND PROCEDURE THEREIN

Admiralty 16
Bankruptcy 51
Equity 150
Federal Civil Procedure 170A

PROCEEDINGS PECULIAR TO CRIMINAL CASES

Extradition and Detainers 166
Fines 174
Forfeitures 180
Grand Jury 193
Indictment and Information 210
Pardon and Parole 284
Penalties 295
Searches and Seizures 349

7. GOVERNMENT

POLITICAL BODIES AND DIVISIONS

Counties 104
District of Columbia 132
Municipal Corporations 268
States 360
Territories 375
Towns 381
United States 393

SYSTEMS AND SOURCES OF LAW

Administrative Law and Procedure 15A
Common Law 85
Constitutional Law 92
International Law 221
Parliamentary Law 286
Statutes 361
Treaties 385

LEGISLATIVE AND EXECUTIVE POWERS AND FUNCTIONS

Bounties 60
Census 72
Commodity Futures Trading Regulation 83H
Customs Duties 114
Drains 137
Eminent Domain 148
Highways 200
Inspection 216
Internal Revenue 220
Levees and Flood Control 235
Pensions 296
Post Office 306
Private Roads 311
Public Contracts 316A
Public Utilities 317A
Schools 345
Securities Regulation 349B
Social Security and Public Welfare 356A
Taxation 371
Weights and Measures 407
Zoning and Planning 414

JUDICIAL POWERS AND FUNCTIONS, AND COURTS AND THEIR OFFICERS

Amicus Curiae 27
Clerks of Courts 79
Contempt 93
Court Commissioners 105
Courts 106
Federal Courts 170B
Judges 227
Justices of the Peace 231
Removal of Cases 334
Reports 336
United States Magistrates 394

CIVIL SERVICE, OFFICERS, AND INSTITUTIONS

Ambassadors and Consuls 26
Asylums 43
Attorney General 46
Coroners 100
District and Prosecuting Attorneys 131
Elections 144
Hospitals 204
Newspapers 274
Notaries 276
Officers and Public Employees 283
Prisons 310
Reformatories 329
Registers of Deeds 330
Sheriffs and Constables 353
United States Marshals 395

MILITARY AND NAVAL SERVICE AND WAR

Armed Services 34
Military Justice 258A
Militia 259
War and National Emergency 402

"Persons") in many different respects. The Key Numbers are assigned as follows: Each Key Number relates to the manner in which a point of law is discussed. This subtopic is represented by a number, also called a "key number." Thus, if a case relates to the prevention of cruelty to an infant, West will title the pertinent headnote **Infants 15**; if a case relates to the effect of marriage of an infant (in a legal sense, an "infant" is simply someone who has not yet attained the age of majority), West will title the pertinent headnote **Infants 10**; and if a case relates to emancipation of an infant by a parent, West will give the pertinent headnote the topic and Key Number **Infants 9**. Each topic name and Key Number combination thus represents a specific point of law and each provides links to other similar cases.

It is unnecessary to commit to memory the classes, subclasses, or topics; it is sufficient if you have a general understanding of West's outline of the law. It may be easiest to understand West's system if you imagine that West possesses an immense chart with all of the topics and Key Numbers listed on it. Every time a portion of *any* case in *any* unit of the *National Reporter System* discusses prevention of cruelty to infants, the headnote will be given the topic name "Infants" and the Key Number 15. The headnote will then be printed initially in the monthly pamphlet *General Digest* and will later be printed in the hardbound copies called *Decennials*. You will be able to locate other cases on this area of the law by taking this topic name and Key Number (**Infants 15**) and inserting it into the various *Decennial* units. You will then be directed to other cases, both federal and state, that discuss this issue and that were decided within specific ten-year periods.

You may have noticed that some of the Key Numbers have been subdivided, such as **Criminal Law 1169.1(5)**. This occurs as an area of the law expands and novel theories are developed. West will categorize its Key Numbers, such as **Criminal Law 1169**, into subdivisions to reflect the varying and developing ways in which this topic is discussed by courts, as shown by the following list:

Criminal Law 1169	Admission of evidence
Criminal Law 1169.1	Admission of evidence in general
Criminal Law 1169.1(5)	Admission of evidence relating to arrest and identification

Similarly, as new causes of action or new defenses arise, West will add new topics, such as "Racketeer-Influenced and Corrupt Organizations," "Abortion and Birth Control," and "Franchises." In this way, West keeps current with case law as it expands and develops.

5. *Locating a Topic and Key Number*

Until now, we have assumed that you knew a topic name and Key Number and inserted it into the various *Decennial* units to locate cases. We will now assume that you are starting your research project from "square one" and that the only information you have is the description of the research problem, for example, the landlord-tenant issue described in the beginning of this chapter. There are three strategies you can use to obtain a topic and Key Number that you can use to locate cases.

a. Descriptive Word Approach

Each of the *Decennial* units includes a volume (or volumes) titled "Descriptive Word Index." West has selected certain words and phrases and listed these alphabetically in its Descriptive Word Indexes. You use these indexes exactly as you do the indexes for U.S.C.A. and U.S.C.S. as described in Chapter 3. That is, you simply think of words and phrases that describe the problem you are researching, such as landlord, tenant, lease. Remember to consider the Who, Where, When, Why, and How questions discussed in Chapter 3 to assist you in developing a list of descriptive words or phrases. Look up these words in any Descriptive Word Index and you will be provided with a topic and Key Number just as you were given a title and section when you located statutes in U.S.C.A. or U.S.C.S.

If you have difficulty thinking of words to use, think of synonyms (renter), antonyms (owner), defenses a party might assert (consent, waiver), the type of relief a party might seek (injunctive relief, damages, rescission of the lease), or the cause of action a plaintiff might plead (breach of contract, negligence). These should assist you in thinking of words to look up in the index. Just as you have seen with the indexes for U.S.C.A. and U.S.C.S., the Descriptive Word Indexes in the *American Digest System* are very "forgiving." Many topics are indexed under more than one entry, making it easy for you to locate the all-important topic name and Key Number.

When attempting to locate a topic name and a Key Number by using this Descriptive Word Index method, you should use the Descriptive Word Index to one of the newer *Decennial* units such as the *Tenth Decennial Digest, Part 2* or *Part 1*. If you cannot locate a topic name and a Key Number in the *Tenth Decennial Digest, Part 2* or *Part 1*, try the *Ninth Decennial* (*Parts 2* and *1*) as it is possible that no cases discussed this particular legal issue during 1986-1996, the time period covered by the *Tenth Decennial Digest*. You could also use one of the Descriptive Word Indexes for the *General Digest*. There is a cumulative Descriptive Word Index in every tenth volume of the *General Digest*.

The Descriptive Word method is the easiest and most reliable way of locating a topic name and a Key Number, and this should be the approach you use until you have become thoroughly familiar with West's *Key Number System*. In fact, West advises that this method of search will generally prove most useful and should always be used first unless the researcher knows the specific topic. See Figure 5-3 for a sample page from the Descriptive Word Index to the *Ninth Decennial Digest, Part 2*, which demonstrates how to locate a topic name and a Key Number through the Descriptive Word approach.

Figure 5-3
Sample Page from Descriptive Word Index

43-9th D Pt 2—77 **LANDLORD**

LANDLORD AND TENANT—Cont'd
GUIDE dogs, waiver of pet restriction inapplicable to dog neither trained nor used as guide dog. **Land & Ten 134(1)**
HABITABILITY. **Land & Ten 125**
Implied warranty—
Coextensive with Residential Rental Agreements Act. **Land & Ten 125(1)**
HEALTH regulations, see this index **Health and Environment**
HEAT, see this index **Heat**
HEAT violation, notice as condition precedent to prosecution. **Health & E 39**
HOLDING over—
Damages—
Landlord's proper measure of damages for tenant's willful holdover. **Land & Ten 144**
Estoppel, effect on. **Land & Ten 62(4)**
Extension by. **Land & Ten 90**
Month to month tenancy. **Land & Ten 115(3)**
Renewal by. **Land & Ten 90**
Rent, amount while holding over. **Land & Ten 200.9**
Sufficiency to create new tenancy. **Land & Ten 90(4)**
Tenancy at sufferance, creation by. **Land & Ten 119(2)**
Tenancy at will, creation by. **Land & Ten 118(4)**
Year-to-year tenancy. **Land & Ten 114(3)**
HOMESTEAD, see this index **Homestead**
HOMICIDE conviction arising from death of tenant's guest—
Due process guarantees. **Const Law 258(3)**
HOTELS—
Duties owed to renter's patrons—
Providing guard for coat rack. **Inn 11(3)**
HUNTING rights. **Land & Ten 134(3)**
HUSBAND and wife—
Lease of community property. **Hus & W 267(3)**
Administration of community. **Hus & W 276(6)**
Separate property of wife, see this index **Separate Estate of Wife**
ICE and snow—
Generally, see this index **Ice and Snow**
ILLUSORY tenancy—
Effect—
Protecting against speculative profiteering by tenants of rent controlled apartment. **Land & Ten 278.4(6)**
Summary proceedings to dispossess, right to maintain. **Land & Ten 298(1)**
ILLUSORY tenants—
Entering into sublease in order to evade rent stabilization requirements. **Land & Ten 200.16**
IMPLIED contracts, see this index **Implied Contracts**
IMPLIED covenants. **Land & Ten 45**
IMPLIED tenancy, see this index **Implied Tenancy**
IMPROVEMENTS. **Land & Ten 150–161**
Actions. **Land & Ten 159**
Claims for. **Land & Ten 223(7)**

LANDLORD AND TENANT—Cont'd
IMPROVEMENTS—Cont'd
Compensation. **Land & Ten 157(6–8)**
Damages for failure to make. **Land & Ten 223(6)**
Lien. **Land & Ten 157(10)**
Ownership in general. **Land & Ten 157(2)**
Reimbursing tenant for repair of boiler made at request of tenant. **Impl & C C 40**
Remedy for failure to make. **Land & Ten 159**
Removal. **Land & Ten 157(4)**
INCOME tax, see this index **Income Tax**
INCUMBRANCES. **Land & Ten 145–149**
Reasonable rent, incumbrances as factor in determining. **Land & Ten 200.25**
INDEMNITY against liability for negligence. **Indem 8.1(2)**
INDORSEMENT, extension or renewal on lease. **Land & Ten 89**
INFANT'S property, lease of. **Infants 44**
INJUNCTION—
Assessing tenants nonrefundable rental fees. **Inj 136(2)**
Communication by tenant by signs or notices—
Free speech. **Const Law 90.1(1)**
Covenants as to use of leased premises. **Inj 62(2)**
Disturbance of possession of tenant. **Land & Ten 132(2)**
Preliminary injunction, tenant's consent to sale of building's air rights. **Inj 136(2)**
Summary proceedings. **Land & Ten 299**
Unlawful detainer, action for. **Land & Ten 290½**
Violation of laws relating to suspension of right of reentry and recovery of possession by landlord. **Land & Ten 278.16**
Waste. **Land & Ten 55(4)**
INJURIES—
Crops. **Land & Ten 139(4)**
Dangerous or defective condition. **Land & Ten 162–170**
Mobile home parks, see this index **Trailer Parks or Camps**
Employees of tenant. **Land & Ten 165, 169(5)**
Patrons of lessee—
Liability of lessee. **Land & Ten 167(8)**
Premises. **Land & Ten 140–142**
Eviction. **Land & Ten 176**
Property of tenant. **Land & Ten 166**
trance of trespassers and vandals. **Land & Ten 166(6)**
Property of third persons. **Land & Ten 167(9)**
Reversion. **Land & Ten 55**
Scalding of cleaning woman when steam pipe burst—
Liability of tenant. **Land & Ten 167(2)**
Tenants or occupants. **Land & Ten 164**
INNKEEPERS—
See this index **Innkeepers**

LANDLORD AND TENANT—Cont'd
INNKEEPERS—Cont'd
Membership in metropolitan hotel industry stabilization association. **Inn 2**
INSANE persons, see this index **Mental Health**
INSOLVENCY, termination of lease. **Land & Ten 101½**
INSURANCE—
Covenants to insure. **Land & Ten 156**
Insurable interest. **Insurance 115(4)**
Landlord's liability insurance—
Risks and causes of loss. **Insurance 435.34**
Nature and cause of injury or damage. **Insurance 435.35**
Lessee's good-faith efforts to obtain—
Preventing cancellation of lease. **Land & Ten 103(1)**
Right to proceeds. **Insurance 580(4)**
INTERFERENCE with—
Possession of tenant. **Land & Ten 131–133**
Relationship. **Land & Ten 19**
Use of premises. **Land & Ten 134(4), 172(2)**
INTERVENTION, see this index **Intervention**
INTOXICATING liquors, see this index **Intoxicating Liquors**
INTRUDER—
Lessor's liability for lessee's injuries inflicted by. **Land & Ten 164(1)**
INVALIDITY as affecting action for unlawful detainer. **Land & Ten 290(4)**
JOINT tenants, implied tenancy between. **Land & Ten 8**
JUDGMENT—
Conclusiveness. **Judgm 684**
Recovery of possession, action for. **Land & Ten 285(6)**
Summary proceedings for possession, post
Unlawful detainer, action for. **Land & Ten 291(17)**
JURISDICTION, see this index **Jurisdiction**
Justices of the Peace
KEY to leased premises, see this index **Keys**
KNOWLEDGE of defects affecting liability for injuries. **Land & Ten 164(6, 7), 165, 166(10)**
LACHES, affecting rescission of lease. **Land & Ten 34(4)**
LANDLORD'S title, estoppel dependent on. **Land & Ten 62(2)**
LARCENY of property from landlord or tenant, see this index **Larceny**
LEASES. **Land & Ten 20–49**
Bankruptcy proceedings. **Bankr 3086–3088**
Farm lease. **Land & Ten 322**
Female tenant's right to possession of apartment though not married to signing tenant—
Civil R 11.5
Land & Ten 43
Nonassignment clauses—
Restraints on alienation, policy against. **Perp 6(17)**
Protection leases—
Nature of. **Mines 56**

Subtopic Heading

Topic Name and Key Number

b. Topic Approach

You may recall that in locating statutes, the topic approach calls for you to bypass the general index at the end of a set of statutes and go directly to the appropriate title and begin examining the statutes. The topic approach to locating a topic name and a Key Number is exactly the same. Thus, if you were using the topic approach for the landlord-tenant problem described herein, you would bypass the Descriptive Word Index and go immediately to the "L" volume of a *Decennial* unit such as the *Ninth Decennial Digest, Part 2*, and look up the phrase "Landlord and Tenant." Prior to the digest listing of the headnotes (**Landlord and Tenant 1, Landlord and Tenant 2**, and so on) you will be given an overview of the coverage of this topic, Landlord and Tenant, much like a book's table of contents. All of the Key Numbers digested under **Landlord and Tenant** will be described in an index or outline fashion, and you may then scan the entries to determine the appropriate Key Number and proceed to look up and examine the headnotes listed or digested under **Landlord and Tenant**. To select topics, you can review an alphabetical list of more than 400 digest topics that appears in the front of any West Digest volume.

Just as the topic method should be used with caution to find statutes, it should be used with caution to locate topic names and Key Numbers because you may miss other topics and Key Numbers under which this area of the law may be digested. Because West's *American Digest System* has more than 400 topics, this method should be used only after one has become thoroughly familiar with West's Key Number classification system. Each topic discussion begins with an overview of its coverage as well as an identification of subjects included and subjects excluded, which will help ensure you are searching within the correct topic. See Figure 5-4 for a sample page from the *Ninth Decennial Digest, Part 2*, showing a partial list of Key Numbers within the topic Landlord and Tenant.

c. Table of Cases Approach

If you know the name of a case, you can look it up in an alphabetically arranged Table of Cases, which will provide you with the citations to the case and a list of the topics and Key Numbers under which it has been digested. For example, if you have the name of the case *DeGracia v. Huntingdon Associates, Ltd.*, and you know it was decided between 1981 and 1986, you can use the Table of Cases in the *Ninth Decennial Digest, Part 2* (which covers the time period 1981-1986). When you look up this case, you will be given all citations to the case, the history of the case (whether it has been affirmed or reversed), and all of the topics and Key Numbers under which it is digested or classified. See Figure 5-5.

Each *Decennial* unit and each volume of the *General Digest* contains a Table of Cases listed alphabetically by plaintiff. The Table of Cases is usually located after the last volume in a *Decennial* set. Some of West's digests contain an additional Table of Cases, the Defendant-Plaintiff Table, so if you know only the name of a defendant, you can determine the

Figure 5-4
Sample Page from *Ninth Decennial Digest, Part 2*

VII. PREMISES, AND ENJOYMENT AND USE THEREOF.—Cont'd

(D) REPAIRS, INSURANCE, AND IMPROVEMENTS.

⇐150. Right and duty to make repairs in general.
- (1). In general.
- (2). Duty to rebuild on destruction of property.
- (3). Landlord's right of entry to make repairs.
- (4). Rights of subtenants.
- (5). Right of tenant to repair at landlord's cost.

151. Statutory provisions.

152. Covenants and agreements as to repairs and alterations.
- (1). In general.
- (2). Consideration for agreement.
- (3). Construction and operation of covenants in general.
- (4). Nature of repairs included in covenant or agreement.
- (5). Duty to rebuild on destruction of property.
- (6). Right of landlord to notice that repairs are necessary.
- (7). Agreement by landlord to pay for repairs.
- (8). Rights and liabilities of assignees and subtenants.
- (9). Waiver of claims under or stipulations in covenant or agreement.
- (10). Right of tenant to repair and recover cost.
- (11). Alterations by tenant.

153. Mode of making repairs.

154. Remedies for failure to make repairs and alterations.
- (1). Nature and form of remedy.
- (2). Right of action and defenses.
- (3). Pleading and evidence.
- (4). Damages.
- (5). Trial.

155. Maintenance of boundaries and fences.

156. Covenants and agreements as to insurance.

157. Improvements by tenant and covenants therefor.
- (1). Covenant by lessee to make improvements.
- (2). Ownership of improvements in general.
- (4). Right to remove and agreements for removal of improvements.
- (5). Forfeiture or waiver of right to remove improvements.
- (6). Right to compensation in general.
- (7). Covenants and agreements to pay for improvements.
- (8). Liabilities of successors of lessor.
- (9). Mode of termination of tenancy as affecting right to compensation.
- (10). Lien for value of improvements.
- (11). Determination of compensation.
- (12). Actions for compensation.

158. Improvements by landlord and covenants therefor.

159. Remedies for failure to make improvements.
- (1). Actions for breach of tenant's covenant to make improvements.
- (2). Actions for breach of landlord's covenant to make improvements.

160. Condition of premises at termination of tenancy.
- (1). In general.
- (2). Covenants and agreements as to condition of premises on termination of tenancy.
- (3). Duty of tenant to rebuild or replace personal property.
- (4). Actions for breach of covenant.

161. Personal property on premises at termination of tenancy.
- (1). Rights and liabilities as to property on premises in general.
- (2). Care of property left on premises by outgoing tenant.
- (3). Actions to recover property or value.

(E) INJURIES FROM DANGEROUS OR DEFECTIVE CONDITION.

⇐162. Nature and extent of landlord's duty to tenant.

163. Mutual duties of tenants of different portions of same premises.

164. Injuries to tenants or occupants.
- (1). Injuries due to defective or dangerous condition of premises in general.
- (2). Injuries due to failure to repair.
- (3). Injuries due to negligence in making repairs.
- (4). Injuries due to unlighted passageways.
- (5). Liability for injuries to subtenant.
- (6). Liability of landlord as dependent on knowledge of defects.
- (7). Notice to or knowledge of tenant as to defects.

165. Injuries to employé of tenant.
- (1). Injuries due to defective or dangerous condition of premises in general.
- (2). Injuries due to failure to repair.
- (3). Injuries due to unlighted passageway.
- (4). Liability of landlord as dependent on knowledge of defects.
- (5). Failure to guard dangerous places.
- (6). Operation or condition of elevators.
- (7). Notice to or knowledge of tenant as to de-[illegible]

166. Injuries to property of tenant on premises.
- (1). Nature and extent of the duties of landlord and tenant respectively.
- (2). Injuries due to defective condition of premises in general.
- (3). Injuries due to failure to repair.
- (4). Injuries due to negligence in making repairs.
- (5). Injuries due to defective water pipes or drains.
- (6). Injuries due to negligent acts of landlord.
- (7). Injuries due to negligence of third persons in general.
- (9). Injuries due to negligence of cotenant.
- (10). Liability of landlord as dependent on knowledge or notice of defects.

Outline of topics and key numbers listed under "Landlord & Tenant"

[illegible]
- (1). Duties of landlord and tenant to third persons.
- (2). Injuries due to defective or dangerous condition of premises in general.
- (3). Injuries due to failure to repair.
- (4). Failure to light or guard dangerous places.
- (5). Injuries due to openings, defects, or obstructions in walks or streets.
- (6). Injuries caused by fall of snow or ice from roof.
- (7). Injuries due to the negligence of tenant.

Figure 5-5
Sample Page from Table of Cases to *Ninth Decennial Digest, Part 2*

References are to Digest Topics and Key Numbers

DeFulmer, People ex rel., v. Scully, NYAD 2 Dept, 487 NYS2d 401, 110 AD2d 671. See People ex rel. DeFulmer v. Scully.

de Furgalski v. Siegel, DCIll, 618 FSupp 295.—Civil R 13.3(1), 13.4(1), 13.5(1), 13.10, 13.12(3); Courts 100(1); Equity 67, 72(1), 84; Fed Cts 425.

DeFusco v. Giorgio, RI, 440 A2d 727.—Judgm 90, 91, 344; Usury 104; Witn 198(2), 205.

DeGarcia v. I.N.S., CA9, 783 F2d 931. See Magallanes-Damian v. I.N.S.

DeGarmo v. State, TexCrApp, 691 SW2d 657, cert den 106 SCt 337, 474 US 973, 88 LEd2d 322.—Crim Law 409(5), 662.-65, 983, 986.2(2), 1134(1), 1144.13(6), 1213.8(1), 1213.8(8); Homic 253(1), 342.

DeGase v. DeGase, MoApp, 690 SW2d 485.—App & E 80(4), 1008.1(5), 1010.-1(6), 1012.1(1); Partners 328(3), 336(3).

De Gasperis v. De Gasperis, NYAD 2 Dept, 469 NYS2d 469, 98 AD2d 758.—Compromise 21.

DeGay v. State, TexApp-Beaumont, 711 SW2d 419, review gr.—Const Law 75; Crim Law 982.9(1).

DeGay v. State, TexApp 9 Dist, 663 SW2d 459.—Ind & Inf 166; Weap 17(4).

Degelos, Succession of, LaApp 4 Cir, 450 So2d 682.—Ex & Ad 92; Spec Perf 106(3).

Degelos, Succession of, LaApp 4 Cir, 446 So2d 412.—Des & Dist 109; Wills 11.

Degen v. General Coatings, Inc., TexApp 14 Dist, 705 SW2d 734.—Courts 81, 85(1); Pretrial Proc 587.

Degenaars v. Degenaars, NJSuperCh, 452 A2d 222, 186 NJSuper 233.—Divorce 87; Infants 18.

Degenaars Co. v. U.S., ClCt, 2 ClCt 482.—U S 70(21), 73(15), 74(11).

Degenaars Co. v. U.S., ClCt, 1 ClCt 129, 555 FSupp 403.—Fed Cts 1101.

Degener, In re Marriage of, IllApp 2 Dist, 75 IllDec 878, 458 NE2d 46, 119 IllApp3d 1079.—Divorce 72, 252.3(4).

Degeneres v. Burgess, LaApp 1 Cir, 486 So2d 769.—Contracts 108(1), 186(3), 205.15(3), 280(3), 322(4), 324(1); Damag 123, 188(1); Evid 445(1); Lim of Act 32(1); Neglig 1; Sales 391(3), 394; Subrog 30; Ven & Pur 3(1).

DeGenova v. Board of Review, Ohio App, 493 NE2d 287, 24 Ohio App3d 125, 24 OBR 196.—Social S 473.

DeGeorge v. Bernier, CAFed, 768 F2d 1318.—Pat 90(1), 99, 106(2), 106(3), 314(5), 328(2).

Degerlia v. First Bank and Trust Co., IllApp 5 Dist, 77 IllDec 238, 460 NE2d 97, 121 IllApp3d 658.—Venue 2, 8(2), 22(1).

DeGette v. Mine Co. Restaurant, Inc., CAColo, 751 F2d 1143.—Lim of Act 95(1).

De Gevulde Hoorn, Matter of, BkrtcyAla, 44 BR 23. See Childers, Matter of.

De Giacomo v. Regan, NYAD, 444 NYS2d 273, 84 AD2d 629.—Offic 101.-5(2).

Degideo v. Com., Unemployment Compensation Bd. of Review, PaCmwlth, 433 A2d 607, 61 PaCmwlth 263.—Social S 728.

DeGidio v. Perpich, DCMinn, 612 FSupp 1383.—Civil R 13.3(1), 13.7, 13.12(6); Fed Civ Proc 172, 181, 186.10; Fed Cts 265, 266, 267, 268, 269; Judgm 567.

DeGier v. Commissioner of Public Safety, MinnApp, 387 NW2d 908.—Autos 144.1(1); Const Law 262.

DeGirolamo v. U. S., DCNY, 518 FSupp 778.—Lim of Act 55(3), 95(1); U S 113, 125(6).

Degiman v. Degiman, SC, 281 SE2d 123, 276 SC 600.—Divorce 235, 240(2), 240(4), 286(3), 287.

Deglopper, In re, BkrtcyIdaho, 53 BR 95.—Bankr 396(5), 399(1); Home 80.

Degnan v. Executive Homes, Inc., Mont, 696 P2d 431.—Contracts 188.-5(1), 205.35(2), 205.40, 322(1); Torts 1.

Degnan v. Monetti, NJSuperAD, 509 A2d 277, 210 NJSuper 174.—Zoning 487, 489, 512, 610, 623, 709.

Degolyer Co., Inc. v. Standard & Poor's Corp., CATex, 672 F2d 433. See Municipal Bond Reporting Antitrust Litigation, In re.

DeGraaf v. General Motors Corp., MichApp, 352 NW2d 719, 135 MichApp 141, appeal den.—Prod Liab 96.5.

DeGrace v. Shelby Tp. Police and Fire Civil Service Com'n, MichApp, 389 NW2d 137, 150 MichApp 587.—Mand

DeGracia v. Huntingdon Associates, Ltd., GaApp, 336 SE2d 602, 176 GaApp 495.—Judgm 185(3), 185.3(14); Land & Ten 164(1).

phone Co., KanApp, 687 P2d 1380.—App & E 930(1), 931(1), 989, 994(1), 1001(1), 1010.1(6); Damag 50, 50.10; Neglig 136(14); Pub Ut 103; Tel 278, 284.

DeGraff, Matter of Compensation of, OrApp, 630 P2d 895, 52 OrApp 1023.—Work Comp 1545.

DeGraff v. Kaplan, IllApp, 65 IllDec 75, 440 NE2d 930, 109 IllApp3d 711.—App & E 984(5); Costs 173(1); Evid 455; Partners 81, 86, 121.

DeGraff's Estate, Matter of, MoApp, 637 SW2d 277.—Ex & Ad 218, 459, 495(3), 496(1), 501; Jury 19(7).

DeGraffenreid v. Curtwright, MoApp, 652 SW2d 310.—Judgm 334.

DeGraffenreid, State ex rel. v. Keet, MoApp, 619 SW2d 873. See State ex rel. DeGraffenreid v. Keet.

de Graffenried v. U.S., ClCt, 2 ClCt 640.—Fed Cts 1112; Pat 203, 292.1(2), 292.2, 328(2).

DeGrand v. Alton Tel. Printing Co., Inc., BkrtcyIll, 15 BR 367. See Alton Tel. Printing Co., Inc., In re.

Degree v. Degree, NCApp, 325 SE2d 36, 72 NCApp 668, review den 330 SE2d 607, 313 NC 598.—Hus & W 279(2), 281; Stip 3.

De Gregorio v. CBS, Inc., NYSup, 473 NYS2d 922, 123 Misc2d 491.—Const Law 90.1(8); Damag 50.10; Libel 6(1); Torts 1, 8.5(6), 8.5(8).

De Gregorio v. Pennsylvania Public Utility Com'n, PaCmwlth, 481 A2d 1241, 85 PaCmwlth 354.—Autos 87, 106; Pub Ut 194.

DeGrio v. American Federation of Government Employees, Fla, 484 So2d 1.—Courts 489(1); Labor 221.

DeGroat v. Ingles, CalApp 1 Dist, 191 CalRptr 761, 143 CA3d 399.—Judgm 181(2), 181(6), 183.

DeGroat v. New York State Higher Educ. Services Corp., NYAD, 456 NYS2d 159, 90 AD2d 616.—Lim of Act 66(11).

Degroat v. State, FlaApp 5 Dist, 489 So2d 1163, review den 496 So2d 142.—Crim Law 986.2(4), 1208.1(3).

DeGroff v. Bethlehem Cent. School Dist., NYAD, 460 NYS2d 630, 92 AD2d 702.—Mun Corp 741.1(8); Schools 112.

DeGroot v. American Legion Post No. 1247, IllApp 1 Dist, 86 IllDec 199, 475 NE2d 5, 130 IllApp3d 735. See Monsen v. DeGroot.

DeGroot v. Arizona Racing Com'n, ArizApp, 686 P2d 1301, 141 Ariz 331.—Admin Law 349, 360, 669, 754, 760, 763, 786, 791; Const Law 287.2(1), 318(1); Theaters 3.10.

DeGroot v. Employment Sec. Com'n, SCApp, 328 SE2d 668, 285 SC 209.—Admin Law 791; Const Law 278.7(3); Social S 584.5, 660.

DeGrow v. DeGrow, MichApp, 315 NW2d 915, 112 MichApp 260.—Divorce 303(6), 303(7); Infants 19.3(6); Parent & C 2(3.4).

De Gryse v. De Gryse, Ariz, 661 P2d 185, 135 Ariz 335.—App & E 982(2); Divorce 163, 165(2), 194, 252.3(4); Hus & W 279(2); Judgm 346.

Deguffroy & Associates, Inc. v. W.C.A.B. (Bianchetti), PaCmwlth, 503 A2d 994, 94 PaCmwlth 566.—Work Comp 504, 1981.

DeHart v. A.C. and S. Co., Inc., DelSuper, 484 A2d 521. See Sheppard v.

DeHart v. Aetna Life Ins. Co., Ohio, 431 NE2d 644, 69 Ohio St2d 189, 23 003d 210.—App & E 962, 1092; Courts 78, 85(1); Pretrial Proc 551.

DeHart v. Diversified Services, NYAD, 442 NYS2d 255, 83 AD2d 685.—Work Comp 1536, 1676, 1939.8.

DeHart v. Moore, DCFla, 424 FSupp 55.—Exchanges 11(11).

DeHart v. Ritenour Consolidated School Dist., MoApp, 663 SW2d 332.—Deeds 144(1); Quiet T 46; Schools 65.

DeHart v. R/S Financial Corp., NCApp, 337 SE2d 94, 78 NCApp 93, review den 342 SE2d 893.—App & E 263(1); Evid 267, 402; Judgm 199(1), 199(3.9); Pretrial Proc 44; Trial 139.1(5), 143, 178; Usury 117.

DeHart v. R/S Financial Corp., NCApp, 311 SE2d 694, 66 NCApp 648, appeal after remand 337 SE2d 94, 78 NCApp 93, review den 342 SE2d 893, 316 NC 376.—Plead 427; Trial 139.1(16), 168, 178; Usury 11, 119.

DeHart v. State, IndApp 3 Dist, 471 NE2d 312, reh den; transfer den.—Const Law 199; Crim Law 150; Health & E 25.5(5), 25.5(5.5), 37, 39, 41; Statut 190.

DeHart v. State, OrApp, 637 P2d 1311, 55 OrApp 254.—Const Law 268.1(6).

DeHart v. U.S., BkrtcyPa, 50 BR 685. See Metropolitan Metals, Inc., In re.

DeHaven v. Dan-Co FS Co-op., WisApp, 383 NW2d 509, 128 Wis2d 472.—Social S 241.

DeHaven v. DeHaven, La, 412 So2d 537.—App & E 185(1); Divorce 387; Hus & W 279(2); Parent & C 3.3(8); Ven & Pur 1.

DeHaven v. DeHaven, LaApp, 401 So2d 418, writ gr 406 So2d 624, rev 412 So2d 537.—App & E 185(1); Courts 37(2), 39, 472.1; Divorce 297, 311.5; Hus & W 279(2); Parent & C 3.1(8), 3.3(8).

DeHaven v. Gant, WashApp, 713 P2d 149, 42 WashApp 666, review den.—App & E 232(2), 241, 754(1); Evid 555.-10; Phys 18.80(3); Trial 388(3).

DeHaven v. Thomas D. Gant, M.D., P.S., WashApp, 713 P2d 149, 42 WashApp 666. See DeHaven v. Gant.

De Hay v. Town of West New York, NJSuperAD, 460 A2d 157, 189 NJSuper 340, certification den 468 A2d 227, 94 NJ 591.—Equity 72(1); Mun Corp 191, 220(8).

Note topics and key number under which case is digested

exact case name and parallel citations. This may be useful if you wish to locate other cases involving a certain defendant.

d. "Case on Point" Approach

If you have already located a case on point, its headnotes will display applicable topic names and Key Numbers. If one of these headnotes is relevant to your research, you can then use that headnote to locate other similar cases by inserting your topic name and Key Number into the various units of the *Decennial Digest System*. For example, review pages 98–102 of this text, where the case *Coughlin v. George Washington University Health Plan*, 565 A.2d 67 (D.C. 1989), appears. Note headnote number 5. given the topic name **Damages** and the Key Number **50**. If you read the *Coughlin* case and determine that this section of the case relating to damages is relevant to your research, you can take the topic name and Key Number **Damages 50** and insert it into the *Decennials* to locate other similar cases.

6. Using Digests

Once you have obtained a topic and a Key Number, such as **Landlord & Tenant 166(1),** you merely insert this into the various units of the *American Digest System* and you will unlock the door to cases from 1658 until last month, all of which relate to injuries to a tenant's property. Because the *Decennials* are arranged alphabetically, you simply retrieve the "L" volume in any of the *Decennial* units and look up **"Landlord & Tenant 166(1)."** At this point, West will do more than merely list the digest headnotes in a haphazard fashion. West has carefully arranged the entries, giving you federal cases, first from the highest federal court, the United States Supreme Court, through cases from the United States courts of appeal to the lowest federal courts, the United States district courts. After all of the federal cases have been digested, you will be given digests for state court cases. Again, West will impose order and list the states alphabetically, making it easy for you to quickly locate cases from Arkansas, Louisiana, Minnesota, and South Carolina. West's listing of cases from South Carolina will be in order of the South Carolina court hierarchy and then in reverse chronological order so you will proceed from the newer South Carolina Supreme Court cases to the older South Carolina Supreme Court cases and then from the newer South Carolina Appellate Court cases to the older South Carolina Appellate Court cases. See Figure 5-6 for a sample page from the *Ninth Decennial Digest, Part 2*, showing the digesting of cases.

In inserting your topic and Key Number into the *Decennial* units, you should start with the most recent *Decennial* unit. If you cannot find the cases you need, proceed to the earlier *Decennial* units. You should never exclusively rely on the brief summaries or digests of the cases. While they are usually very clearly and concisely presented, you must read a case in full to really understand it. Similarly, you should *never* cite a digest

Figure 5-6
Sample Page from *Ninth Decennial Digest, Part 2,* Showing Digests of Cases

⚷166. Injuries to property of tenant on premises.

Library references

C.J.S. Landlord and Tenant § 423 et seq.

⚷166(1). Nature and extent of the duties of landlord and tenant respectively.

Note alphabetical arrangement of cases from states and arrangement from higher to lower courts within a state

Cal.App. 1 Dist. 1983. Where lessee of storage space was afforded option, by operator of space, of greater monthly payments under lease with insurance or of purchasing insurance elsewhere, and she was not subjected to an adhesive contract under which she had to accept exculpatory clause or forego lease, storage lease did not involve the public interest so as to render exculpatory clause in lease invalid under Civil Code section providing, inter alia, that all contracts which have as their object to exempt anyone from responsibility for his own fraud or willful injury to person or property of another are against policy of the law. West's Ann.Cal.Civ. Code § 1668.—Cregg v. Ministor Ventures, 196 Cal.Rptr. 724, 148 C.A.3d 1107.

Cal.Super. 1982. Apartment building owners and managers had no affirmative duty to secure parking facilities, which they never represented as being protected, merely because they had notice of previous instances of vandalism to parked cars and thus tenant could not recover from owners and managers for destruction by fire of tenant's automobile in building parking area.—Jubert v. Shalom Realty, 185 Cal.Rptr. 641, 135 C.A.3d Supp. 1.

D.C.App. 1983. Exculpatory clause in lease which purported to relieve landlord of liability for personal property damage caused by any source, including defective roofing and plumbing, was ineffective to bar recovery of damages from landlord inasmuch as clause amounted to waiver or modification of tenant's rights under implied warranty of habitability.—George Washington University v. Weintraub, 458 A.2d 43.

Kan. 1982. Landlord, having leased premises in their entirety to tenants, did not have control over portion of premises wherein fire started and had no duty to inspect same, and thus failure of landlord to inspect wiring and failure to discover and correct latent defect on premises could not, as a matter of law, constitute negligence.—Moore v. Muntzel, 642 P.2d 957, 231 Kan. 46.

There were no warranties flowing from landlord to tenants on which liability for fire damage could be predicated.—Id.

La.App. 4 Cir. 1982. Alleged failure of lessee to present evidence of negligence by ultimate building owner or lessor had no effect on her right to recover for loss of personal property destroyed in fire at apartment under statutes which base liability on status, either as owner or lessor, rather than on personal fault. LSA-C.C. arts. 2322, 2695.—Barnes v. Housing Authority of New Orleans, 423 So.2d 750.

Minn.App. 1984. Lease provision exculpating landlords from liability for water damage was not ambiguous, even though contract's reference to "premises" varyingly referred to entire building or to first floor and basement.—Fena v. Wickstrom, 348 N.W.2d 389.

N.Y.A.D. 1982. Where the tenant had notice that water would be turned off in building on a Friday and knew that water would be turned on before he reopened his shop on the following Monday, and where building owner did not have access to tenant's premises, it was tenant's responsibility to be particularly careful in closing all the faucets, and his failure to do so was proximate and sole cause of flooding.—Arthur Richards, Inc. v. 79 Fifth Ave. Co., 450 N.Y.S.2d 13, 88 A.D.2d 517, reversed 455 N.Y.S.2d 596, 57 N.Y.2d 824, 441 N.E.2d 1114.

Pa. 1986. Exculpatory clause in commercial lease agreement relieving lessor of liability for injury or damage to personal property in premises caused by fire in any part of building of which demised premises was a part, was valid and enforceable; the clause did not contravene any policy of the law, commercial lease related entirely to parties' own private affairs, there was no disparity in bargaining power between parties, and clause, as modified, spelled out intention of parties with particularity.—Princeton Sportswear Corp. v. H & M Associates, 507 A.2d 339, 510 Pa. 189, appeal after remand 517 A.2d 963, 358 Pa.Super. 325.

Pa.Super. 1984. Exculpatory clauses in lease were valid and enforceable where lease was commercial lease, there was no disparity in bargaining power between the parties, exculpatory clauses had been reviewed, negotiated and modified by both parties and their counsel, and clauses, as modified, evidenced clear and unambiguous intent to release landlords from liability for damages caused by fire when such fire was not the result of any negligence on landlords' part.—Princeton Sportswear Corp. v. H & M Associates, 484 A.2d 185, 335 Pa.Super. 381, reversed 507 A.2d 339, 510 Pa. 189, appeal after remand 517 A.2d 963, 358 Pa.Super. 325.

Landlords were not liable for damages tenant suffered as result of fire which damaged building's power center and thereby deprived tenant of heat, electricity and water, where under exculpatory clauses in lease, it was clear that landlords were not liable for any property damage caused by fire in any portion of the building of which demised premises was a part unless such fire was caused by landlords' negligence, power center constituted portion of building in which demised premises was a part, and lower court specifically found that landlords' conduct was not tortious.—Id.

⚷166(2). Injuries due to defective condition of premises in general.

C.A.La. 1983. Not every defect in leased premises will serve as a basis for a claim of damages against lessor under Louisiana law; instead, vices and defects must be substantial and of such nature as are likely to cause injury to a reasonably prudent individual. LSA-C.C. art. 2695.—Volkswagen of America, Inc. v. Robertson, 713 F.2d 1151.

D.C.App. 1983. While landlords clearly bear burden of maintaining rented premises in compliance with housing code provisions, liability is not imposed upon landlords for losses arising from all conditions that violate the code.—George Washington University v. Weintraub, 458 A.2d 43.

Fla.App. 1 Dist. 1984. Lessee's complaint, which alleged making of the lease and lessor's covenant to keep the roof in good repair, the undertaking by lessor through services of a roofing contractor to keep the roof in good repair, a breach of that covenant by reason of the roof collapsing during course of repairs due either to defects in the structure or to overloading of the roof by the contractor, and resulting damages to lessee's property, was sufficient to state cause of action against lessor for breach of contract.—Cisu of Florida, Inc. for Use and Benefit of Aetna Cas. and Sur. Co. v. Porter, 457 So.2d 1118.

Ill.App. 1 Dist. 1985. Under common law, landlord is not liable for injury to property of tenant caused by defects in demised premises absent express warranty as to condition of premises or covenant to repair.—Wanland v. Beavers, 86 Ill.Dec. 130, 474 N.E.2d 1327, 130 Ill. App.3d 731.

Ill.App. 1982. Warranty of habitability implied in lease of building does not give rise to a cause of action for permanent injuries or property damage.—Auburn v. Amoco Oil Co., 61 Ill. Dec. 939, 435 N.E.2d 780, 106 Ill.App.3d 60.

La.App. 1 Cir. 1986. Lessee and its property insurer were not required to show negligence on the part of the lessor in order to recover damages resulting from a fire caused by a defect in the premises. LSA-C.C. arts. 2322, 2695.—Great American Surplus Lines Ins. Co. v. Bass, 486 So.2d 789, writ denied 489 So.2d 245.

Even if lessee assumed responsibility for the electricity, lessor was liable for damages resulting from the destruction of the lessee's property due to a fire caused by a defect in the building's electrical system where there was no proof of negligence on the part of the lessee and where the lessor knew or should have known of the defect. LSA-R.S. 9:3221.—Id.

La.App. 3 Cir. 1985. Under LSA-C.C. art. 2695, lessor is liable to lessee for any losses sustained as result of "vice and defects" in premises, provided they did not arise as result of lessee's fault.—Freeman v. Thomas, 472 So.2d 326.

La.App. 3 Cir. 1984. Mere fact that common wall between premises leased for jewelry store purposes and adjacent premises was constructed of sheetrock and thus susceptible to breach by burglars did not render the condition a "vice" under statute so as to render owner lessor liable to lessees for damages arising out of the burglary. LSA-C.C. arts. 2322, 2703.—Hall v. Park Dell Terrace Partnership, 452 So.2d 342.

La.App. 4 Cir. 1985. Tenant's allegation that security services provided by landlord were inadequate did not provide basis for landlord's liability for arson damage, where all security services promised in lease were provided.—U.S. Fidelity and Guar. Ins. Co. v. Burns Intern. Sec. Services, Inc., 468 So.2d 662, writ denied 470 So.2d 882.

Implied warranty of fitness for intended use and freedom from defects, applicable to leased office building, did not extend to fire damage caused by arson, in light of provisions in lease waiving landlord's liability for damage caused by fire or unauthorized persons.—Id.

La.App. 4 Cir. 1984. Clause in lease clearly and unambiguously transferred liability of lessor to lessee for damage caused by leaks in roof, and thus lessor and its managing partner could not be held liable to lessee for damage which occurred when roof of premises failed under the burden of a heavy rainstorm.—St. Paul Fire & Marine Ins. Co. v. French Eighth, 457 So.2d 35, writ denied 462 So.2d 195 and Oreck v. French Eighth, 462 So.2d 195, reconsideration not considered 462 So.2d 1240, two cases.

La.App. 4 Cir. 1983. Tenants of building destroyed by fire were entitled to recover damages from landlord, despite fact that defect in leased premises was alleged not to have been in building in which tenants leased premises, but within the building, owned by same landlord, next door to tenants' building, unless landlord could exculpate himself. LSA-C.C. arts. 660, 2322.—Broome v. Gauthier, 443 So.2d 1127, writ denied 445 So.2d 449.

N.J.Super.A.D. 1982. Exculpatory clause in commercial lease which exempted landlord from liability for damage or injury resulting from carelessness or negligence or improper conduct of landlord or others, but did not exclude liability for damage flowing from defective design and construction of major structural aspects of building, did not immunize landlord from liability for water damage to tenant's computer equipment caused by defective design of roof.—Ultimate Computer Services, Inc. v. Biltmore Realty Co., Inc., 443 A.2d 723, 183 N.J.Super. 144, 30 A.L.R.4th 963.

Where exculpatory clause did not clearly express intention to exclude liability for injuries resulting from improper construction, landlord, in

For references to other topics, see Descriptive-Word Index

as legal authority. Its sole function is to locate cases for you, not to serve as support for an assertion you make.

In your review of the various West publications, you may have observed that there are diagrams or drawings of "keys" on the spines of many books in the law library. This diagram indicates the volume is a participant in West's Key Number System.

7. *Other West Digests*

As you have seen, the *American Digest System* is the most comprehensive digest system, with its coverage of all federal and state cases. It is entirely likely, however, that you may not need such extensive coverage. In this regard, there are several specialized digests published by West that will assist you in locating cases from a specific region, jurisdiction, or state. The following digests are kept up to date by annual cumulative pocket parts.

a. *United States Supreme Court Digest*

This digest is published by West and classifies its headnotes according to the Key Number System. As its name indicates, this set provides brief summaries, or digests, only to United States Supreme Court cases. A Defendant-Plaintiff Table of Cases is included.

b. Federal Practice Digests

There are several West digests that serve as casefinders for cases from all federal courts—for example, the United States Supreme Court, the United States Courts of Appeal, and the United States District Courts. Each digest covers a specific time period, similar to the manner in which the *Decennials* each cover a ten-year period.

Federal Digest: Federal Courts (1754-1938)
Modern Federal Practice Digest: Federal Courts (1939-1961)
West's Federal Practice Digest 2d: Federal Courts (1961-1975)
West's Federal Practice Digest 3d: Federal Courts (1975-1983)
West's Federal Practice Digest 4th: Federal Courts (1983-Date)

Thus, if you are interested only in recent cases from the Third Circuit, you could consult West's *Federal Practice Digest 4th* and West's *Federal Practice Digest 3d.* Cases are arranged in groups by court, circuits, and districts, making it easy for you to locate cases from the United States Supreme Court, cases from the Third Circuit, or cases from the United States District Court for the Eastern District of Pennsylvania. All of the *Federal Practice Digests* include a Defendent-Plaintiff Table of Cases.

c. Regional Digests

West has created regional digests for some of its regional geographic units.

Atlantic Digest—digests cases reported in the *Atlantic Reporter*
North Western Digest—digests cases reported in the *North Western Reporter*
Pacific Digest—digests cases reported in the *Pacific Reporter*
South Eastern Digest—digests cases reported in the *South Eastern Reporter*

Thus, if you were interested in locating cases from several states, you could consult the *North Western Digest*, which would assist you in finding cases from North Dakota, South Dakota, Nebraska, Minnesota, Iowa, Wisconsin, and Michigan. Again, the *Digest* will arrange the cases for you so that under **Criminal Law 1169.1(5)** all of the digest headnotes for Iowa cases are grouped together, all of the digest headnotes for North Dakota cases are grouped together, and all of the digest headnotes for Wisconsin cases are grouped together.

You will note there are no current digests for the *Southern Reporter*, *South Western Reporter*, and *North Eastern Reporter*. This should not be considered a drawback, however, as cases from states within these reporters are included within the all-inclusive *American Digest System* and also in state digests.

d. State Digests

West publishes digests for 47 of the states and the District of Columbia. Only Delaware, Nevada, and Utah do not have a digest. Additionally, Virginia and West Virginia are combined in one digest, as are North Dakota and South Dakota. Even though there is no separate digest for Delaware, Nevada, or Utah, you may locate cases from these states in the appropriate regional digest (*Atlantic Digest* or *Pacific Digest*) as well as in the comprehensive *Decennial* units, which arrange the digests or summaries of the cases alphabetically by state.

The state digests are all similarly named (*Alabama Digest, Missouri Digest, Tennessee Digest*), and each digests cases from a particular state according to West's Key Number System. Moreover, these state digests include cases decided by the lower federal courts and the United States Supreme Court that arose in that state jurisdiction or that were appealed from that state.

There is overlap and duplication in the digest entries. For example, a digest entry for a 1985 California case will be located in the *California Digest*, the *Pacific Digest*, and the *Ninth Decennial Digest, Part 2*. Which digest should you use? Generally, if your issue involves California law, start with the *California Digest*. If you do not find helpful cases, perhaps because the issue is one of first impression in California, expand your search by using the *Pacific Digest* and then the *Decennial* units. The state digests also include a Defendant-Plaintiff Table of Cases.

e. Specialized Digests

In addition to the digests for federal court cases, the regional digests, and the state digests, West publishes various specialized digests, each of which digests cases from a particular court. The function of each specialized digest is fully described by its name. These specialized digests are as follows:

West's Bankruptcy Digest
West's Military Justice Digest
United States Claims Court Digest
West's Education Law Digest
United States Merit System Protection Board Digest

8. *Common Features of West's Digests*

a. Uniform Classification

All of West's digests are classified to West's uniform topic and *Key Number System.* Thus, once a legal issue is assigned the topic and Key Number **Landlord & Tenant 166(1)**, later cases that deal with this issue will also be digested under **Landlord & Tenant 166(1)**, whether they appear in a *Decennial* unit, *West's Federal Practice Digest 4th*, the *South Eastern Digest*, or the *Wyoming Digest.*

b. Descriptive Word Indexes

All of West's digests include Descriptive Word Indexes arranged in similar fashion that provide you with topic names and Key Numbers, which you then insert into the pertinent digest.

c. Table of Cases

All of the West digests contain a Table of Cases by plaintiff, so you may look up a case by the plaintiff's name and be provided with parallel citations, the topic names, and Key Numbers under which it has been digested, and the subsequent history of the case. Additionally, the *Ninth* and *Tenth Decennial Digests*, the *United States Supreme Court Digest*, the *Federal Practice Digests*, the state digests, and the specialized digests also contain a Defendant-Plaintiff Table of Cases listing the defendant's name first, so if you know a case only by the defendant's name, you will still be able to locate the case. These tables are usually located after the last volumes in a set.

d. Table of Words and Phrases

Many of the digests (the *United States Supreme Court Digest*, the *Federal Practice Digests*, the state digests, and the specialized digests) contain a Table of Words and Phrases, which alphabetically lists words and phrases that have been construed or defined by cases. Thus, if you look up the word "conspiracy" in the *Colorado Digest*, you will be provided with citations to all of the cases in Colorado that define or interpret this word.

e. Supplementation

The *United States Supreme Court Digest*, the *Federal Practice Digests 3d* and *4th*, the regional digests, and the state digests are kept current by annual cumulative pocket parts and supplemental pamphlets. The *American Digest System*, of course, is supplemented by the *General Digest*. If a pocket part or supplement exists, you must consult it to locate more recent cases and to determine if any new topics have been added.

f. Cross-Referencing

Because West's Key Number System is a truly integrated research approach, other West publications will give you topic names and Key Numbers, allowing easy access into the system. Thus, West's encyclopedias (discussed in Chapter 6) *Corpus Juris Secundum* (C.J.S.) and *American Jurisprudence, Second Series* (Am. Jur. 2d) routinely provide you with topic names and Key Numbers. Similarly, West's set *American Law Reports* (also discussed in Chapter 5) directs you to relevant topic names and Key Numbers. Finally, the Key Number System is also used in West's computer-assisted research system called Westlaw. Thus, this cross-referencing by West continually helps you gain access to its digests to allow you to find all other cases on a similar point of law.

9. Other Digests

While West is the largest publisher of digests and while its Key Number System provides easy access to all reported cases relating to a particular legal issue, it is not the only publisher of digests. The best known of the non-West digests is the *Digest of the United States Supreme Court Reports Lawyers' Edition* published by LEXIS Publishing. This digest uses its own classification scheme to direct readers to cases in *United States Supreme Court Reports, Lawyers' Edition* because only West may use its copyrighted Key Number System. Use the descriptive-word approach or table of cases approach to access this digest. Because this digest is published by LEXIS Publishing, it provides references to other LEXIS publications.

There are also several state digests published by companies other than West, such as McKinney's *California Digest* and Michie's *Virginia and West Virginia Digest*. These non-West digests also use their own classification schemes. Nevertheless, the basic system is the same: The researcher locates topics and subtopics and uses those to find citations to relevant cases.

B. *American Law Reports*

1. Introduction

The *American Law Reports* ("A.L.R.") is a product of West that publishes selected appellate court decisions as well as comprehensive and objective essays relating to the legal issues raised in a case. For this reason, the A.L.R. forms a logical bridge between the primary sources (cases, constitutions, and statutes), which have been discussed, and the secondary sources (encyclopedias, law review articles, treatises, and so on), which will be discussed in the next chapters. A.L.R. combines features of primary sources (in that it publishes cases) with features of secondary sources (in that it publishes essays, called "annotations," which explain and expand upon the issues raised by the cases published in A.L.R.).

The lawyer-editors review both state and federal appellate court decisions from all over the country and publish certain selected decisions that they believe have general significance. You may recall that West's *American Digest System* digests *all* reported cases. A.L.R., on the other hand, does not have such a goal. Its aim is to publish only leading cases rather than cases of purely local interest or those that do not represent a new trend in the law.

The significance of A.L.R. does not lie in the fact that it publishes cases. After all, if A.L.R. selects a recent California Supreme Court case to be published, that case will already be published officially in the *California Reports* and unofficially in both the *Pacific Reporter* and *California Reporter*. The true value of A.L.R. lies in its scholarly and comprehensive articles (called "annotations"), which follow each case A.L.R. selects to publish. Often the case that is published is of average length—perhaps seven or eight pages. The annotation that explains and analyzes the issues raised in the case may exceed 150 pages. Not all annotations are this long, although all are thorough and well-researched.

For example, if a case relating to the liability of a blood bank for providing tainted blood is decided by an appellate court, A.L.R. will publish it. Immediately following the case is an exhaustive analysis of the development of this area of law and how courts in other jurisdictions are treating this subject. The editors may spend months researching this legal issue and writing the annotation, which in many respects is a scholarly monograph thoroughly examining this area of the law and looking at both sides of the issue.

If you are researching a certain area of the law and an A.L.R. annotation has been written regarding your topic, you should immediately retrieve the annotation and view it as "free research," as seldom, if ever, will you have the luxury of being able to devote as much time to an analysis of a legal topic as the editors have in their annotations. In fact, the publisher of A.L.R. reports that A.L.R. is quoted from and cited more often than any other secondary authority.

2. *A.L.R. Organization*

A.L.R. is published in six series and consists of more than 500 volumes.

A.L.R. This set consists of 175 volumes and covers federal cases and state appellate court cases decided between 1919 and 1948.

A.L.R.2d. This set consists of 100 volumes and covers federal cases and state appellate court cases decided between 1948 and 1965.

A.L.R.3d. This set consists of 100 volumes and covers state appellate court cases decided between 1965 and 1980 and federal court cases decided between 1965 and 1969.

A.L.R.4th. This set consists of 90 volumes and covers state appellate court cases from 1980 to 1992.

A.L.R.5th. This set was introduced in 1992 and covers state appellate court cases from 1992 to date.

A.L.R. Federal. This set was introduced in 1969 and, as its name indicates, exclusively covers federal court cases from 1969 to date.

As you can see, until A.L.R. Federal ("A.L.R. Fed.") was introduced in 1969, federal court cases were published and analyzed in A.L.R., A.L.R.2d, and A.L.R.3d. A.L.R. Fed. follows the format of the other A.L.R. series: Significant federal court cases are selected for publication and following the case is an annotation, which thoroughly analyzes the legal topics raised in the case and discusses the treatment of this topic by other federal courts.

A.L.R. is not published in advance sheets and the first volumes that appear on the library shelves are hardbound.

3. *Features of A.L.R.*

The following are all current features of the *American Law Reports*. Note, however, that not all features are found in all of the six units comprising A.L.R. The set was recently purchased by West from Lawyers Co-op, and thus newer volumes in the A.L.R. sets direct you to relevent West Digest topic names and Key Numbers and give you tips on using Westlaw, while earlier volumes do not because Lawyers Co-op would never direct its users to a West publication.

Cases. All of the volumes in each A.L.R. series publish contemporary cases illustrating new developments or significant changes in the law. A brief synopsis of the case is provided together with headnotes summarizing the issues in the case.

Annotations. Immediately following the representative case, a complete essay or annotation analyzing the case and the issues therein is presented. In A.L.R. 5th, and A.L.R. Fed. after approximately 1992, the cases analyzed are collected together in the back of each volume, following the annotations.

Research References. Before the annotation begins, you will be directed to additional sources relating to the topic to be discussed, including other books, law review articles, encyclopedias, and texts. Additionally, you will be given suggestions for drafting search queries so you can find additional information on Westlaw and LEXIS, the computerized research systems. Finally, you are directed to relevant West topic names and Key Numbers so you can gain access to West's digests to find other similar cases.

Outline. An outline is presented that shows how the annotation is organized so you can easily locate and read the sections that may be of the most interest to you.

Index. An alphabetical word index is presented for each annotation, which references the various issues and topics discussed in the annotation, enabling you to readily locate the sections of the annotation that are relevant to the issues of most interest to you.

Jurisdictional Table of Cited Statutes and Cases. Because you may be more interested in the manner in which the topic under discussion has been treated in some jurisdictions than in others, you will be provided with a table showing you which sections discuss cases and statutes from individual states. Analogous information in A.L.R. Fed. is found in its Table of Cases.

Scope Section. The annotation begins with a section titled "Scope," which briefly describes the matters discussed in the annotation and then refers to earlier annotations discussing the topic that are superseded.

Related Annotations Section. This section directs you to other annotations or other sources such as cases, law reviews, or textbooks dealing with topics related to the annotation.

Summary. A concise and useful summary of the entire annotation is presented, setting the stage for the extensive annotation that follows. Additionally, annotations often contain "practice pointers," which provide practical tips on how to handle a case dealing with the subject matter under discussion.

See Figure 5-7 for features of A.L.R.

4. *Finding A.L.R. Annotations*

a. Index or Descriptive-Word Approach

A multi-volume alphabetical index called *A.L.R. Index* exists that directs you to annotations in A.L.R.2d, A.L.R.3d, A.L.R.4th, A.L.R.5th, and A.L.R. Fed. Using this index is similar to using any other index. You simply insert words or phrases that describe the problem or issue you are researching and you will be directed to the appropriate annotation. The *A.L.R. Index* is another "forgiving" index allowing you to locate an annotation by using various words or phrases rather than requiring you to reduce the legal issue to one perfect word. For example, if your research task is to determine whether an obscene movie constitutes a nuisance, you simply look up the word "nuisance" in the *A.L.R. Index*, and you will be directed to the appropriate annotation. See Figure 5-8 for a sample page from the *A.L.R. Index*. After using the *Index*, check the pocket supplement located in the back of each volume of the *A.L.R. Index*, which will provide you with references to more recent annotations.

The *A.L.R. Index* also contains a Table of Laws, Rules, and Regulations directing you to annotations that cite particular federal and state

Figure 5-7
Sample Pages from A.L.R. Annotation Showing Features of Annotations

ANNOTATION

Annotation usually follows the reported case

EXHIBITION OF OBSCENE MOTION PICTURES AS NUISANCE

by

Jack W. Shaw, Jr., J.D.

Annotation usually outline/scheme shows overall organization of annotation

TOTAL CLIENT-SERVICE LIBRARY® REFERENCES

4 AM JUR 2d, Amusements and Exhibitions § 37; 50 AM JUR 2d, Lewdness, Indecency and Obscenity § 26

18 AM JUR PL & PR FORMS (Rev ed), Nuisances §§ 1 et seq.

8 AM JUR PROOF OF FACTS 527, Nuisances; 18 AM JUR PROOF OF FACTS 465, Obscenity—Motion Pictures

10 AM JUR TRIALS 1, Obscenity Litigation

ALR DIGESTS, Amusements, etc. § 1; Indecency, etc. § 3

US L ED DIGESTS, Amusements, etc. § 1; Indecency, etc. § 1

ALR QUICK INDEX, Amusements, Exhibitions, Shows and Resorts; Indecency, Lewdness, and Obscenity; Motion Pictures; Nuisances

FEDERAL QUICK INDEX, Amusements and Exhibitions; Lewdness, Indecency, and Obscenity; Motion Pictures; Nuisances

TCSL box providing references to other helpful sources (no longer printed)

Consult POCKET PART in this volume for later case service

Figure 5-7 (*Continued*)

Scope section describes topics to be discussed

§ 1. Introduction

[a] Scope

This annotation collects those cases considering whether the exhibition[1] of motion pictures[2] alleged to be of an obscene, lewd, or indecent nature constitutes a nuisance sufficient to support an action for damages by those injured thereby, or to support a civil action of abatement.[3]

This annotation deals with or states relevant statutory law only insofar as it is reflected in the reported cases which are within its scope, and the reader is advised to consult any applicable statutes of the jurisdiction in which he is interested.

Related matters section refers you to other annotations, cases, and sources

[b] Related matters

Modern status of rules as to balance of convenience or social utility as affecting relief from nuisance. 40 ALR3d 601.

Punitive damages in actions based on nuisance. 31 ALR3d 1346.

Comment Note.—Validity of procedures designed to protect the public against obscenity. 5 ALR3d 1214.

Modern concept of obscenity. 5 ALR 3d 1158.

Drive-in theater or other outdoor dramatic or musical entertainment as nuisance. 93 ALR2d 1171.

Power of municipality in respect of inspection and censorship of motion-picture films. 126 ALR 1363.

What amounts to obscene play or book within prohibition statute. 81 ALR 801.

Constitutionality of regulation of obscene motion pictures—federal cases. 22 L Ed 2d 949.

Constitutionality of federal and state regulation of obscene literature—federal cases. 1 L Ed 2d 2211, 4 L Ed 2d 1821.

§ 2. Background, summary, and comment

Brief summary of annotation

[a] In general

As a matter of federal constitutional law, matter is said to be obscene only if (1) the dominant theme of the material taken as a whole appeals to prurient interest in sex; (2) the material is patently offensive because it affronts contemporary community standards relating to the description or representation of sexual matter; and (3) the material is utterly without redeeming social value.[4]

A nuisance may be broadly defined as that which unlawfully annoys or does damage to another, and anything wrongfully done or permitted which injures or annoys another in the enjoyment of his legal rights; and the term is applied to that class of wrongs which arises from the unreasonable, unwarrantable, or unlawful use by a person of his own property, which produces such material annoyance, inconvenience, discomfort, or hurt that the law will presume a consequent damage.[5]

These concepts must be kept clearly in mind in determining whether the exhibition of an allegedly obscene motion picture constitutes either a public nuisance (one that affects the public at large or such of the public as may come in contact with it) or a private nuisance (affecting the individual or a limited number of individuals only).[6] Since mo-

1. Only those cases dealing with the exhibition of such motion pictures, rather than their private possession or their sale, are included herein.

2. Cases involving live theatrical productions and the like are not included herein, as involving potentially different questions.

3. Cases involving criminal prosecutions for the maintenance of a public nuisance have been included on a merely illustrative basis in the exercise of editorial discretion.

4. 50 Am Jur 2d, Lewdness, Indecency, and Obscenity § 4.

5. 58 Am Jur 2d, Nuisances § 1.

6. 58 Am Jur 2d, Nuisances § 6.

Figure 5-8
Sample Page from *A.L.R. Index*

NUISANCES—Cont'd

Lewdness, indecency, and obscenity —Cont'd
- porno shops or similar places disseminating obscene materials as nuisance, 58 ALR3d 1134

Life tenant's right of action for injury or damage to property, 49 ALR2d 1117

Lights and lighting, casting of light on another's premises as constituting nuisance, 5 ALR2d 705

Limitation of actions, when statute of limitations begins to run as to cause of action for nuisance based on air pollution, 19 ALR4th 456

Liquors, see group Intoxicating liquors in this topic

Litter and debris, what constitutes special injury that entitles private party to maintain action based on public nuisance—modern cases, 71 ALR4th 13

Livestock, see group Animals in this topic

Location, funeral home as private nuisance, 8 ALR4th 324

Loudspeakers
- bells, carillons, and the like as nuisance, 95 ALR3d 1268
- use of phonograph, loud-speaker, or other mechanical or electrical device for broadcasting music, advertising, or sales talk from business premises, as nuisance, 23 ALR2d 1289

Massage parlor as nuisance, 80 ALR3d 1020

Merry-go-round as nuisance, 75 ALR2d 803

Mines and Minerals (this index)

Minors, see group Children in this topic

Motel or hotel as nuisance, 24 ALR2d 571

Motion pictures
- drive-in theater as nuisance, 93 ALR2d 1171
- obscene motion pictures as nuisance, 50 ALR3d 969

Motor vehicles, see group Automobiles in this topic

Moving of buildings on highways as nuisance, 83 ALR2d 478

NUISANCES—Cont'd

Mufflers or similar noise-preventing devices on motor vehicles, aircraft, or boats, validity of public regulation requiring, 49 ALR2d 1202

Municipal corporations
- attractive nuisance doctrine, liability of municipality for injury to children by fire under, 27 ALR2d 1194
- dump, municipal liability for maintenance of public dump as nuisance, 52 ALR2d 1134
- rule of municipal immunity from liability for acts in performance of governmental functions as applicable to personal injury or death as result of, 56 ALR2d 1415
- swimming pools, public swimming pool as a nuisance, 49 ALR3d 652

Music and musicians
- bells, carillons, and the like as nuisance, 95 ALR3d 1268
- drive-in theater or other outdoor dramatic or musical entertainment as nuisance, 93 ALR2d 1171
- use of phonograph, loud-speaker, or other mechanical or electrical device for broadcasting music, advertising, or sales talk from business premises, as nuisance, 23 ALR2d 1289

Neighborhood, see group Residential area or neighborhood in this topic

Noise or sound
- air conditioning, existence of, and relief from, nuisance created by operation of air conditioning or ventilating equipment, 79 ALR3d 320
- bells, carillons, and the like as nuisance, 95 ALR3d 1268
- carwash as nuisance, 4 ALR4th 1308
- coalyard, noise caused by operation of, as nuisance, 8 ALR2d 419
- dogs, keeping of dogs as enjoinable nuisance, 11 ALR3d 1399
- electric generating plant or transformer station as nuisance, 4 ALR3d 902
- special injury, what constitutes special injury that entitles private party to maintain action based on public nuisance—modern cases, 71 ALR4th 13
- windmill as nuisance, 36 ALR4th 1159
- zoo as nuisance, 58 ALR3d 1126

1086 **Consult POCKET PART for Later Annotations**

statutes, rules, and regulations. Thus, if you are researching 42 U.S.C.A. § 2487 (West 1994), you can look this up in the Table of Laws, Rules, and Regulations, and you will be directed to any annotation that mentions or discusses this statute.

West also provides a one-volume index called *Quick Index*, which is easy to use and directs you to annotations in A.L.R.3d, A.L.R.4th, and A.L.R.5th. A similar index called *A.L.R. Federal Quick Index* will direct you to annotations dealing with the federal law collected in A.L.R. Fed. and is usually shelved after the last volume in A.L.R. Fed.

b. Digest Approach

Multi-volume digests for A.L.R. and for A.L.R.2d as well as a combined digest for A.L.R.3d, A.L.R.4th, A.L.R. 5th, and A.L.R. Fed. organize areas of the law into more than 400 topics and present them alphabetically. For example, if you look up the topic "nuisance" in the digest to A.L.R.3d, A.L.R.4th, A.L.R.5th, and A.L.R. Fed., you will be presented with detailed summaries of the various annotations relating to this topic.

c. Miscellaneous Approaches

You will see in Chapter 6 that another of West's publications, its encyclopedia Am. Jur. 2d, often refers readers to A.L.R. annotations. Similarly, when you Shepardize a case or check its validity through West's electronic updating service called "KeyCite," as discussed in Chapter 9, you will be informed whether the case has been published in any of the A.L.R. series. If A.L.R. has published a case you are interested in, this is a signal that an exhaustive and analytical annotation will be provided immediately after that case.

5. *Updating A.L.R. Annotations*

If a case was decided in 1960 and an annotation was prepared that year analyzing that case, it is possible that a case may have been decided after 1960 that has modified or limited the original case or that a newer annotation has been prepared that discusses the changes in the law since 1960. The publisher has developed systems to help you locate newer cases or newer annotations relating to the topic you have researched. In fact, after you have located an annotation, you *must* update it to determine if the annotation remains an accurate interpretation of the law.

A.L.R. If you have read an annotation in A.L.R. (that is, an annotation written between 1919 and 1948), you update it by checking a source named *A.L.R. Blue Book of Supplemental Decisions*. These volumes are usually located close to the A.L.R. volumes. Thus, if you have read an annotation at 168 A.L.R. 204, you simply look up this reference in the *A.L.R. Blue Book of Supplemental Decisions*, and you will be informed if the annotation has been supplemented or superseded by any later annotation in any A.L.R. series. You will also be directed to cases decided after the date your annotation was published and that relate to the issues discussed in your annotation.

A.L.R.2d Annotations written between 1948 and 1965 and that appear in A.L.R.2d are updated by a set of books called *A.L.R.2d Later Case Service* and are typically located near A.L.R.2d. If your annotation was located at 80 A.L.R.2d 368, you simply look up that citation in the *A.L.R.2d Later Case Service*, and you will be directed to cases decided after 80 A.L.R.2d 368 that relate to the issues discussed in that annotation. These cases will be briefly summarized so you may easily determine which cases will be most helpful to you. The *A.L.R.2d Later Case Service* will also direct you to more recent annotations relating to the subject matter discussed by the annotation at 80 A.L.R.2d 368. *A.L.R.2d Later Case Service* is itself updated by annual pocket parts placed in the back of each volume that must be consulted.

A.L.R.3d, A.L.R.4th, A.L.R.5th, and A.L.R. Fed. Updating annotations in A.L.R.3d, A.L.R.4th, A.L.R.5th, and A.L.R. Fed. is easier than updating annotations in A.L.R. or A.L.R.2d (which require you to use separate books) because these sets are kept current by the more conventional method of updating: annual cumulative pocket-part supplements inserted in the back of each volume. After you read an annotation in A.L.R.3d, A.L.R.4th, A.L.R.5th, or A.L.R. Fed., you simply turn to the pocket part in that volume, which will direct you to more recent annotations and more recent cases relating to the topic discussed by your annotation. See Figure 5-9.

Annotation History Table. The last volume of the *A.L.R. Index* contains the Annotation History Table. This table will inform you whether the annotation you have been researching has been "supplemented," meaning that additional information has been collected in a later annotation, or whether it has been "superseded," meaning that the topics discussed in your annotation have been so significantly changed by later cases that only the new annotation should be relied upon. See Figure 5-10 for a sample page from the Annotation History Table.

Figure 5-9
Updating A.L.R. Annotations

Location of Annotation	*Method of Updating*
A.L.R.	*A.L.R. Blue Book of Supplemental Decisions*
A.L.R.2d	*A.L.R.2d Later Case Service*
A.L.R.3d	Pocket Part in each volume
A.L.R.4th	Pocket Part in each volume
A.L.R.5th	Pocket Part in each volume
A.L.R. Fed.	Pocket Part in each volume

Figure 5-10
Sample Page from Annotation History Table

29 ALR3d 1021
Superseded 13 ALR4th 52

29 ALR3d 1407
Superseded 96 ALR3d 195
24 ALR Fed 808

29 ALR3d 1425
§ 3[a], 3[b], 3[g], 3[i] Superseded 100 ALR3d 1205

30 ALR3d 9
§ 6 Superseded 76 ALR3d 11
§ 14.1 Superseded 90 ALR4th 859
§ 16, 19[d] Superseded 67 ALR3d 308
100 ALR3d 10
100 ALR3d 940
§ 19[c] Superseded 99 ALR3d 807
99 ALR3d 1080
§ 25 Superseded 7 ALR4th 308
§ 26[c] Superseded 11 ALR4th 241
§ 29 Superseded 69 ALR3d 1162

30 ALR3d 203
§ 18 Superseded 46 ALR3d 900

30 ALR3d 1352
Superseded 110 ALR Fed 211

32 ALR3d 508
Superseded 22 ALR4th 294

32 ALR3d 1446
Superseded 20 ALR4th 63

33 ALR3d 1417
Superseded 38 ALR4th 538

34 ALR3d 1256
§ 5 Superseded 81 ALR4th 259
§ 6 Superseded 85 ALR4th 19
§ 8, 11, 13, 15 Superseded 74 ALR4th 388
§ 14 Superseded 71 ALR4th 638

35 ALR3d 412-486
§ 19 Superseded 27 ALR4th 568

35 ALR3d 692
Superseded 4 ALR5th 1000

Indication that annotation at 35 A.L.R. 3d 692 has been superseded or replaced by a later annotation

35 ALR3d 1129
§ 3, 4 Superseded 2 ALR5th 475
§ 6 Superseded 12 ALR4th 611

35 ALR3d 1404
§ 10.5 Superseded 8 ALR5th 463

36 ALR3d 405
§ 7, 8 Superseded 85 ALR4th 979

36 ALR3d 735
Superseded 43 ALR4th 1062

36 ALR3d 820
Superseded 74 ALR4th 277

37 ALR3d 1338
Superseded 22 ALR4th 237

38 ALR3d 363
Superseded 61 ALR4th 27

39 ALR3d 222
Superseded 68 ALR4th 294

39 ALR3d 1434
Superseded 1 ALR5th 132

40 ALR3d 856
Superseded 85 ALR4th 365

41 ALR3d 455
§ 3[e, f] Superseded 91 ALR Fed 547

41 ALR3d 904
Superseded 6 ALR4th 1066

42 ALR3d 560
§ 8 Superseded 96 ALR3d 265

44 ALR3d 1108
Superseded 58 ALR4th 402

45 ALR3d 875
§ 13 Superseded 58 ALR4th 559

45 ALR3d 1181
§ 1-4 Superseded 61 ALR4th 615
§ 5-7 Superseded 61 ALR4th 464

45 ALR3d 1364
Superseded 20 ALR4th 136
24 ALR4th 508

46 ALR3d 680
Superseded 50 ALR4th 787

46 ALR3d 733
Superseded 46 ALR4th 220

46 ALR3d 900
§ 11 Superseded 58 ALR4th 902

46 ALR3d 979
§ 7[b] Superseded 35 ALR4th 225

46 ALR3d 1024
§ 5 Superseded 52 ALR4th 18

46 ALR3d 1383
Superseded 53 ALR4th 231

47 ALR3d 909
Superseded 47 ALR4th 134

47 ALR3d 971
Superseded 47 ALR4th 100

47 ALR3d 1286
Superseded 81 ALR3d 1119

49 ALR3d 915
Superseded 97 ALR3d 294

49 ALR3d 934
Superseded 49 ALR4th 1076

50 ALR3d 549
§ 4 Superseded 70 ALR4th 132

51 ALR3d 8
§ 2 [b] Superseded 65 ALR4th 346

51 ALR3d 520
Superseded 65 ALR4th 1155

52 ALR3d 636
§ 9 Superseded 87 ALR Fed 177

52 ALR3d 1289
Superseded 48 ALR4th 229

52 ALR3d 1344
Superseded 76 ALR4th 1025
79 ALR4th 171

53 ALR3d 731
Superseded 4 ALR5th 273

53 ALR3d 1285
Superseded 97 ALR3d 528

53 ALR3d 1310
Superseded 2 ALR5th 396

55 ALR3d 581
§ 9[c,d] Superseded 86 ALR3d 1116

57 ALR3d 584
§ 5 Superseded 86 ALR Fed 866

58 ALR3d 533
Superseded 45 ALR4th 949

59 ALR3d 138
Superseded 76 ALR4th 22

59 ALR3d 321
§ 5, 6, 13 Superseded 83 ALR4th 1056

1180 **Consult POCKET PART for Later Entries**

Toll-free Number. The front of each softcover pocket-part supplement in A.L.R.3d, A.L.R.4th, A.L.R.5th, and A.L.R. Fed. will provide you with a toll-free telephone number (1-800-225-7488), which you can call to obtain the most recent information regarding annotations.

C. *Words and Phrases*

In the mid-1980s in Southern California, two young men attended a party at which one of them consumed a great deal of an alcoholic beverage. This individual, recognizing he should not drive, asked his friend to drive him home and slid into the passenger side of the vehicle. Before the driver could get into the car, however, the car began rolling down the hill on which it was parked. The passenger grabbed wildly for the steering wheel and managed to move his leg enough to apply the brake. Nevertheless, the car struck another vehicle, and the passenger was issued a citation by the police officer who arrived at the scene for "driving while under the influence of an intoxicating liquor," a violation of the California Penal Code.

The entire case depended on the interpretation of the word "driving," for if the passenger was not "driving," he could not be in violation of the statute. The definition of the word "driving" can obviously be found in any dictionary. How this word has been defined and construed in a legal sense by case law can be found in a 46-volume set of books published by West called *Words and Phrases*. It arranges words and phrases in alphabetical order from Volume 1 ("A" to "Accident") to Volume 46 ("Willfulness" to "Zygoma"), making the set as easy to use as any dictionary. *Words and Phrases* aims at providing the definition of words and phrases as interpreted by cases from 1658 to the present time. *Words and Phrases*, like digests, is thus an excellent casefinder. It contains no narrative treatment as secondary sources do, but rather focuses exclusively on locating cases. It is the last "bridge" to the secondary sources to be discussed in Chapters 6 and 7.

In the case described above, a review of the definition of the term "driving" revealed that "driving" required one to have control of a vehicle. The court hearing the case in California determined that the passenger was not "driving" under the meaning of the California statutes because he had no true ability to control the vehicle. The case was dismissed.

Once again, West will do more than merely list all cases defining words such as "assessment," "clemency," "distress," "guardian," or "petition." *Words and Phrases* will provide you with a brief summary of the cases that have defined these words so you may easily determine which cases you should read in full.

Words and Phrases is kept current by annual cumulative pocket parts. Thus, once you have reviewed the cases in the main volume that define a word—for example, "guardian"—examine the pocket part to determine if newer cases have interpreted or construed the word "guardian." See Figure 5-11 for a sample page from *Words and Phrases*.

Figure 5-11
Sample Page from West's *Words and Phrases*

it. Merritt v. Victoria Lumber Co., 35 So. 497, 500, 111 La. 159.

"Protect" is defined as follows: "To guard; shield; preserve." Webst.Int.Dict. "To cover or shield from danger, harm, damage, trespass, exposure, insult, temptation, or the like; defend; guard; preserve in safety. Synonyms: Defend; shield; screen; secure." Cent.Dict. "To cover, shield, or defend from injury, harm, or danger of any kind." Enc.Dict. An instruction that a servant could presume that the master would use ordinary care to "protect" the servant placed too great a burden upon the master, since he is only bound to use reasonable care to provide a reasonably safe place of work, reasonably safe appliances, and to use reasonable care in selecting fellow servants. Reino v. Montana Mineral Land Development Co., 99 P. 853, 855, 38 Mont. 291.

A patrolman whose chief duties were to guard prisoners and to keep part of a building in order does not, because of his duties, become a turnkey or janitor, but retains his position as a public officer, and Greater New York Charter, §§ 292, 354, 355, Police Department Rule 597, having provided for the relief of injured patrolmen and for relief of their dependents in case of their death, such patrolman, though he suffered injuries in attempting to remove a light bulb, cannot be deemed entitled to compensation under the Workmen's Compensation Law, § 2, group 42, as added by Laws 1916, c. 622, and group 44, as added by Laws 1917, c. 705, including "persons maintaining buildings," and "keepers," "guards," or "orderlies" in prisons. Ryan v. City of New York, 126 N.E. 350, 351, 228 N.Y. 16.

A "railroad cattle gap" or "guard" is a contrivance to restrain cattle. In a sense it is a "fence," but the construction of the gap or guard itself is not limited in its dangerous quality, as is a fence. To be at all effective and serviceable, it cannot be a barrier erected perpendicular to the surface of the ground, and rising above it, but must, in order to answer the purpose in view, be so constructed that its appearance of dangerousness will, under ordinary circumstances, deter cattle from attempting to pass over it; and, in so ordering the gap or guard, a really dangerous contrivance may be properly installed without, in the event of injury to cattle attempting to cross it, rendering the railway company liable, if the fact of its want of safety for that purpose is the proximate cause of the injury. Carrollton Short Line Ry. Co. v. Lipsey, 43 So. 836, 837, 150 Ala. 570.

GUARDED

Cross References

Appropriately Guarded
Sufficiently Guarded

GUARDIAN

Cross References

Action to Remove a Guardian
Agent
Committee
De Facto Guardian
Discharge
Express Trust
General Guardian
Legal Guardian
Legal Representative
Natural Guardian
Next Friend
Occupant; Occupier
Owner
Quasi Guardian
Special Guardian
Trustee of Express Trust
Unsuitable Guardian
Voidable

In general

A guardian is one who is entitled to the custody of the person of an infant. Wilson v. Me-ne-chas, 20 P. 468, 469, 40 Kan. 648.

A guardian is a person upon whom the law imposes the duty of looking after the pecuniary interests of his ward. Sparhawk v. Allen, 21 N.H. 27, 1 Fost. 27.

The term "guardian", as defined in statute governing adoptions, embraces within its meaning the custodial guardianship resulting from a final committal of dependent or neg-

D. Citation Form

Digests and *Words and Phrases* are used solely to locate cases. You may never cite to them. You may, however, cite to an A.L.R. annotation:

> Francine L. Harris, Annotation, *The Battered Spouse Syndrome as a Defense in Manslaughter Cases*, 96 A.L.R.4th 797 (1988).

Technology Tips

Neither West's digests nor A.L.R. annotations are available on the Internet. Nevertheless, both may be found via computer-assisted legal research.

Westlaw, West's electronic research system, allows you to search for cases using West's topics and Key Numbers. When you see a topic and Key Number in a case you are reading in any of West's reporters, you can immediately locate other cases classified under the same topic and Key Number by running a topic and Key Number search on Westlaw (as opposed to inserting the topic and Key Number into a print digest).

Annotations in A.L.R. are available both on Westlaw and on LEXIS, Reed Elsevier's computerized legal research system. One helpful feature of locating A.L.R. annotations online is that the supplementation is completely integrated with the annotation. Using A.L.R. in conventional print form requires that you supplement and update A.L.R. annotations using either separate books or pocket parts. When you access A.L.R. online, the supplements or updates are included together with the annotation, saving you time and effort.

Words and Phrases is not available on the Internet.

Computer-assisted legal research will be fully discussed in Chapter 11.

Writing Strategies

In any research project, remember the key distinction between primary and secondary authorities: If on point, primary authorities must be followed and are binding, while secondary authorities are persuasive at best. Therefore, you should always cite at least one primary authority to support each of your arguments. Secondary authorities such as A.L.R. annotations should be used only in conjunction with primary authorities, namely, as "extra" support for a contention.

Use some variety in the manner in which you discuss your authorities. If each paragraph begins with the phrase "In [case name] or [authority], . . ." or if each paragraph discusses a topic and always concludes with a citation, your writing will have a rigid and structured appearance. Introduce citations, paragraphs, and sentences in varying ways. This variety will enhance readability. Your project must not only be right — it must be read.

Assignment for Chapter 5

1. Use the Tables of Cases to the *Tenth Decennial, Part 2*. Under which topic and Key Numbers are the following cases digested?
   a. *Sims v. Westminster Investing Club*
   b. *Island v. Department of Corrections*
   c. Give a citation to a case in which the defendant's name is "Dorchak."
2. Use the Descriptive Word Index to the *Tenth Decennial, Part 2*.
   a. Which topic and Key Number discuss banishment as a condition of parole?
   b. Look up this topic and Key Number. Which 1995 case from Alabama discusses this?
3. Use the Descriptive Word Index to the *Ninth Decennial, Part 2*.
   a. Which topic and Key Number discuss larceny of mail matter?
   b. Look up the topic and Key Number. Which 1986 case from Pennsylvania (3d Cir.) discusses this?
4. Use the Descriptive Word Index to the *Tenth Decennial, Part 1*.
   a. Which topic and Key Number discuss admissibility of blood tests for children born out of wedlock?
   b. Look up the topic and Key Number. What Colorado case discusses this?
   c. What 1996 Idaho case updates this?
5. Use West's *Federal Practice Digest, 4th Series*.
   a. Which topic and Key Number discuss airports as nuisances?
   b. Review this topic and Key Number. Which Eastern District of Virginia case ruled on this issue?
   c. Review the case. Did evidence show that noise from aircraft had an adverse effect on property values in the vicinity of the airport?
6. Use West's set *United States Supreme Court Digest*. Give the citation to the case *Offutt v. United States* and list the topics and Key Numbers under which it is digested.
7. Use West's *Atlantic Digest*.
   a. Which topic and Key Number discuss divorce on the grounds of sleeping late?
   b. Review the topic and Key Number. Give the citation to the Pennsylvania Superior Court case that discusses this issue and tell whether sleeping late is grounds for divorce.
8. Use the A.L.R. *Quick Index* for A.L.R. 3d, A.L.R. 4th, and A.L.R. 5th. Find and cite annotations dealing with the following:
   a. Driving under the influence of cough medicine as an intoxicating liquor under a DUI statute.
   b. Liability of a swimming pool facility operator for injury or death caused by the condition of a deck or bathhouse.
   c. Physician's withdrawal of life support from a comatose patient as aiding and abetting suicide.
9. Review each of the above annotations in Question 8 and answer the following questions:

a. For (a), what electronic search query does A.L.R. provide you to obtain additional information about this topic via computer-assisted legal research? Give the first ten words only.
b. For (b), what is the most recent case from the Ohio Appellate Court that relates to this topic? Give case name only.
c. For (c), cite a 1985 New Jersey case that relates to this topic.

10. Use West's set, *Words and Phrases*. What case(s) construe the meaning of the term "locus delicti"? Give case name(s) only.

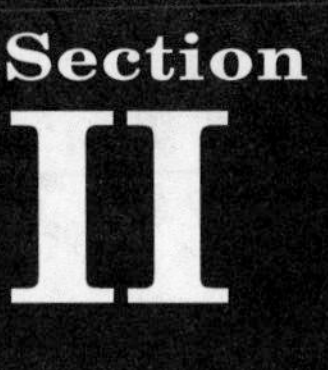

Legal Research: Secondary Authorities and Other Research Aids

Chapter 6

Encyclopedias, Periodicals, Treatises, and Restatements

Chapter Overview

Section I of this text discussed the major primary legal authorities: statutes, constitutions, and cases. Administrative rules and regulations are discussed in Chapter 10. All other sources are secondary authorities. In general, the secondary sources serve to explain, summarize, and locate primary sources.

If you know a legal question can be answered by a statute, you can and should begin your research in one of the annotated codes by locating and reading the statute and then examining the annotations following it to find cases that interpret and construe the statute. Often, however, when presented with a legal issue, you may not know where to begin. In these instances, many experts recommend that you start your research projects by using a secondary source. Secondary sources provide you with a concise analysis of an issue and then direct you to the relevant primary authorities.

Always keep in mind that primary sources are binding on a court or tribunal. If on point, these primary authorities must be followed. Secondary sources lack this mandatory authority. While often highly respected, the secondary sources are persuasive only. A court may elect to adopt a position set forth in a secondary authority or may reject it. Thus, your goal is always to locate relevant primary sources. The secondary authorities will assist you in this task.

The secondary authorities discussed in this chapter are those most frequently used: encyclopedias, periodicals, treatises, and restatements. The following chapter will discuss miscellaneous secondary authorities, including opinions of attorneys general, dictionaries, directories, form books, uniform laws, looseleaf services, and jury instructions.

A. Encyclopedias

1. *Introduction*

Just as *Encyclopaedia Britannica* or *The World Book* encyclopedia are reference works that alphabetically arrange topics ostensibly covering all human knowledge, legal encyclopedias exist that alphabetically arrange topics related to legal issues, from abandonment to mortgages to zoning. Legal encyclopedias are easy to use and serve as an excellent introduction to an area of the law. In addition to providing summaries of hundreds of legal topics, encyclopedias will direct you to cases through the use of footnotes. That is, as you read about an area of the law such as corporations, deeds, or trusts, you will be referred continually to cases dealing with these areas of the law. Generally, the narrative statements or summaries of the legal topics will cover the top half of each page in the set, and the bottom half of each page will be devoted to case citations that support the narrative statements of the law.

One of the hallmarks of encyclopedias is their noncritical approach, meaning that encyclopedias explain the law as it is, without any critical comment or recommendations for changes in the law. Many other secondary sources offer critical opinion and suggestions for change in the law.

The treatment of legal topics in encyclopedias is general and somewhat elementary. For this reason, encyclopedias are seldom cited in court documents such as briefs. They are rather most useful for providing an overview of an area of law and sending you to cases that will provide more thorough analysis. Encyclopedias are excellent casefinders (although the cases you are sent to are often criticized for being older cases) and tools for introducing you to an area of law. Moreover, they are readily available; even small law libraries usually have one, if not both, of the general sets.

It is unlikely that you will need to use both sets. Your choice of which set to use may depend upon convenience or habit.

There are three types of encyclopedias: general sets, local sets, and special subject sets.

2. *General Encyclopedias*

A general or national encyclopedia is a set that aims at discussing all of American law, civil and criminal, state and federal, substantive and procedural. That is, a discussion of false imprisonment will include a complete overview of this area of the law, including summaries of the majority and minority views and then send you to federal cases as well as various state cases dealing with this topic.

There are two general or national encyclopedias: *Corpus Juris Secundum* (C.J.S.) published by West, and *American Jurisprudence 2d* (Am. Jur. 2d) previously published by Lawyers Co-op and now also published by West.

a. C.J.S.

C.J.S. is an encyclopedia consisting of more than 100 dark blue volumes, which discusses in excess of 400 different topics of the law. These topics are arranged alphabetically, making it easy for you to locate the discussions on covenants, franchises, or trial.

C.J.S. is an extremely thorough and comprehensive set, which aims at providing you with references to all cases that support any narrative statement of the law. The narrative material is articulately presented and is easy to understand. The cases that support the narrative statements are arranged in the footnotes alphabetically by state so you can readily locate cases from your jurisdiction or from neighboring states. Often, the "leading case" in an area of the law is summarized briefly for you.

Each topic begins with a thorough outline to provide you with quick access to the most pertinent parts of the discussion. Each section within a topic begins with a boldface "Black Letter" summary of the rule discussed in the section. By reading this preview of the section, you can quickly determine whether you should proceed to read the section in full.

As its very name indicates (*Corpus Juris Secundum*, meaning "Body of Law Second"), C.J.S. was preceded by an earlier set, *Corpus Juris*. While many law libraries still maintain *Corpus Juris* (C.J.), it is unlikely you will use this older set, and you should always begin your research in C.J.S. rather than C.J.

C.J.S. contains a multi-volume index, usually found after the last volume in the set, and is kept current by annual cumulative pocket parts, which will inform you if the narrative statement of the law found in the main volume has changed and will refer you to newer cases supporting the text statement.

Because C.J.S. is a West publication, it is a participant in West's *Key Number System*. As each discussion begins, in a section called "Library References," West provides you with the pertinent topic and Key Number to enable you to locate all cases on this area of the law, particularly the most recent cases, through the use of West's *General Digest*. See Figure 6-1 for a sample page from C.J.S.

b. Am. Jur. 2d

American Jurisprudence 2d (Am. Jur. 2d) consists of more than 80 green volumes, which discuss more than 400 areas of the law. Similar to the arrangement of C.J.S., Am. Jur. 2d arranges its topics (or "titles") alphabetically, enabling you to quickly locate the discussion you need. While C.J.S. aims at directing you to all cases that support any legal principle, Am. Jur. 2d will direct you to a representative cross-section of cases that support a legal principle. In fact, its editors pride themselves on "weeding out" irrelevant, redundant, or obsolete cases and selecting the best cases

Figure 6-1
Sample Page from C.J.S.

§ 182. Abandonment and Nonuser

a. Abandonment in general
b. Nonuser
c. Miscellaneous acts or omissions
d. Operation and effect
e. Evidence

Summary of rule discussed in section to follow

a. Abandonment in General

Trade-marks and trade-names may be lost by abandonment; abandonment requires the concurrence of both an intention to abandon and an act or omission by which such intention is carried into effect.

The title to a trade-mark or trade-name acquired by adoption and user may be lost by an abandonment of such use,[5] although abandonment is not favored.[6] An actual intention permanently to give up the use of a name or mark is necessary to constitute abandonment of it.[7] Abandonment requires the concurrence of both an intention to abandon and an act or omission by which such intention is carried into effect.[8] Abandonment must have been voluntary,[9] and an involuntary deprivation of the use of the name or mark does not in itself constitute abandonment.[10] Failure to affix a trade-mark to goods through inadvertence is not abandonment where no intention to abandon is shown;[11] nor can an undisclosed intention constitute abandonment.[12] Despite the fact that abandonment depends in a large part on the intention of the parties, an ineffective attempt to assign a trade-mark ordinarily results in its abandonment.[13]

b. Nonuser

Nonuser of a trade-name or trade-mark is not of itself an abandonment thereof; however, where intention to abandon is shown by other circumstances and conditions, nonuser is a sufficient act of relinquishment and effectuates the abandonment.

While trade-marks and trade-names may be lost through nonuser,[14] mere disuse, although for a con-

5. U.S.—Greyhound Corp. v. Rothman, D.C.Md., 84 F.Supp. 233, affirmed, C.A., 175 F.2d 893—G. F. Heublin & Bro. v. Bushmill Wine & Products Co., D.C.Pa., 55 F.Supp. 964—Bisceglia Bros. Corp. v. Fruit Industries, D.C.Pa., 20 F.Supp. 564, affirmed, C.C.A., Fruit Industries v. Bisceglia Bros. Corp., 101 F.2d 752, certiorari denied 59 S.Ct. 1043, 307 U.S. 646, 83 L.Ed. 1526.
Ky.—**Corpus Juris cited in** Stratton & Terstegge Co. v. Stiglitz Furnace Co., 81 S.W.2d 1, 4, 258 Ky. 678.
N.Y.—Winthrop Chemical Co. v. Blackman, 268 N.Y.S. 647, 150 Misc. 229.
Wash.—Foss v. Culbertson, 136 P.2d 711, 17 Wash.2d 610—Seattle Street Railway & Municipal Employees Relief Ass'n v. Amalgamated Ass'n of Street Electric Railway & Motor Coach Employees of America, 101 P.2d 338, 3 Wash.2d 520.
63 C.J. p 523 note 17.

6. U.S.—Du Pont Cellophane Co. v. Waxed Products Co., D.C.N.Y., 6 F. Supp. 859, modified on other grounds, C.C.A., 85 F.2d 75, certiorari denied E. I. Dupont De Nemours & Co. v. Waxed Products Co., 57 S.Ct. 194, 299 U.S. 601, 81 L.Ed. 443.

7. Ky.—**Corpus Juris cited in** Stratton & Terstegge Co. v. Stiglitz Furnace Co., 81 S.W.2d 1, 4, 258 Ky. 678.
N.Y.—Neva-Wet Corp. of America v. Never Wet Processing Corp., 13 N.E.2d 775, 277 N.Y. 163.
63 C.J. p 523 note 18.

Letter assuring noncontest
Where plaintiff ordering trade-marked razors from manufacturer sent to lender a letter which consented to manufacturer's pledge of razors as security for loan to manufacturer and which stated that plaintiff would not assert any claims contrary to lender's right to realize on security in event of nonpayment of loan, letter was abandonment of all plaintiff's trade-mark and fair trade rights.—Stahly, Inc. v. M. H. Jacobs Co., C.A.Ill., 183 F.2d 914, certiorari denied 71 S.Ct. 239, 340 U.S. 896, 95 L.Ed. 650.

8. U.S.—E. I. Du Pont De Nemours & Co. v. Celanese Corp. of America, 167 F.2d 484, 35 C.C.P.A., Patents, 1061, 3 A.L.R.2d 1213—Greyhound Corp. v. Rothman, D.C.Md., 84 F. Supp. 233, affirmed, C.A., 175 F.2d 893—Hygienic Products Co. v. Judson Dunaway Corp., D.C.N.H., 81 F. Supp. 935, vacated on other grounds, C.A., 178 F.2d 461, certiorari denied 70 S.Ct. 802, 803, 339 U.S. 948, 94 L.Ed. 1362—Colonial Radio Corp. v. Colonial Television Corp., D.C.N.Y., 78 F.Supp. 546—Coca-Cola Co. v. Dixi-Cola Laboratories, D.C.Md., 31 F.Supp. 835, modified on other grounds, C.C.A., Dixi-Cola Laboratories v. Coca-Cola Co., 117 F.2d 352, certiorari denied Coca-Cola Co. v. Dixi-Cola Laboratories, 62 S.Ct. 60, 314 U.S. 629, 86 L.Ed. 505—Bisceglia Bros. Corp. v. Fruit Industries, D.C.Pa., 20 F. Supp. 564, affirmed, C.C.A., Fruit Industries v. Bisceglia Bros. Corp., 101 F.2d 752, certiorari denied 59 S.Ct. 1043, 307 U.S. 646, 83 L.Ed. 1526—Du Pont Cellophane Co. v. Waxed Products Co., D.C.N.Y., 6 F. Supp. 859, modified on other grounds, C.C.A., 85 F.2d 75, certiorari denied E. I. Dupont De Nemours & Co. v. Waxed Products Co., 57 S.Ct. 194, 299 U.S. 601, 81 L.Ed. 443.
Ky.—Stratton & Terstegge Co. v. Stiglitz Furnace Co., 81 S.W.2d 1, 258 Ky. 678.
Wash.—Foss v. Culbertson, 136 P.2d 711, 17 Wash.2d 610.
63 C.J. p 524 note 19.

9. U.S.—E. I. Du Pont De Nemours & Co. v. Celanese Corp. of America, 167 F.2d 484, 35 C.C.P.A., Patents, 1016, 3 A.L.R. 2d 1213—DuPont Cellophane Co. v. Waxed Products Co., C.C.A.N.Y., 85 F.2d 75, certiorari denied E. I. DuPont De Nemours & Co. v. Waxed Products Co., 57 S.Ct. 194, 299 U.S. 601, 81 L.Ed. 443.

10. U.S.—Fraser v. Williams, D.C. Wis., 61 F.Supp. 763—Reconstruction Finance Corp. v. J. G. Menihan Corp., D.C.N.Y., 28 F.Supp. 920.
Md.—American-Stewart Distillery v. Stewart Distilling Co., 177 A. 473, 168 Md. 212.
Wash.—Washington Barber & Beauty Supply Co. v. Spokane Barbers' & Beauty Supply Co., 18 P.2d 499, 171 Wash. 428.

11. U.S.—Chrysler Corp. v. Trott, Cust. & Pat.App., 83 F.2d 302.

12. Wash.—Olympia Brewing Co. v. Northwest Brewing Co., 35 P.2d 104, 178 Wash. 533.

13. D.C.—Old Charter Distillery Co. v. Ooms, D.C., 73 F.Supp. 539, affirmed Continental Distilling Corp. v. Old Charter Distillery Co., 188 F.2d 614, 88 U.S.App.D.C. 73.

14. U.S.—G. F. Heublin & Bro. v. Bushmill Wine & Products Co., D. C.Pa., 55 F.Supp. 964—Bisceglia Bros. Corp. v. Fruit Industries, D. C.Pa., 20 F.Supp. 564, affirmed, C.C. A., Fruit Industries v. Bisceglia Bros. Corp., 101 F.2d 752, certiorari denied 59 S.Ct. 1043, 307 U.S. 646, 83 L.Ed. 1526.

518

that support the narrative summaries of the law. As stated in the Foreword in volume one of Am. Jur. 2d, "We do not devote pages to listing multiple citations to mere platitudes which no court would deny or doubt."

Many of the features of Am. Jur. 2d are similar to those seen in C.J.S. That is, the narrative statements of the law are clearly and concisely presented in an easy-to-read manner. The cases you are sent to in the footnotes are often briefly summarized for you. Each title begins with an outline to allow you to locate readily the parts of the discussion of greatest interest to you.

Am. Jur. 2d is the successor to *American Jurisprudence* (Am. Jur.), which is still in existence but seldom used due to the expanded coverage of Am. Jur. 2d. Am. Jur. 2d contains a multi-volume general index and, similar to C.J.S., is kept current by annual cumulative pocket parts, which describe changes in the law and send you to newer cases than those found in the main hardbound volumes. Like C.J.S., Am. Jur. 2d also includes "Research References," which lead you to other West publications, including the valuable A.L.R. annotations discussed in Chapter 5.

Am. Jur. 2d also features two unique books in its encyclopedia system:

Am. Jur. 2d Desk Book. This book serves as a legal almanac and is a unique collection of miscellaneous legal and historical information. The Desk Book contains the text of the United States Constitution, the Declaration of Independence, the United Nations Charter, and the Monroe Doctrine. Additionally, there are diagrams showing the organization of various federal agencies, such as the Departments of Labor and Transportation, and directories with addresses, telephone numbers, and Web site addresses of the agencies and of the United States Courts of Appeal, United States District Courts, and United States Bankruptcy Courts. Various statistical charts are given, such as suicide rates, life expectancy tables, and marriage and divorce statistics. The Desk Book also contains other miscellaneous tables, data, charts, diagrams, statistics, and glossaries of terms of interest in the legal profession.

Am. Jur. 2d New Topic Service. The New Topic Service is a looseleaf binder volume of pamphlets designed to provide you with information relating to new and emerging areas of the law, such as Alternative Dispute Resolution, the Americans with Disabilities Act, and Real Estate Time-Sharing. The articles discussed in the pamphlets are merged into the appropriate hardbound volumes when volumes are replaced or revised.

See Figure 6-2 for a sample page from Am. Jur. 2d.

c. Features Common to C.J.S. and Am. Jur. 2d

The following features are common to both C.J.S. and Am. Jur. 2d:

(i) Both C.J.S. and Am. Jur. 2d discuss more than 400 topics of the law, which are arranged alphabetically (Abandonment, Assault, Banks, Contracts, Deeds, and so forth).

Figure 6-2
Sample Page from Am. Jur. 2d

successor by one with knowledge of his former proprietorship, even though the proprietor had never transacted business with him.[82]

Ordinarily, the right to the use of a trademark or tradename acquired by purchase may be further transferred or assigned by the purchaser.[83] Where, however, a contract merely gives to one person the right to use the name of another, which right is personal, it cannot in the absence of an express stipulation be assigned or transferred by the purchaser to a third party.[84]

§ 27. —Restrictions on use; transfer of mark only.

One who has developed a trademark as a guaranty of the quality of his merchandise should not be permitted to license its use apart from his business to those who may sell an inferior product.[85] Thus, since the object of a trademark is to indicate, by its meaning or association, the origin or ownership of the article, when a right to its use is transferred to others, either by act of the original appropriator or by operation of law, the fact of its transfer should be stated in connection with its use, for otherwise a deception would be practiced on the public.[86] For the same reason, purchasers of trademarks and labels which consist largely of the name, residence, etc., of the former owner should not use them without change, if they indicate that the articles to which they are applied are made by the vendor. Words should be added to show that the vendor has retired and the goods were made by his successors.[87]

While the transfer of a name without a business may not be enough to entitle the transferee to prevent others from using it, it may constitute a license that may be sufficient to put the licensee on the footing of the licensor as against a third person.[88]

C. Abandonment

1. In General

§ 28. Generally.

Rights in a trademark or tradename may be lost by abandonment.[89] Ordinarily, intention to abandon a trademark or tradename is an essential element of abandonment at common law.[90] Abandonment requires not only the intention

82. Hendley v Bittinger, 249 **Pa** 193, 94 A 831.

83. Bagby & R. Co. v Rivers, 87 **Md** 400, 40 A 171; Cowan v Fairbrother, 118 **NC** 406, 24 SE 212.

84. Bagby & R. Co. v Rivers, 87 **Md** 400, 40 A 171.

85. Broeg v Duchaine, 319 **Mass** 711, 67 NE2d 466.

86. Manhattan Medicine Co. v Wood, 108 **US** 218, 27 L Ed 706, 2 S Ct 436.

87. Symonds v Jones, 82 **Me** 302, 19 A 820.

88. L. E. Waterman Co. v Modern Pen Co. 235 **US** 88, 59 L Ed 142, 35 S Ct 91.

89. Hanover Star Milling Co. v Metcalf, 240 **US** 403, 60 L Ed 713, 36 S Ct 357; Browning King Co. v Browning King Co. (CA3 Pa) 176 **F2d** 105; E. I. Du Pont de Nemours & Co. v Celanese Corp. of America, 35 Cust & Pat App (Pat) 1061, 167 **F2d** 484, 3 ALR2d 1213; Rockowitz Corset & Brassiere Corp. v Madame X Co. 248 **NY** 272, 162 NE 76, reh den 248 **NY** 623, 162 NE 550.

Annotation: 3 ALR2d 1226, 1232, § 3.

Note reference to A.L.R annotation

90. Hanover Star Mill. Co. v Metcalf, 240 **US** 403, 60 L Ed 713, 36 S Ct 357; Baglin v Cusenier Co. 221 **US** 580, 55 L Ed 863, 31 S Ct 669; Saxlehner v Eisner & M. Co. 179 **US** 19, 45 L Ed 60, 21 S Ct 7; Heaton Distributing Co. v Union Tank Car Co. (CA8) 387 **F2d** 477; Neva-Wet Corp. v Never Wet Processing Corp. 277 **NY** 163, 13 NE2d 755.

Annotation: 3 ALR2d 1226, 1233, § 3.

721

(ii) Because both sets are arranged by topic, neither set contains a table of cases.

(iii) While there is some discussion of statutes in the narrative discussions of the law, neither C.J.S. nor Am. Jur. 2d provides in-depth analyses of statutes. Detailed discussion of all state and federal statutes on each of the more than 400 areas of the law discussed would make the sets too cumbersome and unwieldy to use. In general, Am. Jur. 2d stresses statutory law more than C.J.S. Each set, however, includes a separate volume called "Table of Statutes, Rules, and Regulations Cited," which directs you to specific sections within each set that discuss or cite federal statutes, the *Code of Federal Regulations*, and Uniform Laws.

(iv) The narrative statements of the law are presented concisely in both sets. The style of writing is similar, and the discussion of the law is straightforward. For this reason, it cannot be said that one set is clearly superior to the other. Each set has its advantages, and your choice of which set to use will be based largely on habit and personal preference. While the sets do have some distinguishing features, they are more alike than not, and for most purposes you should research in either C.J.S. or Am. Jur. 2d, but not both. Moreover, now that both sets are published by West, both provide you with West topics and Key Numbers and give references to other West resources.

(v) Each set contains a multi-volume general index usually located after the last volume in the set and each of the more than 400 topics or titles begins with its own table of contents or index allowing you to locate quickly the sections of the discussion of greatest interest to you.

(vi) Each topic discussion in both sets begins with a "scope" paragraph, which briefly outlines what will be discussed in the topic and what specific subjects may be treated or discussed elsewhere in the set. These "scope notes" enable you to determine rapidly whether you are researching the correct topic or whether you should direct your attention to some other topic in the set.

(vii) Both sets support the narrative discussion of the law with footnotes that provide citations to cases, although, as discussed previously, C.J.S. purports to send you to all cases that support any statement of the law, while Am. Jur. 2d will send you to selected leading cases. You will first be sent to federal cases and then to state cases, listed alphabetically by state to allow easy access to the law of selected states and jurisdictions. When presented with a statement of the law and numerous case citations that support it, there are some techniques you can use effectively to select cases when time or budget constraints prevent you from examining all cases. Select and read cases from your jurisdiction before reading cases from other jurisdictions; review newer cases before older cases; and review cases from higher courts before those from lower courts. Do not misinterpret these guidelines as saying "old cases are bad." Old cases are *not* bad; however, when presented with numerous cases and when pressed for time, you should develop effective research strategies, and these guidelines will help you research more efficiently. After all, it may not be productive to review cases from the 1930s only to discover that the law substantially changed in the 1990s, rendering the earlier cases outmoded or invalid statements of the law.

(viii) Both sets will refer you to other sources to enhance your understanding of the law. C.J.S. will provide you with pertinent topic names and Key Numbers, while Am. Jur. 2d will also refer you to other sources, notably A.L.R. annotations.

(ix) Each set is kept current by annual cumulative pocket parts and by replacement volumes when needed. For example, because the law relating to internal revenue and federal taxation changes so often, both C.J.S. and Am. Jur. 2d replace their tax volumes on an annual basis. Moreover, new topics, such as "Pipelines," "Products Liability," and "Energy" are often added to the sets, and these additions necessitate replacement volumes.

(x) Both sets are cited in the same manner:
1A C.J.S. *Actions* § 9 (1985).
1 Am. Jur. 2d *Actions* § 9 (1994).

d. Total Client-Service Library

Lawyers Co-op, the former publisher of Am. Jur. 2d, created a number of other sets of books, which it referred to as the Total Client-Service Library (TCSL), which are now published by West. The books in TCSL are designed to be used with Am. Jur. 2d, although they are not encyclopedias. One of the sets in TCSL has already been discussed (the A.L.R. system). Most of the remaining units of the TCSL deal primarily with litigation and trial practice. Many are available in CD-ROM as well as print form (see Chapter 11). These very practical sets routinely refer you to Am. Jur. 2d and are as follows.

(1) Am. Jur. Proof of Facts

This set of more than 130 volumes (*Proof of Facts*, *Proof of Facts 2d*, and *Proof of Facts 3d*) is designed to assist in the preparation for and proving of facts at trials, both civil and criminal trials. The set is also available in CD-ROM form. The articles in *Proof of Facts* are kept current by pocket parts and the addition of new volumes each year. *Proof of Facts* provides practical information regarding conducting client interviews, preparing witnesses for trial, conducting discovery, negotiating settlements, examining witnesses, and introducing evidence at trial. Each article provides background information regarding certain types of cases, for instance, personal injury or wrongful death cases—and will then succinctly set forth the elements of such a case, which must be proved to prevail at trial. Sample interrogatories (written questions directed at parties in litigation) will be provided together with sample questions for examining witnesses. Each article includes a checklist providing an outline of the essential facts that must be established to prevail in a case or in asserting a defense.

Access to this useful and practical guide to trial techniques is gained through a multi-volume General Index. You only need to think of words that describe the issue or case you are researching and you will be directed to the appropriate article. That is, use the descriptive word approach to gain access to a pertinent article in this set.

(2) Am. Jur. Trials

This set of books consists of more than 70 volumes that focus on trial tactics and strategies. The articles in *Am. Jur. Trials* are authored by experienced litigators and provide a step-by-step approach to trial practice.

The first six volumes of the set, titled "Practice, Strategy, Controls," are devoted to matters common to all trials, such as fee agreements, investigating cases, discovery, settlement, jury selection, and closing arguments. Information is often presented by easy-to-follow checklists, which outline steps to be taken in litigation matters.

The remaining volumes in *Am. Jur. Trials* are titled "Model Trials" and are devoted to specific kinds of cases, such as elevator accident cases, dental malpractice cases, or contact sports injury cases and will analyze in depth the strategy of conducting trials of these specific types of cases. The articles in *Am. Jur. Trials* are kept current by pocket-part supplements.

Access to the articles is achieved through the General Index, which is best utilized through the descriptive word approach. To locate a pertinent article, simply look up words or phrases that describe your research problem or trial, and the General Index will direct you to the appropriate volume and page of an article. Remember to use the supplement to the General Index.

West also offers this set in CD-ROM form.

(3) Am. Jur. Pleading and Practice Forms Annotated

This set of books consists of more than 50 volumes that provide forms for every stage of state and federal litigation, including forms for complaints, answers, interrogatories, jury instructions, motions, and appeals. These forms are extremely useful and serve as excellent guides to drafting forms. Practical checklists are included to remind you of items to be included in various forms. If your state does not have its own sets of form books, this set will provide several examples of litigation documents, which you can tailor to your state's requirements. If you are asked to prepare a complaint or a set of interrogatories, consult *Am. Jur. Pleading and Practice Forms Annotated*, which contains numerous forms you can use as models. Case notes indicate the proper usage for each form and references to topic names and Key Numbers and other West resources, such as A.L.R. annotations, help you expand your research. More than 36,500 forms are included in this set, which is kept up to date by pocket-part supplements. To locate a form, retrieve the multi-volume General Index to the set and then use the descriptive word technique. You will then be directed to the appropriate form.

(4) Am. Jur. Legal Forms 2d

There are many documents prepared in the legal profession that are not litigation-oriented. These documents are often used in connection with a client's personal or business needs, such as a will, a trust, a lease, or minutes of corporate meetings. *Am. Jur. Legal Forms 2d* provides more than 23,000 such forms together with checklists, tips, and advice for preparing various forms and documents. For example, if you are drafting a lease, *Am. Jur. Legal Forms 2d* will provide you with a list setting forth the elements required for a valid lease. As is the case with *Am. Jur. Pleading and Practice Forms Annotated*, described above, you should feel free to customize the forms you find to comply with the client's needs or your state statutes. Often, optional or alternative clauses are provided, allowing you to pick and choose clauses to construct the best document for the client. A "caution" section is included to help you avoid common errors in document drafting. Tax checkpoints and information are also included. References to West's Key Number system, A.L.R., and other West resources are provided.

As in the other sets in TCSL discussed herein, this set is kept current by the use of pocket parts, which will provide new forms, checklists, or other pertinent material. Locating an appropriate form is accomplished by using the General Index to the set and then inserting words or phrases that describe the problem or matter with which you are dealing. You will then be directed to the appropriate form. See Figure 6-3 for a sample page from *Am. Jur. Legal Forms 2d.*

e. Research Strategies for Using General Encyclopedias

There are two primary techniques used in locating the discussion of an area of law in C.J.S. or Am. Jur. 2d. These research techniques, the descriptive word approach and the topic approach, are ones you are already familiar with and that you have used before in locating statutes.

(1) Descriptive Word Approach

The editors at West have selected certain words and phrases that describe the topics discussed in the encyclopedias and have listed these

Figure 6-3
Sample Page from *Am. Jur. Legal Forms 2d*

Cross reference: For form of acknowledgment, see § 7:46. For forms of acknowledgments under the Uniform Recognition of Acknowledgments Act, see §§ 7:281 et seq.

§ 87:77 Connecticut—Quitclaim deed

Quitclaim deed made on __1______, 19_2_. To all people to whom these presents come, greeting:

Know ye, that I, __3______, of __4______ *[address]*, City of __5______, County of __6______, State of __7______, for the consideration of __8______ Dollars ($____) received to my full satisfaction, do remise, release, and forever quitclaim unto __9______, of __10______ *[address]*, City of __11______, County of __12______, State of __13______, his heirs, and assigns forever, all the right, title, interest, claim, and demand whatsoever that I have or ought to have in or to the following premises which are situated in the City of __14______, County of __15______, State of Connecticut: __16______ *[set forth legal description of property]*.

To have and to hold the premises, with all the appurtenances, unto the releasee, his heirs, and assigns forever, so that neither I, the releasor, nor my heirs nor any other person under myself or them shall hereafter have any claim, right, or title in or to the premises or any part thereof, but therefrom I and they are by these presents forever barred and excluded.

In witness whereof, I have hereunto set my hand and seal on the day and year first above written.

[Signature]
[Seal]

[Attestation]

[Acknowledgment]

☑ **Tax Notes:**

(See Tax Notes following § 87:61)

☑ **Notes on Use:**

(See also Notes on Use following § 87:61)

Statutory reference: This form reflects generally the provisions of **Conn** Gen S § 47-5. Statutory deed forms have not been enacted in Connecticut.

Text reference: For general discussion of drafting requirements of deeds, see 23 Am Jur 2d, Deeds §§ 18–40.

Cross reference: For form of acknowledgment, see § 7:46. For forms of acknowledgments under the Uniform Recognition of Acknowledgments Act, see §§ 7:281 et seq.

(For Tax Notes and Notes on Use of form, see end of form)

alphabetically in the general indexes to C.J.S. and Am. Jur. 2d. To use this approach, simply think of words or phrases that describe the issue you are researching. Look up these words in the volumes of the general index for C.J.S. or Am. Jur. 2d and you will be directed to the appropriate topic and section. You should read the section to which you are referred for the background information relating to your legal issue and then begin reading in full the cases cited in support in the footnotes. Be sure to supplement your research by checking the pocket part to ensure that the narrative statement of the law is correct and to locate cases more recent than those cited in the footnotes in the main volume. See Figure 6-4 for a sample page from the index to Am. Jur. 2d.

Because volumes in Am. Jur. 2d are replaced as needed, and because the replacement volumes may add new sections and discussions, it is possible that the General Index may send you to a section in an older volume that does not exist in the newer replacement volume. In such a case, check the Table of Parallel References found in the front of each volume, which will convert the old section number to the new section you should read in the replacement volume.

(2) Topic Approach

Because the more than 400 legal topics discussed in C.J.S. and Am. Jur. 2d are arranged alphabetically, it is often possible to use the topic approach successfully in locating a discussion of the area of law in which you are interested. To use the topic approach, simply think of the area of law related to your issue, for instance, Corporations, Landlord and Tenant, or Partnerships—and immediately retrieve that volume from the shelf. You should then examine the "scope note" to ensure that the specific issue you are interested in is included in the discussion to follow. The next step is to review the outline of the topic under discussion, which will quickly refer you to the appropriate section.

(3) Table of Statutes Approach

Because both Am. Jur. 2d and C.J.S. include a separate volume titled "Table of Statutes, Rules, and Regulations Cited," you can use this volume to look up specific statutes, administrative regulations, or Uniform Laws in which you are interested, and you will be directed to the appropriate volume, topic, and section within the encyclopedia set. The Table is usually shelved at the end of the set.

3. *Local or State Encyclopedias*

a. Introduction

You have seen that C.J.S. and Am. Jur. 2d are general encyclopedias that provide a national overview of more than 400 areas of the law. It is pos-

Figure 6-4
Sample Page from Index to Am. Jur. 2d

AMERICAN JURISPRUDENCE 2d

TRADEMARKS AND TRADENAMES —Cont'd

Determination of abandonment of trademarks and tradenames, Trademark § 30
Device, trademark as consisting of, Trademark § 40
Devise, transfer of rights by, Trademark § 24
Diamond, outline of, as trademark, Trademark § 42
Dictionary, misspelled or malformed words or terms used to comprise trademark as affected by, Trademark § 54
Dilution of trademark or tradename, Trademark § 125
Direct competition between parties, protection against infringement and unfair competition as requiring, Trademark §§ 124, 125
Discontinuance. Abandonment, supra
Disposition or use of containers, governmental control and regulation as to, Trademark § 11
Dissolution, Corp §§ 2874, 2892; Partn § 902
Distinctions
- doctrine of unfair competition distinguished from law of trademarks, Trademark § 84
- duty to distinguish name, mark or other indicia, Trademark § 111
- label distinguished from trademark, Trademark § 4
- patent and trademark, Trademark § 1
- tradename and trademark, Trademark § 2

Distributor, abandonment as affected by placing name on marked goods, Trademark § 31
District court. **Federal Practice and Procedure** (this index)
Documentary use of notation apart from goods as constituting technical trademark use, Trademark § 12
Doing business in state, Partn §§ 64-68; Trademark § 135
Domicil and residence
- purchaser of trademarks and labels consisting of residence or name of former owner, Trademark § 27
- territorial extent of protection as affected by residence of trader, Trademark § 138

Drawing of mark, federal registration, Trademark §§ 72, 73
Drugs and narcotics. Medicinal preparations, infra
Due process of law, statute forbidding sale of product for original package labeled with trademark coupled with false representation as affected by, Trademark § 11
Duration
- estoppel to deny validity of trademark of licensor, expiration of license as affecting, Trademark § 26
- prior user of tradename or trademark, duration of use as affecting protection of, Trademark § 85
- secondary meaning, period or duration of use of, Trademark § 67

Elements of trademarks and tradenames, Trademark §§ 5-7
Employees. Officers, directors, employees, and agents, infra
Engineering, use in corporate name, Corp § 278
Estoppel and waiver
- abandonment of mark, failure to take action against infringement as estopping owner from denying, Trademark § 39

886

TRADEMARKS AND TRADENAMES —Cont'd

Estoppel and waiver—Cont'd
- cancellation of federal registration, application of principle of estoppel to, Trademark § 80
- consent or acquiescence, supra
- license, estoppel to deny validity of licensor's trademark as expiring with, Trademark § 26

Eviction of foreign corporation from state for unfair competition, Trademark § 145
Evidence
- abandonment, clear and convincing evidence as required to prove, Trademark §§ 30, 31
- certificate of registration upon principal register as prima facie evidence of validity of registration, Trademark § 74
- damages, sum agreed by parties for use of trademark and business name as evidence of, Trademark § 150
- documentary evidence, Fed R Evid §§ 289, 298, 307
- hearsay, Fed R Evid § 230; Trademark § 70
- infringement and unfair competition, Trademark §§ 170-171.1
- likelihood of confusion, proof of, Trademark § 119
- multiplicity of similarities as evidence of conscious imitation, Trademark § 96
- opposition to registration, evidence in, Trademark § 78
- parol evidence, Evid § 1053
- possession of containers belonging to another as prima facie evidence of statutory violation, Trademark § 11
- presumptions and burden of proof, infra
- registration, Trademark §§ 83, 153
- secondary meaning, evidence in action under doctrine of, Trademark §§ 169, 172, 173

Examination of application for federal trademark registration, Trademark § 73
Exclusiveness
- appropriation by one person, trademark as requiring, Trademark § 5
- lack of exclusive right as affecting right to relief, Trademark § 161
- right to use trademark, exclusiveness of, Trademark § 16
- secondary meaning, exclusiveness of use of, Trademark § 66

Execution sale, transfer of rights by, Trademark § 23
Executor or administrator, transfer of decedent's trademark or tradename to, Trademark § 24
Exemplary damages. Punitive damages, infra
Expansion of business or trade
- diversion of trade not in actual competition but forestalling, Trademark § 125
- doctrine of right to, Trademark § 139

Expenses
- action for infringement, costs of, Trademark §§ 150, 175
- advertising expenses, evidence as to, Trademark § 171.1
- amount of profits, deduction for general expenses in computing, Trademark § 152
- burden of proving element of cost or deduction in assessment of damages under Federal Trademark Act, Trademark § 168
- cancellation of falsely registered trademark, expenses of proceeding as included in damages recoverable in, Trademark § 81

TRADEMARKS AND TRADENAMES —Cont'd

Expenses—Cont'd
- secondary meaning, large expenditures for advertising as evidence of, Trademark § 172

Expiration. Duration, supra
Fabrics, colored strands or threads in, as trademark, Trademark § 41
Facsimiles, filing with application for registration, Trademark §§ 72, 73
Factors, secondary meaning, Trademark § 65
Fact questions. Questions of law and fact, infra
Fair trade laws, Fair Tr §§ 1, 2
Family names. Personal or family names, infra
Famous names as subject of, Trademark § 58
Fanciful words or names
generally, Trademark §§ 47, 49, 53, 58, 59
- scope of protection against infringement or unfair competition as affected by distinctiveness of mark or name, Trademark § 126

Federal Practice and Procedure (this index)
Federal Rules of Evidence. Evidence, supra
Federal Tort Claims Act, exclusion of claim based on refusing importation of goods, Fed Tort § 15
Federal Trademark Act, generally, Trademark §§ 10, 69-81
Fees
- accounting, amount of license fee as evidence in, Trademark § 152
- attorney's fee, supra
- registration fee under Federal Trademark Act, Trademark § 72

Fictitious name. Assumed name, supra
Field of business, extent of right or trademark rights with respect to, Trademark § 19
Figure, trademark as consisting of, Trademark § 40
Financial condition. Bankruptcy or insolvency, supra
Firm name, duration of use required for acquisition of secondary meaning by, Trademark § 67
Flag of nation or state, prohibition against trademark using, Trademark § 45
Food
- restaurant names as subject of trademark or tradename, Trademark § 60
- sale of meat under false or deceptive name, trademark, or tradename, Food § 36

Foreign commerce. Interstate and foreign commerce, infra
Foreign corporations evicted for unfair competition, Trademark § 145
Foreign country
- commerce. Interstate and foreign commerce, infra
- Federal Trademark Act as providing rights and remedies stipulated by treaties between United States and foreign countries, Trademark § 10
- generic name, effect of use in foreign country, Trademark § 48
- "in commerce" requirements of federal statute on infringement, infringing activities in foreign country as covered by Trademark § 94
- injunctive relief against violation of trademark used in, jurisdiction of Federal District Court to award, Trademark §§ 146, 164

sible, however, that you may not need such broad coverage of a topic and are interested only in the law for your particular state. In this instance, you should consult an encyclopedia for your state, *if* one is published for your state. Not every state has its own encyclopedia. Generally, you will find encyclopedias published for the more populous states.

To determine if an encyclopedia exists for your state, check the card catalog in the law library, ask a reference librarian, or simply look at the shelves in the law library devoted to the law of your state. Carefully examine the books you find, as some state encyclopedias label themselves "digests."

Some state encyclopedias are published by West, such as *Illinois Law and Practice*, *Maryland Law and Practice*, and *Michigan Law and Practice*. Because these encyclopedias are West publications, they are arranged similarly to C.J.S. Other state encyclopedias previously published by Lawyers Co-op, such as *California Jurisprudence 3d*, *Florida Jurisprudence 2d*, *New York Jurisprudence 2d*, *Ohio Jurisprudence 3d*, and *Texas Jurisprudence 3d*, are now published by West. As West replaces earlier volumes, references to other West resources, such as Westlaw topic names and Key Numbers, are given.

A few state encyclopedias, such as *Jurisprudence of Virginia and West Virginia*, are published by other publishers, such as LEXIS Publishing. If your state does not have a local encyclopedia, use C.J.S. or Am. Jur. 2d and research your state's law by locating cases in the footnotes from your state.

b. Features Common to State Encyclopedias

The following features are common to most state encyclopedias:

(i) *Coverage.* The discussion of the law presented will relate only to the law of a particular state, and the cases you will be directed to will be from that state or from federal courts that have construed that state's law.

(ii) *Arrangement.* The various topics covered in a state encyclopedia are arranged alphabetically. The narrative statements of the law are clearly presented, and you will be directed to cases and other authorities through the use of supporting footnotes.

(iii) *Table of Cases.* Unlike C.J.S. and Am. Jur. 2d, which do not contain a table of cases, many local sets will contain tables that alphabetically list the cases discussed or cited in the set. Thus, if you know the name of a case in your state, you can readily locate the text discussion of it or the area of law with which it deals by using the Table of Cases.

(iv) *Table of Statutes.* While C.J.S. and Am. Jur. 2d refer you only to selected federal statutes or uniform laws, many state encyclopedias contain a detailed table of statutes, which will direct you to a discussion or reference of a statute in which you are interested. Thus, if you are interested in Section 50 of the California Probate Code, you simply look this up in the table of statutes, and you will be referred to any titles and sections in Cal. Jur. 3d where this statute is discussed.

(v) *Indexing.* Most state encyclopedias have a multi-volume general index usually located after the last volume in the set. Additionally, many encyclopedias precede the discussion of a topic with an index or outline of the various subjects discussed within the topic.

(vi) *Supplementation.* State encyclopedias are supplemented or kept up to date in the same manner as the general encyclopedias, C.J.S. and Am. Jur. 2d, that is, by cumulative pocket parts and replacement volumes.

c. Research Strategies for Using State Encyclopedias

The research techniques used to access the state or local encyclopedias are as follows:

(i) *Descriptive Word Approach.* By selecting words and phrases that describe the issue you are researching and then inserting these into the general index, you will be directed to the appropriate topic and section.

(ii) *Topic Approach.* Think of the topic or area of law your issue deals with and then retrieve this specific volume from the shelf. Examine the outline of the topic preceding the narrative discussion of the law to determine the specific section you should read.

(iii) *Table of Cases Approach.* If you are interested in a discussion of a particular case from your state, look up the case name in the Table of Cases for your set, and you will be referred to the topic and section that discuss it.

(iv) *Table of Statutes Approach.* If you are researching a particular statute in your state, you can look it up in the table of statutes, and you will be directed to the relevant topic and section in the encyclopedia.

4. *Special Subject Encyclopedias*

The encyclopedias previously discussed, C.J.S., Am. Jur. 2d, and the local encyclopedias, discuss hundreds of areas of the law. There are, however, a few encyclopedias that are devoted to just one area of the law. For example, *Fletcher Cyclopedia of the Law of Private Corporations* contains more than 30 volumes and discusses in depth the law relating to corporations. Check the card catalog at your law library to determine if an encyclopedia exists for a particular subject. Many of these "encyclopedias," however, are more accurately classified as treatises, as discussed in Section C of this chapter. The best research strategy to employ when using a special subject encyclopedia is the descriptive word approach. The encyclopedia will contain either a separate index volume or the index will be found in the last volume of the set. The alphabetically arranged index will contain numerous words and phrases describing topics discussed in the set and will refer you to the appropriate volume and section of the set describing the area of law in which you are interested.

5. *Summary*

Encyclopedias provide excellent introductions to numerous areas of the law as well as easy-to-understand summaries of the law. You must remember, however, to read the primary sources you are directed to by the encyclopedias, as these mandatory authorities *must* be followed by courts, and the encyclopedias are merely persuasive authorities, which *may* be followed. If you are assigned a research project and you are uncertain where or how to begin, begin with an encyclopedia. Be sure this is the beginning, however, and not the end of your research, as the information presented to you in encyclopedias is generally introductory rather than analytical. While you may readily rely on encyclopedias to provide an accurate overview of the law, you should not cite an encyclopedia as authority in any brief or project you prepare unless there are no primary authorities or no other more creditable secondary authorities, such as Restatements, treatises, or law review articles on which to rely. Although encyclopedias are helpful resources, they are not sufficiently scholarly to serve as the sole support for an argument you advance. If you remember these guidelines, encyclopedias will serve as excellent starting points for your legal research.

B. Legal Periodicals

1. *Introduction*

Just as you might subscribe to a periodical publication such as *Time Magazine*, *People Weekly*, or *Sports Illustrated*, law firms, legal practitioners, paralegals, law libraries, legal departments of businesses, and agencies subscribe to a variety of publications that are produced on a regular or periodic basis and which discuss a wide range of legal topics.

There are four broad categories of legal periodicals: publications of law schools; publications of bar associations and paralegal associations; specialized publications for those in the legal profession sharing similar interests; and legal newspapers and newsletters. All of these publications are secondary sources. While many of them, particularly the publications of law schools, are very well respected and scholarly, they remain persuasive authorities whose views *may* be followed rather than primary or mandatory authorities that *must* be followed, if relevant.

The periodical publications serve many functions. Some provide extensive analyses of legal topics; some serve to keep practitioners current on recent developments in the law; and some provide practical information relating to problems and issues facing those in the legal profession.

2. *Law School Publications*

Most law schools produce a periodical publication generally referred to as a "law review," such as the *Montana Law Review*, *University of Cincinnati Law Review*, or *William and Mary Law Review*, although a few title their publications "journals," such as the *Emory Law Journal*, *Tulsa Law Journal*, and *Yale Law Journal*. These are typically published four or more times each year, initially in softcover pamphlet form and later in hardbound volumes. More than 100 law schools publish these reviews, which contain articles on a variety of legal topics. Because the law reviews are published so frequently, they often provide topical analysis of recent cases or recently enacted legislation.

The law reviews are published by law students who have been selected to write for the law review based on academic distinction or writing samples submitted to the board of editors of the law review. These editors are typically second- and third-year law students who bear the primary responsibility for editing and publishing the law review, although faculty members often advise the students. Despite the fact that the law reviews are principally the product of students, they have a high degree of respectability due to the exacting and rigorous standards of the editors. Do not equate these law reviews with the newspapers or newsletters produced at a college. The law reviews provide scholarly analysis of legal topics and are routinely cited with approval by courts. The law reviews differ greatly from encyclopedias, which are noncritical in their approach and usually focus on merely explaining the law. The law reviews offer a critical approach and often advocate reform and change in the law.

A law review usually has several sections:

(i) *Articles*. "Articles" are usually scholarly monographs or essays written by professors, judges, or practicing attorneys. Often exceeding 30 pages in length, an article examines a topic in depth. The topics explored are diverse and may range from an analysis of the California Agricultural Relations Act to a study of discrimination against handicapped persons to an examination of the legal rights of the mentally ill. Despite the fact that these articles are authored by professors, judges, and attorneys, the students on the review's board of editors edit the articles, check the accuracy of the citations in the article, and make suggestions for revisions.

(ii) *Comments* and *Notes*. "Comments" and "Notes" are generally shorter pieces authored by students. These shorter analyses typically examine diverse legal topics, such as warranties in the sale of goods, conflicts of interest for former government attorneys, or tort liability for defective products.

(iii) *Case Comments/Recent Cases/Recent Developments.* This section is also authored by students and examines the impact of a recent case or newly enacted legislation.

(iv) *Book Reviews.* Just as *Newsweek Magazine* reviews recent works of fiction in each issue, most law reviews contain a section that reviews books or texts relating to legal issues, such as *Hazardous Product Litigation*, *Handbook of the Law of Antitrust*, or *Justice by Consent: Plea Bargains in the American Courthouse.* A critical analysis of the book is provided together with an identification of the publisher and the price of the book.

Almost all law schools publish one of these general types of law reviews; that is, a review containing articles on a variety of topics, such as corporate law, civil law, criminal law, trademark law, and so forth. In addition to these general law reviews, many law schools also provide other law reviews devoted to a specific area, such as international law or civil rights. For example, Boston College Law School publishes the following reviews in addition to its general law review, called the *Boston College Law Review*:

Boston College Environmental Affairs Law Review
Boston College International and Comparative Law Review
Boston College Third World Law Journal

Often law reviews are arranged alphabetically in a law library, so that the *Akron Law Review* is followed by the *Alabama Law Review*, which is then followed by the *Alaska Law Review*, and so forth, making the task of locating a law review easy and efficient. Law reviews are cited as follows:

Article: Carl L. Vacketta & Thomas C. Wheeler, *A Government Contractor's Right to Abandon Performance*, 65 Geo. L.J. 27 (1976).

Student Note: Sylvia T. Parker, Note, *Debtors' Rights to Debt Counseling*, 98 Tul. L. Rev. 1604 (1988).

See Figure 6-5 for a sample page of a law review.

3. *Bar Association and Paralegal Association Publications*

Each state and the District of Columbia has a bar association. Usually an attorney cannot practice law in a jurisdiction without becoming a member of that state's bar association. The dues paid to the association often fund various legal programs such as services for indigents, disciplinary

Figure 6-5
Sample Cover from Law Review

VOLUME 85 JUNE 1997 NUMBER 6

THE GEORGETOWN LAW JOURNAL

ARTICLES

INTEGRATING NORMATIVE AND DESCRIPTIVE CONSTITUTIONAL THEORY: THE CASE OF ORIGINAL MEANING
BY MICHAEL C. DORF

RESPONSES

ON READING RECIPES . . . AND CONSTITUTIONS
BY GARY LAWSON

THE PUZZLING PERSISTENCE OF BELLBOTTOM THEORY: WHAT A CONSTITUTIONAL THEORY SHOULD BE
BY LAWRENCE LESSIG

ORIGINAL MEANING WITHOUT ORIGINALISM
BY JAMES E. FLEMING

REPLY

RECIPE FOR TROUBLE: SOME THOUGHTS ON MEANING, TRANSLATION AND NORMATIVE THEORY
BY MICHAEL C. DORF

MORAL FOUNDATIONS FOR A DISCOURSE ON SAME-SEX MARRIAGE: LOOKING BEYOND POLITICAL LIBERALISM
BY CARLOS A. BALL

SAVING CONSTRUCTIONS
BY ADRIAN VERMEULE

NOTES

A PRIVILEGED CHARACTER? THE PRESIDENT AND JOINT DEFENSE
BY MARK MILLER

MANDATORY GENETIC DOGTAGS AND THE FOURTH AMENDMENT: THE NEED FOR A NEW POST-*SKINNER* TEST
BY ROBERT CRAIG SCHERER

CONSTRUCTING SAFE COMMUNITIES: MEGAN'S LAWS AND THE PURPOSES OF PUNISHMENT
BY BRIAN J. TELPNER

1789

proceedings, and the periodical publication of a journal for the members of the bar. Some bar associations publish monthly journals while others publish every other month. The *American Bar Association Journal* is a very professional-looking publication that is sent to members of the American Bar Association 15 times per year.

These publications usually offer a very practical approach to practicing law in a jurisdiction and feature articles on ethics; changes in local court rules, local cases, or local legislation; provide human interest biographies of judges or practitioners in the state; publish lists of attorneys who have been suspended or disbarred from the practice of law; and review books, software, and other publications of interest to practitioners. These journals usually resemble nonlegal publications such as *Time Magazine* or *Newsweek Magazine*. Their size (8½″ × 11″) is the same as the popular press publications, and they usually feature a photograph of a judge or lawyer on a glossy front page. A table of contents is included as well as a variety of advertisements for products and services aimed at the legal profession, such as office furniture, software programs, seminars, and books.

The articles published in these bar association publications are far more practical in their approach than the academic articles published in law reviews. For example, an article in a law review relating to child support might well examine the development and evolution of cases and legislation in that area of the law and analyze the social policies served by child support. In contrast, an article in a bar association publication might be titled "How to Calculate Child Support" and would provide no such scholarly analysis, but rather would focus on the practical aspects of the process of calculating the amount of child support a noncustodial parent should pay.

Just as there are state bar associations, many local jurisdictions will often have city or county bar associations, such as the Montgomery County, Maryland, Bar Association. Many specialized groups may form local associations, such as the Women's Bar Association of the District of Columbia. These associations also produce periodical publications: Some are pamphlets, and others are informal newsletters or flyers. Generally, these publications are very practical and informal in approach. Articles relate solely to local matters, such as changes to the local rules of court, and they often serve to inform the membership of educational or social functions.

In summary, the publications of bar associations tend to focus on practical guidelines for law practice. It is unlikely that you would conduct substantive research using these publications. It is far more likely that your use of these publications will be aimed at keeping you current on legal issues facing your jurisdiction. See Figure 6-6 for a sample cover and page from a bar association periodical.

Just as bar associations are composed of attorneys and produce a periodical publication, there are associations composed of legal assistants that produce periodical publications. For example, the National Association of Legal Assistants publishes a newsletter every other month called *Facts and Findings*. Other periodicals and journals exist for paralegals

Figure 6-6
Sample Cover and Page from Bar Association Periodical

Figure 6-6 (*Continued*)

FEATURES (cont'd)

p. 41

p. 28

TECH

COLUMNS

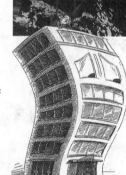

DEPARTMENTS

CALIFORNIA LAWYER

CALIFORNIA LAWYER (ISSN 0279-4063) Volume 17, Number 8. Published monthly by Daily Journal Corporation, 915 E. First St., Los Angeles, CA 90012. SUBSCRIPTIONS: $63 per year for subscriptions within the United States. Periodicals postage paid at Los Angeles, California, and at additional mailing offices. POSTMASTER: Please send address changes to CALIFORNIA LAWYER Circulation, 915 E. First St., Los Angeles, CA 90012.

and are published independently of any association. One of the better-known publications is *Legal Assistant Today*. These publications publish articles of interest to paralegals, such as information on licensing and certification issues; articles offering practical approaches to paralegal tasks such as interviewing, document control, and discovery; and data on average salaries and benefits. Advertisements feature books, software, and seminars. If you belong to a local paralegal association, you will see that its newsletter will undoubtedly contain announcements of job vacancies.

Similar in approach to the journals and periodicals published by bar associations, the journals and periodicals published for legal assistants share a practical focus and are oriented to providing useful information to practicing paralegals.

4. *Specialized Publications*

Just as individuals who are interested in fashion might subscribe to *Vogue*, individuals interested in home decorating might subscribe to *Better Homes and Gardens*, and individuals interested in aviation and defense might subscribe to *Aviation Week and Space Technology*, legal practitioners who have an interest in a specialized area of the law might subscribe to a specialized periodical. Thus, numerous journals and periodicals exist to provide practitioners who focus on a certain area of the law with the information of most interest to them. The numerous specialized periodicals vary in their approach, with some being more analytical and academic, such as the *Computer/Law Journal*, which contains scholarly articles on trade secrets and the protection of proprietary computer software, and others being more practical in approach such as the *Medical Trial Technique Quarterly*, which contains useful articles on topics such as how to cross-examine an expert cardiologist or how effectively to review medical records. Other examples of specialized periodicals are the *American Bankruptcy Law Journal*, the *Human Rights Quarterly*, the *Entertainment and Sports Law Journal*, the *Insurance Law Journal*, the *Trial Lawyer's Guide*, the *Practical Real Estate Lawyer*, and the *Journal of Taxation*. Practitioners interested in keeping current with developments in these fields subscribe to these publications.

Additionally, many periodicals are published for individuals who may share common interests, such as the *Chicano Law Review*, the *Catholic Lawyer*, the *Women's Rights Law Reporter*, the *Black Law Journal*, and the *American Indian Law Review*. Some periodicals focus on the interplay between law and other fields of endeavor, such as the *Journal of Law and Health*, the *Review of Clinical Psychiatry and the Law*, the *Journal of Law & Politics*, and the *Journal of Environmental Law and Practice*. These journals or periodicals focus on issues that have implications for the legal field as well as some other field.

5. *Legal Newspapers and Newsletters*

In large cities such as New York and Los Angeles, you will find daily legal newspapers such as the *New York Law Journal* and the *Los Angeles Daily Journal*. These newspapers, published every weekday, contain the text of recent appellate cases from the state, publish the court calendar or docket for the courts in that locality, and contain articles of general interest to lawyers and paralegals practicing in that jurisdiction. They usually contain extensive classified advertisements and serve as a useful source of job announcements and vacancies.

Other smaller metropolitan areas, such as San Diego, often publish a newspaper every weekday that combines information about law with general business information. Thus, the *San Diego Daily Transcript* contains the court docket, information, and articles of interest to those in the legal profession as well as information relating to bankruptcy filings, the recording of mechanics' liens, and bidding dates for various construction projects in the area.

Some legal newspapers do not restrict their coverage to any locality; they are national in scope, such as the *National Law Journal*, which is published weekly. This weekly newspaper for legal professionals includes articles on a variety of legal topics including ethics, law school admissions, and criminal law matters. Additionally, recent state court and federal court decisions are highlighted. Professional announcements such as those relating to law firm mergers or formations and advertisements for career opportunities are included. A weekly newspaper, *Legal Times*, and a monthly newspaper, *The American Lawyer*, are similar in their coverage.

In addition to legal newspapers, more than 2,000 legal and law-related newsletters are published in the United States. Some of these newsletters are one-page bulletins; others are multiple-page newsletters; and others are looseleaf reporting services, which are stored in ringed binders. Some newsletters offer only short articles, while others provide in-depth analysis of legal issues. Examples of these newsletters include *Environment Week* (which reports news on environmental policy, legislation, pollution, waste disposal, and global warming), the *American Indian Law Newsletter* (published six times per year and containing articles on Indian law), *Jury Trials and Tribulations* (published twice per month and containing summaries of civil jury trials in Florida), and *Bank Bailout Litigation News Newsletter* (a publication reporting on bank closings and related banking matters).

6. *How to Locate Periodical Articles*

While each issue of a law review, bar association publication, specialized periodical, or legal newspaper will contain its own table of contents, it would be extremely ineffective to conduct research by retrieving each of these hundreds of publications and scanning its table of contents in the hope that you will eventually stumble upon an article of interest to you. To locate an article in a periodical publication, you must consult one of several published indexes that will direct you to articles published in periodicals. There are several well-known indexes you can use.

a. *Index to Legal Periodicals and Books*

If you think back to the research you did for high school or college term papers, you may recall using *The Reader's Guide to Periodical Literature*, which directed you to articles in the popular press such as *Time Magazine*, *U.S. News and World Report*, or *Forbes Magazine*. Your technique was to think of words and phrases that described the topic you were researching and look those up in *The Reader's Guide*. You would then be directed to a relevant article in a particular issue of a periodical.

The *Index to Legal Periodicals and Books* is substantially similar in format to *The Reader's Guide*. In fact, both are published by the same company, so if you have used *The Reader's Guide*, you will be comfortable using the *Index to Legal Periodicals and Books* (I.L.P.). I.L.P. indexes articles and books published in the United States, Australia, Canada, Great Britain, Ireland, and New Zealand. The articles, case notes, and biographies must be at least two pages in length to be included. I.L.P. is initially published in softcover monthly pamphlets that are later bound in hardcover volumes.

To locate an article you may use any of the following techniques:

(i) *Subject-Author Approach.* The subject approach calls for you to think of words describing the topic you are interested in, such as bankruptcy, divorce, or emotional distress. Look for these words in I.L.P.'s alphabetically arranged Subject and Author Index. You will then be directed to periodicals that have published articles regarding this topic. Alternatively, if you happen to know that Deborah L. Rhode is an expert on gender bias, you can look up "Rhode" in this Index and you will be directed to articles written by her.

(ii) *Table of Cases Approach.* If you want to read articles that have discussed certain cases, such as *United States v. Nixon*, you can look up this case name in I.L.P.'s Table of Cases. Case names can be located by either the plaintiff's or the defendant's name. You will then be directed to pertinent periodical articles written about this case.

(iii) *Table of Statutes Approach.* If you are interested in whether any articles have analyzed a particular statute, you can look the statute up in I.L.P.'s Table of Statutes, which will direct you to articles discussing this statute.

(iv) *Book Review Approach.* If you are looking for a review of a certain book, locate the title of the book in the Book Review Index in I.L.P., and you will be directed to periodicals that have reviewed this book.

See Figure 6-7 for sample pages from I.L.P.

Figure 6-7
Sample Pages from *Index to Legal Periodicals and Books*

SUBJECT AND AUTHOR INDEX **165**

Eminent domain—*cont.*
A requiem for public purpose: Hawaii Housing Authority v. Midkiff [104 S. Ct. 2321]. D. L. Callies. 1985 *Inst. on Plan. Zoning & Eminent Domain* 8.1-.31 '85
Richard Epstein on the foundations of takings jurisprudence. 99 *Harv. L. Rev.* 791-808 F '86
State regulation of substandard housing and the fifth amendment taking clause: Devines v. Maier [728 F.2d 876]. 29 *Wash. U.J. Urb. & Contemp. L.* 263-76 Wint '85
Taking clause v. technology: Loretto v. TelePrompter Manhattan CATV [102 S. Ct. 3164], a victory for tradition. 38 *U. Miami L. Rev.* 165-85 N '85
Thoughts on the White River Junction manifesto: a reply to the "gang of five's" views on just compensation for regulatory taking of property. [Discussion of The White River Junction manifesto. N. Williams, Jr., R. M. Smith, C. Siemon, D. R. Mandelker, R. F. Babcock. 9 *Vt. L. Rev.* 193-245 Fall '84] M. M. Berger, G. Kanner. 19 *Loy. L.A.L. Rev.* 685-753 My '86
Vertical and horizontal aspects of takings jurisprudence: is airspace property?. 7 *Cardozo L. Rev.* 489-518 Wint '86
Wetlands and agriculture: environmental regulation and the limits of private property. G. Torres. 34 *U. Kan. L. Rev.* 539-76 Spr '86
Emmerson, J. McL.
Computer software: detailed enquiry needed before legisla- [illegible] *Inst. J.* 514-15+ My '84

Entry by author

Emond, D. Paul
[illegible] nature: a new foundation for environmen- [illegible] *Osgoode Hall L.J.* 323-48 Summ '84

Entry by subject

Emotional distress
[illegible] [461 N.E.2d 843 (N.Y.)]: the standards for emotional distress. J. H. Wilson. 57 *N.Y. St. B.J.* 42-4 N '85
Cooper v. Superior Court [200 Cal. Rptr. 746]: the judiciary's distress over emotional distress. 12 *W. St. U.L. Rev.* 917-28 Spr '85
Emotional distress in tort law. J. R. Twiford. 3 *Behavioral Sci. & L.* 121-33 Spr '85
The emotional trauma of hijacking: who pays?. 74 *Ky. L.J.* 599-622 '85/'86
Exposure to hazardous substances and the mental distress tort: trends, applications, and a proposed reform. F. L. Edwards, A. H. Ringleb. 11 *Colum. J. Envt'l L.* 119-39 '86
Guidelines remain arbitrary for bystander recovery for emotional distress: Ochoa v. Superior Court [703 P.2d 1 (Cal.)]. 20 *U.S.F.L. Rev.* 361-73 Wint '86
Illinois law in distress: the "zone of danger" and "physical injury" rules in emotional distress litigation. E. A. McCarthy. 19 *J. Mar. L. Rev.* 17-47 Fall '85
Intentional infliction of emotional distress in the employment at will setting: limiting the employer's manner of discharge. 60 *Ind. L.J.* 365-88 Spr '85
Intentional infliction: should section 46 be revised?. W. H. Pedrick. 13 *Pepperdine L. Rev.* 1-22 D '85
Jaensch v. Coffey [58 Austl. L.J.R. 426]. A. O'Connell, R. Evans. 15 *Melb. U.L. Rev.* 164-9 Je '85
Molien v. Kaiser [616 P.2d 813 (Cal.)]: remedy for an odious diagnostic error. 14 *U. West L.A. L. Rev.* 61-88 '82
Negligent infliction of emotional distress: new tort problem for the mass media. R. E. Drechsel. 12 *Pepperdine L. Rev.* 889-917 My '85
Negligent infliction of emotional distress—Illinois moves into the zone of danger. Rickey v. Chicago Transit Authority, 457 N.E.2d 1 (Ill.). 1984 *S. Ill. U.L.J.* 497-510 '84
Negligent infliction of mental distress upon a bystander in Texas. S. A. Mendel. 26 *S. Tex. L.J.* 305-38 Summ '85
Negligently caused nervous shock—an Antipodean perspective. F. A. Trindade. 5 *Oxford J. Legal Stud.* 305-11 Summ '85
The new English approach to emotional distress: should American courts declare their independence?. 19 *Cornell Int'l L.J.* 65-85 Wint '86
Ochoa v. Superior Court of Santa Clara County [703 P.2d 1 (Cal.)]: new grounds or old guidelines?. 17 *Pac. L.J.* 1027-44 Ap '86
Photojournalism and the infliction of emotional distress. M. D. Sherer. 8 *Com. & L.* 27-37 Ap '86
Recovery for cancerphobia and increased risk of cancer. F. J. Gale, III, J. L. Goyer, III. 15 *Cum. L. Rev.* 823-44 '84/'85
Recovery for emotional distress in strict products liability. J. B. Silverman. 61 *Chi.-Kent L. Rev.* 545-73 '85
Recovery for mental harm under article 17 of the Warsaw Convention: an interpretation of lésion corporelle. 8 *Hastings Int'l & Comp. L. Rev.* 339-64 Spr '85
Recovery for psychic harm in strict products liability: has the interest in psychic equilibrium come the final mile?. S. M. Mead. 59 *St. John's L. Rev.* 457-527 Spr '85
Tort law—emotional distress—a plaintiff has a cause of action for emotional distress induced by witnessing the physical injury or death of a family member caused by a defendant's negligence if the negligence also created an unreasonable risk of bodily harm to the plaintiff. Bovsun v. Sanperi, 461 N.E.2d 843 (N.Y.). 62 *U. Det. L. Rev.* 345-61 Wint '85
Tort law—parents of abducted child denied recovery for negligent infliction of emotional distress—Johnson v. Jamaica Hospital, 467 N.E.2d 502 (N.Y.). 19 *Suffolk U.L. Rev.* 751-8 Fall '85
Torts—an action for intentional infliction of emotional distress will lie where a parent has been psychologically damaged by a former spouse's effort to destroy the relationship between parent and child. Such an action is not barred by either the domestic relations exception to federal diversity jurisdiction, nor the statutory elimination of a cause of action for alienation of affection. Raftery v. Scott, 756 F.2d 335. 24 *J. Fam. L.* 362-7 Ja '86
Torts—damages for mental anguish over the injuries of a third person—Louisiana law prohibits a bystander from recovering damages for mental anguish suffered because of another's injury or death. LeConte v. Pan American World Airways, Inc., 736 F.2d 1019. 50 *J. Air L. & Com.* 351-74 '85
Torts—New Mexico establishes a cause of action for negligent infliction of emotional distress to a bystander: Ramirez v. Armstrong [673 P.2d 822 (N.M.)]. 15 *N.M.L. Rev.* 523-35 Summ '85
The twilight zone of danger: negligent infliction of emotional distress as an actionable tort. 15 *Cum. L. Rev.* 519-39 '84/'85
Warsaw Convention—federal jurisdiction and air carrier liability for mental injury: a matter of limits. J. M. Grippando. 19 *Geo. Wash. J. Int'l L. & Econ.* 59-107 '85
Workers' compensation: the exclusive remedy rule is alive and well in Kansas [Hormann v. New Hampshire Insurance Co., 689 P.2d 837 (Kan.)]. 25 *Washburn L.J.* 192-202 Fall '85
Employee ownership
The benefits of employee stock ownership plans. W. K. Racusin. 124 *Trusts & Est.* 42-6 Ag '85
ESOPs after the Tax Reform Act of 1984. L. E. Irish. 43 *N.Y.U. Inst. on Fed. Tax'n* 1.1-.37 '85
ESOPs and economic distortion. R. L. Doernberg, J. R. Macey. 23 *Harv. J. on Legis.* 103-57 Wint '86
ESOPs and sec. 401(k) plans—a marriage made in heaven?. J. M. Connor. 16 *Tax Adviser* 640-4 O '85
The false promise of worker capitalism: Congress and the leveraged employee stock ownership plan. 95 *Yale L.J.* 148-73 N '85
Planning for ESOPs under DEFRA. W. E. Mattingly, Z. O'Hagin. 37 *Inst. on Fed. Tax'n* 3.1-.22 '85
Recent changes in employee ownership laws: employers may not own their inventions and confidential information. R. B. Coolley. 41 *Bus. Law.* 57-75 N '85
Employer and employee
See also
Agency
Income tax—Employee benefits
Industrial diseases
Labor law
Advice to California employers: an overview of wrongful discharge law and how to avoid potential liability. 13 *Pepperdine L. Rev.* 185-99 D '85
The applicability of the constitution to the employer-employee relations of government contractors. G. D. Ruttinger. 15 *Pub. Cont. L.J.* 309-24 Jl '85
Balancing the rights of the alcoholic employee with the legitimate concerns of the employer: reasonable accommodation vs. undue hardship. 46 *Mont. L. Rev.* 401-18 Summ '85
Choosing a standard for constructive discharge in title VII litigation. 71 *Cornell L. Rev.* 587-617 Mr '86
The common law of employment at-will in New York: the paralysis of Nineteenth Century doctrine. G. Minda. 36 *Syracuse L. Rev.* 939-1020 '85
A comparative, attitudinal, and analytical study of dismissal of at-will employees without cause. F. S. Forbes, I. M. Jones. 37 *Lab. L.J.* 157-66 Mr '86
Contract theory and employment reality. H. Carty. 49 *Mod. L. Rev.* 240-5 Mr '86

Figure 6-7 (*Continued*)

Entry by case name

Kerr-McGee Corp.; Silkwood v., 104 S. Ct. 615
26 *B.C.L. Rev.* 727-44 My '85
1 *Pace Envtl. L. Rev.* 166-79 '83
36 *S.C.L. Rev.* 689-716 Summ '85
Keyes v. Guy Bailey Homes, Inc., 439 So. 2d 670 (Miss.)
5 *Miss. C.L. Rev.* 121-34 Fall '84
Khanna v. Microdata Corp., 215 Cal. Rptr. 860
Kimberly-Clark Corp. v. Johnson & Johnson, 745 F.2d 1437
34 *Am. U.L. Rev.* 779-98 Spr '85
4 *Can. J. Fam. L.* 514-20 N '85
King v. Murphy, 424 So. 2d 547 (Miss.)
4 *Miss. C.L. Rev.* 331-52 Spr '84
King; Norbrook Laboratories Ltd. v., 1984 Indus. R.L.R. 200
6 *D.U.L.J. (n.s.)* 192-9 '84
King & Spalding; Hishon v., 104 S. Ct. 2229
30 *Loy. L. Rev.* 1008-24 Fall '84
15 *U. Balt. L. Rev.* 197-206 Fall '85
Kirchner v. Crystal, 474 N.E.2d 275 (Ohio)
14 *Cap. U.L. Rev.* 681-705 Summ '85
12 *N. Ky. L. Rev.* 369-90 '85
17 *U. Tol. L. Rev.* 255-94 Fall '85
Kizer v. Commonwealth, 321 S.E.2d 291 (Va.)
8 *GMU L. Rev.* 369-87 Spr '86
Klamath Indian Tribe; Oregon Dep't of Fish and Wildlife v., 105 S. Ct. 3420
64 *Or. L. Rev.* 701-26 '86
Klein v. Raysinger, 470 A.2d 507 (Pa.)
23 *Duq. L. Rev.* 1121-48 Summ '85
Kline; Barnes v., 759 F.2d 21
70 *Minn. L. Rev.* 1149-84 My '86
59 *Temp. L.Q.* 151-97 Spr '86
Klinicki v. Lundgren, 695 P.2d 906 (Or.)
22 *Willamette L. Rev.* 163-73 Wint '86
Knapp v. Simmons, 345 N.W.2d 118 (Iowa)
34 *Drake L. Rev.* 561-7 '84/'85
Knight; Minnesota State Bd. for Community Colleges v., 104 S. Ct. 1058
72 *Va. L. Rev.* 91-138 F '86
Koelsch; Ferraro v., 124 Wis. 2d 154
58 *Wis. B. Bull.* 10+ N '85
58 *Wis. B. Bull.* 11+ N '85
Koeppler's Will Trusts, Re, [1985] 2 All E.R. 869
1985 *Conv. & Prop. Law. (n.s.)* 412-15 N/D '85
136 Supp. *New L.J.* 12+ Ap 25 '86
Koire v. Metro Car Wash, 209 Cal. Rptr. 233
12 *W. St. U.L. Rev.* 895-906 Spr '85
Koke v. Phillips Petroleum Co., 731 F.2d 211
9 *Mar. Law.* 297-312 Fall '84
Kolender v. Lawson, 103 S. Ct. 1855
30 *N.Y.L. Sch. L. Rev.* 443-66 '85
Kooragang Invs. Pty., Ltd. v. Richardson & Wrench Ltd., [1981] 3 All E.R. 65
33 *N. Ir. Legal Q.* 182-5 Summ '82
Korell; State v., 690 P.2d 992 (Mont.)
21 *Willamette L. Rev.* 944-53 Fall '85
Kovacs; Ohio v., 105 S. Ct. 705
34 *Am. U.L. Rev.* 1263-300 Summ '85
14 *Cap. U.L. Rev.* 631-61 Summ '85
85 *Colum. L. Rev.* 870-93 My '85
13 *Fla. St. U.L. Rev.* 419-31 Summ '85
34 *De Paul L. Rev.* 1069-88 Summ '85
18 *U.C.C. L.J.* 254-71 Wint '86
54 *U. Cin. L. Rev.* 1101-11 '86
Kremer v. Chemical Constr. Corp., 102 S. Ct. 1883
16 *Loy. U. Chi. L.J.* 209-72 Wint '85
13 *N.Y.U. Rev. L. & Soc. Change* 411-63 '84/'85
54 *U. Cin. L. Rev.* 649-64 '85
Krenzelak v. Krenzelak, 469 A.2d 987 (Pa.)
46 *U. Pitt. L. Rev.* 1123-39 Summ '85
Krenzelak; Krenzelak v., 469 A.2d 987 (Pa.)
46 *U. Pitt. L. Rev.* 1123-39 Summ '85
Krusen; Nelson v., 678 S.W.2d 918 (Tex.)
37 *Baylor L. Rev.* 513-27 Spr '85
16 *Tex. Tech. L. Rev.* 765-93 '85
The Kusu Island, Judgment of Dec. 2, 1983 (High Ct. Singapore)
1985 *Lloyd's Mar. & Com. L.Q.* 309-13 Ag '85
KUTV v. Wilkinson, 686 P.2d 456 (Utah)
1985 *Utah L. Rev.* 739-57 '85

L

Lady Skiffington; Prangnell-O'Neill v., 1984 S.L.T. 282
1985 *Jurid. Rev.* 138-40 Je '85
LaFrance; State v., 471 A.2d 340 (N.H.)
18 *Suffolk U.L. Rev.* 809-14 Wint '84
Lahue; Briscoe v., 103 S. Ct. 1108
1984 *S. Ill. U.L.J.* 687-701 '84
Laker Airways Ltd.; British Airways Bd. v., [1984] 3 All E.R. 39
20 *Wake Forest L. Rev.* 951-74 Wint '84
Laker Airways Ltd.; Midland Bank v., slip op. (C.A. July 30, 1985)
26 *Va. J. Int'l L.* 91-108 Fall '85
Laker Airways Ltd. v. Pan Am. World Airways, Inc., 604 F. Supp. 280
79 *Am. J. Int'l L.* 1069-71 O '85
Laker Airways Ltd. v. Sabena, Belgian World Airlines, 731 F.2d 909
11 *Brooklyn J. Int'l L.* 181-236 Spr '85
71 *Cornell L. Rev.* 645-67 Mr '86
50 *J. Air L. & Com.* 931-67 '85
17 *Law & Pol'y Int'l Bus.* 157-76 '85
Lalande v. State, 676 S.W.2d 115 (Tex.)
26 *S. Tex. L.J.* 621-9 Fall '85
Lamar Outdoor Advertising, Inc. v. Mississippi State Tax Comm'n, 539 F. Supp. 817
5 *Miss. C.L. Rev.* 89-106 Fall '84
Lancaster County Tax Claim Bureau; First Pennsylvania Bank v., 470 A.2d 938 (Pa.)
30 *Vill. L. Rev.* 1191-233 S '85
Lance W., In re, 694 P.2d 744 (Cal.)
12 *Pepperdine L. Rev.* 1059-113 My '85
13 *W. St. U.L. Rev.* 9-26 Fall '85
Land; Sykes v. 271 E.G. 1264
48 *Mod. L. Rev.* 460-5 Jl '85
Land Nordrhein-Westfalen; Von Colson and Kamann v. Case 14/83 (Court of Justice of the E.C.)
101 *Law Q. Rev.* 491-6 O '85
Landreth; Landreth Timber Co. v., 105 S. Ct. 2297
23 *Hous. L. Rev.* 1039-65 Jl '86
11 *Vt. L. Rev.* 1-31 Spr '86
Landreth Timber Co. v. Landreth, 105 S. Ct. 2297
23 *Hous. L. Rev.* 1039-65 Jl '86
11 *Vt. L. Rev.* 1-31 Spr '86
Landsberg v. Scrabble Crossword Game Players, Inc., 736 F.2d 485
27 *Ariz. L. Rev.* 485-91 '85
Langenegger v. United States, 756 F.2d 1565
79 *Am. J. Int'l L.* 1060-3 O '85
Language Rights under the Manitoba Act 1870, Reference Re, 19 D.L.R.4th 1
31 *McGill L.J.* 93-103 D '85
35 *U.N.B.L.J.* 201-10 '86
Lanjani; Peyman v., [1984] 3 All E.R. 703
1985 *Conv. & Prop. Law. (n.s.)* 408-11 N/D '85
Largo Corp.; Crespin v., 698 P.2d 826 (Colo.)
57 *U. Colo. L. Rev.* 419-43 Wint '86
Lastarmco, Inc. v. Commissioner, 737 F.2d 1440
16 *Tax Adviser* 758-62 D '85
Lath; Mitchill v., 160 N.E. 646 (N.Y.)
34 *Emory L.J.* 93-116 Wint '85
Latt v. Superior Court, 212 Cal. Rptr. 380
13 *W. St. U.L. Rev.* 297-310 Fall '85
Lattauzio; United States v., 748 F.2d 559
34 *U. Kan. L. Rev.* 175-90 Fall '85
Lauer; Andrade v., 729 F.2d 1475
85 *Colum. L. Rev.* 1121-39 Je '85
Laventhall v. General Dynamics Corp., 704 F.2d 407
79 *Nw. U.L. Rev.* 780-808 N '84
Law Soc'y of Manitoba v. Giesbrecht, [1984] 1 W.W.R. 430
15 *Man. L.J.* 117-23 '85
Lawrence v. Lawrence, [1985] 1 All E.R. 506
48 *Mod. L. Rev.* 465-71 Jl '85
Lawrence; Lawrence v., [1985] 1 All E.R. 506
48 *Mod. L. Rev.* 465-71 Jl '85
Lawrence v. Lawrence, [1985] 2 All E.R. 733
44 *Cambridge L.J.* 378-81 N '85
35 *Int'l & Comp. L.Q.* 170-8 Ja '86
101 *Law Q. Rev.* 496-505 O '85
Lawrence; Lawrence v., [1985] 2 All E.R. 733
44 *Cambridge L.J.* 378-81 N '85
35 *Int'l & Comp. L.Q.* 170-8 Ja '86
101 *Law Q. Rev.* 496-505 O '85
Lawson; Kolender v., 103 S. Ct. 1855
30 *N.Y.L. Sch. L. Rev.* 443-66 '85

Because I.L.P. is cumulated on an annual basis, you may need to check several pamphlets and several bound volumes for the years you are interested in. Thus, if you are interested in nuisances, you may have to check the softcover pamphlets for this year, looking up "nuisance" in each one, and then continue by looking up "nuisance" in last year's bound volume of I.L.P., then the previous year's bound volume of I.L.P., and so forth. While this process may seem a bit time-consuming, it will yield great rewards, as I.L.P. indexes more than 600 periodicals and dates back to 1908. When using I.L.P., start with the current issues and work backward in time.

I.L.P. is also available in CD-ROM. If your library has purchased I.L.P. in CD-ROM, this will make your search easier by eliminating the need to look at several pamphlets or volumes of the set.

b. *Current Law Index, Legal Resource Index*, and *LegalTrac*

Current Law Index. (C.L.I.) is a comprehensive index of more than 875 legal periodicals from the United States, Australia, Canada, Ireland, New Zealand, and the United Kingdom. C.L.I. is published in monthly softcover pamphlets that are cumulated at year end. C.L.I. indexes all articles from the periodicals it covers, unlike I.L.P., which does not index shorter articles. There are four approaches to locating articles in C.L.I.

(i) *Subject Approach.* The Subject Index lists entries alphabetically by subject name, such as contracts, franchises, or health insurance. By looking up the subject you are interested in you will be referred to a relevant periodical article.

(ii) *Author-Title Approach.* The Author-Title Index alphabetically indexes articles written by certain authors, such as Laurence H. Tribe. When you look up the author's name, you will be directed to periodicals containing articles by that author. This section also indexes book reviews by title of the book and the author's name.

(iii) *Table of Cases Approach.* If you are interested in cases that have been the focus of an article, you can look up the case in the Table of Cases by either the plaintiff's name or the defendant's name, and you will be directed to pertinent periodical articles.

(iv) *Table of Statutes Approach.* If a statute has been analyzed in depth in an article, you can locate it in the alphabetically arranged Table of Statutes, which will refer you to any article that has concentrated on treating that statute.

The company that publishes C.L.I., Gale Group, offers on microfilm the same information found in the conventional books that make up C.L.I. as well as articles from legal newspapers and articles in the popular press that are related to law. The microfilm version of C.L.I. is called *Legal Resource Index*. Its database is available on LEXIS, Westlaw, and DIALOG. The material and information indexed in *Legal Resource Index* is also available on an optical disk information system (CD-ROM) called *LegalTrac*.

One of the advantages of *Legal Resource Index* (or *LegalTrac*) over C.L.I. has to do with cumulation. C.L.I. (the conventional printed set) is arranged very similarly to I.L.P., thus requiring you to look at several pamphlets and hardbound volumes to find articles of interest to you. Because the microfilm version of C.L.I., *Legal Resource Index* (and its CD-ROM version, *LegalTrac*) is completely cumulative, once you locate the topic, author, case, or subject you are interested in, you will be presented with all relevant articles written since 1980, the year this index was created.

Some libraries provide desktop computer access to *Legal Resource Index*. Simply type in the subject matter you are interested in, the author's name, or the title of the periodical, and you will be directed to the relevant publication, which you can then retrieve from the stacks.

While C.L.I. covers several hundred more periodicals than I.L.P., it does have one drawback: It was created in 1980, and therefore its coverage does not extend to any article written before 1980. To locate articles before 1980, use I.L.P. or one of the other indexes discussed herein.

c. Other Indexes

While I.L.P. and C.L.I. (and its microfilm version, *Legal Resource Index*, and CD-ROM version, *LegalTrac*) are the most comprehensive indexes because they send you to hundreds of periodicals, there are several other indexes you should know about that may help you locate periodical articles.

(i) *Index to Periodical Articles Related to Law.* The indexes previously discussed will direct you only to legal publications. It is possible, however, that articles related to law may appear in the popular press such as *Time Magazine*, *U.S. News and World Report*, or *Fortune*. The *Index to Periodical Articles Related to Law*, published quarterly, will direct you to such articles through its indexes arranged alphabetically by subject and author.

(ii) *Index to Foreign Legal Periodicals.* You may have noticed that I.L.P. and C.L.I. index articles from common law countries. The *Index to Foreign Legal Periodicals* will direct you to periodical articles from countries other than the United States and the British Commonwealth. This index is issued quarterly and indexes articles longer than four pages that relate to international law, comparative law, and the municipal law of non-common law countries. Access is gained through an alphabetically arranged subject index (which is in English), a geographical index, and an index by author. If you are interested in reviewing articles written in foreign countries, the *Index to Foreign Legal Periodicals* is an excellent starting place.

(iii) *Current Index to Legal Periodicals.* This weekly publication provides very rapid access to recent periodical articles.

(iv) *Jones-Chipman Index to Legal Periodicals.* As you know, I.L.P. will index and direct you to periodical articles written since 1908. To locate articles written before 1908, consult this index.

(v) *National Legal Bibliography.* This monthly publication will inform you of recent acquisitions of major law libraries. If you need to obtain an article from a lesser known periodical, such as the *Hastings Communications and Entertainment Law Journal*, and it is not available at your law library, you can consult the *National Legal Bibliography* to determine which law libraries subscribe to this periodical and then ask the reference librarian at your library to arrange an interlibrary transfer so you can review the article. Because all law libraries should have facsimile machines, it may be possible to obtain a copy of a needed article within an hour or two of your request.

d. Special Subject Indexes

There are numerous other indexes, some of which index articles related to specific legal topics such as the following: *Criminal Justice Periodical Index*; *Index to Federal Tax Articles*; *Index to Canadian Legal Periodical Literature*; *KINDEX: An Index to Legal Periodical Literature Concerning Children*; and *Public International Law: A Current Bibliography of Articles*. These indexes typically are arranged alphabetically by subject.

e. Other Finding Techniques

Often you may be directed to a particular law review or periodical article in the course of your research. For example, following a statute in U.S.C.S. is a "Research Guide," which typically recommends various A.L.R. annotations and law review articles relating to the statute you are researching. These references to law reviews are found in U.S.C.A. and other annotated codes as well. Similarly, when you Shepardize or KeyCite cases or statutes, you will be directed to periodical articles written about them. Additionally, after you locate an article, you can Shepardize it and be directed to later cases and other articles that have mentioned the article you have read, leading to an ever-increasing collection of legal resources. Shepardizing and KeyCiting are discussed in Chapter 9. Periodical articles can also be located through LEXIS and Westlaw, the computer-assisted research systems discussed in Chapter 11.

Finally, an increasing number of articles are available on the Internet. For example, the Duke Law Journal offers the full text of each published issue online (at www.law.duke.edu/journals/dlj). Moreover, a number of specialty journals exist only on the Internet, as discussed in Chapter 12.

7. *Summary of Legal Periodicals*

All of the legal periodicals (law reviews, bar association and paralegal journals, specialized periodicals, and newspapers and newsletters) are secondary authorities. A court is not required to adhere to the view expressed in a periodical, though it may be persuaded to do so. Periodicals range in approach from the scholarly law reviews to the more practical bar association and paralegal association journals to brief bulletins and newsletters. Locating periodical articles is best accomplished by using one of the separately published comprehensive indexes such as the *Index to Legal Periodicals* or the *Current Law Index*. You may use the descriptive word approach, the author approach, the table of cases approach, or table of statutes approach to locate relevant articles.

Generally, if a periodical article has been written about a topic of interest to you, you should view it as "free research," because the article may well examine the area of law in depth, comparing and contrasting cases in various jurisdictions and analyzing all facets of the topic, thus reducing your research tasks. You can then Shepardize or KeyCite the article to locate newer articles or cases that mention the article you have read. Although periodical publications are not primary authorities, they are frequently cited (especially the authorative academic journal articles) in briefs and court documents to clarify and lend support to primary authorities such as cases.

C. Texts and Treatises

1. *Introduction*

Texts written by legal scholars that focus on one topic of the law are referred to as treatises. Treatises comment upon and analyze an area of law. They do not include cases or statutes and are thus secondary sources. The authors may be academics or practicing attorneys. Treatises vary a great deal in scope and depth. A treatise may be a one-volume work on a fairly narrow legal topic, such as *Evaluating and Settling Personal Injury Claims*, or an analysis of a newly emerging area of the law, such as *Sexual Harassment in the Workplace: Law and Practice*, or an extremely well-known multi-volume set on a broader topic, such as the 15-volume set *Collier on Bankruptcy*.

As you have seen, an encyclopedia typically examines hundreds of topics of law from abatement to zoning and provides introductory information on these topics. Treatises, on the other hand, are devoted to one area of the law and usually examine it in depth. For example, if you were to read all of the sections of C.J.S. on Contracts, you would be presented with approximately 2,000 pages of material. If you were to review a well-known treatise on contracts, titled *Treatise on the Law of Contracts* by Samuel Williston, you would be presented with 15 volumes and approximately 14,000 pages of material.

You may recall that encyclopedias are noncritical summaries of the law, meaning that the information you are given merely summarizes the law relating to that topic. Treatises, however, may be "critical" in the sense that they may boldly criticize case law or question the logic of a judicial opinion. For example, the following language is found in 2 J. Thomas McCarthy, *McCarthy on Trademarks and Unfair Competition* § 18:56 (4th ed. 1997): "A small number of cases appear to have held that a contractual stipulation for quality control is sufficient, even though the licensor failed to exercise the right. In the author's opinion, such cases miss the point that not only must there be a right to control, but that right must be discharged by the licensor." While this comment may not strike you as overly harsh or critical, it is far different in tone from the encyclopedias, which merely present the law without any such disapproving commentary.

The narrative statements found in a treatise are typically more analytical than those found in encyclopedias. One feature treatises share in common with encyclopedias, however, is that they serve as casefinders. The format of most treatises is also similar to that of encyclopedias: Narrative discussions of the law are found on the top portion of each page with case citations located through the use of supporting footnotes in the lower portion of each page. One particular type of treatise is called a "hornbook," a one-volume text devoted to one area of the law, such as contracts, torts, or real property. Hornbooks are primarily designed for use by law students and offer broad and fairly academic coverage of a topic. Cases discussed tend to be the landmark cases in the field.

Remember that texts and treatises come in many forms: from one volume to a multi-volume set; from analysis of very narrow topics, such as *Standby Letters of Credit*, to analysis of a broader topic, such as criminal law, corporations or bankruptcy; from recently published analysis of newer legal topics, such as *Americans with Disabilities Act Handbook*, to the extremely well-known and respected treatise, *Prosser and Keeton on the Law of Torts*, which was first published in 1941 and is still the premier authority on torts; and from volumes that are in hardbound form to loose-leaf binders to softcover pamphlets. Many treatises are now available in CD-ROM form. See Figure 6-8 for a sample page from a treatise.

In fact, if you are unsure what "category" a law book falls in, it is probably a treatise. No matter what kind of treatise it may be, however, it remains a secondary authority, meaning that while a court may choose to follow a position advanced by a well-known and highly regarded treatise such as John H. Wigmore's *Evidence in Trials at Common Law*, the court is not required to do so. Courts have, however, cited numerous treatises with approval, and some treatises such as *Prosser and Keeton on the Law of Torts* have been cited hundreds of times, partly because of the caliber of the authors. You should feel free to rely upon and quote from

Figure 6-8
Sample Page from a Treatise

position that such a statute is not a mandate but a permissive pronouncement, and that the trial judge has discretion under his inherent power to exclude evidence of little value, though relevant and admissible, if its prejudicial quality outweighs its evidentiary value.[67]

§ 26:21. Inquiry as to Believing Witness Under Oath

The propriety of asking a witness who has testified to the bad reputation of another person for truth and veracity, whether the witness would believe such person under oath, is a subject of dispute. It is urged, as an objection to the question, that the opinion of the witness should not be substituted for that of the jury, that the admission of such an opinion is a departure from the usual rules of evidence, and that the inquiry affords opportunity to bring improperly before the jury the prejudices, feelings and hostility of witnesses.[68]

On the other hand, it is contended in favor of the practice, that witnesses frequently misunderstand the nature of impeaching questions, and that, if the question of credit is thus directly presented, the witness will better understand the nature of the inquiry and more carefully weigh the answer. It is reasoned, too, that the reputation of the witness who is sought to be impeached is not a mere matter of opinion but one of fact as to which ordinary witnesses may

or the expiration of probation or parole or sentence, whichever is the later.

67. Brown v United States, 125 App DC 220, 370 F2d 242.

Following § 21 of the Uniform Rules of Evidence it was held that evidence of a plaintiff-motorist's 12-year-old pandering conviction has so little probative value for impeachment purposes that it was inadmissible, and that the trial court's discretionary admission of the evidence was reversible error because of its highly prejudicial effect. McIntosh v Pittsburgh Rys. Co. 432 Pa 123, 247 A2d 467.

68. Benesch v Waggner, 12 Colo 534, 21 P 706; Phillips v Kingfield, 19 Me 375.

Practice Aids: Believing witness under oath. 3 Am Jur Proof of Facts 175, 183, Character and Reputation (Comment Note).

[224]

treatises in memoranda and briefs that you prepare so long as you also have at least one "on point" primary authority to support your position. If you are unsure as to the credibility of the treatise, you can consult a source titled *Who's Who in American Law* and review the author's credentials. Alternatively, you can look up the author's name in the *Index to Legal Periodicals and Books* or in the *Current Law Index* to determine if the author has produced other writings on this topic, or you can ask the reference librarians in your law library for their opinions on the expertise of the author and the treatise's overall reputation in the courts. Finally, if the treatise has been published in multiple editions, this is a signal it is widely accepted and used.

2. Common Features of Treatises

Treatises usually share the following features:

(i) *Format.* Treatises are essentially "expert opinions" on one topic of the law. The analysis of the law is presented in narrative form, and readers are usually directed to cases through the use of footnotes.

(ii) *Index.* An index to the treatise consisting of an alphabetical arrangement of the topics, subjects, words, and phrases discussed in the treatise will be located in the last volume of the set or as a separate index volume after the last volume in the set.

(iii) *Table of Contents.* A table of contents will usually be presented in the front of each volume showing how the discussion of this area of the law is arranged by chapter.

(iv) *Table of Cases.* Most treatises contain an alphabetically arranged table of cases so you may readily locate a discussion of a certain case.

(v) *Table of Statutes.* Some treatises contain a table of statutes so you can locate the discussion of a certain statute.

(vi) *Appendices.* Many treatises include the text of statutes and regulations that are relevant to the area of law covered by the treatise. For example, the appendix to the treatise *McCarthy on the Law of Trademarks and Unfair Competition* includes the full text of the United States Trademark Act.

(vii) *Updating.* Most treatises are maintained by the traditional method of updating of legal books: an annual cumulative pocket part. If the treatise consists of looseleaf binders, it will be updated by periodically issued supplements placed in the binder or by replacement pages sent to the law library on a periodic basis. The law library will be provided with a set of instructions to, for example, "replace old page 41 with new page 41 and discard old page 41." Some treatises are kept current by a separate softcover supplement, which will be placed next to the main volume(s) of the treatises. Check the copyright year of any hardback volumes to make sure they are current.

You must *always* check the pocket part or supplement to determine if the narrative statement of the law presented in the main hardbound volume is still an accurate statement of the law and to locate cases more current than those found in the footnotes in the hardbound volume.

3. *Use of Treatises*

While encyclopedias serve as excellent introductions to a wide variety of legal topics, a treatise usually serves as a thorough examination of one area of the law. Although you are discouraged from citing encyclopedias, you are encouraged to cite treatises, particularly those with established reputations. For a comprehensive analysis of a topic with thoughtful evaluation of case law, consult a treatise.

If you are unsure whether a treatise has been written regarding the topic of law you are interested in, you can try various strategies:

(i) Check the catalog in your law library for your topic (bankruptcy, contracts, trusts, and so forth). The catalog, which may be in print or microfiche format or online, will list every treatise the library contains relating to this topic and will direct you to the particular "stack" where the treatise is located.

(ii) You can also go directly to the shelves where the books relating to this area of law are maintained. For example, all of the books relating to criminal law are generally shelved together, and all of the books relating to real property are generally shelved together. By skimming the titles of the books in the stacks and randomly inspecting these books, you may well "stumble upon" an excellent treatise.

(iii) Ask the reference librarian for assistance. Even if your law library does not contain the treatise you need, you may be able to obtain one via an interlibrary transfer, that is, a "loan" from another library.

(iv) Because many treatises are in high demand, check the reserve room at your law library, which may keep the most frequently consulted treatises on reserve.

4. *Research Strategies for Treatises*

There are several alternative methods you can use to locate a discussion in a treatise on an issue in which you are interested. Most of these are familiar to you.

(i) *Descriptive Word Approach.* This method simply calls for you to select a word or phrase describing the issue you are researching and locate this word or phrase in the index. The index will then direct you to the appropriate volume, paragraph, or section in the treatise.

For example, if the index directs you to **4:12**, this is a signal for you to review section 12 of volume 4 of the set. As always, the descriptive word approach is the most reliable research technique for beginning researchers.

(ii) *Topic Approach.* If you are relatively familiar with the treatise or subject matter you are researching, you may elect to bypass the index to the treatise and proceed directly to the table of contents. You would then scan the list of chapter titles and subdivisions and proceed immediately to the appropriate chapter.

(iii) *Table of Cases Approach.* If you are interested in locating a discussion of a particular case, you can look up the case name in the alphabetically arranged table of cases, which will direct you to that section of the treatise that analyzes, evaluates, and discusses that case. Similarly, if your treatise includes a table of statutes, it will direct you to text discussion of specific statutes.

(iv) *Other Approaches.* It is possible that you may be referred to a treatise through another source entirely. Thus, if you are reading a pertinent case on an issue you are researching and the case comments favorably and relies upon a treatise, you should then retrieve and examine the cited treatise. Similarly, other sources (encyclopedias, periodical articles, and library references found in U.S.C.A. and U.S.C.S.) may refer you to a treatise.

D. Restatements

1. Introduction

In 1923, a group of law scholars established the American Law Institute, which is composed of judges, law professors, eminent lawyers, and other jurists. The Institute was created in response to the ever-increasing volume of court decisions, which the members of the Institute believed produced both uncertainty and complexity in the law. The Institute's solution to this mass of irreconcilable and ambiguous case law was to "present an orderly statement of the general common law of the United States."

To accomplish this task, legal scholars called "Reporters" were appointed by the Institute for various subject matters such as torts, property, contracts, conflict of laws, and agency. Each Reporter, together with his or her assistants and advisors, was assigned to one of these topics of the law to analyze carefully the assigned subject matter and thoroughly examine pertinent cases. Restatements do not exist for all areas of the law but only for selected topics. See Figure 6-9 for a chart of Restatements.

Figure 6-9
Chart of Restatements

Topic	*Series*
Agency	First and Second
Conflict of Laws	First and Second
Contracts	First and Second
Foreign Relations Law of the United States	Second and Third
Judgments	First and Second
Law Govering Lawyers	Third
Property (includes landlord and tenant, wills and donative transfers, mortgages, and servitudes)	First, Second, and Third
Restitution	First
Security	First
Suretyship and Guaranty	Third
Torts	First and Second
Trusts	First, Second, and Third
Unfair Competition	Third

The Reporters then prepared and presented preliminary drafts restating American common law in a terse and nearly rule-like fashion to the Institute. Various revisions to the drafts were made, and ultimately the Institute directed the publications of various final "Restatements," such as Restatement of Torts, Restatement of Contracts, and Restatement of Agency. Some of the Restatements have been updated or newly created in a second or third series, such as Restatement (Second) of Torts, Restatement (Second) of Contracts, and Restatement (Third) of Foreign Relations Law of the United States. For example, the newly created Restatement (Third) of the Law Governing Lawyers (dealing with regulation of the legal profession and the attorney-client relationship) was created in 2000 in its third series with no preceding first or second edition or series. All of the series of Restatements are subject to rigorous drafting and review, making them highly credible and reputable.

The goal of the Institute, to restate American case law in a clear and certain manner, has largely been accomplished due to the authority and repute of the members of the Institute. While the initial focus of the Institute was merely to restate American case law in an unambiguous manner, the current emphasis is on predicting what courts might do in the future as well as restating what courts have held in the past.

2. *Arrangement of Restatements*

Each Restatement typically consists of three to five volumes. Each volume is arranged in chapters, and the chapters are arranged in sections. Each section relates a principle of the law in clear straightforward language printed in bold typeface. These Restatement sections are followed by "comments" and "illustrations." The comments section provides general analysis of the legal principle previously given. The illustrations section exemplifies the legal principle by providing articulately written examples demonstrating the application of the principle. The Reporter's Notes then complete each section by providing general comments and explanations, together with references to cases that support the Restatement position. Each Restatement includes appendix volumes that direct you to cases that have cited Restatement sections. See Figure 6-10 for a sample page from Restatement (Second) of Torts.

3. *Research Strategies*

To locate a pertinent Restatement provision, you can use either the descriptive word approach or the topic approach. To use the descriptive word approach, consult the alphabetically arranged index to the pertinent Restatement generally found in the last volume of the Restatement set. Look up words or phrases that describe your research problem and you will be directed to the appropriate section of the Restatement. Alternatively, you can use a one-volume index published for all of the Restatements in the First Series.

To use the topic approach, simply scan the table of contents located in the first volume of any Restatement volume. By quickly viewing the table of contents you will be sent to the pertinent section.

Because there is an alphabetical Table of Cases for the newer Restatements, you can use this to locate pertinent Restatement sections. The Table of Cases is usually located in the Index volume for the relevant Restatement. Look up case names in the Table of Cases and you will be directed to particular Reatement sections that mention or cite those cases.

Alternatively, you may be directed to a Restatement section in the course of your research. For example, a case you may be reading may refer to a Restatement section. In this instance you should review the section mentioned.

Be sure to check the appendix volume for the section you are researching and the pocket part therein to determine if the Restatement section has been modified or limited and to locate cases supporting the Restatement section.

4. *Effect of Restatements*

The Restatements are a secondary source. Courts are not required to adopt or follow the Restatement positions. Nevertheless, the Restatements have been cited in cases more than 100,000 times. In fact, to determine if a Restatement section you are interested in has been cited by a court, you can consult a set of books entitled *Restatement in the Courts*, which indicates cases that have cited Restatement sections. Updating of *Restatement in the Courts* ceased in 1976. For more recent cases, consult

Figure 6-10
Sample Page from Restatement (Second) of Torts

as a secondary consequence illness or other bodily harm, such as a miscarriage, by its internal operation upon the well-being of the other. As to acts which are negligent because they are intended or likely to cause an emotional disturbance which the actor should recognize as likely so to affect the action of the other or a third person as to cause bodily harm to the other, see § 303. As to acts which threaten bodily harm, but result in emotional disturbance alone, see § 435 A. As to acts which otherwise threaten bodily harm, but result in such harm only through emotional disturbance, see § 436. As to emotional disturbance as an element of damages where there is other harm, see § 905.

§ 312. Emotional Distress Intended

If the actor intentionally and unreasonably subjects another to emotional distress which he should recognize as likely to result in illness or other bodily harm, he is subject to liability to the other for an illness or other bodily harm of which the distress is a legal cause,

(a) although the actor has no intention of inflicting such harm, and

(b) irrespective of whether the act is directed against the other or a third person.

See Reporter's Notes.

Comment:

a. The rule stated in this Section does not give protection to mental and emotional tranquillity in itself. In general, as stated in § 436 A, there is no liability where the actor's conduct inflicts only emotional distress, without resulting bodily harm or any other invasion of the owner's interests. The emotional disturbance is important only in so far as its existence involves a risk of bodily harm, and as affecting the damages which may be recovered if the bodily harm is sustained. See § 905.

b. There is a considerable degree of duplication between the rule stated in this Section and that stated in § 46, which deals with the intentional or reckless infliction of emotional distress by extreme and outrageous conduct. In most of the cases in which the intentional infliction of emotional distress results in foreseeable bodily harm, the known risk of such bodily harm is sufficient in itself to make the act one of extreme out-

either the appendix to the pertinent Restatement or Shepard's *Restatement of the Law Citations*, both of which will direct you to federal and state cases, as well as other authorities, that have cited Restatement provisions. Many legal experts believe the Restatements are the most highly regarded of all of the secondary authorities, and you are encouraged to rely upon them and cite to them in research projects you prepare. In fact, in ordering citations to secondary authorities, only the model codes are cited before the Restatements, according to the *Bluebook* (Rule 1.4(i)), which provides rules for citation form. This preeminence of the Restatements in the order of listing secondary materials confirm their authority.

E. Citation Form

Encyclopedias:

46 C.J.S. *Mechanics Liens* § 121 (1986).

79 Am. Jur. 2d *Trusts* § 42 (1980).

Periodicals:

Stanley L. Paul, *Due Process*, 41 Dick. L. Rev. 1091 (1985).

Treatises:

Susan L. Baker, *Federal Sentencing Guidelines* § 12:06 (2d ed. 1988).

Restatements:

Restatement (Second) of Torts § 13 (1976).

Technology Tips

Encyclopedias and Treatises

Encyclopedias are not available on the Internet. Neither is C.J.S. available on Westlaw, West's computerized legal research system. Nevertheless, C.J.S. provides tips on how to construct queries on Westlaw so you can readily retrieve information.

Both A.L.R. and Am. Jur. 2d are available on CD-ROM (see Chapter 11).

Am. Jur. 2d is available on LEXIS, Reed Elsevier's online legal research system. Moreover, LEXIS provides access to a number of state-specific encyclopedias, such as Cal. Jur., New York Jur., and Fla. Jur.

Due to their voluminous content, treatises are not generally available either on the Internet or LEXIS or Westlaw. While numerous articles and law-related discussions are available on the Internet, there has been no effort to put these comprehensive collections on the Internet, likely due to authors' reluctance to have their materials distributed globally with a concurrent loss of royalty revenue.

Periodicals

Following are Internet addresses that will allow you to retrieve various articles relating to law.

http://www.law.indiana. edu/ v-lib/	The World Wide Web Virtual Law Library is a comprehensive site offering free access to hundreds of legal periodicals
http://www.lectlaw.com	Inter-Law's 'Lectric Law Library offers access to a variety of legal periodicals
http://www.law.com	Law.com provides access to numerous newspapers and journals publishing law-related articles.
http://www.findlaw.com	The FindLaw Web site offers access to a wide variety of legal materials. To locate periodicals, select "Students" and then "Law Reviews."
http://www.lawcourse.com/ also/usa.cgi?usj	The Web site of American Law Sources Online provides direct links to hundreds of law reviews and journals.
http://www.hg.org/ journals.html	The Web site Hieros Gamos is a comprehensive law and government portal with links to hundreds of law reviews and journals.
http:// www.ll.georgetown.edu	The Web site for Georgetown University Law Center provides access to numerous legal and law-related journals. Select "Guide to Legal Journals."
http://www.usc.edu/dept/law-lib/legal/journals.html	The Web site for University of Southern California Law School provides links to numerous law reviews and journals as well as to ABA journals and newsletters.

(continued)

Technology Tips (*Continued*)

http://www.ilrg.com/journals.html	The Web site of the Internet Legal Research Guide provides access to hundreds of law-related publications and journals.
http://www.law.cornell.edu	The Web site for Cornell Law School offers access to legal periodicals. Select "Directories" and then "Journals."

Restatements

The Restatements are not available on the Internet. All of the Restatements currently in print are, however, available on LEXIS in a single file called RESTAT. The Restatements are also available on Westlaw. Nevertheless, the Web site of the American Law Institute (http://www.ali.org) lists the Restatements currently in print and discusses the status of Restatements under consideration and in the drafting or revising process.

Writing Strategies

Writing is neither as mechanical nor as precise as mathematics. You cannot write by formula, assuming that "one primary authority plus one secondary authority equals one argument." In fact, constructing a writing using such an approach will result in a rigid and choppy project.

There is no easy answer to the question, "how many authorities are enough?" For some straightforward issues, a reference to one statute may be sufficient. Complex issues will require more in-depth analysis and expanded discussion of authorities.

Vary the authorities you rely upon. If your entire writing consists of references only to the Restatements, the reader will assume you are a lazy researcher who is uninterested in thoroughly researching the issues and content to rely upon one source. Thorough analysis calls for a combination of primary and secondary sources.

If you are relying upon primary sources as well as secondary sources to discuss an issue, analyze the primary authorities first. After you have shown the reader why the statutes, regulations, cases, or constitutional provisions control, enhance your discussion by providing additional support from a periodical, Restatement, annotation, or treatise.

Assignment for Chapter 6

1. Use Am. Jur. 2d.
   a. Which volume, title, and section deal with whether checks are copyrightable?
   b. Review this section. Are checks copyrightable?
   c. Cite a case from the Northern District of Georgia supporting your answer. Give case name only.
   d. Which volume, title, and section deal with duties of teachers with regard to extracurricular activities?
   e. Review the above section. Are teachers generally required to supervise pupils at extracurricular sports events? Cite a case supporting your answer.
2. Use C.J.S.
   a. Which volume, title, and section discuss waiver of a jury by contract?
   b. Review this section. Which case held that such a waiver may not be valid if it is buried deep in a long contract?
   c. Which volume, title, and section state that in determining custody of a child in a divorce proceeding, the health of the child is an important consideration?
   d. Cite an Illinois Appellate Court case that discusses the above topic.
   e. Define "drunkard."
3. Use the appropriate state-specific encyclopedia.
   a. Which title and section discuss N.Y. Gen. Bus. Law § 597?
   b. Read the section. What does this topic deal with?
   c. What title and section within this set discuss the case *Estate of Wellaver?*
4. Use *Am Jur. Proof of Facts 3d.*
   a. Give the cite to an article relating to adverse reactions to the drug Halcion.
   b. Review this article. What is the alleged annual cost of treating the effects of drug toxicity?
5. Use *Index to Legal Periodicals and Books* to answer the following questions.
   a. Find an article written by Paul K. Blunt in 1998 relating to selective breeding and the patenting of living organisms. Give the citation.
   b. Find an article written in New York in the fall of 1997 relating to homelessness. Identify the author and give the citation.
   c. Find an article published in the summer of 1999 in which the defendant's name is "Boy Scouts of America." Give the citation.
6. Use the *Current Law Index* for 2000 and give the citation to an article relating to press release hoaxes.
7. a. Give the title and the author of the Summer 2000 law review article located at 73 Temp. L. Rev. 681.
   b. Where and when did the author receive her J.D.?

8. Use *Collier on Bankruptcy* (15th ed., revised):
   a. What section in the set discusses the case *Browning v. Navarro*?
   b. Review the section of the treatise that discusses the case. Give the citation to the case and briefly discuss what the case held.
9. Use *Williston on Contracts* (4th ed.), edited by Lord.
   a. What section discusses the case *In re Hub Recycling, Inc.*?
   b. Read the section. Generally, what principle does the case discuss?
   c. What Restatement section supports this?
10. a. Use Restatement (Second) of Torts. What is the effect of consent to a crime?
    b. If *A* and *B* engage in a boxing match that is criminal because there is no license for the match, what is the result?

Chapter 7

Miscellaneous Secondary Authorities

A. Attorneys General Opinions
B. Legal Dictionaries
C. Directories
D. Form Books
E. Uniform Laws
F. Looseleaf Services
G. Jury Instructions
H. Summary
I. Citation Form

Chapter Overview

The previous chapter discussed the most frequently used secondary authorities: encyclopedias, periodicals, treatises, and Restatements. There are, however, several other authorities that are used by legal researchers.These include opinions of attorneys general, dictionaries, directories, form books, uniform laws, looseleaf services, and jury instructions.

These sources summarize and explain the law as well as assist you in locating primary sources. The sources discussed in this chapter are often more practical in their approach and content than encyclopedias, periodicals, treatises, and Restatements. For example, dictionaries help you find the meaning of a word in its legal sense; form books provide information so you can effectively draft complaints, contracts, and other legal documents; and looseleaf services provide an "a" to "z" approach to understanding certain specialized areas of the law.

At the conclusion of this chapter you will be familiar with all of the tools you will need to have in order to locate answers for most research questions.

A. Attorneys General Opinions

1. Introduction

An attorney general is the chief law officer in a government. The United States attorney general is appointed by the president and is confirmed by the United States Senate. The United States attorney general is the head of the Department of Justice and serves as a member of the president's Cabinet. Each of the 50 states also has an attorney general. In most states, the attorney general is elected by the voters. As the chief law enforcement officer, an attorney general issues written opinions on a variety of legal topics, including the interpretation of statutes and the duties and operations of government entities. These opinions typically are written in response to questions by legislators, the executive branch, or other government officials.

Any large law library in your area will collect the opinions of the United States attorney general. However, your law library will likely collect only the opinions of the attorney general from your state and will not have any of the attorneys general opinions from the other 49 states.

The opinions of attorneys general are secondary authority because they are not cases, constitutions, or statutes. Thus, a court is not required to follow an opinion of an attorney general. Because, however, these opinions are written by the chief legal advisor to the executive branch, whether federal or state, and are usually followed, they are highly persuasive, and you should feel free to rely upon them and cite them in briefs and memoranda that you write because courts view them as respectable and creditable commentaries on case law and legislation.

2. *Research Strategies*

Most sets of opinions of attorneys general will have an index, which you can use by the descriptive word approach; that is, by selecting words that describe the issue you are researching, looking up these words in the alphabetically arranged index, and then being directed to the appropriate opinion. Unfortunately, these indexes are often not well-maintained and may be out of date.

It is more likely that you will be directed to a pertinent attorney general opinion by another source you are using. For example, if you are researching a particular statute in U.S.C.A. or U.S.C.S., you will be provided with a reference to any attorney general opinion that has interpreted or construed this statute. Similarly, when you are researching a state statute in your state's annotated code, you may be directed to a state attorney general opinion analyzing this state statute. Additionally, as you will see in Chapter 9, when you Shepardize or KeyCite a case, you will be directed to any attorneys general opinions that have mentioned this case.

B. Legal Dictionaries

Just as you would use a standard dictionary to determine the spelling, pronunciation, and meaning of a word with which you are unfamiliar, you can use a legal dictionary to determine the spelling, pronunciation, and meaning of a legal word or phrase with which you are unfamiliar. Thus, if you need to know the meaning of a word in its legal sense, such as "negligence," or the translation of a Latin phrase such as *damnum absque injuria* ("harm without injury in the legal sense"), or the meaning of a phrase such as "watered stock," you should consult a legal dictionary, which is an alphabetical arrangement of legal words and phrases. Many legal dictionaries will not only provide the definition of a word but will then give you a citation to a case or secondary authority in which the word was defined. So if you look up the word "mistrial" in a legal dictionary, you will not only be given its meaning but will be directed to a case that defines the word "mistrial." This is another example of a secondary source not only explaining the law but directing you to primary sources. Remember that when you define a word in a research project, cite to the case defining the word rather than the dictionary if the case is relevant and on point.

Perhaps the best known of the legal dictionaries is *Black's Law Dictionary*, a one-volume book published by West, which has been in existence since 1891. *Black's* not only includes more than 20,000 definitions but also provides a guide to pronunciation of Latin terms, a table of common legal abbreviations, a chart showing the composition of the United States Supreme Court from 1789 to date, definitions of legal maxims, a Table of British Regnal Years listing the sovereigns of England for the last 900 years, and the text of the United States Constitution. *Black's Law Dictionary* is available in hardcover, paperback, and on Westlaw. A new edition is released every several years. See Figure 7-1 for a sample page from *Black's Law Dictionary* (6th ed. 1990).

Another of the well-known legal dictionaries is *Ballentine's Law Dictionary*, a one-volume book published by the former Lawyers Co-op, which defines more than 45,000 words and phrases. Like *Black's*, *Ballentine's* also contains guides to pronunciation of Latin terms. Moreover, because it was formerly a Lawyers Co-op publication, it contains thousands of references to the Lawyers Co-op publications, *United States Supreme Court Reports, Lawyers' Edition*, A.L.R., and Am. Jur. 2d. *Ballentine's*, however, has not released a new edition since 1969, and thus *Black's* is far more current and should likely be consulted in preference to *Ballentine's*.

There are numerous other legal dictionaries that you can use, including specialized dictionaries such as Ralph De Sola's *Crime Dictionary*, which provides definitions of crimes in legal terms, slang, and street usage. Most legal dictionaries are located in the reference section of the law library, and you should make a point of browsing the shelves in the reference section to discover which dictionaries are available.

You may recall that the set *Words and Phrases* will provide you with definitions of words and phrases. Its coverage, however, is limited to words and phrases that have been defined in cases and therefore you will not be able to find a word in *Words and Phrases* unless it has been the subject of court action. Moreover, because *Words and Phrases* is a multi-volume set, it is more unwieldy than the more standard one-volume legal dictionaries such as *Black's* and *Ballentine's*. One of the advantages of *Words and*

Figure 7-1
Sample Page from *Black's Law Dictionary* (6th ed. 1990)

Unilateral mistake. A mistake by only one party to an agreement and generally not a basis for relief by rescission or reformation.

Mister. A title of courtesy. A trade, craft, occupation, employment, office.

Mistery. A trade or calling.

Note reference to case interpreting "mistrial"

Mistrial. An erroneous, invalid, or nugatory trial. A trial of an action which cannot stand in law because of want of jurisdiction, or a wrong drawing of jurors, or disregard of some other fundamental requisite before or during trial. Trial which has been terminated prior to its normal conclusion. A device used to halt trial proceedings when error is so prejudicial and fundamental that expenditure of further time and expense would be wasteful if not futile. Ferguson v. State, Fla., 417 So.2d 639, 641. The judge may declare a mistrial because of some extraordinary event (*e.g.* death of juror, or attorney), for prejudicial error that cannot be corrected at trial, or because of a deadlocked jury.

"Mistrial" is equivalent to no trial and is a nugatory trial while "new trial" recognizes a completed trial which for sufficient reasons has been set aside so that the issues may be tried de novo. People v. Jamerson, 196 Colo. 63, 580 P.2d 805, 806.

Misuse. As defense in products liability action, requires use in a manner neither intended nor reasonably foreseeable by manufacturer. Smith v. Sturm, Ruger & Co., Inc., 39 Wash.App. 740, 695 P.2d 600, 604.

Misuser /misyúwzər/. An unlawful use of a right. Abuse of an office or franchise. 2 Bl.Comm. 153.

Mitigating circumstances. Such as do not constitute a justification or excuse for the offense in question, but which, in fairness and mercy, may be considered as extenuating or reducing the degree of moral culpability. For example, mitigating circumstances which will reduce degree of homicide to manslaughter are the commission of the killing in a sudden heat of passion caused by adequate legal provocation. People v. Morrin, 31 Mich.App. 301, 187 N.W.2d 434, 438.

Those that affect basis for award of exemplary damages, or reduce actual damages by showing, not that they were never suffered, but that they have been partially extinguished.

In actions for libel and slander, refer to circumstances bearing on defendant's liability for exemplary damages by reducing moral culpability, or on liability for actual damages by showing partial extinguishment thereof. The "mitigating circumstances" which the statute allows defendant in libel action to prove are those which tend to show that defendant in speaking the slanderous words acted in good faith, with honesty of purpose, and not maliciously. Roemer v. Retail Credit Co., 44 C.A.3d 926, 119 Cal.Rptr. 82, 91.

See also Comparative negligence; Extenuating circumstances; Extraordinary circumstances.

Mitigation. To make less severe. Alleviation, reduction, abatement or diminution of a penalty or punishment imposed by law.

Mitigation of damages. Doctrine of "mitigation of damages," sometimes called doctrine of avoidable consequences, imposes on party injured by breach of contract or tort duty to exercise reasonable diligence and ordinary care in attempting to minimize his damages, or avoid aggravating the injury, after breach or injury has been inflicted and care and diligence required of him is the same as that which would be used by man of ordinary prudence under like circumstances. Darnell v. Taylor, La.App., 236 So.2d 57, 61. Mitigation of damages is an affirmative defense and applies when plaintiff fails to take reasonable actions that would tend to mitigate his injuries. Mott v. Persichetti, Colo.App., 534 P.2d 823, 825. See Restatement, Contracts § 336(1) U.C.C. § 2–603. *See also* Avoidable consequences doctrine.

Mitigation of punishment. A judge may reduce or order a lesser sentence in consideration of such factors as the defendant's past good behavior, his family situation, his cooperation with the police and kindred factors.

Mitior sensus /mishiyər sénsəs/. Lat. The more favorable acceptation.

Mitius imperanti melius paretur /míshiyəs impəræ̃ntay míyl(i)yəs pəríytər/. The more mildly one commands, the better is he obeyed.

Mitter. L. Fr. To put, to send, or to pass; as, *mitter l'estate*, to pass the estate; *mitter le droit*, to pass a right. These words are used to distinguish different kinds of releases.

Mitter avant /mítər əvǽnt/. L. Fr. In old practice, to put before; to present before a court; to produce in court.

Mittimus /mítəməs/. The name of a precept in writing, issuing from a court or magistrate, directed to the sheriff or other officer, commanding him to convey to the prison the person named therein, and to the jailer, commanding him to receive and safely keep such person until he shall be delivered by due course of law. State v. Lenihan, 151 Conn. 552, 200 A.2d 476, 478. Transcript of minutes of conviction and sentence duly certified by court clerk. United States ex rel. Chasteen v. Denemark, C.C.A.Ill., 138 F.2d 289, 291.

Old English law. A writ enclosing a record sent to be tried in a county palatine; it derives its name from the Latin word *mittimus*, "we send." It is the jury process of these counties, and commands the proper officer of the county palatine to command the sheriff to summon the jury for the trial of the cause, and to return the record, etc.

Mixed. Formed by admixture or commingling; partaking of the nature, character, or legal attributes of two or more distinct kinds or classes.

As to *mixed* Action; Blood relations *(Mixed blood)*; Contract; Government; Jury; Larceny; Marriage; Nuisance; Policy; Presumption; Property; Tithes; and War, see those titles.

Phrases, however, is that it is supplemented by pocket parts, easily allowing for the addition of new words that enter the legal field. *Black's* and *Ballentine's* are similar to other traditional dictionaries and are not supplemented on an annual basis.

Many legal dictionaries such as *Black's* publish an abridged softcover version at a moderate price. These dictionaries are excellent resources for beginning researchers.

A recent trend is publication of glossaries of legal terms on the Internet. For example, the Web site for "Court TV" offers a glossary of legal terms at http://courttv.com/glossary.html. The credibility of such Internet sources is debatable. As of the date of this text, such glossaries are not particularly comprehensive. They may, however, be helpful in providing you with a quick understanding of a legal term or Latin phrase.

C. Directories

1. *Introduction*

A directory is simply a list of lawyers. Some law directories, such as the extremely well-known and highly regarded *Martindale-Hubbell Law Directory*, aim at listing all lawyers admitted to all jurisdictions. Other directories are more limited in coverage and may list only lawyers in a particular geographic region or locality. Still other directories focus on law schools, law libraries, or courts. Law directories are usually kept in the reference section of a law library.

2. Martindale-Hubbell Law Directory

a. Overview of *Martindale-Hubbell*

The best known law directory in the United States is *Martindale-Hubbell Law Directory*, which has been in existence for more than a century. The initial goal of the directory was to publish an address for a lawyer, a banker, and a real estate office in every city in the United States. *Martindale-Hubbell* is currently published annually in hardbound volumes and is also available on CD-ROM. Additionally, the set is available online through LEXIS and on the Internet. (See Chapter 12.) The CD-ROM disks enable one to find attorneys solely by name without requiring the user to know the city in which the attorney practices. In fact, search criteria can be constructed so that you can readily locate an attorney who graduated from a specific school, such as Yale Law School, is fluent in French, and concentrates in the field of health law. The CD-ROM set costs approximately $1,000 and is updated quarterly. Finally, much of the information in *Martindale-Hubbell* is free on the World Wide Web (http://www.martindale.com).

There are more than 20 volumes in *Martindale-Hubbell*, arranged alphabetically by state. For instance, Volume 1 covers the states Alabama, Alaska, Arizona, and Arkansas. Within the listing for each state, cities are arranged alphabetically from Abbeville, Alabama, to Wetumpka, Alabama. Within each city, law firms and attorneys are arranged alphabetically as well. Thus, if you were interested in locating a firm in Minneapolis, Minnesota, to handle a transaction for you or to refer a case to, you could scan through the law firms located in Minneapolis and select a firm that you believe could best represent the client's interests. See Figure 7-2 for a sample page from the *Martindale-Hubbell Law Directory*.

Each firm that has an entry will list its attorneys and provide biographical information about them. The date of birth, colleges and universities attended, honors awarded, and articles authored by the attorneys in the firm are given. Moreover, the firm's address, phone number, Web site, a sample of its representative clients, and the areas in which it practices will be noted. By reviewing *Martindale-Hubbell* you may be able to select a firm that focuses on a particular practice area such as franchise law, securities litigation, or white-collar criminal defense. Law firms pay a fee for these biographical entries, and therefore not every firm or attorney may elect to participate.

On the other hand, the front of each volume of *Martindale-Hubbell* contains a list of all attorneys licensed to practice in the states covered by that volume. Attorneys are listed in this section free of charge, and the biographical information given is limited to name, address, education, date of bar admission, and the area of practice specialized in by the attorney. *Martindale-Hubbell* includes a rating of legal ability and a general recommendation rating for the attorneys listed. *Martindale-Hubbell* also lists corporate law departments by company name and indicates the city and state in which the corporate law department is located. In 1995, *Martindale-Hubbell* began assigning identification numbers to the more than 850,000 attorneys in its database, including former President Clinton and Chief Justice William Rehnquist. These universal numerical identifiers are designed to make it easier to track attorneys disciplined for misconduct.

These features of *Martindale-Hubbell* make it an excellent source of information for career opportunities. You should consider directing a resume to a law firm that focuses on an area of law in which you are interested. There is no point in applying for a position with a law firm that is exclusively engaged in bankruptcy work if you have no interest in this area of law. Similarly, before interviewing with a firm, always review *Martindale-Hubbell* to familiarize yourself with the firm's practice areas, its office locations in other cities, and the general profile of the firm.

Because many law firms now maintain sophisticated Web sites with biographies of their attorneys, some are reconsidering their decision to list with *Martindale-Hubbell*. For example, in early 2000, Chicago's Sidley & Austin, a mega-firm with more than 900 attorneys, decided not to list in *Martindale-Hubbell*, a savings of $110 per attorney per year. The firm decided that its Web site provided identical information and thus did not renew its *Martindale-Hubbell* listing.

Figure 7-2
Sample Page from *Martindale-Hubbell Law Directory*

TION: Insurance Law; Administrative Hearing and Appeals; Legislative Practice.

(Biographical data on Members of the Firm, Counsel, Of Counsel and Associates, in Washington, D.C.; Albany, New York; New York, New York; Boston, Massachusetts; Harrisburg, Pennsylvania; Hartford, Connecticut; Los Angeles, California; Salt Lake City, Utah; San Francisco, California; Jacksonville, Florida; Raleigh, North Carolina; London, England; Brussels, Belgium and Moscow, Russia are listed in the respective Biographical Sections)

LEVITAN AND FRIELAND

THE LEGAL CENTER, FIFTH FLOOR
ONE RIVER FRONT PLAZA
NEWARK, NEW JERSEY 07102
Telephone: 201-565-0011
Telecopier: 201-565-0451

New York, N.Y. Office: 600 Third Avenue, Seventeenth Floor. Telephone: 212-432-3800.

Areas of practice

General Civil Practice. Corporate, Commercial, Business, Equipment Leasing, Collection, Bankruptcy, Real Estate, Probate, Immigration, Matrimonial and Negligence Law. Trials and Appeals.

MEMBERS OF FIRM

PHILIP I. LEVITAN, born Brooklyn, New York, October 7, 1934; admitted to bar, 1959, New Jersey; 1966, U.S. Supreme Court; 1981, New York. *Education:* New York University (B.S., 1956; J.D., 1959). Tau Epsilon Phi. Editor of Commercial Law Issue, August, 1986. Real Estate Broker, New Jersey, 1959. Author: "Retail & Commercial Collections," New Jersey Lawyers, February, 1980; "Replevin," August, 1986. Acting Prosecutor, Attorney to Planning Board, Special Township Attorney for Township of Hillside, 1965-1969. Appointed to New Jersey Supreme Court Task Force on Small Claims, 1981. *Member:* Essex County (Secretary, 1974-1975; Chairman, Consumer Affairs Committee, 1975-1976), New Jersey State and American (Member, Committee on Commercial Transactions Litigation Section, 1981) Bar Associations; International Association of Jewish Lawyers and Jurists; Commercial Law League of America.

HARRY FRIELAND, born Newark, New Jersey, March 6, 1942; admitted to bar, 1966, New Jersey; 1966, U.S. District Court, District of New Jersey; 1972, New York; 1976, U.S. Supreme Court. *Education:* University of Pennsylvania (B.S., 1963); Rutgers University (LL.B., 1966). Phi Delta Phi. Author: "Tax Sales and Tax Sale Certificates The Unknown Wealth Builders," Tax Sales Certificates, Copyright, 1988 and 1989; "Mortgage Foreclosures-Are They Too Good To Be True?" November 1991; "Section 1031-How To Avoid Taxation of Gain From The Sale of Investment Real Estate," July 1991. *Member:* Essex County, New Jersey State, New York State and American Bar Associations; The American Judicature Society.

ASSOCIATE

DAVID GOODMAN, born Brooklyn, New York, January 31, 1954; admitted to bar, 1980, New Jersey and U.S. District Court, District of New Jersey; 1985, Israel. *Education:* University of Connecticut (B.A., 1975); Rutgers University (J.D., 1979). Phi Beta Kappa; Phi Kappa Phi. *Member:* Essex County Bar Association (Secretary, Board of Trustees, Legal Aid Association, 1986—); Israel Bar Association; American Immigration Lawyers Association. ***LANGUAGES:*** Hebrew.

Representative clients

REPRESENTATIVE CLIENTS: American Express; Chemical Bank; Midlantic Bank; Macy's; Saks Fifth Avenue; Bloomingdale's; Bergdorf Goodman; Nieman Marcus; Beneficial Finance Co.; Financial Collection Agencies; Norwest Financial Credit Corp.; Government Employees Financial Corp.; Citytrust; Fleet Financial; C.U.S., Inc.; Equitable Acceptance Corp.; Industrial Acceptance Corp.; Prudential Mortgagee Corp.; A-Leet Leasing Corp.; Motor Club of America Insurance Co.; Fairfield Lease Corp.; U-Vend, Inc.; Zenith Financial Corp.; Acron Corp.; Educational Industrial Facilities, Inc.; Nationwide Security Patrol Service; Paul Stuart; Crystal Geyser Water Co.; General Equipment Co.; International Vintners; National Publishing Service, Inc.; Big Apple Credit Corp.; Lord & Taylor; Unicyn Financial Corp.
REFERENCES: Midlantic National Bank; Broad National Bank; First Fidelity Bank, N.A.

LEVY, EHRLICH & KRONENBERG

A PROFESSIONAL CORPORATION
Established in 1955
60 PARK PLACE
NEWARK, NEW JERSEY 07102
Telephone: 201-643-0040
Telecopier: 201-596-1781

Tax, Probate and Trust, Business and Corporate Law, Litigation, Real Estate, Negligence and Matrimonial Law. Securities and Collection Law.

IRA A. LEVY, born Elizabeth, New Jersey, August 25, 1928; admitted to bar, 1953, District of Columbia; 1955, New Jersey; 1960, U.S. Supreme Court, U.S. Court of Military Appeals and U.S. District Court, District of New Jersey; 1965, U.S. Tax Court; 1974, New York; 1983, U.S. District Court, Southern District of New York. *Education:* Rutgers University; University of California at Los Angeles (B.A., 1950); Rutgers University (J.D., 1953); New York University (LL.M. in Taxation, 1960). Coordinating Editor, Rutgers University Law Review, 1952. Co-Author: "The Economic Recovery Tax Act of 1981," The Essex County Bar Association Chronicle, Vol. VIII, No. 3, Nov. 1981. *Member:* Essex County (Chairman, Taxation Committee, 1980-1982) and New Jersey State Bar Associations. ***CONCENTRATION:*** Tax; Corporate; Real Estate; Matrimonial.

ALAN EHRLICH, born Washington, D.C., February 6, 1949; admitted to bar, 1975, New Jersey and U.S. District Court, District of New Jersey; 1976, New York; 1977, District of Columbia; 1981, U.S. District Court, Southern District of New York; 1983, U.S. Tax Court. *Education:* Fairleigh Dickinson University (B.S., cum laude, 1971); New York Law School (J.D., 1975). Co-Author: "The Economic Recovery Tax Act of 1981," The Essex County Bar Association Chronicle, Vol. VIII, No. 3, Nov. 1981. Certified Public Accountant, New Jersey, 1973. *Member:* Essex County (Vice-Chairman, Taxation Committee, 1984-1985; Chairman, Taxation Committee, 1985-1986), New Jersey State and New York State Bar Associations; District of Columbia Bar; New Jersey Society of Certified Public Accountants. ***CONCENTRATION:*** Tax; Corporate; Probate.

ARTHUR KRONENBERG, born New York, N.Y., February 20, 1931; admitted to bar, 1957, New York; 1961, U.S. Supreme Court, U.S. Court of Appeals, Third Circuit and U.S. Tax Court; 1963, New Jersey. *Education:* New York University (B.A., 1953); Harvard University (J.D., 1957); New York University (LL.M., in Taxation, 1961). Member, Bergen County District IIA Ethics Committee, 1983-1987. *Member:* Bergen County and New Jersey State Bar Associations; Bergen County Estate Planning Council. ***CONCENTRATION:*** Tax; Corporate; Securities.

JOHN J. PETRIELLO, born Paterson, New Jersey, July 27, 1951; admitted to bar, 1978, New Jersey and U.S. District Court, District of New Jersey; 1980, New York; 1982, U.S. District Court, Southern and Eastern Districts of New York; 1988, U.S. Court of Appeals, Third Circuit and U.S. Tax Court. *Education:* Rutgers University (B.A., with distinction, 1973; J.D., 1977). ***CONCENTRATION:*** Litigation.

DAVID L. EISBROUCH, born Valley Stream, New York, February 18, 1960; admitted to bar, 1989, New Jersey and U.S. District Court, District of New Jersey. *Education:* University of Buffalo (B.S., 1982); Hofstra University School of Law (J.D., 1985). *Member:* New Jersey State and American Bar Associations; Commercial Law League of America. ***CONCENTRATION:*** Creditor's Rights; Collection Law.

JANET EDELMAN, born Brooklyn, New York, December 9, 1940; admitted to bar, 1976, New Jersey; 1977, New York. *Education:* Queens College of the City University of New York (B.A., 1961); Seton Hall University (J.D., cum laude, 1976). *Member:* New Jersey State Bar Association. ***CONCENTRATION:*** Real Estate.

BRUCE E. GUDIN, born Queens, New York, February 1, 1964; admitted to bar, 1989, New Jersey; 1990, New York. *Education:* Fairleigh Dickinson University; Long Island University, C.W. Post (B.S., magna cum laude, 1986); Benjamin N. Cardozo School of Law (J.D., 1989). Recipient, Wall Street Journal Award. *Member:* New York State, New Jersey State and American Bar Associations. ***CONCENTRATION:*** Litigation.

MINDY J. SHEPETIN, born Brooklyn, New York, January 2, 1960; admitted to bar, 1985, New York; 1988, New Jersey and U.S. District Court, District of New Jersey. *Education:* University of Maryland at College Park (B.A., 1981); Pace University School of Law (J.D., 1984). Phi Alpha Delta. *Member:* New York State and New Jersey State (Member, Young Lawyers

(This Listing Continued)

NJ361B

Most law firms maintain Web sites with biographies, photos of attorneys, office locations, descriptions of firm practice areas, summaries of recent "wins," and listings of articles written by attorneys in the firm. Thus, these Web sites provide more information than is available in *Martindale-Hubbell* and can be readily updated as attorneys leave or join a firm.

b. *Martindale-Hubbell* Law Digest Volumes

In addition to *Martindale-Hubbell's* directory list of lawyers, the set contains numerous other features that make it a useful and practical research tool.

(1) State Digests

Martindale-Hubbell contains two volumes providing a brief overview of some of the laws of all 50 states, the District of Columbia, Puerto Rico, and the Virgin Islands. While *Martindale-Hubbell* will not provide all of the laws of these jurisdictions, it will provide a summary of some of the more common laws of each state together with references to pertinent state statutes. For example, you will be able to determine the fees for creating a limited partnership in a state, how many individuals are needed to witness execution of a will, residency requirements to obtain a divorce, information relating to discovery in litigation actions, what the statute of limitations is for personal injury actions, and other items of information commonly needed. Thus, if a client is interested in incorporating a business in another state and you do not have ready access to that state's code, *Martindale-Hubbell's* Law Digest volumes will provide you with a concise summary of the corporate laws for that state. Moreover, these Law Digest volumes will provide you with forms for documents and instruments commonly used by a certain state, such as a form for acknowledging the veracity of an instrument. See Figure 7-3 for a sample page from the Law Digest volume of *Martindale-Hubbell* for Wisconsin.

(2) International Law Directory

The print version of *Martindale-Hubbell* includes three volumes referred to as the International Law Directory. Volumes I and II contain profiles of lawyers and law firms from more than 160 countries, organized alphabetically within major geographic regions. Volume 1 covers Europe, Asia, Australasia, the Middle East, and Africa. Volume 2 covers North America, the Caribbean, and Central and South America. Volume 3 is an index. Another volume provides summaries or digests of the laws of more than 80 countries, such as Canada, El Salvador, Japan, and Saudi Arabia. Once again, all of the laws of a foreign country will not be provided but rather only those laws that are most likely to be needed by practitioners. Descriptions of the organization of the government and legal systems are also given. See Figure 7-4 for a sample page from the *Mexico Law Digest*.

Figure 7-3
Sample Page from *Martindale-Hubbell Law Digest*

Ref. to page 24 of *Wisconsin Law Digest*

WI - 24 MARTINDALE-HUBBELL LAW DIGEST

DEPOSITIONS AND DISCOVERY . . . *continued*
pleading; (3) court deems cause sufficient; (4) when required for use on any hearing. Commission must be signed and sealed by clerk. (887.26).

Compelling Attendance of Witnesses.—Nonparty deponent served by subpoena within state and party served with notice may be compelled to give deposition within 100 miles of residence, place of employment, or where nonparty deponent transacts business or at any other place fixed by court order. Plaintiff may also be compelled to give deposition in county of state where action is commenced or is pending. Nonresident defendant may be compelled by subpoena to give deposition in any Wis. county in which he is personally served. (804.05[3]). Witness fees: $5 per day before municipal judge, arbitrator, or any officer, board or committee, $16 per day before any other court and 20¢ per mile travel expense. (814.67).

Examination of Witnesses.—Examination and cross-examination of deponents proceeds as permitted at trial. (804.05[4]). However, it is not grounds for objection that testimony will be inadmissible at trial if testimony appears reasonably calculated to lead to discovery of admissible evidence. (804.01[2]).

Errors in notice for taking of deposition are waived unless written objection promptly served upon party giving notice. Objection to taking of deposition because of disqualification of officer before whom it is to be taken is waived unless made before taking of deposition begins or as soon thereafter as disqualification becomes known or could be discovered through reasonable diligence. (804.07[3]). Objections to competency of witness or to competency, relevancy or materiality of testimony are not waived by failure to make them before or during taking of deposition, unless ground of objection might have been obviated or removed if presented at that time. Similar rule applies as to errors or irregularities occurring in manner of taking deposition, in form of questions or answers, in oath or affirmation, or in conduct of parties and errors of any kind which might be obviated if objection were seasonably made. Errors and irregularities as to completion and return of deposition are waived unless motion to suppress is made with reasonable promptness. (804.07[3]).

Return.—Person recording testimony must certify on deposition that witness was duly sworn by him and that deposition is true record of testimony given by deponent, must then securely seal deposition in envelope endorsed with title of action and marked "Deposition of (here insert name of deponent)" and must promptly serve it upon attorney requesting deposition or send it by registered or certified mail to attorney requesting deposition and give notice of service to all parties and court. (804.05[7]).

Production of Documents and Things.—Any party may serve on any other party request to produce any designated documents for inspection and copying or to inspect any tangible things or to enter land or other property for inspection, provided matter sought to be inspected is within scope of 804.01(2). Party upon whom request is served must respond within 30 days of service. (804.09).

Interrogatories.—Any party can serve on any other party written interrogatories, which, unless objected to, must be answered fully under oath within 30 days. Interrogatories may relate to any matter within scope of 804.01(2). When answer to interrogatory can be ascertained from business records and burden of ascertaining answer is same for either party, it is sufficient to specify appropriate records and provide opportunity for inspection and copying. (804.08).

Physical and Mental Examination.—Upon motion by party court can order party whose physical or mental condition is at issue to undergo physical or mental examination. (804.10[1]). In personal injury actions, court may also order claimant to permit any party to inspect X-rays taken in course of treatment or diagnosis and any hospital, medical or other records concerning claimed injuries. (804.10[2]). Evidence obtained pursuant to 804.10 is only admissible if five copies of reports of examination are provided to other party within ten days of receipt. (804.10[3]).

Admissions.—Party may serve on any other party written request for admission of truth of any discoverable matter. Matter is admitted unless answer or objection is served within 30 days of service of request. Matter admitted is conclusively established unless court permits withdrawal or amendment. (804.11). If party fails to admit matter which is subsequently established, requesting party may recover reasonable cost of establishing matter, including attorney's fees. (804.12[3]).

Discovery Sanctions.—Variety of sanctions, including order compelling discovery, order deeming certain factual matters established, striking claim for defenses, dismissal of action, and default judgment, are available under certain conditions for failure to comply with discovery rule. (804.12).

DESCENT AND DISTRIBUTION:

Real Estate.—All property descends as follows: (1) Spouse takes entire estate if no surviving issue, or if surviving issue are all issue of surviving spouse and decedent; if there are surviving issue any one of whom are not issue of surviving spouse, spouse takes one-half of decedent's estate not disposed of by will consisting of decedent's property other than marital property; (2) issue take share of estate not passing to spouse or entire estate if there is no surviving spouse; issue in same degree of kinship take equally but if they are of unequal degree then take by representation; (3) if there is no surviving spouse or issue, property descends as follows: (a) parents or surviving parent; (b) brothers and sisters, descendants of deceased brothers and sisters taking by representation; (c) grandparents; (d) next of kin of equal degree. If potential heir dies within 72 hours of death of decedent, property of decedent passes as if person had predeceased decedent. (852.01). Interest in home is assigned to surviving spouse as part of his or her share unless surviving spouse requests otherwise. (852.09). Person to whom property would otherwise pass may disclaim all or part of property by filing signed declaration of disclaimer with court and serving copy on personal representative or holder of legal title to property within nine months after date of decedent's death. (852.13; 853.40).

Degrees of kindred are computed according to the rules of the civil law. (852.03[2]).

Surviving spouse takes as indicated in subhead Real Estate, supra.

Half Blood.—Kindred of half blood inherit equally with whole blood. (852.03[3]).

Posthumous persons may be heirs if conceived before decedent's death. (852.03[4]).

Nonmarital child inherits from and through mother and also from person who has been adjudged to be father or has admitted in open court or in writing signed by him that he is father. (852.05[1]). If nonmarital child dies intestate without surviving spouse or issue, estate descends as provided in 852.01 except that father and his kindred can inherit only if father has been adjudicated to be father. (852.05[2]).

Adopted Children.—See topic Adoption.

Determination of Heirship.—Upon petition to probate court six years or more after death of intestate, descent of property may be determined. (867.05).

Advancements to an heir are considered as a part of estate of intestate so far as it regards division and distribution among issue and must be taken as part of his share of estate. (852.11). Gift by decedent during life is advancement only if there is writing by decedent so stating or if heir states in court or in writing that gift was advance. If any prospective heir so advanced dies before intestate, leaving issue, advancement is taken into consideration in division and distribution of estate and amount allowed to issue of heir so advanced in like manner as if advancement had been made directly to them. (852.11).

Election.—See topic Wills.

Escheat.—See topics Absentees, subhead Escheat: Banks and Banking, subhead Unclaimed Deposits: Wills, subhead Unclaimed Legacies.

Renunciation.—Heir can disclaim in writing within nine months after decedent's death. (852.13; 853.40).

DESERTION: See topic Husband and Wife.

DISSOLUTION OF MARRIAGE: See topic Divorce.

DIVORCE:

Grounds for Absolute Divorce.—This subject governed by 767.001 et seq. Grounds for divorce exist if marriage is irretrievably broken. Marriage is irretrievably broken if: (1) Both parties by petition or otherwise under oath or affirmation so state; (2) one party so states and parties have voluntarily lived apart continuously for at least one year prior to commencement of action; or (3) if only one party so states and parties have not voluntarily lived apart one year, court either finds no prospect of reconciliation or, after court finds prospect of reconciliation and adjourns hearing, at adjourned hearin[illegible]der oath or affirmation that marriage is irretrievably broke[illegible] (767.07; 767.12[2]).

Grou[illegible]ation.—Grounds for legal separation exist if marriage is irretrievably broken (767.07; 767.12[2]), or if both parties by petition or otherwise state under oath or affirmation that marital relationship is broken (767.12[3]).

Citizenship Requirements.—None.

Residence Requirements.—Either party must have been bona fide resident of state for at least six months and of county in which action is brought for at least 30 days prior to commencement of action for divorce. (767.05[1m]).

Jurisdiction.—Circuit Courts have jurisdiction. (767.01).

Venue.—See topic Venue.

Process.—If one party initiates action, service of summons accomplished as in civil actions. If both parties initiate action, service of summons not required. (767.05[1]; 767.085[3]). See topic Process.

Pleading.—Action is initiated by petitioner or joint petitioners. Responding party is respondent. (767.05[3]). Petition is entitled "In re the marriage of A.B. and C.D." (767.05[5]). Petition must state name, birthdate, and social security number of parties, occupations, date and place of marriage, facts relating to residence of parties, name and birthdate of minor children of parties and other children born to wife during marriage, whether wife is pregnant, if petition not filed under 767.12(3), that marriage is irretrievably broken, or, alternatively, that both parties agree it is irretrievably broken, whether action for divorce or legal separation was ever commenced by either party or is pending, whether either party was previously married, manner in which prior marriage terminated, and if terminated by court judgment, name of court and time and place of judgment, whether parties have entered into any written agreements as to support, custody, visitation of children, maintenance and property division (attach copy of agreement to petition), relief requested and, whenever petition requests order affecting minor children, request that Department of Health and Social Services provide services on behalf of minor children. (767.085[1]). If legal separation requested, petition must state specific reason for request (767.085[1][f]), and if petition filed under 767.12(3) petition must state that both parties agree marital relationship is broken (767.085[1][cm]). Commencement of action affecting minor child constitutes application to Department of Health and Social Services for services on behalf of child. (767.02[3]).

Practice.—All hearings and trials to determine whether judgment shall be granted are before court, except may be before court commissioner when both parties state that marriage is irretrievably broken and that all material issues are resolved or when one party does not participate. (767.12[1]; 767.13[5][a]). Unless nonresidence in state shown by competent evidence, or service is by publication, or court otherwise orders, both parties must appear at trial. Order to that effect must be procured and served by moving party on nonmoving party before trial. (767.125). Each party must, within 20 days after service on other party of petition or pleading or before filing same in court, serve copy on Family Court Commissioner. Commissioner may appear when appropriate and must appear when requested by court (767.14). Commissioner must inform parties of availability of counseling services. (767.081). If both parties agree, court may suspend action for 90 days for reconciliation. (767.082).

Judgment.—Judgment of divorce is effective immediately. Neither party may remarry for six months. (767.37[3]; 765.03[2]).

Overview of divorce laws in Wisconsin with references to Wisconsin statutes

See note at head of Digest as to 1992 legislation covered.

See Topical Index in front part of this volume.

Figure 7-4
Sample Page from Law Digest Volume of *Martindale-Hubbell*

MEXICO LAW DIGEST

Revised for 1992 edition by

CURTIS, MALLET-PREVOST, COLT & MOSLE, of the New York Bar.

(Abbreviations used are: C. C., Civil Code of Federal District; Com. C., Commercial Code; C. C. P., Code of Civil Procedure of Federal District. References are to articles of these Codes. See also topic Statutes.)

ABSENTEES: See topic Death.

ACKNOWLEDGMENTS:

Certificates of acknowledgment are unknown in Mexican law, since all documents which in the United States would ordinarily require a certificate of acknowledgment are executed before a notary public who certifies in the instrument itself to the facts which, in the United States, are usually expressed in a certificate of acknowledgment.

Documents executed in the United States should be acknowledged in the usual manner if they are to be used in Mexico. A certificate of the county clerk or other competent official as to the power of the notary to take the acknowledgment should be attached and a certificate of a Mexican consular or diplomatic officer should then be obtained to the effect that the signature of the county clerk or other official is authentic and that he is qualified to act. When the Minister of Foreign Relations of Mexico has attached a certificate regarding the qualifications of the consular or diplomatic officer the document may be recorded in the protocol of a Mexican notary by order of a competent court and is then duly recognized.

ACTIONS:

Actions for Death.—See topic Death, subhead Actions for Death.

Limitation of.—See Prescription.

ADMINISTRATION:

See Executors and Administrators.

ADOPTION:

A person over 25 years of age, free of marriage, and in full exercise of his civil rights may adopt one or more minors or an incapacitated minor or adult; in any case adopting party must be 17 years older than adopted. Individual exercising actual "Patria Potestad" must give his/her consent. Adopting party must prove: (a) Sufficient means to support them; (b) that adoption is beneficial to them; and (c) that he is person of good morals. Adopted party shall have rights and obligations of son. Husband and wife may also adopt when both agree to consider adopted as their own children, and when they are 17 years older than adopted. Adopted persons may use name of adopting party. Adoption can be revoked: (a) When both parties agree to do so, if adopted is over 18 years of age, and (b) in case of ingratitude of adopted. Ingratitude is deemed to exist when: (a) adopted commits intentional crime against adopting party or his family, or (b) if adopted brings criminal action against adopting party. (C. C. 390-410).

ADVERSE POSSESSION: See Prescription.

AGENCY: See Principal and Agent.

ALIENS:

According to Constitution of 1917 aliens have same individual guaranties as citizens. Guaranties are elaborately defined.

Aliens may not intervene in politics, and Federal Executive may require any alien to leave the country immediately and without trial in case his presence in Mexico is deemed undesirable. (Const., art. 33). Ministry of any cult may be exercised only by native Mexicans. (Const., art. 130). Practice of professions is restricted to Mexican citizens by Law of Professions (May 26, 1945; Regulations of Sept. 27, 1945) but not by Constitution. Amparo suit may be filed against law of professions in order to practice. Marriage in Mexico of aliens to Mexicans must be authorized by Department of Interior. Marriage and divorce must be authorized by Ministry of Interior. Entry of aliens is governed by General Law of Population of Dec. 11, 1973, am'd by Decree of Dec. 29 of 1974 and its Regulations of Nov. 12, 1976 as am'd.

Naturalization is governed by Nationality and Naturalization Law of Jan. 20, 1934, as am'd.

Rights of aliens in lands agd waters are governed by art. 27 of Constitution and by law of Dec. 31, 1925, and regulations thereof dated Mar. 22, 1926, as am'd Aug. 1, 1939. Only Mexicans and Mexican companies may acquire ownership of lands, waters and their appurtenances, or obtain concessions to develop mines or waters. State may grant same right to aliens, provided they agree before Ministry of Foreign Relations to be considered Mexicans in respect to such property and not to invoke protection of their governments in respect thereto, under penalty of forfeiture of property to nation. No alien may under any conditions acquire direct ownership of lands or waters within a zone 100 kilometers wide along frontiers and 50 kilometers wide along coasts, nor be a member of a Mexican company acquiring such ownership within these zones. Foreigners may acquire use of property in said zone through trust as beneficiaries only. In order to hold interest in Mexican company owning lands, waters and their appurtenances, or concessions to develop mines or waters within Republic, alien must make above mentioned agreement before Ministry of Foreign Relations with respect to his interest. Ministry will not grant permission to alien if result would be to give aliens total interest of over 50% in company holding property for agricultural purposes. Aliens holding 50% or more of capital of any companies owning properties for agricultural purposes prior to Dec. 31, 1925, may retain their interests until their death, in case of physical persons, or for ten years, in case of legal entities. Provisions do not apply to colonization contracts made with Federal Government prior to operation of this law. Rights legally acquired by aliens prior to this law may be held by them until their death. Should alien acquire by inheritance rights, acquisition prohibited to aliens, Ministry of Foreign Relations will grant permit for acquisition and for registration of corresponding deed. Office of Foreign Relations may also permit alien to hold property, acquisition of which is prohibited by law, if property was acquired in good faith prior to date of law. In both of foregoing cases permission will be granted on condition that rights be disposed of within five years to person authorized to acquire them. Aliens who acquired rights enumerated in this law before law took effect were required to make statement of rights to Ministry of Foreign Relations prior to Jan. 21, 1927, in default of which property is considered to have been acquired after law took effect.

Employment of Aliens.—(Labor Law, effective May 1, 1970). Objective is to obtain equilibrium and social justice in labor-management relations; to work is both right and social obligation. These concepts are to be considered in interpreting law, and in case of doubt, interpretation most favorable to worker takes preference. In every enterprise or business at least 90% of workers must be Mexican. Technical and professional employments requiring special skills not available in country may be filled temporarily by foreign workers, but these may not be more than 10% of total number of workers engaged in each specialization area. Employer and foreign workers must be jointly responsible for training Mexican workers. Doctors on duty in factories or enterprises must be Mexicans. Provisions shall not be applicable to directors, administrators and/or general managers. Employment of aliens for maritime industries is prohibited.

See also topic Corporations, subhead Property.

Legal Rights for Foreigners to Reside in Mexico.—Under Mexican Constitution and laws enacted in accordance with it, every person is accorded right to enter and depart from Mexico, to travel in its territory, and to make changes of residence without need for authorization or documentation of any kind.

In practice, however, exercise of these rights is subordinated to limitations imposed by immigration, population, and public health laws of Republic as well as to authority of Federal Executive summarily to ban or eject from country any foreigner whom government considers to be "persona non grata".

Art. 1 of Constitution of the United Mexican States provides that every person shall enjoy guarantees granted by that instrument; and principle of equality between nations—between Mexican and foreigners—is recognized in specific legislation.

Principle of equality between nationals and foreigners is subject to restrictions and limitations imposed by Constitution, regulatory laws that implement Constitution, and other legislation.

Migration to Mexico or entry for any purpose other than tourism is fraught with restrictions arising from statutes, administrative regulations, and internal policy. Latter, as fixed by Secretariat of Interior (Secretaria de Gobernación), General Bureau of Population (Direccion General de Población), and Department of Immigration (Departamento de Migración), is not always written.

Mexican Immigration Code is Federal in nature, administered and enforced through Secretariat of Interior (Gobernación), which also is charged with responsibility for civil peace and tranquility of nation.

Another important power relating to foreigners stems from Art. 33 of Constitution under which President of United Mexican States is clothed with exclusive authority to deport summarjly any alien from national territory without hearing if in judgment of Federal Executive his presence in Mexico is deemed disadvantageous ("inconveniente") for nation. Mexico's Supreme Court has ruled—and after five like decisions by Supreme Court on same point of law it becomes jurisprudence and therefore mandatory on lower courts—that President may act without alien having been granted hearing or without any finding of fact to support his decision.

In contrast Ministry of Interior in moving to expel alien must act on finding of fact and one that falls within causes for expulsion set out in General Law of Population (Ley General de Población). These are that alien has entered country illegally, hidden his previous expulsion (if any); failed to obey previous order from Ministry to leave country; committed illicit or dishonest act; concealed or been accomplice to concealment of alien who has committed any of previously described acts; claimed immigration status different from that actually possessed; or made false declaration in order to enter or remain in Mexico.

Immigration Categories.—Fact that alien is subject to these administrative proceedings points to differences between status of foreigner and that of citizen.

Foreigners are divided into three broad categories for purposes of immigration and according to which documentation is issued to them to legalize their presence in country. Each of these categories is further divided into sub-categories of immigration status.

General Law of Population establishes three general categories under which aliens may enter Mexico temporarily, or reside here as case may be, namely: (a) Nonimmigrant ("no-inmigrante"), (b) immigrant ("inmigrante"), and (c) one who has immigrated ("inmigrado").

Letters and numbers following Spanish designation of each sub-category is pertinent form number used to document status.

Nonimmigrant Status ("No-Inmigrante").—Nine sub-categories included under this general heading are following:

1. Tourist ("Turista" F.M.T.) status is extended to individual who comes to Mexico for pleasure, recreation or health or for activities of scientific, or artistic nature or to participate in sports. Amateur athletes are usually documented as tourists. No person so documented may be remunerated from or by source in Mexico. Maximum life of tourist permit is 180 days.

See Topical Index in front part of this volume.

(3) International Conventions

Martindale-Hubbell also provides the text of several international conventions or treaties to which the United States is a party, such as the United Nations Convention on Contracts for the International Sale of Goods, the Convention on the Civil Aspects of International Child Abduction, and the Convention on the Taking of Evidence Abroad in Civil or Commercial Matters.

(4) Uniform Acts, Rules, and Court Information

The complete text of some of the better known Uniform Acts is also provided, including the Uniform Commercial Code, the Uniform Arbitration Act, and the Uniform Probate Code.

Finally, *Martindale-Hubbell* contains the Model Rules of Professional Conduct of the American Bar Association and the Code of Judicial Conduct.

3. Local Directories

Directories may be available for a particular region or locality. For example, some local bar associations may publish a booklet listing members of the association. Other local directories may be published by private publishers. An example of a local directory is the "District of Columbia Bar's Lawyer Directory." Some local directories provide only the attorney's name, address, and telephone number, while others may provide brief biographical sketches and even photographs of the lawyers listed in the directory.

4. Specialized Directories

A number of directories provide lists of attorneys who concentrate in specialized practice areas or contain information relating to a certain specialized topic. Examples include the following:

Directory of Entertainment and Sports Attorneys (a guide for locating attorneys specializing in the areas of entertainment and sports).

Directory of Corporate Counsel (a directory of personnel of the law departments of corporations, both for-profit and not-for-profit, in the United States).

The Federal Legal Directory (a guide to the legal offices and key personnel of the United States government).

Want's Federal-State Court Directory (a directory of general information about federal and state courts).

American Association of Law Libraries Directory and Handbook (a directory of information about American law libraries).

5. *Internet Directories*

Much of the information found in the conventional hardbound print volumes of *Martindale-Hubbell* can also be located through the Internet at its site "Martindale-Hubbell Lawyer Locator" at http://www.martindale.com/locator/home.html. The site provides free access to comprehensive listings of 900,000 lawyers and law firms around the world. Searching is easily accomplished by selecting a practice area, city, or state.

Other free legal directories also exist on the Internet. For example, "*Law*Office.com" is offered at http://www.lawoffice.com by West Group. The site provides basic legal information on hundreds of legal topics and a searchable directory of more than 1 million lawyers and law firms, including international counsel, corporate counsel, and government attorneys.

D. Form Books

1. *Introduction*

One of the typical tasks performed by paralegals is drafting legal documents. Some of the documents may be for use in litigation, such as forms for complaints, answers, notices of depositions, or interrogatories. Other forms may relate to transactional aspects of law practice, such as leases, partnership agreements, or corporate bylaws. Seldom, if ever, do attorneys or paralegals draft documents "from scratch." Generally they rely on forms or models, which have proven useful in other instances.

If you are asked to draft a legal document, there are several alternatives you can pursue. The office you work in may have a central form file, which contains forms for commonly used documents. In such a case you would review the form provided and modify it to suit your needs. Alternatively, you can ask another paralegal, a secretary, or an attorney if any individual client files might have a comparable form you can use as a guide. If these strategies are not helpful, you can consult a form book (sometimes called a "practice set").

A form book is a single volume or, more typically, a multi-volume set that contains forms for use in the legal profession. Some sets of form books contain forms that can be used in any aspect of legal practice and include litigation forms as well as forms used in practice areas not related to litigation. Other books provide forms related solely to one state or to one area of the law. An example of such a specialized set of form books is *Murphy's Will Clauses*, a multi-volume set containing numerous forms used in connection with drafting wills.

2. *Well-Known Form Books*

Some of the better known sets of form books are as follows:

American Jurisprudence Legal Forms 2d. This set consists of more than 25 alphabetically arranged volumes of forms and provides forms for contracts, wills, and leases as well as for hundreds of other topics.

American Jurisprudence Pleading and Practice Forms, Revised. This set consists of more than 30 volumes of forms and provides more than 36,000 forms relating to litigation, such as forms for complaints, answers, discovery procedures, motions for change of venue, motions for new trial, and appeals.

Bender's Federal Practice Forms. This more-than-15-volume set also contains forms for use in federal practice.

Current Legal Forms with Tax Analysis by Rabkin and Johnson is a multi-volume set of forms for general law practice.

Federal Procedural Forms, Lawyers Edition. This set consists of more than 25 volumes and provides forms for use in federal practice.

Forms of Discovery by Matthew Bender is a multi-volume set of forms related solely to discovery matters such as interrogatories, depositions, requests for production and inspection, and medical discovery.

West's Legal Forms 2d. This set of books, consisting of more than 30 volumes, contains a variety of forms for general law practice, such as bankruptcy forms, forms for purchase and sale of real estate, and forms relating to business organizations, including partnerships and corporations.

Some publishers have produced sets of form books devoted strictly to forms for use in that state. For example, a set commonly used in California for business or transactional matters is Matthew Bender's *California Legal Forms: Transaction Guide.* If your state does not have a set of books containing forms specifically tailored for your state, use one of the "general" sets of form books, such as *West's Legal Forms, 2d* or *Am. Jur. Legal Forms 2d*, which are designed to provide forms for use in any state. You may also encounter a set of form books for one specific legal topic, such as trademark forms, bankruptcy forms, and so forth.

There are two recent form books prepared strictly for paralegals: *Paralegal Preparation of Pleadings* by Cynthia B. Monteiro, which contains more than 100 forms for use in litigation, and *Paralegal Litigation: Forms and Procedures* by Marcy B. Fawcett, which includes more than 60 forms, checklists, and procedures for drafting litigation documents.

Another source of forms is treatises, which often contain sample documents and forms. For example, one of the best known treatises on bankruptcy, *Collier on Bankruptcy*, contains forms to complete its thorough analysis of bankruptcy practice. Additionally, the Law Digest volumes of *Martindale-Hubbell* contain some forms for use in various states. Finally, some state annotated codes contain forms. See Figure 7-5 for samples of forms.

The Internet offers thousands of legal forms. As with many offerings on the Internet, however, it is unknown who authored the forms or whether they have been subjected to the rigorous checking and editing that accompanies print publications. Thus, they should be used with extreme caution. Such forms may nevertheless provide a useful starting place. References to Internet sites offering forms are provided at the end of this chapter.

Some states now offer various forms on their official Web sites. For example, all states now provide comprehensive forms banks for organizing, maintaining, and dissolving business entities (such as corporations, limited partnerships, and limited liability companies). The forms can be downloaded and printed for free and are generally available on the home page for the state's secretary of state.

3. *Locating Form Books*

To locate form books, check the card catalog in your law library, browse the shelves, or consult your law librarian. Often form books are located near other related books. For example, the books containing forms related to federal practice are usually found near the sets of books containing federal cases. Similarly, sets of books containing forms for use in criminal law practice are often located in the "criminal law" section of the law library or the stack that also contains treatises on criminal law and case books devoted solely to criminal law cases. Thus, the easiest way to locate form books is often to browse the stacks devoted to a certain legal topic.

4. *Research Strategies*

When you have located a set of form books that is pertinent to the legal issue you are researching, you can locate the form you need by either the descriptive word approach or the topic approach.

To use the descriptive word approach, locate the index to the set, generally found in the last volume of the set. The index is alphabetically arranged. You should look up words or phrases that describe or relate to the form you are drafting (contract, trust, complaint, bylaws, venue) and you will then be directed to the appropriate volume and page for the form you need.

To use the topic approach, scan the chapter headings and subheadings in the set. You can then examine the particular form that seems most appropriate.

One of the useful features of many form books is that they are annotated. This means that you will be referred to cases that have approved

Figure 7-5
Sample Page from *West's Federal Forms*

VI. PERMISSIVE JOINDER WHERE CLAIMS BASED ON SAME TRANSACTION AND COMMON QUESTIONS OF LAW OR FACT INVOLVED

Library References:

C.J.S. Federal Civil Procedure §§ 94 et seq., 113–118.
West's Key No. Digests, Federal Civil Procedure ⇐241 et seq.

§ 2911. Complaint Joining Several Plaintiffs Asserting Rights to Relief Severally Arising Out of Automobile Collision

[F.R.C.P. Rule 20(a)]

[*Title of Court and Cause*]

First Count

1. [*Allegation of jurisdiction.*]

2. Plaintiff L_______, who was duly appointed administrator ad prosequendum of the Estate of E_______ and the Estate of A_______, both deceased, by the _______ of the County of _______ and qualified as such pursuant to statute, for the benefit of the parents and next of kin of E_______, and of A_______, both deceased, brings this action and alleges:

3. On [*date*], E_______, deceased, A_______, deceased, and the plaintiff F_______ were passengers in an automobile which was proceeding in a westerly direction upon and along _______ Road and came to a stop at _______ Street, both being public highways in the Town of _______, County of _______ and State of _______.

4. At the same time and place the defendant R_______ was operating a truck and trailer in a westerly direction upon and along _______ Road.

5. The defendant R_______ negligently, carelessly and improperly maintained, drove, operated and controlled the truck and trailer into and against the automobile in which E_______, A_______ and F_______ were passengers.

6. As a result E_______ suffered serious bodily injuries from which she died.

7. The plaintiff's intestate, E_______, left surviving her as next of kin _______, all of whom suffered pecuniary loss and injuries because of her death.

Wherefore plaintiff L_______ as administrator ad prosequendum of the Estate of E_______, deceased, demands judgment

171

Figure 7-5 (*Continued*)
Sample Page from *Fletcher Corporate Forms Annotated*

§ 3276.4. Resolution of directors authorizing any two officers to borrow money for corporation.

Resolved that until otherwise ordered by the board of directors any two officers of the company be and they hereby are authorized to borrow money for the account of this company from ——— or ——— or both of them, and for that purpose and as evidence thereof to execute and deliver all necessary promissory notes or other obligations of this company including but without limitation, judgment notes, payable on demand or otherwise and at a rate of interest not exceeding ———% per annum, and as security for the payment thereof to pledge, assign, mortgage or grant a security interest in any property including, but not limited to, real estate, stocks, bonds or other securities, accounts receivable, chattels, or inventories of the company, and to execute and deliver all agreements or instruments necessary therefor; provided, however, that neither ——— nor ——— shall as an officer of the company execute or deliver any instrument creating any indebtedness of the company hereunder, or securing the payment thereof with respect to any particular borrowing wherein he is the lender.

Further resolved that any such borrowing or borrowings made, or any such indebtedness, incurred, on or about ———, 19—, is hereby ratified, approved and confirmed.[1]

[1] In re Trimble Co., 479 F2d 103 (parties specified were majority stockholders whose "loans" were construed as contributions to capital).

§ 3277. Resolution of stockholders authorizing borrowing of money, etc.

Resolved, that the president and treasurer of this company be, and they are hereby, authorized and directed to borrow for the use and benefit of this corporation, ——— dollars, and to cause to be duly executed and delivered to the person or persons loaning the said ——— dollars, the bonds of this company of the par value of ——— dollars, payable ——— years after date, and redeemable at any time after ——— years from date at the pleasure of this company, with interest at ——— percent per annum, payable semiannually, the money so borrowed to be applied as follows: ———.

337

or supported language used in the form. Moreover, many form books provide analysis and commentary on use of the forms and practical aids such as checklists, providing items to consider in drafting a certain type of form.

Most form books are kept current by pocket parts. Therefore, after reviewing a form, check the pocket part to determine if language used in the form has been revised or if new annotations and comment have been provided.

One of the recent developments in form books is for the publisher to put the forms on disk for use with various software programs. For example, a recent set published by Bancroft-Whitney and titled *California Civil Practice* not only contains forms arranged by topic but provides disks containing the forms for use with the software program WordPerfect, allowing you to download forms to your word processor for customizing and to print or copy forms with a simple keystroke. Disks are usually updated annually.

5. *Summary*

Form books provide an excellent starting point for drafting legal documents. You should not view drafting documents as merely an exercise in finding a form and then "filling in the blanks." Carefully review the form to ensure it is appropriate for the document you need to prepare. Feel free to revise the form to make it fit your purposes so long as these revisions are consistent with the law in your jurisdiction. Often you may combine features or elements of several forms to create the best document. Be alert to forms prepared by others in your office as well as other firms and start collecting your own set of forms of documents and pleadings you believe are well drafted and effective. In sum, exercise discretion in using form books. "Cut and paste" until you have a form that is best suited to your needs.

E. Uniform Laws

1. *Introduction*

You have seen that the Restatements were produced as a result of concern by legal scholars that case law was overly complex and uncertain. At about the same time that the American Law Institute (the "Institute") was formed to produce the Restatements, legal scholars became concerned over the great disparity in state statutes on areas of the law that could be treated similarly or uniformly among the states.

The result of this concern was the formation of the National Conference of Commissioners on Uniform State Laws in 1892. The Conference is composed of more than 300 practicing attorneys, judges, law professors, and other legal scholars who are usually appointed by the governor of each state and meet on an annual basis to draft proposed legislation on various areas of the law. These proposed laws, which are the result of considerable time and effort, are then presented to the legislatures of the 50 states with the hope and expectation that the state legislature will pass the Conference's version of the law on that particular legal topic. The Conference can only propose uniform laws. No Uniform Law is effective until a state legislature specifically enacts it.

For example, after studying statutes relating to partnerships from various states, the Conference drafted its proposed set of partnership statutes, titled the Uniform Partnership Act, and began persuading the various state legislatures in the 50 states to adopt the Uniform Partnership Act in place of their divergent partnership statutes. Once a state adopts a Uniform Law, it is then a primary authority in that state. Until they are adopted, however, Uniform Laws have no such legal effect and thus assume the characteristics of secondary authority. Once adopted, a Uniform Law is published in the state's annotated codes together with other statutes in that state. After printing the text of the Uniform Law, the state code will usually provide you with the text of the Conference's comments about the law and with an explanation as to how the state version of the Uniform Law differs from the original version drafted by the Conference. Cases interpreting the Uniform Law will follow.

Some states, after holding hearings, debates, and other legislative proceedings, just as for any other state law, will adopt the uniform act "as is." Other states may reject the act, while others may revise the act, adding certain provisions and omitting others. Thus, while the goal of the Conference is to produce a statute that will be uniform from state to state, the end result is a statute that nearly always has some variation from state to state. Nevertheless, many of an act's provisions will be retained intact or with only minor revisions so there will be resulting overall uniformity among the states that adopt a uniform act.

The Conference has approved more than 200 uniform laws, ranging from perhaps the best known, the Uniform Commercial Code (relating to commercial practices and sales), which took ten years to complete and has been adopted by every state but Louisiana, to the Uniform Adoption Act, to the Uniform Brain Death Act.

The Conference also drafts proposed legislation known as "Model Acts." While a Uniform Law is one whose adoption is urged in every state by the Conference, a Model Act is one for which uniformity among the states is not as necessary or desirable. An example is the Model Penal Code. Typically, the way crimes are defined and the punishments for committing a crime are matters of greatest concern to the jurisdiction within whose borders the crime was committed. While the Model Penal Act serves as a source to which states can look for guidance in enacting penal statutes, it is unlikely that all states will adopt identical statutes relating to crimes. In sum, Model Acts are intended as guidelines that states can borrow from while Uniform Acts are intended to be adopted exactly as written. The Conference often works with the Institute in developing uniform and model legislation.

2. *Research Strategies*

Uniform Laws Annotated, Master Edition. To locate the text of the more than 200 Uniform Laws and the Model Acts, you can consult West's *Uniform Laws Annotated, Master Edition.* This multivolume set not only provides the text of Uniform Laws and Model Acts but also provides official comments of the drafters explaining the intent and purpose of each Uniform Law, a list of the states that have adopted each particular Uniform Law, the date the Law was adopted, brief descriptions of how various states have modified the Uniform Law, references to law review articles regarding the Uniform Law, annotations or brief summaries of cases interpreting the Uniform Law, references to topics and Key Numbers to enable the reader to access West's Key Number System, and references to sections of C.J.S., which discuss that area of the law. The set is kept current by pocket parts and supplements. See Figure 7-6 for a sample page from the *Uniform Laws Annotated, Master Edition.*

While *Uniform Laws Annotated, Master Edition* thus provides an overview of all uniform legislation, it lacks a comprehensive general index or table of contents. The Uniform Laws and Model Acts are, however, grouped together by general subject matter. Additionally, a pamphlet published regularly in conjunction with the *Master Edition*, titled *Directory of Uniform Acts and Codes*, lists all Uniform Laws alphabetically and will direct you to the location of the Law in the *Master Edition.* In effect, this directory serves as an index to the *Master Edition.* The directory also lists each state and the particular Uniform Laws it has adopted. See Figure 7-7 for a sample page from the *Directory of Uniform Acts and Codes.*

Am. Jur. 2d Desk Book. The Am. Jur. 2d Desk Book does not print the text of Uniform Laws, but it will provide a list of which states have adopted which Uniform Laws.

Am. Jur. 2d and *C.J.S.* The one-volume "Table of Statutes, Rules, and Regulations Cited" in Am. Jur. 2d and C.J.S. will refer you to sections in each of the encyclopedias that discuss Uniform Laws.

Martindale-Hubbell. The complete text of several of the better known and more widely adopted Uniform Laws, such as the Uniform Commercial Code, the Uniform Arbitration Act, and the Uniform Probate Code can be found in *Martindale-Hubbell.*

Westlaw. The text of all uniform and model acts contained in the Master Edition is also available on Westlaw.

Internet. Some Uniform Laws are available on the Internet. See Technology Tips at the end of this chapter.

Figure 7-6
Sample Page from the *Uniform Laws Annotated, Master Edition*

wife which listed as a possible heir the illegitimate child of appellant. In re Raso's Estate, Fla.App.1976, 332 So.2d 78.

Trial court abused its discretion in denying appellant's motion to vacate default judgment where appellant properly alleged excusable neglect for her failure to timely respond to petition for determination of heirs and where appellant properly alleged a meritorious defense. Id.

Section 2-102. [Share of the Spouse.]

The intestate share of the surviving spouse is:

(1) if there is no surviving issue or parent of the decedent, the entire intestate estate;

(2) if there is no surviving issue but the decedent is survived by a parent or parents, the first [$50,000], plus one-half of the balance of the intestate estate;

(3) if there are surviving issue all of whom are issue of the surviving spouse also, the first [$50,000], plus one-half of the balance of the intestate estate;

(4) if there are surviving issue one or more of whom are not issue of the surviving spouse, one-half of the intestate estate.

COMMENT

This section gives the surviving spouse a larger share than most existing statutes on descent and distribution. In doing so, it reflects the desires of most married persons, who almost always leave all of a moderate estate or at least one-half of a larger estate to the surviving spouse when a will is executed. A husband or wife who desires to leave the surviving spouse less than the share provided by this section may do so by executing a will, subject of course to possible election by the surviving spouse to take an elective share of one-third under Part 2 of this Article. Moreover, in the small estate (less than $50,000 after homestead allowance, exempt property, and allowances) the surviving spouse is given the entire estate if there are only children who are issue of both the decedent and the surviving spouse; the result is to avoid protective proceedings as to property otherwise passing to their minor children.

See Section 2-802 for the definition of spouse which controls for purposes of intestate succession.

Law Review Commentaries

How the family fares. Donald L. Robertson. 37 Ohio S.L.J. 264 (1976).

Modern Wills Act. John T. Gaubatz. 31 U.Miami L.Rev. 497 (1977).

Probate change. 20 Boston Bar J. No. 11, p. 6 (1976).

59

Figure 7-7
Sample Page from *Directory of Uniform Acts and Codes*

DIRECTORY OF UNIFORM ACTS

List of Uniform Acts or Codes, in alphabetical order, showing where each may be found in Uniform Laws Annotated, Master Edition.

The designation "Pocket Part" under the page column indicates that the particular Act or Code is complete in the Pocket Part. The designation "Pamphlet" under the page column indicates that the particular Act is complete in a Supplementary or Special Pamphlet. The user should always, of course, consult the Pocket Part or Pamphlet for changes and subsequent material when an Act or Code appears in the main volume.

Title of Act	Uniform Laws Annotated Volume	Page
Abortion Act, Revised	9, Pt. I	1
Absence as Evidence of Death and Absentees' Property Act	8A	1
Acknowledgment Act	12	1
Notarial Acts, Uniform Law on	14	125
Administrative Procedure Act, State (1981) (Model)	15	1
Administrative Procedure Act, State (1961) (Model)	15	137
Adoption Act	9, Pt. I	11
Aircraft Financial Responsibility Act	12	21
Alcoholism and Intoxication Treatment Act	9	79
Anatomical Gift Act (1987 Act)	8A	Pocket Part
Anatomical Gift Act (1968 Act)	8A	15
Ancillary Administration of Estates Act	8A	69
Antitrust, State Antitrust Act	7B	711
Arbitration Act	7	1
Attendance of Witnesses From Without a State in Criminal Proceedings, Act to Secure	11	1
Audio-Visual Deposition Act [Rule]	12	Pocket Part
Brain Death Act	12	Pocket Part
Canada—U.S. Transboundary Pollution Reciprocal Access Act	9B	625
Certification of Questions of Law Act	12	49
Child Custody Jurisdiction Act	9, Pt. I	115
Children and minors,		
Abortion Act, Revised	9, Pt. I	1
Adoption Act	9, Pt. I	11
Child Custody Jurisdiction Act	9, Pt. I	115
Civil Liability for Support Act	9, Pt. I	333
Gifts to Minors Act (1966 Act)	8A	181
Gifts to Minors Act (1956 Act)	8A	225
Interstate Family Support Act	9, Pt. I	Pocket Part
Juvenile Court Act	9A	1
Parentage Act	9B	287
Paternity Act	9B	347
Putative and Unknown Fathers Act	9B	Pocket Part
Reciprocal Enforcement of Support Act (1968 Act)	9B	381
Reciprocal Enforcement of Support Act (1950 Act)	9B	553
Revised Abortion Act	9, Pt. I	1
Status of Children of Assisted Conception	9B	Pocket Part
Transfers to Minors Act	8A	Pocket Part

1

3. *Use of Uniform Laws*

If you are researching a state statute that has been adopted as a Uniform Law and there are no cases interpreting it, you should review the Official Comment to the Uniform Law and cases from another state that has also adopted the Uniform Law. As you will recall from Chapter 1, while cases from one state are never binding in another state, cases from another state interpreting Uniform Laws may be highly persuasive inasmuch as such cases would be interpreting statutory provisions that are similar or identical to those enacted in your state.

A Uniform Law or Model Act drafted and approved by the Conference is secondary authority. The official comments of the drafters related to the background, purpose, and effect of a Uniform Law are also secondary authority, and while these comments provide credible insight into the goals of a Uniform Law and the ills it is designed to remedy, they need not be followed by a court. Once a Uniform Law or Model Act is adopted by your state legislature, however, it is primary authority that must be followed in your state.

F. Looseleaf Services

1. *Introduction*

You have seen that law books are usually published in a hardbound version or in softcover pamphlets, supplements, or advance sheets. Yet another method of publication is "looseleaf," meaning a ringed binder (or a book with removable covers and pages stacked on posts) with individual looseleaf sheets of paper, which are easily removed and replaced. These are the looseleaf services. The major looseleaf publishers are Commerce Clearing House, Bureau of National Affairs, Clark Boardman Callaghan, and Matthew Bender.

The looseleaf services are a variety of treatise and may consist of one volume or several volumes devoted to one topic of the law, such as labor law, securities, environmental law, Social Security compensation, bankruptcy, tax, criminal law, or family law. In general, looseleaf services are used for areas of the law that are subject to frequent change. For example, revisions are constantly being made to our tax laws. To publish information relating to taxation in hardbound sets of books would not be efficient or cost-effective, as the hardbound volumes would be out of date almost as soon as they would be placed on library shelves. Even frequent updating by pocket parts will not keep pace with our changing tax laws. Therefore, the looseleaf service binder sets are purchased by law firms and law libraries. As changes occur in the law or as new cases are decided, the publisher will send packets of replacement pages to the subscriber with an instruction to remove and destroy certain pages in the set and replace them with the new pages provided by the publisher. In this manner, the books are kept current to reflect accurately the status of the law without being cost-prohibitive to the subscriber. Some looseleaf services are updated as frequently as once a week.

Many of the looseleaf services are devoted to rules and regulations promulgated by our federal agencies, such as the service titled Occupational Safety and Health Reporter. These will be discussed in greater detail in Chapter 10. Several of the looseleaf services, however, report on areas of the law for which no particular agency is responsible but for which there is general interest, such as criminal law or family law. There are hundreds of looseleafs covering nearly every legal topic.

A typical looseleaf service will include primary and secondary authorities. Primary authority will be found in the statutes governing a certain area of the law, which are set forth in full text as well as in the court decisions, which are often included. Often summaries or digests of court cases related to this area of the law are given. Secondary authority is found in the commentary and discussion of this topic and of recent developments in this area of the law as well as practice tips and notices of upcoming seminars or meetings of legal professionals or proposed legislation related to this area of law. The looseleafs then function to provide a complete treatment of an area of the law, bringing together all information on a legal topic in one set. Some experts call the looseleafs "mini-libraries" because they are comprehensive collections of current legal materials devoted to one area of the law and brought together in one source.

Although a treatise may appear in binder or looseleaf form (such as the six-volume binder set, *McCarthy on Trademarks and Unfair Competition*), a true looseleaf service is distinguishable from such a treatise because the looseleaf service will contain primary authority, such as cases, statutes, and administrative regulations as well as secondary authority. A treatise usually includes only comment and analysis of an area of the law with no cases (although statutes may be included in an appendix to the set).

You should feel free to cite a looseleaf service in a memorandum or brief that you prepare. Often, however, the looseleaf services function more as "finding" tools, which provide general background information on a certain area of law and direct you to the primary authorities (statutes and cases) in the field, which you would then cite.

2. *Arrangement of Looseleaf Services*

There is no one uniform pattern for arrangement of looseleaf services. Different publishers arrange the discussion of the law in different ways, and each service is different from another. Often the best way to determine the arrangement of the service to enhance your research efforts is simply to invest 20 to 30 minutes in reading the editor's introduction to the service and then browsing through the set to familiarize yourself with its features and structure.

In general, however, looseleaf services will consist of multiple ringed binders, each of which has several sections, divided by colorful marked tabs. For example, one tab is usually marked "How to Use." This section provides an overview of the service and guidelines for using the set. Other tabs may be marked "Topical Index," "Table of Cases," "State Laws," "Federal Laws," "Cumulative Index," and "New Developments."

3. *Research Strategies*

To determine if a looseleaf service exists for an area of the law you are researching, for instance, labor law, consult the card catalog in your law library or ask the reference librarian. Alternatively, you could locate the stacks in the law library that contain labor law materials and simply scan the shelves to determine if a looseleaf service exists.

Each looseleaf service will have a general index, which will alphabetically list the topics and subjects discussed in the service. Use the descriptive word approach to locate words in the index that describe your research issue. The index will then refer you to the appropriate paragraph or section. Alternatively, you can use the table of cases to locate cases reported or discussed in the set. Review the cases to which you are directed.

Note that references in the index are seldom to *pages*. It is typical of looseleaf services that paragraph or section references are used rather than references to pages, as this facilitates the addition of new replacement sheets in the set. Many looseleaf services also use subsections and decimals such as a reference to "¶ 10060.101" to accommodate the insertion of new pages. Thus, it may take you a bit of time to become accustomed to the organization of the looseleaf services. Invest the time it takes to understand how to use looseleaf services because these mini-libraries provide a comprehensive discussion of relevant legal topics.

G. Jury Instructions

1. *Introduction*

At the conclusion of a trial, a judge will "charge" the jury by providing it with instructions for reaching a decision. Preparing instructions for the jury is done by attorneys and paralegals. Until approximately 60 years ago, new jury instructions were developed for each trial. Often the instructions were erroneous statements of the law, and an appellate court would order a new trial due to the improper instruction. For example, if judges were free in criminal trials to develop their own definitions for "reasonable doubt," convictions of criminal defendants would be based upon differing standards.

Recognizing the duplication of effort required in preparing jury instructions for each trial and the waste of time and excessive cost involved in new trials due to erroneous instructions, a movement for pattern or form jury instructions emerged. Just as there are forms for leases, contracts, and motions for change of venue, there are now form books that contain jury instructions.

The jury instructions are typically drafted by committees of legal scholars or bar associations who study cases and then prepare accurate, brief, and easily understood instructions regarding the law. A new development is the drafting of jury instructions in "plain English" to improve jurors' comprehension. In many states, the standard jury instructions are so highly regarded that rules of court for the state recommend or require that the trial judge read the applicable instruction. In other instances, jury instructions may be modified to state the law accurately.

Paralegals often play a major role in preparing jury instructions. While the primary role of a jury instruction is to provide an accurate statement of the law for a judge to communicate to a jury, a secondary role is to provide research sources. Many sets of jury instructions not only provide the actual text of an instruction but follow it with commentary directing you to cases, statutes, or treatises that support the language used in the instructions or provide additional information relating to that area of the law. This commentary is an excellent secondary authority source. Moreover, the instruction itself is a source of useful information for researchers. For example, if you were writing a memorandum on a contract matter and needed to list the elements of a cause of action for breach of contract, a jury instruction will likely set them forth. That is, when you read the jury instruction relating to contracts, you will see language similar to the following:

> Ladies and Gentlemen, if you find from your consideration of all the evidence that there was an agreement between the parties, that the defendant without justification or excuse breached the agreement, and that this breach was the cause of damage to the plaintiff, then you should find the defendant liable for breach of contract.

By analyzing the statement, you can easily see that a cause of action for breach of contract arises when three elements exist: an agreement; a breach of the agreement by one party; and damage caused by the breach. Thus, jury instructions serve to provide a quick summary of the key elements of many areas of the law, including contracts, fraud, negligence, infliction of emotional distress, assault, and battery.

2. *Research Strategies*

To locate the jury instructions in your law library, check the card catalog or ask a reference librarian for assistance. Some law libraries keep the materials on trial practice in one section, and in such instances you may be able to locate the jury instructions in that section. There may be a set of jury instructions for use strictly in your state. For example, the sets commonly used in California are *Book of Approved Jury Instructions* for civil cases and *California Jury Instructions Criminal* for criminal cases.

If there is no set of jury instructions specific to your state, consult the set *Am. Jur. Pleading and Practice Forms, Annotated.* As you will recall from Chapter 6, this multi-volume set contains thousands of forms and documents for use in all phases of litigation and also contains standard jury instructions. For federal cases you may consult a set titled *Modern Federal Jury Instructions*, which provides jury instructions for both civil and criminal cases. Some sets are available in both conventional bound volumes and in CD-ROM form.

When you have located the books containing jury instructions, consult the general index to the set. As is typical of indexes, it is usually found at the end of the last volume of the set and lists alphabetically the topics covered by the set.

Use the descriptive word approach and locate words describing the issue you are researching, such as burglary, misrepresentation, or perjury. You will then be directed to the instructions used in such cases. Most sets of jury instructions are updated by pocket parts. See Figure 7-8 for sample jury instructions for a copyright infringement case.

H. Summary

All of the sources discussed in this and the preceding chapter are secondary authorities, meaning that while you may refer to these sources and cite them in memoranda or briefs, courts are not required to follow them. While secondary authorities are often highly reputable, they remain persuasive at best and lack the force of the primary authorities of cases, constitutions, statutes, and administrative regulations. Keep in mind that some of the secondary authorities such as Restatements and law review articles are highly regarded and often cited, while others, such as encyclopedias, are viewed as elementary in approach and are seldom cited. One of the best indications of the strength of a secondary source is found in Rule 1.4 of the *Bluebook*, which provides the following hierarchical order when string-citing numerous secondary authorities: model acts; Restatements; treatises and books; works in journals, such as law review articles; annotations; magazine and newspaper articles; and electronic sources. Encyclopedias are not listed. All of the secondary authorities do an excellent job of providing commentary on the law and typically direct you to the primary authorities that you should rely upon and cite in your memoranda and briefs. A summary of the secondary sources is provided in Figure 7-9.

Figure 7-8
Sample Jury Instructions from *Jury Instructions in Intellectual Property Cases*

You may also consider CBS' contention that all three television broadcasting networks regularly broadcast obituary tributes to deceased celebrated personages, including celebrated motion picture performers, within 48 hours of their deaths usually, at approximately 11:30 p.m., immediately following the eleven o'clock news programs, and that film clips from those persons' motion picture performances are customarily included in such obituary tributes, and that such film clips are usually provided to the networks for use without charge for the rights of copyright involved. [4/82]

Source: *Roy Export Co. v. Columbia Broadcasting System, Inc.*, 503 F.Supp. 1137, 208 U.S.P.Q. 580 (S.D. N.Y. 1980), 673 F.2d 1045, 215 U.S.P.Q. 289 (2d Cir. 1982).

40:64:11 Nature of the Copyrighted Work

[See also instruction 40:20:03, *supra*.]

Jury instruction

In determining whether particular copying was fair or unfair use you may consider that the extent of fair use is somewhat broader for a collection of facts assembled through diligence rather than a literary work resulting from intellectual creativity. [8/84]

Annotation to case supporting language used in instruction

Source: *National Business Lists, Inc. v. Dunn & Bradstreet, Inc.*, 552 F.Supp. 89, 215 U.S.P.Q. 595 (N.D. Ill. 1982).

The second factor that you should consider in applying the fair use doctrine is the nature of the copyrighted work itself, here, the Chaplin films. In this action, CBS claims that in order to present the public with a full and complete retrospective view of Chaplin's motion picture life it had to include the excerpts or clips from those Chaplin films in issue. CBS also claims that plaintiffs refused to give it any access at all.

If you believe that the evidence supports the defendant's contention that it had no reasonable alternatives to the use of plaintiff's copyrighted materials, this should weigh in CBS' favor in your determination of whether its use was fair. [4/82]

Source: *Roy Export Co. v. Columbia Broadcasting System, Inc.*, 503 F.Supp. 1137, 208 U.S.P.Q. 580 (S.D. N.Y. 1980), 673 F.2d 1045, 215 U.S.P.Q. 289 (2d Cir. 1982).

40:64:13 Amount and Substantiality of Use

The third factor which you should consider in determining if the defendant's use of the Chaplin films was a fair use is the substantiality, both quantitatively and qualitatively of those excerpts actually broadcast in relation to the particular Chaplin film from which each excerpt was taken. As you know, plaintiff Roy Export owns separate renewal copyrights in each separate Chaplin film.

Therefore, in determining whether the defendant's use was a fair use, you should ask yourselves how much from each film was broadcast when measured against the entirety of the original Chaplin motion picture film

Figure 7-9
Chart of Secondary Sources

Secondary Source	*Overview*	*Description of Set*	*Supplementation*	*Research Techniques*	*Research and Use Notes*
Encyclopedias	Alphabetically arranged narrative statements of hundreds of areas of the law supported by cases and other authorities found in footnotes	Multi-volume general sets: C.J.S. and Am. Jur. 2d Multi-volume state sets Special subject sets	Annual cumulative pocket parts	Descriptive word approach Topic approach	Excellent introductory information. Be cautious about citing to encyclopedias, as they are considered elementary in approach.
Legal Periodicals	Publications produced on a periodic basis discussing a wide variety of legal topics	Law school publications Bar association and paralegal association publications Specialized publications Legal newspapers and newsletters	No supplementation. Each periodical issue is complete.	Index to Legal Periodicals Current Law Index and online retrieval Other separately published indexes	Periodicals range from the very scholarly and well respected law reviews to the more practical and seldom cited bar association publications and newsletters.

Texts and Treatises	Texts written by legal scholars on one legal topic that discuss cases and statutes in the narrative statements	Multi-volume sets that contain thorough and often critical analysis of an area of the law	Annual cumulative pocket parts or softcover supplements	Descriptive word approach Topic approach Table of cases or statutes approach	Many treatises are highly regarded, and you should feel free to refer and cite to them.
Restatements	Statements of the law in clear and unambiguous language	Multi-volume sets on selected areas of the law such as torts, agency, or property	Appendix volumes with pocket parts	Descriptive word approach Topic approach	Restatements are probably the most highly regarded of all of the secondary authorities.
Attorneys General Opinions	Written opinions by United States attorneys general and state attorneys general on a variety of legal topics	Multi-volume sets for United States attorneys general opinions and opinions of state attorneys general	No supplementation. Each volume is complete.	Descriptive word approach References from other sources	Attorneys general opinions are strongly persuasive and highly respected.
Legal Dictionaries	Books providing definitions of legal words and phrases and references to cases so defining a word	One-volume alphabetical arrangement of words, phrases, Latin and other foreign terms	No supplementation. Each volume is complete.	Alphabetical approach	While many dictionaries are well known and authoritative, you should cite to and rely on the cases you are directed to rather than the dictionary's definition of a word or phrase.

Figure 7-9 (*Continued*)

Secondary Source	*Overview*	*Description of Set*	*Supplementation*	*Research Techniques*	*Research and Use Notes*
Law Directories	Lists of lawyers	General directories such as *Martindale-Hubbell* contain lists of all attorneys and other useful features such as law digests. Specialty directories list attorneys specializing in certain practice areas or certain geographical regions.	Generally, no supplementation. Replacement sets issued annually or as needed.	Alphabetical approach by state, city, attorney's and firm's name.	Used primarily to obtain information about attorneys and law firms. *Law Digests* of *Martindale-Hubbell* provide summaries of laws of 50 states and more than 140 foreign countries.

Form Books	Sets of books containing standard or pattern forms for general use or for use in certain practice areas. Often annotated and containing useful commentary and practice guides.	Multi-volume sets of books containing forms for general legal practice or specialty areas such as criminal law, corporate law, etc.	Pocket parts	Descriptive word approach Topic approach	Used primarily to assist in drafting documents. Seldom, if ever cited, though used with great frequency.
Uniform Laws	Drafts of statutes proposed by legal scholars for certain areas of the law.	Multi-volume set, *Uniform Laws Annotated, Master Edition*, containing text of *Uniform Laws*, commentary, references to other sources, etc.	Pocket parts and supplements	Use *Directory of Uniform Acts and Codes* to locate a Uniform Law.	Cases interpreting a Uniform Law, even those from another state, may be highly persuasive in your state if your state has also adopted the Uniform Law.

Figure 7-9 (*Continued*)

Secondary Source	*Overview*	*Description of Set*	*Supplementation*	*Research Techniques*	*Research and Use Notes*
Looseleaf Services	A variety of treatise devoted to one area of the law (usually a frequently changing area) containing both primary and secondary authority	Multi-volume sets of books, arranged in ringed binders containing statutes, cases, case digests, and commentary on one topic of the law	Replacement pages	Descriptive word approach Consult "how to use" section	Looseleaf services provide a thorough overview of an area of the law though their arrangement and use can be awkward.
Jury Instructions	Sets of books containing instructions for charging the jury in civil and criminal trials as well as commentary and annotations	One-volume or multi-volume sets specific to one state or general in nature	Pocket parts	Descriptive word approach	Useful in obtaining a "snapshot" of an area of the law, though seldom cited in research projects.

I. Citation Form

You sould never cite to a directory. Other secondary sources are cited as follows:

1. Attorneys General Opinions:
   46 Op. Att'y Gen. 496 (1997).
2. Dictionaries:
   Black's Law Dictionary 908 (7th ed. 1999).
3. Uniform Acts:
   U.C.C. § 2-216 (1977).
4. Looseleaf Services:
   8 Lab. L. Rep. (CCH) ¶ 6107 (Nov. 8, 1999); or *In re Pillowtex Textiles Co.,* 4 Bankr. L. Rep. (CCH) ¶ 16,041 (Bankr. D.N.J. Mar. 10, 1999).
5. Jury Instructions:
   Sean T. Moore, *Federal Jury Instructions* 12 (4th ed. 1992).

Technology Tips

Attorney General Opinions

http://www.usdoj.gov/ag/index.html	The Web site for the United States Attorney General provides a great deal of information about the Attorney General's duties as well as the text of speeches but does not provide opinions of the Attorney General.
http://www.washlaw.edu	Some states post their state attorney general opinions on their Web sites. This site provides a direct link to the home page for each state so you can search the site to determine if it offers attorney general opinions.

Dictionaries

http://www.courttv.com/glossary.html	This site provides a brief glossary of many legal terms.
http://www.wwlia.org/diction.htm	Attorney Lloyd Duhaime offers a law dictionary online.
http://www.lawoffice.com/pathfind/orans/orans.asp	*Oran's Law Dictionary*, a well-known law dictionary, is offered by West at this online site.
http://findlaw.com	To access FindLaw's legal dictionary, select "Reference Resources" and then "Dictionary."

Directories

http://www.lawoffice.com	This Web site offered by West provides a searchable directory of more than one million lawyers and law firms.
http://martindale.com	This Web site offered by Martindale-Hubbell offers a searchable directory of law firms and lawyers.

Forms

http://www.lectlaw.com/form.html	The Web site of 'Lectric Law Library offers a variety of forms, including many used for litigation, business, real estate, wills, trusts, and corporations.
http://findlaw.com	FindLaw offers a wide variety of legal materials. Select "Forms."
http://www.uscourtforms.com	U.S. CourtForms publishes over 40,000 legal forms, including forms for both state and federal courts.

(continued)

Technology Tips *(Continued)*

Uniform Laws

http://www.nccusl.org	The official Web site of the National Conference of Commissioners on Uniform State Laws provides information and legislative status on Uniform Laws and discussion of projects under consideration.
http://www.law.upenn.edu/bll/ulc/ulc.htm	The Web site of the University of Pennsylvania provides the text of most Uniform Laws and Model Acts and discusses projects currently under consideration.
http://www.law.cornell.edu	The Web site of Cornell Law School provides links to Uniform Laws on the Internet.

Jury Instructions

There is no one site to locate jury instructions. Some states, however, post their state-specific jury instrucions on their home pages. To locate home pages, access http://www.findlaw.com, then select "U.S. State Resources" and then select the paricular state in which you are interested. The following sites may be helpful as well.

http://www.netlawlibraries.com	This site provides civil jury instructions that can be used in California.
http://www.ce9.uscourts.gov/web/sdocuments.nsf/civ	This site provides a "Manual of Model Civil Jury Instructions" for use in the Ninth Circuit.

Writing Strategies

There is a great temptation in using secondary sources such as *Black's Law Dictionary* or form books to use the very language you are provided. While the use of a definition from a legal dictionary or the use of certain language given in a form book may be technically correct, it may result in "legalese." Legalese produces a document that is difficult for the reader to understand because its meaning is buried in a sea of redundant phrases and archaic word forms.

When discussing the secondary sources explained in this chapter, be on the alert for the following signs of legalese:

archaic words	hereinabove, erstwhile, albeit, opine
Latin or foreign phrases	*inter alia*, *res gestae*
redundancies	final result, basic fundamentals
nominalizations	"inspection" rather than "inspect," "harassment" rather than "harass," "decision" rather than "decide"
overuse of negatives	"notwithstanding anything to the contrary discussed herein, you must not refrain from paying your rent"

Assignment for Chapter 7

1. Use *Black's Law Dictionary* (7th ed. 1999).
   a. What is the first definition of "moral rights"?
   b. What authority is cited in support of the definition?
2. Use the most current edition of *Martindale-Hubbell Law Dictionary*.
   a. An attorney named Harry R. Hauser is with the Boston, Massachusetts, firm of Gadsby & Hannah, L.L.P. Where and when did Mr. Hauser attend law school?
   b. Review the Corporate Law Departments section. What corporation is Amy E. Hamilton with?
   c. An attorney named Maria Allessandra Livi is with the Rome, Italy, law firm Studio Legale Tosato. Where did she receive her J.D.?
   d. What is the filing fee in Illinois for filing articles for a limited liability company?
   e. Review the ABA Model Rules of Professional Conduct. What Rule relates to attorney advertising?
   f. What is the legal rate of interest in Ireland in the absence of any contract?
   g. Review the Uniform Probate Code. What does § 3-801 deal with?
3. Use *Am. Jur. Pleading and Practice Forms Annotated*.
   a. What form provides a notice of time and place of oral examination (a deposition) of an officer of a corporate party?
   b. What federal rule is this form based on?
   c. What form relates to a complaint for wrongful death on a roller coaster?
   d. Review the form. What does paragraph 1 allege?
4. Use the General Index to *Am. Jur. Legal Forms 2d*.
   a. What form provides a general application for reservation of a corporate name?
   b. Review the form. What Am. Jur. 2d reference are you directed to?
5. Use *Uniform Laws Annotated*.
   a. Has Vermont adopted the Limited Liability Company Act (1995)?
   b. If so, give the citation to Vermont's statute.
   c. Review the Act. What does § 112 deal with?
   d. Has South Carolina changed this definition? If so, in what way?

Chapter 8

Legal Citation Form

Chapter Overview

Paralegals are routinely assigned the task of "cite-checking." Cite-checking comprises two components: verifying that citations given in a project are accurate and in compliance with rules for citation form (often called "bluebooking") and then verifying that the authorities cited in a project are still "good law." The guidelines and rules relating to the form of citations will be discussed in this chapter and the method of ensuring that authorities relied upon are still correct statements of the law, usually called "Shepardizing" or "KeyCiting," will be discussed in the following chapter.

This chapter will review the history of the *Bluebook*, the best known guide to citation form, and will provide examples of citations for the primary authorities of cases, constitutions, and statutes as well as the secondary authorities of encyclopedias, legal periodicals, treatises, Restatements, and other authorities. Moreover, this chapter will provide information on more intricate citation tasks, such as punctuation, quotations, and the use of signals such as *id.*, *supra*, and *infra*. Note that while numerous examples of citations are provided in this chapter, most are fictitious and are provided solely for the purpose of illustrating citation rules. References to *Bluebook* notes are given in parentheses. Finally, many examples of citation form are found in other chapters. For example, illustrations of citation form for international materials and court rules are found in Chapter 10, which discusses those subjects.

Additionally, a newer and simpler form of citation was developed in 2000, primarily by the Association of Legal Writing Directors ("ALWD") and will be discussed as well. Although the ALWD citation system is becoming more widely accepted at the time of the writing of this text, the *Bluebook* remains the predominant citation system in the United States and thus it is the focus of this chapter.

A. Introduction to Citation Form

You may have already observed that legal writings are filled with references to cases, statutes, annotations, and numerous other authorities. The reason for this is that statements about the law must be attributed to their sources. You cannot simply make an assertion such as stating that a trial by jury is waived unless it is requested by a party. Such statements must be supported by legal authority; that is, by primary authorities or secondary authorities. These supporting authorities appear as "citations" or "cites" within the body of your work. Moreover, these citations must appear in a standard and consistent format so that any judge, attorney, paralegal, or other reader, upon viewing your citation, will be able to retrieve the legal authority you cited and verify that you have accurately represented the status of the law.

Because citations communicate information to a reader, it is essential that legal professionals communicate using the same "language" or citation form. You should be able to prepare a legal argument and present it to any court in the United States with confidence that a reader will be able to locate the authorities you cite. If legal professionals cited cases, statutes, and other authorities in varying ways, this would not only impede communication but would dilute the strength of your argument. When you present a persuasive argument, you do not want to distract the reader from the argument by using disfavored or incorrect citation form.

Newcomers to the legal field often inquire what will happen if citation form is incorrect in a brief or other document. Improper citation form has an effect similar to spelling errors in a writing: Such errors will not transform an otherwise winning argument into a losing one. Rather, they result in a loss of respect for the author, and cause readers to question the integrity and analysis of an argument. Many readers will conclude that if an author cannot be depended upon to cite or spell correctly, the author likely cannot be depended upon to conduct thorough legal analysis.

B. The *Bluebook*

1. *Overview of the* Bluebook

The best known rules for citation form are found in a small ringed publication titled *The Bluebook: A Uniform System of Citation* (Columbia Law Review Ass'n et al. eds., 17th ed. 2000) [hereinafter the *Bluebook*], which is now in its 17th edition. Its front and back covers are bright blue, and it is the most commonly used guide to citation form. The *Bluebook* was originally produced in the 1920s by the editorial boards of the *Columbia Law Review*, the *Harvard Law Review*, the *University of Pennsylvania Law Review*, and the *Yale Law Journal*. As time has passed, the editors of these law reviews have updated the *Bluebook*, and the newly revised 17th edition was published in late 2000 by the same consortium. Questions and comments about the *Bluebook* can be addressed to The Harvard Law Review Association, Gannett House, 1511 Massachusetts Avenue, Cambridge, Massachusetts 02138. Its Web site is http://www.legalbluebook.com.

While there are other guides to citation form, the most notable of which is the *Chicago Manual of Legal Citation*, usually referred to as *The Maroon Book*, and used primarily in the Chicago metropolitan area, and the new ALWD citation system discussed in this chapter, the *Bluebook* is the oldest and best known guide. Another excellent guide is *Bieber's Dictionary of Legal Citations* (Mary Miles Prince ed., 5th ed. 1997), which alphabetically lists hundreds of examples of legal authorities cited in accordance with the *Bluebook* rules. *Bieber's Dictionary* is an invaluable tool for cite-checkers. It is published by William S. Hein & Co., Inc., of Buffalo, New York (800/828-7571). The examples given are in the form for practitioners rather than in the form used for law review footnotes and text, and thus no adaptation of typeface is required. Unless you are specifically directed to use some other system of citation rules or unless your jurisdiction has its own system of citation, however, follow the *Bluebook* because it is universally known and accepted. If local citation rules exist for your jurisdiction, they must be followed.

Do not rely on the way books and cases refer to themselves. For example, if you consult one of the first pages in any volume of U.S.C.A., it will instruct you, "Cite This Book Thus: 42 U.S.C.A. §1220." This form is incorrect according to the *Bluebook*, which clearly provides the correct citation form: 42 U.S.C.A. § 1220 (West 1994). Similarly, many court decisions in California use the incorrect abbreviation "C.A." rather than the correct abbreviation "Cal. App." to refer to cases from the California appellate courts. Therefore, you should always rely on the *Bluebook* rules rather than the citation forms you may observe in other books or case reports.

Law students, paralegals, and practitioners have long bemoaned the organization of the *Bluebook*, its confusing index, its dearth of sufficient examples, and its lack of articulate explanation of certain citation rules. While each edition of the *Bluebook* attempted to respond to such criticisms, each new edition seemed to create as much confusion as it resolved. The 15th edition, released in 1991, however, reorganized the *Bluebook*, making it easier to use and of more benefit to practitioners, who often believed the *Bluebook* devoted far too much attention to citation form for various obscure publications and far too little attention to citation problems commonly encountered by practitioners. All of the information provided in this chapter (except that relating to the ALWD citation form) is based upon the *Bluebook* rules, 17th edition.

In sum, there are few jurisdictions that require use of *Bluebook* form. For example, the rules of the United States Supreme Court impose requirements for nearly every aspect of documents submitted to the Court, from size of paper used to font size for footnotes, yet are silent on citation form. Use of the *Bluebook* is simply expected and traditional.

2. *Typeface Conventions*

Perhaps the single most important fact you should know about the *Bluebook* is that almost all of the examples given in the white pages of the *Bluebook* show how to cite authorities as if you were writing a law review article. Because your cite-checking work as a paralegal will in all likelihood relate to authorities cited in court documents and legal memoranda, you must convert the examples you are given by the *Bluebook* that relate to law review format to those suitable for practitioners.

The *Bluebook* includes a special section on light blue paper called "Practitioners' Notes," which shows you how to adapt the examples you find in the body of the *Bluebook* to the format needed for court documents and memoranda. For example, if you were citing a text in a law review, it would appear as follows:

> 1 J. THOMAS MCCARTHY, MCCARTHY ON TRADEMARKS AND UNFAIR COMPETITION § 3:1 (4th ed. 1997).

On the other hand, if you were to cite this same text in a court document or a legal memorandum, it would appear as follows:

> 1 J. Thomas McCarthy, *McCarthy on Trademarks and Unfair Competition* § 3:1 (4th ed. 1997).

The obvious difference between these two citation forms is that the first, used for law reviews, uses a style of large and small capitals for the author's name and treatise title, while the second format, used by practitioners, uses initial capital letters only. It is common for law reviews to use large and small capitals for statutes, book titles, periodicals, and other materials. This format, however, is not used by practitioners. In fact, the 17th edition of the *Bluebook* (P.1 (b)) clearly instructs practitioners, "[d]o not use large and small capitals," and Rule 2 notes that "[l]arge and small capitals do not appear in court documents and legal memoranda." Thus, when you see an example given in the *Bluebook* such as the reference to the Florida Law Review as "FLA. L. REV.," you will need to adapt the format to that used by practitioners, namely, "Fla. L. Rev."

Many experts believe that the use of large and small capitals in law reviews is a holdover from the time law review articles were manually typeset. Because documents prepared by practitioners were typed rather than typeset and typewriters could not change fonts to make one capital letter larger than another, practitioners never used large and small capitals (even though the advent of word processing has made this possible). Thus, every time you encounter an example in the *Bluebook*, ask yourself, "Could this format be reproduced on an old-fashioned typewriter?" If not, it is a signal to you that the form is for law reviews, not for practitioners' documents. This dual system of citation (the use of large and small capitals for law reviews and the use of ordinary roman type by practitioners) has continued to exist long past any need for it. Because word processors can readily use a large and small capital format, practitioners could adopt that method of citation, and the dual citation system could be scrapped. Why do two separate systems continue to exist, each with its own rules and requirements? No one knows.

Other useful guides to showing you the differences in citation form between law review format and the style used for court documents and legal memoranda are on the inside front and back covers of the *Bluebook*. The inside front cover is titled "Quick Reference: Law Review Footnotes" and gives you several examples for citation form for use for law review footnotes. The inside back cover is titled "Quick Reference: Court Documents and Legal Memoranda" and gives you the same examples for use in legal writings for practitioners.

Be sure to refer often to the inside back cover. Do not become confused and assume that because an example appears in the body of the *Bluebook* it is correct. It may well be correct—but only for a law review. After viewing an example in the body of the *Bluebook*, check the Practitioners' Notes and the inside back cover of the *Bluebook* and adapt the typeface for use in a court document or legal memorandum. Remember that practitioners never use large and small capitals.

Another difference you will note between citations shown on the inside front cover (for law review footnotes) and those shown on the inside back cover (for use by practitioners) is that in most instances case names are neither underscored nor italicized in law review footnotes and yet they are always underscored or italicized by practitioners. Moreover, hundreds of examples throughout the white pages in the *Bluebook* show case names in ordinary roman type (without underscoring or italicization). Do not become confused by the examples shown in the white pages throughout the *Bluebook*. Unless you are preparing footnotes for a law review article, case names will always be underscored or italicized.

3. *Organization of the* Bluebook

While it would be unnecessarily time-consuming to read the *Bluebook*, you should become familiar with its overall arrangement and should skim at least the first 100 pages or so. The *Bluebook* is composed of six major sections:

Preface. The Preface provides a summary of the changes initiated in the 17th edition of the *Bluebook*.

Introduction. The Introduction discusses the structure of the *Bluebook* and general principles of citation.

Practitioners' Notes. This section of the *Bluebook* is printed on light blue paper for easy reference, discusses the differences in typeface conventions for law review footnotes, as opposed to court documents and legal memoranda, and gives several examples of citation forms for such court documents and legal memoranda. References in this chapter to Practitioners' Notes will be shown as "P."

General Rules of Citation and Style. This section, printed on white paper, provides general standards of citation and style used for legal writings and then sets forth specific rules of citation for primary authorities (cases, constitutions, and statutes) and secondary authorities (books, periodicals, foreign materials, and so on). References in this chapter to Rules will be shown as "R."

Tables. The *Bluebook* contains 17 tables printed on light blue paper for easy access showing how cases and statutes from federal courts and each state court are cited and providing abbreviations for court documents, geographical terms, months, and various periodicals.

Index. An alphabetically arranged Index is found at the end of the *Bluebook*. When you have a question or concern regarding citation form, use the descriptive word approach to access the Index, which will refer you to the pertinent page for the citation rule you need.

4. Revisions to the 17th Edition of the **Bluebook**

The 17th edition of the *Bluebook* retains the same basic approach to citation form as earlier editions. Nevertheless, it does contain some changes, primarily in the use of some signal words, the rules relating to abbreviating words in case citations, and guidance for citing materials on the Internet. While these changes are discussed in detail in the preface to the *Bluebook* and throughout the *Bluebook*, and in this chapter, some of the more significant changes are as follows:

(i) Rule 1.2, relating to the use of signals, has been revised. *Contra*, a signal indicating contradiction, had disappeared from the 16th edition of the *Bluebook* but has now been restored. Similarly, the use of "no signal" to introduce a citation and the use of the signal *see* have been changed from the 16th edition of the *Bluebook*.

(ii) For nearly 75 years, the first word in a case name (with a few minor exceptions) could not be abbreviated. The 17th edition of the *Bluebook* now requires that the first word in a case name be abbreviated in stand-alone citations.

(iii) The *Bluebook* provides additional information on formats for public domain citations. Additionally, Table 1 shows examples for those states that have adopted a public domain citation format.

(iv) Rule 18 provides extensive information on citation to electronic sources (namely, the electronic databases LEXIS-NEXIS and Westlaw) and the Internet. The basic citation principle, however, is that the *Bluebook* requires the use and citation of traditional printed sources except when the information is unavailable in printed form or if the traditional source is obscure or difficult to locate. Thus, there is a strong preference against citing to LEXIS-NEXIS, Westlaw, or the Internet.

(v) Table 1 now provides a reference to each state's judicial Web site, making it easy to locate each state's cases and court rules.

(vi) Table 10, providing abbreviations for words used in legislative documents (such as abbreviations for Committee, Congress, and Resolution) has been added.

C. Citation Rules and Examples for Primary Authorities

1. Cases

a. Introduction

A typical case citation includes the following components:

- Case name
- References to the set(s) of case reports that published the case and the page on which the case begins
- The year of decision and the court that decided the case if not apparent from the citation itself
- The subsequent history of the case, if any (Rule 10.1).

Thus, a typical citation to a case cited in a court document in Nevada is as follows:

Smith v. Jones, 68 Nev. 101, 104, 329 P.2d 411, 414 (1979).

b. Case Names

The *Bluebook* contains numerous rules regarding case names in citations. Carefully review Rules 10.2, 10.2.1, and 10.2.2 in the *Bluebook* for a full discussion of these rules. Some of the more common guidelines you should be aware of are as follows:

(i) Cite only the last names of the parties to an action.

Correct: *Talbert v. Carver*
Incorrect: *Luisa N. Talbert v. Jay Carver*

Note, however, that many corporations use an individual's name as part of the business name. In such a case, include the full name of the business entity.

Correct: *Ruiz v. Edward N. Pauley, Inc.*
Incorrect: *Ruiz v. Pauley, Inc.*

(ii) If more than one party is listed, omit all but the first party.

Correct: *Hart v. Ward*
Incorrect: *Hart v. Ward, Schiff, and Newley*

(iii) If several actions have been consolidated into one decision, omit all but the first listed action.

Correct: *Marrien v. Jacobson*
Incorrect: *Marrien v. Jacobson, Taylor v. Reynolds*

(iv) Omit any indication of multiple parties.

Correct: *Galinda v. Dubek*
Incorrect: *Galinda v. Dubek, et al.*

(v) Omit indications of legal status or other descriptive terms.

Correct: *Brumer v. Crawford*
Incorrect: *Brumer v. Crawford, Executor*
Incorrect: *Brumer v. Crawford, d/b/a The Green Grocer*
Incorrect: *Brumer v. Crawford, Defendant*

(vi) Do not abbreviate "United States" in a case name and omit the phrase "of America."

Correct: *United States v. Souther*
Incorrect: *U.S. v. Souther*
Incorrect: *United States of America v. Souther*
Incorrect: *USA v. Souther*

(vii) For criminal cases decided by your state, cite as follows:

Correct: *State v. Eagan*
Incorrect: *State of Kansas v. Eagan*
Correct: *Commonwealth v. Nelson*
Incorrect: *Commonwealth of Pennsylvania v. Nelson*

If the case was not decided by a court in your state (if, for example, the case was later appealed from the Kansas Supreme Court to the United States Supreme Court), cite as follows:

Correct: *Kansas v. Eagan*
Incorrect: *State v. Eagan*
Correct: *Pennsylvania v. Nelson*
Incorrect: *Commonwealth of Pennsylvania v. Nelson*

(viii) Omit the second "business signal" such as "Inc.," "Co.," or "Corp." if the case name already contains one business signal.

Correct: *Smith v. Auto Service Corp.*
Incorrect: *Smith v. Auto Service Corp. Inc.*

(ix) Omit prepositional phrases of location unless they follow the word "City" or a similar word.

Correct: *Brown v. Board of Education*
Incorrect: *Brown v. Board of Education of Topeka, Kansas*

(x) When a citation appears in a textual sentence, for example, when it appears as a grammatical component of a sentence, abbreviate only the following words in a case name and widely known acronyms (such as FBI, CIA, and NLRB) (Rule 10.2.1):

and	&
Association	Ass'n
Brothers	Bros.
Company	Co.
Corporation	Corp.
Incorporated	Inc.
Limited	Ltd.
Number	No.

When a citation appears by itself, rather than functioning as a grammatical component of a sentence, always abbreviate any word in the case name that is listed in Table 6 of the *Bluebook* (Rules 10.2.1. (c) and 10.2.2). The word is abbreviated even if they are the first word in a case name or the only word in a party's name.

Examples

Textual Sentence: In *Franklin Hospital Guaranty Co. v. Latham Division Ltd.*, 780 F. Supp. 91 (W.D. Tex. 1990), the court held that fraud requires a material misrepresentation.

Stand-alone Citation: Fraud requires a material misrepresentation. *Franklin Hosp. Guar. Co. v. Latham Div. Ltd.*, 780 F. Supp. 91 (W.D. Tex. 1990).

This rule is one of the least understood rules in the *Bluebook* and requires you to focus on the location of a citation before you determine which words can be abbreviated in a case name. For simplicity, use this rule: If a citation appears as a textual part of a sentence (meaning the cite is needed to make sense of the sentence), you may abbreviate only widely known acronyms and the eight well-known and commonly used abbreviations provided in Rule 10.2.1., such as "Co." and "Inc." On the other hand, if a citation stands alone in a clause or after the end of a sentence and is not needed to make sense of a sentence, you must abbreviate any of the nearly 170 words listed in Table 6, even if they are the first word in a party's name or the only word in a party's name. Why? Many experts believe that because readers are unused to seeing abbreviations in the middle of sentences, to abbreviate any words other than very commonly used words would be distracting. On the other hand, if a citation stands by itself, readers will not be disconcerted by seeing abbreviations such as "Indem." or "Sur."

The rule requiring abbreviation of the first word in a party's name that appears as a "stand-alone" citation is new to the 17th edition and is causing some confusion. For nearly 100 years, practitioners have been firmly instructed, "never abbreviate the first word in a party's name." Thus, the change in the 17th edition will require some effort for existing practitioners to become familiar with, particularly when the citation might read *Allen v. W.*, 520 U.S. 13, 16 (1998).

(xi) Generally, omit the word "The" as the first word of a party's name.

Correct: *May Co. v. Lorenzi*

Incorrect: *The May Co. v. Lorenzi*

(xii) Entities that are widely known (for example, NAACP, SEC, FCC, FDA) may be referred to as such in case names, without periods.

Correct: *SEC v. Garcia*

Incorrect: *S.E.C. v. Garcia*

Incorrect: *Securities and Exchange Commission v. Garcia*

The *Bluebook* (R. 6.1 (b)) gives only a few examples of such entities. Generally, however, if an entity is referred to in spoken language by its initials rather than its full name (for example, one usually says, "*Friends* is on NBC" rather than *Friends* is on the National Broadcasting Company"), it may be used in its abbreviated form without periods.

(xiii) The "v." in a case citation stands for "versus" and always appears in lower case form. While you may see some other form for "versus" in a pleading such as a complaint or answer, in citation form always use a lower case "v" followed by a period.

Correct: *Marksen v. Sigler*

Incorrect: *Marksen V. Sigler*
Incorrect: *Marksen vs. Sigler*

(xiv) Always underline or italicize the name of a case in a citation, including the "v.," and any procedural phrases such as "In re." Use a solid unbroken line. Either underlining (also called "underscoring") or italicizing is appropriate (P.1). Years ago, underlining was most popular, as few typewriters were capable of producing italics. With the advent of word processors, which are capable of italicizing, this technique became very popular. Many legal writers, however, continue to prefer underlining because it is very noticeable and dramatic on a white sheet of paper. Moreover, the examples given in the Practitioners' Notes section of the *Bluebook* show underlining, indicating a slight preference for such. Practioners' Notes (P.1) confirms that underscoring is more common in practice. Note these rules for underlining:

- The line should be unbroken.
- The line should be placed underneath the entire case name, including any periods.

Correct: Peters v. Swanson & Johnson Co.

Incorrect: Peters v. Swanson & Johnson Co.

Whichever method you select, be consistent. Check your firm or office practice for preferences.

(xv) The case name should always be followed by a comma. The comma is not underlined.

Correct: Jeffries v. Purvis,

Incorrect: Jeffries v. Purvis,

(xvi) Note that the correct abbreviation for "second" is 2d and the correct abbreviation for "third" is 3d, rather than 2nd or 3rd, which are commonly encountered in nonlegal writings.

(xvii) Note that the page given in a case citation is the page on which a case begins and is not introduced with an abbreviation such as "p." which is often used in nonlegal writings.

c. Parallel Cites

(1) Old Rule

Until relatively recently, citation rules required that all citations to all state court cases include all parallel cites; that is, references to the official report and the unofficial reporter(s) that published the case. The parallel citations were provided as a courtesy to the reader because the writer would not know if the reader had access to the official reports or the unofficial reporter(s). The writer would thus provide *all* citations so the reader could easily locate the cited case no matter which set of books or case reports the reader used.

Example

Liston v. Alpha Co., 129 Va. 109, 381 S.E.2d 12 (1980)

This requirement of providing all parallel cites made citation form awkward and difficult for the writer because the writer would have to obtain all parallel cites and then, if quoting from a certain page in the text, would have to indicate the exact page the quote appeared on in each case report. For California, Illinois, and New York cases, which often have three parallel cites, this rule made the difficult task of citation form even more complicated.

(2) New Rule

Bluebook Rule 10.3.1 and Practitioners' Notes Section P.3 govern parallel citations for state court cases. The *Bluebook* first notes, as always, that citations to state court cases should conform to local rules. Although not clearly stated, the examples given in Practitioners' Notes Section P.3 indicate that when citing a state court case in a document submitted to a court in the state that originally decided that case, one should include all parallel cites, with the official citation preceding the unofficial citation(s). In any other instance, for example, when citing the case in an internal office memorandum, a letter to a client, and documents submitted to another state or to a federal court, cite only to the relevant unofficial, regional reporter (A., P., S.E., and so forth) and include information about which state and court decided the case in the parenthetical along with the date.

Although Practitioners' Notes Section P.3 and Rule 10.3.1 clearly indicate that when citing a state court case in a document submitted to a state court in the state that decided the case one should include all parallel citations, Table 1 of the *Bluebook* does not reiterate this rule and seems to suggest that merely citing to the unofficial, regional citation will always be sufficient. Nevertheless, based on the fact that practitioners should always follow the citation formats given in the Practitioners' Notes section, and the fact that it will always be easier for state court judges to locate a case when they are given parallel citations, follow the format shown in Practitioners' Note Section P.3 and described above.

If you are citing state court cases in a document for a court in that state, you must place the citations in a certain order: official cite first, then the unofficial cite(s). For California, Illinois, and New York cases cited in documents for courts in California, Illinois, and New York, respectively, include all three parallel cites, if available, in the correct order as required by the *Bluebook*. For example, if you are citing a California case in a document submitted to a California court, the correct citation form is as follows:

Stein v. Springer, 69 Cal. 2d 101, 461 P.2d 409, 102 Cal. Rptr. 806 (1968).

If, on the other hand, you are referring to this case in a letter to a client, a memorandum prepared for use in your office, or a document submitted to any court other than a California state court, the correct citation form is as follows (assuming there are no special court rules governing citation form):

Stein v. Springer, 461 P.2d 409 (Cal. 1968).

Likewise, in a brief to Michigan court, cite a Michigan case as follows:

Green v. Hall, 68 Mich. 2d 802, 301 N.W.2d 604 (1979).

In all other instances, cite:

Green v. Hall, 301 N.W.2d 604 (Mich. 1979).

Although the *Bluebook* rule does not require parallel cites in an internal law office memorandum, many practicing legal professionals will include the parallel cite knowing that if the memorandum later becomes the basis for a brief submitted to a court, such as a motion for change of venue or a trial brief, the parallel cite would be required for that document. Thus, including it in an earlier memo will save time later by eliminating the need to return to the law library to track down the parallel cite. Follow your firm or office practice.

As you will recall from Chapter 4, 21 states and the District of Columbia no longer publish their cases officially, and cases from those jurisdictions appear only in the relevant regional reporter. If you are citing a case from one of these states decided after the date official publication ceased, the correct citation form will refer the reader only to the regional reporter and will include information about the court that decided the case parenthetically as follows:

Gray v. Donoghue, 704 P.2d 118 (Colo. 1989).

To determine which states no longer publish officially and when those states discontinued their official publications, consult the chart in Chapter

4 herein or Table 1 of the *Bluebook*, which alphabetically lists all 50 states and provides information about correct citation form for each state.

Do not forget that if a citation refers to the name of a jurisdiction (Cal., Mass., Vt.) and does not include any other information, you should assume the case was decided by the highest possible court in that state (*Bluebook* Rule 10.4 (b)). For example, the case cite *Guevara v. Herndon*, 168 Or. 904, 221 P.2d 84 (1975), signals that the case is from the Oregon Supreme Court. If it were from another court in Oregon, the citation would have so indicated, as follows: *Henley v. Gabriel*, 128 Or. App. 324, 201 P.2d 29 (1971). Thus, if you are citing a case in any document other than one filed with your state court, be sure to correctly indicate parenthetically the state *and* the court of decision (unless the court is the highest court in the state) because this information will be significant to the reader.

Examples

Guevara v. Herndon, 168 Or. 904, 221 P.2d 84 (1975). This is the correct citation form for a case from the Oregon Supreme Court when referred to in a document filed with an Oregon Court.

Henley v. Gabriel, 128 Or. App. 324, 201 P.2d 29 (1971). This is the correct citation form for a case from the Oregon Court of Appeals when referred to in a document filed with an Oregon court.

Guevara v. Herndon, 221 P.2d 84 (Or. 1975). This is the correct citation form for a case from the Oregon Supreme Court when referred to in any document other than one filed with an Oregon court.

Henley v. Gabriel, 201 P.2d 29 (Or. Ct. App. 1971). This is the correct citation form for a case from the Oregon Court of Appeals when referred to in a document other than one filed with an Oregon court.

Some states (Maine, Montana, Nevada, New Hampshire, Rhode Island, South Dakota, Vermont, West Virginia, and Wyoming) have no intermediate appellate courts. In those states, all citations are to the state supreme court, and the parenthetical would always display only the abbreviation of the state (such as "Wyo.") and never any abbreviation that would indicate an appellate court (such as "Wyo. Ct. App.").

Finally, in a few states (including Arizona, Idaho, New Mexico, South Carolina, and Wisconsin), cases from the state supreme court are published in the same volumes as those from the lower intermediate court of appeals. For example, the set *New Mexico Reports* includes cases from the New Mexico Supreme Court and the New Mexico Court of Appeals. Citations to cases from these states may need parentheticals identifying the deciding court. For example, when citing a case from the New Mexico Court of Appeals, show this as follows: *Cruz v. Harley*, 94 N.M. 861, 729 P.2d 14 (Ct. App. 1993). Without the parenthetical, the reader would assume the case is from the New Mexico Supreme Court. If the case is, in fact, from the New Mexico Supreme Court, the parenthetical need only include the date; it need not include any reference to "S. Ct." Allow the reader to assume it is from the highest court in New Mexico. In sum, if the name of the reporter contains the name of the state, omit the state abbreviation in the parenthetical.

Do not indicate the department, division, county, or district in citing a case from a state court unless that information is of particular importance.

Correct: *Crandall v. Brown*, 291 So. 2d 481 (La. Ct. App. 1981)

Incorrect: *Crandall v. Brown*, 291 So. 2d 481 (La. Ct. App. 4th Dist. 1981)

(3) Public Domain Format

As difficult as the *Bluebook*'s rules are, legal professionals have had, until recently, only this one source to learn. The proliferation of legal materials on electronic databases and the Internet, however, is likely to add further to the confusion already associated with citation form. A controversy currently rages with regard to citation form: how to adapt the traditional citation systems advanced for 70 years by the *Bluebook* to an increasingly technological age.

Current citation rules require citations to conventional print forms, the majority of which are published by West, requiring legal professionals to purchase West sets even though cases and other materials are easy and inexpensive to access on the Internet. Thus, many legal professionals and consumers advocate the implementation of what is usually referred to as a public domain, "format-neutral" or "vendor-neutral" citation system, meaning that the citation looks the same whether the reader has accessed the case by conventional print format or by electronic methods, such as CD-ROM, LEXIS, Westlaw, or the Internet. These groups argue that the *Bluebook* rules requiring citation to West sets, such as the *Federal Reporter* and the *Federal Supplement*, give West a near monopoly and discourage other legal publishers from entering the market, which would ultimately lead to increased competition with resulting lower costs.

While the text of cases and statutes are public domain materials and are thus not subject to copyright protection, when a publisher such as West compiles these materials, adds headnotes, indexes, and other features, it can copyright the resulting product. To end what is perceived as West's unfair market advantage obtained through citation rules requiring or preferring citation to West books, both the American Bar Association and the American Association of Law Libraries as well as numerous professionals support the development of a vendor-neutral citation scheme.

In August 1996, despite objections by state justices and many of its own members, the ABA approved a resolution calling for state and federal courts to develop a uniform or standard format-neutral citation system that would replace the present citation rules (requiring references to sets of books and pages) with one requiring references to cases and paragraphs identified by sequential numbers.

If the ABA proposal is ultimately adopted and approved by the various states and federal courts, and professionals can cite freely to the Internet, cases and other legal authorities will be even more widely disseminated on the Internet. Many law librarians view this as a public service and a key to opening the Internet to widespread and practical use by legal professionals.

At the time of the writing of this text, the following states have adopted a public domain citation format: Arizona, Colorado, Louisiana, Maine, Mississippi, Montana, New Mexico, North Dakota, Oklahoma, South Dakota, Utah, and Wisconsin. Other states are considering doing so. With regard to federal courts, only the Sixth Circuit has presently adopted a public domain format for citations to its cases, and its use is optional. Citation to Sixth Circuit cases is discussed later in this chapter, in Section C.1.g. When states adopt a public domain citation format, it is prospective only and effective only after a certain date (clearly indicated in Table 1 in the *Bluebook*). Citations to cases decided before the date a state adopts a public domain format would follow the standard citation format previously described in Section C of this chapter.

The *Bluebook* (R. 10.3.3) requires that for public domain citations, one give the case name, year of decision, that state's two-character postal code, the court abbreviation (unless the court is the state's highest court), the sequential number of the decision, and, if a parallel citation is available, it must be provided. A pinpoint paragraph rather than a pinpoint page is given. If the case is unpublished, a capital "U" should be placed after the sequential number of the decision.

Example

Albert v. Tinley, 1998 ME 116, ¶ 3, 710 A.2d 14, 17.

In the above example, the case name is *Albert v. Tinley*, the case was the 116th case decided in 1998 by the Maine Supreme Court, and the relevant information is located in paragraph 3 of the case. The remaining information is the usual unofficial citation. Thus, the public domain citation replaces only the official citation in state court cases. If available, the unofficial or regional citation must be given as well to ensure easy access to the case by readers.

Table 1 of the *Bluebook* clearly indicates which states have adopted the public domain citation format, and Rule 10.3.3 provides citation rules. As in all citations, if a jurisdiction has adopted its own rules as to citation form, they supersede the *Bluebook* rules, and the same is true for public domain citation format. The *Bluebook's* Web site (http://www.legalbluebook.com) and the Web site of the American Bar Association (www.abanet.org/citation/home.html) provide additional information on jurisdictions that have adopted a public domain format. A state's own judicial Web site (see Table 1 in the *Bluebook*) may provide court rules giving instruction as to citation presenation. There is a great deal of discrepancy among the adopting states as to spacing in the citations so carefully follow the examples you are given.

d. Recent Cases

(1) Unofficial Cite Unavailable

West typically publishes its cases a bit quicker than the official publishers. If you wish to cite to a very recent case and the official report is not yet available, you may cite as follows:

Hunter v. Hoffman, ___ Conn. ___ , 417 A.2d 704 (1999)

The "blank" lines serve as a signal to a reader that an official citation will exist but it is not yet available. This form is not provided by the *Bluebook* but is commonly used by practitioners.

(2) Slip Form

When a case is not yet reported and is available only in slip or looseleaf form, give the case name, the docket number, the court, and the exact date (Rule 10.8.1(b)).

Correct: *Miller v. Pritchett*, No. 00-201 (N.D. Cal. Dec. 9, 2000)

(3) Cases Available on Electronic Databases (Rule 18.1.1)

A case may be cited to a widely used electronic database such as LEXIS or Westlaw if it is not available in reported print or slip form. Provide the name of the case, docket number, identification of the database (with sufficient information to allow a reader to locate the case), name of court, and the full date of the most recent disposition of the case. If screen or page numbers have been assigned, they should be preceded by an asterisk.

Examples

Gruber v. Edwards, No. 00-829 (E.D. Va. Sept. 14, 2000) (LEXIS, Genfed Library, Dist. File)

McKnight v. Walter, No. 99-10426, 1999 U.S. App. LEXIS 4221, at *4 (4th Cir. Apr. 14, 1999)

Thomas v. Bowman, No. 99-6040, 1999 WL 65102 (S.D. Cal. July 17, 1999)

Neely v. Younger, No. 99-4091, 1999 WL 46723, at *3 (D.C. Cir. 1999)

(4) Cases Available on the Internet (Rules 18.2 and 18.2.2)

Although there are now hundreds of thousands of cases available on the Internet, the *Bluebook* requires the use and citation of traditional printed sources, except when the information is not available in a printed source, or if the traditional source is difficult to find and citation to the Internet will substantially improve access to the information. Because nearly all cases appear in traditional print form within a matter of days after they are decided, the *Bluebook* seems to suggest that citing to the Internet would be exceptional, for example, only for newly released decisions. In fact, Rule 18.2.2 (a) confirms this by providing that a case must be cited first to a traditional source or electronic database, except that the Internet source may be cited when the information is not available in a traditional source or electronic database. Thus, in the hierarchy of citation form, cite cases first to a traditional print source. If the case is not available in the traditional print source, you may cite it to an electronic database such as LEXIS-NEXIS or Westlaw. Only when the case is not available in either of those sources, should you then cite to the Internet.

The basic citation rule is that citation to Internet sources should clearly and unambiguously indicate the source actually used or accessed by the writer. An additional citation in the form of a parallel citation may be provided.

In general, a citation to a case located through the Internet should include the following elements:

- The available information about the authority being cited.
- The appropriate explanatory phrase (if any) to indicate which source was accessed by the writer.
- The provider responsible for the Internet site (if this is not apparent from the Uniform Resource Locator ("URL"), which is the address of the information on the Internet).
- The Uniform Resource Locator.
- A date parenthetical.
- Any explanatory parenthetical.

There are a number of additional, difficult citation principles set forth in the *Bluebook*. For example, if the case is available both in traditional print form and on the Internet, the citation should introduce the Internet cite with the explanatory phrase "*available at*." If the writer located the case or material solely through the Internet, no explanatory phrase is given. Finally, if the material is located exclusively on the Internet and not in traditional sources (for example, some materials are published exclusively online), one should use the explanatory phrase "*at*."

The date parenthetical is also subject to a variety of difficult rules. If the citation is solely to an Internet source and no traditional print source is given, the date parenthetical follows the URL (except in the case of an online journal, when the date parenthetical precedes the URL).

Examples

Recent United States Supreme Court case accessed solely through the Internet: *Seling v. Young*, No. 99-1185 (U.S. Jan. 17, 2001), http://www.supremecourtus.gov/opinions/00pdf/99-1185.pdf.

United States Supreme Court case accessed in print form but available on the Internet: *United States v. Alaska*, 530 U.S. 1 (2000), *available at* http://www.supremecourtus.gov/opinions/99pdf.84orig.pdf.

Second Circuit case accessed in print form but available on the Internet: *Baker v. Dorfman*, 115 F.3d 118 (2d Cir. 2000), *available at* http://tourolaw.edu/2ndCircuit/September00/99-7528.html.

The *Bluebook* provides information on citing statutes, books, and journals to Internet locations. Examples of each of these will be found in Section E.9 of this chapter.

e. Abbreviations in Case Citations

Do not assume that you know the correct abbreviations for Colorado, Idaho, or Oklahoma. While you may know the correct abbreviation for a state for purposes of addressing a letter, the *Bluebook* contains some surprising abbreviations for commonly known geographical terms. Review Table 11 in the *Bluebook* to determine the required abbreviations for the 50 states and for other geographical locations. Similarly, rely upon Table 13 for the correct abbreviations for months of the year.

f. Spacing (*Bluebook* Rule 6.1 (a))

The print in the *Bluebook* is very small, and it is next to impossible to simply look at the examples given and determine the appropriate spacing in a citation. Therefore, you must memorize three spacing rules given as Rule 6.1 of the *Bluebook*:

- Do not put a space between adjacent single capital letters. For purposes of this rule, the abbreviations for "2d" and "3d," and so forth are viewed as single capitals.

Examples

N.W.2d
S.W.
P.2d
F.3d
U.S.

Each of the examples given here shows adjacent single capital letters. Therefore, do not put spaces between them.

- Multiple letter abbreviations are preceded and followed by a space:

Examples

So. 2d
F. Supp. 2d
L. Ed. 2d
Cal. 2d
Ill. App.
S. Ct.

Each of the examples given here includes a multiple letter abbreviation. Therefore, put a space before it and after it.

- In abbreviations of the names of legal periodicals, close up adjacent upper case letters except when one or more of the upper case letters refers to a geographical or institutional entity. In this case separate the upper case letter referring to the entity from other adjacent single letters with a space (*Bluebook* Rule 6.1 (a)).

This rule is confusing. Perhaps the best guide when citing legal periodicals is simply to mimic carefully Table 14 of the *Bluebook*, which provides more than 700 abbreviations for periodicals.

Examples

B.U. L. Rev.

Because the "B.U." in this abbreviation refers to an institutional entity, for example, Boston University, the capital letters for this entity are separated from the other adjacent single letters.

Loy. L.A. L. Rev.

Because the "L.A." in this abbreviation refers to a geographical entity, namely, Los Angeles, the capital letters for such are separated from the next adjacent single letter, "L," which stands for "Law."

Note that Table 14 shows the abbreviations as "B.U. L. REV." and "LOY. L.A. L. REV.," using large and small capitals, as would be used for law review typeface style. Practitioners should always follow the rules on typeface conventions and convert the large and small capitals to ordinary type, specifically "B.U. L. Rev." and "Loy. L.A. L. Rev."

With regard to presentation of citations within your project, the *Bluebook* does not offer any guidelines whatsoever. Most experts suggest that you "break" your citation from one line to the next at a "natural" break point, that is, one that is pleasing to the eye and doesn't strike the reader as awkward in appearance.

g. Federal Cases (*Bluebook* Table 1)

(1) United States Supreme Court Cases

Despite the fact that cases from the United States Supreme Court are published in permanent hardbound volumes in three different sets of books (U.S., S. Ct., and L. Ed.), the *Bluebook* rule is to cite only to the official set, *United States Reports* (U.S.).

This rule of requiring a single citation to U.S. and ignoring the sets S. Ct. and L. Ed. is the reason "star paging" was developed, namely, to allow a reader to read a case in S. Ct. or L. Ed. and yet cite to the official *United States Reports*. (See Chapter 4 for discussion of star paging.)

Correct: *Leroy v. Holden*, 368 U.S. 46 (1975).

Incorrect: *Leroy v. Holden*, 368 U.S. 46, 96 S. Ct. 101, 109 L. Ed. 2d 14 (1975).

You may recall that the *United States Reports* have only had that title since 1875 and that before that date, the sets were named after the individual primarily involved in editing the set (for example, Dallas, Cranch, Wheaton, Peters). Thus, if you see an awkward looking case citation such as *Carter v. Lee*, 4 U.S. (2 Dall.) 16 (1798), you should simply recognize that this is a very old case.

If you cannot cite to U.S. because the official report is not yet available, cite to S. Ct., L. Ed., or U.S.L.W., in that order.

Examples

Hogue v. Davidson, 241 S. Ct. 902 (2000).
Hogue v. Davidson, 289 L. Ed. 2d 101 (2000).
Hogue v. Davidson, 63 U.S.L.W. 1226 (U.S. May 19, 2000).

Remember that you should never give a parallel cite for cases from the United States Supreme Court.

(2) United States Courts of Appeals Cases

There are no official citations for cases from the United States Court of Appeals; therefore, cases should be cited only to West's *Federal Reporter* (F., F.2d, or F.3d). The reader will need to know the circuit that decided the case. Not only will circuit information confirm the case on point (for example, arguments submitted to the Eighth Circuit Court of Appeals should rely on precedents from the Eighth Circuit), some circuits may have established reputations in deciding certain kinds of cases. Thus, this information must be provided to the reader in the parenthetical with the date. *Bluebook* Rule 10.4 clearly requires that every case citation must indicate which court decided the case unless this information is unambiguously conveyed by the name of a reporter (such as is the case with *United States Reports* or *California Reports*). The information must appear in the parenthetical before the date. Thus, because a reference to "F.2d" tells a reader only that a case is from one of the United States courts of appeal, the parenthetical must identify the particular circuit, as follows:

Correct: *Rose v. Capwell Co.*, 721 F.2d 806 (3d Cir. 1988).

The Sixth Circuit (covering Kentucky, Michigan, Ohio, and Tennessee) has adopted a public domain citation format for cases after December 31, 1993, but its use is optional in the Sixth Circuit. Table 1 of the *Bluebook* shows the following example for a public domain citation for a case from the Sixth Circuit:

Equality Fund v. City of Cincinnati, 1997 FED App. 0318P (6th Cir).

(3) United States District Court Cases

There are no official citations for cases from the United States District Courts; therefore, cases should be cited only to West's *Federal Supplement* (F. Supp. and F. Supp. 2d). For the same reasons that readers need to know which circuit court decided a case, readers need to know which district court decided a case. Thus, identify the district court (but not the division of the district court).

Correct: *Simon v. Parker*, 760 F. Supp. 918 (E.D. Ark. 1988).
Correct: *Arnold v. Kenney*, 697 F. Supp. 2d 746 (D. Ariz. 1999).

See Figure 8-1 for abbreviations for our more than 90 district courts.

h. Subsequent History (*Bluebook* Rule 10.7)

Whenever you cite a case you are required to provide its subsequent history. Do not, however, give history relating to:

- denials of *certiorari* or denials of similar discretionary appeals unless the decision is less than two years old or is particularly relevant; or
- history on remand or any denial of a rehearing unless it is particularly relevant.

The rule instructing writers to omit history relating to denials of *certiorari* (unless less than two years old or particularly relevant) is new since 1996 and has caused some disagreement. Many practitioners take the position that the refusal of the United States Supreme Court to grant "cert" and take a case is always relevant because it confirms that the decision is thus final and not subject to further review. Therefore, many practitioners simply ignore the rule and always note that "cert" has been denied. Consult your firm or office to determine its policy on this much-criticized change.

Figure 8-1
Abbreviations for District Courts

State / District	Circuit
ALABAMA	11th Cir.
M.D. Ala.	
N.D. Ala.	
S.D. Ala.	
ALASKA	9th Cir.
D. Alaska	
ARIZONA	9th Cir.
D. Ariz.	
ARKANSAS	8th Cir.
E.D. Ark.	
W.D. Ark.	
CALIFORNIA	9th Cir.
C.D. Cal.	
E.D. Cal.	
N.D. Cal.	
S.D. Cal.	
COLORADO	10th Cir.
D. Colo.	
CONNECTICUT	2d Cir.
D. Conn.	
DELAWARE	3d Cir.
D. Del.	
DISTRICT OF COLUMBIA	D.C. Cir.
D.D.C.	
FLORIDA	11th Cir.
M.D. Fla.	
N.D. Fla.	
S.D. Fla.	
GEORGIA	11th Cir.
M.D. Ga.	
N.D. Ga.	
S.D. Ga.	
HAWAII	9th Cir.
D. Haw.	
IDAHO	9th Cir.
D. Idaho	
ILLINOIS	7th Cir.
C.D. Ill.	
N.D. Ill.	
S.D. Ill.	
INDIANA	7th Cir.
N.D. Ind.	
S.D. Ind.	
IOWA	8th Cir.
N.D. Iowa	
S.D. Iowa	
KANSAS	10th Cir.
D. Kan.	
KENTUCKY	6th Cir.
E.D. Ky.	
W.D. Ky.	
LOUISIANA	5th Cir.
E.D. La.	
M.D. La.	
W.D. La.	
MAINE	1st Cir.
D. Me.	
MARYLAND	4th Cir.
D. Md.	
MASSACHUSETTS	1st Cir.
D. Mass.	
MICHIGAN	6th Cir.
E.D. Mich.	
W.D. Mich.	

Figure 8-1 (*Continued*)

MINNESOTA 8th Cir.
D. Minn.

MISSISSIPPI 5th Cir.
N.D. Miss.
S.D. Miss.

MISSOURI 8th Cir.
E.D. Mo.
W.D. Mo.

MONTANA 9th Cir.
D. Mont.

NEBRASKA 8th Cir.
D. Neb.

NEVADA 9th Cir.
D. Nev.

NEW HAMPSHIRE 1st Cir.
D.N.H.

NEW JERSEY 3d Cir.
D.N.J.

NEW MEXICO 10th Cir.
D.N.M.

NEW YORK 2d Cir.
E.D.N.Y.
N.D.N.Y.
S.D.N.Y.
W.D.N.Y.

NORTH CAROLINA 4th Cir.
E.D.N.C.
M.D.N.C.
W.D.N.C.

NORTH DAKOTA 8th Cir.
D.N.D.

OHIO 6th Cir.
N.D. Ohio
S.D. Ohio

OKLAHOMA 10th Cir.
E.D. Okla.
N.D. Okla.
W.D. Okla.

OREGON 9th Cir.
D. Or.

PENNSYLVANIA 3d Cir.
E.D. Pa.
M.D. Pa.
W.D. Pa.

RHODE ISLAND 1st Cir.
D.R.I.

SOUTH CAROLINA 4th Cir.
D.S.C.

SOUTH DAKOTA 8th Cir.
D.S.D.

TENNESSEE 6th Cir.
E.D. Tenn.
M.D. Tenn.
W.D. Tenn.

TEXAS 5th Cir.
E.D. Tex.
N.D. Tex.
S.D. Tex.
W.D. Tex.

UTAH 10th Cir.
D. Utah

VERMONT 2d Cir.
D. Vt.

VIRGINIA 4th Cir.
E.D. Va.
W.D. Va.

WASHINGTON 9th Cir.
E.D. Wash.
W.D. Wash.

Figure 8-1 (*Continued*)

WEST VIRGINIA 4th Cir.
N.D.W. Va.
S.D.W. Va.

WISCONSIN 7th Cir.
E.D. Wis.
W.D. Wis.

WYOMING 10th Cir.
D. Wyo.

MISCELLANEOUS

CANAL ZONE 5th Cir.
D.C.Z.

GUAM 9th Cir.
D. Guam

N. MARIANA ISLANDS 9th Cir.
D.N. Mar. I.

PUERTO RICO 1st Cir.
D.P.R.

VIRGIN ISLANDS 3d Cir.
D.V.I.

U.S. COURT OF APPEALS FOR THE FEDERAL CIRCUIT Fed. Cir.

U.S. COURT OF FEDERAL CLAIMS Fed. Cl.

Correct: *Bernard v. Scott*, 761 F.2d 902 (8th Cir. 1986), *aff'd*, 106 U.S. 921 (1988)

Correct: *Dowell v. Wong*, 629 F.2d 809 (2d Cir. 1999), *cert. denied*, 410 U.S. 466 (2001)

Note that if any subsequent history occurred in the same year as the lower court case was decided, give the year only once, in the last parenthetical.

Correct: *Walker v. Whiteley*, 701 F.2d 416 (9th Cir.), *rev'd*, 430 U.S. 906 (1985)

A list showing the appropriate abbreviations for subsequent history such as "reversed," "affirmed," "modified," "rehearing granted," all of which must be underlined or italicized, is provided in Table 9 of the *Bluebook*. You will be informed of the subsequent history of a case when you Shepardize or KeyCite it. Shepardizing and KeyCiting are discussed in Chapter 9.

i. Prior History (*Bluebook* Rule 10.7)

There is no ethical obligation to give the prior history of a case. The *Bluebook* states only that you should give prior history of a case if it is relevant to the issue you are discussing or if the case you are citing does not fully describe the issues (such as a memorandum opinion) and therefore you are relying on the lower court case for a full analysis of the issues involved in the case.

This citation rule is logical and eliminates needless citations. For example, virtually all United States Supreme Court cases got to the Supreme Court from some other court and thus have a prior history. Some, in fact, have three or even four prior histories. To include these citations would be confusing and unnecessary because the decision by the United States Supreme Court is the one that is determinative under our system of stare decisis, as discussed in Chapter 1.

j. Parenthetical Information (*Bluebook* Rule 10.6)

If you are relying upon or quoting from any part of an opinion other than the majority opinion, you must so indicate in your citation. A reader will always assume that you are relying upon the majority opinion unless you indicate otherwise. While it is acceptable to cite a dissent or a concurring opinion, remember that only the majority opinion is binding. Dissents and concurring opinions are persuasive only.

Correct: *Wu v. Bradley*, 490 U.S. 102 (1985) (White, J., dissenting).

Similarly, if you wish to give more information about the case (for example, 7-2 decision, author of opinion) do so parenthetically as follows:

Parker, Inc. v. Simpson, 504 U.S. 66 (1989) (7-2 decision).

If the citation you rely on quotes from another case, present that information as follows:

Costello v. McCarty, 490 U.S. 102, 106 (1985) (quoting *Lyons v. Wagner*, 488 U.S. 66, 75 (1983)).

Parentheticals must be given in a certain order. Parenthetical information relating to the weight of a decision (whether it is a 6-3 decision or *per curiam* decision) must precede parenthetical information explaining something about the decision, for example, a phrase such as "following the exclusionary rule." Parentheticals should precede any references to prior or subsequent history (Rule 10.6.2).

k. Different Case Name on Appeal (*Bluebook* Rule 10.7.2)

You may recall that if a case is instituted by a plaintiff, Jones, against a defendant, Smith, and Smith loses the case and appeals, some courts reverse the order of the parties and refer to the case on appeal as *Smith v. Jones*. If the parties' names are merely reversed on appeal, retain the original order, here, *Jones v. Smith*.

l. Order of Preference for Citations

Bluebook Rule 10.3.1 provides an order of preference for citing cases: If a case is not available in an official or preferred unofficial reporter or as a public domain citation, cite to another unofficial reporter, to a widely used computer database (such as LEXIS or Westlaw), to a looseleaf service, to a slip opinion, to an Internet source, or to a newspaper, in that order of preference.

2. *Statutes*

a. State Statutes (*Bluebook* Rule 12 and Table 1)

Citations to state statutes must include the name of the code; the section, paragraph, or article number(s) of the statute; and parenthetically the year of the code, as follows: Miss. Code Ann. § 1401 (1986). The "year of the code" is not necessarily the year the statute was enacted but the year that appears on the spine of the volume, the year identified on the title page, or the latest copyright year, in this order of preference (*Bluebook* Rule 12.3.2).

You may recall from Chapter 3 that some states have codes that classify statutes by title, such as an Agriculture Code, a Civil Code, a Corporations Code, an Evidence Code, or a Probate Code. Usually the more populous states have arranged their codes in such titles. The states that have such subject matter codes are California, Kansas, Louisiana, Maryland, New York, and Texas. If your state organizes its statutes in such a manner, you must indicate the name of the title. Otherwise, if you refer to "Cal. § 301," the reader does not know whether to review Cal. Civil Code § 301, Cal. Evid. Code § 301, or Cal. Prob. Code § 301. The other 44 states and the District of Columbia do not organize their statutes by subject matter, and therefore you follow the standard statute citation rule and identify the name of the code; the section/paragraph/article number; and the date.

Cite to the official code, if possible. If no official code exists, cite to the unofficial or privately published code, but then indicate the publisher parenthetically with the date. If you cite a statute to an electronic database (because the official or unofficial code or privately published session laws are not available), give parenthetically the name of the database (LEXIS or Westlaw) and information relating to the currency of the database as provided by the database itself (Rule 18.1.2).

Example

Cal. Evid. Code § 52 (West, WESTLAW through 1999 Legis. Sess.).

Table 1 of the *Bluebook* lists all 50 states alphabetically and gives examples of how to cite statutes from every state. For those states such as California, New York, Texas, and the others that classify their statutes by subject matter, be sure to properly abbreviate the subject matter according to Table 1. For example, in Texas, the abbreviation for the Family Code is "Fam.," the abbreviation for the Insurance Code is "Ins.," and the abbreviation for the Property Code is "Prop."

Examples for states that do not have subject matter codes:

Official Codes:	Mont. Code Ann. § 1401 (1996). N.C. Gen. Stat. § 1401 (1998). Utah Code Ann. § 1401 (1996).
Unofficial Codes:	Ark. Code Ann. § 5-601 (Michie 1996). Fla. Stat. Ann. § 1401.03 (West 1997). Ohio Rev. Code Ann. § 1401 (Anderson 1999).

Examples for states that organize their statutes by subject matter:

Cal. Evid. Code § 1401 (West 1996).
La. Code Crim. Proc. Ann. art. 1024 (West 1998).
N.Y. Educ. Law § 1401 (McKinney 1994).
Tex. Lab. Code Ann. § 1401 (Vernon 1996).

Remember that the examples given in the *Bluebook* show large and small capitals, for example, "TEX. LAB. CODE ANN. § 1401 (Vernon 1996)," the format used for law reviews. As a practitioner, you will need to adapt the style as follows: "Tex. Lab. Code Ann. § 1401 (Vernon 1996)."

b. Federal Statutes (*Bluebook* Rule 12.3)

You will recall from Chapter 3 that all federal statutes are published officially in the *United States Code* (U.S.C.) and unofficially in *United States Code Annotated* (U.S.C.A.), published by West, and *United States Code Service* (U.S.C.S.), now published by LEXIS Publishing. The elements of a citation for a federal statute are the title, name of set, section number, and year of the code. Once again, the "year of the code" is the date that appears on the spine of the volume, the date shown on the title page, or the most recent copyright year of the volume, in that order. In most cases, this date will *not* be the date the statute was enacted.

Cite federal statutes to the current official code (U.S.C.) if possible. If you cannot cite the federal statute to the official code because it is not available at your law firm or local law library, cite to the unofficial codes (U.S.C.A. or U.S.C.S.). Cite to the actual set in which you located the statute. That is, do not merely drop the "A" of U.S.C.A. to produce an official cite. When you cite to the unofficial codes, you must identify the publisher in the parenthetical before the year of the code.

Examples

U.S.C.	42 U.S.C. § 1246 (2000).
U.S.C.A.	42 U.S.C.A. § 1246 (West 1996).
U.S.C.S.	42 U.S.C.S. § 1246 (LEXIS Publ'g 2000).

If a statute is commonly known by a popular name or such information would assist the reader, you may include the popular name as follows:

Norris-LaGuardia Act § 161, 29 U.S.C. § 221 (1986).

c. Miscellaneous Rules Regarding Citation of Statutes

(1) Spacing

A space should appear between the signal for the section (§) and the number of the statute because the section sign is an abbreviation or replacement for the word "section." A space should also be placed before the parenthetical.

41 U.S.C. § 1982 (1988).

*(2) Internal Revenue Code (*Bluebook *Rule 12.8.1)*

There are special rules for citing to Title 26 of the *United States Code*, entitled "Internal Revenue." For Internal Revenue statutes, drop "26 U.S.C." and replace it with "I.R.C."

Correct:	I.R.C. § 501 (1988).
Incorrect:	26 I.R.C. § 501 (1988).

*(3) Pocket Parts and Supplements (*Bluebook *Rules 3.2 (c) and 12.3.1 (e))*

If the statute appears only in a pocket part or supplement, indicate as follows:

Alaska Stat. § 1401 (Michie Supp. V 1998).
17 U.S.C. § 101 (Supp. III 1997).

If the original statute appears in the hardbound volume and an amendment to it appears in a pocket part or supplement, cite as follows:

17 U.S.C. § 102 (1994 & Supp. I 1996).

*(4) Multiple Sections (*Bluebook *Rule 3.4 (b))*

Because of the often awkward numbering system used for statutes, you must be precise when referring a reader to a group of statutes. For example, if you referred a reader to Tenn. Code Ann. § 1764-66 (1996), the citation is ambiguous. The reader is unsure whether to read sections 1764,

1765, and 1766 or whether there is one particular statute identified as section 1764-66.

While it is common in references to page numbers to drop repetitious digits, do not do so for statutes. If you wish the reader to review sections 1764 through 1766 indicate as follows:

Correct:	Tenn. Code Ann. §§ 1764-1766 (1996).
Incorrect:	Tenn. Code Ann. §§ 1764-66 (1996).

For clarity, follow these rules:

- When referring a reader to one section, use one section symbol (§).
- When referring a reader to more than one section, use two section symbols (§§) and do not drop any digits.
- When referring a reader to more than one section, do not use the term "et seq.," a Latin term for "and the following." Such a reference is too imprecise as it does not tell the reader when to stop reading. For example, the citation 28 U.S.C. §§ 4201 et seq. (1998), strictly interpreted, tells the reader to read the thousands of statutes in the United States Code following section 4201 of title 28.

*(5) Section Reference (*Bluebook *Rule 3.4)*

In a citation, use the sign "§" for the word "section." Most word processors include this symbol, so if it is available, use it. Otherwise, use the word "section." However, spell out the word "section" in a narrative discussion of a statute (except when referring to a provision of the U.S. Code) as follows: The court's interpretation of section 1110 was confined to an analysis of the meaning of the term "compensation." (R.6.2(c)).

*(6) Publisher (*Bluebook *Rule 12.3.1 (d))*

While you may be tempted to omit the parenthetical identification of publisher and/or year in citing statutes, and while practitioners commonly omit such information, the *Bluebook* is unambiguous in requiring such information.

Correct:	16 U.S.C. § 141 (1994).
	16 U.S.C.A. § 141 (West 1996).
	16 U.S.C.S. 141 (Law. Co-op. 1996) or (LEXIS Publ'g 2000).
Incorrect:	16 U.S.C. § 141.
	16 U.S.C.A. § 141.
	16 U.S.C.S. 141.

3. *Rules* (Bluebook *Rule 12.8.3)*

Cite rules of evidence and procedure without any section sign or date, as follows:

Fed. R. Civ. P. 56(a).
Fed. R. Crim. P. 12.
Fed. R. Evid. 210.

4. *Constitutions* (Bluebook *Rule 11)*

a. State Constitutions

The correct form for citing a state constitution is shown on the inside back cover of the *Bluebook*. Note that you do not include a date unless the provision you are citing has been repealed, amended, or superseded.

Correct: Cal. Const. art. XXII.

b. United States Constitution

Cite current provisions of the United States Constitution without dates.

Correct: U.S. Const. art. III, § 8.
U.S. Const. amend. I.

While the earlier editions of the *Bluebook* stated that parts of the United States Constitution were not to be capitalized when referred to in a narrative discussion, the *Bluebook* (R.8) now requires capitalization of parts of the United States Constitution when discussed in textual sentences.

Correct: First Amendment
Equal Protection Clause
Fifth Amendment

Incorrect: first amendment
equal protection clause
fifth amendment

D. Citation Rules and Examples for Secondary Authorities

Examples for citing secondary authorities will be discussed in the order in which those authorities were discussed in Chapters 6 and 7.

1. *Annotations (*Bluebook *Rule 16.6.5)*

For A.L.R. annotations give the author's full name, identify the item as an "annotation," give the title of the annotation (underlined or italicized), the reference to the volume and page of A.L.R. in which it can be found, and the year it was written. A.L.R. annotations are cited as follows:

Jack W. Shaw, Jr., Annotation, *Exhibition of Obscene Motion Pictures as Nuisance*, 50 A.L.R.3d 969 (1978).

2. *Encyclopedias (*Bluebook *Rule 15.7 (a))*

Because the encyclopedias are weak secondary sources and are used primarily to give you introductory explanations of the law and to help you locate cases, you should not cite encyclopedias in support of a contention unless you have no primary authorities or stronger secondary authorities. The correct citation form is as follows:

1 C.J.S. *Abandonment* § 14 (1984).
1 Am. Jur. 2d *Abandonment* § 14 (1986).
6 Cal. Jur. 3d *Contracts* § 221 (1988).

Be sure to include and underscore the title in your citation (*Abandonment, Contracts, Deeds*). Otherwise a citation to 1 C.J.S. § 14 (1984) leaves the reader wondering whether to read Abandonment § 14 or Administrative Law § 14, both of which titles or topics are found in Volume 1 of C.J.S.

3. *Periodical Materials (*Bluebook *Rule 16)*

For periodical articles, give the author's full name, the title of the article (underscored or italicized), the reference to the periodical in which it appeared (abbreviated according to Table 14 in the *Bluebook*), the page on which the article begins, and the date of publication. Be sure to convert the law review format form of large and small capital letters you see in Table 14 to ordinary typeface.

Law Review Articles (*Bluebook* Rules 16.1, 16.5). Steven A. Peterson, *Plea Bargaining in Federal Courts*, 68 Loy. L. Rev. 1421 (1975).

Student-written Articles. Elizabeth A. Brandon, Comment, *Philosophy of Law*, 48 Ariz. L. Rev. 123 (1998).

Bar Association Publications. Lori B. Andrews, *Surrogacy Wars*, Cal. Law., Oct. 1998, at 42.

Special Subject Publications. Andrew P. Neil, *Thrift Regulations*, 16 Inst. on Sec. Reg. 411 (1998).

Legal Newspapers. Joan M. Cheever & Joanne Naiman, *The Deadly Practice of Divorce*, Nat'l L.J., Oct. 12, 1999, at A1.

Note that a comma is used after the title of the article.

4. *Books, Texts, and Treatises* (Bluebook *Rule 15)*

For texts and treatises, give the volume the material appeared in (if there is more than one volume to the set), the author's full name as the author gives it, the title of the text, the page/paragraph/section that the reader should review, and in parentheses the edition (for any edition after the first edition) and date of publication, as follows:

2 J. Thomas McCarthy, *McCarthy on Trademarks and Unfair Competition* § 18:18 (4th ed. 1997).

If the book has two authors, give the full names of both in the order they are listed on the publication, separated by an ampersand (&). If there are more than two authors, you may give the first author's name, followed by "*et al.*," or you may list all authors if relevant.

Refer to later editions and pocket parts as follows:

6 Daniel R. Donoghue, *Maritime and Admiralty Law* § 7.09 (3d ed. Supp. 1992).

Note that there is no comma after the title of a book, text, or treatise, although a comma is given after the title of a periodical article.

5. *Restatements* (Bluebook *Rule 12.8.5)*

Restatements should be cited to the title of the Restatement, the edition being referred to, the section the reader should review, and the date of publication.

Restatement (Second) of Torts § 312 (1976).
Restatement (Second) of Agency § 24 cmt. a (1979).

6. *Uniform Laws* (Bluebook *Rule 12.8.4)*

If you are referring to a Uniform Law as adopted by a state, use the standard statutory citation form for that state, as follows:

Cal. Com. Code § 2-216 (West 1996).

If you are referring to the actual Uniform Law adopted by the Commissioners, cite as follows:

U.C.C. § 2-216 (1977).

If you are referring to the set *Uniform Laws Annotated*, cite as follows:

Unif. Com. Code § 2-216, 10 U.L.A. 109 (1992).

7. *Dictionaries (*Bluebook *Rule 15.7)*

Dictionaries should be cited to the name of the dictionary, the page on which the definition appears and, parenthetically, the edition and year of publication, as follows:

Black's Law Dictionary 679 (7th ed. 1999).
Ballentine's Law Dictionary 415 (3d ed. 1969).

8. *Attorneys General Opinions (*Bluebook *Rule 14.4)*

Cite opinions of attorneys general by title of opinion (if desired), the volume, title of set, first page of opinion, and year, as follows:

State attorneys general opinions:
64 Op. Md. Att'y Gen. 104 (1995)
or
Pharmaceutical Standards, 64 Op. Md. Att'y Gen. 104 (1995).

United States Attorneys General Opinions:
47 Op. Att'y Gen. 16 (1985)
or
Treasury Regulations, 47 Op. Att'y Gen. 16 (1985).

9. *Looseleaf Services (*Bluebook *Rule 19)*

Cite looseleaf services by volume, title of the service (using appropriate abbreviations (see Table 16)), publisher, section/subdivision/paragraph, and date, as follows:

1 Bus. Franchise Guide (CCH) ¶ 3202 (1988).

To cite cases in looseleaf services, cite as follows, unless the case is also published in an official reporter in which case you should cite to it.

Anderson v. CFFC Franchise Corp., 2 Bus. Franchise Guide (CCH) ¶ 8904 (S.D.N.Y. 1992).

E. Special Citation Issues

1. *Introduction*

Learning the various citation rules can be difficult, and the task is made even more complicated by the work of integrating citations into your legal writing. While citations for law review and other academic articles appear in footnotes, citations in other legal writings such as legal memoranda or court documents appear in the body of your narrative text. Because you will typically be preparing or checking cites appearing in text, the information presented in this chapter relates to citing in text. Citations do not exist alone. They appear as part of sentences that must be correctly punctuated, as support for quotations, and together with certain signals that give readers information about the level of support the citation provides for the assertion of law you have made. This section of the chapter will address these special citation issues such as punctuation, quotations, signals, and short form citations you can use when you have once cited an authority in full and now wish to refer to it again. Examples provided will be shown in the form used for legal memoranda.

2. *Punctuation (*Bluebook *Practitioners' Note P.2)*

There are three punctuation marks that may follow a citation: a period; a comma; or a semicolon.

a. Citation "Sentences"

Citations appear in legal writings in two ways: as complete "sentences" or as clauses set off by commas within a sentence. If you have made an assertion about the law, it must be supported by legal authority. You cannot make a statement about the law without attributing it to the appropriate authority. If the statement that you have made about the law is a sentence, the citation that follows the sentence will appear as though it were a "sentence" itself.

Example

> Landlords are required to provide written notice to tenants before commencing actions for eviction. *Williams Co. v. Sanders Eng'g Enter.*, 428 P.2d 102 (Alaska 1996).

In this example, a statement about the law was made in a complete sentence. The citation that supports this legal assertion also appears as a "sentence" in that it starts with a capital letter and ends with a period. The citation informs the reader that the entire preceding sentence is supported by the case *Williams Co. v. Sanders Eng'g Enter*. Note that the words "Engineering" and "Enterprise" have been abbreviated according to Table 6 because the citation stands alone.

b. Citation "Clauses"

Authorities that support (or contradict) only a portion of a sentence appear in a citation format set off by commas, which immediately follow the statement they support (or contradict).

Example

> While it has been held that landlords must provide notice to tenants before commencing eviction actions, *Williams Co. v. Sanders Eng'g Enter.*, 428 P.2d 102 (Alaska 1996), the amount of time provided by the notice may vary from three to ten days, *Hill v. Irwin*, 432 P.2d 918 (Alaska 1997).

This example informs the reader that *Williams Co. v. Sanders Engineering Enterprise* requires landlords to give notice to tenants and that *Hill v. Irwin* provides that the length of time set forth in the notice may vary. Note that because the *Williams* case cite is not needed to make sense of a sentence or clause, it is viewed as a stand-alone cite rather than as part of a textual sentence. Thus, words such as "engineering" and "enterprise" can be abbreviated.

Do not place a citation in parentheses or brackets. Try to vary your placement of citations. If your writing consists of a series of sentences each of which is followed by a citation, your project will be choppy. Besides varying citations so that some appear as sentences and some appear as clauses, another technique used by many legal writers to achieve variety and interest in their writing is occasionally to use citations in introductory clauses.

Example

> According to *Williams Co. v. Sanders Engineering Enterprise*, 428 P.2d 102 (Alaska 1996), landlords must provide written notice to tenants before commencing actions to evict those tenants.
>
> or
>
> One of the first cases to address the issue of default notices was *Williams Co. v. Sanders Engineering Enterprise*, 428 P.2d 102 (Alaska 1996), which held that landlords must provide written notice to tenants before commencing actions to evict those tenants.

These phrases provide a different technique for introducing citations and add interest to a project. Again, however, do not fall into the lazy habit of always introducing your legal authorities in the same manner. Occasionally students start each and every paragraph in a project with the phrase "In *Williams v. Sanders* . . ." or "In *Hill v. Irwin* . . ." The reader, on looking at the page, is presented with a series of paragraphs each of which commences with the word "in" followed by a case citation, giving the project a rigid look and a style lacking in interest and variety.

3. *String Citing (*Bluebook *Rule 1.4)*

a. Introduction

Another manner in which citations appear in legal writing is in "strings" or groups of several citations. If you cite more than one authority in support of a proposition, separate each citation from the next by a semicolon and follow the last citation with the appropriate punctuation mark, usually a period.

Example

> Courts from all over the country are in agreement in requiring landlords to provide notice to tenants before commencing actions to evict those tenants. *Samson v. Oak Tree Apts., Inc.*, 761 P.2d 118 (Cal. 1980); *Allen v. Carwood*, 421 A.2d 181 (N.J. 1976); *Fulton v. Garden Apts., Ltd.*, 388 S.W.2d 200 (Tex. 1977).

In general, "string citing" is disfavored. Courts prefer that you select the best authority that supports a proposition and cite it rather than cluttering your writing with citations that do not add anything. In certain situations, however, string citing is acceptable. Thus, as shown in the preceding example, if you need to demonstrate to a reader the breadth and variety of authorities that are in agreement, or if your state has no authorities for a certain issue and you wish to persuade the court to adopt a view espoused by several jurisdictions, you may wish to string cite.

b. Order of Citations in String Cites

When you string cite, however, you must place the citations in a certain order. The *Bluebook* (Rule 1.4) provides that if one authority is more helpful or authoritative than the others, it should be placed first. Absent this or some other substance-related rationale, you should list the citations in the following order (see *Bluebook* for complete list):

(i) Constitutions (list federal Constitution first, then state constitutions, alphabetically by state).
(ii) Statutes (list federal statutes first by order of U.S.C. title, then state statutes alphabetically by state).
(iii) Cases (list federal cases first, ordering by United States Supreme Court, United States courts of appeal, United States district courts, then state cases, alphabetically by state and from highest court to lowest court).

(iv) Secondary authorities (in this order: Model codes, Restatements, books, law review articles, annotations, and electronic sources).

If you have several cases from the same state, for example, Missouri—cite from highest court to lowest court and within each group from newer cases to older cases.

If you have several cases from the United States courts of appeal or the United States district courts, cite by date, giving the newer cases first.

Example

Landlords must provide notice to tenants before commencing actions for eviction. *Alan v. Anderson*, 421 F.2d 101 (4th Cir. 1985); *Darwin v. Balboa Gardens*, 415 F.2d 222 (8th Cir. 1984); *Swanson v. Trudeau*, 399 S.W.2d 14 (Ark. 1988); *McNenly v. Trainor*, 346 S.W.2d 606 (Ark. 1981); *Harrison v. J.T. Alton, Inc.*, 394 S.W.2d 102 (Ark. App. 1986).

4. *Quotations* (Bluebook *Rule 5*)

a. Introduction

You may find in the course of legal writing that you wish to quote directly from a case, treatise, law review article, or other legal authority. Your decision to quote a legal authority rather than merely summarize or paraphrase it may stem from your desire to emphasize a certain point or perhaps your determination that the judge's or author's manner of expressing a legal principle is so articulate that you wish to present the material in its original form rather than weaken its force by summarizing it. Quoting from legal authorities is certainly acceptable so long as it is not overdone and so long as the citation is in correct form.

You must *always* indicate the exact page a quote appears on to allow a reader to review the original source and ensure that you have correctly reproduced the material and have not altered the meaning of the quotation by omitting or adding material. This reference to the exact page on which the quoted material appears is often called a "spot cite," or a "pinpoint cite," as you are pinpointing the reader's attention to a specific page, or a "jump cite," as you are asking the reader to "jump" from the first page of a legal authority to a specific page within that authority.

The reference to quoted material is placed immediately after the page on which the case or article begins, separated by a comma.

Examples

Case: *Goodman v. Gray*, 429 F.2d 109, 114 (7th Cir. 1979). This informs the reader that the case begins at page 109, and the quoted material is found at page 114.

Article: Susan L. Hoffman, *The Juvenile's Right to Counsel*, 47 N.C. L. Rev. 411, 446 (1985). This informs the reader that the article begins at page 411, and the quotation is found at page 446.

Recall that for state court cases decided by your state and cited in court documents submitted to courts in your state, you must give all parallel citations, if they exist. This requirement imposes the additional burden of informing the reader on which page a quote occurs in each parallel cite. In some instances, you will have to locate the quote in several sources.

Examples

"A landlord must provide a notice to a tenant before commencing an action to evict the tenant." *Tapper v. Savage*, 201 Wis. 2d 191, 196, 299 N.W.2d 47, 52 (1986).

"It is incumbent upon the prosecution to prove defendant's guilt beyond a reasonable doubt." *State v. Harrison*, 262 Cal. 3d 104, 106, 461 P.2d 201, 204, 189 Cal. Rptr. 966, 968 (1979).

If the quote spans more than one page, provide the inclusive page numbers but separate them by a hyphen. Retain the last two digits but omit any other repetitious digits. (R. 3.3 (d)).

Examples

Patterson v. Crowley, 88 U.S. 407, 414-16 (1989).

Signorelli v. Stanley, 98 F. Supp. 1069, 1071-73 (N.D. Cal. 1986).

If you are citing from individual scattered pages from a source, indicate the separate pages as follows (R. 3.3 (d)).

Example

Bailey v. Pridewell, 412 F.2d 109, 114, 121 (9th Cir. 1978).

While you are only required to give the exact page on which material appears if you are quoting, most attorneys and paralegals routinely give the exact page even if they are summarizing or paraphrasing, rather than quoting directly. This practice is a courtesy to readers to enable them to locate easily that portion of the authority you are discussing. If your research is accurate and the legal authority does in fact say what you claim it does, there is no reason not to provide a reference to a specific page. This is the position suggested by the *Bluebook* (R. 3.3(a)), which states that when referring to "specific material" within a source, one should include both the page on which the source begins and the pinpoint.

If a point is continually made throughout a source, use *passim*, a Latin word meaning "everywhere" and interpreted as "scattered here and there," as follows (R. 3.3 (d)).

Example

Taft v. Alpert, 429 S.E.2d 616 *passim* (W. Va. 1988).

If your specific material appears on the first page of a source, repeat the page number (R. 3.3 (a)), as follows:

Example

Allison P. Page, *Statutory Construction*, 46 BYU L. Rev. 109, 109 (1998).

b. Indicating Quotations in Text

The *Bluebook* rules regarding quotations conform to the rules regarding quotations that you have been familiar with since high school, that is, that quotations of 49 or fewer words appear in the text of your writing while quotations of 50 or more words are indented.

*(1) Non-Indented Quotations (*Bluebook *Rule 5.1 (b))*

Quotations of 49 or fewer words should appear in the body of your text without indentation. Indicate the beginning and ending of the quotation by quotation marks ("/"). If your quote then relies on or incorporates other quoted material, indicate such by a single quotation mark ('). Commas and periods must be placed inside the ending quotation mark. Other punctuation marks such as question marks or exclamation points appear inside the ending quotation mark only if they are part of the matter quoted.

Example

In one recent case, the court ruled that the defendant could properly be found to have been carrying a knife for use as a dangerous weapon and held as follows: "Although appellant was attempting to check the knife when arrested, his statements permitted the inference that he was prepared to use it, should the occasion arise, but prior to entering and, after retrieving the briefcase, immediately upon leaving the Longworth Building." *Monroe v. United States*, 598 A.2d 439, 441 (D.C. App. 1991).

*(2) Indented Quotations (*Bluebook *Rule 5.1 (a))*

Quotations of 50 words or more should be indented (typically ten spaces), left and right, and appear without quotation marks. This "block" quote should be single-spaced. A reader is alerted to the fact that material is being quoted by the indentation itself. If your quotation quotes from some other source or authority, indicate such with quotation marks ("/"). That is, retain all punctuation marks and quotation marks as they appear in the original quote. This is quite different from a non-indented quote, which requires you to use a single quotation mark (') when it is quoting from another source.

To determine whether you should indent a quote and place it in block form, you must count the words in the quote. While this is somewhat time-consuming, it must be done. There are, however, a few word processing programs, such as SpellCheck, that will count the words in a quote for you.

Some legal writers indent quotes of fewer than 50 words to emphasize the indented material and make it stand out from the remainder of the narrative. Avoid this practice, as it not only violates *Bluebook* rules but has been overdone, with the result that some readers "skip over" short indented material. Your writing should be sufficiently forceful in itself without resorting to "tricks" to draw emphasis.

One of the mistakes most commonly made by legal writers relates to placement of the citation that supports the quote. The citation does *not* appear within the block indentation. Placement of the citation within the indention indicates that it is part of the quote. The citation should be placed at the left margin on the line that follows the quote.

Correct:
XXXXXXXXXXXXXXXXXXXXXX
XXXXXXXXXXXXXXXXXXXXXX
XXXXXXXXXXXXXXXXXXXXXX
XXXXXXXXXXXXXXXXXXXXXX

Monroe v. United States, 598 A.2d 439, 441 (D.C. App. 1991).

Incorrect:
XXXXXXXXXXXXXXXXXXXXXXX
XXXXXXXXXXXXXXXXXXXXXXX
XXXXXXXXXXXXXXXXXXXXXXX
Monroe v. United States, 598 A.2d
439, 441 (D.C. App. 1991).

After you have placed your citation at the left margin, continue your narrative. If you begin a new paragraph, skip to the next line (or skip two lines if you are double spacing) and indent as usual to show a new paragraph is beginning.

c. Alterations of Quotes (*Bluebook* Rule 5.2)

Anytime you alter a quote in any way, whether by pluralizing a word, inserting a word, capitalizing a word that was not capitalized in the original quote, or some other alteration, you must always alert the reader that you have changed the quote. When you change a letter from lower case to upper case, or vice versa, enclose it in brackets. Similarly, substituted words or letters or other inserted material should be bracketed. If a letter has been omitted, indicate such with empty brackets—for example "boy[ ]" for "boys."

If the original quote was, for example, "The factfinder must consider circumstances surrounding the possession and use of the dangerous weapon," you must indicate an alteration of the quoted material as follows: "The factfinder [should have] consider[ed] circumstances surrounding the possession and use of the dangerous weapon."

If a mistake or misspelling has occurred in the original material, indicate such by following the mistake by the word *sic*, a Latin word meaning "thus; so; in such manner." For example, if the original quoted material provides, "Defendants was convicted in the Superior Court," indicate the error in the original as follows: "Defendants was [sic] convicted in the Superior Court."

d. Adding Emphasis (*Bluebook* Rule 5.2)

If the material you are quoting is emphasized in the original by italics, underscoring, or otherwise, retain the original emphasis but do not otherwise indicate such. Thus, do not state "emphasis in original." By including the italicized or underscored word or phrase in the quotation, the reader will assume this emphasis occurred in the original. If, on the other hand, you wish to emphasize something that was *not* so emphasized in the original, you must indicate your alteration of the quote by a parenthetical explanation.

For example, assume the original quote read as follows:

> "The court refused to hold that merely possessing a dangerous weapon was a violation of the statute." *Franklin v. James*, 681 F.2d 102, 106 (8th Cir. 1988).

If you wish to emphasize any of the words or phrases in the original material, do so as follows:

> "The court refused to hold that *merely possessing* a dangerous weapon was a violation of the statute." *Franklin v. James*, 681 F.2d 102, 106 (8th Cir. 1988) (emphasis added).

e. Omitting Citations (*Bluebook* Rule 5.2)

It is possible that the quotation you wish to include is peppered with other citations, resulting in a quote that is disrupted by these intervening cites, weakening the force and effect of the quotation. To eliminate these intrusive citations and yet remain faithful to the original quoted material, simply indicate to the reader that you have omitted citations.

Example

> The court relied on numerous precedents in refusing to hold that "merely possessing a dangerous weapon was a violation of the statute." *Franklin v. James*, 681 F.2d 102, 106 (8th Cir. 1988) (citations omitted).

If readers wish to review the other cases whose citations have been omitted, they may easily do so by locating page 106 of the case *Franklin v. James*, located at volume 681 of the *Federal Reporter, Second Series*.

f. Use of Ellipses (*Bluebook* Rule 5.3)

If you omit a word, phrase, or sentence from quoted material, you must indicate this omission by the use of an ellipsis, three periods separated by spaces from each other and set off by a space before the first period and after the last period. An ellipsis signals that words have been omitted from the middle of a quotation or the end of a quotation. Do not use an ellipsis to begin a quotation. If you have altered a word or omitted words at the beginning of a quotation, indicate such by changing the first letter of the word now beginning your quote from a lowercase letter to an uppercase letter and enclosing it in brackets. This will signal the reader that you have altered the beginning of a quote.

For example, assume your quote is as follows:

> "In order to prove a violation of the statute, the prosecution must prove defendant's intent."

If you wish to omit the first part of the quote, do so as follows:

> "[T]o prove a violation of the statute, the prosecution must prove defendant's intent."

g. Omissions from the Middle of the Quote

To indicate that you have omitted language from the middle of a quote, use the ellipsis, three periods separated by spaces:

> Example: "In order to prove a violation . . . the prosecution must prove . . . intent."

h. Omissions from the End of a Quote

To indicate that you have omitted language from the end of a quote, use three periods separated by spaces followed by the final punctuation of your quote, typically a period.

> Example: "Although Appellant was attempting to check the knife when arrested, his statements permitted the inference that he was prepared to use it . . . ."

i. Using Quoted Language as a Phrase

When using quoted language as a phrase or clause rather than as a full sentence, you need not use an ellipsis.

Example

> Justice O'Connor stated that malice and recklessness "will give rise to punitive damages."

j. Paragraph Structure

If you have indented a quote of 50 or more words and this quote commenced a paragraph, indent further to let the reader know that your quote is from the beginning of a paragraph.

Example

XXXXXXXXXXXXXXXXXXXXXXX
XXXXXXXXXXXXXXXXXXXXXXXXXXXX
XXXXXXXXXXXXXXXXXXXXXXXXXXXX
XXXXXXXXXXXXXXXXXXXXXXXXXXXX
XXXXXXX.

If you continue to quote another paragraph, skip a line and once again indent the second quote to indicate it commenced a paragraph.

Only indent your block quote(s) if the original quote began a paragraph. Quotations from the middle of paragraphs appear in block style with no additional indentations.

If you are quoting one paragraph of 50 words or more and then wish to omit or skip a paragraph and then continue quoting another paragraph of 50 words or more, use four indented periods on a new line to signal that you have omitted an entire paragraph.

Example

XXXXXXXXXXXXXXXXXXXXXXX
XXXXXXXXXXXXXXXXXXXXXXXXXXXX
XXXXXXXXXXXXXXXXXXXXXXXXXXXX
XXXXXXXXXXXXXXXXXXXXXXXXXXXX
XXXXXXX.

. . . .

XXXXXXXXXXXXXXXXXXXXXXX
XXXXXXXXXXXXXXXXXXXXXXXXXXXX
XXXXXXXXXXXXXXXXXXXXXXXXXXXX
XXXXXXXXXXXXXXXXXXXXXXXXXXXX
XXXXXXX.

To signal an omission at the beginning of a second or subsequent paragraph, use an ellipsis (even though you may never use an ellipsis to begin a quotation).

Example

XXXXXXXXXXXXXXXXXXXXXXX
XXXXXXXXXXXXXXXXXXXXXXXXXXXX
XXXXXXXXXXXXXXXXXXXXXXXXXXXX
XXXXXXXXXXXXXXXXXXXXXXXXXXXX
XXXXXXXXXXXXXXXXXXXXXXXXXXXX
XXXXXXX.

...XXXXXXXXXXXXXXXXXXXXXXX
XXXXXXXXXXXXXXXXXXXXXXXXXXXX
XXXXXXXXXXXXXXXXXXXXXXXXXXXX
XXXXXXXXXXXXXXXXXXXXXXXXXXXX
XXXXXXXXXXXXXXXXXXXXXXXXXXXX
XXXXXXX.

5. *Citation Signals (*Bluebook *Rule 1.2)*

Legal writers often use certain citation signals as a shorthand method of indicating to the reader the manner in which an authority supports or contradicts an assertion. If a citation does anything other than directly state a proposition, identify the source of a quotation, or identify an authority referred to in text, a signal indicating such should be used before the citation. These signals can be very confusing and often there are only very subtle shadings of difference between one signal and another. Moreover, the use of signals is complicated by the fact that their use and meaning have shifted from one edition of the *Bluebook* to the next. See Figure 8-2.

(i) *No signal.* If, after having made an assertion, the author immediately cites a legal authority, this indicates the legal authority directly states the proposition, identifies the source of a quotation, or identifies an authority referred to in text.

(ii) *Accord.* The word *accord* is used after one case has been given and introduces a second case agreeing with the first.

Example

"Landlords are required to provide notice to tenants before commencing actions to evict tenants." *Li v. Carr*, 420 U.S. 20, 29 (1994); *accord Smith v. Jones*, 681 P.2d 104, 107 (Cal. 1990).

(iii) *See.* The signal *see* is used when the citation clearly supports the proposition. *See* is used when the proposition is not directly stated by the authority you rely upon but obviously follows from it. The use of *see* has shifted over time, and the 17th edition of the *Bluebook* reverts to the position taken by the 15th edition, which omits the confusion caused in the use of *see* by the 16th edition of the *Bluebook* from 1996-2000. See Figure 8-2.

(iv) *See also.* This signal is used to show additional legal authorities that support a proposition. The *Bluebook* encourages you to use a parenthetical explaining the relevance of the authorities.

(v) *Cf.* The signal *cf.*, meaning "compare," is used to indicate legal authority supporting a proposition that is different from the main proposition but that is analogous to the main proposition. The *Bluebook* strongly recommends that when using

Figure 8-2
The Evolution of Citation Signals in the *Bluebook*

	[No signal]	*See*	*Contra*
Fifteenth Edition (1991-1996)	Citation clearly states the proposition or identifies the source of a quotation or authority referred to in text.	Citation clearly supports the proposition.	Citation directly states the contrary of the proposition.
Sixteenth Edition (1996-2000)	Citation identifies the source of a quotation or authority used in text.	Citation clearly states or clearly supports the proposition.	*Contra* did not exist in the Sixteenth Edition of the *Bluebook*.
Seventeenth Edition (2000-date)	Citation directly states the proposition or identifies the source of a quotation or authority referred to in text.	Citation clearly supports the proposition.	Citation directly states the contrary of the proposition.

this signal, the writer explain parenthetically how the cited authority supports the proposition.

(vi) *Contra*. The signal *contra* indicates contradiction and is used when the cited authority directly states the contrary of the proposition you have made. Like "no signal" and *see*, the use of *contra* has shifted over time, and, in fact, was omitted entirely from the 16th edition of the *Bluebook*. It has been revived in the current 17th edition.

(vii) *But see*. This signal is used when the legal authority you cite clearly supports a proposition contrary to the main proposition.

(viii) *But cf.* The signal *but cf.* is used when the legal authority you cite supports a proposition analogous to the contrary of the main proposition. The *Bluebook* strongly recommends a parenthetical explanation as to the relevance of the authority you cite.

(ix) *See generally*. The signal *see generally* indicates that the legal authority you cite provides helpful background material related to the proposition. The *Bluebook* recommends an explanatory parenthetical.

These signals are given before your citation. They may or may not be capitalized, depending on the context in which they are used. Capitalize a signal beginning a sentence and do not capitalize a signal that is part of a sentence. The signals are underscored or italicized unless they are used as verbs in ordinary sentences, and an unbroken line is used for signals composed of two words, such as *see generally*.

Most individuals find these signals confusing and very difficult to distinguish. Typically, they are used more often in academic legal writing, such as law review articles, which provide a complete analysis of an issue, including cases in support of a proposition and cases in contradiction to a proposition, rather than in court documents and legal memoranda, which often use citations with no or few introductory signals.

6. *Short Form Citations*

Once you have cited an authority in full, to save time you may use a short form on subsequent occasions when you refer to it in your writing. The *Bluebook* (P.4) provides that a short form may be used if it will be clear to the reader which citation has been shortened, the earlier full citation appeared in the same general discussion, and the reader will be able to locate readily the earlier full citation.

a. Cases (*Bluebook* Rule P.4 (a))

Assume your full citation is *Singer v. Bryant*, 219 N.E.2d 409, 411 (Ind. 1987). Once you have given this full citation, you may use any of the following short forms:

Singer, 219 N.E.2d at 411.
219 N.E.2d at 411.
Id. at 411.

If you have fully referred in a court document to a case from a state that has parallel citations such as *Lowell v. Allen*, 204 Ga. 102, 104, 68 S.E.2d 19, 21 (1976), you may use any of the following short forms:

Lowell, 204 Ga. at 104, 68 S.E.2d at 21.
204 Ga. at 104, 104 68 S.E.2d at 21.
Id. at 104, 68 S.E.2d at 21.

The *Bluebook* also provides that if you have given a full case citation and later refer to the case in the same general discussion, you may use one of the parties' names without including any further citation (Rule 10.9 (b)).

Example

In *Lowell*, the court also held that punitive damages are recoverable in fraud actions.

Generally, use the plaintiff's name in a short form unless the plaintiff is a common litigant such as the United States, "People" or some government agency, in which case use the more distinctive defendant's name.

b. Statutes (*Bluebook* Rule P.4 (b))

Once you have given a full citation to a statute, you may later use any short form that clearly identifies the statute.

First reference:	Ohio Rev. Code Ann. § 101 (Anderson 1988).
Later reference:	Ohio Rev. Code Ann. § 101.

c. Constitutions (*Bluebook* Rule P.4 (c))

Do not use any short form other than *id.* for constitutions.

d. Books and Periodical Materials (*Bluebook* Rule P.4 (d))

Use *id.* or *supra* to refer to these materials after you have given a full citation to them.

7. *Use of* Id., Supra, Infra, *and Hereinafter*

a. *Id.* (*Bluebook* Rule 4.1)

(1) Introduction

Id. is an abbreviation for *ibidem*, a Latin word meaning "in the same place." You may recall using *ibid.* or *id.* in high school or college term papers to avoid having to repeat information in a footnote and to signal the reader that your material originated from the same source as that indicated immediately before.

Id. functions the same way in legal writing. A court document or legal memorandum may rely almost exclusively on one case, which you discuss over the course of several pages. To avoid having to repeat and retype the citation each time you make an assertion, you can elect to use the signal *id.* to refer the reader to the immediately preceding authority. Note that while the signal *ibid.* is acceptable in some writings, it is not acceptable in legal writing. Only *id.* may be used.

Id. may be used for any legal authority. That is, *id.* may be used to direct a reader to a preceding case, statute, treatise, law review article, or other legal authority. *Id.* will be capitalized if it "stands alone" or begins a sentence or it will be introduced with a lower case letter if it is part of a citation clause or sentence. If underscoring, underscore the period in id. (P.1 (f)).

If you have cited a case or some other authority and you then wish to direct the reader to that immediately preceding citation, use *id.*

Example

In order to prove a violation of the statute, the government must demonstrate only that the defendant carried a dangerous weapon, and intended to carry a weapon. *Monroe v. United States*, 598 A.2d 430, 439 (D.C. App. 1991). There is no requirement that a defendant evidence a specific intent to use the weapon for a wrongful purpose. *Id.*

The use of the signal *id.* in the example indicates to the reader that *Monroe v. United States* is the source of the assertion that there is no requirement that the government prove that a defendant had a specific intent to use a weapon for an unlawful purpose.

(2) "Id. *Plus*"

Use *id.* alone if you wish to direct the reader to the exact source and page/section/paragraph as the preceding citation. If, however, you wish to direct the reader to the preceding source, but to a different page/section/paragraph within that source, use "*id.* plus" the change:

Example

"A landlord is required to provide written notice to a tenant before instituting an action to evict the tenant." *Jasper v. Schick*, 92 P.2d 106, 109 (Wash. 1984). "This notice must be hand-delivered to a tenant at least three days before the action is commenced." *Id.* at 114.

The reader has been directed to *Jasper v. Schick* but to a different page within that source.

Examples

First reference to a case: *Daly v. Chu*, 661 F.2d 918, 920 (10th Cir. 1986).
Next reference: *Id.* or *Id.* at 921.
First reference to a statute: 42 U.S.C. § 1604 (1986).
Next reference: *Id.* or *Id.* § 1606.
First reference to a treatise: 1 J. Thomas McCarthy, *McCarthy on Trademarks and Unfair Competition* § 18:18 (4th ed. 1997).
Next reference: *Id.* or *Id.* § 18:22.
First reference to a law review article: Carolyn L. Gray, *Tariff Restrictions*, 40 Mo. L. Rev. 161, 166 (1982).
Next reference: *Id.* or *Id.* at 169.

Note that when you are directing a reader to a different page you use "*Id.* at ______." When, however, you direct a reader to a different section or paragraph, you simply use "*Id.* § ______" or "*Id.* ¶ ______." The *Bluebook* expressly states that the word "at" is not used before a section or paragraph symbol. (Rule 3.4).

Correct:	*Id.* § 314.
	Id. ¶ 14.120.
Incorrect:	*Id.* at § 314.
	Id. at ¶ 14.120.

(3) Parallel Citations

Remember that for cases decided in your state and cited in court documents submitted to a court in your state, you must include parallel citations if they exist. This requirement makes the use of *id.* somewhat more complicated because you must use the following form:

First cite	*Garde v. Whetsell*, 209 Ariz. 106, 108, 309 P.2d 309, 311 (1986).
***Id.* reference**	*Id.* at 110, 309 P.2d at 313.

Note that only the official citation is replaced with *id.* The regional reporter citation is repeated.

(4) The Use of "Id." in Footnotes

The signal *id.* may be used to refer to an immediately preceding authority within the same footnote or to an immediately preceding footnote when that preceding footnote contains only one authority. If the preceding footnote contains more than one source, later use of *id.* does not tell the reader which of the preceding sources is being referenced (R. 4.1).

b. *Supra* (*Bluebook* Rule 4.2)

(1) Introduction

Supra means "above" and informs a reader to look at preceding authorities (although not *immediately* preceding sources, for which you should use *id.*) for the information desired. For example, if you are searching an index for entries related to tenants, you may find the following:

Tenant, see Landlord, *supra*.

This is an instruction that the information you need is arranged and presented under the heading "Landlord," which appears "above" or earlier in the volume, rather than being arranged under the heading "Tenant."

Often in a legal writing you may refer to one authority, for example, a treatise, then refer to various other authorities and then wish to refer to the treatise again without repeating the entire citation. In this situation you cannot use *id.* because there are citations that intervene between your first reference to the treatise and your current reference to it. In this instance, use *supra*, which informs the reader that you have given the citation previously in your project, although it was not given immediately preceding.

The *Bluebook* is quite clear that you may not use *supra* when referring to primary authorities (cases, constitutions, statutes, legislative materials, or regulations) "except in extraordinary circumstances," such as when the name of the case or other authority is very long (Rule 4.2). If you have referred to a case, constitution, or statute and then discussed other authorities and then wish to refer again to the case, constitution, or statute, you may not use *supra*. You must use a "short form" citation, discussed previously in Section E.6, *supra*.

This prohibition against using *supra* to refer to previously cited cases is a commonly violated *Bluebook* rule. Practicing attorneys and paralegals routinely use *supra* to refer to previously cited cases. Before joining the majority and embarking on such a violation, determine what the common practice is in your firm or agency. Some firms, usually the larger ones, will rigidly adhere to the *Bluebook* and would view your use of *supra* to refer to a preceding case as an unforgivable gaffe, while other firms would view such a use of *supra* as a practical and effective citation form.

Supra does not "stand alone" like *id.* It must appear with other identification, usually the last name of an author, or, if there is no author, the title of a work.

Examples

First cite:	Carolyn L. Gray, *Tariff Restrictions*, 40 Mo. L. Rev. 161, 164 (1982).
Intervening cite:	*Powell v. Silvers*, 661 F.2d 918 (10th Cir. 1986).
***Supra* cite:**	Gray, *supra*.

To indicate a variation, use "*supra* plus" the variation, such as *Gray, supra*, at 166. If you are underscoring, underscore the word *supra* but not any punctuation following it.

The examples given in the *Bluebook* for practitioners show a comma after *supra* when the "*supra* plus" form is used to refer a reader to a book or article such as Gray, *supra*, at 166 (P.4(d)).

Examples of Short Forms in a Brief or Court Document

Page 1.	*Taylor v. Ellis*, 501 U.S. 621, 626 (1994).
Page 2.	*Id.*
Page 3.	*Id.* at 629.
Page 4.	6 Judith N. Hunter, *Intellectual Property* § 104 (3d ed. 1991).
Page 5.	*Id.*
Page 6.	*Id.* § 107.
Page 7.	a. *Taylor*, 501 U.S. at 630 *or* b. 501 U.S. at 630 *or* c. In *Taylor*, the Court also held . . .
Page 8.	Hunter, *supra* or Hunter, *supra*, § 108.

(2) *Internal Cross-References* (Bluebook *Rule 3.6)*

It is possible that you may have cited a book or treatise very early in your project and then wish to refer to it many pages later. If your only direction to the reader is "Gray, *supra*," the reader may have to thumb through several pages to find the original citation. As a courtesy to the reader you may wish to include a reference to the specific page in your project on which the original citation appeared. Use "p." or "pp." to direct your reader to the first page in your project on which the full citation originally appeared.

Examples

Gray, *supra* p. 3

Gray, *supra* p.3, at 168. (This signal directs the reader to page 168 of the article written by Carolyn L. Gray and informs the reader that the full citation appears on page 3 of your project.) Follow *supra* with a comma when you direct a reader to the page or section of the previously cited legal authority. No comma is used after *supra* when you refer a reader to a previous page or section within your project.

c. *Infra*

Infra is a Latin word meaning "below" or "beneath." It is used to direct a reader to material that will appear later in a project. For example, if you were directed to review some chapter appearing after this one, the signal would be "Chapter 10, *infra*." *Infra* is the direct opposite signal of *supra* and you should follow the guidelines discussed previously for *supra* in using *infra*. Note that neither *supra* nor *infra* may be used to refer to the primary authorities of cases, constitutions, statutes, legislative materials, or regulations.

As you can imagine, *infra* is not used very often in documents or memoranda prepared by practitioners. It makes little sense to state a legal principle and then give the reader the following citation: Gray, *infra*, meaning that you will be giving the full cite to the article by Carolyn L. Gray later in the project. It is more likely that your use of *infra* will relate to directing a reader to a later section in your document. In this case, use the following form: *See infra* Section V.

d. Use of "Hereinafter" (*Bluebook* Rule 4.2 (b))

If an authority would be difficult to identify repeatedly due to an extremely long name or title, you may identify it in full the first time you cite it and then inform the reader that thereafter you will be referring to it by a shorter name or form.

Earlier editions of the *Bluebook* required that writers identify a session number for a Congress when citing to bills, hearings, committee reports, and other documents. Because astute readers know that the first session of a Congress (1st Sess.) always occurs in odd-numbered years and the second session (2d Sess.) always occurs in even-numbered years, the *Bluebook* no longer requires a reference to a congressional session for any materials published after the 60th Congress in 1907.

Examples

First citation: *Proposed Amendments to the Federal Fair Franchising Practices Act of 1992: Hearings on H.R. 5961 Before the House Comm. on Energy and Commerce*, 102d Cong. 41 (1992) [hereinafter *Hearings*]

Later citations: *Hearings*, *supra*.

8. Capitalization in Court Documents and Other Legal Memoranda

Bluebook Rule 8 and Practitioners' Note 6 require that in headings and titles of documents submitted to courts you should capitalize the initial word, the word following a colon, if any, and all other words except articles (a, an, the), conjunctions of four or fewer letters (or, but, and), and prepositions of four or fewer letters (of, up, to). Additionally, capitalize the following:

- Act—when you are referring to a specific act of a legislature, as in "the Lanham Act."
- Circuit—when you use the word with a circuit number, as in "the Eighth Circuit."
- Court—when you name any court in full, as in "the California Supreme Court"

  —whenever you refer to the United States Supreme Court.

  —in a court document when referring to the court that is receiving the document, as in "this Court is respectfully urged to grant Plaintiff's motion."
- Party designations—when referring to the parties in a matter that is the subject of the court document, as in "Defendant's argument to this Court misstates the law."
- Judge, Justice—when referring to a specific judge or justice, as in "Justice Smith" or any reference to any of the justices of the United States Supreme Court, as in, "The Justices were unanimous in their decision."
- State—when it is part of the full title of the state, such as "State of Florida"; when the wording it modifies is capitalized, as in "the State Attorney General"; or when referring to a state as a litigant, such as "the State argues for conviction."

*9. Electronic Sources, Databases, and the Internet (*Bluebook *Rule 18)*

The 17th edition of the *Bluebook* includes a new rule (Rule 18) devoted solely to citation form for electronic media. Once again, however, the *Blue-*

book evidences a bias against citing to electronic media, stating flatly that *Bluebook* rules require the use and citation of traditional printed sources, except when the information is not available in print form, or if the traditional source is difficult to find and provision of an Internet source will significantly improve access to the information. The traditional source should be used and cited whenever possible, and the electronic source may then be given as a parallel citation using the following explanatory phrases:

- *available at* (to indicate that the traditional source was used but the material is also available on the Internet).
- *at* (when the material is found exclusively on the Internet).
- [no explanatory phrase] (when the author accessed only the Internet to find the material but the material is available in a traditional printed source).

a. Statutes and Constitutions (*Bluebook* Rule 18.2.3)

Statutes and constitutions must be cited first to a traditional source and then to an electronic database (such as LEXIS or Westlaw). If the information is not available in a traditional source or electronic database, one may cite to the Internet.

Examples

Statute accessed in print form but Internet citation is available: 3 U.S.C. § 101 (1998), Cornell Legal Info. Inst., *available at* http://www4law.cornell.edu/uscode/3/101.text.html.

Statute available in print form but author accessed only the Internet: 15 U.S.C. § 1022c (1998), http://caselaw.lp.findlaw.com/casecode/uscodes/15/chapters/21/sections/section_1022c.html.

b. Books, Journals, and Magazines (*Bluebook* Rule 18.2.6)

As always, cite books, journals, and magazines first to a traditional source and only to the Internet when the information is not available in a traditional format or electronic database. Very few books are available in their entirety on the Internet, but there are now a variety of journals and articles that are published exclusively online and are not available in print form.

If the citation is only to an Internet source, a date must be provided (before the URL in the case of an online journal, namely, a journal that is published exclusively online and not in print form). The date provided in other cases should be one of the following in order of preference:

- The date of the article as specified in the information itself.
- The date the Internet site was last modified.
- The date the Internet site was last visited.
- If no date is indicated anywhere in the information, indicate such as follows: (n.d.).

Examples

Journal available in print form but also available through the Internet: Eugene Volokh, *Freedom of Speech and Information Privacy*, 52 Stan. L. Rev. 1049 (2000), *available at* http://www.law.ucla.edu/faculty/volokh/privacy.htm.

Journal available in print form but accessed only through the Internet: Eugene Volokh, *Equal Treatment Is Not Establishment*, 13 Notre Dame J.L. Ethics & Pub. Pol'y 341 (1999), http://www.law.ucla.edu/faculty/volokh/equal.htm.

Journal or article available only on the Internet: Thomas J. Field, Jr., *Intellectual Property: The Practical and Legal Fundamentals, at* http://www.fplc.edu/tfield/plfip.htm (last visited Jan. 22, 2001).

Dated journal or article available only on the Internet: (including pinpoint): Vicki L. Gregory, *UCITA: What Does It Mean for Libraries?*, 25 Online 1, ¶ 3 (Jan. 2001), *at* http://www.onineinc.com/onlinemag/OL2001/gregory1_01.html.

At this time, no one is entirely certain what direction legal citation form will take. In general, practitioners are in favor of the speed and lower costs associated with locating and citing cases to electronic sources such as the Internet, while judges and their clerks prefer the traditional method of citation. The ABA Special Committee on Citation Issues and ABA Section of Science and Technology as well as the Judicial Conference's Committee on Automation and Technology continue to meet and discuss citation form in the digital age. As of now, however, cases are relatively easy to locate on the Internet but hard to cite to in legal documents.

F. ALWD Citation System

Although the *Bluebook* is the best known manual for citation form, a recently published citation manual, the *ALWD Citation Manual*, created in 2000 by the Association of Legal Writing Directors ("ALWD," pronounced "all wood") in association with Professor Darby Dickerson of Stetson University College of Law, is rapidly drawing interest. The intent of *ALWD* is to provide a citation system that is easy to use and learn.

Because *ALWD* has not gained widespread endorsement at the time of writing of this text and because the legal profession is notoriously slow to change (even when a change seems compelling, as is clearly the case with the difficult-to-use *Bluebook*), this text provides only basic information regarding *ALWD* citation format. In many instances the *ALWD* format is identical to *Bluebook* format. For example, the format for lower federal court cases, most statutes, constitutions, journals and periodicals, and encyclopedias is identical. Rules for spacing are identical, and most short forms are identical. There are, however, differences in many abbreviations for periodicals. Until judges and attorneys learn about and adopt the *ALWD* format, however, the *Bluebook* will continue to be the gold standard in citation form. The *ALWD Citation Manual* can be obtained at most law school bookstores and from its publisher, Aspen Law & Business, at http://aspenpubl.com.

Some of the more significant differences between *ALWD* and the *Bluebook* are shown in Figure 8-3.

G. Tips for Effective Cite-Checking

Whenever you are presented with a cite-checking assignment, there are several practical tips you should consider to ensure you perform your task accurately and efficiently.

(i) Ask the individual who assigned the project to you when the deadline is so you can be sure you do the cite-checking in a timely fashion. Often cite-checking is one of the last tasks performed in legal writing projects, and you may need to start working immediately on the project so it can be filed timely.

(ii) Highlight all citations in the document as soon as it is given to you and while you are fresh, so you will readily be able to find citations and check them even after several hours have passed and your energy level is low.

(iii) If the document is being filed with a court, you must obtain a copy of the court rules so you can determine whether the court requires a specific citation form. Some courts insist that documents follow non-standard citation form. For example, some courts in California require that papers submitted show citations in the following format, even though it is unsupported by the *Bluebook* or any other guideline: *Atwell v. Jay* (1985) 142 Cal. 2d 109. If court rules dictate a specific format, you must adhere to that format. To obtain a copy of the rules of the

Figure 8-3
Differences in *ALWD* and *Bluebook* Citation Formats

Topic	*ALWD Format*	*Bluebook Format*
Parallel Citations for State Court Cases	Do not use parallel citations unless required by local rule.	Follow local rules. In absence of rules, give all parallel cites when citing a state court case in a document submitted to a state court but not in other documents.
Parallel Citations for United States Supreme Court Cases	*ALWD* permits parallel citations for United States Supreme Court cases.	The *Bluebook* does not permit parallel citations for United States Supreme Court cases.
Case Names	• Numerous words in case names are abbreviated even if the citation appears in a textual sentence. • If the United States is a party, cite as "U.S."	• Words in case names are only abbreviated if the citation appears as a stand alone and not as part of a textual sentence. • If the United States is a party, cite as "United States."
Treatises and Dictionaries	Publisher of treatise is included in parenthetical with date.	Publisher of treatise is not included in parenthetical with date.

Figure 8-3
Differences in *ALWD* and *Bluebook* Citation Formats *(Continued)*

Topic	*ALWD Format*	*Bluebook Format*
A.L.R. Annotations	The word "Annotation" is omitted from the citation.	The word "Annotation" is given after the author's name.
Signals	There are many differences in the use of signals between *ALWD* and the *Bluebook*. For example, *ALWD* does not use *see also* or *accord*. See Rule 45.	There are many differences in the use of signals between *ALWD* and the *Bluebook*. For example, the *Bluebook* uses the signals *see also* and *accord*. See Rule 1.2.
Miscellaneous	• When giving pinpoints, one can retain all digits (example: 1014-1019). • One must use the word "at" before any pinpoint, even a section sign or paragraph symbol (example: *Id.* at § 14). • Internet citations are placed in angled brackets. • There are many differences in abbreviations used in *ALWD* and the *Bluebook* (for example, *ALWD* abbreviates "Publishing" as "Publg." while the *Bluebook* abbreviates it as "Publ'g" (with no period following)). • *ALWD* includes local citation rules and forms.	• When giving pinpoints, drop repetitive digits (example: 1014-19). • The word "at" cannot be used before a section sign or paragraph symbol (example: *Id.* § 14). • Internet citations do not appear in angled brackets (although they did in the 16th edition of the *Bluebook*). • There are many differences in abbreviations used in the *ALWD* and the *Bluebook* (for example, *ALWD* abbreviates "Publishing" as "Publg." while the *Bluebook* abbreviates it as "Publ'g" (with no period following)). • The *Bluebook* does not include local citation rules and forms.

court, call the court clerk and inquire. Alternatively, most states and courts publish their court rules on the Internet. For rules for the United States Supreme Court, access http://www.supremecourtus.gov. For lower federal courts, access http://www.law.emory.edu/FEDCTS. For state court Web sites, Table 1 of the *Bluebook* provides a reference to each state's judicial Web site. If no court rules exist with regard to citation form, use *Bluebook* form unless directed otherwise.

(iv) You will quickly learn that some writers are more exacting than others. It is possible that the document you are cite-checking contains complete citations and you need only compare each cite against the *Bluebook* to ensure compliance with *Bluebook* rules. It is equally possible that the document you are given has several omissions and you need to go to the law library to obtain dates of decisions, pages of quotes, and so forth. Therefore, as you review the document, use different colored pens, sticky flags, or different symbols to indicate which cites have been checked and are accurate, which need further information supplied, and those for which you have questions. Determine if the author of the document has any preferences as to format, such as preferring underscoring of case names and signals rather than italicizing. Similarly, determine if the author has any special conventions as to format you should follow in lieu of *Bluebook* format. In the absence of instruction, assume *Bluebook* rules govern.

(v) When you find an error, make the correction by interlineating or crossing out the error and inserting the correct information. You may wish to note in the margin which *Bluebook* rule governs your correction as authors can be notoriously defensive about recognizing errors and you should be ready to support and defend your correction.

(vi) Because the document may be evolving as you work on it and other attorneys and paralegals may be continuing to edit the document, make sure each version is clearly marked with the date and the time it is printed. This will help you ensure you are working on a current version, not one superseded by a later version.

(vii) If the document contains quotations, check each one for accuracy. Quotations must be faithfully reproduced. If alterations and omissions are made, make sure those are indicated by brackets and ellipses. You must also verify that the citation includes the page of a quote.

(viii) Pay attention to short form citations and verify that the author's use of short forms, *id.*, and *supra* are correct. Because the document may be subject to revising and editing at the eleventh hour, you must always check the accuracy of signals in the final version of the document.

(ix) Make sure that you look beyond the body of the document and also check the cites in any appendices, footnotes, table of contents, or index of authorities.

(x) Be consistent. If you underscore case names, underscore book titles and signals such as *id.* and *supra*. If you italicize case names, italicize book titles and signals.
(xi) After the document is resubmitted for revision and correction, review to ensure that your corrections were incorporated.
(xii) Validate all primary authorities listed in the document, either manually or online (see Chapter 9).

It is possible that the author might wish you to do more than simply correct errors in citation format and might ask that you confirm the accuracy of the author's conclusions. Thus, if the author has cited *Jones v. Smith*, 421 A.2d 91 (Pa. 1986), for the proposition that a landlord is required to provide notice to a tenant before commencing an action to evict the tenant, you will have to review this case to verify that it does in fact support the author's conclusion. Similarly, checking citation signals such as *see*, *cf.*, and *accord* requires that you read the cited source to confirm the author has used the correct signal. This extensive type of cite-checking is far less common than the usual cite-checking assignment, which typically requires you only to correct errors in citation form and then to Shepardize or KeyCite. Unless you are directed otherwise you should assume that if someone asks you to cite-check a document you are expected only to verify that the citations are in correct form and to Shepardize.

H. Quick Reference for Citations (*Bluebook* Form)

1. *Cases*

(i) State Cases

Sidley v. Steinman, 201 N.C. 118, 429 S.E.2d 16 (1984) [for cases cited in documents filed in North Carolina courts].
Sidley v. Steinman, 429 S.E.2d 16 (N.C. 1984) [in all other instances].

(ii) Federal Cases

United States Supreme Court:

LaPointe v. Sullivan, 98 U.S. 396 (1984).

United States Courts of Appeals:

Lawrence v. Mather, 691 F.2d 114 (8th Cir. 1984).

United States District Court:

Blakely v. Yost, 742 F. Supp. 908 (D.R.I. 1986).

2. *Statutes*

(i) **State:** Ariz. Rev. Stat. Ann. § 104 (West 1986).
N.Y. Gen. Bus. Law § 308 (McKinney 1988).
(ii) **Federal:** 17 U.S.C. § 101 (1994).
17 U.S.C.A. § 101 (West 1996).
17 U.S.C.S. § 101 (Law. Co-op. 1988) or (LEXIS Publ'g 2000).

3. *Constitutions*

(i) **State:** N.M. Const. art. III.
(ii) **United States:** U.S. Const. amend. X.

4. *Encyclopedias*

68 C.J.S. *Trusts* § 302 (1988).
54 Am. Jur. 2d *Trusts* § 114 (1989).

5. *Law Review Articles*

Allan A. Sanders, *The Juvenile's Right to Counsel*, 46 Colum. L. Rev. 891 (1988).

6. *Texts and Treatises*

Joy N. Hildebrand, *Securities Review* § 421 (2d ed. 1991).

7. *Restatements*

Restatement (Second) of Contracts § 112 (1992).

8. *Dictionaries*

Black's Law Dictionary 1172 (7th ed. 1999).

9. *Attorneys General Opinions*

State: 65 Op. Cal. Att'y Gen. 104 (1995).
United States: 49 Op. Att'y Gen. 918 (1988).

10. *Summary of Special Citation Issues*

(i) **Quotation**: Always give the page of a quotation. As a courtesy to readers, always include a pinpoint cite even for material paraphrased. Quotations of fewer than 49 words should appear in text with quotation marks. Place periods and commas inside quotation marks. Quotations of 50 words or more should appear indented or in "block" form without quotation marks. Retain the original paragraph structure of a block quotation.

(ii) **Short forms**: Once you have cited a case in full you may use a short form.

First cite:	*Parsons v. Geneva*, 92 U.S. 104 (1982).
Short form:	*Parsons*, 92 U.S. at 106.
	92 U.S. at 106.
	Id. or *Id.* at 108.
	In *Parsons*, . . .

(iii) ***Id.***: Use *id.* or "*id.* plus" to refer a reader to the immediately preceding cite.

(iv) ***Supra***: Use *supra* to refer the reader to a previous cite that is not the immediately preceding cite. *Supra* may not be used to refer to cases, constitutions, statutes, legislative materials, or regulations. *Supra* must appear with the name of an author or title of a work.

11. *Internet Citation Form*

(i) **Case accessed in print form but available on the Internet:** *Hill v. Colorado*, 528 U.S. 13, 15 (2000), *available at* http://www.supremecourtus.gov/opinions/99pdf/98-1856.pdf.

(ii) **Statute available in print form but accessed solely on the Internet:** 35 U.S.C. § 101 (1998), http://www4.law.cornell.edu/uscode/35/101.text.html.

(iii) **Article available solely on the Internet:** Kevin E. Grady & H. Suzanne Smith, *Antitrust Issues for Hospital Mergers, at* http: //www.alston.com/docs/Articles/199709/Antitrust.htm (last visited Feb. 12, 2001).

Technology Tips

www.legalbluebook.com	This Web site of the *Bluebook* provides an overview of changes to the 17th edition of the *Bluebook*, asks for comments and corrections, allows ordering of the *Bluebook*, and provides introductory material about the *Bluebook*.
http://www.abanet.org/tech/ltrc/research/citation/home.html	The American Bar Association Web site has information devoted to neutral, public domain, or universal citation form and provides the ABA resolution regarding this issue as well as lists of states that have adopted public domain citation formats and those considering adoption.
http://www.law.cornell.edu/citation.table.html	Educator Peter W. Martin of Cornell Law School offers a complete citation primer based on the 17th edition of the *Bluebook*. *Bluebook* rules are explained and numerous examples are provided.
http://www.ualr.edu/~smbarger/shortform.htm	This Web site provides basic information about constructing and using short form citations.
http://www.citeit.com	The Web site of CiteIt! provides a free tutorial showing how its citation formatting system works.

Citation Software Programs

At this time, there is no absolutely reliable way to put your citations in proper *Bluebook* form other than for you to do the task the old-fashioned way: manually. Nevertheless, LEXIS offers a service called CiteRite II, which will put your citations in proper *Bluebook* or California citation format. While it is unclear whether CiteRite II can understand all of the idiosyncracies of citation form (such as when you can abbreviate the word "Surety" in a case name and when you cannot), it is clear that CiteRite II will notify you of improper underlining in a cite, missing parallel cites, or improper punctuation (such as the failure to put a period after the word "Supp").

Additionally, computer-assisted legal research offers some quick approaches to ensure that at least the name and numbers in a case cite have been reproduced accurately.

Use LEXIS's CheckCite to verify the accuracy of the name of a case and the volume and page numbers you have indicated. You will be informed whether *Shepard's* agrees with you or whether it reports different volume numbering or pagination for a case. Westlaw's KeyCite citation research service also provides citation verification information such as correct case name and parallel citations.

A company in Massachusetts, Sidebar Software, has created a software program called CiteIt!, which purportedly formats all citations to *Bluebook* rules (17th edition). When you wish to enter a citation into your document, you choose a citation source and then select the appropriate citation from ones displayed.

(continued)

Technology Tips (*Continued*)

Even such a system, however, presupposes some familiarity with the *Bluebook*; otherwise, how would one be able to select the "correct" citation when several are given? Law firms can purchase separate individual licenses, which are approximately $170 each. Although there is some special pricing, a law firm with 100 legal professionals could expect to pay approximately $17,000 for licenses, all of which may be outdated with the next edition of the *Bluebook*. Contact http://www.citeit.com for additional information.

When citing authorities in a brief, avoid "string citing" (citing more than one authority to support a contention). Too many citations clutter your project and disrupt the flow of your narrative. Moreover, string cites must be in a specific order according to the *Bluebook*, making string citing even more difficult.

Similarly, avoid footnotes in writing projects. Upon encountering footnotes, most readers will either stop reading the narrative while they jump to the footnote or will skip over the footnote entirely. Neither result is desired; the first causes a disruption of your argument, while the second renders your research ineffective. Some experts contend that if something is not significant enough to be included in the main body of a text, it should be omitted, and thus there is never a need for footnotes.

To some extent, the overuse of quotations may also result in the reader skipping over them. Use quotations sparingly, in those situations in which what the court has said is so authoritative and persuasive that paraphrasing the statement would dilute its impact. Judicious use of quotations adds drama and variety to your project. Overuse of quotations may cause the reader to wonder if you have taken the easy way out by simply reproducing another's words rather than analyzing those words.

Assignment for Chapter 8

CITATION FORM

There is at least one thing wrong with each fictitious citation below. Correct the citations using the current edition of the *Bluebook*. You may need to supply missing information such as dates. Punctuation is not needed after the citations. Unless otherwise indicated, use the form for memoranda and court documents and assume that the citations appear in textual sentences rather than as "stand alone" citations. There is no need to include "pinpoints," unless otherwise directed.

1. Timothy Graves vs. A.L. Smithson, Jr., a 1998 New Hampshire case located at volume 230 and page 145 of the relevant reporter.
2. Harvey Manufacturing Company v. Allison Stanley, a 1990 case from the Supreme Court of Texas, located in volume 890 at page 770.
3. Andrew Jacobs versus June Jacobs, a 1999 case from the California Court of Appeal, located in volume 114 of the relevant reporter, page 309, with quoted material on pages 314 to 315.
4. Jackson Engineering Enterprises, Corp. v. Hollis and Hollis Brothers, 469 United States Reports at page 116, 450 Lawyers' Edition (Second Series) page 14, 509 Supreme Court Reporter page 690.
5. Central Intelligence Agency vs. Henry Wagner, Executor, 114 Federal Reporter, Third Series, page 116, decided in 1999.
6. USA v. John Roberts, Susan Black, and Lisa Harding, 809 Federal Supplement 161, decided in 1994.
7. Franklin Association v. Talbot, James, a 1994 case decided by the United States Supreme Court.
8. Title 35, United States Code, Sections 114 through 117.
9. Title 42, United States Code Annotated, Section 2223(a).
10. Title 3, United States Code Service, Section 103.
11. Section 8-241 of Virginia's Code.
12. Section 1160 of the California Business and Professions Code.
13. Fifth Amendment to the United States Constitution.
14. Restatement, Second Series, of Torts, Section 13.
15. An article by Janice Hopkins and Barry H. Cooper, entitled "Antitrust Issues in Health Care" and published in volume 34, at page 1101, of the New Mexico Law Review, with a quotation from pages 1115 through 1119.
16. Volume 4, Section 10:4 of the treatise entitled "Sports and Entertainment Law" authored by Erin Donoghue, Third Edition, 2000.
17. Assume the following case is cited in a brief to a Georgia court: Kyle Davis v. Robertson, 331 Georgia Appellate Court 144 (1994). Give the appropriate citation.
18. Assume the following citation appears as a "stand alone" citation: the 1998 United States Court of Appeals Case, Second Circuit, Lawson Construction Company vs. Southern Industrial Construction Commission.

There are numerous errors in the fictitious citations in the following brief memorandum. Correct citation errors using the current edition of the *Bluebook*. You may need to supply missing information. You need not include pinpoints unless otherwise directed.

MEMORANDUM

Generally, partnership law provides that each partner in a general partnership is liable for debts and obligations incurred by other partners. 4 *Partnership Law,* by David A. Lowell, pages 114-119. Moreover, the liability is joint and several, meaning that any one partner can be held liable for the entire debt or obligation. Id., page 159. In a limited partnership, however, only the general partners face such exposure; the liability of limited partners is limited to their contribution to the enterprise. Sanders v. Sunset Gardens Partnership, 499 United States reports 607 (1995).

The ability to determine in advance one's maximum liability is a distinct advantage for limited partners in limited partnerships; however, the price paid for such limitation of liability is that limited partners may not manage or control the limited partnership business. Western Gardens Partnership vs. Harrison, 401 Cal. Reports, third series, page 119 (1998). While limited partners may consult in the business and have a right to be informed as to its activities, they cannot engage in management functions. *Partnership Law, supra*, at page 204. A variety of cases have considered whether limited partners are engaging in permissible advising and consulting or impermissible managing and operating. *Fleet Brothers v. Henderson*, 256 Mich. 119, 679 N.W. 2nd 14 (1995), *Talbot v. Grayson Enterprise Association*, 301 Mich. App. 114, 692 N.W. 2nd 333 (1998), *Chemical Trust Co. v. Atlantic Technology, Inc.*, 244 Mich. 901, 644 N.W.2nd 104 (1994). The most important factor to be considered is whether the limited partner is engaging in decision-making functions. *Sanders, id.* If so, liability will attach. *Id.*, page 614.

According to David Lowell, supra, page 301, the newly developed form of business enterprise, the limited liability company, provides distinct advantages over both the general partnership and the limited partnership. In limited liability companies, the members generally have no liability for the acts of their co-members and yet may engage in management activities. *Id.*, page 301. Thus, limited companies combine the best features of both corporate and partnership principles, allowing one to manage and yet limit one's financial exposure. Moreover, liability is limited not only as to actions arising in tort, such as negligence, but to actions arising in contract. Harrison Incorporated vs. Jacobs Publishing, 790 Federal Supplement 104, 109 (Eastern District Michigan) (1997). Members, however, retain liability for acts they commit as well as those committed by others under their supervision and control. Id. pages 116-119. This principle is consistently applied throughout all states. John Gibson, *Limited Liability Companies*, volume 108 New York University Law Review, page 614. The new limited liability companies thus continue the trend of hybrid business entities that combine the best features of partnerships with the best features of corporations. Id. page 622. In sum, members of limited liability companies enjoy “distinct advantages over partners in general partnerships as well as partners in limited partnerships.” *Harrison*, 790 Fed. Supp., page 114.

Chapter

9

Updating and Validating Your Research

Chapter Overview

The task of cite-checking has two components: ensuring that the format of the citations meets *Bluebook* or local standards and then verifying that the primary authorities cited are still valid. This second component of updating and validating your authorities can be conducted manually, using *Shepard's Citators* (published in conventional print form, in CD-ROM, and available online through LEXIS, the owner of *Shepard's* database of more than 146 million references) or using KeyCite, West's online citation service. Validating your authorities through the use of *Shepard's* products is called "Shepardizing."

Until recently, the only method of updating authorities was Shepardizing. In the late 1990s, however, West lost the right to use *Shepard's* database and launched its own online citation service, called KeyCite. In sum, there are now two methods of updating and validating your research: using *Shepard's* (in print, CD-ROM, or online) or using KeyCite (offered exclusively online). In this chapter, *Shepard's* and KeyCite will be referred to as "citators" because they both provide citations to other authorities that update, validate, and comment on the sources you cite.

This chapter focuses on techniques for effective and efficient Shepardizing and KeyCiting as well as the use of these citators as research tools. Once you thoroughly understand the technique of Shepardizing or KeyCiting, you will readily see why a citation is much more than a merely mechanical way to check that primary authorities are still "good"; it is also an excellent way to expand your research and locate other references dealing with the issue you are researching.

This chapter will initially discuss Shepardizing cases and will then explain the procedure of Shepardizing statutes, constitutions, and ordinances. You will also be introduced to other citators produced by the publishers of *Shepard's* for specialized research needs. Updating authorities online is far more common than using conventional print forms of *Shepard's*. Thus, this chapter will address updating through the use of *Shepard's* online and through KeyCiting. However, a thorough grounding in the way the conventional print versions of *Shepard's* work will enhance your understanding of the techniques and value of online updating. Thus, it is discussed first.

A. Introduction to Updating and Validating

In the course of your research efforts thus far, you may have noticed that there are often several alternative paths you can follow to obtain an answer to a research issue. That is why there are so few "rules" for legal research. You may, however, recall one inflexible rule from Chapter 3: Whenever a book has a pocket part or a supplement, it must be examined. Neglecting a pocket part or supplement might cause you to rely on outdated law. For example, the pocket parts to U.S.C.A. and U.S.C.S. inform you of changes in statutes, whether those changes are amendments to a statute or a complete repeal of a statute. Moreover, the pocket part will direct you to cases interpreting a statute that are more recent than those annotated in the main volume.

Even if you rely on cases from the most recent issue of a pocket part, however, it is still possible that the case may have been overruled or reversed or somehow limited since the pocket part was published. You must therefore determine the current status of every primary authority on which you rely. To do this, you can use sets of books called *Shepard's Citations*. The technique of using *Shepard's* to check whether the authorities you wish to cite are still "good law" is called "Shepardizing." *Shepard's Citations* are now the product of LEXIS and were first introduced more than 100 years ago. They have developed from gummed stickers solely devoted to Illinois cases to hundreds of bound volumes as well as online services devoted to cases and other legal authorities from every jurisdiction. Alternatively, you can use West's product, KeyCite, available exclusively online.

If the first inflexible rule of legal research is to check the pocket parts, the second is that you must update every primary authority you cite. Updating and validating must be done not only for briefs that you file with a court but for internal office memoranda, letters to clients, and other writings.

You cannot simply validate most of the cases in a brief, or only older cases, or gamble that the cases you refer to are still good. You must validate each and every case, statute, and constitutional provision. You should assume that your adversary will be validating the authorities you cite to ensure that your brief or argument is valid. It would not only be an acute embarrassment to rely on an outdated case and have this called to your attention by an adversary or a judge, it would be a clear breach of the duty imposed on legal professionals to represent a client's interests adequately by performing accurate legal research. According to at least one judge, "without belaboring the point, we remind the bar that, as this case so dramatically shows, cases must be Shepardized . . . ." *Glassalum Eng'g Corp. v. 392208 Ontario Ltd.*, 487 So. 2d 87, 88 (Fla. App. 1986). Numerous other cases include similar statements by judges clearly indicating there is a legal duty to check the validity of the authorities one cites.

One of the advantages of updating is that not only are you given the assurance that the authorities you rely on are valid, but that *Shepard's* and KeyCite can be used as additional research tools. These citators will provide you with parallel citations and references to other sources in the law library that mention or discuss your case, statute, or constitutional provision, such as law review articles, annotations, and attorneys' general opinions. While some individuals view updating solely as a means to determine whether authorities are still valid, you should remember this other function of a citator: It will serve as an excellent research tool by directing you to numerous authorities that discuss your case, statute, or constitutional provision.

B. Shepardizing Cases

1. *Locating* Shepard's Citations

Assume the case you are interested in updating is *Gose v. Monroe Auto Equipment Co.*, 409 Mich. 147, 294 N.W.2d 165 (1980), and you have decided to Shepardize it using conventional print sources. Before you can begin the actual task of Shepardizing, you must gather the volumes of *Shepard's* that you need. There is a set of *Shepard's Citations* for each set of case reports. Thus, there are sets called *Shepard's Arizona Citations, Shepard's Idaho Citations, Shepard's Massachusetts Citations*, and *Shepard's Washington Citations*. Moreover, there are sets of *Shepard's* for cases reported in West's regional reporters, such as *Shepard's Atlantic Reporter*

Citations, *Shepard's Northwestern Reporter Citations*, and *Shepard's Southern Reporter Citations*. Similarly, there are sets of *Shepard's* for federal cases such as *Shepard's United States Citations* (covering United States Supreme Court cases), and *Shepard's Federal Citations* (covering cases from the United States courts of appeal, published in the *Federal Reporter* and cases from the United States district courts, published in the *Federal Supplement*).

Most law libraries place the volumes of *Shepard's* immediately after the last volume in a set of case reports. Thus, the volumes of *Shepard's New Jersey Citations* are usually located after the final volume of the *New Jersey Reports*; the volumes of *Shepard's Pacific Reporter Citations* are usually located after the final volume of the *Pacific Reporter*; and the volumes of *Shepard's United States Citations* are usually located after the final volume of the *United States Reports*.

Some law libraries, however, maintain all of the volumes of *Shepard's* in one central location. In such a case, the volumes may comprise several stacks. Many law libraries, realizing the critical importance of Shepardizing, keep duplicate sets of *Shepard's* on reserve. If you cannot find the volumes you need, ask a law librarian for help.

Often locating the appropriate volumes of *Shepard's* is more difficult in a law school library than it would be in a law firm or other office. This is because many law students will be using *Shepard's* and they may be somewhat careless with the *Shepard's* volumes, leaving them in a study room or carrel. In a law firm, however, more care will be taken, and the volumes of *Shepard's* will seldom leave the confines of the firm's library. The volumes of *Shepard's* are typically quickly used and then returned to the shelves. They are not meant to be perused or read at a leisurely pace.

You will usually be using two or three hardbound volumes of *Shepard's* and one or two softcover advance sheets. All of the hardbound volumes of *Shepard's* are deep maroon in color. The softcover advance sheets or supplements are white (issued approximately every six weeks), bright red (issued quarterly), or gold (issued annually or semi-annually). *Shepard's* also issues blue "express" supplements. Eventually, the softcover supplements are accumulated into hardbound volumes, and new supplements will be issued to provide the treatment of the case you are relying on by recently decided court decisions.

To be sure that you have all of the volumes of *Shepard's* you need, look at the most recent softcover supplement. The front of each supplement displays a box or notice labeled "What Your Library Should Contain," which lists the volumes of *Shepard's* you will need to complete your task. If the supplement you are using is more than three months old (dates are provided at the top of each supplement), consult a reference librarian as there should always be a *Shepard's* volume marked with a date within the past calendar quarter. You cannot simply proceed to Shepardize assuming that it is sufficient if you have most of the volumes you need. Incomplete Shepardizing is the equivalent of not Shepardizing at all. See Figure 9-1 for a sample cover sheet from *Shepard's*.

Figure 9-1
Sample Cover Sheet from *Shepard's*

VOL. 83 SEPTEMBER, 1992 NO. 12

Shepard's Michigan Citations

ANNUAL CUMULATIVE SUPPLEMENT
CASES AND STATUTES

(USPS 656870)

IMPORTANT NOTICE

Do not destroy the September, 1992 gold paper-covered Annual Cumulative Supplement until it is removed from the "What Your Library Should Contain" list on the front cover of any future supplement.

WHAT YOUR LIBRARY SHOULD CONTAIN

1987 Bound Volume, Cases (Parts 1 and 2)*
1987 Bound Volume, Statutes (Parts 1 and 2)*
1987-1990 Bound Supplement*
**Supplemented with:*
–Sept., 1992 Annual Cumulative Supplement Vol. 83 No. 12
Subscribers to Shepard's Michigan EXPRESS Citations should retain the latest blue-covered issue.

DESTROY ALL OTHER ISSUES

Reference to books needed to Shepardize

RECYCLE YOUR OUTDATED SUPPLEMENTS

When you receive new supplements and are instructed to destroy the outdated versions, please consider taking these paper products to a local recycling center to help conserve our nation's natural resources. Thank you.

SEE TABLE OF CONTENTS ON PAGE III

SEE "THIS ISSUE INCLUDES" ON PAGE IV

SHEPARD'S
McGRAW-HIL

2. *Locating* Shepard's *References to Your Case*

Because the case you are Shepardizing is a Michigan case, you will need to locate the volumes of *Shepard's Michigan Citations*. Open the first volume of *Shepard's Michigan Citations* and scan the upper corners of each page looking for a reference to **Vol. 409**, the volume in which *Gose v. Monroe Auto Equipment Co.* is reported. This process is similar to looking at the guide words in the upper corners of each page in a dictionary or telephone directory to determine which page will contain the word or name you need.

When you have located the page or pages for **Vol. 409**, scan this page looking for the black boldfaced typed reference **- 147 -** because this is the page on which *Gose v. Monroe Auto Equipment Co.* begins. There are three possibilities:

(i) There may be no reference at all to **- 147 -**. There may be a reference to **- 126 -**, followed by a reference to **- 217 -**. Lack of a reference to your page is an indication that during the period of time covered by that issue of *Shepard's*, no case or other authority mentioned *Gose v. Monroe Auto Equipment Co.* in any manner. For instance, assume you are looking in one of *Shepard's* gold yearly supplements. If no entry for **- 147 -** is found, it merely means that during this one-year period, *Gose v. Monroe Auto Equipment Co.* was not discussed or referred to in any way, either favorably or unfavorably. If this occurs, close this volume of *Shepard's* and examine the next volume, once again looking for a reference to **Vol. 409** in the upper corners of each page and then scanning the page for a reference to **- 147 -**.

(ii) There may be citations appearing in parentheses immediately below **- 147 -**. These are parallel cites for *Gose v. Monroe Auto Equipment Co.* You may recall from Chapter 4 that if you have an official cite and wish to obtain an unofficial cite (or vice versa), you can consult the Table of Cases in your state digest or the *National Reporter Bluebook* (or the *State Blue and White* book) or you can Shepardize your citation. *Shepard's* will provide you with parallel citations for your case, and provides perhaps the easiest and most efficient way of locating parallel citations. You will be given a parallel citation in the first volume of *Shepard's* published after the parallel cite becomes available. To save space, the parallel cite will not be repeated in subsequent volumes or supplements.

If your case has been selected by the publishers of A.L.R. as a leading case about which an annotation has been written, this will be indicated by a reference to A.L.R. in parentheses immediately below the parallel cite also given in parentheses. When you see such a reference, consider stopping further research until you read the annotation; it may provide you with a thorough review of a legal topic, eliminating the need for you to conduct much of your own research.

(iii) There may be cites below **- 147 -** that do not appear in parentheses. These are references to the history of *Gose v. Monroe Auto Equipment Co.* as it has traveled through the courts and sources that have mentioned, discussed, or commented upon *Gose v. Monroe Auto Equipment Co.* in any manner whatsoever.

3. Analysis of References in Shepard's

a. Abbreviations

You may have already observed that the presentation of citations in *Shepard's* is not in *Bluebook* format. In fact, the citations given you by *Shepard's* have a uniquely peculiar appearance such as follows:

38LE106

132Az991

  2
182NW282

These examples are correctly interpreted as follows:

38 L. Ed. 106
132 Ariz. 991
182 N.W.2d 282

Because *Shepard's* is tasked with presenting so much information as efficiently as possible, it has developed its own "shorthand" references for cases and other legal authorities. You will quickly learn how to interpret correctly the citations given you by *Shepard's*. If you have any difficulty, each volume of *Shepard's*, whether a hardcover volume or a softcover supplement, will contain a Table of Abbreviations placed in the front of each volume identifying these abbreviations. Cases that have not yet been published in a case reporter are temporarily identified by a condensed LEXIS citation, as in "2001 Mich LX 14."

b. History References

Shepard's will provide you with a history of *Gose v. Monroe Auto Equipment Co.*, meaning that you will be informed whether a rehearing of *Gose v. Monroe Auto Equipment Co.* has been denied, whether *certiorari* was denied, whether *Gose v. Monroe Auto Equipment Co.* has been affirmed, or whether it has been reversed.

The first references provided by *Shepard's* under **- 147 -** (after the parallel citations) relate to the history of *Gose v. Monroe Auto Equipment Co.*, that is, how this case has been dealt with as it has progressed through the courts. Often this history must be included in your citation because the *Bluebook* (Rule 10.7) requires that the subsequent history of a case be included in its citation.

For instance, if upon Shepardizing *Jones v. Smith*, 681 F.2d 911 (4th Cir. 1986), you discover it was reversed on appeal to the United States Supreme Court, you are obligated by the *Bluebook* (Rule 10.7) to indicate this in the citation, as follows:

> *Jones v. Smith*, 681 F.2d 911 (4th Cir. 1986), *rev'd*, 482 U.S. 601 (1988)

Shepard's provides you with this information relating to the history of *Gose v. Monroe Auto Equipment Co.* by means of an identifying abbreviated letter placed immediately before the citation. Most of the letters are easy to understand. For example, "a" means "affirmed"; "r" means "reversed"; and "m" means "modified." If, however, you cannot remember the meaning of a history letter, each volume of *Shepard's* contains a Table of Abbreviations in the front identifying each letter and providing a brief explanation. See Figure 9-2 for the most common abbreviations relating to the history of a case.

c. Treatment References

Shepard's Michigan Citations will not only inform you how *Gose v. Monroe Auto Equipment Co.* has been dealt with by higher courts but will also refer you to every other case as well as selected law review articles, annotations, and attorneys general opinions that discuss or even mention *Gose v. Monroe Auto Equipment Co.* in passing. *Shepard's* does more than merely refer you to these authorities. These sources have been thoroughly analyzed, and *Shepard's* will inform you how *Gose v. Monroe Auto Equipment Co.* has been treated by other sources, namely, whether it was followed by a later case, mentioned in a dissenting opinion, or criticized or questioned by a later authority.

Shepard's provides you with this information relating to the treatment of *Gose v. Monroe Auto Equipment Co.* by means of an identifying abbreviation letter placed immediately before the reference. Once again, most of the letters are easy to interpret (such as "o" for "overruled" or "f" for "followed"), but each volume of *Shepard's* will provide you with a Table of Abbreviations in the front of the volume, which will explain the abbreviations. See Figure 9-3 for the most common abbreviations relating to treatment of cases.

Pay careful attention in examining the treatment of a cited case. If the case you are relying on is continually being questioned or criticized, you may wish to reevaluate your research strategies and attempt to locate a case that is more authoritative. Conversely, if the case you are relying upon has been followed by later cases on a number of occasions, this indicates the opinion has a certain amount of precedential weight and you may wish to inform a reader of this significance. If your case is mentioned

Figure 9-2
Abbreviations for History of Case

a	(affirmed)	Your case has been affirmed on appeal by a higher court.
cc	(connected case)	The citing case is related to your case in some way. Either it involves the same parties or arises out of the same subject matter.
D	(dismissed)	A case that has been appealed to a higher court has been dismissed or discontinued without further hearing.
Gr	Rev./Rehearing granted	The citing case grants review or *certiorari* in the case you are Shepardizing.
m	(modified)	The lower court's decision is modified in some way. For example, a lower court decision that is affirmed in part and reversed in part is shown as "modified."
Nu	(nullified)	Your case has been designated as without precedential value or effect.
r	(reversed)	Your case has been reversed on appeal to a higher court.
ReG	Reh./Recon. granted	The case you are Shepardizing has been granted a rehearing or reconsideration.
ReD	Reh./Recon. denied	The case you are Shepardizing has been denied a rehearing or reconsideration.
s	(same case)	The case is your case, although at a different stage of proceedings.
S	(superseded)	A subsequent opinion has been substituted for your case.
v	(vacated)	Your case has been rendered void and has no precedential force or effect.
W	(withdrawn)	Your case has been withdrawn by either the court or the publisher.
US	cert den	The United States Supreme Court has denied *certiorari* for your case.
US	cert dis	The United States Supreme Court granted *certiorari* and then dismissed cert.
US	reh den	The United States Supreme Court has denied a rehearing of your case.
US	reh dis	The United States Supreme Court granted a rehearing of your case and then dismissed it.
US	app pndg	An appeal of your case is pending before the United States Supreme Court.
US	cert gran	The United States Supreme Court has granted *certiorari* for your case.
lv	app den	Leave to appeal has been denied to your case.

in dissenting opinions, you should review these. If your case is the view of a bare majority and dissenting justices are challenging it, a change in the composition of the court could result in your case being overruled.

The difference between the *history* of a case and the *treatment* of it is readily illustrated by comparing "reversed" (relating to the history of a case) with "overruled" (relating to the treatment of a case). Assume *Smith v. Jones* was decided in 1990 by the United States District Court for the Southern District of Georgia. If Smith loses the case and appeals the decision to the Eleventh Circuit Court of Appeals, which decides that an error of law was committed at the trial, it may *reverse* the case. On the other hand, it is possible that in 2000, several years after *Smith v. Jones* is decided, the Eleventh Circuit, in hearing an entirely unrelated case titled *Gray v. Hill*, may decide that the reasoning in *Smith v. Jones* was

Figure 9-3
Abbreviations Relating to Treatment of a Cited Case

c	(criticized)	The court is disagreeing with the soundness of the opinion in your case.
d	(distinguished)	The case cited is significantly different from your case, either in the facts or issues involved.
e	(explained)	Your case is being explained or interpreted in a significant manner.
f	(followed)	Your case is being relied upon as controlling or persuasive authority.
h	(harmonized)	The cases differ in some way. Nevertheless, the court has found a way to reconcile or harmonize the differences.
j	(dissenting opinion)	Your case is mentioned in a dissenting opinion.
L	(limited)	The court restricts the application of the opinion in your case. Generally, the court finds that the reasoning in your case applies only in specific instances.
o	(overruled)	The court has determined that the reasoning in your case is no longer valid, either in part or in its entirety.
p	(parallel)	The case cited is "parallel" to or "on all fours" with your case, meaning your case is being relied upon as controlling or persuasive authority.
q	(questioned)	The soundness of your case is being questioned.
~	(concurring opinion)	Your case is mentioned in a concurring opinion.

erroneous and *Gray v. Hill* may *overrule Smith v. Jones*. Thus, a reversal refers to later history of a case, that is, what was decided by a higher court relating to that very case. An overruling refers to how a case was treated by some entirely different case, perhaps years after the original case was decided. For example, *Brown v. Board of Education*, 347 U.S. 483 (1954), overruled the much earlier case of *Plessy v. Ferguson*, 163 U.S. 539 (1896).

Shepard's has recently added a few abbreviations. Moveover, the abbreviations may vary in some states. For example, the following abbreviations are found in *Shepard's California Citations:*

GP Review granted and case ordered published.

RE Republished (Reporter of Decisions directed to publish opinion previously ordered not published).

Citing reference may be of questionable value as precedent because review was granted by California Supreme Court or case was ordered not published.

d. No Indication of Treatment

You may have observed that several of the references listed in *Shepard's* have no letters whatsoever preceding them. In fact, it is far more common for entries to appear without identifying letters than for letters related to treatment to be included. The absence of an identifying letter before a reference means that the later case has mentioned your case in some fashion, but the editors at *Shepard's* have not made any judgment as to the effect of this later case on your case.

4. *Arrangement of Later Cases*

The references in *Shepard's* to cases mentioning your case will be arranged in a fashion similar to the following:

226P2108
231P2414
239P2106
239P2109
239P2111
246P2901

These are all references to cases in the *Pacific Reporter, Second Series*, that have mentioned your case. These references are arranged in chronological order so you are first sent to earlier cases mentioning your case and then to more recent cases. If a later case mentions your case on several different pages, *Shepard's* will direct you to each and every page within that case on which your case is discussed. Although *Shepard's* does not provide a date for the later cases that discuss your case, by carefully examining the entries you can easily select more recent cases. You will also be directed to cases from the federal courts that mention your case.

You will recall that a standard case citation always directs you to the page on which a case begins. *Shepard's* references, however, are precise and direct you to the very page within a case on which your case is being discussed. This is far more efficient than merely being directed to the page on which a lengthy case begins, which you might have to read through to locate the reference to your case. If you retrieve one of the cases listed in *Shepard's* and you cannot locate a reference to your case on the page *Shepard's* directed you to, check any footnotes that appear on the page because it is possible that the discussion or mention of your case is not in the main body of the later case but instead is in a footnote.

5. *Other Identifying Letters*

When Shepardizing you may come across two lowercase letters placed after an entry. A lowercase "n" placed at the end of an entry indicates that the reference to your case appears in an A.L.R. annotation or an annotation in *United States Supreme Court Reports, Lawyers' Edition.* A lowercase "s" placed at the end of an entry indicates that the reference to your case appears in a supplement (either a pocket part or a softcover supplement) to an annotation.

6. *References to Headnotes*

You will recall from Chapter 4 that when a case is reviewed by editors at a publishing company, they will assign headnote numbers for each legal issue in the case. For example, if the case deals with 11 different issues, there will be 11 headnotes; if the case deals with six different legal issues, there will be six headnotes.

It is possible that you are relying on only a portion of a case in a brief or argument you have written. That is, you may be referring to a case only with reference to the issue discussed in headnote 4 of that case. *Shepard's* will not only provide you with information relating to the treatment by later cases of your case, it will focus on cases that have discussed specific headnotes of your case.

These references are accomplished by small elevated numbers placed immediately after the name of the case reporter. For example, when Shepardizing *Gose v. Monroe Auto Equipment Co.*, you observe one of the *Shepard's* entries is 125McA^{4}474. This indicates that page 474 of Volume 125 of the *Michigan Court of Appeals Reports* discusses the point of law discussed in headnote 4 of *Gose v. Monroe Auto Equipment Co.* This feature of *Shepard's* allows you readily to locate later cases discussing the specific points of law discussed in your case.

Thus, if you relied solely upon the issue discussed in the second headnote of *Gose v. Monroe Auto Equipment Co.*, you could quickly run your finger down the column of *Shepard's* entries looking for elevated "2s" because these will direct you to later cases that mentioned *Gose v. Monroe*

Auto Equipment Co. with regard to the point of law discussed in its headnote 2. Similarly, if, when you Shepardize, you discover that only headnote 4 of *Gose v. Monroe Auto Equipment Co.* has been criticized or questioned, and you are relying solely upon the point of law discussed in headnote 3 of *Gose*, you may be able to bypass those references with elevated number 4s. Because some cases have been mentioned or discussed by subsequent cases on hundreds of occasions, you can use this feature of *Shepard's* to save time and eliminate cases that are not relevant to the particular issue you are researching.

It is possible that some entries in *Shepard's* contain no elevated (or "superscript") numbers. This is an indication that a later case discusses *Gose v. Monroe Auto Equipment Co.* only in some general fashion rather than focusing on a specific legal issue discussed in any particular headnote.

7. *References to Sources Other than Cases*

a. Attorneys General Opinions

When you Shepardize a case in one of the state sets such as *Shepard's Illinois Citations*, after *Shepard's* directs you to every case that has mentioned or discussed your case, it will refer you to the specific page of any opinion of that state's attorney general that mentions your case.

b. Law Review Articles

When you Shepardize a case in one of the sets of *Shepard's* for state cases, you will be provided not only with a list of every case from your state decided after your case that mentions or discusses your case, you will be provided with references to leading law review articles or periodicals that mention your case (such as the *Columbia Law Review, Stanford Law Review*, or *Yale Law Journal*). References are given to the specific page of an article that mentions your case.

You should read any article that discusses your case because it may well provide a thoughtful and complete analysis of your case or the issues presented in your case, saving you precious research time.

c. Annotations

The state *Shepard's* will also direct you to any A.L.R. annotations that mention your case and will indicate if your case has been selected by the publisher of A.L.R. as a "leading" case about which an annotation has been written. This is accomplished by a reference to A.L.R. in a parenthetical immediately following the parenthetical for the parallel cite. Remember that a small "n" appearing after the A.L.R. citation indicates that your case has been cited in an annotation. A small "s" appearing after the A.L.R. citation indicates that your case is mentioned in a pocket part or softcover supplement. See Figure 9-4 for a sample page from *Shepard's Michigan Citations*.

8. *Using* Shepard's

As you can see, *Shepard's* provides a vast amount of information about your case, from its history as it progresses through the court system, to its treatment by later cases that mention or discuss it, to other sources such as attorneys' general opinions, law review articles, and A.L.R. annotations that mention your case. It is possible that a controversial or well-known case such as *Brown v. Board of Education*, 347 U.S. 483 (1954), has been mentioned hundreds of times by other cases and by attorneys' general opinions, law review articles, and A.L.R. annotations.

Beginning researchers typically wonder whether they are required to read each and every one of these cases or other references that mention a case they have updated. The answer to this question is a typical legal response: It depends. If you have been specifically directed by your supervisor to retrieve and review every case or other reference that mentions your case, you must do so. If you are pleased with your research project and you believe the cases cited in your writing clearly and articulately support the arguments you have made, Shepardizing can be reduced to the fairly easy task of simply locating the entries in *Shepard's* for your case and looking for "bad" letters, such as "r" (reversed), "m" (modified), "o" (overruled), "L" (limited), "c" (criticized), or "q" (questioned). If your updating does not disclose any such negative history or treatment of your case, your task is complete and you need not read and analyze the entries that refer to your case. Conversely, if your case is being consistently followed by later cases, you may wish to read a few of these and mention this in your document as a means of further enhancing the strength of your arguments and conclusions.

It is possible, however, that you are not entirely pleased with the cases you have located. Perhaps the cases are a bit older than you would prefer, or from your state appellate court rather than from your state supreme court, or the cases are not clearly presented. In this case, use *Shepard's* as a research tool to locate newer cases, cases from a higher court, or cases that more clearly or articulately explain a legal issue. When you Shepardize, look for such newer cases or cases that have followed your case. Remember to use the elevated numbers to locate only those cases dealing with the issues presented in the relevant headnotes from your case.

If the issue you are researching is an uncertain area of the law or a newly emerging legal topic, you should probably read some of the cases listed in *Shepard's* to obtain better insight into this area of the law.

9. *Analyzing Negative Letters*

If your Shepardizing reveals one of the "negative" letters, especially "r" (reversed), "m" (modified), "c" (criticized), "o" (overruled), "L" (limited), or

Figure 9-4
Sample Page from *Shepard's Michigan Citations*

Volume number

Vol. 409

MICHIGAN REPORTS

Page number

Parallel citation

e148McA[2]24
j148McA7
d149McA647
f149McA[24]
[647
149McA[14]648
d149McA[16]
[650
151McA[5]168
Cir. 6
564FS355
61MBJ558
61MBJ563
27WnL972
28WnL915
29WnL815
30WnL707
ICD§ 6.03
28A3551s
20A41112n
23A419n
23A446n
25A420n
25A458n
28A4424n
30A4181n
30A4183n
30A4194n

—67—
(293NW315)
s409Mch1102
[illegible]
j409Mch868
f409Mch885
j412Mch892
106McA[2]223
115McA[10]786
28WnL703
28WnL1153
29WnL419
29WnL1034

—110—
(293NW588)
s406Mch1009
s86McA5
410Mch884
e418Mch[2]6
j418Mch126
99McA[2]559
f101McA471
107McA280
107McA[4]742
111McA[4]743
118McA690
119McA[5]557
131McA[2]674
27WnL428
27WnL665
28WnL707
28WnL745

—126—
(293NW332)
s403Mch845
s406Mch1008
s77McA411
e409Mch[6]736
410Mch[5]864
410Mch920
411Mch852
411Mch[5]858
f411Mch946
414Mch952
d416Mch[1]244
416Mch[6]587
d416Mch[7]600
99McA[6]741
d101McA[5]582
d103McA[3]713
d105McA[8]638
108McA[6]627
j108McA631
110McA[1]289
110McA346
111McA[8]49
112McA[2]649
d112McA[6]787
f115McA[1]437
115McA[5]438
e125McA[6]110
e126McA[1]299
e127McA[5]639
f130McA612
139McA[7]804
d139McA[8]809
d143McA[5]583
143McA[3]589
150McA[5]747
Cir. 6
741F2d[6]838
741F2d[8]838
27WnL666
28WnL746
30WnL450
31WnL444

—147—
(294NW165)
s80McA190
412Mch[2]583
414Mch112
414Mch[3]589
101McA[2]160
105McA[2]130
114McA[2]383
115McA[2]747
116McA392
118McA[2]49
119McA[3]478
120McA[1]151
123McA[2]439
125McA[4]474
125McA[3]670
126McA[2]572
133McA[2]789
135McA[2]263
136McA[2]394
d139McA[2]181
147McA[2]75
j147McA76
f148McA[2]753
149McA[2]350
Cir. 6
758F2d[1]1145
512FS[1]1165
512FS[2]1165
564FS[2]1301
611FS[2]854
631FS1520
64MBJ1093
28WnL1195
29WnL407
30WnL335
31WnL347

—217—
(293NW341)
409Mch913
417Mch[1]1050
99McA[6]786
100McA[1]743
j103McA771
104McA[1]112
e117McA135
f129McA[1]282
143McA312
147McA[6]421
28WnL484
28WnL642
28WnL661
31WnL635

—231—
(293NW594)
s405Mch826
s405Mch827
s83McA207
409Mch887
414Mch10
418Mch[5]647
418Mch[5]662
f100McA172
103McA[4]39
110McA[4]137
115McA679
118McA[1]808
121McA771
125McA[1]125
134McA194
137McA699
137McA811
139McA[1]61
154McA[7]327
1983MiAG53
28WnL918
27A4178n

—262—
(293NW346)
s409Mch1102
61JUL58

—271—
(294NW194)
s403Mch832
s90McA399
419Mch[2]926
f119McA582
Cir. 6
e653F2d[3]269
754F2d168
d567FS[1]65
64MBJ174
28WnL936

—279—
(294NW571)
s83McA153
f409Mch916
f411Mch[1]705
j411Mch709
d110McA569
d110McA[5]569
118McA[1]445
f128McA[2]576
Cir. 6
551FS[1]1282
28WnL1133
88A3926s

—299—
(294NW578)
s406Mch1011
s89McA564
410Mch868
410Mch876
414Mch647
422Mch[1]90
101McA[3]397
f103McA[4]783
111McA444
142McA[3]717
146McA[1]420
151McA[1]695
151McA[2]695
1981MiAG
[494
1981MiAG
[757
59JUL117
64MBJ1067
64MBJ1068
27WnL855
28WnL969
22A41118n

—346—
(294NW197)
s407Mch873
s409Mch1102
s93McA579
412Mch87
116McA[1]419
122McA273
d143McA778
28WnL761
29WnL551

—356—
(294NW202)
410Mch[4]899
109McA[3]311
d113McA[4]624
118McA[1]249
125McA[2]234
125McA[3]234
28WnL882

—364—
(294NW827)
s402Mch926
420Mch[12]161
420Mch[3]171
420Mch[4]171
e420Mch[11]171
f107McA[9]481
113McA[1]61
113McA[2]61
113McA[4]61
113McA[5]61
j113McA64
27WnL425
28WnL713
RLPB§ 4.13
48A21436s

—401—
(295NW50)
s409Mch1116
s79McA639
413Mch[2]590
414Mch[25]573
416Mch[25]224
416Mch[1]225
j416Mch231
420Mch[16]260
420Mch[11]263
421Mch136
422Mch[2]600
422Mch[7]600
422Mch[9]600
422Mch[12]601
422Mch[13]604
422Mch[11]620
422Mch[13]620
422Mch[2]627
423Mch572
f100McA[6]688
f100McA[7]688
f100McA[1]689
f100McA[2]689
f100McA[3]689
f100McA[4]689
f100McA[5]690
j100McA842
102McA[2]647
102McA[7]649
e103McA[11]
[348
f103McA[11]
[515
104McA[10]68
104McA[8]72
107McA[12]451
f110McA[3]423
110McA[8]511
f111McA[7]149
114McA[1]182
114McA[3]182
114McA[2]185
f116McA[12]
[119
117McA706
118McA[8]629
119McA[8]236
j119McA542
120McA[1]217
120McA[2]218
f121McA[1]21
f121McA[2]23
121McA[1]733
123McA[8]171
f123McA[9]524
f123McA[10]
[525
f123McA[11]
[525
f123McA[15]
[525
f123McA[4]525
f123McA[1]526
f123McA[2]526
j123McA528
124McA[8]268
e124McA[1]476
e124McA[2]476
124McA[11]478
125McA[11]249
127McA[2]458
d128McA[1]170
f129McA[1]216
f129McA[5]216
f129McA[7]216
f132McA[11]
[106
f134McA[2]606
135McA[12]50
d135McA598
138McA[7]432
f139McA[13]
[606
141McA[1]112
141McA[11]621
141McA[1]682
f142McA[1]635
f142McA[2]635
f142McA[5]635
e143McA[11]
[425
e143McA[13]
[426
146McA[2]498
150McA[28]754
151McA[11]636
152McA[11]121
Cir. 3
570FS[2]620
Cir. 6
695F2d[12]234
716F2d[2]388
741F2d[1]877
f772F2d276
503FS[11]845
503FS[11]1059
f506FS[6]636
f506FS[7]636
f506FS[8]636
f506FS[9]636
510FS348
f510FS[2]349
f517FS[5]224
564FS[1]358
d576FS[2]543
f576FS[10]544
583FS[5]1355
635FS[2]1467
642FS[13]36
24BRW159
36BRW[1]438
f36BRW[2]439
Cir. 7
568FS[11]553
Cir. 10
784F2d[2]1057
60JUL120
60MBJ257
60MBJ654
60MBJ745
61MBJ624
62MBJ773
63MBJ599
64MBJ174
27WnL651
27WnL837
28WnL735
28WnL930
29WnL399
29WnL514
29WnL808
30WnL439
30WnL689
33CLA1586
70Cor838
69VaL304
ICD§ 6.36
LPIB§ 3.21
47A3314s
38A41010n

—463—
(295NW354)
s92McA742
410Mch865
e411Mch1044
412Mch687
415Mch449
418Mch[1]109
418Mch942
419Mch310
f105McA[1]659
e107McA[1]338
f107McA[1]466
107McA[1]741
e108McA[1]469
f108McA[1]596
111McA[1]52
114McA[1]669
j115McA542
117McA[2]526
120McA652
120McA[1]772
121McA335
d122McA[1]590
128McA550
129McA[1]474
f131McA[1]629
140McA[1]232
f141McA[1]625
142McA200
142McA575
154McA[1]21
27WnL747
30WnL468
18A3259s

—468—
(295NW491)
134McA674
28WnL1209

—474—
(295NW482)
US cert den
in449US1101
s77McA357
j109McA742
d110McA[3]610
d110McA[4]610
d110McA[5]610
d110McA[6]610
j110McA613
f111McA[6]51
113McA541
f124McA[2]787
f124McA[5]787
133McA635
134McA[1]156
27WnL429
28WnL809

—495—
(296NW813)
s96McA276
106McA589
112McA[1]12
116McA787
c118McA22
119McA83
119McA112
62MBJ429
HCC§ 3.14

—500—
(297NW578)
s79McA63
s80McA721
s116McA791
f421Mch[6]283
113McA[13]438
123McA[13]121
125McA[6]348
130McA713
149McA[6]741
150McA[6]81
64MBJ289
28WnL706
28WnL766
30WnL408
77NwL496
5A4866s

—552—
(297NW115)
s408Mch877
s127McA716
416Mch[3]261
f120McA697
121McA[1]496
130McA[3]151
141McA[3]164
143McA448

—564—
(297NW120)
s92McA427
419Mch[2]307
119McA[2]729
e119McA[2]781
d121McA[2]329
d126McA[2]713
e135McA[2]194
f150McA[2]444
1982DCL909
27WnL659
28WnL752
28WnL764
30WnL460
31WnL455

—569—
(297NW544)
28WnL82
28WnL691

—639—
(297NW387)
s402Mch828
s420Mch463
s74McA237
s96McA92
s88LE223
s89LE294
s92LE504
s106SC224
s106SC1175
s106SC3129
cc54USLW
[5037
410Mch[10]249
410Mch[1]257
410Mch[1]275
413Mch632
120McA320
131McA769
1981MiAG
[617
1985DCL
[1031
28WnL1165
62A3314s
63A388s

—672—
(299NW304)
(13A41180)
s396Mch843
s402Mch938
s403Mch821

Continued

922

"q" (questioned), you should be extremely alert and exercise great caution. It may be premature, however, to assume that your entire document is now incorrect and useless.

In *all* instances, retrieve and read the cases that have been assigned one of these negative abbreviations. It is possible that only a portion of your case has been criticized or overruled and that the remainder of the case is still authoritative. Carefully examine the elevated numbers because it is also possible that only headnote 8 of your case is being criticized or questioned or only the issue discussed in headnote 10 has been overruled. If you are relying solely on headnote 6 from a case, this negative treatment is serious but not devastating. Read the cases listed in *Shepard's* to determine whether your case may still be relied upon.

If the portion of the case you are relying upon is still valid and some other portion has been reversed, you may still cite your case, but you must disclose to the reader the later treatment as follows:

> *Smith v. Jones*, 291 N.M. 103, 418 P.2d 945 (1984), *rev'd on other grounds*, 292 N.M. 646, 419 P.2d 109 (1985).

10. Shepardizing Using a Regional Shepard's

Because many cases are published in both an official report as well as in a West regional reporter such as the *Atlantic Reporter* or the *Pacific Reporter*, you may elect to Shepardize such a case either in a state or regional *Shepard's*. For example, assume your case is cited as follows: *Gose v. Monroe Auto Equipment Co.*, 409 Mich. 147, 294 N.W.2d 165 (1980). You may Shepardize this case using *Shepard's Michigan Citations*, as discussed previously, or by using *Shepard's Northwestern Reporter Citations*.

The process of Shepardizing a case is always the same whether you Shepardize your case in a state *Shepard's* or in a regional *Shepard's*. For example, to use the regional *Shepard's*:

(i) Locate the volumes of *Shepard's Northwestern Reporter Citations*.
(ii) Examine the box or notice labeled "What Your Library Should Contain" to ensure you have all of the *Shepard's* volumes necessary.
(iii) Open a volume of *Shepard's* and examine the upper left and right corners of each page to find a reference to **Vol. 294.**
(iv) Scan down the page looking for a boldface **- 165 -**.
(v) Examine the entries listed.

The first entry given will be the parallel citation to *Gose v. Monroe Auto Equipment Co.* and will be placed in parentheses.

The next entries will be references to the history of the case and then to other cases in the *Northwestern Reporter* that mentioned or discussed

Gose v. Monroe Auto Equipment Co. First you will be directed to cases from Michigan, the state that decided *Gose v. Monroe Auto Equipment Co.* You will then be sent to federal cases and then to cases from other states whose cases are reported in the *Northwestern Reporter*, such as Minnesota, North Dakota, and Wisconsin. Next you will be given citations to cases from other units of the *National Reporter System*, such as the *Pacific Reporter* and *Southern Reporter*, and then you will be directed to any A.L.R. annotations discussing *Gose v. Monroe Auto Equipment Co.*

One of the advantages of Shepardizing *Gose v. Monroe Auto Equipment Co.* in *Shepard's Northwestern Reporter Citations* rather than *Shepard's Michigan Citations* is that you will be directed to cases from states other than Michigan that have mentioned or discussed *Gose v. Monroe Auto Equipment Co.* If you Shepardize *Gose v. Monroe Auto Equipment Co.* in *Shepard's Michigan Citations*, you will only be directed to cases from Michigan that mention or discuss *Gose v. Monroe Auto Equipment Co.*

A disadvantage, however, is that the regional *Shepard's* will not direct you to law review articles or attorneys general opinions that mention *Gose v. Monroe Auto Equipment Co.* If *Gose v. Monroe Auto Equipment Co.* has been overruled, reversed, limited, and so forth, however, you will be provided this information whether you Shepardize in *Shepard's Michigan Citations* or in *Shepard's Northwestern Reporter Citations*. You will be directed to annotations in A.L.R. no matter which set of *Shepard's* you use.

Are you required to Shepardize a case in both *Shepard's Michigan Citations* and in *Shepard's Northwestern Reporter Citations*? For the most complete treatment of *Gose v. Monroe Auto Equipment Co.*, you should Shepardize in both sets, as the state *Shepard's* will direct you to law review articles and attorneys' general opinions, and the regional *Shepard's* will direct you to cases from states other than Michigan that have mentioned *Gose v. Monroe Auto Equipment Co.* In practice, however, most legal professionals will Shepardize in the state *Shepard's* or the regional *Shepard's*, but not both. Because the most critical information provided by *Shepard's* is the history of a case (whether it has been affirmed, reversed, or so forth), and both sets give you this information, Shepardizing in one set rather than both is sufficient for these purposes. Updating electronically eliminates this concern.

After some experience in Shepardizing, you may develop a preference for one method over another. Unless you have a compelling reason otherwise, you should probably Shepardize in the companion *Shepard's* to your case. That is, if you read a case in the *Kansas Reports*, Shepardize it in *Shepard's Kansas Citations*. If you read this same case in the *Pacific Reporter*, Shepardize it in *Shepard's Pacific Reporter Citations*. This procedure will enable you to most effectively use the elevated (superscript) numbers given by *Shepard's* to pinpoint later discussion of the headnotes from your case. That is, because the publisher of the official report may use a different headnote numbering system than West will use when it reports the same case in its regional reporter, Shepardizing is most effective when you use a set of *Shepard's* that will pinpoint the particular

Figure 9-5
Sample Page from *Shepard's Northwestern Reporter Citations*

Volume number

Page number

Parallel cite

25A4 58n
30A4 181n
30A4 194n
ICD§6.03

- 165 -
(409Mch147)
s263NW329
300NW[1]481
306NW[1]421
317NW[1]4
319NW[1]353
321NW[1]799
323NW413
323NW[3]915
324NW[1]777
326NW[1]415
327NW272
328NW[1]22
332NW[1]570
336NW[3]31
337NW[1]267
337NW[1]582
349NW[2]547
351NW[1]921
357NW[1]54
512FS[2]1165
564FS[1]1301

- 194 -
(409Mch271)
s270NW1
s282NW8
f326NW568
355NW[2]110
e653F2d[5]269
d567FS[1]65

- 197 -
(409Mch346)
s286NW909
312NW[1]620
323NW425
332NW[1]466

- 202 -
(409Mch356)
311NW[5]761
d318NW[6]497
324NW[1]592
336NW[3]455
336NW[5]455

- 205 -
(96McA510)
309NW[2]577
309NW[5]582
f311NW[1]756
d311NW[6]758
e313NW347
f316NW[3]430
j316NW431
f325NW[5]560
329NW497
84A3 375s

- 209 -
(96McA524)
v306NW103
j308NW464
60A3 226s

- 215 -
(96McA708)

- 218 -
(96McA714)
44A2 1156s

- 221 -
(96McA726)
(19A4 361)
311NW[3]738
328NW[4]618
f328NW[1]619
f346NW[4]54
Ariz
676P2d622
Wash
685P2d626
86A2 1443s

- 224 -
(96McA763)
r309NW174
c304NW[1]540
q311NW[1]373
335NW115
343NW[3]186
502FS[1]731
q502FS[1]732

- 228 -
(97McA5)
a327NW783
324NW[5]338
324NW613
336NW[5]833
f348NW[10]709
NY
469S2d555
26A4 672n
26A4 687n

- 236 -
(97McA33)
US cert den
in104SC3537
r341NW92
cc244NW619
318NW[3]669

- 241 -
(97McA44)
312NW[1]425

- 243 -
(97McA50)

- 246 -
(97McA56)
s261NW215
299NW[10]374
304NW[10]578
323NW[7]532
357NW[5]814

- 249 -
(97McA92)
e309NW[4]255
350NW[4]269
Fla
435So2d391

- 253 -
(97McA122)
cc241NW260
299NW[12]397
300NW[3]542
318NW[1]482
323NW[7]519

326NW837
j338NW403
339NW[7]498
339NW[8]498
96A2 768s
15A4 715n

- 262 -
(97McA287)
e308NW[7]197
e308NW[8]197
351NW[3]907
86A2 722s
39A3 1000s

- 266 -
(97McA340)
r307NW682

- 269 -
20A3 988s
75A3 616s
RLPB§1.63

- 271 -
356NW[4]849
NM
680P2d609

- 275 -
296NW[1]380

- 280 -
295NW[2]101
295NW[1]546
j295NW547
297NW[2]288
299NW[2]738
302NW[1]31
305NW[2]342
306NW[2]118
349NW[2]296
350NW926

- 286 -
d313NW[1]433
d321NW[1]890
68A3 7s

- 288 -
d298NW[3]356
f309NW[7]44
354NW[5]118
354NW[1]470
716F2d1215

- 297 -
f307NW[23]772
e336NW[2]152
336NW[2]353
343NW[23]709
351NW[18]379
352NW[18]807
d353NW557
355NW[22]302
356NW[21]741
356NW[23]742
512FS941
Colo
679P2d1067

- 312 -
348NW375
73A2 1238s
24A4 939n

- 320 -
313NW[1]388
325NW[1]642

- 321 -
354NW451

- 322 -
Md
439A2d6
Tenn
654SW414
61A3 293s

- 324 -
319NW34
357NW[2]149
17MJ503
45A3 958s

- 327 -
cc270NW758
330NW104
336NW[3]53

- 330 -
(206Neb516)
f330NW[2]744

- 334 -
(206Neb559)
e303NW[5]310
321NW428
328NW[3]179
334NW[2]449
334NW[3]449
343NW[2]758
343NW[3]758
343NW[4]758

- 338 -
(206Neb578)

- 341 -
(206Neb587)

- 343 -
(206Neb599)
320NW[1]102
320NW[3]104

- 347 -
(206Neb615)
333NW[1]404
333NW[2]404
6A2 1244s
42A2 13s
81A2 456s

- 350 -
(206Neb619)
328NW[3]773
96A3 745s

- 354 -
(206Neb625)
300NW[2]23
300NW[3]23
301NW[7]342
336NW[2]604
76A3 163s

- 357 -
(206Neb630)
d295NW273
j304NW677

318NW[6]744
5A4 1033n

- 363 -
(206Neb639)
73A2 1238s
24A4 942n

- 369 -
(206Neb651)
318NW[4]727
329NW101

- 372 -
(206Neb655)
352NW[2]601

- 374 -
(206Neb658)
333NW[1]909
335NW537
352NW[1]585

- 376 -
(206Neb662)
f316NW[5]602

- 379 -
(206Neb666)
cc262NW187
319NW[4]442
15A4 684n

- 382 -
(206Neb670)
s300NW194
d294NW[4]871
357NW[4]205
NH
480A2d186
NY
444S2d415

- 386 -
s261NW399
s264NW888

- 391 -
310NW739
312NW[1]363
d313NW735
336NW[2]112
61A2 1390s

- 397 -
325NW[1]215
Fla
428So2d366
18A3 1376s

- 404 -
302NW[4]783
311NW[6]184
315NW[4]680
315NW[7]681
f315NW[8]681
316NW[2]96
322NW[2]464
e328NW[3]218
e329NW[3]376
331NW[2]17
e340NW[2]175
343NW[3]366
351NW[1]96
82LE[6]326
104SC[6]3144

Fla
400So2d1000
Mass
438NE63
25A2 1407s
31A3 565s

- 411 -
301NW[4]398
576FS[5]809
ICD§6.02

- 416 -
313NW[2]468
328NW259
334NW[2]489
337NW[2]813
346NW[2]307
350NW[2]610
e356NW472
53A2 1102s

- 419 -
303NW[1]356
303NW[2]356
304NW[1]109
304NW[5]111
304NW[2]122
304NW[1]714
310NW[2]785
315NW[1]499
315NW[2]499
329NW[4]888
329NW[5]888
f330NW[5]544

- 426 -
(14A4 773)
Me
461A2d1059
3A3 1072s

- 431 -
504FS[2]1092

- 435 -
f318NW[1]9
f318NW[2]9
338NW[1]292

- 437 -
(97W260)
(13A4 1)
s284NW120
f293NW[5]901
j293NW908
297NW[2]499
297NW[16]500
307NW903
308NW[32]408
311NW[5]223
340NW[14]219
340NW[34]496
342NW[9]54
342NW[29]54
342NW443
343NW[20]427
344NW[30]519
346NW770
347NW[2]603
355NW563
75LE[2]646
103SC[2]1636
655F2d[2]658
665F2d[29]208
686F2d[15]467

686F2d[18]467
686F2d[2]469
717F2d[5]834
717F2d[3]839
727F2d527
727F2d[9]529
e746F2d1241
746F2d
[[33]1241
512FS[11]1280
520FS[6]161
526FS[5]900
536FS467
548FS[22]376
572FS[33]119
f572FS[3]121
572FS[4]121
576FS201
576FS[34]202
Iowa
347NW410
347NW[2]411
Colo
684P2d215
Conn
472A2d312
Fla
403So2d467
426So2d1109
428So2d247
438So2d194
438So2d1068
Ill
427NE616
450NE1207
Ind
460NE184
Kan
666P2d713
NJ
471A2d438
472A2d583
NY
481S2d971
Pa
469A2d662
469A2d671
25A3 1416s
10A4 949n
11A4 1262n

- 473 -
(97W332)
s282NW637
f297NW[2]76
f297NW[3]76
297NW[1]502
e298NW[6]104
d298NW106
298NW410
300NW[2]69
302NW[11]508
d306NW[7]297
f308NW[2]917
f309NW[5]12
314NW[9]323
e314NW[6]324
324NW[1]443
f325NW[5]318
327NW[1]61
327NW[2]61
327NW[5]63
329NW[2]241
331NW[5]607
334NW[2]583
f337NW[2]191

338NW[5]488
f339NW[1]336
348NW[1]153
348NW[3]153
f349NW100
351NW[4]163
535FS666
74A2 984s

- 485 -
(97W485)
US cert den
in449US994
296NW741
298NW555
325NW[24]689
342NW[14]407
348NW[14]562
587FS[24]1481
W Va
314SE398
314SE400

- 501 -
(97W521)
a301NW156
340NW[22]927
508FS[16]222
539FS917
11A3 9s
18A3 10s
18A3 88s
51A3 981s
12A4 108n
13A4 326n

- 528 -
(97W627)
298NW[3]413
313NW[10]823
326NW[1]119
334NW[1]688
345NW[1]514

- 534 -
(97W638)
r303NW608
10A2 22s
11A3 9s
18A3 10s
18A3 170s
12A4 180n

- 540 -
(97W654)
a307NW881
e321NW[1]314
Ind
443NE70

- 547 -
(97W679)
j306NW697
Wash
688P2d149

- 551 -
(97W669)
315NW[3]370

- 555 -
s242NW702
304NW[3]235
322NW[1]302
f322NW[4]308
Continued

headnote of your case that is treated by later cases. See Figure 9-5 for a sample page from *Shepard's Northwestern Reporter Citations.*

11. Shepardizing Public Domain Citations

As you know from reading Chapter 8, several states now assign public domain numbers to cases as they are released, such as "1998 MT 1" for the first Montana case in 1998. These can be Shepardized in the state *Shepard's* in a separate section devoted to public domain opinions as well as in the regional *Shepard's*. Thus, 1998 MT 1 can be Shepardized in *Shepard's Montana Citations* and in *Shepard's Pacific Reporter Citations*.

12. When to Shepardize

When to perform the task of Shepardizing is left to your discretion. You may find that if you have been assigned the task of cite-checking someone else's project, you may be Shepardizing after the final draft has been completed and just before the document is delivered to court or to the adverse party. The obvious hazard of Shepardizing so late in the process is that you run the risk of discovering that a key case cited in the document has been overruled or reversed, causing a last-minute crisis.

If the project is your own writing, you should consider Shepardizing fairly early in the research process for two reasons: first, to eliminate any possibility of a devastating eleventh hour surprise; and, second, to locate other sources to support your argument.

Many legal professionals Shepardize almost concurrently with performing legal research. That is, as they locate cases that appear promising, they immediately Shepardize them so as not to invest time and effort in reading, analyzing, and writing about cases only to discover later they are no longer valid. The other advantage of early Shepardizing is that you will be directed to law review articles, A.L.R. annotations, and attorneys' general opinions. These sources may provide a thorough analysis of the very subject you are researching and can serve as "free research." If you wait to Shepardize until a project is completed, you may miss these valuable research aids.

13. Shepardizing Federal Cases

a. United States Supreme Court Cases

Use *Shepard's United States Citations* to Shepardize cases from the United States Supreme Court. The technique used to Shepardize United States Supreme Court cases is identical to that used to Shepardize state cases.

Assume you are Shepardizing the case *Rabeck v. New York*, 391 U.S. 462 (1968). The first entries *Shepard's* will provide you are parallel references to your case, that is, the references to 20 L. Ed. 2d 741 and 88 S. Ct. 1716. *Shepard's* will then give you references to the history of the case *Rabeck v. New York*, and then entries relating to the treatment of *Rabeck v. New York* by later United States Supreme Court cases and lower federal court cases. These entries are arranged by circuit and state allowing you to easily locate cases from the Ninth Circuit, Fifth Circuit, Alaska, or Connecticut. You will next be sent to annotations that discuss or mention *Rabeck v. New York*.

Shepard's now offers separate sets to Shepardize cases from the United States Supreme Court. Thus, cases published in the official *United States Reports* are Shepardized using one set of *Shepard's*, while cases published in West's *Supreme Court Reporter* are Shepardized using a separate set of *Shepard's*, and cases published in LEXIS' *United States Supreme Court Reports, Lawyers' Edition*, are Shepardized using still another set of volumes.

See Figure 9-6 for a sample page from *Shepard's United States Citations.*

b. Lower Federal Court Cases

Use *Shepard's Federal Citations* to Shepardize cases that appear in the *Federal Reporter*, *Federal Supplement*, or *Federal Rules Decisions*. The technique used to Shepardize cases from the United States courts of appeal and the United States district courts is exactly the same as that used to Shepardize any case.

When you Shepardize a lower federal court case, *Shepard's* will provide you with references to federal cases relating to the history of your case and then cases relating to the treatment of your case. Once again, entries will be arranged by circuit and state so you can readily locate cases from a specific circuit or state that discusses your case. *Shepard's* will also direct you to annotations that mention or discuss your case. See Figure 9-7 for a sample page from *Shepard's Federal Citations.*

14. How Many Volumes to Use When Shepardizing

You have seen that Shepardizing may require you to use more than one volume of *Shepard's.* Often you may need to use one or two hardbound volumes and one or more of the softcover supplements. While you can certainly look up your case citation in each and every one of the *Shepard's* volumes, both hardcover and softcover, that may not be necessary. The front cover or the spine of the *Shepard's* volumes may provide you with information that your case is not covered by that volume. For example, assume the case you need to Shepardize is *Pillsbury Co. v. Conboy*, 459 U.S. 248 (1983). When you retrieve the volumes of *Shepard's*, you may note that the spine or the front of the first hardcover volume states, "Cases

Figure 9-6
Sample Page from *Shepard's United States Citations*

Vol. 391

UNITED STATES SUPREME COURT REPORTS

Dk6 92-3139
741FS649
750FS294
796FS[1]279
796FS[1]296
796FS[1]1091
797FS[1]602
Cir. 7
886F2d[2]888
890F2d[2]914
902F2d540
916F2d1264
717FS[2]1317
735FS[2]254
735FS[2]841
736FS209
740FS[2]512
743FS[2]564
Cir. 8
972F2d[2]895
972F2d946
Cir. 9
797FS792
797FS[2]838
Cir. 10
743FS[2]1445
743FS[2]1462
749FS1058
ClCt
26ClC746
1992MC2731
—308—
Cir. 2
d903F2d[1]153
—367—
Cir. DC
e886F2d[1]413
e886F2d[1]417
d890F2d1190
972F2d[1]373
713FS[1]476
d731FS[1]1126
Cir. 2
Dk2 91-1722
f903F2d148
f903F2d[1]157
j903F2d166
915F2d62
915F2d[1]63
916F2d780
d916F2d[1]781
Cir. 4
921F2d54
973F2d299
Cir. 5
Dk5 92-7291
jDk5 92-7291
911F2d1004
973F2d1257
j973F2d1261
Cir. 6
721FS862
f730FS[1]84
Cir. 7
f879F2d[1]1548
d901F2d633
f901F2d[1]635
Cir. 8
d897F2d[1]921
f897F2d923
j897F2d928
898F2d[1]616
911F2d89
Cir. 9

914F2d1254
d731FS[1]418
f795FS[1]335
Cir. 11
Dk11 91-
[8941
f795FS[1]1092
Calif
3C4th845
12CaR2d709
838P2d231
—404—
Cir. 2
Dk2 91-1077
—418—
Cir. DC
j880F2d533
920F2d[3]61
Cir. 1
973F2d972
—430—
Cir. 4
914F2d534
Cir. 7
896F2d1054
Cir. 8
890F2d[3]69
Cir. 10
fDk10 87-
[1668
Conn
29CtA352
—510—
Cir. 5
Dk5 91-2204
881F2d[1]187
881F2d1278
973F2d[3]1180
Cir. 7
742FS[4]489
Cir. 11
f971F2d1515
Calif
13CaR2d12
838P2d740
Ill
232IlA1005
600NE418
La
604So2d1041
Md
93MdA121
—543—
Cir. DC
711FS[2]643
797FS[2]15
Cir. 2
972F2d35
Cir. 4
975F2d[1]125
Cir. 8
Dk8 92-
[2263NI
973F2d1376
Cir. 10
714FS[2]1154
Cir. 11
890F2d328
Ala
606So2d217
Conn

613A2d300
Tex
834SW367
835SW241
Wash
67WAp97
839P2d354
—563—
494US680
j494US680
Cir. DC
d886F2d[1]415
886F2d[2]417
e886F2d418
Cir. 2
f933F2d[1]1154
Cir. 3
971F2d1021
715FS[1]669
Cir. 4
899F2d[1]287
921F2d[1]54
f973F2d298
Cir. 5
889F2d[1]578
d910F2d[1]210
d910F2d[2]210
d910F2d[3]212
973F2d[1]1270
Cir. 6
887F2d[1]720
Cir. 7
fDk7 91-2157
Dk7 91-2157
fDk7 91-2157
eDk7 91-2288
Dk7 91-2288
973F2d[3]585
730FS1482
d797FS[2]1471
Cir. 8
d903F2d[1]561
e972F2d[1]916
f972F2d[1]995
Cir. 9
888F2d598
924F2d[2]860
j924F2d865
972F2d[3]1137
730FS[1]314
Cir. 10
f881F2d[1]910
f883F2d[1]856
883F2d[3]858
883F2d[1]860
719FS[1]1529
Cir. 11
f888F2d1563
888F2d[1]1564
972F2d[1]1237
j972F2d1238
747FS708
f796FS[1]491
f796FS[3]491
f796FS[2]492
Ky
834SW661
Ore
837P2d510
837P2d516
P R
121DPR717
1992JTS9924
W Va
421SE691

—585—
Cir. 2
728FS[2]263
734FS[2]68
N H
135NH413
Ohio
74OA114
598NE85
Tenn
836SW128
—964—
Case 3
Va
420SE239
—966—
Case 4
Cir. 9
713FS1349
—968—
Case 2
Mass
598NE1146
—971—
Case 4
Cir. 5
972F2d124

Vol. 392

—1—
Cir. DC
892F2d[5]114
e892F2d[4]115
f895F2d[4]1424
f895F2d[5]1424
j895F2d1430
973F2d[5]931
973F2d[5]946
973F2d[6]947
f711FS[4]641
711FS[6]641
734FS[6]39
Cir. 1
j903F2d70
718FS[5]1068
Cir. 2
Dk2 92-1160
972F2d33
f719FS[5]123
f719FS[6]123
728FS264
733FS582
d733FS[1]583
d733FS[5]583
744FS494
797FS216
797FS[6]217
Cir. 3
722FS[6]81
736FS[1]558
736FS[6]560
736FS[4]564
Cir. 4
722FS[6]1298
732FS[6]631
Cir. 5
884F2d818
911F2d[6]1009
714FS812
717FS[4]1223

Cir. 6
f884F2d[6]277
f890F2d[6]860
915F2d215
915F2d[6]216
915F2d[6]216
915F2d[6]218
f974F2d[5]692
e719FS[6]616
Cir. 7
891F2d625
910F2d[4]1508
972F2d841
f974F2d[6]819
f974F2d[10]910
717FS[4]1332
Cir. 8
f890F2d[8]1414
e890F2d[2]1420
891F2d[6]681
900F2d142
915F2d[6]1209
973F2d1386
f974F2d[5]956
796FS1257
f797FS[6]709
f797FS[6]709
Cir. 9
Dk9 91-
[50050
883F2d[6]696
887F2d[4]234
891F2d1420
901F2d819
974F2d[6]1204
975F2d[4]636
f714FS[6]1573
Cir. 10
Dk10 91-
[2225
880F2d[1]1193
892F2d[6]967
f892F2d[6]968
j892F2d971
f973F2d[6]826
712FS866
712FS[6]867
714FS1150
735FS[6]390
Cir. 11
d890F2d327
972F2d1257
716FS1472
716FS[6]1473
Calif
9CA4th1247
12CaR2d337
Conn
29CtA212
613A2d1307
613A2d1319
614A2d1231
D C
612A2d838
614A2d537
614A2d873
Fla
604So2d503
604So2d838
605So2d603
Ga
204GaA484
204GaA576
205GaA436
419SE921
420SE30

Idaho
121Ida493
121Ida496
121Ida497
121Ida525
121Ida726
121Ida932
121Ida936
121Ida966
839P2d42
Ill
231IlA675
233IlA76
233IlA275
233IlA471
233IlA493
233IlA548
598NE427
599NE46
599NE193
599NE514
599NE1338
Ind
598NE531
Kan
17KA2d249
838P2d906
Ky
834SW687
La
604So2d605
604So2d706
605So2d719
Me
614A2d1300
Md
327Md587
93MdA50
93MdA379
93MdA561
613A2d469
Mass
413Mas600
33MaA442
599NE247
600NE1018
Mich
195McA121
489NW170
Mo
835SW408
835SW905
835SW953
836SW487
N H
135NH380
N J
258NJS612
614A2d158
N Y
180NYAD
[586
152NYM964
587NYS2d10
N C
107NCA406
420SE703
N D
488NW603
Ohio
72OA46
72OA52
72OA150
72OA156
72OA285
72OA509

72OA591
74OA166
74OA504
75OA32
75OA525
76OA147
76OA198
598NE729
598NE851
599NE710
599NE860
601NE158
601NE191
Pa
529Pa462
412PaS113
412PaS118
412PaS613
413PaS436
413PaS440
613A2d6
614A2d696
614A2d1380
614A2d1385
Tex
834SW455
835SW104
835SW783
Utah
837P2d11
837P2d988
Vt
614A2d793
614A2d795
Va
14VaA476
14VaA484
14VaA489
26VCO294
421SE4
421SE8
421SE216
421SE666
421SE884
Wash
67WAp46
Wis
171Wis2d751
Wyo
838P2d180
—40—
Cir. 2
Dk2 92-1160
719FS125
744FS497
Cir. 3
910F2d1077
f796FS821
f796FS[1]824
Cir. 5
730FS9
Cir. 6
974F2d694
D C
614A2d538
Ill
233IlA77
598NE428
Md
93MdA296
Minn
489NW795
N Y
181NYAD
[600

586NYS2d
[342
Ohio
72OA508
74OA167
76OA376
598NE730
—83—
Cir. DC
883F2d1041
883F2d[3]1048
j883F2d1055
887F2d[4]283
Cir. 1
721FS388
Cir. 2
885F2d[4]1026
e972F2d[3]471
Cir. 3
894F2d65
796FS[3]120
Cir. 4
902F2d1160
Cir. 6
f711FS[3]374
Cir. 8
f891F2d[3]1356
Cir. 9
f741FS[3]1400
f741FS[4]1401
Cir. 10
882F2d1489
Okla
j838P2d22
P R
1992JTS9931
—134—
Cir. 3
Dk3 91-5613
—157—
Cir. DC
890F2d1183
—206—
Cir. 2
797FS128
Cir. 9
Dk9 92-
[15389
—219—
Tex
837SW641
—236—
Cir. 1
885F2d945
885F2d[1]954
721FS393
Cir. 9
f741FS[1]1392
—273—
Cir. 4
971F2d[1]1082
Cir. 9
907F2d[1]886
f975F2d653
N C
421SE393
Ohio

Continued

Citing cases arranged by circuit and then state

46

Figure 9-7
Sample Page from *Shepard's Federal Citations*

FEDERAL SUPPLEMENT

Vol. 446

Citing cases arranged by circuit and then state

—120—
j446US466
j64LE433
j100SC1785
Cir. 2
596F2d[3]1100
Cir. 5
j597F2d430
Cir. 8
624F2d826
Cir. 10
535FS[2]528
Ill
117IlA518
452NE1388
Minn
280NW25
59ARF840n
59ARF854n
14ARF849s

—124—
j446US466
j64LE433
j100SC1785
Cir. 5
j597F2d430
14ARF849s

—129—
23ARF637s

—131—
s595F2d1209
s646F2d563
60LE[3]936
99SC[3]2330
Cir. 4
560FS[2]782
Cir. 8
579F2d[3]1087
72ARF438n

—136—
Cir. 3
f471FS[4]962
471FS[1]963
565FS[3]1548
Cir. 7
d581FS[2]657
d581FS[5]657
N Y
85NYAD926
446NYS2d
[770

—141—
a577F2d723
cc585F2d7
Cir. 3
555FS[1]693
Cir. 11
68BRW[5]227
68BRW[7]228
P R
109DPR828

—149—
a593F2d1372

—153—
a589F2d39

—160—
(199PQ466)
a599F2d1126
Cir. 2
452FS444
452FS[5]446
469FS680
512FS982
Cir. 7
635FS[2]611

—165—
(201PQ242)
s463FS232
Cir. DC
477FS[5]947
Cir. 3
f482FS[5]17
495FS[5]540
f503FS[5]211
503FS[4]213
509FS[5]351
533FS[5]20
Cir. 11
644FS[5]547

—171—
Cir. DC
f516FS[3]1259
d538FS[4]895
Cir. 4
724FS[4]378
Cir. 7
565FS414
Cir. 9
652F2d[3]917
AgD§ 17.53

—175—
Cir. 2
604F2d794

—178—
r581F2d172
s553F2d51
Mo
cc530SW457
S D
272NW311

—181—
US cert den
in444US926
in100SC265
a598F2d310
Cir. DC
655F2d361
729FS7
Cir. 1
d695FS[6]638
Cir. 2
475FS[7]934
Cir. 5
659F2d[3]709
Cir. 10
595F2d[1]538
716F2d1351
D C
462A2d14
Haw
1HA212
616P2d1030
Ky
598SW471
Mo
643SW14

N J
189NJS574
461A2d190
N C
42NCA228
256SE479
35ARF461s

—186—
Cir. 1
562FS[3]227
Cir. 2
497FS[4]1071
Mo
618SW452
13ARF145s
28ARF266s
28ARF534s

—191—
Cir. 8
d510FS[1]1060
Cir. 9
537FS[1]979
73ARF357n

—193—
US reh den
in449US1028
in101SC601
D449US808
D66LE11
D101SC55
s489FS1248
cc392US83
cc20LE947
cc88SC1942
cc271FS1

—196—
Cir. 3
66BRW[1]395
Cir. 6
15BRW[1]754
59BRW[1]844

—199—
Cir. 6
550FS[5]431
550FS[6]431

—206—
(197PQ903)
Cir. 2
649FS[5]343
649FS[7]345
Cir. 3
495FS[4]317
495FS[6]317
527FS[6]740
539FS[4]161
539FS[6]161
539FS[8]161
d583FS523
632FS[10]2
704FS[6]545
718FS[10]344
Cir. 7
575FS[5]1424
12ARF502s

—209—
Cir. 2
461FS[1]135
601FS[1]725
Cir. 11
666F2d[1]523
Md
54MdA144
458A2d457
64ARF683n
20ARF731s

—210—
Cir. 2
511FS1186
549FS[3]1141
556FS[3]560
Cir. 3
657F2d[3]35
Cir. 6
c500FS[3]1154
Cir. 8
627F2d[3]850
471FS[1]464
e471FS[2]465
e471FS[3]465
627FS[3]850
Cir. 11
533FS[3]88

—212—
Cir. 1
752F2d[1]8
655FS[2]743
Cir. 2
462FS[4]700
562FS824
639FS[3]320
673FS[2]91
696FS[4]961
710FS461
Cir. 9
719FS1517
Cir. 10
520FS[4]1198
Colo
626P2d691

—216—
Cir. DC
q683F2d449
526FS[7]822
Cir. 2
555FS[7]268
Cir. 4
476FS[10]801
Cir. 7
f25BRW267
25BRW[3]268
Ark
266Ark536
588SW694
Colo
42CoA391
595P2d273
61ARF848n
11ARF815s
27ARF602s

—221—
a585F2d22
Cir. 2
488FS[1]516
488FS[4]517
Cir. 9
d815F2d[1]1274

13ARF323s

—226—
Cir. 10
457FS1016
474FS[3]443
480FS[2]262

—232—
Mo
654SW334
29A481n

—236—
a588F2d90

—242—
ML
446FS1268
448FS[1]273
458FS[1]225
483FS[1]825
MFP§ 6.20

—244—
v687F2d14
s636F2d580
s453FS648
s464FS949
cc768F2d1263
cc533FS703
cc89FRD695
Cir. 3
541FS1350
Cir. 4
669F2d[2]949
Cir. 8
720F2d[1]535
720F2d[2]535
Cir. 11
704F2d588
ML
470FS[1]859
Calif
87CA3d760
151CaR433
GMS§ 2.05
PLPD§ 2.37
TT§ 15.08

—248—
ML
464FS[1]966
470FS[1]866
487FS[1]1354

—252—
Cir. 1
834F2d6
Cir. 3
505FS[32]1228
729FS[12]1482
88FRD562
Cir. 4
800F2d440
814F2d956
493FS602
495FS[11]565
592FS[25]441
728FS1273
Cir. 5
722F2d1198
508FS1202
508FS1203
508FS1204
561FS697

Cir. 6
c864F2d[16]424
f503FS[9]797
f503FS[10]797
f503FS[11]797
f503FS[12]797
Cir. 7
d607F2d785
803F2d[36]279
521FS[51]21
521FS[52]21
532FS[50]1133
546FS[88]1140
688FS[35]1323
Cir. 8
633F2d[36]84
633F2d[37]85
641F2d598
c771F2d1120
779F2d[38]436
d779F2d[39]439
819F2d1431
88FRD[88]348
Cir. 9
500FS[66]428
502FS[9]866
Cir. 10
570FS[71]519
575FS340
Cir. 11
704F2d[49]1538
539FS[24]838
13MJ884
16MJ892
22MJ74
75TCt15
Alk
700P2d1307
718P2d141
Ariz
134Az348
656P2d637
Calif
132CA3d926
183CaR501
Conn
180Ct105
429A2d816
D C
422A2d1285
Haw
60Haw245
589P2d520
Ill
68IlA385
385NE853
Ind
441NE472
Iowa
286NW160
286NW221
La
425So2d759
Md
296Md686
296Md707
306Md328
48MdA390
55MdA468
427A2d1046
463A2d293
464A2d1037
464A2d1047
508A2d983
Mass
377Mas202

381Mas734
15MaA402
17MaA708
20MaA120
385NE519
412NE343
446NE91
462NE331
478NE753
Mich
432Mch110
123McA317
175McA765
333NW267
437NW613
438NW659
Minn
292NW769
Mo
609SW434
N J
86NJ535
432A2d91
N M
97NM686
643P2d250
N Y
100NYAD
[465
99NYM871
100NYM388
105NYM845
107NYM233
109NYM77
117NYM754
118NYM237
136NYM736
417NYS2d
[648
419NYS2d
[426
433NYS2d
[542
435NYS2d
[463
437NYS2d
[1020
459NYS2d
[540
460NYS2d
[883
474NYS2d
[987
519NYS2d
[318
N C
315NC85
337SE840
N D
337NW147
Ohio
16OA283
475NE810
Ore
309Ore116
786P2d153
W Va
358SE200
Wyo
638P2d1282
674P2d725
674P2d729
HHb§ 6.01
2LE1686s
15A21152s
5A3763s

5A3819s
37A3612s
19A41213n
48ARF454n
55ARF695n
57ARF960n
60ARF532n
85ARF61n
25ARF723s

—329—
35LE735s

—330—
Cir. DC
579FS[2]166
Cir. 2
d465FS[11]602
493FS[7]40
497FS[12]1086
529FS[8]229
534FS[3]330
582FS[6]1524
609FS[1]79
628FS733
658FS[6]813
83FRD448
20BRW[2]806
N M
93NM117
597P2d302
18LE1685s
38A31102s

—342—
Cir. 5
755F2d[4]1167

—348—
Cir. 2
478FS[1]1064
602FS[8]514
602FS[9]514
603FS[13]373
49ARF403n
72ARF109n
27ARF407s

—357—
s469FS54
s83FRD112
Cir. 5
634F2d[1]290
Cir. 6
f598F2d[1]1024
Cir. 10
489FS1283
49ARF397n

—361—
a588F2d61
Cir. DC
813F2d430
Cir. 1
677F2d[9]161
Cir. 2
630F2d[5]90
474FS[9]1261
483FS[10]341
Cir. 3
q466FS[18]1227
472FS[4]1328
Cir. 4
q454FS1083

Continued

141

to 420 U.S." This would be an indication that your case is not covered by that volume. You would then proceed to examine the next volume of *Shepard's* and determine whether your case will be Shepardized by that volume.

Another tip as to which volume to start in is that *Shepard's* will provide you with a parallel citation in parentheses only the first time the parallel cite is available. After that, the parallel citation will not be repeated in subsequent volumes. Thus, when you find the parallel citation in parentheses, you know that you should Shepardize in that volume and in volumes published thereafter. Similarly, when you Shepardize, if you are never provided with a parallel citation, this should serve as a signal that one of the volumes of *Shepard's* is missing, unless there is no parallel citation for your case.

It does not matter whether you start with the more recent softcover supplements and work backward to the older hardbound volumes or whether you start Shepardizing by using the hardbound volumes and work forward to the recently issued softcover supplements. Use the approach that works best for you so long as you check all the volumes that cover the period of time after your case was decided.

Remember that the softcover supplements are not cumulative. You cannot examine the most recent one and assume it covers every case decided since your case was decided. Each volume of *Shepard's* relates to a separate and distinct period of time. For example, the most recent softcover red supplement for *Shepard's Maryland Citations* will list only those cases decided in the past six weeks that have mentioned or discussed certain cases. Thus, you may need to examine several volumes of *Shepard's*. As a rule of thumb, the older your case is, the more volumes of *Shepard's* you will need to examine.

15. Troubleshooting

There are several events that should serve as hints that something has gone wrong in the Shepardizing process.

(i) If you never find a parallel cite for your case, this may indicate that one of the volumes of *Shepard's* is missing. Do not forget, however, that lower federal court cases have no parallel cites and that many states no longer publish officially. Thus, there are no parallel cites for these cases. Check the box or notice labeled "What Your Library Should Contain" to be sure you have all of the volumes you need.

(ii) If you never see any entry for your case, it is possible that the citation is incorrect. Check to make sure you have not transposed numbers in the citation. It is also possible that you are attempting to Shepardize in the wrong series. This is a common mistake. For example, if your citation is *Jones v. Smith*, 141 Ill. App. 3d 499, 349 N.E.2d 809 (1986), and you are Shepardizing using *Shepard's Illinois Citations*, make sure you have located the pages that Shepardize Volume 141 of *Illinois Appellate Reports, 3d Series*, rather than *Illinois Appellate Reports, 2d Series*, or *Illinois Appellate Reports*. *Shepard's* will contain a Table of Contents directing you to the appropriate pages for the series in which you are interested.

(iii) If the entries in the book look completely unfamiliar to you, it is likely that you have retrieved the volumes of *Shepard's* for statutes rather than cases.

(iv) If one or two of the *Shepard's* volumes do not list your case, this may mean that during the period of time covered by that issue no case or other source mentioned or discussed your case. This is not a cause for concern.

(v) Remember that *Shepard's* is entirely self-correcting. To reassure yourself that your Shepardizing technique is correct, retrieve one of the cases listed by *Shepard's* and verify that it mentions your case. Once you have verified that you are Shepardizing correctly, you will soon feel more confident about your technique.

16. Using Shepard's *to Find Parallel Citations*

While there are usually alternative ways to find a parallel cite for a case (see Chapter 4), Shepardizing is probably the easiest and most efficient. If you have only a single citation to a case and your law library or law firm does not purchase this set, or the volume you need is missing from the shelf, you should immediately Shepardize the citation and obtain the parallel cite, which is given in parentheses. This will enable you to readily locate the case you need. See Figure 9-8 for steps in Shepardizing cases.

C. Shepardizing Statutes

1. Locating Shepard's *for Statutes*

Just as you can Shepardize a case to determine whether it is still "good law," you must Shepardize a statute to determine its history and how it has been treated by later court decisions. The technique of Shepardizing statutes is substantially similar to Shepardizing cases.

You must make sure you have the volumes of *Shepard's* for statutes rather than cases. Some states, usually those with a rich body of case law, such as California, have volumes of *Shepard's* for cases and then entirely separate volumes devoted solely to statutes. Other states have combined the references for cases and statutes in one volume. In these books, the

Shepard's case citations are given first, followed by the statute citations. Within the volumes or sections for statutes are also citations for a state's constitution and usually citations to local ordinances as well as court rules and jury instructions.

Be sure to check the section on the front cover of the latest issue of *Shepard's* entitled "What Your Library Should Contain" and retrieve all of the volumes you need, both hardcover and softcover. Most law libraries maintain the volumes of *Shepard's* for statutes immediately next to the volumes of *Shepard's* for cases. All of the *Shepard's* volumes are usually located immediately after the last volume of reports for state or for federal cases.

2. *Locating* Shepard's *References to Your Statute*

If your state arranges its statutes solely by number, as most states do, open one of the volumes of *Shepard's*, check the upper left and right corners of each page and look for a reference to your statute or one numerically close to it. Then scan down the page looking for a boldfaced reference to your statute.

Figure 9-8
Steps in Shepardizing a Case

- Locate the volumes of *Shepard's* you need (state *Shepard's*, regional *Shepard's*, or federal case *Shepard's*).
- Examine the front cover of the most recent issue of *Shepard's* and read the box labeled "What Your Library Should Contain." Make sure you have all of the volumes needed.
- Select the volumes of *Shepard's* that contain citations to cases decided after your case was decided.
- Examine the upper right and left corners of the pages in *Shepard's* to locate the volume number of the case you are Shepardizing.
- Scan down the page looking for the bold page number identical to the page on which your case begins.
- Carefully examine the entries listed, paying particular attention to the parallel citation, the history of the case as it progressed through the court system, its treatment by other cases, and any other sources, such as annotations and law review articles that discuss your case.
- If desired, verify that you are Shepardizing correctly by checking one or two cites listed by *Shepard's* to ensure your case is, in fact, mentioned by these cites.
- Repeat, as needed, in other volumes of *Shepard's*.
- Examine and analyze troublesome entries, including later cases that criticize or question your case.

If your state arranges its statutes by title, as do California, Maryland, New York, and Texas, locate the title you need by looking at the upper left- and righthand corners of each page. When you have located your title (Agriculture, Business Occupations, or Education), scan down the page to locate the boldfaced reference to your statute. Be sure you are checking the right title and that when you want to Shepardize Education Section 5201, you are not mistakenly Shepardizing Elections Section 5201 or Finance Section 5201.

3. *Analysis of References in* Shepard's

Similar to the way *Shepard's* provides you with information about a case through the use of various abbreviations, it also indicates the history and treatment of a statute you are Shepardizing by the use of abbreviations placed before the entries listed. Do not be concerned that you will not be able to remember or memorize all of the abbreviations. Each volume of *Shepard's Citations for Statutes* will contain a Table of Abbreviations placed near the front of the volume. See Figure 9-9 for the most common abbreviations for history and treatment of statutes.

a. History References

The first entries given will relate to the history of your statute, namely, how it has been treated subsequently by the *legislature*. It is possible that your statute has been amended, repealed, or suspended. *Shepard's* will provide this information to you through the use of identifying letters. For example, a reference to "A1990C37" would mean that your statute had been amended and you would find the amending language in Chapter 37 of your state's session laws for 1990.

b. Treatment References

Following the entries related to the history of your statute in the legislature, you will be given entries related to the treatment of your statute by *cases*. Perhaps a court in your state or a federal court case has interpreted your statute and determined it is unconstitutional or void. This treatment is indicated by letters placed before the citation. For example, if you have Shepardized a statute and you are presented with the entry "U577A2d784," this signifies that your statute was held unconstitutional, and the determinative language is located on page 784 of Volume 577 of the *Atlantic Reporter, Second Series*. If no identifying letters are given, this is simply an indication that a case has mentioned your statute in some generalized fashion.

c. No References to Your Statute

One of the detailed features of Shepardizing a statute is that you will be directed to the history and treatment of each particular subsection of a

Figure 9-9
Abbreviations Relating to Statutes

History in Legislature

A	(amended)	Statute amended
Ad	(added)	Addition of new section
E	(extended)	Provisions of a statute extended to a later statute or additional time allowed for performance of duties required by a statute within a specific time
L	(limited)	Provisions of a statute not extended to a later statute
R	(repealed)	Repeal of an existing statute
Re-en	(re-enacted)	Statute re-enacted
Rn	(renumbered)	Existing sections of a statute renumbered
Rp	(repealed in part)	Repeal of part of an existing statute
Rs	(repealed and superseded)	Repeal of an existing statute and substitution of new legislation
Rv	(revised)	Statute revised
S	(superseded)	Substitution of new legislation for an existing statute not expressly repealed
Sd	(suspended)	Suspension of statute
Sdp	(suspended in part)	Suspension of part of statute
Sg	(supplementing)	Addition of new matter to an existing statute
Sp	(superseded in part)	Substitution of new legislation for part of an existing statute not expressly repealed
Va	(validated)	Statute validated

Judicial Treatment

C	(constitutional)	Statute declared to be constitutional
U	(unconstitutional)	Statute declared to be unconstitutional
Up	(unconstitutional in part)	Statute declared to be unconstitutional in part
V	(void or invalid)	Statute declared to be void or invalid
Va	(valid)	Statute declared to be valid
Vp	(void or invalid in part)	Statute declared to be void or invalid in part
f	(followed)	Case follows statute
i	(interpreted)	Case interprets or construes statute
j	(dissenting opinion)	Statute mentioned in dissenting opinion
na	(not applicable)	Case finds statute not applicable
rt	(retroactivity)	Case discusses retroactivity of statute

statute. For example, if you have cited Section 5201(b) of your state's code, generally you need only examine the references for subdivision (b) of Section 5201. If other portions of the statute have been repealed or ruled unconstitutional, you may still be able to rely upon and cite your particular subdivision. Moreover, you can readily locate cases interpreting the subdivision in which you are interested and bypass the cases or other authorities that mention or discuss other portions of the statute.

If you are Shepardizing your statute in a volume of *Shepard's* and your statute never appears, it is possible that during the period of time covered by that volume of *Shepard's* the legislature did not deal with that statute and no cases or other sources mentioned or discussed your statute. You may then close that volume of *Shepard's* and proceed to examine the next volume.

d. Other References

Just as *Shepard's Citations* for cases will direct you to law review articles, attorneys general opinions, and annotations that mention or discuss a case you are Shepardizing, *Shepard's Citations* for statutes will direct you to law review articles, attorneys general opinions, and annotations that mention your statute. Additionally, *Shepard's* will cite administrative decisions that have mentioned your statute.

4. *Advantages of Shepardizing Statutes*

You may recall from Chapter 3 that statutes are typically updated by cumulative pocket parts or statutory supplements, which will provide you with any changes or amendments to a statute as well as references to newer cases interpreting that statute. Most publishers issue these pocket parts on an annual basis and the supplements on a quarterly basis. Because *Shepard's* issues its new supplements every few weeks, it can offer you the most up-to-date information on your statute. For example, if a case declares your statute unconstitutional, *Shepard's* will usually provide you with a reference to this case well before a new pocket part or supplement to the annotated code is issued.

5. *Analyzing Negative Letters*

If you encounter "negative" letters when you Shepardize your statute (such as "R" for repealed or "U" for unconstitutional), exercise great caution. Carefully examine the *Shepard's* entries. It is possible that only a portion of the statute or some other subdivision of the statute has been repealed or ruled unconstitutional. In all instances, retrieve and read the entries listed in *Shepard's* to determine the exact status of your statute. See Figure 9-10 for a sample page from *Shepard's Alaska Citations for Statutes.*

Figure 9-10
Sample Page from *Shepard's Alaska Citations for Statutes*

ALASKA STATUTES, 1962, (AS AMENDED BY REVISED TITLES TO 1990) AND SUPPLEMENTS, 1990 **12.55.120**

Reference to amendment of subdivision of statute

§ 11.71.020
Subd. a
809P2d926
§ 11.71.030
811P2d318
823P2d671
829P2d841
8AkLR54
Subd. a
A1991C63
¶1
810P2d173
811P2d319
816P2d1386
821P2d134
823P2d18
825P2d905
827P2d455
829P2d1198
833P2d16
837P2d1124
Subd. b
R&Re-en
[1991C63
§ 11.71.040
956F2d893
829P2d841
Subd. a
816P2d126
A1991C63
¶2
799P2d1347
807P2d507
813P2d687
¶3
Cl. A
809P2d926
809P2d942
816P2d908
837P2d1124
Cl. F
809P2d424
816P2d220
Subd. b
R&Re-en
[1991C63
§ 11.71.060
830P2d438
9AkLR280
Subd. a
C830P2d436
¶3
C830P2d436
Subd. b
830P2d441
§ 11.71.190
Subd. b
830P2d436
9AkLR280
§ 11.71.900
Subd. 13
811P2d319
¶A
811P2d320
Subd. 28
Ad1991C63

Subd. 29
Ad1991C63
§ 11.75.110
7AkLR268
§ 11.76.100
Subd. a
A1992C113
Subd. b
R&Re-en
[1992C113
Subd. d
A1992C113
§ 11.76.105
830P2d438
§ 11.76.107
Ad1992C113
§ 11.81.250
810P2d161
§ 11.81.320
815P2d390
7Æ99n
§ 11.81.330
825P2d918
§ 11.81.335
825P2d918
§ 11.81.340
825P2d918
§ 11.81.350
825P2d918
Subd. a
825P2d912
§ 11.81.370
830P2d774
Subd. a
¶1
830P2d776
§ 11.81.400
825P2d913
825P2d918
Subd. a
825P2d911
¶2
825P2d913
§ 11.81.420
825P2d911
829P2d844
Subd. b
829P2d844
¶1
829P2d844
§ 11.81.430
Subd. a
¶1
820P2d1095
§ 11.81.440
815P2d390

§ 11.81.450
815P2d390
821P2d138
§ 11.81.600
Subd. b
Cl. A
808P2d284
¶2
808P2d283
§ 11.81.610
Subd. a
808P2d284
Subd. b
828P2d178
7Æ837n
Subd. c
836P2d958
§ 11.81.620
Subd. a
819P2d908
§ 11.81.630
7Æ837n
§ 11.81.640
828P2d178
§ 11.81.900
810P2d565
835P2d456
Subd. a
¶1
805P2d356
818P2d141
818P2d692
¶2
805P2d356
808P2d282
7Æ837n
¶3
818P2d695
7Æ837n
¶4
805P2d356
Subd. b
¶1
815P2d390
821P2d138
Cl. B
7Æ100n
¶2
960F2d879
¶3
837P2d131
¶11
820P2d1092
823P2d1255
834P2d1252
836P2d958
837P2d134
¶13
834P2d1252
¶17
837P2d133
¶19
816P2d210
¶32
834P2d1259
¶34
800P2d953
A1991C91

¶49
5Æ339n
¶50
836P2d959
5Æ316n
Cl. A
836P2d959
5Æ342n
Cl. B
836P2d959
¶52
810P2d565
Cl. A
Subcl. 1
810P2d565
Cl. B
Subcl. 1
810P2d565
Subcl. 2
810P2d565
¶53
807P2d1097
Cl. A
810P2d568
¶58
Ad1991C59
§ 11.446.660
Subd. a
¶3
960F2d879
§ 11-16-100
et seq.
828P2d178
§ 12.10.010
964F2d1201
A1992C79
§ 12.10.020
Subd. c
A1992C79
§ 12.15.010
805P2d361
§ 12.20.010
825P2d908
§ 12.25.030
825P2d915
Subd. b
A1992C30
§ 12.25.150
809P2d419
Subd. a
8AkLR44
Subd. b
803P2d413
813P2d313
Subd. c
809P2d420
§ 12.25.160
809P2d420
814P2d747
7AkLR383

§ 12.25.180
Subd. a
825P2d915
§ 12.30.010
et seq.
823P2d15
§ 12.30.010
823P2d16
823P2d17
§ 12.30.025
A1991C64
§ 12.30.030
Subd. b
A1991C21
§ 12.30.040
823P2d16
§ 12.30.060
Subd. 1
823P2d14
837P2d720
§ 12.35.010
Subd. b
A1991C60
§ 12.35.015
Subd. a
A1991C60
Subd. b
A1991C60
Subd. c
A1991C60
Subd. d
A1991C60
Subd. e
A1991C60
Subd. g
Ad1991C60
§ 12.35.040
825P2d914
§ 12.40.110
Subd. a
838P2d816
§ 12.45.020
824P2d729
100YLJ791
§ 12.45.045
814P2d739
836P2d381
Subd. a
957F2d1546
§ 12.45.046
111LE684
110SC3168
807P2d1093
7AkLR223
§ 12.45.048
807P2d1088
818P2d689

§ 12.45.049
Ad1992C95
§ 12.47.010
et seq.
828P2d175
§§ 12.47.010
to 12.47.090
828P2d175
§ 12.47.010
828P2d173
§ 12.47.030
140PaL2291
§ 12.47.050
828P2d175
§ 12.47.060
828P2d174
§ 12.47.070
829P2d1208
§ 12.47.095
Subd. a
A1992C10
Subd. f
Ad1992C10
§ 12.47.100
812P2d617
829P2d1208
Subd. a
812P2d617
Subd. b
812P2d618
§§ 12.50.010
to 12.50.080
74MnL154
§ 12.50.020
Subd. b
74MnL155
§ 12.50.101
816P2d175
825P2d928
Subd. a
825P2d921
§§ 12.55.005
to 12.55.185
810P2d161
§ 12.55.005
800P2d958
805P2d964
809P2d932
820P2d300
835P2d1258
8AkLR23
Subd. 1
800P2d957
809P2d934
816P2d219
836P2d383
Subds. 2 to 6
809P2d934

Subd. 4
810P2d161
§ 12.55.015
487US826
108SC2694
835P2d455
Subd. a
¶7
831P2d361
§ 12.55.023
Subd. b
A1991C57
§ 12.55.025
7AkLR289
Subd. c
828P2d1208
829P2d1193
Subd. e
7AkLR289
A1992C79
Subd. g
7AkLR289
¶¶1 to 3
7AkLR289
¶1
7AkLR290
¶¶4 to 6
7AkLR289
¶4
7AkLR290
¶5
7AkLR290
¶6
7AkLR290
Subd. h
835P2d454
7AkLR294
Subd. i
Ad1992C79
§ 12.55.035
835P2d456
Subd. a
A1992C71
Subd. b
¶3
838P2d1258
¶4
830P2d441
¶5
808P2d288
§ 12.55.045
810P2d161
835P2d456
7AkLR334
Subd. a
7AkLR337
A1992C71
Subd. b
7AkLR342
Subd. e
Ad1991C53
Subd. f
Ad1992C71
Subd. g
Ad1992C71

§ 12.55.050
7Æ387n
§ 12.55.051
Subd. a
7AkLR338
A1992C71
Subd. c
7AkLR338
R&Re-en
[1992C71
Subd. d
7AkLR346
§ 12.55.055
835P2d456
Subd. f
Ad1991C53
§ 12.55.080
807P2d517
823P2d17
831P2d361
835P2d456
§ 12.55.085
807P2d517
824P2d1387
8AkLR22
Subd. d
824P2d1387
Subd. e
824P2d1387
§ 12.55.088
Subd. d
A1991C57
Subd. f
A1991C57
Subd. g
A1991C57
§ 12.55.090
823P2d17
Subd. a
807P2d517
Subd. b
807P2d517
§ 12.55.100
823P2d17
Subd. a
¶2
7AkLR342
§ 12.55.115
818P2d1163
823P2d1256
827P2d450
838P2d277
§ 12.55.120
805P2d969
816P2d221
7AkLR270
Subd. a
816P2d223
7AkLR265
Subd. b
838P2d1257
7AkLR270

119

Figure 9-11
Sample Page from *Shepard's Federal Statute Citations*

Cir. 9
984F2d1509
987F2d554
812FS164
Cir. 10
984F2d1568
986F2d1351
112ARF92n
112ARF95n
112ARF101n
§§ 151 to 169
Cir. 3
985F2d1223
Cir. 7
987F2d423
§ 151
Cir. 6
984F2d734
Cir. 9
987F2d556
§ 152
Subsec. 2
122LE578
113SC1198
Cir. 1
983F2d329
Cir. 3
985F2d1223
985F2d1227
Subsec. 3
Cir. 1
984F2d559
Cir. 2
812FS1345
Cir. 8
812FS1003
Subsec. 5
Cir. 3
985F2d1223
812FS510
Subsec. 11
Cir. 2
812FS1345
Cir. 6
987F2d1258
§ 157
122LE574
113SC1194
Cir. DC
987F2d790
Cir. 4
985F2d126
Cir. 6
983F2d701
983F2d1343
Cir. 7
987F2d425
987F2d438
987F2d450
Cir. 8
812FS1002
Cir. 9
984F2d1514
987F2d556
812FS164
§ 158
122LE574
113SC1194
Cir. 6
983F2d1343
984F2d734

Cir. 7
987F2d447
Cir. 8
812FS1002
Cir. 11
813FS794
112ARF640n
Subsec. a
Cir. 7
987F2d447
Subd. 1
Cir. DC
983F2d241
986F2d1435
987F2d778
Cir. 1
984F2d558
Cir. 4
985F2d125
986F2d73
Cir. 5
985F2d803
Cir. 6
983F2d701
983F2d708
985F2d853
987F2d1258
Cir. 7
984F2d867
987F2d425
987F2d434
987F2d449
Cir. 8
987F2d541
812FS1000
Cir. 9
986F2d341
Cir. 10
984F2d1564
986F2d1348
112ARF93n
112ARF97n
112ARF102n
112ARF129n
Subd. 2
Cir. 4
986F2d75
Subd. 3
Cir. DC
983F2d241
986F2d1435
987F2d778
Cir. 1
984F2d558
984F2d560
Cir. 5
985F2d803
Cir. 6
983F2d708
985F2d853
810FS918
812FS755
Cir. 7
984F2d869
987F2d425
987F2d448
Cir. 8
987F2d541
812FS1000
Subd. 5
Cir. DC
983F2d241
Cir. 4
985F2d125
986F2d73
Cir. 7

984F2d867
987F2d425
987F2d434
Cir. 8
812FS1000
Cir. 9
986F2d341
Cir. 10
984F2d1564
986F2d1348
112ARF93n
112ARF97n
112ARF101n
112ARF128n
Subsec. b
Subd. 4
¶ B
Cir. 6
985F2d857
¶ D
Cir. 9
984F2d342
Subd. 6
Cir. 6
984F2d736
Subsec. c
Cir. 7
987F2d436
987F2d449
Cir. 10
986F2d1351
Subsec. d
122LE579
113SC1198
Cir. DC
983F2d241
Cir. 7
984F2d870
112ARF93n
Subsec. e
122LE573
113SC1193
Subsec. f
122LE573
113SC1193
Cir. 1
984F2d556
Cir. 2
809FS191
Subsec. g
112ARF92n
§ 159
Subsec. a
Cir. 2
809FS191
Cir. 3
985F2d1226
Cir. 4
986F2d74
Cir. 6
810FS914
Subsec. c
122LE578
113SC1197
Subsec. e
122LE578
113SC1197
§ 160
Cir. 2
809FS191

Subsec. b
Cir. 2
809FS189
Cir. 6
984F2d734
987F2d1238
811FS316
Cir. 7
984F2d867
Cir. 10
986F2d1354
Subsec. c
Cir. DC
984F2d481
Cir. 5
985F2d804
Cir. 6
983F2d709
Subsec. e
Cir. DC
983F2d244
Cir. 1
984F2d559
Cir. 3
810FS589
Cir. 4
985F2d125
986F2d74
Cir. 5
985F2d803
985F2d805
Cir. 6
983F2d709
Cir. 7
987F2d423
987F2d437
987F2d450
Cir. 10
984F2d1564
986F2d1349
Subsec. f
Cir. DC
986F2d1436
Cir. 1
984F2d559
Cir. 5
985F2d803
Cir. 7
987F2d423
Cir. 10
984F2d1564
986F2d1349
Subsec. k
Cir. 9
984F2d342
§ 161
Cir. 10
985F2d1041
Subsec. l
Cir. 10
985F2d1041
§ 173
Subsec. d
Cir. 3
812FS70
§ 185
et seq.
Cir. 3
812FS68
Cir. 11
986F2d427

§ 185
Cir. 1
983F2d327
811FS42
Cir. 2
809FS190
810FS68
810FS510
Cir. 3
983F2d492
985F2d112
Cir. 4
812FS638
Cir. 5
985F2d231
813FS523
Cir. 6
983F2d726
984F2d735
987F2d1238
810FS911
810FS939
811FS316
812FS756
813FS1329
Cir. 7
985F2d325
Cir. 8
984F2d245
812FS1001
Cir. 9
987F2d560
Cir. 10
985F2d1421
809FS801
809FS809
Subsec. a
Cir. 1
985F2d10
Cir. 2
810FS410
810FS512
813FS197
Cir. 3
985F2d110
985F2d1226
812FS510
Cir. 4
812FS638
Cir. 5
985F2d232
812FS646
Cir. 6
984F2d735
985F2d860
810FS914
810FS939
812FS757
813FS593
Cir. 8
811FS467
812FS949
812FS1005
Subsec. b
Cir. 2
810FS512
Cir. 3
985F2d1225
§ 186
Cir. 2
812FS1318
Cir. 3
985F2d718
Cir. 6
984F2d734

Subsec. a
Cir. 2
812FS1326
Cir. 6
984F2d734
Subd. 2
Cir. 2
812FS1344
Cir. 7
984F2d869
Subsec. b
Cir. 2
812FS1326
Subd. 1
Cir. 2
812FS1329
Cir. 11
813FS794
Subsec. c
Cir. 2
812FS1326
Cir. 6
812FS105
Subd. 1
Cir. 2
812FS1344
Subd. 4
Cir. 2
812FS1347
Cir. 7
984F2d869
Cir. 11
813FS796
Subd. 5
Cir. 2
812FS1328
¶ B
Cir. 11
813FS794
Subd. 6
Cir. 11
813FS794
§ 201
et seq.
USDk 92-1
Cir. 1
813FS895
Cir. 2
987F2d89
810FS531
Cir. 3
145FRD359
145FRD373
Cir. 5
809FS1214
Cir. 7
810FS245
811FS1334
812FS806
Cir. 9
810FS259
Cir. 11
984F2d409
812FS1201
§§ 201 to 219
Cir. 4
985F2d131
Cir. 7
812FS803
Cir. 9
810FS262
811FS508

§ 202
Cir. 9
811FS513
§ 203
USDk 92-1
Subsec. d
USDk 92-1
Cir. 2
985F2d50
Cir. 11
812FS1206
Subsec. e
Cir. 2
987F2d89
Subd. 2
¶ C
Cir. 7
810FS246
Subsec. g
Cir. 2
987F2d89
Cir. 11
812FS1206
Subsec. m
Cir. 11
812FS1212
Subsec. r
USDk 92-1
Cir. 4
985F2d131
§ 206
USDk 92-1
Cir. 2
809FS232
Cir. 4
985F2d131
Cir. 5
984F2d152
809FS1213
Cir. 7
985F2d331
986F2d1160
Cir. 9
811FS508
Subsec. a
Subd. 1
USDk 92-1
Cir. 11
812FS1212
Subd. 5
Cir. 11
812FS1212
Subsec. d
Subd. 1
Cir. 5
984F2d152
809FS1226
§ 207
USDk 92-1
Cir. 1
813FS897
Cir. 4
985F2d131
Cir. 7
810FS248
Cir. 9
811FS508
Cir. 10
986F2d411

Subsec. a
USDk 92-1
Cir. 1
813FS895
ClCt
27FedCl 670
Subd. 1
Cir. 7
810FS246
Subsec. e
Cir. 1
813FS902
Subd. 5
Cir. 1
813FS902
Subsec. f
Cir. 1
813FS896
Subsec. o
USDk 92-1
Subd. 2
USDk 92-1
¶ A
USDk 92-1
Cl. 1
USDk 92-1
Cl. 2
USDk 92-1
§ 211
Subsec. c
Cir. 4
985F2d131
§ 213
Subsec. a
Subd. 1
Cir. 7
810FS246
811FS1335
§ 215
Subsec. a
Subd. 2
Cir. 4
985F2d132
Subd. 3
Cir. 7
984F2d791
812FS803
ClCt
27FedCl 670
Subd. 5
Cir. 4
985F2d132
§ 216
Cir. 3
145FRD359
Cir. 4
985F2d134
Subsec. b
Cir. 1
813FS896
813FS902
Cir. 3
145FRD359
Cir. 4
985F2d134
Cir. 5
984F2d670
809FS1214
Cir. 7
985F2d370
Continued

Citing cases arranged by circuit

49

6. *Shepardizing Federal Statutes*

The process of Shepardizing a federal statute is virtually identical to that of Shepardizing a state statute. Assume that you are interested in Shepardizing 29 U.S.C. § 216 (1988). Locate the volumes of *Shepard's* entitled *Shepard's Federal Statute Citations.* Examine the section entitled "What Your Library Should Contain" to ensure you have all of the volumes of *Shepard's* you need. Look in the upper right- and left-hand corners of the pages for references to Title 29. Then scan down the page to locate a boldfaced reference to Section 216.

You will now be presented with references to the history of this statute (for example, what treatment it has received from the United States Congress), references to the treatment of this case by federal cases (arranged by circuits and districts), references to annotations, and to articles, texts, and treatises that have mentioned this case. See Figure 9-11 for a sample page from *Shepard's Federal Statute Citations.*

7. *When to Shepardize*

Just as you have seen with regard to Shepardizing cases, the decision when to Shepardize statutes is left to your discretion. Shepardizing fairly early in the research process, however, may save you time by alerting you to any problems with your statute and may provide you with valuable research sources by referring you to cases, annotations, and law review articles that discuss your statute.

8. *How Many Volumes to Use When Shepardizing a Statute*

There are usually fewer volumes of *Shepard's* for statutes than for case citations. When you first begin Shepardizing a statute, use all volumes. As you become more experienced, you may be able to skip some volumes by realizing that a newly enacted statute will only appear in the most recently issued softcover *Shepard's* supplements.

9. *Troubleshooting*

If you Shepardize a statute and you never find any entries to it, this may indicate that your statute has never been subsequently dealt with by the legislature or any later cases. It may also indicate a problem in the Shepardizing process. If this occurs:

(i) Examine your citation to make sure you have cited it correctly and have not transposed any numbers.

(ii) Examine the box on the most recent softcover supplement labeled "What Your Library Should Contain" to ensure you have all of the appropriate volumes.

(iii) Review the entries in *Shepard's* to verify that you are Shepardizing Probate Code Section 52 rather than Public Utilities Section 52, if your statute is cited by a title as well as a number.

See Figure 9-12 for steps in Shepardizing statutes.

D. Shepardizing Constitutions

1. *Shepardizing Provisions of State Constitutions*

The volumes of *Shepard's* that enable you to Shepardize statutes from your state will also contain references to the history and treatment of provisions of your state's constitution. To Shepardize provisions of your state's constitution, retrieve all of the volumes of *Shepard's Citations* for statutes for your state. Remember that some states have separate volumes of *Shepard's* for cases and for statutes. Other states will combine the citations for cases and statutes in the same volumes. Check the Table of Contents in the front of each volume of *Shepard's* which will direct you to the appropriate pages containing references to the state constitution.

Examine the upper left- and right-hand corners of each page for references to specific articles or amendments to the state constitution. Scan down the page looking for boldfaced references to specific provisions of your constitution. A typical entry would appear as follows:

Art. 3
§9
741FS341
576A2d517
68TxL982

When you locate the specific provision of the constitution in which you are interested, you will be provided with the history of that provision (for example, whether it has been amended or repealed) and then with citations to state cases, federal cases, attorneys general opinions, law review articles, and annotations that have cited, mentioned, or discussed that provision of the constitution. You should then read and analyze the references as needed.

2. *Shepardizing Provisions of the United States Constitution*

Citations to the United States Constitution appear in the volumes of *Shepard's* that contain citations to our federal statutes, that is, *Shepard's Fed-*

eral Statute Citations. After you make sure you have all of the volumes you need, check the Table of Contents in the front of each volume so you will know on which page the citations to the United States Constitution begin. Check the upper right- and left-hand corners of each page for references to the articles or amendments you are Shepardizing and then scan down the page to find the particular provision in which you are interested. When you locate the pertinent provision you need to Shepardize, you will be presented with references to United States Supreme Court cases, lower federal court cases, and annotations that have cited, mentioned, or discussed that particular provision of the United States Constitution. Read and analyze these references, as needed. See Figure 9-13 for a sample page showing citations to the United States Constitution.

E. Shepardizing Administrative Regulations

Chapter 10 discusses the enactment and publications of regulations of administrative agencies such as the FDA, FCC, and FAA. It is possible to Shepardize administrative regulations published in the *Code of Federal*

Figure 9-12
Steps in Shepardizing a Statute

- Locate the volumes of *Shepard's* you need (*Shepard's* [*State*] *Citations for Statutes, Shepard's Federal Statute Citations*).
- Examine the front cover of the most recent issue of *Shepard's* and read the box labeled "What Your Library Should Contain." Make sure you have all of the volumes needed.
- Examine the upper right and left corners of the pages in *Shepard's* to locate the article or title of the statute you are Shepardizing.
- Scan down the page looking for a boldfaced entry for the particular section in which you are interested. If your statutes are arranged by title, exercise caution to be sure you are Shepardizing the correct title.
- Carefully examine the entries listed, paying particular attention to the history of the statute by the legislature, its treatment by cases, and any other sources, such as law review articles and annotations that cite your statute.
- If desired, verify that you are Shepardizing correctly by checking one or two cites listed by *Shepard's* to ensure your statute is in fact mentioned by these other cites.
- Repeat the process in all volumes of *Shepard's*.
- Analyze troublesome entries.

Figure 9-13
Sample Page of Citations to United States Constitution

Citing cases arranged by article and section

UNITED STATES CONSTITUTION

Amend. 4

Art. 1
Cir. DC
811FS701
Cir. 2
811FS798
Cir. 7
986F2d1108
150BRW692

§ 1
122LE17

§ 2
122LE14
122LE398
113SC1079
Cl. 2
Cir. 11
813FS831
Cl. 5
122LE10

§ 3
122LE19
Cir. 11
813FS825
Cl. 3
Cir. 11
813FS824
Cl. 6
122LE7
Cl. 7
122LE12

§ 4
Cir. 11
813FS825
813FS828
Cl. 1
Cir. 11
813FS824
813FS828
813FS832

§ 5
122LE14
Cl. 2
122LE22

§ 6
Cl. 1
Cir. DC
809FS142

§ 8
122LE16
Cir. 8
985F2d1385
Cir. 10
985F2d1455
812FS201
36MJ1101
Cl. 1
146FRD342
Cl. 3
122LE20
122LE434
122LE564
113SC1098
113SC1189
146FRD342
Cir. DC
987F2d785
Cir. 2
986F2d620

810FS119
Cir. 3
809FS1177
811FS205
811FS1050
Cir. 4
985F2d165
Cir. 5
986F2d759
810FS754
813FS502
Cir. 7
986F2d1059
813FS668
Cir. 8
985F2d1383
809FS718
Cir. 9
983F2d913
811FS518
Cir. 10
985F2d1466
Cir. 11
814FS84
Cl. 7
Cir. 3
810FS609
Cl. 9
Cir. 2
984F2d90
Cl. 10
Cir. 2
813FS976
Cl. 11
122LE444
113SC1110
Cl. 18
Cir. 2
812FS21

§ 9
Cir. 6
810FS842
Cir. 9
812FS1545
Cir. 10
811FS575
Cl. 2
Cir. 3
809FS325
Cir. 5
985F2d793
Cl. 3
146FRD342
Cir. 1
811FS764
Cir. 4
983F2d608
984F2d122
813FS1181
Cir. 5
984F2d654
986F2d880
Cir. 6
810FS842
814FS30
Cir. 7
985F2d1345
Cir. 8
983F2d882
Cir. 9
987F2d577
Cir. 11
813FS816

Cl. 7
121LE485
Cir. Fed.
985F2d1581

§ 10
Cir. 2
983F2d417
Cir. 3
809FS325
Cir. 7
810FS993
111LE844n
Cl. 1
146FRD342
Cir. 1
811FS764
Cir. 4
984F2d122
813FS1184
Cl. 2
122LE438
113SC1098

Art. 2

Cir. DC
983F2d297
Cir. 7
986F2d1108

§ 2
Cir. DC
811FS701
813FS92
Cl. 1
122LE11
122LE224
Cl. 2
122LE444
113SC1110
Cir. DC
811FS701
36MJ1016
36MJ1021
36MJ1032
36MJ1044

§ 3
122LE444
113SC1110
Cir. DC
813FS84

Art. 3

122LE100
USDk 92-484
Cir. DC
986F2d511
809FS145
810FS1312
811FS701
813FS890
Cir. 1
986F2d613
811FS744
Cir. 2
984F2d91
985F2d1153
809FS1118
812FS20
Cir. 3
983F2d489
987F2d168
813FS390

813FS1138
Cir. 4
811FS1145
812FS624
812FS1412
813FS420
813FS1161
Cir. 6
145FRD454
Cir. 7
984F2d828
985F2d382
986F2d1108
809FS1344
811FS1347
812FS1518
150BRW692
150BRW1002
Cir. 9
984F2d1538
985F2d1410
145FRD529
149BRW621
Cir. 10
985F2d1425
986F2d403
810FS1164
Cir. 11
811FS673
Cir. Fed.
986F2d1403

§ 1
Cir. 2
984F2d90
Cir. 7
150BRW692

§ 2
121LE470
Cir. 1
984F2d1279
811FS39
Cir. 2
985F2d1153
813FS216
Cir. 3
809FS325
Cir. 4
984F2d104
Cir. 6
983F2d724
Cir. 7
811FS1308
CIT
810FS321
Cl. 1
USDk 92-484
Cir. DC
986F2d527
Cir. 1
986F2d613
Cl. 3
122LE20

Art. 4

Cir. 9
811FS518

§ 1
Cir. 3
810FS653
Cir. 6
983F2d693

§ 2
122LE51
122LE86
Cir. 4
985F2d738
Cir. 9
813FS1432
111LE886n
Cl. 1
146FRD342
Cir. 3
811FS205
Cl. 2
112ARF486n

Art. 5

36MJ1065

Art. 6

Cir. DC
813FS95
Cir. 1
983F2d1132
Cir. 2
986F2d617
810FS1336
Cir. 10
986F2d375
112ARF508n
Cl. 1
Cir. 3
809FS325
Cl. 2
122LE188
122LE429
122LE515
122LE574
113SC1098
113SC1158
113SC1194
Cir. 1
983F2d1133
984F2d1273
987F2d67
812FS1291
Cir. 2
986F2d617
810FS1336
813FS185
Cir. 3
809FS1185
Cir. 5
984F2d1419
813FS502
Cir. 7
984F2d213
985F2d912
150BRW433
Cir. 8
809FS718
Cir. 9
987F2d644
811FS1441
811FS1462
Cir. 10
985F2d1447
986F2d375
809FS1483
149BRW992
Cir. 11
985F2d1491
Cir. Fed.
984F2d1195
112ARF489n

112ARF500n
Cl. 3
Cir. 5
809FS509

Art. 7

Cir. 3
813FS1119

Amendments

Amends. 1 to 10
Cir. 1
811FS53
Cir. 4
812FS599
Cir. 5
985F2d780
Cir. 6
813FS560
Cir. 11
985F2d1509
811FS671
36MJ1081

Amend. 1

121LE502
121LE564
121LE672
122LE52
113SC1507
146FRD211
Cir. DC
983F2d295
984F2d436
986F2d538
810FS1303
810FS1310
Cir. 1
983F2d313
983F2d335
984F2d12
984F2d1321
811FS33
812FS1288
Cir. 2
984F2d36
984F2d578
985F2d96
809FS176
809FS189
809FS276
809FS1023
809FS1122
811FS893
811FS994
812FS25
812FS323
812FS408
812FS432
813FS135
813FS151
813FS228
813FS1035
145FRD293
Cir. 3
983F2d464
984F2d1361
985F2d121
985F2d710
987F2d193

809FS383
809FS1144
809FS1196
810FS144
811FS184
813FS340
813FS1077
145FRD368
145FRD380
Cir. 4
983F2d589
984F2d605
985F2d1290
809FS398
809FS426
810FS710
811FS1122
811FS1138
811FS1145
812FS79
812FS640
Cir. 5
984F2d1413
985F2d205
986F2d772
986F2d886
986F2d957
986F2d963
810FS779
813FS1265
Cir. 6
983F2d691
983F2d723
985F2d256
986F2d159
810FS213
810FS869
810FS929
811FS1223
813FS559
Cir. 7
983F2d747
984F2d789
984F2d877
985F2d307
985F2d895
985F2d1363
986F2d1059
986F2d1144
809FS585
809FS1316
810FS973
811FS1325
811FS1346
812FS807
812FS830
145FRD482
Cir. 8
985F2d966
986F2d261
986F2d296
986F2d1182
986F2d1198
810FS1063
810FS1449
811FS434
811FS453
813FS678
Cir. 9
984F2d1509
985F2d1413
986F2d1255
986F2d1522
987F2d643
809FS749
810FS1488

811FS546
811FS555
811FS1436
811FS1447
812FS1034
812FS1096
Cir. 10
986F2d1345
810FS1524
811FS1482
812FS1161
Cir. 11
983F2d1028
983F2d1546
985F2d1569
987F2d710
809FS952
810FS1560
811FS667
811FS670
813FS824
111LE843n
111LE845n
111LE893n
112ARF20n
112ARF311n
112ARF576n

Amend. 2

Cir. 8
985F2d990
Cir. 11
985F2d1510

Amend. 3

Cir. 1
150BRW872
Cir. 11
985F2d1510

Amend. 4

121LE457
122LE52
122LE192
122LE480
122LE522
122LE564
122LE739
113SC1133
113SC1161
113SC1189
113SC1359
USDk 92-207
Cir. DC
983F2d290
985F2d1096
Cir. 1
987F2d11
810FS352
811FS745
812FS17
812FS1293
813FS98
813FS117
150BRW873
Cir. 2
983F2d452
984F2d57
986F2d639
809FS294
809FS1004

Continued

3

Regulations by using *Shepard's Code of Federal Regulations Citations.* This set will also enable you to research presidential proclamations and executive orders.

The technique of Shepardizing a federal regulation is substantially similar to Shepardizing a case, statute, or constitutional provision. Retrieve the appropriate volumes and check the Table of Contents to be directed to the page on which references to the regulations begin. Locate the pertinent administrative regulation by examining the upper right- and left-hand corners of the pages and then scan the boldfaced entries on that page. When you locate the entry for your regulation, you will be provided with citations to cases, periodicals, and annotations that discuss your regulation.

F. Shepardizing Local Ordinances

The process of performing municipal or local research relating to your city, county, or town will be discussed in the next chapter. You will see that while city or county ordinances are compiled and published for municipalities, the sets of books are rarely annotated, making it difficult to find cases interpreting local law. The easiest way to locate cases that interpret, mention, or discuss local ordinances is to Shepardize the ordinances.

Use the volumes of *Shepard's* for your state statutes. Make sure you have all of the volumes you need and then check the Table of Contents to be directed to the specific page(s) you need to review. *Shepard's* usually arranges the references alphabetically by municipality so that first you would find references to ordinances of Allegheny County, then Kent County, then Washington County. Examine the upper right- and left-hand corners of each page to look for the county in which you are interested and then scan the page to locate the pertinent title or section, presented in boldface, in which you are interested. You will then be presented with references to state cases, federal cases, articles, and annotations that discuss or interpret local ordinances. See Figure 9-14 for a sample page showing *Shepard's* citations to ordinances.

G. Shepardizing Court Rules

Rules of Court are discussed in Chapter 10. You can Shepardize these court rules to locate cases, law review articles, and annotations that refer to these rules, such as Rules of the Supreme Court of the United States, Federal Rules of Evidence, or the Federal Rules of Civil Procedure. To Shepardize state court rules, use the volumes of *Shepard's* for your state's statutes. To Shepardize federal court rules, use *Shepard's Federal Statute*

Figure 9-14
Sample Page from *Shepard's* Citations to Ordinances

ORDINANCES

ALLAKAKET

Alcoholic Beverages
Regulations
4AkLR228

ANCHORAGE

Aircraft
Operation–Breath Test
815P2d392

Chemical Breath Test
Consent
815P2d392

Initiative and Referendum
Provisions
9AkLR279
Use Restrictions
9AkLR288

Labor
Arbitration–Emergency Services–Expiration of Contract–Minimal Negotiation Period
839P2d1082
–Emergency Services–Impasse Procedures
839P2d1082
–Neutral Mediator
839P2d1082
–Selection of Fact Finder
839P2d1082
–Specified Rules
839P2d1088
Arbitrator–Authority–Limits
839P2d1082
–Decision Based on Fact
839P2d1087
–Final Decision–Binding
839P2d1081
–Pre-emptory Challenges
839P2d1086
Employee Relations–Appropriate Compensation
839P2d1088
–Harmonious–Orderly
839P2d1089
–Negotiation
C839P2d1081
–Negotiation–Binding Arbitration
C839P2d1082
–Tenure–Variables
839P2d1088
Employees–Emergency Services–Strikes and Slowdowns–Prohibited
839P2d1082
Negotiation During Arbitration
839P2d1087

Motor Vehicles
Driving While Intoxicated
823P2d11
–Chemical Tests
823P2d12
–Prohibition
749P2d376
803P2d412
838P2d817
–Second Time Offenders–Provisions
823P2d11
–Second Time Offenders–Sentencing
823P2d11
Intoxication–Chemical Tests–Refusal
803P2d412
Operation–Driving While Intoxicated–Breath Test
815P2d392

Municipal Code
Severability Clause
803P2d884
Trespassing–Criminal–Prohibition
3ARS5th541n

Offenses
Assault–Prohibition
812P2d233
Trespassing–Provisions
803P2d880
–Public or Private Property–Prohibited
803P2d880

Parking Lots
Trespassing–Provisions
803P2d880

Public Employees
Emergency Services
839P2d1082
Services–Classification–Necessity
839P2d1081

Watercraft
Operation–Breath Test
815P2d392

FAIRBANKS

Taxation
Motel and Hotel Tax–Provisions
818P2d1153
–Revenues–Disbursement
818P2d1154

KENAI

City Council
Authority–Assessments–Benefitted Real Property
821P2d718
–Assessments–Capital Improvements
821P2d718
–Assessments–Private Real Property
821P2d719

Lottery
Land Sale
810P2d158

Utilities
Electric–Agreement–City and Homer Electric Association, Inc.
816P2d183
–Agreement–City and Homer Electric Association, Inc.–Requirements–Relocation
816P2d187

KENAI PENINSULA BOROUGH

Taxation
Assessments–Appeals–Procedure
807P2d491

KODIAK ISLAND BOROUGH

Zoning
Parking–Professional Office Buildings–Requirements
827P2d1122
Variances–Purpose
827P2d1124
–Requests–Investigation–Required
827P2d1123

TENAKEE SPRINGS

Zoning
Permits–Encroachment Permits–Issuance
821P2d457
–Encroachment Permits–Provisions
821P2d460

TYONEK

Tribal Members
Homes–Leasing–Non Members–Violation
957F2d633
Territorial Boundaries–Non Members–Violations
957F2d633

Village Territory
Leasing–Non-Tribal Members–Prohibited
953F2d1179
Non-Tribal Members–Presence–Prohibited
953F2d1179

Citing cases arranged alphabetically by locality

169

Citations. The technique of Shepardizing a court rule is analogous to Shepardizing cases, statutes, and other sources.

H. Specialized Citators

There are several other sets of books published by *Shepard's* that cover more specialized topics. Among the more commonly used sets are the following:

(i) *Shepard's Acts and Cases by Popular Name—Federal and State*. If you know a federal or state statute or a federal or state case by its popular name, for example, the Fireman's Tenure Act or the Macaroni Case, you can look up the statute or case in the alphabetically arranged lists in this book, which will then provide you with the correct citation to the statute or case.

(ii) *Shepard's State Case Name Citators*. *Shepard's* has developed a state case name citator for each state. For example, there is a *Shepard's Florida Case Name Citator* and a *Shepard's Wisconsin Case Name Citator*. These citators arrange cases from your state alphabetically by plaintiff and defendant. If you need to locate a Colorado case and all you know is the plaintiff's name or the defendant's name, look it up in *Shepard's Colorado Case Name Citator* and you will be provided with the citation(s) to the case, the date of decision, and an identification of which court in Colorado rendered the decision. *Shepard's* also publishes regional case name citators, such as *Shepard's Pacific Reporter Case Name Citator*.

(iii) *Shepard's Federal Case Name Citators*. *Shepard's* has developed books that contain tables of all lower federal court cases since 1940 and all United States Supreme Court cases since 1990. If all you know about a federal case is the plaintiff's name or the defendant's name, the full citation can be located in the alphabetically arranged Table of Cases. There are separate *Federal Case Name Citators* for each of the 11 numbered circuits and for the Federal Circuit and District of Columbia Circuit. Each citator is updated four times a year with supplements. See Figure 9-15 for a sample page from *Shepard's Federal Circuit Case Name Citator*.

(iv) *Shepard's Restatement of the Law Citations*. If you are relying upon a Restatement in a document you are preparing, you can Shepardize the Restatement provision. You will be referred to federal and state cases as well as other authorities, including law reviews and annotations, that have mentioned or cited a particular Restatement section.

(v) *Shepard's Law Review Citations*. If you have read an interesting law review article, you can locate cases and other law review articles that have mentioned or cited your law review article by Shepardizing it in *Shepard's Law Review Citations.*

I. Miscellaneous Citators

Shepard's publishes nearly 200 different citators whose titles describe their coverage. Among them are the following:

Bankruptcy Case Names Citator
Bankruptcy Citations
Code of Federal Regulations Citations
Corporation Law Citations
Criminal Justice Citations
Federal Energy Law Citations
Federal Labor Law Citations
Federal Occupational Safety and Health Citations
Federal Rules Citations
Federal Tax Citator
Immigration and Naturalization Citations
Insurance Law Citations
Intellectual Property Law Citations
Medical Malpractice Citations
Military Justice Citations
Ordinance Law Annotations
Partnership Law Citations
Products Liability Citations
Professional and Judicial Conduct Citations
Uniform Commercial Code Citations
United States Administrative Citations

J. Shepard's *Daily Update Service*

Law firms, agencies, and law libraries that subscribe to any of *Shepard's* citators may take advantage of a unique service offered by *Shepard's* titled "Daily Update Service." This service provides up-to-the-minute information on cases and statutes you may be Shepardizing, so you can find out what has happened to your authority since the last softcover supplement was published. Information may be as current as 24-48 hours from the time of decision from the courts. Subscribers can call *Shepard's* and ask for the most recent history and treatment of statutes or cases being Shepardized. Call (800) 899-6000 for the "Daily Update Service."

Figure 9-15
Sample Page from *Shepard's Federal Circuit Case Name Citator*

K

Cases arranged alphabetically by plaintiff and defendant

Kaasa v Mekler 97 F.2d 612, 25 C.C.P.A. 1303, 38 U.S.P.Q. 107, 1938 C.D. 718 (1938)

Kaase, In re 140 F.2d 1016, 31 C.C.P.A. 932, 60 U.S.P.Q. 565, 1944 C.D. 271 (1944)

Kabushiki Kaisha Wako, Wagner Shokai Inc. v 699 F.2d 1390, 217 U.S.P.Q. 15, 217 U.S.P.Q. 98 (Fed. Cir. 1983)

Kachurin Drug Co. v United States 26 C.C.P.A. 356, C.A.D. 41 (1939)

Kachurin Drug Co., United States v 39 C.C.P.A. 36, C.A.D. 459 (1951)

Kachurin Drug Co. v United States 39 C.C.P.A. 223 (1951)

Kacprowicz v Office of Personnel Management 740 F.2d 1552 (Fed. Cir. 1984)

Kacprowicz v Office of Personnel Management 769 F.2d 756 (Fed. Cir. 1985)

Kademann v Bollmann 421 F.2d 1372, 57 C.C.P.A. 907, 164 U.S.P.Q. 630 (1970)

Kadin Corp. v United States 782 F.2d 175 (Fed. Cir. 1986)

Kagawa & Co., United States v 5 C.C.A. 388, Treas. Dec. 34934 (1914)

Kaghan, In re 387 F.2d 398, 55 C.C.P.A. 844, 156 U.S.P.Q. 130 (1967)

Kahlen v United States 2 C.C.A. 206, Treas. Dec. 31947 (1911)

Kahn v Phipard 397 F.2d 995, 55 C.C.P.A. 1284, 158 U.S.P.Q. 269 (1968)

Kahn & Co., United States v 13 C.C.A. 57, Treas. Dec. 40881 (1925)

Kaisling, In re 44 F.2d 863, 18 C.C.P.A. 740, 7 U.S.P.Q. 134, 1931 C.D. 35 (1930)

Kalart Company Inc. v Camera-Mart Inc. 258 F.2d 956, 46 C.C.P.A. 711, 119 U.S.P.Q. 139, 1958 C.D. 432 (1958)

Kalich, W. B. Roddenberg Co. v 158 F.2d 289, 34 C.C.P.A. 745, 72 U.S.P.Q. 138, 1947 C.D. 79 (1946)

Kalman v Kimberly-Clark Corp. 713 F.2d 760, 218 U.S.P.Q. 781 (Fed. Cir. 1983)

Kalm, In re 378 F.2d 959, 54 C.C.P.A. 1466, 154 U.S.P.Q. 10 (1967)

Kalter, In re 125 F.2d 715, 29 C.C.P.A. 858, 52 U.S.P.Q. 483, 1942 C.D. 302 (1942)

Kalter, In re 316 F.2d 747, 50 C.C.P.A. 1191, 137 U.S.P.Q. 347, 1963 C.D. 441 (1963)

Kalter Mercantile Co., United States v 11 C.C.A. 540, Treas. Dec. 39680 (1923)

Kamal, In re 398 F.2d 867, 55 C.C.P.A. 1409, 158 U.S.P.Q. 320 (1968)

Kamikawa Bros. v United States 15 C.C.A. 12, Treas. Dec. 42130 (1927)

Kamlet, In re 185 F.2d 709, 38 C.C.P.A. 776, 88 U.S.P.Q. 106, 1951 C.D. 95 (1950)

Kamm, In re 452 F.2d 1052, 59 C.C.P.A. 753, 172 U.S.P.Q. 298 (1972)

Kamp v Houghtaling 376 F.2d 971, 54 C.C.P.A. 1354, 153 U.S.P.Q. 634 (1967)

Kamrath, In re 67 F.2d 928, 21 C.C.P.A. 787, 20 U.S.P.Q. 61, 1934 C.D. 128 (1933)

Kanamaru, Griffith v 816 F.2d 624, 2 U.S.P.Q.2d 1361 (Fed. Cir. 1987)

Kander, In re 312 F.2d 834, 50 C.C.P.A. 928, 136 U.S.P.Q. 477, 1963 C.D. 180 (1963)

Kangaroos U.S.A. Inc. v Caldor Inc. 778 F.2d 1571, 228 U.S.P.Q. 32 (Fed. Cir. 1985)

Kanmak Textiles Inc. v Carnac Inc. 189 F.2d 1006, 38 C.C.P.A. 1148, 90 U.S.P.Q. 105, 1951 C.D. 467 (1951)

Kansas Jack Inc. v Kuhn 719 F.2d 1144 (Fed. Cir. 1983)

Kanter, In re 399 F.2d 249, 55 C.C.P.A. 1395, 158 U.S.P.Q. 331 (1968)

Kanthal Corp., United States v 554 F.2d 456, 64 C.C.P.A. 89, C.A.D. 1188 (1977)

Kaplan Bros. v United States 12 C.C.A. 586 (1925)

Kaplan Bros. v United States 21 C.C.P.A. 87, Treas. Dec. 46396 (1933)

Kaplan, In re 110 F.2d 670, 27 C.C.P.A. 1072, 45 U.S.P.Q. 175, 1940 C.D. 410 (1940)

Kaplan, In re 789 F.2d 1574, 229 U.S.P.Q. 678 (Fed. Cir. 1986)

Kaplan Products & Textiles Inc. v United States 51 C.C.P.A. 2, C.A.D. 828 (1963)

Karlson, In re 311 F.2d 581, 50 C.C.P.A. 908, 136 U.S.P.Q. 184, 1963 C.D. 71 (1963)

Karnofsky, In re 390 F.2d 994, 55 C.C.P.A. 940, 156 U.S.P.Q. 682 (1968)

Karoware Inc. v United States 564 F.2d 77, 65 C.C.P.A. 1, C.A.D. 1197 (1977)

243

K. Electronic Updating of Legal Authorities

1. *Introduction to Electronic Updating*

For nearly one hundred years, legal researchers updated their legal authorities through the use of conventional print versions of *Shepard's*. Electronic updating, however, provides more up-to-date validation of legal authorities and is easily accomplished. There is no need to learn quirky abbreviations. Negative history, such as reversal of a case, appears in plain English. Electronic updating eliminates the worry that you do not have all of the print volumes in a set of *Shepard's* because all of the citing references to your case or statute appear in a single location. Moreover, there is no need to gather together numerous bulky sets of *Shepard's* if your document cites federal cases, federal statutes, California cases, California statutes, and Nevada cases. You need not worry that you should check the status of a Michigan case in both *Shepard's Michigan Citations* and in *Shepard's Northwestern Reporter Citations* because all of the authorities that mention your Michigan case will be consolidated in a single result online. Updating and checking your opponent's citations are easily accomplished. Finally, references are available online far more quickly than the print versions of *Shepard's* are published, thus directing you to the most recent treatment of your authorities. Consequently, updating electronically is the preferred method for many, if not most, legal professionals.

Although *Shepard's* is available in CD-ROM form, the most common way citation updating is now performed is through the use of *Shepard's* online or through the use of West's online product, KeyCite.

One of the newest developments in electronic updating is updating and validating by wireless access. Both *Shepard's* and KeyCite are available through handheld PDAs (personal digital assistants), such as Palm devices. Users can review the full history, negative history, or citations to legal authorities, making updating and validating easier and entirely portable. Legal professionals can now update their cases in their cabs on the way to the courthouse!

2. *Shepardizing Online*

a. How to Shepardize a Case Online

Assume the case you are updating and validating is *United States v. Falstaff Brewing Corp.*, 332 F. Supp. 970 (D.R.I. 1973) (hereinafter called *Falstaff*). If you are viewing the case online using LEXIS, there will be a *Shepard's* signal indicaor displayed on the screen. If you click it, *Falstaff* will be immediately Shepardized. If you are not currently viewing *Falstaff* on your screen but are instead perhaps validating a written brief that mentions *Falstaff*, follow these steps:

- Sign on to lexis.com.
- Click the tab called "Check a Citation" at the top of your screen.
- Type in your citation (332 fs 970) in the open field.
- Select one of the following options: "*Shepard's* for Research" also called "FULL," which will list every authority that mentions *Falstaff*) or "*Shepard's* for Validation" (also called "KWIC," which will provide you with negative history only, rather than all authorities that mention *Falstaff*).
- Click the word "Check" at the bottom of your screen. (See Figure 9-16.)

You are now ready to interpret your results. You will be informed, in plain English, whether *Falstaff* has been distinguished, criticized, followed, and so forth. If you are interested in one of these references, you simply click on it, and you will be immediately transported to that reference, thereby eliminating the need for you to run around the library collecting authorities that distinguish, criticize, or follow *Falstaff*.

Shepard's uses "Signal Indicators" to inform you at a glance of the precedential status of your case. These signal indicators appear at the top of your *Shepard's* results. A graphic is given along with citations. The

Figure 9-16
Shepardizing Online

RESEARCH STEPS FOR CASES

This case is on point for your issue: *McNeil v. Economics Laboratory, Inc.*, 800 F.2d 111 (7th Cir. Ill. 1986). Is *McNeil* still good law? You can *Shepardize* 800 F. 2d 111 to find out—and to find more cases that discuss the issue for which you plan to cite *McNeil.*

There are two ways to *Shepardize* a citation on the *lexis.com* service. If you are not viewing the case, click the **Check a Citation** tab. If you want to *Shepardize* the document you are viewing, click the ***Shepard's* Signal indicator**.

Since you are not viewing 800 F. 2d 111,
HERE'S WHAT YOU DO:

1. Establish an Internet connection and sign on to ***lexis.com***.
2. Click the **Check a Citation** tab at the top of the screen.
   Shepard's (the default setting) is ready for your citation.
3. **Type your citation** (e.g., *800 f2d 111*) in the open field. Make sure to choose *Shepard's* for Research (FULL) to see the complete universe in which your case has been cited. Then click **Check** at the bottom right corner to start your research.

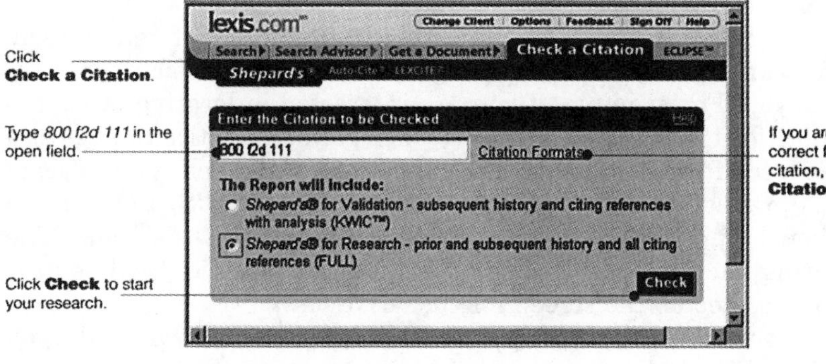

4. **Review your results.**

following signal indicator graphics are used: a red "stop sign" is a warning that an authority contains strong negative history or treatment of your case (for example, your case has been overruled or reversed); a yellow "yield sign" is used to indicate that there may be some negative history or treatment of your case (for example, your case is being criticized or questioned); a green "plus sign" tells you that your case has positive history (for example, it has been affirmed or followed); an "A" in a circle tells you that your case has been analyzed in a neutral manner (for example, it has been explained); and an "i" in a circle informs you that other citation information is available, such as law review articles that mention your case.

These signal indicators make Shepardizing online extremely easy because they tell you at a glance that either your citation is in trouble or it is cleared for your use. You can immediately retrieve the authorities that accompany the signal indicators by clicking on them.

When *Shepard's* lists other cases that mention *Falstaff*, they will be organized by jurisdiction and court, and sorted by date, with the most recent decisions appearing first in each category. (See Figure 9-17.)

b. Features of *Shepard's* Online

Shepard's provides a number of tools that help you maximize your research efforts.

- Full citation. *Shepard's* will list the full citation for your case, including all parallel citations.
- FULL. Selecting the FULL option will provide you with all of the prior history of your case, all subsequent appellate history, every citing reference to your case (including cases, law reviews, periodicals, statutes, and A.L.R. annotations), and the ability to do a "FOCUS" search (described below). Thus, FULL helps you find other sources to assist with your research efforts.
- KWIC. Selecting the KWIC option provides a quick answer to the question, "Is my authority still valid?" You will not be directed to law reviews and annotations that mention your authority; you will only be given subsequent appellate history and the ability to do a FOCUS search. Use KWIC when you are satisfied with your research efforts and only want to confirm that your authority is still good law.
- FOCUS. By clicking "FOCUS Search" at the top of your screen, you can find authorities dealing with the issues or facts confronting you. For example, if you are interested in locating other authorities that discuss whether it is legal malpractice to neglect a statute of limitations, you can type in your search terms ("legal malpractice," "statute of limitations"), click FOCUS, and you will then be provided with authorities dealing with this issue. The terms you have searched, such as "legal malpractice," will appear highlighted on the screen for ease of review.
- Custom Restrictions. *Shepard's* allows you to tailor the results you desire by selecting groups of citations to review. For example, you can elect to see only those cases that explain *Falstaff*, only those

Figure 9-17
Reviewing *Shepard's* Results

INTERPRETING YOUR *Shepard's* RESULTS

Shepard's unique combination of expert editorial analysis and powerful navigational tools helps you organize, prioritize and narrow your research. These tips for interpreting *Shepard's* results use *McNeil v. Economics Laboratory, Inc.*, 800 F.2d 111 (7th Cir. Ill. 1986)

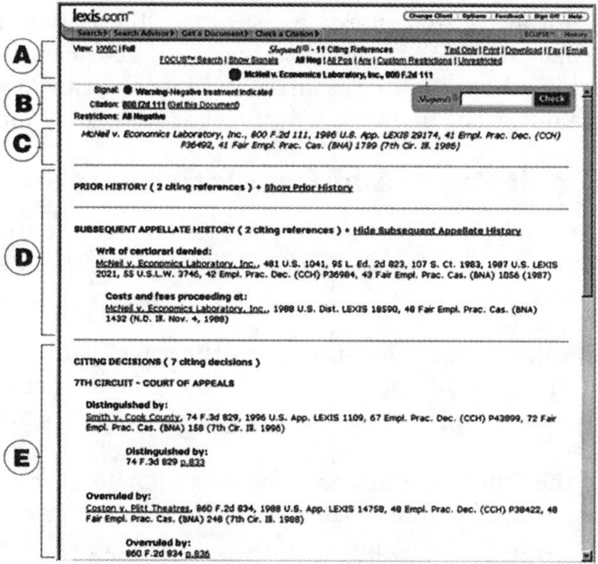

(A) Shows the number of **citing references** for the current viewing mode (**All Neg** for *McNeil*) and provides links to Custom Restrictions, FOCUS search and other navigational tools. Also gives the short-form citation for the authority you are *Shepardizing*.

(B) Shows ***Shepard's* Signal indicator** (graphic and descriptive text), which indicates that citing references to *McNeil* contain strong negative history. Click on the underlined citation to remove any restrictions; click **Get this Document** to display the full text of *McNeil*. The restrictions field tells you if there are any restrictions (e.g., **All Negative**). To *Shepardize* another citation, enter a citation in the *Shepard's* box and click **Check**.

(C) Lists the **full citation**, including parallel citations, for *McNeil*.

(D) Provides the **Prior and Subsequent Appellate History**.
Click the underlined links to show or hide these fields. Always be sure to check the case history before using Custom Restrictions to preview and narrow citing references that are not part of the direct history.

(E) Shows **citing references outside the direct history** of your case.
Citing decisions are organized by jurisdiction and court, and sorted by date with more recent decisions appearing first in each category. Also included are citations from secondary sources, including law reviews and annotations. Treatment analysis codes assigned by a *Shepard's* legal editor (distinguishes, follows, overrules, etc.) precede the citation. Click on a case name, *Coston v. Plitt Theatres*, for example, to link to the first page of a citing decision on *lexis.com*. Click on the page number in the indented reference to the *Coston* citation and link directly to the overruling language. Many citing decisions will have multiple analysis codes, for example, when the court follows on one point of law and criticizes on another.

cases from the Third Circuit that mention *Falstaff* after 1990, or only law review articles that mention *Falstaff*.

- Auto-Cite. *Shepard's* Auto-Cite service is much like the KWIC option described above. When you access *Shepard's* online (after you click "Check a Citation"), you can select "Auto-Cite" by clicking on it. Type your citation in the open field, click "Check," and you will be informed whether your case is still good law. You will be sent not to every authority that mentions your case but only to those authorities that affect the precedential value of your case. Thus, if you are satisfied with your research and merely want a quick answer to the question, "Is my case still good?" use Auto-Cite.

c. Shepardizing Statutes and Regulations Online

Shepardizing statutes and regulations online is similar to Shepardizing cases online. To Shepardize 18 U.S.C. § 2124 (1998), follow these steps:

- Sign on to lexis.com.
- Click the tab called "Check a Citation" at the top of your screen.
- Type in your citation (18 usc 2124) in the open field (there is no need to use a section sign or the word "section" or "sec" before the section number).
- Select one of the following options: "*Shepard's* for Research" (also called "FULL," which will list every authority that mentions your statute) or "*Shepard's* for Validation" (also called "KWIC," which will provide you with negative history only rather than all authorities that mention your statute).
- Click the word "Check" at the bottom of your screen.

You will now be informed whether your statute has been held unconstitutional by a later case, amended by the legislature, and so forth. Just as with cases, you can use Custom Restrictions to narrow your results, such as to review only legislative materials that amend your statute or only authorities that mention your statute after a certain date. Similarly, you can use the FOCUS feature to locate authorities dealing with your particular issues and facts. The graphic signal indicators used with cases (the stop sign, and so forth) are not used with statutes.

Shepardizing a regulation and other materials is accomplished much the same way as Shepardizing a case or statute. Directions are easy to follow, and the *Shepard's* Daily Update Service is available to find the most recent authorities that mention the case or legal authority you are citing in your document.

d. Other *Shepard's* Products

(1) Automatic Citation Validation Through CheckCite

One of the most significant advances in validating citations is software programs that automatically check whether legal authorities you rely on and cite are still good law. Consider the task of checking the validity of 25 separate citations in a 50-page brief. Although Shepardizing online will be considerably faster than manual Shepardizing (especially if you use Auto-Cite or KWIC to determine whether the authorities are still valid), keying in 25 separate entries and examining the screen for 25 separate results can be time-consuming.

Shepard's offers a software program called CheckCite (at present, called "CheckCite 2000"), which automatically checks all citations in your brief, without the necessity of your keying in a single citation. The program "reads" your brief, locates your citations, and checks them, and then provides you with the results of the citation-checking either on the screen or in a separate printed report. You can customize the results so your citations can be fully Shepardized or merely Auto-Cited. CheckCite also checks your quotations for accuracy and locates discrepancies in case names, dates, and page numbers. CheckCite is also useful for checking your adversary's documents, allowing you to spot weaknesses in the opponent's arguments.

(2) CD-ROM

Shepard's offers a CD-ROM version of its citators, which is highly similar to Shepardizing online. A companion product to the CD-ROM, called "CiteFinder," is a search engine that uses the databases in the CD-ROM to generate a statistically ranked list of relevant authorities for you. You enter up to five citations, and CiteFinder Shepardizes them and then returns a ranked list of the authorities that most often cite the cases and/or statutes you have entered. Another feature offered with the CD-ROM version of *Shepard's* is "Extract," a tool that automatically extracts all citations in your document and Shepardizes them for you. Thus, Extract is similar to the CheckCite software program.

(3) CiteRite II

CiteRite II is a citation-checking software program that checks your citations for proper form using the *Bluebook* rules (or the *California Style Manual*). You will be provided with parallel cites and informed of errors in punctuation (such as neglecting the period after "Cal"), incorrect reporter abbreviations, improper underscoring, and other errors. In addition to checking the format of case cites, statutes, books, and law review articles, signals and short forms can also be checked. It is unclear, however, whether CiteRite II can thoroughly master the intricacies of citation form, such as when you may abbreviate "Western" and when you may not. Nevertheless, it is a valuable tool for checking citation form errors in both primary and secondary authorities. It does not, however, validate your authorities by telling you whether they are still "good law."

3. *KeyCite*

a. How to KeyCite Cases

KeyCite is West's service, launched in 1997, that updates and validates your legal authorities. KeyCite can be accessed through WestMate software or on the Web at www.westlaw.com. Although there are some differences between Shepardizing online and KeyCiting online, the services are probably more alike than different. Assume you want to KeyCite the *Falstaff* case. If *Falstaff* is presently displayed on your screen, you will be given a case status flag at the top of the case (red, yellow, or blue) or the word "update" and you simply click it to access KeyCite. Alternatively, there will be a "KC" displayed in the tool bar. Click it to access KeyCite. If you are not presently viewing a case to KeyCite it, follow these steps:

- Sign on to westlaw.com.
- Click the KeyCite button on the main button palatte (labeled "KC") or select "Services" from the toolbar and then select "KeyCite a Citation." Type in your citation in the box displayed and click "OK."

You are now ready to interpret your results. The first thing that appears is any negative history of the case. Like *Shepard's* online, KeyCite uses graphics to instantly convey information to you about the status of the case. A red flag informs you the case is no longer good law (it has likely been reversed or overruled); a yellow flag indicates there is some negative history (for example, the case has been criticized or limited); a blue "H" indicates there is some direct history for the case (such as that the case is being explained). The absence of a flag means that there is no direct history or negative indirect history for the case.

You can easily jump to cases that mention *Falstaff* by double-clicking on them. (See Figure 9-18.)

b. Features of KeyCite

KeyCite offers the following features to assist you with your citation updating and validating:

- Full citation. KeyCite will provide you with the full citation to the case, including all parallel cites.
- Citation history options. You can customize your KeyCite results to display different types of case history for your case. By clicking on "Show Full History," you will be given the complete history of your case; by selecting "Negative History Only," you will be provided only the subsequent history that negatively affects your case; finally, you can select "Omit Minor History," to suppress minor procedural history of your case.
- Citations to the Case. By clicking on the wording "Citations to the Case," you will be able to retrieve the citing references to *Falstaff*, namely, cases, law review articles, helpful Am. Jur. 2d references, and A.L.R. annotations that mention *Falstaff*. The citations that are most likely to be helpful are listed first. Thus, the cases that might negatively affect *Falstaff* are given first, followed by those that treat *Falstaff* positively.
- Limit Citations. By selecting the "Limit Citations" button, you can restrict the number of citing references KeyCite will give you. You

Figure 9-18
Sample KeyCite Screen

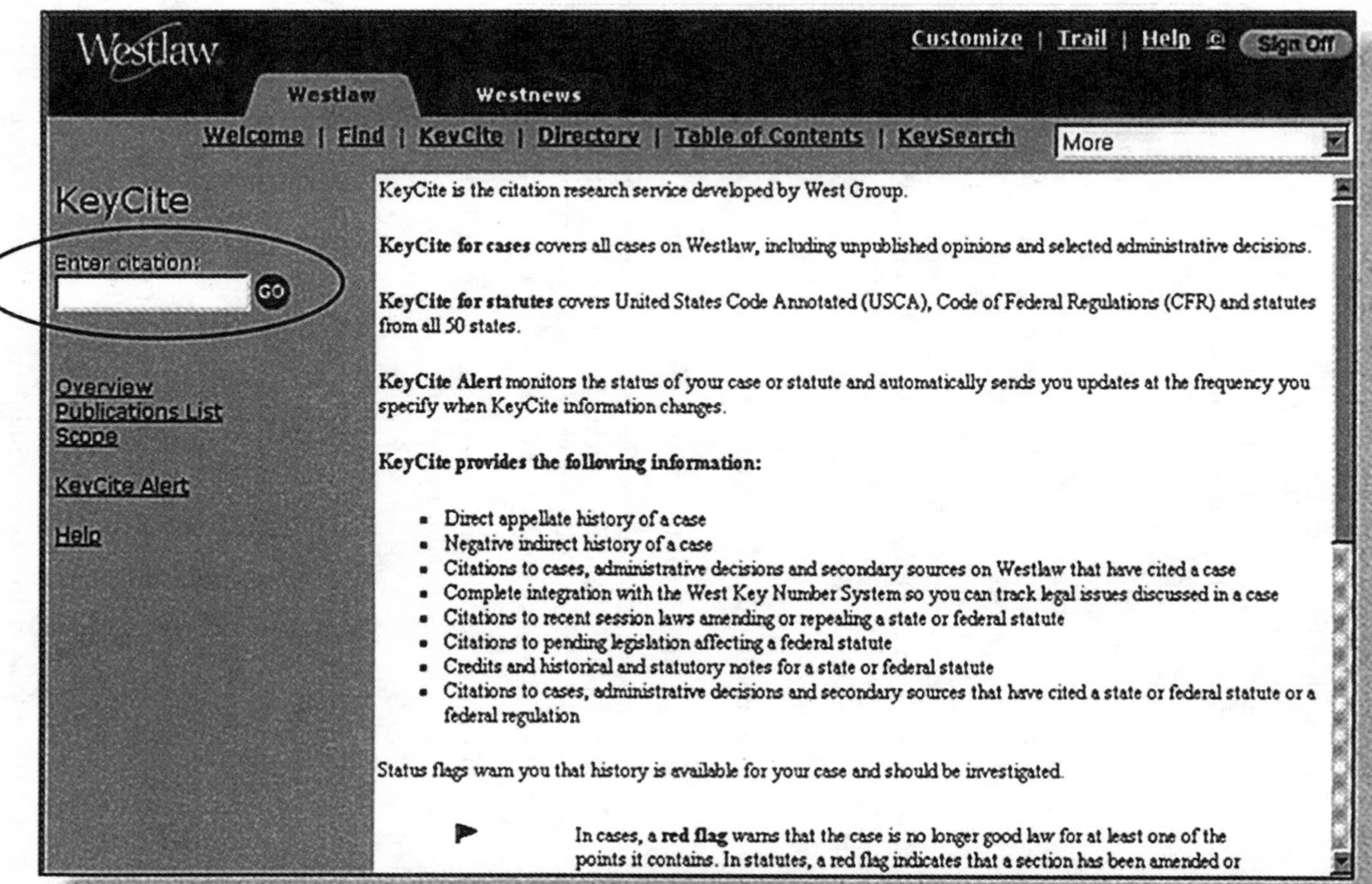

can elect to view only those authorities that explain *Falstaff*, only Ohio cases that mention *Falstaff*, those cases that discuss headnote 2 of *Falstaff*, those that mention *Falstaff* after a certain date, those that discuss *Falstaff* in a dissenting opinion, and so forth.

- Depth of treatment stars. As KeyCite lists the cases that mention *Falstaff*, a number of green stars will be displayed above each citation. These stars tell you how much a citing case discusses *Falstaff*. Four green stars means that the case that follows examines *Falstaff* in depth; three stars indicates that there is significant discussion of *Falstaff*, two stars means that there is some very brief discussion of *Falstaff*, and one star indicates that *Falstaff* was mentioned in passing, probably in a string citation.
- Quotation marks. If KeyCite displays quotation marks (") after a case citation, it means that the case quotes from *Falstaff*.
- Headnote references. *Falstaff's* headnote references are clearly displayed. Thus, a reference to "HN2" means that the case discusses the point of law discussed in headnote 2 of *Falstaff*.
- KeyCite Alert. KeyCite Alert is a clipping service that automatically notifies you of any changes in the treatment of *Falstaff*. You can restrict its coverage so that, for example, you are only notified of later negative treatment of *Falstaff* rather than every time *Falstaff* is later mentioned by some other authority. You can elect to be notified daily, weekly, and so forth.

c. KeyCiting Statutes and Regulations

If you are viewing a statute on Westlaw, the upper left corner of the screen is labled "Update." You may select this to update your statute. Alternatively, your statute may appear with a red or yellow flag, indicating there is negative treatment of your statute. Click on the flag to be directed to the negative history.

If you are not presently viewing a statute on the screen, update the statute by taking the following steps:

- Sign on to westlaw.com.
- Click the KeyCite button on the main buttton palette (labeled "KC"), or select "Services" from the toolbar and then select "KeyCite a Citation." Type in your citation in the box displayed and click "OK."

After you enter your statute citation in KeyCite, the history of the statute is displayed, including links to recent session laws that amend or repeal your statute and historical and statutory notes describing the legislative changes affecting your statute.

After viewing the history of the statute, click the "KC Citations" tab to view citations to cases, administrative materials, and secondary sources that mention your statute. You can use KeyCite Alert to automatically notify you of any changes in the statute. KeyCiting regulations in C.F.R. is accomplished in the same manner as KeyCiting statutes.

d. Other West Products

(1) Automatic Citation Validation Through WestCheck

Similar to LEXIS' CheckCite, West offers a software program called WestCheck, which automatically extracts citations from your document, checks their validity, and produces a printed report with the results of the check. The advantage of using WestCheck rather than KeyCite is that WestCheck automatically "reads" and validates your citations, thus saving you the time of keying in each citation you wish to check.

The process is easily accomplished. Once the software is "loaded" onto your computer, you merely open your brief or other document that contains the citations you wish to check and then click the WestCheck button on your toolbar. WestCheck is launched and automatically extracts the citations. The extracted citations will be displayed on the screen. Click "Verify" to determine that the case law citations in the list are valid.

You may customize the results you desire by directing WestCheck to KeyCite the results (limiting or restricting options as you desire), or by using a companion service called "QuoteRight," you can ensure your quotations are accurate. Launch these services by selecting "Run."

(2) Table of Authorities

While KeyCite lists cases that mention your case, West's product "Table of Authorities" lists the cases cited by your case. Thus, if *Falstaff* relies upon six federal cases, Table of Authorities will list them and inform you whether they are subject to negative history or treatment. Table of Authorities is useful for finding weaknesses in cases relied upon by an adversary as well as in the cases you rely upon.

4. Comparing Shepardizing Online with KeyCite

In most instances, researchers elect to Shepardize online because they are most familiar with *Shepard's* or LEXIS, or they select KeyCite because they are most familiar with Westlaw. Costs are approximately equivalent, and it is impossible to make absolute statements as to pricing and fees. Most large law firms afford desktop access to both LEXIS and Westlaw, realizing their legal professionals have distinct preferences. Moreover, these firms have negotiated pricing schedules with LEXIS and Westlaw, often "in bulk," so that everyone in the firm could be signed on to LEXIS or Westlaw all day long and the fee would be the same. Nevertheless, fees for Shepardizing online of KeyCiting are usually assessed on a per-case basis. Generally, it costs about $2.50 to check any one citation. Thus, in a document with 25 citations, the cost merely for accessing the databases will be $62.50. Additional fees will be charged to the client for your time in performing the updating and reviewing results and for the attorney's time as well. Because fees are roughly equivalent, a decision whether to Shepardize online or KeyCite is not ususally based upon cost.

Beginning researchers often wonder, "Which service is better?" Advertising material for *Shepard's* clearly touts its superiority, while that for KeyCite does the same. Both offer many of the same features: rapid and easy citation validating; the use of easy-to-understand, colorful graphics (signs and flags) to tell you at a glance that your citation is in trouble; the ability to limit or restrict your results; and the ability to immediately jump to an authority that mentions your case or statute. Both services offer automatic citation updating so you need not key in citations. West's product KeyCite Alert is valuable for notifying you of later changes in your case or statute. While *Shepard's* does not offer a similar service, it does offer its Daily Alert Service, which allows you to check the status of a citation by a toll-free telephone number. *Shepard's* also offers CiteRite II, its service that assists in putting citations in *Bluebook* format. Thus, each provider offers some unique products.

A recent advertisement for KeyCite announced that in an independent head-to-head review of KeyCite and LEXIS' *Shepard's*, KeyCite was named the better citator. On the other hand, the home page for *Shepard's* directs readers to a study showing that *Shepard's* is more current and complete than KeyCite. In sum, the use of *Shepard's* online or KeyCite is usually a matter of habit, convenience, or preference. For most citation updates and validation purposes, the systems are equally proficient.

5. *Other Services*

Although LEXIS and Westlaw are the giants in computer-assisted legal research systems, three other systems provide citation updating: Law Office Information Systems, Inc. (called "LOIS") of Arkansas; JuriSearch.com of California; and VersusLaw Inc., of Washington. LOIS, JuriSearch, and VersusLaw generally aim their services at smaller firms or sole practitioners and charge reasonable fees, but they offer much smaller databases than LEXIS or Westlaw. In fact, JuriSearch's focus is primarily on California law. LOIS' citator is called GlobalCite and JuriSearch.com's citator is called CheckMate. Their use is similar to that of Shepardizing or KeyCiting online, but, in general, they offer fewer enhancements and features for customization. VersusLaw offers only rudimentary updating.

L. Summary

Updating and validating your primary authorities is the second component of cite-checking. After you have corrected citations in a document so they conform to *Bluebook* or local form, you must verify that the primary authorities you rely on are still "good law." While the foremost function of updating is to check the status of your primary authorities, a secondary function is to allow you to tap into additional legal research by providing you with references to cases, periodicals, attorneys general opinions, and annotations that mention or cite the authority being updated.

The determination of when to perform the task of updating is a matter of individual discretion, although updating early in the research process will not only alert you to an invalid or weakened case, statute, or constitutional provision but will enhance your efforts by directing you to additional research sources.

If you elect to update manually after a project is completed, you may want to arrange the authorities in some order before you begin. On a separate piece of paper, list all cases from the same jurisdiction together so that you update all United States Supreme Court cases and then move on to update lower federal court cases, then state court cases, and so on. This will enhance your efficiency and save you from constantly running around the library from one set of *Shepard's* to the next. Update statutes and constitutional provisions in the same ordered fashion.

Most researchers prefer the ease and convenience of updatng electronically, either by using *Shepard's* online by LEXIS or by using KeyCite online, offered by West. These services provide easy and very recent validation of legal authorities. Moreover, the new software programs offered by LEXIS and West, CheckCite and WestCheck, respectively, offer automatic updating, eliminating the necessity of keying in any citations. Thus, many law firms and legal departments no longer subscribe to the print versions of *Shepard's*, and there are numerous working paralegals who have never updated "manually"; they have only checked their authorities using *Shepard's* online or by KeyCiting online. Thus, at some point, the print versions of *Shepard's* may be relics.

Once you have Shepardized or KeyCited a few times, you will quickly get the hang of it and will find that while it is a routine task, it is quickly accomplished. Do not assume that because Shepardizing and KeyCiting are easy and routine that they are unimportant. On the contrary, updating is one of the most critical aspects of legal research, and no project is complete until every reference to a case, statute, or constitutional provision has been updated and validated.

Technology Tips

http://www.shepards.com	The Web site for *Shepard's* fully explains all of its products, both print and other versions; describes new products; and usually offers free tutorials.
http://helpcite.shepards.com	This reference desk, provided by *Shepard's* (for print products only) will inform you of the most current supplement available from *Shepard's* so you can ensure your library has complete sets of *Shepard's*.
http://www.westgroup.com	The Web site of West provides information about its products, including KeyCite and WestCheck, and often offers free tutorials.
http://www.JuriSearch.com	The Web site of JuriSearch describes its citation service, CheckMate.
http://www.pita.org	The Web site of LOISLaw describes its citation service, called "GlobalCite."
http://www.versuslaw.com	The Web site of VersusLaw describes its databases and fees, and provides basic information about updating cases.
http://www.lectlaw.com/files/lwr17.htm	This Web site of the 'Lectric Law Library offers an excellent description on "How to Shepardize."

Writing Strategies

Be sure to update any citations in an adversary's written project. It is possible that while the cases cited may still be "good law," they may have lost some of their strength by being criticized or questioned. You will then be able to point this out in your project or response as follows: "While Plaintiff relies upon *Caldwell Co. v. Baldwin Emporium Inc.*, 688 F. Supp. 101 (S.D.N.Y. 1990), that case has been subject to increasing criticism . . . ."

Similarly, if a case cited by an adversary is limited to its own particular facts, point this out to the reader: "The case relied upon by Plaintiff, *Ellers v. McGrath*, 692 F. Supp. 946 (D. Mass. 1991), has been specifically limited to written lease agreements. *Warren v. Chesterton*, 719 F.2d 101 (1st Cir. 1992). Because the present case involves an option to purchase real property and not a written lease, Plaintiff's reliance on *Ellers* is misplaced."

Use updating as a way of enhancing your own writing. If a case you rely on is followed by a later case, bring this to the reader's attention: "In *Satterly v. Jespersen*, 718 F.2d 906 (9th Cir. 1992), the court [noted with approval] or [endorsed] or [followed] the test for defamation set forth in *Handler v. Jacobson*, 689 F. Supp. 614 (C.D. Cal. 1990)."

Assignment for Chapter 9

In this assignment, you will Shepardize cases, statutes, and other sources. Provide the answer as *Shepard's* gives it to you. You need not use *Bluebook* form.

1. Shepardize 566 A.2d 227.
   a. Give the parallel citation.
   b. Review the abbreviations in the front of this volume. What does "CS" stand for?
2. Locate *Shepard's* first reference to 29 N.W. 425.
   a. Give the parallel citation.
   b. What is the first case that follows headnote 2 of 29 N.W. 425?
   c. What is the first A.L.R. annotation to mention this case?
   d. Review the abbreviations in the front of the volume. What does "Ia" stand for?
3. Shepardize 639 N.E.2d 1003.
   a. Give the parallel citations.
   b. Has this case ever been overruled? If so, give citations.
4. Locate the first time *Shepard's* discusses 674 P.2d 145.
   a. Give the parallel citation.
   b. What negative subsequent history is given for headnote 16 of 674 P.2d 145 in this volume?
5. Shepardize 937 S.W.2d 35.
   a. Give the name of the case.
   b. Give the citations to the denial of *certiorari* for 937 S.W.2d 35.
6. Use *Shepard's Southeastern Reporter Citations, Cases and Case Names* (hardbound supplement for 1994-1997).
   a. Give the citations for the case *Simpson v. Sanders.*
   b. Using this same volume, Shepardize *Simpson v. Sanders*.
      (i) What case followed headnote 2 of *Simpson v. Sanders*?
      (ii) What is the most recent case that discusses headnote 2?
7. Use *Shepard's Federal Citations* and Shepardize 163 F.3d 1354. Has *certiorari* been denied in this case? If so, give citations to denial of *certiorari*.
8. Use *Shepard's Federal Citations* for the first time *Shepard's* mentions 33 F.3d 754.
   a. What Seventh Circuit case followed 33 F.3d 754?
   b. What Fifth Circuit case mentions this case in a dissent?
   c. Review the Fifth Circuit case to which you are referred. Where is your case mentioned or discussed?
9. Use *Shepard's Federal Citations* for the first time *Shepard's* mentions 52 F. Supp. 913.
   a. Give the case name.
   b. Has the case ever been reversed? If so, give the citation.
10. Use *Shepard's United States Citations* for the first time 524 U.S. 399 is mentioned and Shepardize 524 U.S. 399. What A.L.R. Fed. annotation discusses this case?

11. Use *Shepard's United States Citations* for the first time 476 U.S. 409 is mentioned and Shepardize 476 U.S. 409. What was the first case from the Ninth Circuit to mention this case?
12. Use *Shepard's Federal Citations* for 1996, Volume 5, for the United States Code and Shepardize 45 U.S.C. § 764.
    a. Give the negative history for this statute.
    b. Go to the source to which you are referred. What was the general topic of the statute you Shepardized?
13. Use *Shepard's Federal Citations* for 1996, Volume 4, for the United States Code and Shepardize 28 U.S.C. § 6514(b). Which Seventh Circuit case mentions this statute?
14. Use *Shepard's Federal Statute Citations* for 1996, Volume 1, for the United States Constitution. Shepardize Article 6 of the Constitution. What is the first Third Circuit case to discuss clause one of Article Six?
15. Use *Shepard's Federal Statute Citations* for 1996, Volume 6, for Tariff Schedules, Statutes at Large and so forth.
    a. Shepardize Volume 30 of *U.S. Treaties and Other International Agreements* 3409. Give the history.
    b. Shepardize Rule 45 of the Rules of the Supreme Court of the United States. What Eighth Circuit case discusses this rule?
16. Use *Shepard's Acts and Cases by Popular Names (Federal and State)*, 1999, Part 1.
    a. Give the citation to the Alcoholic Habit Act.
    b. Give the citations to the *Santa Claus* case.

Chapter 10

Special Research Issues

A. Legislative History
B. Executive Materials
C. Administrative Law
D. International Law
E. Municipal Research
F. Rules of Court
G. Citation Form

Chapter Overview

Most legal research problems can be solved by examining and analyzing the conventional sources of primary authorities and secondary authorities. There are, however, a few types of legal research tasks that lie outside those usual approaches to legal research and that involve sources arranged and published differently from the typical primary and secondary authorities.

This chapter will examine these special research issues and will provide information on legislative histories, presidential documents, administrative law, international law, local and municipal law, and court rules. Although research in many of these unique areas will not be required often, should you need to do any especially thorough research project or should you be employed by a firm concentrating on international or administrative law, you will use the research techniques described herein. A brief introduction to these specialized tasks is needed so you will be able to conduct research efficiently and effectively in these areas if you are asked to do so.

A. Legislative History

1. *Introduction to Federal Legislative History Research*

It is possible that in the course of your research of an issue you realize that the statute relating to the issue is unclear. Usually you would then read and analyze the cases interpreting the statute to determine its meaning. Not all statutes have been subject to court interpretation, however, and you may still be faced with an ambiguous statute and no guidance in determining its meaning. It is equally possible that the cases interpreting the statute are contrary to the position you need to assert on behalf of a client.

In these instances, you should examine the various documents that reflect the activity of the legislature that enacted the statute to assist you in determining the intent of the legislature. This process is referred to as preparing or compiling a legislative history. By examining the various versions of the bills, the testimony given before the committee, the committee report, and the debates, you may be able to resolve ambiguities in a statute or argue that a court's prior interpretation of a statute is contrary to the intended purpose of a statute.

While a well-constructed argument relating to a legislative history and the legislature's intent and purpose may be useful and instructive to a court, a court is not required to adopt an interpretation of a statute based upon the legislature's intent in enacting the law. In fact, many courts view legislative history arguments with skepticism. Typically, courts will not examine the legislative history of a statute if the meaning of the statute is clear or "plain" from a reading of it. Only when a court cannot determine the plain meaning of a statute will it resort to reviewing the legislative history of the statute. Supreme Court Justice Antonin Scalia is vehemently opposed to relying on legislative history. He prefers that legislative intent be determined from the plain meaning of a statute itself.

Alternatively, you may be monitoring a piece of legislation as it progresses in order to better assist clients or your employer. This section will first discuss legislative histories for federal statutes and then legislative histories for state statutes. You may wish to review Chapter 3, which discusses the process by which legislation is enacted. In brief, a bill is introduced, referred to a committee, which hears testimony and issues a report, and then the bill is voted on after debate. This procedure is then duplicated in the second chamber of a legislature.

There are three excellent published guides explaining and describing the background of legislative histories, the documents to be examined when compiling a legislative history, and the actual process of assembling a legislative history. Review the following for introductory information and links to relevant materials and Web sites:

- Carold D. Davis, *How to Follow Current Federal Legislation and Regulation,* CRS Report for Congress 96-473 (May 20, 1996), *at* http://www.house.gov/rules/96-473.htm.
- Richard J. McKinney, Law Librarians' Society of Washington, D.C., Inc., *Federal Legislative Research: A Practitioner's Guide to Compiling the Documents and Sifting for Legislative Intent, at* http://www.llsdc.org/sourcebook/fed-leg-hist.htm (last modified Feb. 9, 2001).
- University of Michigan Documents Center, *Legislative Histories—United States Congress, at* http://www.lib.umich.edu/govdocs/legishisnew.html (last visited July 22, 2001).

2. Documents Comprising Federal Legislative History

There are several documents you may analyze in the process of compiling a legislative history. Each one of these documents may help you achieve your goals of determining the purpose and intent of a statute.

a. Versions of a Bill

One of the steps in compiling a legislative history is examining the various versions of a bill. By studying the evolution of a statute, you may be able to make certain inferences about the intent of the legislature in enacting a law. For example, assume a bill as introduced allows certain benefits for veterans, their spouses, and dependents. Its first amendment limits the benefits to veterans and their spouses, and its second amendment limits the benefits solely to veterans. You may be able to argue that the legislature considered extending the benefits to various groups of people but then narrowed the groups, and therefore the benefits should be limited solely to the veterans themselves and not to the spouses, dependents, or ex-spouses of the veterans. That is, comparison of the language of the various versions of the bill as it proceeds through the enactment process may enable you to draw certain conclusions regarding the intent and purpose of the law. Additionally, the bill may include a preamble or introductory section that explains its purpose and intent.

b. Transcripts of Committee Hearings

You will recall that after a bill is introduced it is assigned to a committee, which holds hearings and receives testimony regarding the proposed legislation. Usually a transcript of the testimony is prepared and published. Keep in mind that while some of the individuals who testify may be neutral and independent consumers, scientists, or experts, others may be celebrities or may be lobbyists paid to advance a particular viewpoint persuasively. Thus, while the testimony received by the committee may influence the legislators, courts often view the testimony given at committee hearings with a certain amount of skepticism. You may wish to conduct additional research to determine the credibility and reputation of a party who testified before a committee before you advance an argument based on that person's testimony.

c. Committee Reports

After the committee has concluded the hearings, it will issue a report with its recommendations and its reasons therefor. The committee report is published and reflects the views of the majority of committee members after a thorough analysis of the bill and after the often lengthy hearing process. The committee report usually includes the text of the legislation, an abstract of it, and the committee's findings and recommendations. A committee report is viewed by courts as considerably more credible than transcripts of committee hearings. Those members of the committee who disagree with the majority may issue a minority report, which will provide a different point of view on the subject of the legislation. If the bill was sent to a conference committee, it will also issue a report, including the text of the compromise legislation and an analysis of how the compromise was reached.

d. Debates

If debate is held on a bill, the remarks of the speakers will be published in the *Congressional Record*, a publication prepared for each day Congress is in session. It is possible that the sponsor of the legislation may discuss the intent or purpose of the bill or that interested parties may explain certain provisions of the legislation. These remarks, published in the *Congressional Record*, form part of a legislative history and may be used to persuade a court as to the intent of the legislature when it enacted a statute. Remarks and statements made by sponsors of legislation may carry more weight than remarks made by other legislators, who may enter material into the *Congressional Record* for purely political reasons.

Moreover, the use of debates as a guide to legislative intent is subject to criticism because members of Congress have the right to "revise and extend" their remarks by altering the *Congressional Record*. Although the intent of this right is to allow members to "dot their i's" and "cross their t's," to eliminate minor errors, in some instances members have made more substantive changes, resulting in a *Congressional Record* that is not a verbatim transcript but a revised version of proceedings on the floor of the House and Senate.

3. *The Process of Compiling a Legislative History*

Many researchers have difficulty compiling a legislative history because the documents are diverse and are seldom located together. Often you will be required to search many sources. This is especially true because a statute may have been enacted one year and then amended on several occasions thereafter. You may have to compile a legislative history for each version of the statute. Moreover, the material is voluminous. Congress's committees produce more than 500,000 pages of material each year. Do not be shy asking a reference librarian for help. Reference librarians are aware that conducting legislative history research can be difficult and that few researchers are familiar with the various sources to be used. There are, however, several steps you can take to gather the documents you need.

a. Examining the History of a Statute

After you read a statute in U.S.C., U.S.C.A. or U.S.C.S., you will be provided with historical notes giving information about the enactment of the statute. For example, immediately following a statute in U.S.C.A., you will be provided with information such as the following:

> Pub. L. 106-78, Title I, Oct. 22, 1999, 113 Stat. 1139.
> In the section immediately beneath the statute, called "Historical and Statutory Notes," you are directed to "see 1999 Cong. and Adm. News, p. 198."

Thus, West also refers you to its publication *United States Code Congressional and Administrative News Service* (USCCAN), a monthly pamphlet that is later compiled into hardbound volumes, which includes the public laws recently enacted, the legislative history of selected bills, a summary of pending legislation, presidential proclamations and executive orders, various federal regulations, and court rules. Perhaps the most important information you are given is that the statute in question was introduced as Public Law 106-78, that is, it was the 78th bill enacted by the 106th Congress. This public law number will assist you in tracking the legislative history of your statute. You are also informed that the legislation was enacted October 22, 1999, and can be found at 113 United States Statutes at Large 1139.

If U.S.C.A. directs you to USCCAN, immediately review the materials you are directed to because they are generally excellent sources of legislative intent and nearly always include committee reports and presidential signing statements. Although only U.S.C.A. sends you directly to the pertinent legislative material in USCCAN, U.S.C. and U.S.C.S. will provide you with the public law number for the statute you are researching. The public law number appears immediately following the statute. You can then use the public law number to access USCCAN and the other sources discussed below. U.S.C. and U.S.C.S. also provide a citation to *United States Statutes at Large*.

If for some reason you do not have or know the public law number for a particular statute but you know the general subject matter of a statute, you should use the subject matter index for USCCAN for the congressional session during which the statute was enacted. Look up the subject matter of the statute (environment, crimes, social security) and you will be given the public law number and other important legislative information pertaining to this statute, which you can then use to locate legislative history materials in USCCAN.

b. Using a Public Law Number

Once you have obtained the critical public law number, you can locate the documents comprising legislative history by using a variety of sources.

(1) USCCAN

At the end of a congressional session, the monthly USCCAN pamphlets are cumulated into bound volumes. USCCAN is subscribed to by many law firms and is readily available at almost all law libraries.

Use USCCAN's Table of Legislative History (known as Table 4) and insert the public law number of the statute you are researching. This easy-to-read Table will inform you what bill number was originally assigned to the statute when it was introduced, such as H.R. 289, meaning the 289th law introduced in the House of Representatives, or S. 741, meaning the 741st bill introduced in the Senate. You will then be given a reference to which committee report to examine as well as the dates the House of Representatives and Senate considered and passed the bill. You can use these references to locate the pertinent committee reports as well as the debates published in the *Congressional Record*. USCCAN will provide you with the dates of consideration and passage for each public law. Official committee reports, conference reports, and statements by legislative leaders on major bills are provided, explaining the background, history, and purpose of the legislation. Read the materials provided to determine legislative intent. Some material that is duplicative or unnecessary is omitted from USCCAN. Nevertheless, USCCAN usually provides excellent legislative history materials, including discussion of the background and purpose of the legislation in question.

(2) Congressional Information Service

Congressional Information Service (CIS), part of the LEXIS family, is published in monthly pamphlets, which are ultimately cumulated in three bound volumes for each year. Many experts consider CIS the most thorough source for compiling a legislative history because it will refer you to all the documents needed for a complete legislative history. One of the volumes is titled *CIS Annual Abstracts of Congressional Publications*; one is called *CIS Annual Legislative Histories*; and the third is an annual Index to the yearly set.

Each CIS yearly set includes a comprehensive index, which allows you to access documents through a variety of methods. You can look up materials by subject matter (environment, crimes, social security), by name of any witness who testified at committee hearings, by bill number, by popular name of a statute, and by the name of a committee chairperson. The indexing by witness name allows you to check the credibility of a witness by determining other hearings at which the witness has testified.

The CIS index will then refer you to the appropriate pages in the CIS Annual Abstracts volume, which contains summaries or "abstracts" of the bill as introduced, the testimony given at committee hearings, the committee reports, and references to the particular days debates were held so you can readily locate these in the *Congressional Record*. Not only will you be provided with these abstracts, you will be given references or citations to the exact documents you will need (for example, "House Report 106-451") so you may obtain and analyze the document in full, if desired. CIS's annual volume, titled *CIS Annual Legislative Histories*, is arranged by public law number. By "plugging in" your public law number (found immediately after your statute in U.S.C., U.S.C.A., and U.S.C.S.), you will be directed to a brief summary of the law and references to the documents you need to compile your legislative history. For example you will be directed to House and Senate Reports, committee hearings, and the debates that appear in the *Congressional Record*. CIS then publishes these documents in microfiche in its CIS/Microfiche Library so you can easily locate the documents you need. CIS also makes its database available through LEXIS-NEXIS, on CD-ROM, and on the Internet through its source called "Congressional Universe." Congressional Universe, a Web-based tool, offers more than 25 years of congressional information. Searching is easily done by bill number, subject matter, committee name, or public law number. Seamless linking is made to the full range of legislative resources, including bills, hearing transcripts, committee reports, and the *Congressional Record*. Most materials created since the mid-1980s are available. Additional information about Congressional Universe can be found at http://www.lexis-nexis.com/congcomp or http://www.cispubs.com.

Alternatively, to obtain documents, you can call CIS ((800) 227-2477) and, for a fee, simply order the documents you need from its service called "CIS Documents on Demand."

In the event that your law library does not maintain the CIS/Microfiche Library, CIS will provide you with the stock number of the Government Printing Office documents so you can contact the GPO ((202) 512-1808) and order the documents you need. In this way, CIS is a complete reference tool for compiling a legislative history.

(3) CCH Congressional Index

Commerce Clearing House (CCH) is the publisher of *Congressional Index*, a looseleaf service, which issues weekly pamphlets. A two-volume set of binders is available for each congressional session. Each set contains an index to all public laws introduced in that session. This set will direct you to the specific documents you need to examine but does not itself reproduce them in the set. You can access the index by the name of the legislator who sponsored the bill or by subject matter. If you need to obtain a bill number, use the Subject Index to the set.

When you have a bill number, you can look it up in the section called "Status of House Bills" or "Status of Senate Bills." You will then be given a chronological record of actions taken on the bill, including the date it was introduced, when it was referred to a committee, when hearings were held, when amendments were adopted, when it was passed, and when it was sent to and signed by the president. You will also be informed of the bill's public law number and its citation in *United States Statutes at Large*. You can also take your bill number and insert it into a section called "House Bills" or "Senate Bills," which gives a brief description of the legislation, identifies its chief sponsor and the committee to which it was sent. The *Congressional Index* also includes a variety of other information, such as membership rosters for House and Senate committees and subcommittees, information relating to presidential vetoes, and the voting records relating to bills. Moreover, *Congressional Index* is useful in tracking pending legislation.

Congressional Index does not provide references to the *Congressional Record*, meaning that you will be unable to locate debates through the use of *Congressional Index*.

4. *Using Electronic Sources and the Internet to Compile a Legislative History*

a. LEXIS

The computerized legal research system LEXIS offers easy access to legislative information. After you sign on, select the LEXIS database or "Library" called "Legis." You can search by Congress number (such as the 104th Congress), by a bill number, public law number, topic of the legislation, committee report number, and so forth. You will then be given the full text of the bill, selected hearing transcripts, committee reports, the *Congressional Record* since approximately 1985, and compiled legislative histories for selected legislation of widespread public interest. LEXIS provides hypertext links that allow you to jump from one source or document to another.

Alternatively, after you sign on, you can click on "Get a Document" and then enter the citation to your bill number, the public law number, or to the reference to the *Congressional Record*. You will then be immediately transported to the relevant document.

b. Westlaw

Westlaw, West's computerized legal research system, operates nearly identically to LEXIS. Westlaw offers compiled, full legislative histories for some statutes and other acts of public interest, such as the Family and Medical Leave Act. After you sign on, select the pertinent database. For example, Billcast (enter "BC") provides information on current bills in Congress. Billcast Archives (enter "BC-OLD") provides information on public laws introduced in previous sessions of Congress. The database BILLS provides the full text of bills pending in Congress. The *Congressional Record* (enter "CR") is available since 1985, and legislative history for selected statutes is available by accessing the database called Legislative History (enter "LH").

c. THOMAS

Although LEXIS and Westlaw are easy to use and provide extensive legislative materials, they are fee-based subscription services. Since 1995, it has been possible to obtain many items of legislative history for free, 24/7, through a source called THOMAS. In 1995, the Library of Congress initiated THOMAS, its online database of congressional information and materials named for Thomas Jefferson and located at http://thomas.loc.gov. THOMAS provides a wealth of information, including the following:

- Descriptions of how our laws are enacted.
- Historical documents (including the Federalist Papers, Declaration of Independence, and the U.S. Constitution).
- House and Senate Directories (alphabetical lists of House and Senate members, including their addresses, phone numbers, links to their Web pages, and lists of their committee assignments).
- Committee home pages (providing information about the composition and work of House and Senate committees).
- Committee schedules and calendars of upcoming hearings.
- "Congress in the News," a service with direct links to legislation that is discussed in the media.
- Direct links to other legislative agencies, including the Government Printing Office, Library of Congress, and others.

More important, THOMAS offers easy access to many documents of legislative history. When you access THOMAS, you will be provided with search boxes into which you can enter a bill number or public law number. You will then be given access to the exact text of the bill or public law, a summary of it, and its status (such as the date when it was introduced, when it was referred to a committee, when it was voted upon, and when it was sent to and signed by the president).

If you do not know or have a bill number or public law number, you can search by word or phrase (such as "patent infringement") or by popular name (such as "Family and Medical Leave Act"). In general, searching is done by particular congressional sessions (104th, 105th, 106th, and so forth). Thus, searching can be a bit time-consuming if you do not know in which congressional session legislation was introduced. THOMAS also provides references to the *Congressional Record*.

THOMAS allows one to view, download, and print the entire text of a bill or *Congressional Record* article.

THOMAS provides the following legislative history coverage:

- Bill Summary & Status: a summary of all bills since 1973 is available.
- Bill Text: the full text of all bills since 1985 is available.

- Transcripts of Committee Hearings: selected hearing transcripts are available for some House committees since 1997. At the time of writing of this text, transcripts of Senate hearings were not yet available.
- Committee Reports: the full text of nearly all House and Senate Committee Reports since 1985 is available, and the Reports are searchable by word/phrase, report number, bill number, and committee name.
- *Congressional Record*: the full text of the daily edition of the *Congressional Record* is available since 1989, searchable by member of Congress, date of debate or remarks, or word/phrase.

THOMAS offers an easy, free, and highly reliable way to compile a legislative history, particularly for legislation enacted in the past five to ten years. Once you locate the bill you are interested in, you can track its progress, locate committee reports, and find references to it in the *Congressional Record* through easy-to-use hyperlinks. Simply click on the topics and documents in which you are interested, and you will be immediately transported to that information. THOMAS is updated several times each day, making the information extremely current. Generally, information about a bill's summary and status is available 24 to 48 hours after any action is taken on the bill. (See Figure 10-1 for a sample page from THOMAS.)

d. GPO Access

The Government Printing Office offers numerous official publications through its comprehensive and easy-to-use Internet site, called "GPO Access," at http://www.access.gpo.gov. Congressional bills, transcripts of hearings, committee publications, the *Congressional Record*, and public laws are available, together with a great deal of other congressional and legislative history information. Most materials since the early 1990s are available. Searching is easily done by bill number, public law number, key words or subject titles, or *United States Code* citation. Questions or comments can be directed to a toll-free number at (888) 293-6498.

5. *Obtaining Documents Needed for Legislative Histories*

a. Bills and Their Amendments

You can obtain the text of bills and later amendments to bills in committee reports or in the microfiche collection of CIS titled "Congressional Bills on Microfiche" or through THOMAS or GPO Access.

b. Transcripts of Committee Hearings

Transcripts of the hearings held by congressional committees and subcommittees are available in pamphlet form as well as in microfiche through

Figure 10-1
Sample Page from THOMAS

House Floor This Week | House Floor Now | Senate Schedule

Search 106th CONGRESS for Text of Bills:

By Bill Number [ ] By Word/Phrase [ ] Search Clear

What's New in THOMAS?

Frequently Asked Questions (FAQ)

107th Congress:
House Directories
Senate Directories

Congressional Internet Services:
House - Senate
Library of Congress
GPO - GAO - CBO
AOC - OTA - More

Library of Congress Web Links:
Legislative
Executive
Judicial
State/Local

The Legislative Process:
House
Senate
Summary of Congressional Activity

Historical Documents

LEGISLATION

Bill Summary & Status
93rd - 107th

Bill Text
101st - 107th

Public Laws By Law Number
93rd - 107th

CONGRESSIONAL RECORD

Most Recent Issue

Text Search
101st - 107th

Index
104th - 107th

Roll Call Votes:
House
Senate

COMMITTEE INFORMATION

Committee Reports
104th - 107th

House Committees:
Home Pages,
Schedules,
and Hearings

Senate Committees:
Home Pages,
Schedules,
and Hearings

Status of FY2001 Appropriations Bills

Consolidated Appropriations Act for FY2001 Conference Report

Consolidated Appropriations Act for FY2000 Conference Report

National Bipartisan Commission on the Future of Medicare.

H.R. 4328 The Omnibus Appropriations Bill for FY 1999.

FirstGov. gov: Comprehensive links to U.S.Government websites.

Library of Congress
101 Independence Ave.S.E.
Washington, D.C. 20540

Feedback | About THOMAS

Please Read Our Legal Notices

Library of Congress Links:
Library of Congress Home | American Memory | LC Bicentennial | Copyright Office | Global Legal Information Network | Exhibitions | The Library Today

CIS/Microfiche Library. Some are available through THOMAS or GPO Access.

c. Committee Reports

Congressional committees and subcommittees issue their reports in conventional pamphlet form. These reports are published in a bound set of books called the "*Serial Set*." USCCAN also reprints selected committee reports. CIS produces committee reports in microfiche in its CIS/Microfiche Library. Finally, reports since 1995 are available through THOMAS and many are available through GPO Access.

d. Debates

Debates are published in the *Congressional Record*, a "newspaper" issued daily when Congress is in session. The *Congressional Record* is initially issued in pamphlet form and is finally published in bound volumes at the end of a congressional session. CIS also publishes the *Congressional Record* in microfiche. If you do not already know the date any debates occurred, look up the bill number in the *Record's* History of Bills and Resolutions. This will cite the date of any debate on the bill that you are researching. The spine of each volume clearly indicates the dates covered by the volume, making it very easy to access the set. Once you know the date debate occurred, you simply match this date with the date appearing on the spine of a volume of the *Congressional Record*. The full text of the *Congressional Record* since 1989 is available through THOMAS and since 1995 is available through GPO Access.

6. *Alternate Methods of Obtaining Legislative History for Federal Statutes*

a. Compiled Legislative Histories

A compiled legislative history is a "pre-packaged" legislative history. That is, it is possible that a legislative history may already have been compiled on the statute in which you are interested, thereby eliminating the need for you to perform the task of legislative research yourself. USCCAN provides legislative histories for selected federal laws in its monthly pamphlets. Since 1979, CCH has done the same.

Public Laws — Legislative Histories on Microfiche is published by CCH. Beginning with the 96th Congress in 1979, this source provides all of the elements of a legislative history except transcripts of committee hearings. By using the index to the service (accessible by subject matter, public law number, and bill number), you will be provided the bill as well as transcripts for any committee report and floor debates. You should also consult *Sources of Compiled Legislative Histories*, a looseleaf service published by AALL Publishers, which will direct you to the publisher of any legislative history already compiled for federal statutes. Consult the card catalog at your law library to determine whether these sources are available. Generally, compiled legislative histories exist for legislation of public importance. As discussed earlier, both LEXIS and Westlaw offer some compiled legislative histories, especially for significant legislative enactments.

b. Legislative History Worksheets

Recognizing that legislative history can be difficult and time-consuming, some law libraries have worksheets for you to use that provide a step-by-step approach and clear instructions for compiling a legislative history. Ask the reference librarian at your law library if the library provides such a worksheet.

c. Commercial Services

There are several commercial services that will assist you in obtaining documents or in monitoring legislation. Check your local phone book or local legal directory to obtain information about private companies that will obtain government documents for you for a fee. Following is a partial list of some of these companies or services:

(i) BNA Plus, a division of the Bureau of National Affairs, Inc., in Washington, D.C., will obtain bills and congressional testimony as well as court opinions, agency decisions, or foreign treaties. The toll-free telephone number is (800) 452-7773 or visit http://www.bna.com/bnaplus/docret.html.

(ii) Washington Document Service of Washington, D.C., will locate various federal and regulatory documents for a moderate fee. The address is 400 7th Street, N.W., Suite 300, Washington, D.C., 20004. The toll-free number is (800) 728-5201, and the Web site is http://www.wds.docs.

(iii) StateNet, a well-known company that recently acquired Legi-Slate, another leader in the field of providing legislative information, will provide legislative materials for Congress and all 50 states. Contact its office at 444 N. Capitol Street, N.W., Suite 725, Washington, D.C., 20001. The telephone number is (202) 638-7999, and the Web site is http://www.state.net.com.

(iv) Federal Information Service will obtain any public document from any government agency or court system, whether federal, state, or local. The toll-free number is (800) 728-5201.

(v) Congressional Information Service, Inc., will obtain all documents for a legislative history. The telephone number in Bethesda, Maryland, is (301) 654-1550.

(vi) Legislative Intent Service, a well-known company established in 1974, will obtain federal legislative history as well as legislative history for any state. This service also provides expert analysis of materials obtained. Call (800) 666-1917, or visit the Web site at www.legintent.com.

(vii) Commerce Clearing House, the publisher of *Congressional Index,* if available, and for a fee that varies with the number of pages involved, will provide copies of bills, committee reports, and hearing testimony. Call CCH at 1-800-TELL-CCH or write to CCH Incorporated, 2700 Lake Cook Road, Riverwoods, IL, 60015.

d. Reference Assistance

Legislative history research is a unique and specialized method of attempting to determine the intent of the legislature when it enacted a statute by reviewing the documents that are part of the legislative process. A bill may be introduced in one congressional session and not enacted and then may be re-introduced the next congressional session with a different bill number. A bill may be reported out of a committee, voted upon, and then referred to conference if the House of Representatives and Senate pass differing versions. Amendments may be made to the statute in several different years.

These complexities make legislative history research a difficult task, especially to the uninitiated. If you encounter difficulty, ask a law librarian for assistance. Large law libraries and law firms often designate an individual to field inquiries and offer assistance in the area of legislative history research. Law librarians are well aware of the complex nature of gathering the documents needed to compile a legislative history and will not be surprised if you ask for help.

e. Congressional Assistance

Members of the House of Representatives and Senate have office staff assistants whose job it is to perform a variety of tasks, including responding to requests for information by constituents. Call the office of your congressional representative and ask for copies of the bill, the committee report, or other pertinent materials. If you cannot recall the name of your representative, check your telephone directory, as this information is often provided in the first few pages of telephone books. Alternatively, check the House and Senate rosters in THOMAS. Often you will be mailed copies of the materials needed within a few days. If you do not receive the materials you need, call and ask again.

House of Representatives: If you have a bill number, call (202) 226-5200 to check on availability. You may mail a request for a copy of a bill to:

House Document Room
B-18 Ford House Office Building
(House Annex II)
Washington, D.C. 20515
FAX (202) 226-4362

United States Senate: If you have a bill number, call (202) 224-7860 to check on availability. You may mail a request for a copy of a bill to:

Senate Document Room
B-04 Hart Senate Office Building
Washington, D.C. 20510

If you are looking for a bill but do not have a bill number, call the Congressional Legislative Office at (202) 225-1772 and provide as much information about the statute as possible, such as subject matter, sponsor's name, and date introduced.

f. Law Reviews and Annotations

It is possible that a law review or A.L.R. annotation has already performed the task of legislative history research for you. That is, a law review or other periodical publication may contain a thorough analysis of the statute you are researching and already may have examined the bill, the transcripts of the committee hearings, the committee reports, and the debates and may summarize this legislative history for you.

The best way to determine if an article or annotation discusses your statute is to Shepardize or KeyCite it. If *Shepard's* or KeyCite identifies a law review article or annotation as discussing the pertinent statute, examine these sources to determine if they have deduced the intent of the legislature in enacting the statute by examining all of the documents that comprise a legislative history.

Alternatively, you could examine the "Table of Laws, Rules and Regulations" in A.L.R.'s Index to Annotations. This table will direct you to annotations in A.L.R. that cite or analyze federal statutes.

7. *Introduction to State Legislative History*

You will recall that the process of enacting state statutes is substantially similar to that of enacting federal statutes. Just as there may be ambiguity in a federal statute that would result in a need to research the intent of the United States Congress in enacting a federal law, there may be ambiguity in a statute enacted in your state. If there are no cases interpreting the state statute, you may wish to perform state legislative history research to determine the intent of your state legislature when it enacted the statute.

The process of compiling a legislative history for a state statute is substantially similar to that for federal statutes. Unfortunately, collecting the actual documents involved can be frustrating because many of them are not published and some are available only at the state capitol.

8. *Documents Comprising State Legislative History*

The documents involved in compiling a legislative history for a state statute are identical to those needed for compiling a legislative history for a federal statute: the original bill, together with any of its later versions, transcripts of committee hearings, committee reports, and floor debates.

9. The Process of Compiling a State Legislative History

After you have read a state statute, carefully examine the historical notes following it to determine the derivation of the statute. For instance, you may be presented with information such as the following:

Derivation Stats. 1996, c. 141, p. 621

This would indicate the statute was enacted in 1996 and was initially published at Chapter 141 of the state's session laws and can be found at page 621 of the session laws for 1996.

Consult your law librarian to determine if a legislative service exists for your state. Such a legislative service will operate similarly to USCCAN, CIS, or CCH *Congressional Index* in that it will provide you with a bill number for your state statute and information regarding the committee that considered the bill.

Once you have a bill number or the name of the committee that considered the bill, you can contact the chairperson of the committee or a legislative staffer at your state capitol and ask for copies of the pertinent documents. Unfortunately, many states do not maintain many of the documents needed for state legislative histories. While the bill and its versions will be available, the proceedings of committee hearings are rarely transcribed, committee reports are rarely published, and debates are rarely reported. Thus, in many states, the only documents available to you in preparing a legislative history are the various versions of the bill as it proceeds through the state legislature.

To determine what documents are available in your state, consult the following: Mary Fisher, *Guide to State Legislative and Administrative Materials* (4th ed. 1988). This source provides a state-by-state outline of the documents available for each of the 50 states and the District of Columbia.

10. Alternate Methods of Obtaining Legislative History for State Statutes

Due to the difficulties in compiling a legislative history for state statutes, you may find that the following alternate methods of legislative history are the most effective.

Compiled Legislative Histories. Some well-known state statutes may already have been the subject of a legislative history. Your law librarian may assist you in locating these.

Legislative History Worksheets. Check with your law librarian to determine if a worksheet or checklist has been prepared to assist individuals compiling legislative histories of state statutes.

Commercial Services. There may be private companies that will perform state legislative history for you. Because many of the documents are available only at the state capitol, these private companies are often located in the capital city of a state.

Due to the difficulty of compiling a legislative history for a state statute, making arrangements with a private company to obtain the needed documents may well be the most effective way of obtaining a complete legislative history. Often the fees charged by these companies are moderate, and you may be provided with the documents you need within a matter of days.

To determine if such a company exists in your state, check with a reference librarian, consult a directory of legal services, call directory information at the capital city, or contact an attorneys' service.

Following are some fee-based commercial services that provide state legislative history information and documents:

- LegAlert, a state legislative history service provided by NETSCAN iPublishing, provides all proposed state legislation, enacted legislation, and related documents for all 50 legislatures, Committee reports are also available from some states. Contact NETSCAN iPublishing, Inc., at 8-3 W. Broad Street, Suite 110, Falls Church, VA, 22046. The toll-free telephone number is (800) 982-2177, and the Web site is http://www.legalert.com.
- StateNet, located at 444 N. Capitol Street, N.W., Suite 725, Washington, D.C., 20001, provides legislative materials for all 50 states. Its telephone number is (202) 638-7999, and its Web site is http://www.statenet.com.
- LEXIS and Westlaw both provide bill text and bill tracking for all 50 states.
- CIS State Capitol Universe, offered through LEXIS-NEXIS, provides summaries and full text of state laws, articles about policy issues, links to Web sites with useful information about the states, and bill tracking for all 50 states. Contact CIS at its toll-free telephone number, (800) 638-8380, or access http://www.cispubs.com and select "State Capitol Universe." CIS State Capital Universe provides state legislative history information, while CIS Congressional Universe, discussed earlier, provides federal legislative history information.

Internet Searching. The Wed site of the National Conference of State Legislatures (http://www.ncsl.org) is a gateway to state legislative sites, allowing direct linking to the legislative site in each state. Although the site is designed as a source for lawmakers and their staffs, it also provides public users with many reports, meetings schedules, direct linking to the home page for each state's legislative body, and a method of ordering publications.

Reference Assistance. Be sure to ask your law librarian for assistance if you encounter difficulty in locating the documents you need. You should also check the card catalog at your law library to determine if there are any books or publications that will provide guidance in compiling a state legislative history.

Legislative Assistance. Contact your state legislators or representatives and ask for assistance or for copies of documents.

Law Reviews and Annotations. Shepardize or KeyCite the particular statute you are researching to determine if it has been the subject of any law review article, A.L.R. annotation, or attorney general opinion. If *Shepard's* or KeyCite directs you to any of these sources, review them because they may provide a convenient summary of the information you need.

11. Tracking Pending Legislation

If you are in the process of tracking pending legislation rather than reviewing legislative history for statutes already enacted, there are a variety of sources that will assist you:

- CCH *Congressional Index* (discussed earlier in this chapter) describes action on a bill, allowing you to track when action is taken on pending legislation. Once you have a bill number (easily obtained from the Subject Index to the set), you can "plug it in" the sections called "Status of House Bills" or "Status of Senate Bills" to determine the most recent action taken on the legislation.
- CIS's Congressional Universe provides bill tracking.
- LEXIS' service, called "Eclipse," will provide you with daily, weekly, or monthly updates on your legislation. You can be notified by e-mail or view the results online. A database entitled Billtrack (enter "BLTRCK") will also provide bill tracking and a report for you.
- Westlaw's database, called US-Billtrack (enter "US-BILLTRK"), provides tracking of pending legislation.
- THOMAS does not automatically alert you to changes in legislation in which you are interested, but by routinely checking the status and summary of a bill, you can determine the progress it is making through Congress. Search by bill number or by word/phrase and then select "Bill Summary and Status."
- StateNet, the commerical service described earlier, will provide bill tracking service for a fee.

To track the progress of state legislation, use LEXIS, Westlaw, or StateNet. Alternatively, some states automatically provide you with e-mail updates on the status of pending legislation. For example, in California the legislature provides a bill status updating service to keep you informed as bills you are interested in move through the legislature. The free tracking service automatically e-mails you when there are changes in the bill or changes in its status.

12. *Summary of Legislative History Research*

The primary purpose of compiling a legislative history is to aid a court in interpreting an ambiguous statute that has not yet been the subject of judicial interpretation. If there are no cases interpreting a statute, you may wish to compile a legislative history to present to a court as evidence of what the legislature intended the statute to accomplish.

The use of legislative history to interpret statutes is often criticized. Perhaps one of the most vocal critics is United States Supreme Court Justice Antonin Scalia. Justice Scalia has stated that using legislative history is "not merely a waste of research time and ink [but] a false and disruptive lesson in the law." Moreover, Justice Scalia has remarked that the use of "frankly partisan statements" by lawmakers can and should in no way be viewed as reflective of some consensus in Congress. Demanding that legislatures draft statutes more clearly, many judges believe that when courts go beyond the plain meaning of a statute by relying on legislative history they exceed their function as interpreters of the law and are in danger of making law, which is the exclusive province of legislatures.

Keep in mind that, at best, a legislative history is a secondary source. It is not a case, constitution, or statute, which is binding on a court and which therefore must be followed. A court may elect to follow the recommendation of a committee report or the sponsor of the legislation in determining the purpose or effect of the statute. Some courts, however, are reluctant to rely on legislative history and view many of the documents as the product of a political process rather than a careful and reasoned analysis of the statute. That is, remarks made at committee hearings or at debates may be the result of political bias or may be made by legislators who are not totally familiar with the legislation. In such cases, over-reliance on legislative history may be misplaced. Nevertheless, if you have no other argument to advance, you should definitely perform the research needed for a legislative history, present it to the court as clearly and persuasively as possible, and hope for the best. With no other guidance to interpret an ambiguous statute, a court may be persuaded to rely upon legislative history as evidence of the purpose or intent of a statute.

B. Executive Materials

1. *Introduction*

The conventional view of the three branches of our government is that the legislative branch makes our laws, the judicial branch interprets our laws, and the executive branch enforces our laws. The executive branch, however, does issue certain directives and documents that affect all of us, although they are of varying legal effect.

2. *Proclamations*

A proclamation is a statement issued by the president that has no legal effect. Proclamations are often issued for ceremonial, public relations, or public awareness reasons. For example, Presidential Proclamation No. 6459 declared a certain week to be Lyme Disease Awareness Week. Other proclamations are Presidential Proclamation No. 6461, announcing Buffalo Soldiers Day, and Presidential Proclamation No. 7347, announcing National Disability Employment Awareness Month. See Figure 10-2 for a sample Presidential Proclamation.

Presidential proclamations have no legal effect because they do not command or prohibit any action, and no punishment or liability accrues as a result of any "violation" of a presidential proclamation. Proclamations are published in a number of sources:

- USCCAN.
- *Federal Register*, the daily weekday newspaper published by the Office of the Federal Register.
- Title 3 of C.F.R. (the annual codification of the *Federal Register*).
- *Weekly Compilation of Presidential Documents*, a weekly pamphlet containing all messages and statements released by the White House.
- U.S.C.S. advance pamphlets.
- *United States Statutes at Large*, the bound volumes containing all public and private laws passed by the United States Congress.
- LEXIS and Westlaw.

Title 3 of C.F.R. and *Weekly Compilation of Presidential Documents* are both available for free, on the Internet, from the Government Printing Office at the following Web site: http://www.access.gpo.gov/nara/cfr/index.html. Searching can be done by inserting key words in search boxes or by browsing through tables of contents.

3. *Executive Orders*

An executive order has more legal effect than a proclamation. Executive orders are regulations issued by a president to direct government agencies. These executive orders have the force of law (unless, of course, a court rules to the contrary) and require no action by Congress. An example of an executive order is Executive Order No. 12812 for the Declassification and Release of Materials Pertaining to Prisoners of War and Missing in Action. Executive orders can be located in the same sources as proclamations, including through GPO Access at http://www.access.gpo.gov and through the National Archives Records at http://www.nara.gov/fedreg/eo/html, except they are not located in *United States Statutes at Large*.

The National Archives and Records Administration provides executive orders and information about executive orders for all presidents since

Figure 10-2
Sample Presidential Proclamation

72 *Jan. 10 / Administration of George Bush, 1992*

After thorough review, I have determined that, given that an embargo is currently in effect and given the negotiations towards an international dolphin conservation program in the ETP, sanctions will not be imposed against intermediary nations at this time. Costa Rica, France, Italy, Japan, and Panama will continue to be certified, and we will review their status as intermediary nations under the Marine Mammal Protection Act, if requested for 1992. I will make further reports to you as developments warrant.

Sincerely,

George Bush

Note: *Identical letters were sent to Thomas S. Foley, Speaker of the House of Representatives, and Dan Quayle, President of the Senate.*

Proclamation 6399—Year of the Gulf of Mexico, 1992

January 10, 1992

By the President of the United States of America

A Proclamation

More than a vast repository of marine and wildlife and other natural wonders, the Gulf of Mexico is also a major factor in the economic life of the United States. This year, we reaffirm our commitment to protecting and preserving this magnificent body of water.

The Gulf of Mexico enchants because it is full of life and beauty. A vital habitat for shorebirds and for much of the Nation's migratory waterfowl, the Gulf region is replete with colors and sounds that are as rich and varied as each evening's sunset. Indeed, few sights can compare to that of majestic whooping cranes winging over Gulf waters to wintering grounds on the Texas coast. Many a visitor has been delighted to watch fishing boats dock at the bustling ports of Florida, Louisiana, Mississippi, and Alabama—only to unload the day's catch and to prepare for another turn at sea. Even amateur anglers know the thrill of casting into Gulf waters, and millions of vacationing Americans have enjoyed the region's warm, sandy beaches.

While we celebrate the natural splendor and the unique cultural heritage of the Gulf coast and barrier islands, we also acknowledge their vital role in our Nation's economy. The fishing, naval defense, and other maritime industries that employ millions of people from Brownsville, Texas, to Key West, Florida, also help to promote the economic prosperity and security of our entire country. Natural gas and oil extracted from the Gulf floor are vital sources of energy for our homes, farms, factories, and automobiles. A significant percentage of all U.S. shipping passes through ports on the Gulf of Mexico, and each year the region generates billions of dollars in revenue through travel and tourism. To ensure that the Gulf remains a viable natural resource for future generations, the United States is determined to reconcile legitimate needs for economic development with our responsibility to protect its beaches, estuaries, fisheries, and wildlife.

The Congress, by Public Law 102–178, has designated 1992 as the "Year of the Gulf of Mexico" and has authorized and requested the President to issue a proclamation in observance of this year.

Now, Therefore, I, George Bush, President of the United States of America, do hereby proclaim 1992 as the Year of the Gulf of Mexico. I invite all Americans to observe this year with appropriate programs, ceremonies, and activities.

In Witness Whereof, I have hereunto set my hand this tenth day of January, in the year of our Lord nineteen hundred and ninety-two, and of the Independence of the United States of America the two hundred and sixteenth.

George Bush

[*Filed with the Office of the Federal Register, 4:01 p.m., January 10, 1992*]

Note: *This proclamation was published in the Federal Register on January 14.*

Dwight Eisenhower at the following Web site: http://www.nara.gov/fedreg/eo.html. As discussed above, GPO Access also provides Title 3 of C.F.R. and *Weekly Compilation of Presidential Documents* on its Web site, and both of these include executive orders.

4. Weekly Compilation of Presidential Documents

One of the best sources for materials relating to the executive branch is a set of books entitled *Weekly Compilation of Presidential Documents*. This weekly publication of the Office of the Federal Register contains the following presidential items:

(i) addresses and remarks such as remarks made at luncheons or ceremonies
(ii) announcements such as those recognizing certain programs
(iii) appointments and nominations such as one announcing the assistant secretary for science and education for the Agriculture Department
(iv) bill signings, bill vetoes, and communications to the United States Congress
(v) communications to federal agencies
(vi) executive orders and proclamations
(vii) interviews with news media

Access to the *Weekly Compilation* is gained through a regularly published index. See Figure 10-3 for a sample page from the *Weekly Compilation of Presidential Documents*. *Weekly Compilation of Presidential Documents* is also available for free online from GPO Access. Documents since 1993 are available. Searching is usually done by key words or search terms entered in search boxes. Access the following site: http://www.access.gpo.gov/nara/nara003.html.

Numerous other sources provide executive materials. Browse the shelves in the reference section of your law library. You may also consult *Codification of Presidential Proclamations and Executive Orders,* which compiles presidential proclamations, executive orders, and other presidential documents, such as administrative orders and reorganization plans. Unfortunately, this source was temporarily suspended in 1989. For more current information, consult Title 3 of C.F.R.

C. Administrative Law

1. Introduction to Federal Administrative Law

In the first half of the 20th century, it became evident that Congress' lawmaking ability could not keep pace with the demands of modern so-

Figure 10-3
Sample Page from *Weekly Compilation of Presidential Documents*

Week Ending Friday, March 20, 1992

Exchange With Reporters Aboard Air Force One
March 16, 1992

Iraq

Q. Mr. President, exactly what is your approach towards Iraq at this point? There are constant stories about desires to take action, to put carriers—[*inaudible*]. Where do you stand now?

The President. We stand that we are just insisting in every way we can that Iraq comply with the United Nations resolutions. And I'm not discussing options. All options are open. And we're consulting our allies as we have in various phases of the Iraq situation. So I wouldn't read too much into the movement of a carrier, inasmuch as we have carrier elements up in the Gulf from time to time. But on the other hand, I think it's fair to say we are determined that they follow through on what they said they'd do, serious business here. And the United Nations is saying firm—our Ambassador up there put it very well. And so we're watching and hoping they will fully comply.

Q. Does that mean that action is not imminent? That you are willing to give them time?

The President. I just would leave it where I stated it, Charles [Charles Bierbauer, Cable News Network].

Q. What did you think about Tariq 'Aziz's appearance at the United Nations? Did he seem to be foot-dragging?

The President. Yes, bobbing and weaving.

House Bank Controversy

Q. How much do you think this check scandal's going to hurt the House? Do you think people should vote based on whether or not a Member bounced a bunch of checks?

The President. No, I think you've got to look at the whole situation. But it is—people are outraged by it. And I think each individual case has to be viewed as to its content. But I'm waiting and watching it unfold. I think it's an institutional thing. I think people are very concerned, but I'm not jumping on any individual. I mean, I think everyone has his own case, his or her own case to make to their constituents or to the people.

Q. Will you support Congressman Gingrich's call for a special prosecutor?

The President. Well, I haven't even talked to our attorneys about that.

Illinois and Michigan Primaries

Q. What do you look for in Michigan and Illinois?

The President. Victory.

Q. What kind of victory? How big?

The President. No, no, no. Never try to say how high the high bar should be on these primaries. I haven't done it. I've been very pleased. They seem to be getting better and better. But I'm just—keep working to try to, one, get the message out on the primaries, but two, try to address myself to the problems facing this country. And I am doing that. And I'm just going to keep on doing that.

Q. Are you going to offer any goodies to the people of Illinois and Wisconsin today, any Federal aid, Federal——

The President. Well, got a good program for them in terms of this economy. I just hope that they can use their influence with a recalcitrant Senate and House.

Well, welcome aboard. It's just a pleasure having you fellows here. It's a little long trip, but it will be a good one.

Presidential Medal of Freedom

Q. An early one tomorrow, too.

The President. What?

Q. An early one tomorrow.

The President. Look, I'm very much looking forward to that tomorrow. I have a very high regard for Sam Walton and what he's done and the way in which he's done it. And so to me, that one, I know some will say it's political, it is purely nonpolitical. It is to honor a great American. And that one I'm

483

ciety. As a result, Congress delegated certain tasks to agencies, each created to administer a body of law. For example, the use of air waves to communicate information by radio led to the creation of the Federal Communications Commission in the 1930s.

You will recall that the typical view of our system of government is that each of the three branches of government (legislative, judicial, and executive) exercises one function (making law, interpreting law, and enforcing law, respectively). The administrative agencies are an apparent contradiction to this principle of separation of powers in that the agencies act quasi-legislatively (like a legislature) in enacting their own rules and regulations and also act quasi-judicially (like a court) in settling disputes.

Despite these seeming sweeping powers, there are some constraints on the agencies' powers: Congress, in creating an agency, typically enacts legislation directing how the agency should operate and also exercises some oversight and supervision of the agency to ensure it properly fulfills its function and does not exceed its authority as set forth in the enabling statute that created the agency.

Each agency administers or regulates a body of law. For example, the Federal Aviation Administration (FAA) regulates aviation, the Federal Communications Commission (FCC) regulates communication, and the National Labor Relations Board (NLRB) regulates labor practices. Note that agencies have different titles, with some being referred to as "Administrations," some referred to as "Boards," and others "Agency," "Commission," "Service," or "Corporation."

While you may be under the impression that these agencies are far removed from you and exercise only a minor role in your daily life, in actuality these agencies affect you every day in numerous ways. For instance, every time you listen to a radio or watch television, the FCC is playing a role. For every item of food you eat or aspirin you take, the FDA (Food and Drug Administration) is playing a role. Perhaps the most pervasive agency and the one that affects you in a dramatic way each and every day is the IRS (Internal Revenue Service).

The individuals who head the agency as well as members of their staffs are usually experts in the area of law that the agency regulates, such as aviation, communication, or securities. The agency heads are selected by the president, are approved by the United States Senate, and serve for a specified term of office.

Because legal practitioners tend to specialize and because administrative law research is highly technical, it is possible that you will never need to conduct administrative law research. On the other hand, you may work for one of the administrative agencies or for a company that engages in a highly regulated field, such as the environment, franchising, or securities. You may be employed by a law firm that specializes in communications law or labor law. In such instances, you will likely become highly familiar with the agencies, their rules and regulations, and the books that publish administrative law. In any event, all legal professionals should be able to conduct competent legal research in the field of administrative law to respond to client or employer needs.

You will need to become familiar with the terminology of administrative law in order to conduct research efficiently in this field of law.

While the product of a legislature is a "law" or "statute," the product of an administrative agency is a "rule" or "regulation." Rules or regulations are issued by an agency to implement and carry out the policies and tasks assigned to the agency by the enabling statute. The terms "rule" and "regulation" are used synonymously. Violation of a rule or regulation can subject one to punishment just as can violation of a statute. Administrative agencies are often referred to as "regulatory" bodies due to the fact that the function of each agency is to administer or regulate a body of law. Agency rules and regulations are primary law.

2. *Publication of Federal Administrative Law*

Until 1936, there was no official publication of the rules and regulations of administrative agencies. For example, while radio stations were subject to the regulations of the Federal Communications Commission (FCC), the regulations were published sporadically, making it nearly impossible for those companies regulated by the agencies to determine if they were in compliance with the agency's regulations.

This confusing situation reached a climax with the famous case *Panama Refining Co. v. Ryan*, 293 U.S. 388 (1935), in which the defendant company was prosecuted for violation of an administrative regulation. It was not until the case reached the United States Supreme Court that it was discovered that the regulation Panama Refining Company was accused of violating had been revoked before the original prosecution was commenced.

To rectify this situation, the United States Congress enacted the Federal Register Act, which provided for the publication of the *Federal Register*. The *Federal Register* is a pamphlet published weekdays and distributed by the United States Government Printing Office. No agency rule will have legal effect unless it is first published in the *Federal Register*. Thus, the *Federal Register* provides an organized system for making agency regulations available to the public. The *Federal Register* does more than merely recite the language of the agency regulations. It provides a summary of the regulation, its effective date, a person to contact for further information, and background material relating to the regulation. Additionally, as discussed earlier, the *Federal Register* includes various presidential documents. See Figure 10-4 for a sample page from the *Federal Register*.

Because each daily issue of the *Federal Register* is roughly the same size as an issue of *Time Magazine*, and it is published daily, resulting in publication of approximately 50,000 pages each year, researching the *Federal Register* is a daunting task. Therefore, just as our federal statutes published in the *United States Statutes at Large* were better organized or codified into the 50 titles of the United States Code (U.S.C.), so also has the *Federal Register* been codified to better enable researchers to access administrative regulations. In fact, the *Federal Register* has been codified in 50 titles in a set entitled *Code of Federal Regulations* (C.F.R.). These

Figure 10-4
Sample Page from *Federal Register*

Rules and Regulations

Federal Register
Vol. 66, No. 19
Monday, January 29, 2001

This section of the FEDERAL REGISTER contains regulatory documents having general applicability and legal effect, most of which are keyed to and codified in the Code of Federal Regulations, which is published under 50 titles pursuant to 44 U.S.C. 1510.

The Code of Federal Regulations is sold by the Superintendent of Documents. Prices of new books are listed in the first FEDERAL REGISTER issue of each week.

DEPARTMENT OF TRANSPORTATION

Federal Aviation Administration

14 CFR Part 39

[Docket No. 2000–NM–184–AD; Amendment 39–12093; AD 2001–02–09]

RIN 2120–AA64

Airworthiness Directives; Boeing Model 757–200 Series Airplanes

AGENCY: Federal Aviation Administration, DOT.

ACTION: Final rule.

SUMMARY: This amendment supersedes an existing airworthiness directive (AD), applicable to certain Boeing Model 757–200 series airplanes, that currently requires inspections to detect cracking on the free edge of the tang, if necessary, and of the fastener holes in the lower spar chord; and various follow-on actions. That AD also provides for an optional terminating action for the repetitive inspections. This amendment adds inspections to detect additional cracking of the fastener holes in the lower spar chord. This amendment also adds an optional terminating modification. This amendment is prompted by the issuance of new service information. The actions specified by this AD are intended to detect and correct fatigue cracking in the lower spar chord, which could result in reduced structural integrity of the engine strut.

DATES: Effective March 5, 2001.

The incorporation by reference of Boeing Service Bulletin 757–54–0031, Revision 4, dated November 11, 1999, as listed in the regulations, is approved by the Director of the Federal Register as of March 5, 2001.

The incorporation by reference of Boeing Service Bulletin 757–54–0031, Revision 2, dated December 19, 1996, as listed in the regulations, was approved previously by the Director of the Federal Register as of March 28, 1997 (62 FR 11760, March 13, 1997).

ADDRESSES: The service information referenced in this AD may be obtained from Boeing Commercial Airplane Group, P.O. Box 3707, Seattle, Washington 98124–2207. This information may be examined at the Federal Aviation Administration (FAA), Transport Airplane Directorate, Rules Docket, 1601 Lind Avenue, SW., Renton, Washington; or at the Office of the Federal Register, 800 North Capitol Street, NW., suite 700, Washington, DC.

FOR FURTHER INFORMATION CONTACT: Dennis Stremick, Aerospace Engineer, Airframe Branch, ANM–120S, FAA, Seattle Aircraft Certification Office, 1601 Lind Avenue, SW., Renton, Washington 98055–4056; telephone (425) 227–2776; fax (425) 227–1181.

SUPPLEMENTARY INFORMATION: A proposal to amend part 39 of the Federal Aviation Regulations (14 CFR part 39) by superseding AD 97–06–04, amendment 39–9961 (62 FR 11760, March 13, 1997), which is applicable to certain Boeing Model 757–200 series airplanes, was published in the **Federal Register** on October 10, 2000 (65 FR 60129). The action proposed to continue to require inspections to detect cracking on the free edge of the tang, if necessary, and of the fastener holes in the lower spar chord; and various follow-on actions. The action also proposed to continue to provide for an optional terminating action for the repetitive inspections. The action also proposed to require additional inspections to detect additional cracking of the fastener holes in the lower spar chord; and to add an optional terminating modification.

Comments

Interested persons have been afforded an opportunity to participate in the making of this amendment. No comments were submitted in response to the proposal or the FAA's determination of the cost to the public.

Conclusion

The FAA has determined that air safety and the public interest require the adoption of the rule as proposed.

Cost Impact

There are approximately 418 Model 757–200 series airplanes of the affected design in the worldwide fleet. The FAA estimates that 151 airplanes of U.S. registry will be affected by this AD.

The inspections that are currently required by AD 97–06–04 take approximately 52 work hours per airplane to accomplish, at an average labor rate of $60 per work hour. Based on these figures, the cost impact of the currently required actions on U.S. operators is estimated to be $471,120, or $3,120 per airplane.

The new inspections that are required in this AD action will take approximately 4 work hours per inspection, per airplane to accomplish, at an average labor rate of $60 per work hour. Based on these figures, the cost impact of the new requirements of this AD on U.S. operators is estimated to be $36,240, or $240 per airplane.

The cost impact figures discussed above are based on assumptions that no operator has yet accomplished any of the requirements of this AD action, and that no operator would accomplish those actions in the future if this AD were not adopted. The cost impact figures discussed in AD rulemaking actions represent only the time necessary to perform the specific actions actually required by the AD. These figures typically do not include incidental costs, such as the time required to gain access and close up, planning time, or time necessitated by other administrative actions.

Regulatory Impact

The regulations adopted herein will not have a substantial direct effect on the States, on the relationship between the national Government and the States, or on the distribution of power and responsibilities among the various levels of government. Therefore, it is determined that this final rule does not have federalism implications under Executive Order 13132.

For the reasons discussed above, I certify that this action (1) is not a "significant regulatory action" under Executive Order 12866; (2) is not a "significant rule" under DOT Regulatory Policies and Procedures (44 FR 11034, February 26, 1979); and (3) will not have a significant economic impact, positive or negative, on a substantial number of small entities under the criteria of the Regulatory Flexibility Act. A final evaluation has been prepared for this action and it is contained in the Rules Docket. A copy of it may be obtained from the Rules

50 titles represent the areas subject to federal regulation and roughly correspond to the 50 titles of U.S.C. For example, Title 29 of both U.S.C. and C.F.R. is "Labor," while Title 27 of the U.S.C. is "Intoxicating Liquors" and Title 27 of C.F.R. is "Alcohol, Tobacco Products and Firearms." Each of the 50 titles in C.F.R. is divided into chapters. Chapters are further subdivided into "parts" covering specific regulatory areas.

C.F.R. is a softcover set revised annually with one-fourth of the volumes in the set issued on a quarterly basis. Thus, revision of the set is staggered with one-fourth of the set updated or revised each calendar quarter. Titles 1 through 16 are issued each January 1; Titles 17 through 27 are issued each April 1; Titles 28 through 41 are issued each July 1; and Titles 42 through 50 are issued each October 1. The volumes of C.F.R. are always issued in softcover pamphlet form. Each year the pamphlets are published in a color different from the previous year's pamphlets (except Title 3, containing various presidential materials, which is always white or black) so you can readily locate the issues for the year you need. For example, the 2000 edition of C.F.R. was white, while the 2001 edition is purple. See Figure 10-5 for a sample page from C.F.R.

3. Research Techniques for Administrative Law

a. C.F.R.

Because C.F.R. is revised annually, with new volumes issued quarterly, any rule or regulation promulgated a year or more ago can best be located in C.F.R.

There are several methods or indexes you can use to locate information in C.F.R. In many instances you will be directed to the pertinent reference in C.F.R. after you read a federal statute in U.S.C.A. or U.S.C.S. Carefully examine the notes that follow the wording of federal statutes in U.S.C.A. or U.S.C.S. to see if you are directed to sections of C.F.R.

(1) C.F.R. Index and Finding Aids

C.F.R. contains an index volume entitled "C.F.R. Index and Finding Aids." This one-volume index is revised annually and can be accessed by subject matter (pesticides, wildlife management) or by the name of an agency (Agricultural Marketing Service, Atomic Energy Commission). The index will direct you to one of the 50 titles of C.F.R. and then to the part within that particular title. There is also a separate index for each of the 50 titles of C.F.R. located immediately after the last part of each of the 50 titles.

The C.F.R. Index and Finding Aids volume also contains a table entitled "Parallel Table of Statutory Authorities and Agency Rules" (Table I). If you know the citation to the enabling statute that created the agency or by which authority the agency issues its regulations, you can look up this citation in Table I. You will then be directed to the appropriate title

Figure 10-5
Sample Page from C.F.R.

§60.490 **40 CFR Ch. I (7–1–99 Edition)**

CAS No. [a]	Chemical
25013–15–4	Vinyl toluene.
1330–20–7	Xylenes (mixed).
95–47–6	o-xylene.
106–42–3	p-xylene.
1300–71–6	Xylenol.
1300–73–8	Xylidine.

[a] CAS numbers refer to the Chemical Abstracts Registry numbers assigned to specific chemicals, isomers, or mixtures of chemicals. Some isomers or mixtures that are covered by the standards do not have CAS numbers assigned to them. The standards apply to all of the chemicals listed, whether CAS numbers have been assigned or not.

[b] No CAS number(s) have been assigned to this chemical, its isomers, or mixtures containing these chemicals.

[c] CAS numbers for some of the isomers are listed; the standards apply to all of the isomers and mixtures, even if CAS numbers have not been assigned.

Subpart WW—Standards of Performance for the Beverage Can Surface Coating Industry

SOURCE: 48 FR 38737, Aug. 25, 1983, unless otherwise noted.

§60.490 Applicability and designation of affected facility.

(a) The provisions of this subpart apply to the following affected facilities in beverage can surface coating lines: each exterior base coat operation, each overvarnish coating operation, and each inside spray coating operation.

(b) The provisions of this subpart apply to each affected facility which is identified in paragraph (a) of this section and commences construction, modification, or reconstruction after November 26, 1980.

§60.491 Definitions.

(a) All terms which are used in this subpart and are not defined below are given the same meaning as in the Act and subpart A of this part.

(1) *Beverage can* means any two-piece steel or aluminum container in which soft drinks or beer, including malt liquor, are packaged. The definition does not include containers in which fruit or vegetable juices are packaged.

(2) *Exterior base coating operation* means the system on each beverage can surface coating line used to apply a coating to the exterior of a two-piece beverage can body. The exterior base coat provides corrosion resistance and a background for lithography or printing operations. The exterior base coat operation consists of the coating application station, flashoff area, and curing oven. The exterior base coat may be pigmented or clear (unpigmented).

(3) *Inside spray coating operation* means the system on each beverage can surface coating line used to apply a coating to the interior of a two-piece beverage can body. This coating provides a protective film between the contents of the beverage can and the metal can body. The inside spray coating operation consists of the coating application station, flashoff area, and curing oven. Multiple applications of an inside spray coating are considered to be a single coating operation.

(4) *Overvarnish coating operation* means the system on each beverage can surface coating line used to apply a coating over ink which reduces friction for automated beverage can filling equipment, provides gloss, and protects the finished beverage can body from abrasion and corrosion. The overvarnish coating is applied to two-piece beverage can bodies. The overvarnish coating operation consists of the coating application station, flashoff area, and curing oven.

(5) *Two-piece can* means any beverage can that consists of a body manufactured from a single piece of steel or aluminum and a top. Coatings for a two-piece can are usually applied after fabrication of the can body.

(6) *VOC content* means all volatile organic compounds (VOC) that are in a coating. VOC content is expressed in terms of kilograms of VOC per litre of coating solids.

(b) Notations used under §60.493 of this subpart are defined below:

C_a=the VOC concentration in each gas stream leaving the control device and entering the atmosphere (parts per million as carbon)

C_b=the VOC concentration in each gas stream entering the control device (parts per million as carbon)

D_c=density of each coating, as received (kilograms per litre)

D_d=density of each VOC-solvent added to coatings (kilograms per litre)

D_r=density of VOC-solvent recovered by an emission control device (kilograms per litre)

E=VOC destruction efficiency of the control device (fraction)

F=the proportion of total VOC emitted by an affected facility which enters the control device to total emissions (fraction)

362

and part of C.F.R. A list of all 50 C.F.R. titles, chapters, and parts is also found in this index, together with an alphabetical list of agencies. See Figure 10-6 for a sample page from the C.F.R. Index.

(2) Index to the Code of Federal Regulations

The *Index to the Code of Federal Regulations* is a privately published annual index to C.F.R. designed to provide access to C.F.R. by subject matter and by geographic location. Thus, you can look up items by subject matter (port safety, textiles, oil pollution) or by geographic location (California, Boston, Appalachia, Yellowstone National Park). You will be directed to a title and part of C.F.R.

b. The *Federal Register*

Because C.F.R. is issued annually it will not contain newly promulgated rules and regulations, which are published in the *Federal Register*. To access the *Federal Register*, use the *Federal Register Index*, which is issued monthly in cumulative form. Thus, the *Federal Register Index* for June contains all of the information for the previous five months. Entries in this Index are arranged alphabetically by agency (Agriculture Department, Air Force Department, and National Science Foundation).

At the back of each issue of each daily *Federal Register* is a section called "Reader Aids." This section lists any C.F.R. parts affected during the month that issue was published, provides reminders of the rules going into effect that day and within the next few days, identifies the next week's due dates for comments for pending rules, and provides general information for customers needing service and assistance.

Additionally, the United States government periodically offers three-hour free lectures in various locations throughout the United States describing the regulatory process, the relationship between the *Federal Register* and C.F.R., and how to use the *Federal Register*. For dates, locations, and times, check either the inside front or back covers of a few issues of the *Federal Register*.

4. Updating C.F.R. Regulations

Because agency rules and regulations are revised or revoked so frequently, you must always check the current status of any regulation you have found. Updating C.F.R. regulations is a two-step process.

a. *List of C.F.R. Sections Affected*

To bring any regulation up to date, consult a publication titled *List of C.F.R. Sections Affected* ("LSA"). LSA is a monthly softcover publication designed to inform researchers of amendments or changes in any regulation found in C.F.R. By looking up the C.F.R. title and section you are researching, you will be provided a short explanation such as "amended"

Figure 10-6
Sample Page from C.F.R. Index

Reference to C.F.R. title and part

63

or "revised" and you will then be directed to the appropriate page of the *Federal Register* on which the amendatory language or other change is found. See Figure 10-7 for a sample page from LSA.

b. C.F.R. Parts Affected

After you have used LSA (which will update the regulation only through the end of last month), you must further check a regulation by determining its status as of today's date. This is accomplished by reviewing the section titled "Reader Aids" at the back of the most recent issue of the *Federal Register*. Each issue of the *Federal Register* includes a section within "Reader Aids" titled "C.F.R. Parts Affected," which will inform you of any changes to any C.F.R. regulations for the period after the most recent issue of LSA. Just as with LSA, you will be directed to the particular page of the *Federal Register* that contains the revisions to a regulation. If you do not locate any entries for your C.F.R. title and part in either LSA or C.F.R. Parts Affected, this means there are no revisions to your regulation during the period covered.

5. *Electronic and Online Methods of Administrative Law Research*

LEXIS and Westlaw both include the full text of the *Federal Register* and C.F.R. in their easy-to-use and search databases. Both of these services, however, charge a fee for their use. The Government Printing Office now offers for free both the *Federal Register* (since 1994) and C.F.R. (since 1996) on the Internet. Access http://www.access.gpo.gov/nara/cfr/index.html and select either *Federal Register* or *Code of Federal Regulations.* Searching the *Federal Register* can be done by subject or keyword, agency name, citation, or by browsing tables of contents. Searching C.F.R. can be done by keyword, citation, or by browsing your choice of C.F.R. titles or volumes.

Just as a C.F.R. citation located in print must be updated by using LSA and C.F.R. Parts Affected, a C.F.R. section located online must also be updated. In fact, some information is available electronically prior to publication in the monthly print issue of LSA. First, select "Search the LSA." You can then enter your C.F.R. section in the search box. Second, access "Current List of CFR Parts Affected," which lists C.F.R. Parts affected by changes since the last monthly issue of LSA. It is updated daily. Simply scan down the list of parts affected to see if your specific C.F.R. citation has been changed, amended, revised, and so forth.

6. *Decisions*

As discussed earlier, in addition to issuing rules and regulations (acting in a quasi-legislative manner), administrative agencies interpret their

Figure 10-7
Sample Page from LSA

76 **LSA—LIST OF CFR SECTIONS AFFECTED**

CHANGES JULY 3, 2000 THROUGH JANUARY 31, 2001

TITLE 40 Chapter I—Con.

(C), (iii), (iv), (4) and (k)(7) amended **62160**
61.356 (b)(2)(i), (ii), (4), (j)(4), (5), (6) and (8) amended **62161**
61.357 (b), (c), (d) introductory text, (7)(iv)(A), (B), (C) and (E) amended **62161**
61 Appendix B amended **62161**
62.13 (c) added **49881**
62.2350 (b)(7) and (c)(5) added **68908**
62.2370 Undesignated center heading and section added **68908**
62.4179 Undesignated center heading and section added **43704**
62.5160—62.5161 Undesignated center heading and sections added **53608**
62.6357 (d) added **68905**
62.14400—62.14495 (Subpart HHH) Added **49881**
63.7 (c)(4)(i) amended **62215**
[illegible]
63.14 (b) revised **62215**
[illegible]
63.90 Revised **55835**
63.91 Revised **55837**
63.92 Revised **55840**
63.93 Revised **55841**
63.94 Revised **55841**
63.95 Revised **55843**
63.96 Revised **55843**
63.97 Revised **55844**
63.99 (a)(36) added 1591
63.100 (e) introductory text and (j)(4) revised; (q) added 6927
63.101 Amended 6928
63.107 Added 6928
63.110 (i) added **78284**
(a) revised 6929
63.111 Amended **62215**
Amended 6929
63.113 (a) introductory text and (c) introductory text, (1) introductory text, (e) and (g) revised; (a)(3) amended; (i) added 6929
63.114 (a)(3), (4)(ii) and (d) revised 6930
63.115 (a) introductory text , (b) introductory text, (c) introductory text, (4)(i), (ii), (d)(1) introductory text, (iii)(D)(*4*), (2) introductory text, (i), (ii) introductory text and (C) revised; (f) added 6931
63.116 (a), (b)(2), (c)(1)(i)(B), (4)(iv) and (d) introductory text revised 6931
63.117 (a) introductory text, (4)(iv), (6) introductory text and (8) revised 6932
63.118 (a)(3), (e)(1) and (f)(3) revised; (f)(5) amended 6932
63.128 (b) and (h)(1)(ii) revised 6932
63.130 (d)(5) amended 6932
63.132 (a)(3) and (b)(4) revised 6933
63.138 (i) introductory text and (2)(iii) revised; (i)(1) introductory text, (2) introductory text and (2)(i) introductory text amended; (i)(2)(iv) redesignated as (i)(3) 6933
63.140 (c) amended 6933
63.145 (j) revised 6933
63.146 (b)(1) added; (b)(9) introductory text and (d) introductory text revised; (b)(9)(iii) removed 6933
63.147 (b) introductory text, (d) introductory text and (2) revised; (b)(8) and (d)(3) added 6933
63.150 (a) amended; (g)(2) introductory text, (i), (2)(iii)(B)(*2*), (m)(1)(i) and (2)(i) revised 6934
63.151 (b)(1)(iii) and (e)(1) revised 6934
63.152 (b)(6) and (d)(4) added; (c)(4)(iv) revised 6934
63.110—63.152 (Subpart G) Appendix amended **78284**
Appendix G amended 6935
63.160 (g) added **78285**
63.169 (b) revised **78285**
63.171 (a) revised **78285**
63.180 (e) revised 6936
63.160—63.182 (Subpart H) Table 4 added **78285**
63.301 Amended **62215**
63.304 (b)(6)(iii) amended **62215**
63.443 (d)(4) revised **80762**
63.446 (d)(1), (e)(2) and (i) revised **80762**
63.453 (j), (n) and (p) revised **80762**
63.454 (a) revised; (e) and (f) added **80763**
63.455 (e) and (f) added **80763**

NOTE: **Boldface page numbers indicate 2000 changes.**

Reference to revision to C.F.R section

rules and regulations through the process of issuing decisions (acting in a quasi-judicial manner). For example, the Federal Communications Commission issues rules and regulations relating to radio broadcasts. If a radio personality such as Howard Stern allegedly violates those regulations, the FCC will hold a hearing and issue a decision relating to this matter. The hearing held by the agency is somewhat less formal than a trial conducted in a courtroom, but its basic function—to determine facts and render a decision—is the same. There is no jury, and the individual who renders the decision in the proceeding (called an "adjudication") is an administrative law judge ("A.L.J.") who is an expert in this field. Alternatively, the agency can prosecute violators in court, often by referring the matter to the Department of Justice for prosecution. Thus, the Environmental Protection Agency can ensure compliance with its regulations by instituting a civil or criminal action. There are approximately 1,300 A.L.J.s assigned to more than 30 federal agencies.

These decisions rendered by the administrative agencies will be published so you may gain access to them and review them. There is no one set of books containing the decisions of all of the agencies; however, the United States Government Printing Office does publish sets containing decisions for each agency. Table T.1 of the *Bluebook* identifies more than 40 official administrative publications, from *Decisions and Orders of the National Labor Relations Board* to the *Federal Power Commission Reports.* While these publications are official, the sets lack a uniform approach. Indexes are often difficult to use, and the updating can be sporadic. As a result, private publishers such as CCH, BNA, and Matthew Bender have published sets that report agency decisions. Typically, these sets are in looseleaf format (see Chapter 7), and decisions are located through alphabetically arranged Tables of Cases or through the subject matter index for the set, which will direct you to a narrative discussion followed by annotations to cases. To locate the actual case, use the citation given in the annotation. These decisions are often published in separate bound volumes that contain both agency decisions and court decisions. Table T.15 of the *Bluebook* identifies more than 100 of these services, from *Aviation Cases* to the *Environmental Law Reporter*.

If a decision has been rendered by an agency, you can check its current status, namely, Shepardize it, by using *Shepard's United States Administrative Citations*, which provides update information for decisions reported in more than 30 reporters published by federal administrative departments, boards, courts, and commissions. Alternatively, you can KeyCite the case through Westlaw to make sure it is still good law.

Shepard's also publishes *Shepard's Code of Federal Regulations Citations,* which allows you to insert a reference to a particular C.F.R. provision or a presidential proclamation or executive order, and then directs you to state and federal court decisions, law review articles, and annotations that interpret or mention that regulation, proclamation, or executive order.

7. *Review of Agency Decisions*

If a party is dissatisfied with the decision rendered by the A.L.J., in most instances the matter may be reviewed at a higher level within the agency and then appealed to the federal court. Because a "trial" has already occurred at the agency itself, the aggrieved party appeals the agency decision to the United States courts of appeal, the intermediate level of court in our federal system, bypassing the United States district courts, which function as trial courts in our federal system. Further appeal may be made to the United States Supreme Court, assuming certiorari is granted. See Figure 10-8 for a chart showing the appeal process for federal agency decisions.

8. *Locating Federal Cases Reviewing Agency Decisions*

There are several techniques you can use to locate federal cases that have reviewed federal agency decisions. You can Shepardize the agency decision in *Shepard's United States Administrative Law Citations*. This will give you the subsequent history of the agency decision by providing you with the appropriate citations to cases published in the *Federal Reporter* and *United States Reports*, which have reviewed agency decisions.

Because you are now interested in locating cases from the United States courts of appeal and United States Supreme Court that have re-

Figure 10-8
Appeal of Agency Decisions

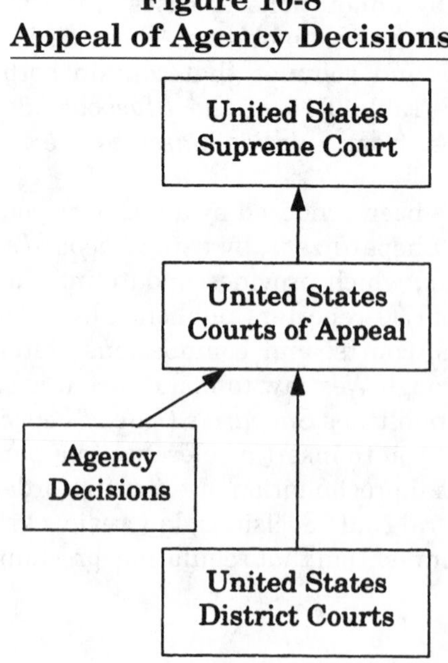

viewed agency decisions, you can also rely on the standard sources you would use to locate federal cases on any topic: digests and annotations.

For all federal court cases, use *West's Federal Practice Digest, 4th Series* (or, if needed, any of the earlier series). To locate United States Supreme Court cases, use West's *United States Supreme Court Digest*. To locate annotations on agency matters, use A.L.R. Fed.

The online source GPO Access offers direct links to some agency decisions. Access the Web site http://www.access.gpo.gov/su_docs/admin.html. Alternatively, you can check the Web sites of the agencies themselves to see if they provide their decisions. For example, when you access the site of the National Labor Relations Board (http://www.nlrb.gov), you are immediately informed that decisions since 1990 are available for viewing, downloading, and printing. Similarly, LEXIS and Westlaw offer decisions of numerous agencies (although fees are charged to access their databases).

9. The United States Government Manual

One book of particular relevance to administrative law is *The United States Government Manual*, referred to as the "Official Handbook of the Federal Government." This softcover book is prepared by the Office of the Federal Register and provides thorough and detailed information on the agencies (such as the Federal Communications Commission), quasi-official agencies (such as the Smithsonian Institution and the Legal Services Corporation), and international organizations in which the United States participates.

For each agency, the *Manual* provides a list of the principal officials, a summary of the agency's purpose, a brief history of the agency, including a reference to the statute that established it, and a description of the activities engaged in by the agency. The *Manual* also provides miscellaneous information about the three branches of government, such as a list of senators and representatives and information about the federal judicial system. The *Manual* displays a variety of diagrams showing the organization of various executive departments, such as the Department of Defense and Department of Justice, making the division of authority and organization of the various offices and divisions within each department readily understandable.

Finally, the *Manual* provides information regarding terminated agencies. For example, when you attempt to find information relating to the Civil Aeronautics Board, you are promptly informed that most functions of the Board were terminated in 1981, 1983, and 1985, and its remaining functions were transferred to the transportation secretary and United States Postal Service.

Since 1995 the *Manual* has been offered for free online by the Government Printing Office at its site, GPO Access. Access http://www.access.gpo.gov/nara/nara001.html. Searching can be done by entering keywords or search terms in the search box provided. Using the *Manual* online is an easy and free way to gain information about various government agencies, their addresses, appointees, staff members, and functions.

10. State Administrative Law

There are agencies in most states, the actions and activities of which often parallel federal agencies. For example, one of the better known federal agencies, the Occupational Safety and Health Administration ("OSHA"), is patterned after the California Occupational Safety and Health Administration ("Cal-OSHA"). While the federal OSHA agency regulates health and safety measures on a national basis, the state OSHA agency may impose additional standards for ensuring that work environments and public buildings are safe. Similarly, many state agencies issue regulations for the practice of certain occupations in the state, such as standards for beauticians, barbers, and real estate agents.

One of the best examples of a state agency is your state department of motor vehicles. While your state statute will set forth the age at which one may drive, testing and licensing procedures as well as other regulations related to the activity of driving typically are determined by the department of motor vehicles.

Some states, usually the more populous ones, publish their agency's rules and regulations in a fashion similar to the publication of administrative law at the federal level; that is, in separate sets of books devoted solely to agency regulations and titled "Administrative Codes." These generally have indexes, which are arranged similarly to other indexes and are easy to use. Simply look up the word or phrase that describes the issue you are researching, and you will be directed to the pertinent administrative code section.

You may also find that after you read a statute in the state code, you are referred to an administrative regulation in the cross-references or library references that follow the statute. In other instances, in the course of reading a case or a local encyclopedia, you may come across a reference to an administrative regulation. In any of these cases, carefully review the administrative regulations, as they typically provide detailed rules, which are subject to strict compliance.

Some state agencies issue decisions. With the exception of tax and unemployment compensation decisions, these are rarely published. Some agencies, however, publish newsletters or other publications that briefly review and summarize their decisions and other activities. These newsletters may be available for subscription or may be available at your law library or through the agency itself.

Both LEXIS and Westlaw offer state agency rules and some state agency decisions. Agency rules and decisions may also be available for free on the Internet. Start with your state's home page and look for links to administrative agencies, rules, and decisions. Your state's home page can be accessed by starting with FindLaw at http://www.findlaw.com and then selecting "states" or by accessing http://www.washlaw.edu and then selecting your state's name from the list provided.

For further information contact the pertinent agency. Usually, the main division or office for an agency is located in the state capital. You should begin your search for information and materials there.

D. International Law

1. *Introduction*

"International law" is broadly defined as the law relating to relations among sovereign nations. While most individuals regard international law as the exclusive province of international lawyers and as an area of law that has no relevance to their daily lives, international law does impact your everyday existence. For example, the fish you order in a restaurant or the tuna fish you may purchase in a supermarket may have been caught in another country's "economic fishing zone" and is available here pursuant to a treaty. Similarly, individuals in the legal profession who practice near Canada or Mexico often need to become familiar with various aspects of international law. The General Agreement on Tariffs and Trade ("GATT") and the North American Free Trade Agreement ("NAFTA") will have implications for those doing business in foreign countries. Moreover, with more and more companies "going global" and the Internet allowing worldwide communication and commerce, it is important for legal professionals to have a basic understanding of international law research.

One often hears that there are two branches of international law: public and private. "Public" international law is what we typically view as international law: the conduct and regulation of nations, usually called the "law of nations." "Private" international law is an older and more archaic term, used primarily in Europe to describe an area of law more properly classified as "conflict of laws." For example, assume a store in your city ordered a shipment of vases from France that arrived broken. The issue as to which jurisdiction's law would apply, that of France or that of your jurisdiction, is a matter of "private international law."

While it is true that international law is a specialized field of law and that most paralegals will not be involved in this practice area, you should become sufficiently familiar with international law sources and research procedures so that, if needed, you can adequately perform a basic research task in this field.

2. *Sources of International Law*

International law is derived from four sources:

(i) International conventions (for example, treaties), which set forth rules for conduct expressly recognized and agreed to by signatory nations
(ii) International custom; that is, some general practice accepted as law or believed to be obligatory
(iii) General principles of law accepted by civilized nations

(iv) Judicial decisions and the teachings of international law experts

3. *Overview of International Law Research Procedure*

If you are presented with an international law research task, you should use the following procedure unless you know the exact source for the answer to your issue or problem: You should first "get your feet wet" by reading some basic or introductory information relating to your issue. This familiarization process will save you time by ensuring that you do not head off in the wrong direction due to a lack of understanding of the issues involved. After you have familiarized yourself with the issue by reviewing some basic materials and sources, you should determine whether a treaty covers this issue and provides a definitive answer to your question. If so, you will need to review the treaty and then determine if it is still "good law," that is, if it is still "in force." Finally, you will need to read analyses and cases interpreting the treaty.

To follow this research process, you need to know which sources to consult. This section of the chapter will provide you with the names of the sets of books you should consult in order to perform international law legal research.

4. *Basic Texts and Sources*

There are several sources to consult to obtain introductory information and background on international law. Law libraries usually collect all international law materials together. You should browse the shelves in this section for other useful materials. Some of the better known general texts relating to international law are as follows:

Green H. Hackworth, *Digest of International Law* (1940)
John B. Moore, *A Digest of International Law* (1906)
Francis Wharton, *A Digest of International Law* (1887)
Marjorie M. Whiteman, *Digest of International Law* (1963)

These digests all provide excellent information relating to international law. In many ways, they resemble an encyclopedia in that they are multi-volume sets that contain articulate narrative statements of the law and citations to cases that are located in footnotes.

Thus, you are not only provided with a description or summary of an issue, but you are directed to cases as well. Access is gained through the alphabetically arranged index found in the last volume of each set.

You should also consult Restatement (Third) Foreign Relations Law of the United States. This Restatement focuses on the foreign relations law of the United States and is an excellent starting place for international law research. The Restatement provides general information on international law, international agreements, and international jurisdiction, judgments, and remedies. The Restatement will also provide you with citations to cases that have interpreted treaties. Additionally, a set of books titled *Foreign Relations of the United States* provides a historical overview of significant foreign policy decisions and diplomatic activities of the United States.

Finally, you should consult an excellent periodical, the *American Journal of International Law*. This quarterly publication contains thoughtful and analytical articles relating to various international law topics. Use the index for the set or use the *Index to Legal Periodicals* (see Chapter 6) to determine if an article has been written relating to the issue you are researching.

5. *Treaties*

Once you have gained some background information relating to your research problem, you need to determine if a treaty governs this issue. A treaty is a formal agreement, usually written, between two or more countries. The history of treaty-making goes back thousands of years. Some treaties have ended wars, others have resolved boundary disputes, and still others deal with trade or economic issues. One type of treaty is referred to as a "convention" and usually relates to one single topic for agreement, such as "The Geneva Convention Relative to the Treatment of Prisoners of War." While treaties may have been signed and agreed to by representatives of the countries involved, they are not effective until they are ratified or officially approved by each government.

In the United States, treaties are negotiated by the Department of State and are entered into by the president with the "advice and consent" of the Senate. Two-thirds of the United States Senate must approve a treaty. There are, however, types of agreements called "executive agreements" that can be entered into by the president without Senate approval. There is often a great length of time between the date a treaty is signed by the representatives of the countries and the date it is formally ratified. For example, in 1954 the United States signed a treaty called, in part, "The Hague Convention for the Protection of Cultural Property." As of the date of writing of this text, the treaty had not been approved. In some cases, years pass between signing and ratification, and it is quite difficult to obtain the text of a treaty during this interim stage.

According to the Constitution, "all Treaties made, or which shall be made under the Authority of the United States shall be the supreme Law of the Land; and the Judges in every state shall be bound thereby, any Thing in the Constitution or Laws of any State to the Contrary notwithstanding." U.S. Const. art. VI. Thus, treaties are "primary" law in that they must be followed.

6. *Sources for Treaties*

a. Pre-Ratification

During the time between signing of a treaty and approval by the United States Senate, treaties can be located in a series entitled *Senate Executive Documents*. Because the United States Senate, namely, the Committee on Foreign Relations, will hold hearings on a treaty and issue a report much the same way hearings are held and reports are issued for legislation, you can review the report by consulting *Congressional Information Service* (CIS) *Index* (see Section A.3 of this chapter). Additionally, CCH's *Congressional Index* contains a table reflecting the status of treaties pending before the United States Senate. Finally, access the Web site of the Senate at http://www.senate.gov/legislative/legis_act_treaties.htm to locate treaties received from the president, treaties approved by the Senate, and a listing of other recent treaty status actions.

b. Post-Ratification

Since 1945, all treaties and executive agreements to which the United States is a party are published as pamphlets in a set titled *Treaties and Other International Acts Series* (T.I.A.S.). Since 1950, all of the pamphlets published in T.I.A.S. are then published in hardbound volumes called *United States Treaties and Other International Agreements* (U.S.T.). To locate treaties in either of these sets, use the index *United States Treaties and Other International Agreements Cumulative Index*. This Index is easily used. You may locate a treaty by country name (Brazil, Canada, Senegal, United States of America) or by topic (health care, extradition, trademarks, navigation).

Another collection of treaties is the *United Nations Treaty Series* ("U.N.T.S."), which publishes treaties filed, registered, or recorded with the Secretariat of the United Nations. Thus, this collection contains numerous treaties to which the United States is not a party. A cumulative index to U.N.T.S. provides access by country and by topic. U.N.T.S. expands at the rate of more than 100 volumes per year.

Until 1950, treaties and executive agreements were also published in *United States Statutes at Large*. A few well-known treaties to which the United States is a party are published in *Martindale-Hubbell Law Directory* in the last International Law Digest volume.

Many treaties are now available on the Internet. The United Nations Treaty Collection offers access to more than 40,000 treaties and international agreements and complete access to U.N.T.S. Access http://untreaty.un.org/English/treaty.asp (or http://www.un.org). All multilateral treaties deposited with the secretary general of the United Nations are available together with a description of their latest status and a link to their full text. Searching for treaties in U.N.T.S. that are posted online can be done by country participant, subject terms or keywords, or by popular name of an agreement. To obtain access to the entire database, law firms and companies pay a moderate fee, but some treaties are available for free viewing and downloading. The United Nations site also offers a glossary of terms relating to treaty actions.

More than 20 treaties related to intellectual property are available for free through the Web site of the World Intellectual Property Organization at http://www.wipo.org, and many recent treaty documents can be located for free through GPO Access. Access the site at http://www.access.gpo.gov/congress/cong006.html, select a Congress (such as the 106th), select "Treaty Documents," and then enter either search terms (such as "hazardous waste") or country name (such as "Canada"). You will then be provided with a summary of the treaty as well as its full text.

7. *Determining the Current Status of Treaties*

After you have read and reviewed a treaty, you should determine whether it is still in force. Sometimes the treaty itself will specify the date until which it will be in force. For example, the treaty might provide as follows: "The treaty enters into force 30 days after ratification and remains in force for a period of 10 years and continues in force thereafter unless terminated by either party by giving one year's written notice to the other." You should also check an annual publication of the State Department entitled *A Guide to the United States Treaties in Force*, which identifies all of the treaties and executive agreements still in force. *Treaties in Force* is easy to use as it is organized both by country and by topic.

Until 1989, the State Department issued a monthly publication titled *Department of State Bulletin*. The *Bulletin* provided a monthly update to *Treaties in Force* to provide current information on the status of treaties. For information after 1989, use the weekly *U.S. Department of State Dispatch*. Review the section called "Treaty Actions" to obtain the most current information on treaties. Alternatively, you may consult a private publication called *Foreign Policy Bulletin*. Because *Treaties in Force* is issued only annually, you must check either the weekly *Dispatch* or the bi-monthly *Foreign Policy Bulletin* to obtain current information on the status of treaties.

Hardbound distribution of *Dispatch* ended in December 1999. All access is now done via the Internet. Access *Dispatch* through the United States State Department Web site at http://www.state.gov/www/publications/dispatch/index.html. You can look up country names or specific treaties in each year's Index and then link to the appropriate issue of *Dispatch* online. For example, when you review the 1999 Index, you can look up "Egypt." You will then be directed to the August/September 1999 online issue of *Dispatch*, which informs you that the Egyptian Investment Incentive Agreement was signed at Washington, D.C., on July 1, 1999, and entered into force that same day.

8. *Interpreting Treaties*

To assist you in interpreting treaties, use both secondary sources and primary sources. For secondary sources that have construed treaties, review the digests and the *American Journal of International Law*, described in Section D.4 of this chapter.

To locate primary sources, for example, cases that have interpreted treaties, check the following two sources:

Shepard's Federal Statute Citations. Be sure you have obtained *Shepard's* for statutes rather than the volumes for cases. Locate the section called "United States Treaties and Other International Agreements." By inserting the volume and page of the T.I.A.S. citation and using the same technique for Shepardizing cases and statutes, you can locate judicial decisions and A.L.R. annotations that have mentioned, discussed, or interpreted your treaty. See Figure 10-9 for a sample page from *Shepard's Federal Statute Citations*.

U.S.C.S. U.S.C.S. contains a separate volume titled "Notes to Uncodified Laws and Treaties," which will provide you with annotations to judicial decisions interpreting treaties.

Once you have located cases construing your treaty, be sure to Shepardize or KeyCite these cases to ensure they are still good law and to help you locate additional pertinent cases.

9. *Citation Form*

The *Bluebook* (Rule 21.4) provides that a citation to a treaty or other international agreement should include the name of the treaty, the date it was signed, the parties to the agreement (although if there are more than three parties, their names need not be given), the particular subdivision of the treaty relied upon (if applicable), and the source(s) in which the treaty is located.

For agreements to which the United States is a party, cite to U.S.T. or T.I.A.S., in that order.

Example

Treaty on Health Care, June 29, 1991, U.S.—Can., 41 U.S.T. 621.

If there are three or more parties to the treaty (including the United States), cite to either U.S.T. or T.I.A.S. in that order as well as to one source published by an intergovernmental organization (such as U.N.T.S.) or one unofficial treaty source.

Example

Treaty on Navigational Waterways, Apr. 14, 1986, 38 U.S.T. 1421, 49 U.N.T.S. 606.

Figure 10-9
Sample Page from *Shepard's Federal Statute Citations*

UNITED STATES TREATIES AND OTHER INTERNATIONAL AGREEMENTS

Vol. 2
—884—
112ARF499n
112ARF536n

Vol. 12
—794—
122LE552
113SC1180
Cir. DC
986F2d529

Vol. 17
—1835—
CIT
813FS841

Vol. 20
—301—
122LE429
113SC1098

Art. 1
122LE430
113SC1099

Art. 2
122LE430
113SC1099

Art. 3
122LE430
113SC1099

—361—
Cir. 11
145FRD607
112ARF251n

Arts. 2 to 6
112ARF284n

Art. 2
112ARF252n

Arts. 3 to 6
112ARF252n

Art. 3
Cir. 11
145FRD608

Art. 5
Cir. 11
145FRD608
112ARF255n
112ARF263n
112AR285n

Art. 6
Cir. 11
145FRD608

Art. 8
112ARF252n
112ARF282n

Art. 10
112ARF266n
112ARF281n
Subsec. a
112ARF252n
112ARF257n
112ARF282n
Subsec. b
112ARF252n
112ARF282n
Subsec. c
112ARF252n
112ARF282n

Art. 11
112ARF252n

Art. 15
Cir. 11
145FRD608

Art. 19
112ARF252n

Art. 21
112ARF252n
112ARF281n

Vol. 22
—407—
112ARF546n

—737—
112ARF522n
112ARF550n

Vol. 26
—1439—

Art. 14
112ARF528n

Vol. 27
—983—
112ARF510n

Vol. 28
—227—
112ARF497n
112ARF499n
112ARF516n
112ARF547n

Vol. 31
—4920—
CIT
813FS863

—5059—
112ARF494n

Vol. 32
—1485—
112ARF553n
112ARF499n

TIAS 10837

Art. 1
Cir. 9
813FS1439

Art. 2
Cir. 9
813FS1439
Subsec. 2
Cir. 9
813FS1440

Art. 10
Cir. 9
813FS1439
Subsec. 3
Subd. a
Cir. 9
813FS1439
Subd. b
Cir. 9
813FS1439
Subd. c
Cir. 9
813FS1439

Art. 12
Cir. 9
813FS1439

79

10. International Tribunals

There are a variety of methods available to nations to resolve disputes. Often one country will agree to act as an informal mediator in a dispute between two countries. For example, in the dispute over the Falkland Islands between Great Britain and Argentina, the United States attempted to avoid the outbreak of hostilities by acting as a mediator or liaison between the two nations.

The Permanent Court of Arbitration was established in 1899 at The Hague, Holland's royal city. Members of this court serve not as judges but as arbitrators, and the court offers a broad range of services, including mediation, arbitration, and fact-finding, for resolving international disputes. It is the oldest institution dedicated to international dispute resolution.

In 1920, the League of Nations established the Permanent Court of International Justice, also at The Hague. This court was renamed the International Court of Justice in 1946 when the United Nations accepted responsibility for its operations. It is often called the "World Court." This court has 15 judges elected for nine-year terms by the United Nations Security Council and the General Assembly voting independently. The World Court also provides advisory opinions upon request of the five organs or 16 specialized agencies of the United Nations. In addition, any United Nations member may bring a dispute before the Court. The Court renders its decision by majority vote. Its decisions are final, and there is no appeal. While the World Court has rendered a number of decisions, including those dealing with war reparations and a ruling that Iranian militants had violated international law by taking 52 American diplomats as hostages, its decisions have often been ignored by the offending nation.

There is no uniform method of enforcing these decisions of the World Court. The United Nations General Assembly may, if the Security Council fails to act on a threat to peace or act of aggression, recommend collective measures, including use of armed force, to maintain or restore peace. The United Nations itself has no permanent police force to resolve international conflicts and will send peacekeeping forces when the United States and other members of the Security Council decide and the disputing countries agree. Since 1948, there have been 49 peacekeeping operations. At the time of the writing of this text, 17 were currently underway.

One of the better known examples of United Nations action occurred subsequent to the invasion of the Republic of Korea by Communist forces from North Korea. The United Nations Security Council agreed to a "police action," and 16 member nations of the United Nations countries sent armed forces to South Korea, with South Korea and the United States providing most of the supplies and troops.

11. International Organizations

There are thousands of international organizations. The best known is the United Nations, established in 1945 and located in New York City.

The United Nations now has 189 member nations, including its original 51 member nations.

Other well-known international organizations include the Organization of American States, the oldest regional international organization in the world, composed of 35 North, Central, and South American nations, Caribbean nations, and the United States; the Organization of African Unity, an association of 55 African nations; the Council of Europe, composed of 40 members; NATO (North Atlantic Treaty Organization); and the European Union, composed of 15 European countries.

E. Municipal Research

1. Introduction

Often a legal question may arise that is entirely of local concern. For example, if a client wishes to install a swimming pool in a backyard, he or she will need to know what requirements are imposed by the local jurisdiction with regard to fencing around the pool. A client who has a two-acre parcel of land may wish to maintain horses on his or her property and will need to know if this is permissible. Similarly, a client may desire to put an addition onto a house, bringing the structure within a few inches of a neighbor's boundary line. These and other similar issues are determined by referring to the requirements imposed by the local jurisdiction or municipality rather than the code of the state. To determine the answer to such questions of local concern, you need to know how to conduct municipal or local legal research.

The following is an example of a city code section. "It shall be unlawful to sell, or offer for sale, any food, beverage or merchandise on any sidewalk within the Central Business District without obtaining a permit pursuant to section 6-193." Richmond, Va., Code § 6-192 (1999).

2. Terminology

Most municipalities operate under a document called a "charter," which sets forth the powers and activities in which the municipality may engage. A charter for a city is similar to a constitution for a state.

Just as your state passes statutes that are the laws for your state, municipalities also engage in lawmaking. These local laws are usually called "ordinances" or "resolutions." Ordinances are passed by the local governing body. This may be a city council, a city council acting with a mayor, a county board of supervisors, or some other local legislative body.

In smaller communities, proposed ordinances are published in the community newspaper, setting forth the text of the proposed ordinance and the time and date of the meeting scheduled to consider and vote on passage of the ordinance. If the measure is passed, its text will also be published in the local newspaper. In larger municipalities, information relating to proposed ordinances and the text of approved ordinances is usually published in a separate journal.

At both the federal and state level, after statutes are passed, they are organized into codes, that is, they are codified. This same process occurs for municipal legislation. The ordinances passed by the local legislature are organized or "codified" so that all of the zoning ordinances are together, all of the health and safety measures are brought together, and all of the animal control ordinances are organized together.

3. *Municipal Research Materials*

One of the most difficult tasks in performing municipal research is finding an up-to-date version of the city or county code. Often the law library in your area will maintain the codes for the surrounding municipalities. You can also check your public library, which will usually have the codes. Unfortunately, public librarians are not as familiar with updating and supplementing materials as are law librarians, and the code at the public library may be outdated.

The best place to review a code may be at the appropriate government office: city hall, city clerk's office, county counsel's office, or city attorney's office. These codes should be current and complete.

4. *Municipal Research Procedure*

Once you have found the code for your municipality, the research techniques used to locate ordinances are similar to the research techniques used to locate federal or state statutes. The most common method of locating ordinances is the descriptive word approach.

Codes are usually maintained in looseleaf binders that contain all of the municipality's ordinances organized according to topic, such as elections, business regulations, and fire protection. An index is provided at the end of the binder. You use this index to locate ordinances just as you would any other kind of index. Think of words and phrases that describe the problem you are researching, look these up in the alphabetically arranged index, and you will be directed to the appropriate ordinance. Most codes also contain the city charter.

5. *Interpretations of Municipal Ordinances*

Municipal codes are rarely annotated. That is, after you read the ordinance relating to the issue you are researching, you are seldom directed to cases interpreting this ordinance. Each ordinance is usually followed only by a brief historical note indicating when the ordinance was enacted.

One of the best places to find cases interpreting municipal ordinances is in *Shepard's Citations* for your state. At the back of each volume (after the entries relating to statutes) is a section that will direct you to cases that have interpreted ordinances. Usually, each county within the state is listed alphabetically. You are then provided with citations to cases that have mentioned, discussed, or construed ordinances from that locality. See Figure 9-14 for a sample page from *Shepard's Citations* listing cases that interpret ordinances. You can Shepardize ordinances through LEXIS.

Moreover, *Shepard's* publishes volumes titled *Ordinance Law Annotations*, which direct you to cases, annotations, and law review articles that cite ordinances. This set is arranged by topic (loitering, taxation, towing, satellite dishes) and will provide digests or brief summaries of all cases that have interpreted ordinances relating to these topics. Thus, if you were to look for ordinances relating to satellite dishes, you would be directed to cases from a variety of states that have interpreted ordinances dealing with this topic.

F. Rules of Court

1. Introduction

As you know, there is an explosion of litigation in this country. If litigants could file their pleadings with courts in any format they liked, on any type of paper they liked, and at any time they liked, the backlog in cases would be even more severe than it presently is. To promote efficient operation, courts are usually empowered to enact certain rules relating to various procedures and administrative matters, such as the correct size of paper to be used, when papers must be filed, and the format of papers presented to the court. In addition to rules relating to such procedural matters, there are rules of evidence.

Courts usually insist on strict compliance with these rules and will refuse to accept pleadings submitted that are not in conformance with these rules promulgated for the orderly administration of justice.

2. Federal Rules

The United States Supreme Court has the power and authority to issue rules for all of the federal courts. The rules of the Supreme Court of the United States, effective May 3, 1999, comprise more than 50 pages of materials relating to matters such as the time allowed for oral argument, the necessity of a table of contents for briefs in excess of five pages, and the availability of the Court's library. The United States Supreme Court has even issued a detailed chart setting forth the required color for the covers of briefs submitted to the Court, for example, white for petitions for writs of certiorari, tan for supplemental briefs, and yellow for reply briefs.

The rules of civil procedure for federal courts are set forth both in U.S.C.A. and U.S.C.S. In U.S.C.A., the Federal Rules of Civil Procedure are located in volumes following the statutes in Title 28, and the Federal Rules of Criminal Procedure are located in volumes following the statutes in Title 18. In U.S.C.S., there are separate unnumbered volumes for the Federal Rules of Civil Procedure and for the Federal Rules of Criminal Procedure, which follow Title 50. After you read the pertinent rule, you will be directed to relevant cases through the use of annotations.

You can locate a pertinent rule by any of the standard research techniques used for locating statutes: the descriptive word approach, the topic approach, or the popular name approach. Once you have located the rule in which you are interested, you can examine the historical notes, library references, and then the annotations after the rule. The annotations will direct you to cases interpreting or construing the rule. Moreover, West's set titled *Federal Rules Decisions,* discussed in Chapter 4, is devoted exclusively to cases that have interpreted the Federal Rules of Civil Procedure or Federal Rules of Criminal Procedure.

Another useful set of books is *Federal Procedure, Lawyers Edition*, published by West, which provides invaluable information relating to matters common to any federal court action such as discovery, pleadings, motions, and trials as well as particular types of federal actions (environmental protection, trademarks, and veterans affairs). A companion set to *Federal Procedure, Lawyers Edition*, is *Federal Procedural Forms, Lawyers Edition*, which provides forms for general matters such as discovery, injunctions, and appeals and for specific actions, such as antitrust actions and civil rights actions.

Even though the United States Supreme Court has promulgated certain rules for the lower federal courts (found in U.S.C.A. and U.S.C.S.) relating to court rules, the lower federal courts themselves are free to enact their own rules as well. That is, each of the approximately 90 federal district courts have rules specific just to that court. Often these rules are administrative and relate to matters such as the maximum length of a brief or citation form. Other rules are substantive and might impose a duty upon counsel to meet and confer regarding disputed issues or to attend a status conference or settlement conference. No matter what the nature of the rule and no matter how insignificant it may seem to you, the court will expect and demand strict compliance with its rules.

With 90 district courts and 13 circuits, determining the specific rules for each court can be a daunting task. One excellent source you should consult is *Federal Rules Service*, which arranges all the rules alphabetically by state. *Federal Procedure, Lawyers Edition*, mentioned earlier, also includes circuit and district court rules.

Additionally, Shepard's set titled *Federal Rules Citations* will direct you to federal and state cases, law review articles, and A.L.R. annotations that interpret or mention federal rules.

Finally, you should Shepardize the federal rules. Use *Shepard's Federal Statute Citations* to locate cases and annotations that have mentioned or interpreted any of the federal rules.

You could also check the library in your law firm or the local law library, which will usually maintain current copies of the court rules for the federal courts in your area. Additionally, copies of court rules are readily obtainable from the clerk of the court. Call the clerk of the court and ask the procedure and fee for obtaining the rules of the court. Usually, these will be mailed to you upon the clerk's receipt of a nominal fee therefor. Finally, most courts publish their rules on their Web sites. Access http://www.uscourts.gov/allinks.html#all for links to federal circuit and district courts.

3. *State Rules*

Just as federal courts may issue rules governing practice and procedure in federal courts, state courts may also issue such rules. Typically, these rules govern procedural matters, such as how many days a defendant has to answer a complaint, when a notice of appeal must be filed, and what defenses may be asserted by a defendant.

Many states have modeled their rules of civil procedure after the Federal Rules of Civil Procedure. These rules are often published together with the state's statutes. For example, in California, the Civil Procedure statutes follow the Civil Code and precede the Commercial Code. You will be provided with historical notes, library references, and annotations, just as for other state statutes. Additionally, many states now publish their rules on their Web sites. See Table T.1 of the *Bluebook* for each state's judicial Web site.

In addition to these rules governing statewide practice, courts within the state may also issue specific rules governing practice before those courts. These local rules tend to be more administrative than substantive and often address such matters as the size and weight of papers accepted by the court, what time the clerk's office closes, whether pleadings are accepted by facsimile transmission or electronically, and the format of citations. Failure to follow the local rules regarding even such minor matters as the type of paper to be used may result in rejection of documents and pleadings. If your pleading is rejected for nonconformance with local rules and the time limit for filing the pleading expires before you can submit an acceptable pleading, the client's rights may be jeopardized, and your firm may be subjected to a claim of professional negligence.

To obtain a copy of the local rules, contact the clerk of the court and arrange to purchase a set of the rules. The fee for obtaining local rules is usually nominal. Changes in local rules are often announced and published in your local legal newsletter or other publication. To ensure you are using a current set of rules, call the court clerk on a periodic basis to inquire if there have been any amendments or revisions to the rules since the time you obtained your set.

G. Citation Form

1. Legislative Materials
   Bill: H.R. 1026, 106th Cong. (1999).
   Committee Hearing: *Child Care Costs: Hearings on H.R. 1249 Before the Subcomm. on Labor*, 105th Cong. 94-96 (1998).
   Committee Report: H.R. Rep. No. 94-506, at 6 (1987), *reprinted in* 1976 U.S.C.C.A.N. 109.
2. Presidential Materials
   Proclamation No. 6361, 3 C.F.R. 906 *reprinted in* 3 U.S.C. § 469 (1999).
   Exec. Order No. 7125, 3 C.F.R. 477 (1981-1985), *reprinted in* 3 U.S.C. § 297 (1994).
   President's Message to Congress Transmitting Nominations, 16 Weekly Comp. Pres. Doc. 768 (Feb. 26, 1989).
3. Administrative Materials
   Water Pollution Standards, 47 Fed. Reg. 8076 (proposed Mar. 13, 1995) (to be codified at 38 C.F.R. pt. 47).
   25 C.F.R. § 1592 (1999)
4. International Materials
   Convention on Nuclear Proliferation, Oct. 18, 1989, U.S.—Can., art. 14, 46 U.S.T. 107, 119.
5. Local and Municipal Materials
   Boise, Idaho, Code § 1409 (1996).
   Baltimore, Md., Code § 7-149 (1988).
6. Court Rules
   Fed. R. Civ. P. 12(b).
   Cal. Sup. Ct. R. 56.
   Sup. Ct. R. 21.

Technology Tips

http://www.access.gpo.gov/nara/cfr/index.html	GPO Access, offering access to C.F.R., the *Federal Register*, public laws, the *United States Government Manual*, the *Weekly Compilation of Presidential Documents*, and United States Congress information
http://www.senate.gov	Web site of the United States Senate
http://www.house.gov	Web site of United States House of Representatives
http://www.whitehouse.gov	Web site of White House
http://thomas.loc.gov	THOMAS, offering text of bills, public laws, committee information, the *Congressional Record*, and other information about the United States Congress
http://www.lib.umich.edu/govdocs/legishisnew.html	Excellent information about legislative histories with links to relevant materials
http://www.llsdc.org/sourcebook/fed-leg-hist.htm	Guide to federal legislative history research
http://www.house.gov/rules/96-473.htm	Guide to following current federal legislation and regulations
http://legintent.com	Web site of Legislative Intent Service, which provides federal and state legislative histories for a fee
http://www.statenet.com	Web site of State Net, a commercial service that provides monitoring and information about federal and state legislation
http://www.wdsdocs.com	Web site of Washington Document Service, which retrieves documents for a fee
http://www.bna.com/bnaplus.docret.html	Web site of BNA Plus, which retrieves documents for a fee
http://www.un.org	Web site of United Nations, offering texts of treaties, glossary of treaty terms, and links to other information and sites related to international law
http://www.lib.uchicago.edu/~llou/forintlaw.html	Primer on conducting international law research on the Internet with links to treaties and Web site of major international organizations
http://www.access.gpo.gov/Congress/cong006.html	Select "Treaty Documents" to obtain text of treaties

(continued)

Technology Tips (*Continued*)

http://www.municode.com/new/about/founder.html	Site of Municipal Code Corporation, providing text of many municipal codes
http://www.uscourts.gov/allinks.html#all	Site offering direct links to federal circuit and district courts
http://www.ll.georgetown.edu/lr/lg/state.html	Site offering links to each state's legal materials

Table T.1 of the *Bluebook* provides each state's judicial Web site

Writing Strategies

When writing about the "special" research projects discussed in this chapter, use the following techniques:

Legislative History: To lend credibility to your legislative history results, always use full titles. Refer to *Senator* Joseph Biden, not Joe Biden. Refer to "the United States Senate Committee on Labor" rather than "the Committee."

Administrative Law: In discussing agency decisions, omit personal pronouns. Do not discuss an agency decision by saying, "he decided . . . ." Instead, state that "the National Labor Relations Board decided . . . ."

International Law: Because treaties are usually cited by their names and those names are often lengthy, unclutter your writing by giving the full name of the treaty only once and then giving it a short descriptive title by saying "hereinafter 'Nuclear Waste Treaty.' "

Municipal Law: Do not use personal pronouns in discussing the entity that enacted municipal legislation. Do not say "*our* ordinance provides . . . ." but rather say "County of Fairfax ordinance 12,345 provides . . . ." or "the relevant City ordinance states . . . ."

Assignment for Chapter 10

LEGISLATIVE HISTORY

1. Use the CIS Annual Index for 1999.
   a. What public law relates to school buses and safety?
   b. Locate the legislative history for this public law.
      (i) When was it approved?
      (ii) What was its designation in the House of Representatives?
      (iii) On what days did debate occur in the House and Senate?
2. Use the CIS Annual Index for 1999.
   a. For what piece of legislation did Carol Hughes testify?
   b. Review the CIS Annual Abstracts for 1999. What day did Carol Hughes testify?
   c. Who is Carol Hughes?
3. Use *United States Congressional and Administrative News Service.*
   a. What does Public Law 106-528 deal with?
   b. Use Table 9 for the 104th Congress, Second Session. Locate information relating to the Veterans Health Care Eligibility Reform Act of 1996.
      (i) Give the Senate Bill Number.
      (ii) Give the House Bill Number.
      (iii) Give the date the bill was reported from the House of Representatives.
      (iv) Give the date the bill was passed by the House of Representatives.
      (v) Give the date the bill was reported from the Senate.
      (vi) Give the date the bill was passed by the Senate.
      (vii) Give the date the bill was approved.
      (viii) Give the public law number.
4. Review legislative history in *United States Code Congressional and Administrative News Service* for the above-described public law.
   a. According to Senate Report 104-262, what does Title IV of this legislation require?
   b. What volume of the *Congressional Record* includes debates relating to this legislation?
5. Review the *Congressional Record* for July 19, 2000.
   a. Who called the House to order?
   b. Which chaplain offered the prayer in the Senate?
   c. Who led the pledge of allegiance in the Senate?
   d. Who was "remembered" in the Senate that day?

ADMINISTRATIVE LAW AND PRESIDENTIAL MATERIALS

6. Use the most recent C.F.R. Index and Finding Aids volume.
   a. What C.F.R. title and part deal with control of scrapie in sheep?

   b. What C.F.R. title and part deal with food grades and standards for bakery products?
      (i) Review this provision and its subparts. If a label bears a picture of an egg, what must the food contain?
      (ii) May water extract of raisin be used in raisin bread?
7. Use *Weekly Compilation of Presidential Documents* for March 2, 2000.
   a. Which NBC interviewer interviewed President Clinton on that day? What topic was discussed?
   b. Use this same volume and review the materials for the week ending March 16, 2000. Which team did the president honor and why?
8. Use the CCH *Labor Law Reporter*.
   a. Use "Topical Index—Wages and Hours." What Paragraph deals with wage-hour coverage for harvesting tomatoes?
   b. Review this Paragraph. Are tomato pickers engaged in producing goods for commerce when tomatoes are later canned and shipped outside the state?
   c. Give the name and the citation to a case from Wisconsin discussing this subject.
   d. Retrieve the case discussing this topic. Is the employment of minors during school hours "oppressive child labor"?
   e. To what compensatory fine was the petitioner entitled?

INTERNATIONAL LAW

9. Use the Cumulative Index, Volume 19, for volumes 1101-1150 for the United Nations Treaty Series. Find the treaty that deals with cooperation between Pakistan and the United States for basic health services. When and where was the agreement signed?
10. Use the Index for volumes 1455-1500 of the United Nations Treaty Series and find the agreement between Australia and the United Arab Emirates regarding trade and economic technical cooperation.
    a. Give the citation to the agreement.
    b. When did the agreement enter into force?
    c. When and where was the agreement signed?
    d. Who signed the agreement for each party?
    e. How long will the treaty remain in force?
11. Use Moore's *International Law Digest*.
    a. What volume and page discuss fishing rights on the Great Lakes?
    b. Review this section. Who has title to land beneath the Great Lakes?
12. Use Whiteman's *Digest of International Law*.
    a. What volume and page deal with the treatment of battle scrap as booty?
    b. Review the material you are referred to. Who owned a German crashed aircraft and why?

Chapter
11

New Technology in Legal Research

Chapter Overview

Legal research can be accomplished by means other than using the conventional sources of bound books and journals. There are several methods that enable you to conduct research efficiently and accurately by using new technology. This chapter will introduce you to some of the new technology in legal research: microforms, sound recordings and videocassettes, floppy disks, CD-ROM, and computer-assisted legal research. Legal research using the Internet is discussed in Chapter 12, which is devoted solely to Internet legal research. Being a competent researcher requires use and familiarity with all media, including traditional print sources, CD-ROM, computer systems, and the Internet, to find the best answer to a legal question in the most efficient manner and at the lowest cost to the client.

A. Microforms

Microforms (sometimes called microtext) are based on the principle of microphotography: Images are reduced and placed on rolls or sheets of film. A microfilm reader is then used to review the images recorded on the film. The readers resemble a television screen and are often equipped with printers so you may obtain a photocopy of the material you have viewed.

There are three principal types of microforms: microfilm, microfiche, and ultrafiche.

1. *Microfilm*

Microfilm is a reel of film that you thread or insert into a reader. The reader enlarges the images on the film and displays them on the screen before you. The film is usually either 16 or 35 millimeters. Because copying the information displayed on the screen is painstaking, most microfilm reader machines are equipped with printers, which enable you to obtain a photocopy of the image or material displayed.

Older versions of microfilm required you to actually thread the film into the reader. Because it was often difficult to thread the film, users would cut or clip a section of the film so they would have a clean, crisp edge to thread. This continual clipping led to the loss of valuable information recorded on the cut film, so the makers of microfilm, for the most part, have converted to cartridges or cassettes, which you simply insert into the reader and which thread themselves, much the same way a cassette tape is played in the tape deck of your car.

Most readers have written instructions for their use attached to them enabling convenient use of the microfilm. Once you have inserted the cassette of film into the reader you may fast-forward or rewind the film to the image you desire. The image displayed on the screen can be fuzzy or grainy, depending on the quality and age of the microfilm and the reader. Some users complain that the fast-forwarding and "jumpiness" of the image can lead to headaches if frequent breaks are not taken.

While microfilm certainly saves storage space, it has not been used to any great extent in the legal world. It is, however, widely used for government records and documents, bank records, and other commercial records and nonlegal publications.

Many counties maintain their records of land transactions on microfilm. If you needed to determine the owner of a parcel of property on a certain date, you would likely examine the chain of title by reviewing the county records on microfilm. Similarly, marriage, birth, and death records are often maintained on microfilm. This not only saves storage space but allows easy access without destroying the original documents.

Public libraries typically preserve older books, journals, magazines, and newspapers on microfilm. If you do estate work you may need to prove the value of stock as of a certain date. To accomplish this, simply go to a public library and ask for the newspaper for the date in question. In most cases, you will be given a microfilm cassette containing the newspaper for a certain time period. After you locate the information you need, obtain a certified copy of it and you may then attach this as an exhibit to whatever document you are submitting to the court. If the reader is not equipped with a printer, ask the librarian or other curator to obtain a copy of the pertinent page. Much of this information and these records are now also available on the Internet (see Chapter 12).

Some courts also preserve their older files on microfilm, and if you need to review a criminal, civil, probate, or family law file you may be directed to a microfilm section. Seldom, however, are conventional legal research sources such as U.S.C.S., Am. Jur. 2d, or A.L.R. maintained on microfilm.

2. *Microfiche*

The word "fiche" means a card or strip of paper or film used in cataloging or archiving documents. Microfiche is a microfilm displayed on a thin transparent celluloid flat sheet rather than on a roll of film. The sheet is usually four inches by six inches and greatly resembles the negatives you receive when you have film developed. Its color is usually either an orange-brown or a bluish-gray-green. The images on the sheet of microfiche are arranged in a block or grid type of pattern. Each sheet of microfiche may contain images of up to 400 pages.

Like microfilm, microfiche is not as widely used for legal sources as it is for nonlegal materials. Some libraries have replaced their conventional card catalog, consisting of drawers with small index cards, with microfiche. Each sheet of microfiche will cover certain sections of the alphabet. To determine if the library has a copy of a certain book or publication, insert the sheet of fiche into a reader, which will display the enlarged image on the screen.

It can take a bit of time to get used to using the reader for microfiche because when you move the card to the right, the image on the screen shifts to the left, and vice versa. Many users are not particularly careful when using the microfiche cards or sheets and often neglect to replace them in their specific slots, making searching difficult and time-consuming.

One well-known use of microfiche is the publication by Congressional Information Service (CIS) of *Congressional Bills, Resolutions & Laws on Microfiche*. This set is used for compiling a legislative history and provides copies of bills and their amendments in microfiche. You will recall from Chapter 10 that the CIS system includes all of the documents you need to compile a legislative history (bills, committee reports, transcripts of committee hearings, and debates) in microfiche. Moreover, the *Federal Register* and the *Code of Federal Regulations* are also on microfiche.

3. *Ultrafiche*

Ultrafiche, or ultramicrofiche, as it is sometimes called, is a sheet of film that is the same size as a sheet of microfiche (4″ × 6″) but that holds a great many more images. As many as 1,400 pages of text can be held on a single sheet of ultrafiche. West has reproduced its National Reporter System in ultrafiche, with each sheet replacing one hardbound volume of the *Atlantic Reporter*, *Pacific Reporter*, and others.

Viewing ultrafiche is identical to viewing microfiche. Simply insert the sheet of ultrafiche into the reader, which will display the image or case on the screen. Most readers are equipped with printers, enabling you to obtain a copy of the case if needed.

4. *Summary of Microforms*

All of the varieties of microform (microfilm, microfiche, and ultrafiche) perform the valuable function of saving storage space. While their use for nonlegal purposes has been broad, their role in legal research has been a bit slower to take hold. Most researchers believe it is easier to simply grab a volume of the *Federal Supplement* from the shelf (or use one of the legal research computers to locate a case) than to retrieve the correct sheet of fiche and insert it into a reader. A notable exception is the use of microfiche for the materials comprising a legislative history.

Even though certain materials and sources may be available in microform, your particular law library may not have purchased the microforms. That is, the fact that microforms are published does not mean that they will be available at your law library. Ask your law librarian what materials are available in microform at your law library.

To determine what materials are published in microform, consult *Guide to Microforms in Print*, which is a cumulative list of journals, books, government publications, newspapers, and other materials currently available from micropublishing organizations. Micropublications are listed in the *Guide to Microforms in Print* alphabetically by title and by author. Each listing will identify the publication, the publisher, the price, and the particular type of microform.

Many libraries maintain their microforms in a separate section of the law library. This is usually an attempt by the library to control access as well as to preserve the microforms by regulating temperature, humidity, and other conditions that may affect them.

The advent of the Internet, with its nearly limitless ability to provide information, may soon make many microforms obsolete.

B. Sound Recordings and Videocassettes

Many continuing legal education programs are offered for those in the legal profession. The programs or seminars are usually held in hotel conference or meeting rooms. Some law firms prefer to purchase a sound recording or videocassette of the program, which will then be available for use by all of the professionals in the firm, rather than send just one person to a seminar. Your firm or office may maintain a library of these sound recording cassettes or videocassettes, which you can take home and review at your leisure.

Some law libraries also maintain a library of tapes, both audio and video, which you can check out and review. These tapes cover a variety of subjects from estate planning to recent changes in the tax laws to how to handle a real estate condemnation action. You may also notice advertisements for audio and videotapes for sale in legal journals, newspapers, and other publications.

Most of the sound recordings and videotape presentations are elementary and introductory in their approach. All, of course, are secondary sources in that they explain, describe, or summarize the law rather than provide a verbatim recitation of a statute, case, or constitution.

There are a few other uses of videotape. Some law firms videotape mock questioning of clients before a trial. This helps sharpen the attorney's skill as an advocate as well as perhaps point out certain characteristics of the client that may affect his or her credibility as a witness, such as fidgeting or refusing to answer directly.

Other firms use videotape presentations to introduce the client to certain routine matters, such as providing the client with basic information about having a deposition taken, the trial process, or the basics of will-drafting. This saves time for the attorneys and paralegals because they do not have to repeat the same information over and over for clients and thus saves the clients' money.

Videotapes are often used at trials as well to show the jury an accident scene, for example, or the layout of a building or for criminal prosecutions when the crime itself (bank robbery, shoplifting) has been videotaped.

C. Floppy Disks and CD-ROM

1. Floppy Disks

In addition to their use in a law office for word processing purposes, floppy disks are also used for legal research. Many publishers now offer books on various areas of practice and research on floppy disks. For example, Bancroft-Whitney offers its set titled *California Civil Practice* in conventional hardbound volumes and on floppy disks. Often the sets available on floppy disks are very practical in their approach and provide forms as well. Thus, you can load the disks into your computer, read about a certain area of the law such as wills, and then begin drafting the will with the aid of the forms provided.

Floppy disks are also used for teaching purposes. Both West and Reed Elsevier provide tutorials on floppy disks to assist individuals in learning to use their computerized research systems, Westlaw and LEXIS, respectively.

The use of disks is decreasing due to the ease of use of CD-ROMs.

2. CD-ROM

One of the significant technologies available to researchers is CD-ROM (compact disk, read-only memory). These CDs look substantially like any other CD and can contain thousands of pages of information. They offer distinct advantages, however, in that they provide full coverage for a variety of legal topics and yet take up little valuable office or library space.

Martindale-Hubbell Law Directory (see Chapter 7) is now available on CD-ROM. More than 900,000 lawyers and law firms worldwide can be located using two disks. Locating the information you need can be incredibly easy. You can locate attorneys by name, firm name, state, city, county, law school, languages, field of law, and several other criteria. For example, if you need to locate an attorney in Raleigh, North Carolina, who speaks Arabic and is engaged in banking law, you type in these criteria and you will be presented with a list of attorneys who fit the criteria you selected. It is also possible to obtain a print of the information shown on the screen. The CD-ROM version of *Martindale-Hubbell* is more expensive than the print version (about $1,000 compared to about $500).

Several major publishers, including West and Matthew Bender, are now making cases, statutes, and practice guides available on CD-ROM. Some sets offer only civil cases, while others offer civil and criminal cases. These compact disks save space and provide easy access to cases. One disk can take the place of hundreds of bound volumes. *Shepard's* offers its *Shepard's Citations* on CD-ROM, making it easy to Shepardize cases and statutes. Various journals and publications, such as the most widely read legal periodical in the United States, *The Business Lawyer,* are also available on CD-ROM. Plans are also underway to publish the *Harvard Law Review* on CD-ROM. One of the best-known treatises, *Collier on Bankruptcy,* is available on CD-ROM from Matthew Bender & Company. Various bankruptcy forms are included as well.

As discussed in Chapter 6, LegalTrac is a CD-ROM version of the *Legal Resource Index*, which provides you with access to legal periodicals.

Check with your law librarian to determine what sources are available on CD-ROM. CD-ROM not only offers the advantage of saving space by making thousands of pages available on one wafer-thin disk but also saves money, as there are no online charges. Once the CDs are purchased they can be used with no further costs, although replacement disks will need to be purchased when updating is done.

The CD can be used with a portable laptop computer and small printer, enabling legal professionals to perform valuable research at home or while commuting or traveling. Their use at trial can be extremely valuable. If adverse counsel cites an unfamiliar case or statute, you can use a computer disk and laptop computer to find and read the case and immediately point out exceptions or limitations. Because compact disks containing cases or statutes need to be updated, most publishers will issue you new disks (for a fee) and take back your old ones at monthly or quarterly intervals. In general, the cost for CD-ROM products is about the same as for their print counterparts.

West offers a wide variety of legal materials in a CD-ROM format. Searching can be done by plain language. Hypertext links allow you to jump within a product. Among the publications offered on CD-ROM are the following:

Am. Jur. 2d, the legal encyclopedia covering all American law.

Am. Jur. Legal Forms 2d, a complete selection of business and legal forms for all aspects of federal and state law practice.

Am. Jur. Pleading and Practice Forms, including forms related to federal and state trial practice.

Am. Jur. Trials, a step-by-step guide through all stages of civil and criminal trials.

A.L.R.3d, 4th, and 5th, including leading cases from state appellate courts and annotations on issues raised by those cases.

A.L.R. Federal, providing case law analysis on federal questions of law.

United States Supreme Court Reports, Lawyers' Edition, reporting United States Supreme Court cases in full.

U.S.C.A., providing full coverage of all federal statutes and annotations to cases interpreting those statutes.

C.F.R., containing the entire *Code of Federal Regulations* on disk.

Federal Register, providing full coverage of administrative agencies, proposed regulations, agency notices, and executive orders.

Other West products offered in CD-ROM include the Restatements, the American Digest System, *Federal Reporter, Federal Supplement,* and various practice sets and treatises such as *Couch on Insurance 3d* and *McCarthy on Trademarks and Unfair Competition.*

D. Computer-Assisted Legal Research

1. *Introduction*

There are two major competing computer-assisted research services: LEXIS, now provided by Reed Elsevier, Inc. (and formerly owned by Mead Data Central, Inc., of Dayton, Ohio) and Westlaw, provided by West Group of Eagan, Minnesota. Other systems, such as FLITE (Federal Legal Information Through Electronics) and JURIS (Justice Retrieval and Inquiry System), are accessible only to federal government employees. Although there are other systems available (which will be discussed later in this chapter), LEXIS and Westlaw remain the best known and most often used computerized legal research systems. LEXIS and Westlaw operate in essentially the same manner. Most users, however, develop a preference for one or the other.

These research systems provide access to a tremendous variety of cases, statutes, administrative regulations, and numerous other authorities, which a law firm, agency, or other employer may not otherwise be able to afford or otherwise be able to set aside shelf space for. Moreover, you can often locate the information you need very rapidly. The more familiar you become with LEXIS or Westlaw, the more efficient you will be at locating the information you need.

Both systems consist of a personal computer, a keyboard used to type in words for searching and locating the information you need, a video display screen, which will display information for you to review, and a printer, which will print the case, statute, or other information you desire.

Each service consists of thousands of databases. The databases include the cases, constitutions, statutes, administrative regulations, and other materials for you to access. LEXIS and Westlaw continually add information and authorities to their databases to bring you as much information as possible.

In general, research using LEXIS and Westlaw is similar. Both allow easy retrieval of cases, statutes, and other materials when you already have a citation. You merely type the citation into an open field and press "Go" or a similar button. When you do not have a citation, you will usually access the appropriate database (such as federal cases or state cases) and then formulate a search question by using Boolean terms and connectors or by using natural language. Neither system is case-sensitive, thus allowing you to use either lowercase or capital letters.

To determine the information is contained in a database, you can consult printed lists published by Reed Elsevier and West, which contain all of the sources contained in the databases, for example, Iowa Court of Appeals cases from 1977, the *Environmental Law Reporter*, and federal bankruptcy and tax materials. Your law librarian will usually have a copy of these printed database lists. Alternatively, you can consult the online directory for each system. As soon as you sign on to either service, you can select a directory listing all of the sources and authorities available. Fees and charges are usually assessed as soon as you sign on, so you may want to become as familiar as possible with the printed list of the database rather than relying on the online directories.

You access these databases in a remote location through a telecommunication device similar to a telephone line. This is why the systems are referred to as "online." The services are now both accessible through the Internet as well. Typically, fees are assessed for each minute online, thus requiring you to research as efficiently as possible. Some law firms and companies, however, pay fixed fees, allowing unlimited access for one fee.

While these computerized research services can provide rapid access to numerous useful authorities, they cannot replace you. It is always your analysis and interpretation of the legal authorities the services provide that is valuable to the client. The computer cannot analyze, evaluate, or consider alternate strategies to achieve a client's goals — only you and your fellow legal professionals can do this.

While it is important to have a basic understanding of the two computerized legal research systems, the best way to learn how to perform computerized legal research is to do it. There is no substitute for "hands on" experience. Both Reed Elsevier and West offer training courses and written materials describing their systems. Often a complete tutorial package will be sent to you consisting of written descriptions of the systems as well as floppy disks to demonstrate use of the system. Contact:

LEXIS-NEXIS
P.O. Box 983
Dayton, Ohio 45401
24-hour toll-free customer service:
1 (800) 543-6862

West Group
610 Opperman Drive
Eagan, MN 55123
Toll-free customer service:
1 (800) Westlaw

It is entirely possible that your employer may not subscribe to LEXIS or Westlaw. Conventional legal research methods are *always* acceptable to obtain answers to research questions. Computerized legal research is simply an alternative tool you can use to find the information you need—it is not the only tool.

The continual updates to the LEXIS and Westlaw databases, the modifications of search strategies, the frequent addition of new features and screens to these computer-assisted legal research ("CALR") systems, make it nearly impossible to provide current information relating to LEXIS or Westlaw. Legal researchers should therefore review publications and materials issued by Reed Elsevier and West as well as advertisements and articles in legal publications to keep informed of new developments in the field of CALR.

2. *LEXIS*

a. Introduction and Organization

LEXIS, introduced in 1973 by Mead Data Central, Inc., was the first computerized legal research service. Its database contains more than 3.2 billion searchable documents. LEXIS is part of LEXIS-NEXIS Group, with LEXIS focusing on legal materials and NEXIS focusing on business and news services.

LEXIS' database consists of a series of "libraries"—materials relating to particular areas of the law, such as the library titled "FEDSEC," which contains cases, statutes, and rulings on federal securities legislation, or the library titled "HEALTH," which contains materials on health issues, or the library titled "GENFED," which contains materials related to general federal matters.

Within each library are "files." For example, the GENFED library contains separate "files" for cases from the United States Supreme Court, cases from the Courts of Appeals, the *Federal Register*, C.F.R., and files for other federal materials.

Getting started usually requires you to sign on to either LEXIS or Westlaw and to type in the identification and password assigned to you by your school or employer. When performing research on the job, you will usually enter a client name or number so that the client can be billed for the time spent conducting the research. LEXIS is often provided by law firms to their legal professionals through a software package allowing desktop computer access.

After you access LEXIS (which can also be accessed through the Web, at http://www.lexis.com), the first screen provides the following research options at the top of your screen:

- Search. Clicking on the "Search" tab allows you to explore sources such as federal authorities, state authorities, secondary authorities, public records, and news.
- Search Advisor. Selecting the "Search Advisor" tab allows you to learn about an area of law and locate cases by legal topic.
- Get a Document. Use the "Get a Document" tab when you know the citation to a case, statute, regulation, or law review.
- Check a Citation. Use "Check a Citation" to Shepardize your cases. (See Figure 11-1.)

b. Constructing a Search

There are two ways to seach for materials on LEXIS if you do not have a citation: the traditional search using Boolean connectors or the newer plain English search method called "Freestyle," or "Natural Language."

Boolean Searching

"Boolean searching" is the term used to describe searches on computers using symbols, word fragments, and numbers rather than plain English.

You will find that the computer is extremely literal. You may believe that the words "tenant" and "lessee" mean essentially the same thing, but to the computer, these are two entirely separate concepts. If you instruct the computer to search for "tenant," it will do so and will not provide you

Figure 11-1
Sample LEXIS Screen

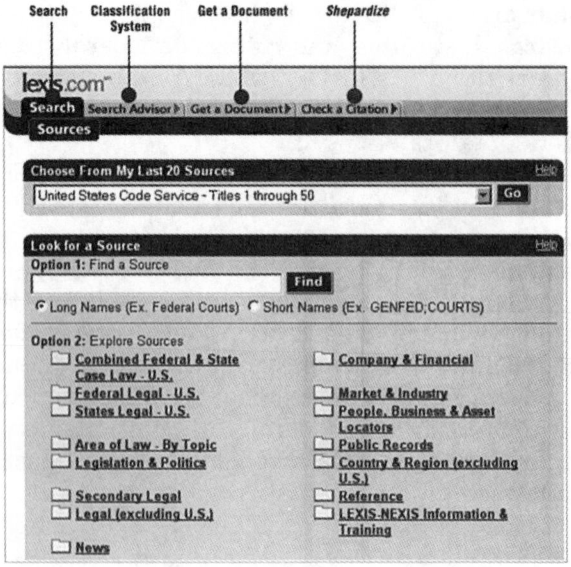

with information relating to a lessee. Thus, you need to know some basic rules of how LEXIS operates so you can search efficiently. First, LEXIS is not sensitive to capital letters unless you specify in your search request that capital letters be read as such. For basic searching, use all lowercase letters.

(1) Plurals

If a word forms its plural by adding "es" or "s" or by changing "y" to "ies," LEXIS will automatically find both forms for you. Thus, if you are searching "tenant" or "baby," LEXIS will automatically search for "tenants" and "babies" as well. LEXIS will not, however, automatically find the plural of irregular plural forms such as "knives" for "knife."

(2) Possessives

LEXIS will also automatically search for singular and plural possessives of a word. If you enter "defendant," LEXIS will search for defendant, defendant's, and defendants'.

(3) Universal Symbols

Because a search for cases containing the word "explode" would not include "exploding" or "explosion," LEXIS offers two universal characters (usually referred to as "root expanders") to help you expand your search:

- An *asterisk* (*) substitutes for any character. Thus, "explo****" will locate "explode," "exploded," "exploding," or "explosion." It will also locate "explore," "explored," and "exploring." An asterisk can be used at the middle or end of a word. Thus, "m*n" will search for "men," "man," or a word containing any other letter that might appear where the asterisk is placed.
- An *exclamation point* (!) substitutes for any number of additional letters at the end of a word. Thus, "expl!" will locate "explode," "exploded," "exploding," or "explosion." Remember, however, that it will also locate "explore," "explored," and "exploring." The "!" may only be used at the end of a word segment, not at the beginning or the middle.

(4) Connectors

Because many concepts are expressed in different ways, LEXIS uses words and symbols called "connectors" to help you locate needed documents. The most common connectors are "or," "/n," "and," and "and not."

- The connector *or* joins words that are synonyms so that a search will locate both words. For example, a search for "tenant or lessee" will locate documents containing either or both of these words. Likewise, a search for "shareholder or stockholder" will locate documents containing either or both of these words.

- The connector */n* instructs the computer to find documents that contain words appearing within a specified number of words of each other. For example, the search instruction "tenant or lessee /50 evict!" instructs LEXIS to locate documents in which the words tenant or lessee appear within 50 words of the word "evict," "eviction," or "evicting." You may select intervening words from 1 to 255. When counting words, LEXIS ignores what it refers to as "noise words," that is, common words such as "the," "and," "of," "is," "are," and "to."
- The connector *and* instructs LEXIS to locate documents containing certain words no matter how far apart those words are. Thus, the search instruction "tenant and default" instructs LEXIS to locate documents in which the words tenant and default occur anywhere in the same document.
- The connector *and not* instructs LEXIS to exclude certain documents. For example, a search for "negligen! and malpractice and not medical" instructs LEXIS to retrieve documents in which the terms "negligence" (or "negligent") or "malpractice" occur, and excludes documents if they also contain the word "medical."

While there are other connectors, the four described herein are the most commonly used. For an explanation of the other connectors, consult any of the published descriptions of LEXIS. Multiple connectors may be used in one search request.

Connectors help you limit your search and make it more manageable. If you simply entered "first amendment," LEXIS would locate thousands of documents containing this phrase. A more effective search would be "first amendment /50 free! and press." This instructs LEXIS to locate only documents that contain the phrase "first amendment" within 50 words of the words "freedom" or "free" and "press."

Constructing a proper search is the most important part of computerized legal research and requires thought and planning before you sign on and start incurring charges. Use a pen and paper and play around with the universal characters and connectors to frame the most efficient search instruction.

If your search does not reveal sufficient results or, conversely, provides you with an abundance of documents, it is possible to modify your search. Simply press "m" and modify your search by using additional connectors such as "or," "/n," or "and." Thus, if your search for "landlord /20 tenant and default" discloses hundreds of cases, press "m" and continue by adding "/20 evict! and rent."

Plain English Searching

Recognizing that many individuals find working with Boolean connectors awkward, LEXIS has introduced "Freestyle," a method of searching that allows researchers to use plain English rather than connectors or root expanders. Freestyle allows you simply to type in your search inquiry in plain English and locate documents that respond to your search request. Click inside the open circle on your screen marked "Natural Language" to select this research format. Then type in your search terms. For example, to locate cases relating to adoption of children by unmarried individuals, first select a library or source from the "Source" menu (such as "Federal Legal-U.S." for all federal cases or "States Legal-U.S." for state sources only). Type your search the way you might describe it to another, for instance, "When can unmarried or single individuals adopt children?" To modify your search, press "m." To conduct a new search, press ".ns." To switch to Boolean searching, click inside the open circle marked "Terms and Connectors." (See Figure 11-2.)

c. Search Advisor

A new service offered by LEXIS, Search Advisor, is designed for research in a known area of law. Search Advisor is an ideal place to begin researching an issue because it assists you in selecting a legal topic and a jurisdiction and will suggest terms and words to search.

To use Search Advisor, click on "Search Advisor" at the top of your screen and then either choose a legal topic (such as antitrust, bankruptcy, or contracts) from the drop-down menu or type in your legal topic in the open search box. You will be presented with a list of more specific subtopics that you can select to explore. Continue clicking and selecting until you are presented with the specific topic you desire. You can select a jurisdiction and then determine whether you prefer to search using Terms and Connectors (Boolean searching) or Natural Language. Click "Search." When documents are retrieved, you can view the full text of a document or case presented or only a portion. When cases are listed, their core terms (key terms used in the case, such as "debtor" or "arrest") will be presented with their citations so you can select the cases of most interest to you. (See Figure 11-3.)

Figure 11-2
LEXIS Search Form

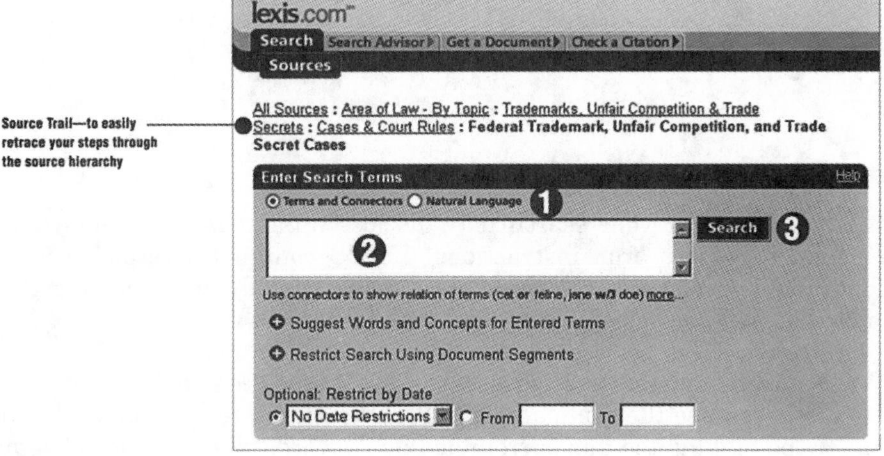

Figure 11-3
LEXIS Search Advisor

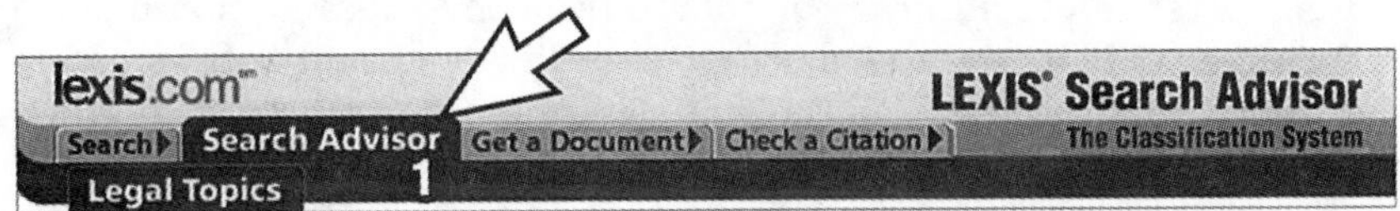

Starting a research project and not sure where to begin?

Search Advisor links treatise articles, law reviews, news, and case law materials within a specific area of law. The following example shows how to use LEXIS Search Advisor to research a summary judgment ruling in a trademark infringement case:

1. Click the *Search Advisor* tab to display a list of practice areas, such as Administrative Law, Bankruptcy Law, Trademark Law, etc.
2. Click *Trademark Law* to display a list of subtopics for trademark law. (See illustration.)
3. Click *Infringement.*
4. Click *Summary Judgment.*
5. Click into relevant treatises, law reviews or legal news on the topic of trademark infringement and summary judgment.

   OR

6. Type search terms in the open field to search on the topic of trademark infringement and summary judgment in case law.

To complete your search, type and select the appropriate information in the fields of the LEXIS Search Advisor template shown below.

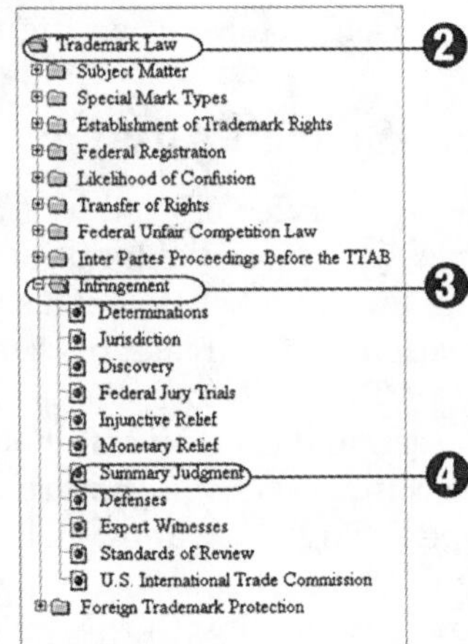

Trademark Sub-Topics (Step 2)

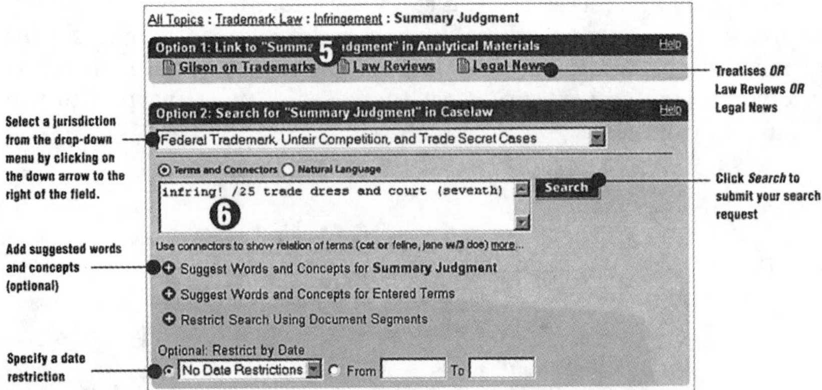

d. Display of Search Results

It is possible that your search may disclose numerous documents that respond to your search instructions. LEXIS contains several features that allow you to review these documents quickly to weed out the ones that will not be helpful to you.

- KWIC (type in ".KW" or select "KWIC" from the top of your screen). If you use the command "KWIC," the search terms you used will be highlighted and surrounded by 25 words on either side of your search terms. This feature allows you to review at a glance that portion of the document that displays your search terms and determine if the document should be bypassed or studied in greater detail.

- FULL (type in ".FU" or select "Full" from the top of your screen). The command "Full" instructs LEXIS to display the full text of the document containing your search terms.
- CITE (type in ".CI" or select "Cite" from the top of your screen). By selecting "Cite," LEXIS will display the citations to the documents or cases containing your search terms. Each document is assigned a number. To review any of these cases, type the number of the document and "transmit." You will then be shown the text of that case in KWIC format (that is, a 25-word band around your search terms).

(See Figure 11-4.)

Figure 11-4
Viewing LEXIS Results

Viewing Results

Cite—displays a bibliographic list of the citations in your answer set

KWIC™—displays 25 words of text around your search terms

Full—displays the full text of your document

Powerful Cite List

1. Case Summaries—for an overview of the procedual posture, legal issues, holding, and outcome of the case
2. Core Terms—for a snapshot view of the case
3. Show Hits—displays each sentence where your terms appear in the case
4. Tag Docs—quickly check the cases you want to print/download
5. *Shepard's*® Signals—click on the warning, caution, or positive treatment signal to *Shepardize* the case

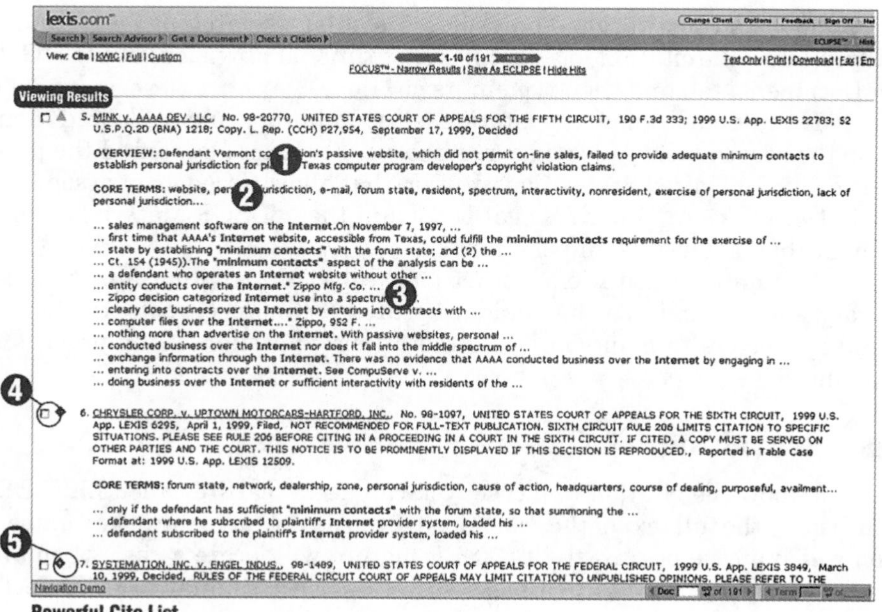

Powerful Cite List

e. Searching for Statutes

If you know the precise citation for a statute, you can find it readily by using and clicking the "Get a Document" tab at the top of your screen. Click on the "Citation" tab. Type in your citation (such as "35 uscs 101") in the open field. Select the open circle called "LEXSTAT." Click "Get." This feature allows you immediately to locate the statute you need without having to select a library and file.

After you have reviewed the particular statute in which you are interested, you can browse through preceding and consecutive sections to determine whether they are of any use to you. To browse, click on "Book Browse" at the top of your screen.

To locate statutes when you do not have a specific citation but know or believe the matter is covered by a statute (such as determining how many days a defendant in Ohio has to answer a complaint or locating federal statutes relating to sex discrimination), you must select a library or source and then construct a search combining descriptive words with root expanders and connectors. For example, to locate the Ohio statute, select or click on "States Legal-U.S." and then "State Statutes" then "Ohio." You might then enter "complaint and defendant /25 answer" to locate Ohio statutes containing the word "complaint" and "defendant" within 25 words of the word "answer."

To find the federal statutes relating to sex discrimination, select or click on "Federal Legal-U.S." and then "USCS Materials." You might then wish to enter "sex! and discriminat!" to locate statutes containing both these terms.

Once you have located a statute, you may browse through preceding or succeeding statutes by selecting "Book Browse."

f. Searching for Constitutions

Searching for constitutional provisions is similar to searching for statutes. If you know the citation to a specific constitutional provision, use the "Get a Document" tab and then type in its citation.

If you do not know the citation, select a library and a file and then use the search techniques discussed above. For example, to find the provision of the United States Constitution that allows freedom of assembly, select or click on "Federal Legal-U.S." and then "USCS Materials." You might then enter "fre! and assemb!"

For state constitutional provisions, select the appropriate state library and file and use the standard search techniques, root expanders, and connectors to help you locate the article or section of the provision you need.

g. Searching for Cases

If you know the citation to a case, you can use a feature called LEXSEE to display the full text of the case. Even if you do not have the page number on which a case begins, the LEXSEE feature will locate a case when all you have is a jump cite to a page within the case. Similar to LEXSTAT,

LEXSEE allows you to view the case without having to select a source. Simply sign onto LEXIS, click the "Get a Document" tab, click on the "Citation" tab, type in your citation (such as "420 US 104") in the open field, and select "LEXSEE." Click "Get."

If you know only the name of the case or even the name of one of the parties, search as follows: Click on the "Get a Document" tab, click on the "Party Name" tab, type in the party name(s) in the open fields, and select "Combined Courts—Federal and State Courts." Click "Search."

To locate cases when you do not have a citation, use LEXIS' "Search Advisor," discussed above. One of the advantages of using LEXIS over conventional research methods is the rapid access it affords to newly decided cases. Often cases are available online within hours after they are decided. Contrast this with the several weeks it usually takes to obtain advance sheets.

h. Shepardizing

As fully dicussed in Chapter 9, Shepardizing is easily accomplished on LEXIS. Use the "Check a Citation" tab at the top of your screen and enter the citation to be checked. Click "Check" at the bottom of the screen. Review your results, paying attention to the signal indicators (red for strong negative history, yellow for cautioning you of possible negative treatment, and so forth). Use "Custom Restrictions" to narrow your results, for example, to find out which Fifth Circuit or Iowa cases mention your case.

i. CheckCite 2000 and CiteRite II

CheckCite 2000, a new software program, now allows you to validate automatically all of the cases in an entire brief. The program "reads" your document and locates all case citations. Your citations are then Auto-Cited or Shepardized, depending upon your instructions. Results are printed in a report, which you can then review to determine the subsequent history and treatment of your cases. CheckCite thus instantly and automatically verifies the validity of all of your cases, saving you from the time-consuming task of inputting each citation separately. CheckCite can also verify the accuracy of quotations from cases, statutes, and law reviews.

Due to the ease of checking the validity of cases online, many law firms have ceased subscribing to the print versions of *Shepard's* and rely exclusively on computer-assisted cite-checking.

CiteRite II, a citation-checking software program provided by LEXIS, checks your citation format against that of the *Bluebook* or California citation form. You will be provided with parallel cites, informed of errors in punctuation (such as a failure to place a period after "Mich"), errors in underlining, and errors in the names of reporters.

j. Segment Searching

Segment searching on LEXIS allows you to find segments or parts of documents. LEXIS has divided documents into segments that reflect naturally occurring parts of the document. For example, you can search cases by names of the parties, the court deciding the case, the judge who wrote the opinion, or the date of the document. Similarly, you may wish to restrict your search to a specific time period, for example, cases after 1990.

When the "Enter Search Terms" template is displayed after you select a source, click on "+ Restrict Search Using Segments." A drop-down menu will allow you to select terms such as "dissent," "concur," or "court" to narrow your research. You can also use date restrictions to locate cases from a certain year or before or after a certain date. A drop-down menu is provided so you can select your desired time period.

These features allow you to isolate cases and retrieve only those from certain courts within specified time periods.

k. Law Reviews

LEXIS contains several libraries or sources of particular interest to researchers, particularly the libraries containing law review and journal articles. LEXIS includes the text of articles from more than 300 journals and law reviews. Use the "Get a Document" feature if you have a citation to an article. If you do not have an article citation, select "Search Advisor" and type in key words about the issue you are researching in the open field. Click "Find." Select the topic that looks like the closest match and select "Law Reviews" and review the sources given.

l. Administrative and Legislative Materials

The GENFED library contains files for C.F.R. and for the *Federal Register* since 1980. If you know the citation to a C.F.R. or *Federal Register* provision, select "Get a Document" and type in the citation. If you do not have a citation, select "Search" at the top of your screen, and then enter "genfed;cfr" (or "genfed;fedreg" for *Federal Register* materials) in the open field called "Look for a Source." Click "Short Names" and then "Find." In the search box presented, select "Terms and Connectors," type in your search terms, and then click "Search."

LEXIS includes public laws, *U.S. Statutes at Large*, transcripts of congressional hearings, conference reports, and the *Congressional Record*. If you have a citation, use ""Get a Document" to obtain the record you wish. If you do not have a citation, follow the steps discussed above for retrieving C.F.R. and *Federal Register* materials. LEXIS also provides bill-tracking reports to show the chronological history of a bill and includes some materials relating to state administrative law.

m. Other LEXIS Features

LEXIS includes a wide variety of other features to make researching easy and customizable, including the following:

- KWIC. Displays 25 words of text in a band around your search terms
- Full. Displays the full text of your document
- Core Terms. Provides a snapshot view of a case

- Case Summaries. Gives an overview of the procedural background, legal issues, holding, and result of a case
- Show Hits. Displays each sentence where your terms appear in a case
- FOCUS. Narrows your results and pinpoints words within your search results by allowing you to type in words in a FOCUS terms box
- More Like This. Allows you to find other cases or authorities similar to the one you have identified as central to your research efforts

n. Affiliated Services

LEXIS offers a variety of services that are complementary to LEXIS and that are frequently used by legal professionals.

NEXIS. The NEXIS library offers the full text of almost 700 general news, business, and financial publications. Select the "News" link under "Explore Sources" and then "Major Newspapers" and "Natural Language." Type in "Bill Gates" and you will be provided with hundreds of articles in which Mr. Gates is mentioned. You may wish to use a date restriction on some NEXIS searches so you are not overwhelmed with articles.

NAARS. The NAARS (National Automated Accounting Research System) provides access to annual reports for more than 4,200 publicly traded companies, thus allowing you instant information pertaining to a company's officers, directors, dividends, and so forth.

LEXIS Financial Information Service. This service offers information relating to the United States economy and the economy of numerous foreign countries, as well as corporate reports and SEC filings.

MEDIS Service. Of particular interest to attorneys in personal injury practice, the MEDIS service contains the full text of almost 100 medical journals, books, and articles.

ECLIPSE. The ECLIPSE (Electronic Clipping Service) feature allows you to follow the development of a topic automatically. The service automatically runs searches and provides updates to you.

FINDER. The FINDER library provides access to nearly 3,500 telephone directories so you can readily locate an individual or business.

INSOLV. The INSOLV library provides information on current bankruptcy petitions, dismissals, and discharges from most districts of the United States Bankruptcy Courts.

ALLVER. ALLVER is a verdicts and settlements file providing information on expert witnesses, verdict and settlement amounts, and jury polls.

MARHUB. The MARHUB library makes the *Martindale-Hubbell Law Directory* available online.

o. Delivering Documents

There are multiple options for the delivery of documents viewed on LEXIS. They can be printed, downloaded, e-mailed, or faxed to yourself or others.

See Figure 11-5 for quick review of LEXIS.

3. Westlaw

a. Introduction and Organization

Westlaw, West Group's computer-assisted legal research system, was introduced in 1975, slightly after LEXIS. Initially, Westlaw contained only headnotes and case synopses of cases rather than the full text of cases. Shortly after Westlaw was introduced, however, West began to include the full text of court decisions.

The information in Westlaw is contained in "databases" (analogous to LEXIS' "libraries" or "sources") and "files." Within each database there may be several files. For example, within the database called "Federal Materials" are files for federal cases and federal statutes.

Generally, to locate materials, either you can use the "Find a Document" feature when you know a citation, or you can construct a search by accessing an appropriate database and entering your search inquiry using Boolean connectors or natural language.

Figure 11-5
Quick Review of LEXIS

Getting Started

1. Turn on the computer.
2. Type in your LEXIS user number, indentification number, and password.
3. Type in the client or billing number.
4. If you know a citation to a case, statute, law review article, or federal regulation, select "Get a Document" at the top of your screen, enter the citation, click on LEXSEE (for cases, law reviews, and the *Federal Register*) or LEXSTAT (for statutes or C.F.R. provisions) and click "Get."
5. If you do not know a citation to a case, use "Search Advisor" to help you select topics. Type your search phrase in natural language and click "Search."
6. If you do not know a citation to a statute, use "Search," select either federal or state sources, and use terms and connectors to construct a search inquiry in the open field. Click on "Search."
7. Examine entries given. Shepardize all primary authorities. Sign off LEXIS.

You can access Westlaw either through the Internet at http://www.westlaw.com or by using WestMate, a software package provided by West that customizes your computer for Westlaw research.

b. Getting Started

When you sign on to Westlaw, the welcome screen will provide you with three choices:

- Find a Document. Enables you to find a document when you have its citation by typing the citation in a search box and clicking "Go"
- KeyCite a Citation. Allows you to enter a citation, click "Go," and update your citation for validity
- Search a Database. Allows you to enter a database identifier (such as ALLFEDS for all federal cases) and access that database for searching

If you do not know your database identifier, the "Welcome" screen has a button called "Westlaw Directory" for access to Westlaw's list of databases. (See Figure 11-6.)

If you are not on the "Welcome" page, locate the drop-down menu at the top of your screen, and select either "Find a Document" or "Type a Query" to begin your Westlaw research efforts.

c. Constructing a Search

To access information in Westlaw when you do not have a citation, you need to construct a search or, in West's terms, formulate a "query." As soon as you access a database by typing a specific database identifier (such as ALLFEDS or USCA), Westlaw will instruct you to enter your query. You may select to search either by "Terms & Connectors" or "Natural Language." The use of Terms & Connectors will be discussed first. Just as when you perform legal research with conventional sources, or when you are using LEXIS, think of words and phrases that describe the research

Figure 11-6
"Welcome to Westlaw" Screen

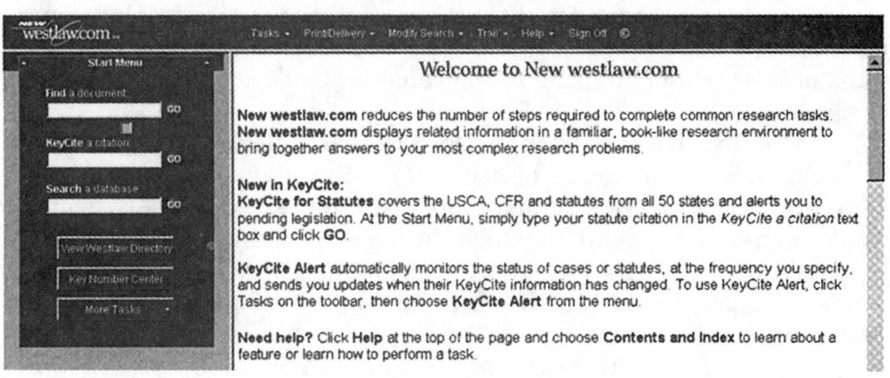

issue that will form the basis of your query. Similar to LEXIS, Westlaw automatically searches for plural words (boys) if you enter a regular singular word (boy), and if you enter a nonpossessive word (landlord) Westlaw automatically searches for the possessive forms (landlord's or landlords').

(1) Universal Symbols

Westlaw uses certain universal symbols to help you expand your query.

An *asterisk* (*) may be placed anywhere in a word and substitutes for a letter. For example, if you enter "franchis*r," Westlaw will retrieve "franchisor" and "franchiser."

An *exclamation point* (!) is used at the end of a word to retrieve all forms of a word. For example, "valu!" would retrieve value, valued, and valuation.

These symbols, sometimes called universal characters, are identical to those used for LEXIS.

(2) Connectors

Westlaw uses certain connectors to help you expand your query. The most common connectors are "or," "and," "/p," "/s," "/n," and "but not."

The *or* connector, represented by a single space, will help you search for alternative terms. Thus, the query "landlord lessor" will retrieve documents containing the terms "landlord" or "lessor."

The *and* (or "&") connector will retrieve documents containing two terms. Thus, the query "landlord and lessor" will retrieve documents containing both terms.

Westlaw features two grammatical connectors. The connector */p* requires search terms to appear in the same paragraph. Thus, a query for "landlord lessor/p evict!" will result in the retrieval of documents that contain either the word "landlord" or "lessor" within the same paragraph as the words "evict," "evicting," or "eviction." The connector */s* requires search terms to appear within the same sentence. For example, a query for "landlord lessor/s evict!" would retrieve documents in which the word "landlord" or "lessor" appear in the same sentence as "evict," "evicting," or "eviction."

The numerical connector */n* requires search terms to appear within a specific number of words of each other. You may select any number between 1 and 255. Thus, a query for "rescission /25 contract agreement" would retrieve documents in which the word "rescission" appears within 25 words of the terms "contract" or "agreement." When searching for words, Westlaw, unlike LEXIS, counts "stop words" such as "and," "to," "but," and "the."

You can exclude terms by using the "but not" connector ("%"). For example, a query such as "divorce dissol! % custody" instructs Westlaw to retrieve documents containing the words "divorce" or "dissolution" but to exclude such documents if they also contain the word "custody."

Once again, invest a bit of time in formulating your query. The time you spend in planning and constructing your query is time well spent because your aim is to retrieve documents quickly that are the most useful in helping you research your issue. (See Figure 11-7.)

Just as you can modify your search in LEXIS, you can edit your query in Westlaw. If you discover that your query resulted in too few documents or too many documents, you can click "Modify Search" on the toolbar and choose "Edit Query."

d. WIN

Since 1992 Westlaw has provided a legal research method called WIN (an acronym for "Westlaw Is Natural"). WIN allows you to enter your issue in plain English and eliminates the need for root expanders, connectors, or other such commands. Using WIN, you need only enter your question in plain English. For example, if the issue you are researching relates to the liability of a tobacco company for injuries caused by smoking, the typical Boolean search query might be as follows: "liab! negligen! /100 tobacco smok! /100 injur! death." With WIN, however, you could simply type the following: "Is a tobacco company liable for injuries or deaths caused by smoking?" While experienced searchers are comfortable constructing searches using root expanders and connectors and can easily construct a search, less experienced users may find WIN far less intimidating and awkward than Boolean searching. Similar to LEXIS' plain English searching through "Freestyle," this natural language search method greatly simplifies the search process.

Figure 11-7
Sample Westlaw Query Screen

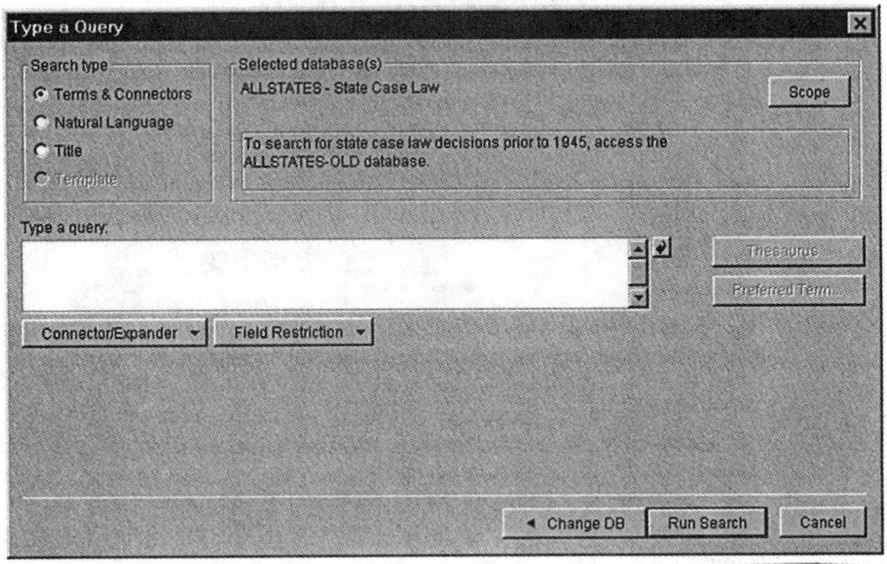

e. Display of Search Results

There are several methods to use to browse the documents you retrieve to determine if they are on point. On the left side of the screen, a list of citations to cases that respond to your query will be listed. Select as desired. The right side of the screen displays the full text of the cases selected. The terms in your query, such as "landlord" or "evict," will be displayed in bold type. To move to the next occurrence of your search terms, click the "Term" arrow on your screen. (See Figure 11-8.)

You can also search the document for a particular term, whether or not that term was part of your query. Thus, if your search results in 50 cases and you wish to see if any of the cases also contain the word "option," select "Locate" from the drop-down menu at the top of the screen and type in "option." Westlaw will then locate any of the cases that contain the word "option."

Cases displayed on the screen are presented in "full-text plus" format. That is, you will be given the full text of the case plus West's editorial feature such as a synopsis of the case, headnotes, and topic names and key numbers.

f. Searching for Statutes

There are two ways to locate statutes. If you know the citation, select the tab "Find a Document," type the citation in the "Enter a Citation" box, and click "Go." Thus, you could enter "35 usca s 105" to retrieve that statute.

If you do not know the citation to a statute, you will need to select a database. For federal statutes, select the database "USC" or "USCA." You will then need to formulate a query using descriptive words, universal characters, and connectors. For state statutes you can select a database

Figure 11-8
Viewing Westlaw Results

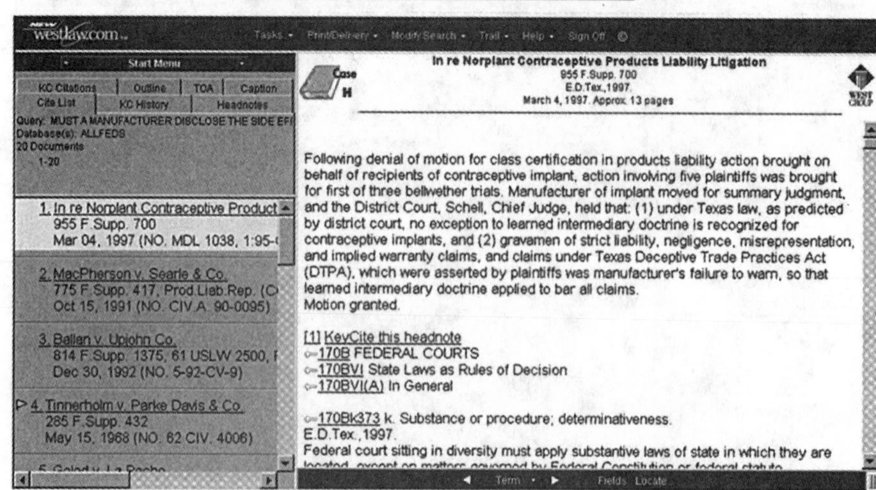

for all 50 states ("ST-ANN-ALL") or for an individual state such as New Jersey ("NJ-ST-ANN"). Once again, formulate a query by using descriptive terms, universal characters, and connectors. To retrieve library references or annotations relating to a statute, enter "RM" ("related materials"). You will then be able to view references to secondary sources discussing your statute or annotations to cases construing your statute.

g. Searching for Cases

There are two primary methods to locate cases through Westlaw. If you know the citation, select the "Find a Document" tab, enter your citation in the search box, and click "Go." If you do not know the citation to a case, select an appropriate database and then formulate a query using natural language descriptive words or universal characters and connectors. For federal cases, you may select specific databases ("SCT" for Supreme Court cases, "DCT" for district court cases), or select ALLFEDS, the database containing federal cases from the United States Supreme Court, United States courts of appeal, United States district courts, and other federal courts.

For state cases, you may select state-specific databases ("AZ-CS-ALL" for Arizona cases, "LA-CS-ALL" for Louisiana cases) or ALLSTATES, which will retrieve cases from all 50 states and the District of Columbia. You can also select one of West's regional reporters, such as the *North Eastern Reporter*. Because cases reported in West's National Reporter System are unofficial, Westlaw includes star paging to inform you of the page number you would be on if you were reading the case in an official report.

Like LEXIS, Westlaw offers rapid access to recently issued cases, enabling you to locate cases within hours after they are decided. Because these recent cases are not yet reported, they are in slip form and do not display the editorial fields of synopses, or topics or key numbers.

h. KeyCiting

The method of updating and validation of primary authorities offered by Westlaw is called "KeyCite." The service and process are fairly similar to Shepardizing on LEXIS, and is fully discussed in Chapter 9. In brief, sign on to Westlaw and select the "KeyCite a Citation" box on the left side of your screen. Type in your citation in the search box, click "Go," and view your results, noting the warning graphics (for example, red flags to indicate strong negative history and yellow flags to indicate caution).

i. WestCheck

Like LEXIS' CheckCite 2000, Westlaw's software program called WestCheck relieves you of the time-consuming and tedious task of inputting each citation in a brief or document to determine whether it is still valid. WestCheck automatically extracts citations from a document or table of authorities and checks the cites. The results of the cite-checking are sent to your choice of a stand-alone printer, attached printer, or computer. See Chapter 9 for additional information about WestCheck.

j. Field Searching/Restrictions

Like LEXIS, Westlaw allows you to retrieve documents by name or date. LEXIS refers to this as "segment searching," while Westlaw refers to this as "field searching" or "restrictions." You must select a database before you search for certain "fields" on Westlaw. For example, if you know that a federal case is titled *Anderson v. D'Antonio Co.*, select a database such as ALLFEDS and enter "ti" (for "title") followed by your search terms in parentheses: "ti (Anderson & D'Antonio)." This instructs Westlaw to search for all federal cases in which the names Anderson and D'Antonio appear in the title.

Using these fields or restrictions to limit your search allows you to search by court, date, judge, or attorney. When your search results are displayed on the screen, a "Restrictions" box is provided. Select and click on the restrictions you desire.

You can also limit your search by date so as to retrieve documents before or after a specific date. Thus, by entering "da" followed by a date you can obtain documents restricted by date. For example, if your query is "landlord tenant/20 default da (aft 1990)" Westlaw searches for cases decided after 1990 containing the words "landlord" or "tenant" within 20 words of the term "default."

k. Additional Databases

Westlaw contains several additional databases that are extremely useful in conducting legal research. These databases include the following:

American Law Reports. Westlaw includes A.L.R. annotations since 1965.

Texts and Periodicals. Westlaw includes selected articles from over 400 law reviews and bar journals. To access this database, enter "TP-ALL."

Index to Legal Periodicals. The Index to Legal Periodicals indexes more than 500 legal periodicals and is updated weekly. To access this database, enter "ILP."

Restatements of the Law. Westlaw includes all of the Restatements. To access the Restatements, type in "REST."

Legal Resource Index. The *Legal Resource Index* will refer you to more than 850 legal publications. To access this, enter "LRI."

Black's Law Dictionary. To determine the correct spelling of a legal word or phrase or to check the definition of a legal word, use *Black's Law Dictionary*, which can be accessed by entering "DI."

Jury Verdict and Settlement Summaries. Westlaw includes the jury verdict and settlement summaries collected by the American Association of Trial Lawyers of America since 1994 in its ATLA-JV database.

Legal Newspapers. Westlaw's legal newspapers database ("LEGALNP") provides access to a variety of legal newspapers, including *The National Law Journal, Chicago Lawyer,* and the *New York Law Journal.*

Texts and Treatises. Westlaw includes a wide variety of materials from various books and treatises. Punch in "TEXTS" to access this database.

Congressional Quarterly's Washington Alert. Enter "CQ-ALERT" to gain access to congressional and presidential actions.

Once you access any of these databases, select the button indicating you wish to use Natural Language (or Terms & Connectors, if you prefer). Type in your query in the search box and click "Go." You will then be directed to the appropriate Restatement, A.L.R. annotation, law review articles, and the like. In some instances (such as for A.L.R. annotations and law review and journal articles), you can search by author's name or title of an annotation or article.

l. Administrative and Legislative Materials

Like LEXIS, Westlaw offers a variety of administrative materials. You can access the *Federal Register* by entering "FR" or access C.F.R. by entering "CFR." If you know the citation to a C.F.R. regulation, you can use the feature "Find a Document" and enter the citation. For example, type "28 cfr 10102" or "38 cfr 2.20." For tracking pending federal regulations, use the database "US-REGTRK." If you do not have a citation to C.F.R. or the *Federal Register*, you will need to formulate a query using descriptive words, universal characters, and connectors. For example, to locate C.F.R. regulations relating to licensing requirements for airline pilots, you could formulate a query similar to the following:

airline pilots /50 licens! test! examin!

Westlaw would then search C.F.R. regulations that included the terms "airline" or "pilots" within 50 words of any form of the words "license," or "test," or "examination."

Westlaw also includes a variety of documents relating to legislative history. For example, Billcast ("BC") provides information on public bills introduced in the current session of the United States Congress. BILLCAST ARCHIVES ("BC-OLD") provides information on public bills introduced in previous sessions of the United States Congress. "BILLTRK" provides current data for tracking pending bills before Congress or any state legislature. The *Congressional Record* ("CR") since 1985 is also available. Moreover, legislative history for selected provisions of the United States Code since 1948 is available by accessing Legislative History ("LH").

The database "BILLS" will provide the full text of bills from all 50 states and summaries of pending bills from all states and the United States Congress. The database LEGIS-ALL provides state legislative information from all 50 states.

m. Affiliated Services

Westlaw offers a wide variety of other publications and services relating to business and economic issues as well as popular press articles and information of general interest to legal professionals. Among these specialized materials are the following:

DIALOG ("DIALOG"): DIALOG contains references, articles, tables, and data from numerous business, medical, scientific, and social fields, news releases, consumer reports, magazine articles, current addresses and information on companies with more than 20 employees, business profiles, and linkage information for 100,000 parent companies and affiliates, credit history for more than 2.5 million companies, SEC filings, and patent and trademark information.

Dow Jones Major Newspapers ("NPMJ"): This database provides access to more than 40 major newspapers from across the country.

Dow Jones News Service ("DJNS"): This service provides business and economic news, general news, the text of the *Wall Street Journal, Barrons,* and 1,500 other publications as well as stock market quotations.

Dun & Bradstreet Business Records PLUS ("DUNBR"): This service provides financial information on over 9 million businesses in the United States.

ExpertNet ("EXPNET"): ExpertNet provides biographical information on experts in the medical malpractice and personal injury field who are available to serve as consultants or expert witnesses.

WestClip: Westlaw's clipping service enables you to stay informed by monitoring topics, people, and companies of interest to you. Select "WestClip Directory" from the drop-down menu at the top of any screen.

n. Document Delivery

Westlaw allows you to print documents on a printer attached to your computer or to send them to a stand-alone printer or fax machine. The documents can also be downloaded for saving in your word processor or e-mailed to yourself or another. Click on the "Westlaw Print/Download" button to display options for document delivery.

o. Key Number Searching

You will recall from Chapter 5 that West has classified more than 400 areas of the law by topic name (liens, rescue, trespass), each of which is further subdivided by the use of key numbers. Westlaw has assigned a number to each topic name (for example, "liens" is 239, "rescue" is 337, and "trespass" is 386). By entering an appropriate query, you can retrieve all cases classified under certain topics, names, and key numbers.

From the Welcome page, click "Key Number Center." If you are not on the Welcome page, select "Key Number Center" from the Services menu. When you access the Key Number Center page, browse the list of topics given to find the topic of interest to you. When you select your topic, you will select a jurisdiction, formulate your query, and click "OK" to run the search. See Figure 11-9 for a quick review of Westlaw.

4. *Final Pointers on Computer-Assisted Legal Research*

a. When to Use LEXIS or Westlaw

Some tasks are best performed by using conventional legal research tools, for example, books, while others are best performed by using LEXIS or Westlaw. Still other tasks might call for you to use conventional tools together with a computer-assisted legal research service. Knowing which method to use requires an analysis of many factors, including the complexity of the task, the costs involved, and time constraints.

If you are called upon to provide an answer to a legal question and you know which statute or case to consult, it may be more efficient for you to simply grab the book containing the statute or case and quickly review it.

On the other hand, if you do not have access to all the books or publications you need and it would be time-consuming to travel to a larger law library to review certain materials, computer-assisted legal research will undoubtedly save you time and provide you access to publications a law firm could neither afford to purchase nor have room to shelve.

Both LEXIS and Westlaw are extremely current. They often provide access to materials within hours after their release or publication. More-

Figure 11-9
Quick Review of Westlaw

Getting Started

1. Turn on the computer.
2. Enter your Westlaw password.
3. Identify the client billing information and press ENTER.
4. At the Welcome page, select "Find a Document" (if you know a citation) and press "Go" to retreive the document. Select "Search a Database" if you do not know a citation. Enter the database identifier (such as "ALLSTATES" for cases from all states) and press "Go." When you access the database, select the particular tools or materials you wish to search and select "Query." In the query box, select to search by Terms & Connectors or Natural Language. Type in your query and select "Run Search." Review the materials presented and KeyCite all primary authorities.
5. Sign off by typing "off." After you sign off, you will be informed of the elapsed time you spent online.

over, the materials are available 24/7 and are never "off the shelves." Small firms may be the biggest beneficiaries of CALR, which provides immediate access to a wide array of materials that small firms and sole practitioners could not otherwise afford. Back issues of materials do not need to be retained or shelved, thereby freeing up valuable office space. Law firms can open up branch offices without investing in duplicate sets of books.

LEXIS and Westlaw enable you to rapidly locate cases that would take hours to find using conventional methods. For example, computer-assisted research allows you to quickly locate cases from the Eleventh Circuit decided between 1975 and 1990, authored by Judge Allen Little and dealing with trespass on federal property. Locating such cases using conventional techniques would be either impossible or so time-consuming as to be grossly inefficient.

Perhaps the best caution regarding computer-assisted legal research is that you should never simply sign on and begin working on formulating your search. Once you are "online," charges may be accruing, and time wasted in working on a query is a costly disservice to an employer or client. Therefore, before you sign on to LEXIS or Westlaw, spend some time getting familiar with your subject. Review C.J.S. or Am. Jur. 2d for background information on your topic and to familiarize yourself with the legal issues involved in your problem. Then take a piece of paper and write out your query. Have a "back-up" plan in mind in case your query does not yield the desired results so you can quickly modify or edit the query and try again. Select the smallest relevant database to eliminate irrelevant documents.

Do not spend valuable time reading the screen. Print your results or jot down citations and review them when you are no longer online. This is not only less costly but will be easier on your eyes, because a screen is never as easy to read as a printed page.

The more you use LEXIS or Westlaw, the more familiar you will become with their features, thus enabling you to research rapidly and effectively. If you find that your search is not providing results, go off-line and think through the steps you took, trying to decide on an alternative strategy.

Finally, do not become so wedded to either conventional research methods or computer-assisted legal research techniques that you will be unable to use an alternative method if you change jobs.

With practice, you can become extremely proficient at computerized legal research. Nevertheless, there are numerous tasks that can be performed as rapidly and more cost-effectively by using conventional techniques. Many researchers prefer to use books for most of a task and then switch to LEXIS or Westlaw to look for other perhaps less-known authorities, to verify the results of their searches, and to Shepardize or KeyCite their primary authorities.

To build confidence when you are first learning CALR, you may wish to re-research an issue to which you already know the answer. By going online, using Boolean terms or connectors, or plain English, and attempting to locate previously known cases, statutes, or other authorities, you will easily be able to verify that your CALR techniques are effective.

b. LEXIS or Westlaw

As you have seen, research strategies are substantially similar for LEXIS and Westlaw. The process of constructing a search or query either in Boolean terms or connectors or natural language is nearly identical, and both services allow you to browse documents, readily locate cases and statutes if you have a citation, Shepardize or KeyCite to validate your authorities, and print the results of your search.

Each service has some advantages over the other. LEXIS, as the owner of Matthew Bender & Co., offers a number of treatises, texts, form books, and practice sets. Westlaw offers A.L.R. annotations and its key number system. Both offer federal and state cases and statutes, administrative and legislative materials, selected law review articles, United States Attorney General Opinions, and numerous other publications and documents.

You may find that due to habit or convenience you prefer one service over the other. Researchers often develop a preference for the service on which they were trained or to which they were first introduced. Just as some people prefer U.S.C.A. over U.S.C.S., and vice versa, some people prefer LEXIS over Westlaw, while others feel equally strongly that Westlaw is preferable to LEXIS. Because both services contain substantially the same materials, it is impossible to declare that one service is superior to the other. The one that is "best" is the one that is best for you.

c. New Developments in LEXIS and Westlaw

LEXIS and Westlaw have both recently been making additional efforts to make their services affordable and attractive to sole practitioners and law firms, which often cannot afford the high costs usually associated with CALR. LEXIS has therefore launched "lexisONE" (http://www.lexisone.com), which offers free access to some of the materials available through the fee-based LEXIS service. Users can search federal and state statutes and recent federal and state cases. To access older cases or to Shepardize, the user must switch to LEXIS and pay a fee. A variety of other practice materials, such as forms, are also available. LEXIS hopes that once users become familiar with the new service they will wish to subscribe to LEXIS. West's competitive service is WestWorks, which offers forms, practice libraries, and other materials through the Web for a monthly per-attorney fee. Because much of the material offered by lexisONE and WestWorks is available for free on the Internet, experts are unsure as to the continued viability of these services.

The other new development offered by LEXIS and Westlaw is availability of some of their legal materials in wireless electronic formats accessible through personal digital assistants, such as Palm Pilots. Both LEXIS and Westlaw offer cases, statutes, and updating (through

Shepardizing or KeyCiting), thus allowing legal professionals on the run immediate access to some materials.

d. Limitations of Computer-Assisted Legal Research

There are some limitations to computer-assisted legal research. These can be briefly summarized as follows:

(1) Literalness

Computers are extremely literal, and if you instruct LEXIS or Westlaw to search for "attorney," it will do so, to the exclusion of "lawyer" or "counselor." This literal approach requires that you construct your search or query as carefully as possible so as to make the most effective use of the computers.

(2) Cost

There are so many pricing variations for LEXIS and Westlaw that it is impossible to summarize them. Special pricing schemes exist for both small firms (to encourage their access to materials they otherwise wouldn't have) and large firms (to obtain the high volume of business generated by a firm with hundreds of legal professionals). Flat rate or subscription pricing exists whereby a firm pays a flat annual or monthly rate for CALR services, allowing unlimited use of CALR materials and enabling firms to have fixed and predictable costs. Hourly pricing can range from $10 to $800 per hour, depending upon the files accessed and the time of day the service is used, with higher fees charged during peak hours.

Another variety of pricing is "transactional" pricing, whereby the user is assessed a per-search charge to work in a file without regard to online time (although flat fees are also assessed for certain adjunct services, for example, $5.00 for each LEXSEE or LEXSTAT search, and $2.50 printing charge per document. Both LEXIS and Westlaw usually assess a connection fee merely to connect to the system.

If your time is billed to the client at $50 per hour, the client may pay a total of approximately $250 per hour for each hour you are online ($50 for your time and $200 for the time online). This $250 equates to five hours of your time if you were engaged in conventional legal research. On the other hand, if you stumble around in the law library or spend valuable time traveling to a larger library, it may well be more cost-effective to research using LEXIS or Westlaw. As you gain experience and familiarity with LEXIS and Westlaw, you will be better able to gauge which technique works best for each particular research issue.

(3) Database Limitations

While the number of publications and documents in the LEXIS and Westlaw databases is truly staggering and while both LEXIS and Westlaw add to their databases every day, there are some limitations to computer-assisted legal research. For example, LEXIS and Westlaw both provide the text of the *Federal Register*, but only since 1980. Similarly, both provide access to the *Congressional Record*, but only since about 1985. While both provide cases from all states, coverage is similarly limited. For example, LEXIS and Westlaw provide cases from the Kansas Supreme Court since only about 1945. To determine the date limitations of publications and materials, consult the database lists published by LEXIS and Westlaw, which will clearly outline the scope and coverage of each database. Alternatively, when using LEXIS, select the Sources library, which will describe the coverage of certain LEXIS libraries. Alternatively, click on the blue dot with an "i" to find out more information about the source. When using Westlaw, use the SCOPE command, coupled with a database identifier to obtain a description of the coverage.

While these restrictions may not significantly hamper your research, you should not make the mistake of thinking either service is a perfect substitute for a large, well-equipped law library.

e. Asking for Help

Both LEXIS and Westlaw are extremely cooperative in training and assisting researchers. Both provide toll-free numbers, which you can call 24 hours a day to ask for help. To assist you in constructing searches and formulating queries, LEXIS publishes a worksheet to help you construct a search step by step. Similarly, West publishes "Query Planners," which serve the same function.

Both LEXIS and Westlaw provide tutorials complete with instructions and floppy disks to help you become proficient with their services.

Westlaw provides its own training database to help you learn the system. Once you sign on to Westlaw you can access the training program, WesTrain ("db wt"), without incurring database charges. When you press "db wt" you will be presented with a menu of training lessons to select such as "Forming Queries," "Field Searching & Special Searches," and KeyCiting. When you select a lesson, you will be given information on this topic and then asked a series of multiple choice questions to help verify your understanding of the lesson. West also offers tours of Westlaw and KeyCite at http://www.westlaw.com/tours.

Similarly, LEXIS offers several interactive training lessons to help you improve your techniques without incurring search or connect charges. The LEXIS training tools are as follows:

CAI (Computer-Assisted Instruction): This lesson provides interactive lessons in using connectors.

TUTOR: TUTOR assists you in reviewing general search strategies and allows you to select specific databases for practice purposes.

PRACT: This lesson allows you to practice your search skills.

Both LEXIS and Westlaw publish numerous materials and publications, including database lists, which fully describe and explain their services. You can obtain these materials by calling or writing Reed Elsevier or West.

Finally, both LEXIS and Westlaw offer training classes, including initial introductions to the systems, refresher courses, and advanced classes. The classes are usually free and are held at training centers or law firms. Call Reed Elsevier or West (at (800) 255-9334 or (800) 328-9352, respectively) to inquire about these training classes and to find out if they are offered in your locality. Often the attendees at the classes are offered the opportunity to conduct free research, and instructors are available to assist with research problems.

E. Other Competitors in Commercial Electronic Research

While LEXIS and Westlaw are the acknowledged giants in the field of computer-assisted electronic research, a number of other companies have begun offering access on a fee basis to legal materials through the Internet. Most charge moderate fees and appeal to small firms and sole practitioners. Among the newcomers are the following:

- VersusLaw (http://www.versuslaw.com). VersusLaw provides access to federal and state court opinions, statutes, and other legal materials for a low monthly fee of approximately $7 per attorney or user. Federal statutes, all federal cases, and cases from each state's higher courts are available.
- LoisLaw (http://www.pita.com). LoisLaw offers case law, statutes, constitutions, administrative law, and court rules for all states and the federal courts. Low monthly flat fees are charged.
- JuriSearch (http://www.jurisearch.com). JuriSearch specializes in California law but offers United States Supreme Court cases as well. Fees are moderate.
- American LegalNet (http://www.americanlegalnet.com). American LegalNet specializes in litigation-related forms and California law and provides its services for about $20 per month. All California court opinions since 1934 are available, as well as court rules, court forms, and other materials.

F. Dead-Tree Publishing

The publishing of legal materials in conventional print form has come to be referred to as "dead-tree" publishing. On occasion, experts ponder whether the new virtual libraries will ultimately replace conventional law libraries with their dead-tree collections. In brief, the more reasoned conclusion is that while the emerging information technologies, especially the Internet, provide excellent tools, they are unlikely to replace books. Consider the following:

- Several years ago, CD-ROMs were touted as the technological marvel that would replace the printed page. Now, most experts recognize their value as complementary sources to conventional printed materials. Many experts view CD-ROMs as interim products whose use is likely to decrease as Internet legal research becomes more familiar to legal professionals.
- Libraries are permanent archives of materials, while the Internet is a temporary host continually being updated, and even replaced, with earlier versions of information sometimes lost forever.
- Certain materials, especially articles, texts, and treatises, are copyrighted and are thus unlikely to appear on the Internet. Their copyright owners, the authors, cannot receive needed royalties if their works are disseminated globally with the touch of a keystroke.
- The Internet is often described as "information chaos," meaning that numerous and sometimes even thousands of "hits" appear in response to certain queries, forcing researchers to undertake the painstaking task of separating useful information from that which is irrelevant.
- While people often read hundreds of pages at a sitting, research shows that most people only read three screens of information before printing it out.

In sum, become familiar with the newly emerging technologies of CD-ROM, CALR, and the Internet. Clients are entitled to the most efficient and accurate research at the lowest cost. These new information technologies, however, should be used in addition to, not in place of, conventional research using print sources. Effective researchers will consider a client's needs carefully and then determine the best approach. If all you need is a copy of a statute, it is far easier and far less expensive to obtain it on the Internet rather than drive to a law library several miles away. On the other hand, if a problem is more complex, you will need to review a variety of sources using a variety of methods: conventional research, computer-assisted research, and the Internet. No one method is best. Combine the best features of each approach to best serve a client's needs.

G. Citation Form

Videotape:	Videotape: Shepardizing Made Easy (Shepard's/McGraw-Hill, Inc., 1994 (on file with Georgetown University Law Center).
LEXIS:	*Bailey v. Carpenter*, No. 93-1402, 1997, U.S. Dist. LEXIS 4098, at *4 (W.D. Tex. Feb. 14, 1997).

Westlaw: *Franklin v. Darling*, No. 97-176, 1997 WL 26197, at *1 (E.D. Va. Oct. 13, 1997).

In summary, computer-assisted legal research is a valuable tool. The computer-assisted research services such as LEXIS and Westlaw provide rapid access to a wide range of materials that no law firm could afford to purchase or shelve. Many tasks such as Shepardizing and KeyCiting are simplified on computer. Nevertheless, computer-assisted legal research may be expensive and will only produce useful results if you understand how to make the system work effectively for you. This takes practice and experience. Neither conventional research nor computer-assisted legal research should be used exclusively. Effective researchers will use a combination of the two methods and employ selectivity to decide which method will yield the best results for a given task.

Strategies and Tips for Using CALR

Use CALR when:

- You already have a citation to a known case or statute.
- You are looking for cases involving a known party, attorney, or judge.
- The area of law is new or evolving.
- You are researching a unique area of law or unique fact situation.
- You are looking for the most current information available.
- You are updating or verifying your primary authorities (such as by Shepardizing or KeyCiting).

Use books when:

- You are researching a complex area of law.
- You are researching statutes and wish to review the annotations that follow them.
- The search terms in your issue are so commonly used that numerous "hits" would be produced using CALR.

Tips for Efficient Use of CALR

- Construct your search or query before you sign on and start incurring costs.
- You need not memorize all of the commands and root expanders. A quick reference sheet is usually provided at each terminal.
- Do not waste time by reading long cases or law review articles on the screen. Such a practice causes strain to the eyes and the wallet. Either print the document or jot down its citation so you can locate it later.
- To save money, use a smaller file or database rather than a larger one. For example, if you are interested only in California cases, use the database just for California ("CA") rather than one for all 50 states ("ALLSTATES").
- Because CheckCite and WestCheck can check cites from a table of authorities, check the cites in an adversary's brief to ensure that the cases relied upon by the adversary are valid and have not been weakened.
- Use the clipping services to track information about clients and then send the clients articles that mention them. Clients are thrilled when their legal team expresses a personal interest in their business.

Technology Tips

http://www.westlaw.com	West's home page provides information about West products and services, including Westlaw
http://www.lexis.com	LEXIS' home page provides information about LEXIS-NEXIS

To obtain a case when you are away from your office and cannot access LEXIS or Westlaw, contact WestFax, a case retrieval service provided by West that is available through any touch-tone phone. Call 1-800-562-2329 and, following the prompts, punch in your cite, credit card number (or West account), and the number of the fax machine to which you would like the case sent. The case will soon be sent to the designated fax machine. KeyCiting of the case is included. The current cost is $7.00 per case and $1.50 per page.

WestDoc is a 24-hour-per-day Internet version of West's fax-back service. Register online or through a toll-free telephone call so charges can be assessed to a credit card. Then merely point your browser to http://www.westdoc.com, type in a case or statute cite, and Westlaw will display the case or statute for you. You can then download or print the case. The cost is $10.00 per document.

Writing Strategies

While computer-assisted legal research is somewhat mechanical, writing about the results you locate online is not. Because the reader of every project you write will be busy, and some readers may be highly critical, you need to produce a written project that is readable.

To enhance interest in your writing:

- Use the active voice because it is more forceful than the passive voice.

- Use lists and quotations to "break up" long narrative passages and add visual impact to your page.

- Use verbs ("conclude") rather than nominalizations ("drew a conclusion") to create interest.

- Use strong words ("unique" rather than "somewhat unusual").

- Use concrete words ("your lease") rather than vague terms ("your situation").

- Use placement to enhance interest by placing stronger arguments at the beginning and end of your project where they will have more impact.

- Use "graphics" such as high-quality paper, headings, and white space to capture the reader's interest.

Assignment for Chapter 11

PART I. LEXIS

1. Select the "Get a Document" button at the top of the screen and then select "Citation." Enter the citation 214 S.W.2d 353.
   a. What is the case name?
   b. Select "More Like This" and then "Search." What is the first statute you are directed to?
   c. Return to the case and select "Shepardize." What case cites your case?
   d. Retrieve the case that cites your case. Who delivered the opinion of the court?
2. Select "Get a Document" and then "Citation." Enter the citation Cal. Civil Code § 2332.
   a. What does this statute refer to?
   b. Are there any A.L.R. annotations relating to this statute?
   c. Retrieve the annotation. What is its title?
3. Select "Get a Document" and then "Party." Select for all state courts. Find a case in which a party's name is Catherine E. Plesich.
   a. What is the citation?
   b. What is the LEXIS citation?
   c. What was the appellee formerly known as?
   d. Select "Shepardize."
      (i) What is the most recent Colorado Court of Appeals case that mentions your case?
      (ii) Retrieve this case. For what particular point of law is your case mentioned?
4. Select "Check a Citation" and enter 308 Ky. 399. Select for "Full" Shepardizing.
   a. What is the case name?
   b. What is the most recent case to mention it?
5. Select "Check a Citation" and enter RCW 18.130.
   a. How many documents in total mention this statute?
   b. How many references are there for § 18.130.020?
6. Select "Get a Document" and then "Citation." Enter 12 C.F.R. § 550.10. What does this section relate to?
7. Select "Get a Document" and then "Docket Number." Select for all state courts. Enter the docket number 79493.
   a. What is the case name?
   b. Retrieve the case and give the Illinois Reports 2d citation.
   c. Shepardize the case. Is there any cautionary note? Explain.
   d. Give the citations to the denial of certiorari by the U.S. Supreme Court for this case.
8. Select "Get a Document" and then "Citation." Select for law reviews and enter 34 J. Marshall L. Rev. 407.
   a. What is the title of the article?
   b. Who are the authors of the article?
9. Select "Search Advisor" and then "Immigration Law," "Immigration Crimes," and then "Marriage Fraud." Select to review all federal im-

migration cases and agency decisions. In the search box, select "Natural Language" and enter "fraudulent marriage."
   a. What is the first case you are directed to?
   b. Retrieve the case. Who represented the petitioner?
10. Select "Search Advisor" and then "Legal Ethics" and "Unauthorized Practice of Law." Select to review only California ethics cases. In the search box, select "Natural Language" and use appropriate language to locate cases determining whether paralegals may give advice during divorce proceedings.
   a. What is the first case you are directed to?
   b. Retrieve the case. What year was it decided?
   c. Shepardize the case.
      (i) How many decisions cite your case?
      (ii) Give the citation to the most recent California Attorney General Opinion that mentions your case.
11. Select "Search" at the top of the screen and then select for all federal and state court cases. Using "Natural Language," locate authorities regarding whether smokers may sue tobacco companies for injury and death.
   a. What is the first case you are directed to?
   b. Retrieve this case. What is its "Outcome"?
   c. Shepardize this case.
      (i) How many citing references mention your case?
      (ii) What 2000 *American Journal of Law and Medicine* article cites your case?
      (iii) Retrieve the article. What is its length? Who is the author? What law school did the author attend?
12. Select "Get a Document" and then "Citation." Enter 18 U.S.C. § 101.
   a. What is the current cite for this statute?
   b. Select the first reference. What does this statute relate to?
   c. Review the "Interpretive Notes and Decisions" and select Note 18. What Fourth Circuit Court of Appeals case are you directed to?
13. Select "Search" at the top of the screen. In the search box, enter "dictionary" and then select "A Dictionary of Modern Legal Usage." In the search box, enter a query to determine the definition of "abandonee." What is the definition of "abandonee"?
14. Select "Search" at the top of the screen and then "Secondary Legal" and then "Combined ALR and Am. Jur. 2d." Select to use "Natural Language" and develop an appropriate query to determine information relating to abandonment of trademarks. Retrieve the Am. Jur. 2d reference you are sent to. What is an essential element of abandonment of a trademark?

PART II. WESTLAW

1. Select the "Welcome" button at the top of the screen and then select "Find this document by citation" and enter the citation, 603 N.E.2d 1.
   a. What is the case name?
   b. How many pages does this case have?

2. Select the "Directory" button at the top of the screen and then select "All state cases after 1944." Select "Search by title" and locate a case in which the name "Eugene Clyatt" appears.
   a. Give the case name and the citation.
   b. Who delivered the opinion of the court?
   c. KeyCite this case by selecting "C" at the top of the case name.
      (i) How many documents are shown that cite this case?
      (ii) Are there any A.L.R. annotations that cite this case relating to joint, split, or shared custody arrangements?
      (iii) Retrieve the A.L.R. annotation. How current is this volume of A.L.R.?
      (iv) Which particular section in the A.L.R. annotation mentions the *Clyatt* case?
3. Select the "Welcome" button at the top of the screen and then select "Find this document by citation" and enter the citation 178 Ill. 2d 215.
   a. What is the case name?
   b. Click on the "yellow flag" shown at the top of the case. Which case distinguishes this case? How many green stars are displayed?
4. Select "Key Search" from the top buttons. Then select "Trademarks" listed within the "Intellectual Property" section. Select "Generic Terms." Select "all federal cases" and then press "Search."
   a. Give the name and citation for the case provided.
   b. What terms within the opinion on the screen are highlighted in yellow bands?
5. Select "Directory" from the top buttons and then select "Jury Instructions" and "California Jury Instructions—Civil." In the "Terms & Connectors" box, type in the appropriate wording to locate California jury instructions that relate to fraud and deceit. Which instructions deal with fraud and deceit?
6. Select "Directory" from the top buttons and then select "KeyCite, ALR and Am. Jur." Select "ALR." Select the option for "Natural Language" and, using appropriate wording, locate an annotation dealing with statutory damages for copyright infringement.
   a. What A.L.R. annotation are you directed to?
   b. How many pages does the annotation have?
   c. Select the section relating to "bank forms" and review. What damages were recoverable to the copyright owner for infringement of its copyright?
7. Select "Directory" from the top buttons. Select "Law Reviews, Bar Journals & Legal Periodicals." Select "Journals & Law Reviews Combined." Select the option to search by using "Natural Language" and use appropriate wording to determine if adults may adopt other adults. Give the name and citation for the article you are sent to.
8. Select the "Welcome" button at the top of the screen and then select "Find this document by citation" and enter the citation to locate 11 U.S.C. § 101.
   a. What does this statute relate to?
   b. How many pages are given?
   c. What is the definition of "debt"?

9. Select the "Welcome" button at the top of the screen and then select "Search These Databases" and find the database for *Black's Law Dictionary*. Using *Black's Law Dictionary*, give the definition for the term "et uxor."
10. Select the "Welcome" button at the top of the screen and then select "Search These Databases" and type in "usca." Using the option for Natural Language, find the citation for the Taft-Hartley Act. What statute are you directed to?
11. Select the "Welcome" button at the top of the screen and then select "KeyCite this Citation" and type in 178 Ill. 2d 174.
    a. What is the parallel citation for this case?
    b. How many documents mention this case?
    c. Which case distinguishes this case? (Give case name only.)
12. Select "Welcome" from the top buttons and select "Search These Databases." Type in "California statutes" and then select "California Statutes Annotated." Using natural language, locate the statute of limitations for breach of contract actions for sales.
    a. What section are you directed to?
    b. What is the statute of limitations in California for breaches of sales contracts?
13. Select "Welcome" from the top screen and then select "Search These Databases" and type in "New York cases." Select "Search by Title" and locate a case in which the defendant's name is Sikorski.
    a. What is the citation?
    b. Give the date of the decision.
    c. What does this case relate to?
    d. The case cites N.Y. Veh. & Traffic § 511(3)(a)(ii). Retrieve this statute. What does § 511 (3)(a)(ii) relate to?
14. Select "Directory" from the top buttons and then select "Headnotes Databases." Select "Delaware Headnotes." In the "Terms & Connectors" box, enter the following words: corporate AND takeover.
    a. What Key Number deals with "management of corporate affairs in general"?
    b. Select this key number and press "Search." What Am. Jur. reference are you sent to?
    c. What A.L.R. annotation regarding hostile takeovers are you sent to? Retrieve this A.L.R. annotation.
        (i) Who wrote the annotation?
        (ii) What New Jersey case is cited in the annotation?
        (iii) Retrieve this New Jersey case. Locate the flag for the case and click on it. Examine the references you are sent to. What 1980 Northen District of New York case distinguished the New Jersey case?
15. Select "Welcome" from the top buttons and then select "Search These Databases." Enter usca in the search box. Select United States Supreme Court cases.
    a. What United States Supreme Court case discusses the Americans with Disabilities Act?
    b. What is the date of decision?

c. How many pages does Westlaw provide for this case?
d. Give the Westlaw citation for this case.
e. From which district court did this case arise?

16. Select the "Welcome" button at the top of the screen. Select "Search These Databases" and then select to search South Carolina statutes. Select "South Carolina Statutes Annotated." Using the Natural Language option, which South Carolina statute deals with a trustee's standard of care?
17. Select the "Welcome" button at the top of the screen and then type in 117 S. Ct. 1032 in the "Find this document by citation" box.
    a. What is the name of this case?
    b. How many pages does Westlaw provide?
    c. From which district court did this case arise?

Chapter
12

Legal Research Using the Internet

A. Introduction
B. Glossary of Terms
C. Conducting Legal Research Online
D. Strategies and Tips for Internet Legal Research
E. Ethical Concerns Regarding Use of the Internet
F. Surf's Up: The Best Internet Legal Research Sites
G. Cautionary Notes on Internet Legal Research
H. Citation Form

Chapter Overview

The best legal researchers know how to use a combination of conventional research methods with computerized and electronic research methods to achieve results. While one need not be a computer guru to satisfy one's duty to perform legal research competently, legal professionals should be sufficiently proficient in using the Internet that they can quickly find a case or statute. The Internet affords researchers the ability to find and review cases, statutes, and a vast array of other materials at no cost, 24 hours each day. Every year more and more materials are available on the Internet. While the Internet will never replace conventional research methods and while there are some significant drawbacks to Internet legal research, it is an extremely efficient and timesaving method for some research tasks.

Although this chapter provides a glossary of Internet-related terms, one need not be conversant with the jargon of computers to be an effective researcher. In fact, the most useful strategy in conducting Internet legal research is to have one good starting place and then use this to branch out to other sites of interest.

This chapter provides a glossary of Internet terms, tips and strategies on conducting legal research on the Internet, and some cautionary notes about over-relying on the Internet. The chapter also provides the "best of the best" sites for various legal research tasks as well as some sites for non-legal research.

A. Introduction

Today's legal professionals have at their fingertips vast amounts of information that is free and available 24 hours each day. Until just recently, a researcher wanting to review a newly issued Supreme Court decision had only two options: drive to a law library or subscribe to a costly computerized legal research service such as LEXIS or Westlaw. The advent of the Internet has dramatically changed legal research, allowing professionals immediate access to cases, statutes, federal regulations, forms, legislative materials, treaties, journal articles, and much more. In some instances, cases are posted to the Internet within hours after their release by the clerk of the court. While the good news is that there is a vast array of legal materials available for your use, the bad news is that the information is so voluminous that making sense of the materials offered can be difficult and confusing.

The Internet was originally developed in the 1970s for military and government use, primarily to provide a secure method of communication in the event of nuclear attack. Use then expanded to the scientific and educational communities and, starting in the late 1980s, people began realizing the Internet's potential for enhancing communication. Use rapidly spread to the commercial sector, which quickly worked to develop the Internet's ability to promote the sale of goods and services. The Internet is now used in nearly every possible field of endeavor, from the military, to the government, to educational institutions, to not-for-profit organizations, to commercial enterprises. Nearly every business, including nearly all large law firms, has a presence on the Internet.

Legal professionals typically use the Internet for the following purposes:

- Communication. Legal professionals use the Internet to communicate with each other and with clients. Through electronic mail ("e-mail"), clients can be kept informed of the progress of their cases. Legal professionals can become involved in "listservs" to keep apprised of topics of interest to them and to continue their legal education. In many instances listservs or newsgroups will automatically e-mail newsletters or bulletins to subscribers, enabling legal professionals to keep current in their fields of interest.
- Marketing. Most law firms have a Web site, which is a marketing brochure about the firm that is published electronically rather than in print form. The site will typically describe the firm, its professionals, areas of expertise, and locations, and may provide articles or newsletters on legal topics. State bar codes regulate

advertising. Thus, firms need to ensure their Web sites are in compliance with those regulations.
- Commerce. Legal professionals can order books, publications, and other materials from publishers and other vendors.
- Research. Legal professionals can use the Internet to conduct research, including legal research. One can determine an adversary's address, a client's exact corporate name, when a company's stock "went public" and who its officers and directors are, and a variety of other research tasks. The Internet can also be used for legal research, including finding cases, statutes, regulations, locating forms, reviewing legal journals and periodicals, and locating legislative documents. This chapter will focus on the use of the Internet to conduct legal research.

Although legal research on the Internet can seem awkward and intimidating to the novice, all legal professionals should strive for some degree of familiarity with Internet legal research. The general duty imposed on legal professionals to have a sufficient level of competence to represent their clients is broad enough to require competence in new and emerging technologies, including the Internet. According to at least one case, a lawyer must "discover those additional rules of law which, although not commonly known, may be readily found by standard research techniques." *Baird v. Pace*, 752 P.2d 507 (Ariz. 1987). Using the Internet will soon be viewed as a standard or common method of conducting research. Moreover, employers and clients are increasingly technologically proficient and will justifiably expect their legal team to be equally proficient, so that clients can be kept apprised of the status of their matters by e-mail, relevant cases can be sent electronically to co-counsel, and others in the firm can be provided immediate access to files and records pertaining to a client's case.

Not only is there a nearly overwhelming amount of information available on the Internet, the technology surrounding Internet legal research continues to develop rapidly. For example, access to certain West materials is now available through wireless communications devices, such as Palm devices, allowing users to retrieve a wide variety of legal materials such as cases and then to KeyCite them to check their continued validity. Similarly, LEXIS offers access to cases, statutes, and Shepardizing through personal digital assistants. In order to best serve their clients, legal professionals need to be conversant with all methods of research, from conventional print materials, to microforms, to CD-ROMs, to computerized legal research systems, to the Internet.

There is, of course, some danger in relying too much on the Internet, primarily because not all legal materials are available online. Nevertheless, learning good Internet research techniques will save you a great deal of time. In most instances, Internet legal research should complement your other research techniques—namely, conventional book research and research using LEXIS and Westlaw.

Finally, be aware that there is an astounding amount of non-legal information on the Internet. Use the Internet as a tool to track clients' stock prices, determine the weather at the client's headquarters, and obtain basic information about clients' industries. Read the press releases issued by clients. Clients will be pleased and flattered that you took the time and effort to do some homework about their business, location, and financial status.

B. Glossary of Terms

Many otherwise confident professionals are intimidated by the Internet, in many cases because terms commonly used when discussing the Internet, such as "browser," "URL," and "hyperlink," are entirely new to them. While this section of the chapter provides you with some basic Internet terms, practically speaking, there is little need to know a great deal about how the Internet works or how specific terms are defined. Most of us have no idea how our cell phones and microwave ovens work and yet are entirely comfortable using these appliances. The Internet should be viewed the same way: It is nice to know some of the terms commonly used, but it is not totally necessary in order to be able to conduct legal research competently.

Following are some of the terms frequently encountered in the electronic world:

Browser: Software that helps access and review information on the Internet and translates HTML-encoded files into text and images that one can read and view. Netscape and Microsoft Explorer are examples of browsers.

Chat room: A location in cyberspace fostering real-time communications among several people.

Cyberspace: The electronic or computer world in which vast amounts of information are available; sometimes used as a synonym for the Internet.

Domain name: The name that identifies an Internet site, such as "www.ibm.com." Domain names have two parts: the "generic top-level domain," which is the last part of the domain, such as "com," or "gov," and which usually refers to the type of provider of the information, and the "secondary domain," which is more specific and is to the right of "www," such as "ibm" in the above example.

Download: Transferring files or information from the Internet to your personal computer files.

E-mail: Electronic mail or messages sent through the computer rather than in physical form (which is often called "snail mail").

Extranet: An internal company or law firm Intranet that provides access to selected outsiders on a case-by-case basis.

FAQ: "Frequently asked questions," often included on Web sites and that respond to the most commonly asked questions about the site or about the information provided by the site.

FTP: File transfer protocol, a common method of moving files or communicating between two Internet sites.

Home page: The first or main page you are sent to when accessing a person's or business's Web site.

HTML: Hypertext markup language, a standard language of computer code.

HTTP: Hypertext transfer protocol, a common method of moving files or communicating between two Internet sites.

Hyperlink: A method of instantaneous transport to another destination. Hyperlinks are often underscored or appear in different color on the computer screen; by clicking the colored line, you will be immediately transferred to that particular site or page.

Internet: A collection of worldwide interconnected computer networks originally developed for defense purposes and linked together to exchange information; the Internet is not owned by any one person or company.

Internet Service Provider (ISP): A company that provides Internet access, such as America Online or Roadrunner, for a monthly fee.

Intranet: A private network inside a company or law firm that provides access only for internal use to those in the company or firm and not to outsiders; for example, a law firm's intranet could be used only by those in the firm and could not be accessed by any member of the general public.

Link: See "Hyperlink."

Listserv: A system that allows groups of people to e-mail each other and participate in group discussions, usually about a topic of common concern. For example, a listserv comprising law students may automatically send one message to all others in the group; sometimes called a "newsgroup."

Log-in: (n.) An account name used to gain entry to a computer system. Unlike a password, it is not secret. Also called a "user name"; log in: (v.) the method of accessing a computer system.

Modem: A device that connects to your computer and to a telephone line allowing the computer to communicate with other computers much the way telephones allow humans to communicate with each other.

Netiquette: The code of etiquette or conduct for the Internet.

Network: The connecting of two or more computers so that they can communicate with each other and share resources and information.

Online: The process of being connected to the Internet through electronic communication.

Password: The secret code used to gain access to a computer system.

PDF: Portable document format, a format that duplicates on a computer screen what a conventional print source looks like.

Posting: Entering information or messages into a network—for example, cases are "posted" to the Web site of the United States Supreme Court, and legal professionals "post" messages on a listserv.

Search box: An initially blank box on a computer screen in which you type or key in the word or terms you are interested in researching.

Search engine: A particular service that helps one locate useful information on the Internet, usually through the use of keywords; common search engines are "Yahoo," "Google," "Lycos," and "AltaVista." A search engine is a Web site that looks for and retrieves other Web sites. Search engines look for words in the millions of Web pages on the Internet and direct you to pages that include the search words or keywords you enter in a search box.

Server: A computer or software package that provides or serves information to other computers.

Spamming: Sending blanket unsolicited messages to others; similar to "junk mail."

Surfing the 'Net: The process of moving or linking from one site to another in the course of reviewing information.

URL: Uniform resource locator, one's address on the Internet. Most Internet addresses begin with "www" or "http://www." The URL of IBM is "www.ibm.com."

User name: See log-in (n).

WWW: World Wide Web, commonly used to refer to the entire collection of resources that can be accessed in cyberspace through the Internet.

Web: See "WWW."

Web page: A particular file or "page" included in a Web site.

Web site: A collection of Web pages; for example, IBM's Web site (www.ibm.com) will consist of numerous Web pages, each of which is devoted to a specific topic. A Web site always begins with a "home page," which is the first screen viewed when the Web site is accessed.

C. Conducting Legal Research Online

1. *Getting Started*

Following are the steps in accessing the Internet so you can begin conducting legal research. In brief, you will be using your modem and telephone line to connect to the server of your Internet service provider. When the communication between your computer and the Internet has been established, you will type in a request or click a link, and your browser will send a request for information to the server. The server will send the information to you, and you will view it in your browser. You will "surf the 'Net" by clicking on hyperlinks and jumping to other sites of interest. You may download files or information for later viewing or printing.

- Turn on your computer and proceed to log in, using your log-in identification (sometimes called your "user name") and your password.
- Look for the icon that identifies your Internet service provider, such as AOL.
- Double click on the icon.
- Enter any identifying log-ins or passwords to access your account.
- Type in the word or term you are researching in the search box (if you are in a general search engine such as http://www.yahoo.com). Alternatively, in the address "box" at the top of the page, type in your favorite starting page, such as http://www.ll.georgetown.edu; http://www.washlaw.edu; or http://www.findlaw.com. Use this page as your jumping-off point and begin double clicking on the links that interest you. (See Figure 12-1.)
- Note that while most Internet addresses begin with "http://www" you may not need to type in the initial "http" information. Some browsers are configured to recognize "www" by itself. Similarly, in most instances the Internet is not "case-sensitive," meaning that you can often type in either upper- or lower-case letters and they will be recognized and read.

2. *Using a Good Start Page*

There is probably no better tip for conducting legal research on the Internet than to always begin your project with one good "start page." Your start page should be reliable and easy to use. It should be formatted in a user-friendly manner so that you can easily read the print on the screen and locate the information you need without confusing graphics, pictures, and distracting scrolling announcements or advertisements. The advantage of always beginning at the same place or start page is that you will quickly become comfortable and familiar with the page and it will serve as an excellent jumping-off place for your research tasks.

While there are many start pages from which you can begin your research, following are some well-known legal favorites:

- http://www.ll.georgetown.edu. This Web site for the Georgetown Law Center will direct you to cases, statutes, journals, and numerous other legal materials. The site has a pleasing appearance and is easy to use, and because it is the site of an educational institution rather than that of a commercial enterprise, it is highly credible. (See Figure 12-2 for a reproduction of the home page for http://www.ll.georgetown.edu.)
- http://www.washlaw.edu. This site of Washburn University School of Law lists legal materials, courts, and states in alphabetical order, making it very easy to locate material of interest. Once again, because it is a site offered by an educational institution, it is highly regarded. Its appearance is plain, nearly stark, without any distracting graphics. (See Figure 12-3.)

Figure 12-1
Home Page for FindLaw

Legal News

Legal Professionals

Students

The Public

Business

MY
MY FindLaw

FREE Official California Case Law! 1934 - Present

LegalEd

FindLaw Career Classifieds
Find Your Dream Job/Employee Today!

search | FindLaw

Channels: Legal Professionals - Students - Business - The Public - News - MYFindLaw
Email@Justice.com - Toolbar - CLE Program Guide - LawCrawler - Library - Supreme Ct Center - FindLaw Australia

Lawyer Search powered by West Legal Directory Name Search | International | Corporate | Advanced
City or ZIP | Select a State | Select a Practice Area | Find Lawyers!

Legal Professionals

Channel Home Page

Legal Subjects
Constitutional, Intel. Prop., Labor ...

Laws: Cases & Codes
US Sup Ct, US Code, Constitution, States ...

Links to Primary Authorities

West LegalEdcenter
FindLaw Online CLE, Elim. Bias, Ethics ...

US Federal Resources
Executive, Legislative, Judicial ...

Legal Careers
For Employers, For Candidates, Salaries ...

US State Resources
California, New York, Texas ...

Consultants & Experts
Investigators, Practice Support ...

Foreign & International
Countries, Int'l Law, Int'l Trade ...

Software & Technology
Case Management, Time Billing ...

Forms
Court, Tax, Sample Contracts ...

Lawyer Marketing
Advertising, Consultants, Strategies ...

Reference Resources
Library, Dictionary, Directories ...

Law Office & Practice
MY FindLaw, Free E-mail, Firm Web Sites ...

Legal Organizations
Nat'l Bars, State Bars, Local Bars ...

Students

Channel Home Page

Law Schools
Law Schools A-Z, Paralegals, Rankings ...

Outlines & Exams
Const. Law, Civil Procedure, Property ...

Law Reviews
General, International, Technology ...

Course Pages
Constitutional Law, Ethics, Evidence ...

Law Student Resources
Study Skills, Publications, Discussion Group ...

Employment
Firm Salaries, Alt. Careers, Insider's Guide ...

Pre-Law Resources
Financing, Preparation, Forums ...

The Bar
Prep-Courses, Bar Results, Bar Exams ...

Business

Channel Home Page

Business Formation
Business Plans, Legal Structure ...

Human Resources
Compensation, Hiring, Firing ...

Legal
Lawsuits, Contracts, Environmental ...

Tech Deals & Contracts
Exec. Compensation, IP Licenses, Acquisitions ...

Finance
Bankruptcy, Funding, Taxes ...

Silicon Valley Center
Finance, Human Resources, Management ...

Intellectual Property
Copyright, Patent, Trademark ...

Lawyers
Lawyer Directory...

Public

Channel Home Page

Housing
Landlord-Tenant, Buying, Selling ...

Family
Adoption, Divorce, Marriage ...

Auto
Accidents, Buying, Repairs ...

Money
Credit, Bankruptcy, Taxes, Wills ...

Personal Injury
Med Malpractice, Negligence, Products ...

Work
Pensions, Termination ...

Crime
Drunk Driving, Identity Theft ...

Immigration
Green Card, H1B, Student, Travel ...

Government and Politics
Issues and Legislation, Write to Congress ...

Lawyers
Lawyer Directory...

Legal Market Center

Experts & Consultants
Legal Investigators
Court Reporters
Process Servers
Practice Support
Software
Hardware & Technology

TODAY IN WRIT

Gary Condit and the Fifth Amendment

Why He Cannot Invoke It and How It Can Be Used Against Him

by JULIE HILDEN

AND "Do Unto Others Before They Sue Onto You:" Religious Discrimination In The Work Place by Sean Carter

MY FindLaw

Email :
Password:
Keep me logged in until I sign out.
Sign In
Forgot Your Password ? click here!
New User? Click Here!

Legal News

- Napster Hearings (MP3)
- Legal Commentary
- Legal TV Reviews
- Sports Legal News

more news...

FindLaw Newsletters

- **Legal Grounds** Daily legal news.
- **US Supreme Court** Case summaries.

Enter Email | sign-up

more newsletters...

Community Boards

- Greedy Associates
- Divorce
- Employment Law
- Immigration Law
- Copyright Law
- Cyberspace Law
- Personal Injury

more boards...

Figure 12-2
Home Page for Georgetown University Law Library

Electronic Collections
- Quick List: Web Databases
- Annotated List of Web Databases
- Subject Guide to Web Databases
- List of CD-ROM Databases
- Access from Off-Campus

Periodicals Research
- Quick List: Journal Indexes & Full Text
- Guide to Legal Journals
- Guide to General Periodicals

Law Related Web Sites
- Federal
- State, Local & Territorial
- Legal Topics, A - Z
- Foreign
- International

Tools for Legal Scholars
- Resources for First-Year Students
- Resources for Research Assistants
- Resources for Cite Checkers
- Archives, Manuscripts and Rare Books NEW
- The Library Catalog (About GULLiver)
- LEXIS-NEXIS Loislaw Westlaw
- Reference Tools
- Legal News
- Legal Organizations and Discussion Groups
- Major Legal Gateways
- Other Libraries' Home Pages
- SEARCH THE WEB

Beyond the Law Library
- Community Intranet
- Law Center Home Page
- Georgetown U. Home Page
- Washington Area Information
- Multicultural Resources
- Travel Information
- General News

| Comments | Statement of Purpose |

The Law Library

Subscription Databases

GULLiver Catalog

Research

- Reference Service
- Interlibrary Loan
- Library Collections
- Research Guides

Information

- Access
- Hours
- Job Opportunities
- Library Classes
- Library Guide
- Public Patrons
- Resident Program
- Staff & Departments
- Tour

- FAQs

Address:
111 G Street, NW
Wash, DC 20001
(202) 662-9160

MAP DIRECTIONS

Figure 12-3
Home Page for Washburn University School of Law

WashLaw WEB

Add your site | Terms & Conditions | Law Application Info | Law School Services | Check your email
Law Library | Library Catalog | Search this site | Send comments

1st Circuit	2nd Circuit	3rd Circuit
4th Circuit	5th Circuit	6th Circuit
7th Circuit	8th Circuit	9th Circuit
10th Circuit	11th Circuit	Aallnet
Alabama	Alaska	All States Information
Arizona	Arkansas	Archives
Area Codes (Domestic)	Area Codes (International)	Bankruptcy
Bar Associations	Bar Exams	Books
Business Directory	CALI	California
City Codes	Colorado	Commercial Sites
Connecticut	Course Materials	Court Current Awareness
Court Rules	Courts	CLE
D.C. Circuit	Delaware	District of Columbia
Directories	Discussion Groups	Documents
Download/FTP	E-Mail Directories	Executive Law
Experts/Consultants	Federal Agencies	Federal Circuit
Federal Caselaw	Federal Legislation	Federal Statutes
Federal Documents	Florida	Foreign Law
Freenet	Full-Text Searches	Georgia
Government	Government Directories	Graduate School
Hawaii	Historic Documents	Humor
Hytelnet	Idaho	Illinois
Indexes	Indiana	International Law
Investigators	Iowa	Judges
Kansas	Kansas Bankruptcy	Kansas Decisions
Kentucky	Law	Law Firms
Law Jobs	Law Journals	Law Library Catalogs
Law Listservs	Law School Labs	Law Professors
Law Schools	Law Search Engines	Law Students
Legal Books	Legal Dictionaries	Legal Forms
Legal Humor	Legal Indexes	Legal Institutes
Legal News	Legal Newsletters	Legal Newspapers
Legal Organizations	Legal Software	Legal Vendors
Lexis/Nexis Service	Listserv Instructions	Listserv Owners
Listservs	Local Law	London Law Studies

Figure 12-3 (*Continued*)

Louisiana	Magazines	Maine
Maps	Maryland	Massachusetts
Michigan	Minnesota	Mississippi
Missouri	Montana	Nebraska
Nevada	New Hampshire	New Jersey
New Law Books	New Mexico	New York
News	Newsgroups	Newspapers
North Carolina	North Dakota	Ohio
Oklahoma	Oregon	Other Law Sites
Pennsylvania	Police	Phone Numbers
Politics	Post-Graduate	Prelaw Students
Publishers	Radio	Reference-Legal
Request Service	Research Guides	Research and Writing
Rhode Island	Rules of Court	Search Law Full-Text
Search Internet	Search State Law Full-Text	South Carolina
South Dakota	State Admin. Law	State Caselaw
State, Court, County	State Legislation	State Statutes
Stock Market	Street Maps	Study Law
Subject Index	Subscriber Instructions	Table of Contents
Television	Tennessee	Texas
Topeka	Topical Index	Travel
U.S. Court of Appeals	Uniform Laws	United States Supreme Court
Usenet News	User Guides	Utah
Vermont	Video Conferencing	Virginia
Washburn Law Catalog	Washburn Law School	Washburn Law Library
Washburn Law - London	Washington	West Virginia
Westlaw Service	Wisconsin	Weather Reports
Wyoming	Zipcodes	

Contacts:

Mark Folmsbee, Managing Editor, zzfolm@washburn.edu

Joe Hewitt, Technical Editor, zzhewitt@washburn.edu

- http://www.findlaw.com. This site, offered by FindLaw, a commercial enterprise, is one of the best known legal sites that directs users to a vast array of legal materials, including cases, statutes, forms, reference materials, and legal periodicals. Links to hundreds of sources of interest to legal professionals are provided, including links to each state's bar association, special links for law students, links to help locate attorneys, experts, and consultants, and numerous other links to legal resources. Although FindLaw is a commercial site, it is highly reliable and easy to use. FindLaw is a specialized legal search engine. You can type in a term in which you are interested in a search box and you will be led to sites that display or use that term. In early 2001, West signed an agreement to purchase FindLaw. (See Figure 12-1.)

Once you choose a "start page" that you are comfortable with, begin your research task with this page and progress from there. After some time, you may encounter other sites that are of more use to you. If you are a beginner in Internet legal research, however, this method of beginning any Internet legal research task with your "one good start page" is the best way to gain expertise on the Internet.

D. Strategies and Tips for Internet Legal Research

It is far easier to get distracted when researching on the Internet than when researching using conventional print volumes. A site piques your interest so you click on it. When you access that site, another site looks promising and you click on it. When you access that site, yet another intriguing link appears. Before you know it, you are no longer researching search and seizure articles but have begun reviewing stock quotes, checking the weather in Seattle, or perusing movie reviews. The vast amount of information on the Internet is a constant source of diversion and distraction. Staying focused is a continuing campaign.

Understand that when you enter a term in a search box—for example, "patent infringement"—and a list of relevant sites is given, the sites are usually listed in order, specifically, in order of how many times your term, "patent infringement," appears on the site, even in coded or hidden form. Thus, the first site identified is not necessarily the best; it is merely the one that uses or displays the term "patent infringement" most often. Because terms can be hidden in Web sites, you may be directed to a site that offers little or no substantive information about patent infringement. In some instances, you are directed to law firm Web sites and you must wade through marketing material before you can locate substantive material on patent infringement.

Why use the Internet rather than LEXIS or Westlaw? While search strategies using LEXIS and Westlaw are generally more focused and produce more targeted results, LEXIS and Westlaw are fee-based services, while the Internet offers free legal research 24/7. LEXIS and Westlaw, however, have far more complete databases. For example, state court cases are available on the Internet only for the past few years, while LEXIS and Westlaw offer access to nearly all state court cases. Moreover, there is no way to check the validity of a case you locate on the Internet, while LEXIS offers Shepardizing and Westlaw offers KeyCiting to determine whether your case is still "good law."

Following are some tips and strategies to help ensure that your Internet research is as efficient and effective as possible:

1. Take notes. Rather than jumping or linking from site to site, jot down the sites that appear promising. You can access other sites after you have come to a dead end in your present research efforts. Moreover, it is possible that you will get disconnected from the Internet. If you have jotted down sites of interest, you will be able to locate them later.
2. Use the history lists. When you research, you will use links to jump from site to site. To return to the immediately previous site, select the "back" arrow at the top of your toolbar. By continually selecting the "back" and "forward" arrows, you can move through the sites you have visited. Alternatively, you can review the sites you have visited by clicking on the "history" button or on the down arrow at the top of your page that displays the URL of the site you are currently visiting. A drop-down menu will be displayed that identifies the most recent sites you have visited. Select the site in which you are interested and you will be transported there.
3. Use bookmarks. When you determine that there are certain sites you continually visit or that provide you with useful information, "bookmark" them so you can readily return to them. When you are at the Web site of interest, select "Favorites" from the top of your toolbar. This site will be bookmarked as your personal favorite. Once you add a bookmark, the page name appears whenever you click the "Favorites" or "bookmark" icon.
4. Do not spend too much time reading the screen. Reading material on a computer screen is very tiring and causes eyestrain. If a long article or case appears promising, print it and read it in hard copy form.
5. Be aware of gaps in the information available on the Internet. While a law library and LEXIS and Westlaw offer all federal court cases, the Internet presently offers only all the United States Supreme Court cases; lower federal cases are available only for the past several years. Thus, research on the Internet cannot be a complete substitute for research using conventional print sources or the computerized research systems LEXIS or Westlaw.
6. Evaluate the credibility of Internet sources. Understand that books published in conventional print form have been subject to rigorous fact-checking and editing and that the authors are usually experts in their field. On the Internet, it is nearly impossible

to judge credibility. Articles often neglect to identify an author or date. Contributors to listservs or newsgroups are anonymous. Consider the following in evaluating credibility:

- Some sites are considered more reliable than others. For example, the "gov" (government) sites are probably most authoritative, followed by the "edu" (educational) sites, followed by the "com" (commercial) and "org" (organization) sites.
- Articles posted on the Internet may become quickly stale. Examine the site to determine if material has been recently updated.
- Well-known experts like to get paid for their work; thus, "free" articles on the Internet may not be authored by the best-known experts in a field.

7. Never completely rely on the Internet. While the Internet provides some excellent information and is often the easiest and cheapest way to find a case or statute, it is not a substitute for a law library. Relying solely on the Internet for legal research will result in a research project that lacks in-depth analysis. The best way to find cases interpreting statutes is still the old-fashioned way: reviewing the annotations following statutes in U.S.C.A., U.S.C.S., or the state codes. The Internet, however, is an excellent tool for locating a quick answer to questions such as, "What is the statute of limitations for medical malpractice actions in California?" or "What is the definition of 'copyright' in federal law?" or "What is the citation to the United States Supreme Court case *Brown v. Board of Education*?" To complete a research project, you will need to supplement your Internet legal research efforts with conventional research methods or with computerized services such as LEXIS and Westlaw.
8. Subscribe to a listserv. Consider subscribing or signing up to receive news bulletins or updates from a law-related Web site. You will then be provided with daily or periodic updates related to topics of interest to you. Be cautious: While many of the update or listserv services (such as those offered through www.findlaw.com) are excellent, subscribing to too many listservs or newsgroups will only result in duplication of materials and a clogged inbox.
9. Consider disclaimers. Review the disclaimer section of a Web site. It will tell you the limitations of the site and will usually indicate if you are permitted to reproduce the material on the site. Unless otherwise indicated, material on a private, educational, or commercial Web site is protected by copyright law, and you cannot copy and use it any more than you could photocopy a well-known treatise and then use it. The "gov" sites, however, including THOMAS, publish materials in the public domain, and any material on these sites is freely available for printing, using, downloading, or other purposes.

E. Ethical Concerns Regarding Use of the Internet

One of the many uses of the Internet is facilitating communication, or e-mail, between legal professionals and their clients. Additionally, in many instances documents are sent to clients for review. Such messages to clients travel over a variety of networks in an essentially open environment. One concern regarding such communications is that of privacy. Legal professionals owe ethical duties to clients to maintain their information in confidence. Electronic communications are vulnerable to interception, misuse, and alteration. Thus, law firms using e-mail must ensure that the means used to communicate information to clients are secure so that the attorney-client privilege is not inadvertently waived. While not every communication between legal professionals and clients needs to be encrypted, some communications may be so sensitive that they should not be sent unless they are protected by encryption software. Before communicating electronically with clients, determine what your firm or office policy is. At a minimum, communications to clients should be accompanied by the type of notice common on facsimile cover sheets, namely, that the communication is intended only for the recipient; it is private and confidential; if it is received in error it should be returned to the sender and may not be copied or disclosed; and so forth. Law firms that market themselves as knowledgeable about the Internet and cyberlaw may be held to a higher standard of care regarding electronic communications.

Another ethical concern that has arisen regarding use of the Internet by legal professionals is whether law firm marketing materials constitute advertising and solicitation. In one instance, a law firm sent an advertisement for its immigration services to thousands of different newsgroups, raising the question whether the advertisement was improper client solicitation. State bar regulations regarding attorney advertising must be carefully reviewed to ensure that all materials posted by a firm on the Internet or sent out to newsgroups is in compliance with state codes regulating advertising and client solicitation.

Similarly, legal professionals should be circumspect about providing any information on the Internet that could be viewed as legal advice. The Web sites of most law firms include broad disclaimers that state that information posted on the site is not legal advice and is provided for general information purposes only.

F. Surf's Up: The Best Internet Legal Research Sites

At the end of each chapter in this text, pertinent Web sites have been given to assist you in your research efforts. As you have noticed, there are hundreds of Web sites available, so many that research using the Internet can seem overwhelming. For example, federal cases can be located through at least ten different Web sites. This section of this chapter will give you brief descriptions of some of the best sites for legal and non-legal research.

1. *Best Start Sites*

As mentioned earlier, the best way to conduct efficient legal research on the Internet is to have a reliable and user-friendly starting place. Among the best starting places are the following:

• http://www.ll.georgetown.edu	Site serving as a gateway or portal to numerous other sites providing primary and secondary law.
• http://www.washlaw.edu	Site offering direct links to cases, statutes, journals, international materials, regulations, and numerous other legal resources by alphabetically arranged links for easy access.
• http://www.findlaw.com	Commercial site, devoted to legal topics, offering easy and direct linking to cases, statutes, journals, and a wide variety of other law-related materials, including bar associations, codes of ethics, directories of lawyers, legal reference materials (such as dictionaries), and numerous other law-related sources.
• http://www.hg.org/hgfr.html or http://www.hg.org	Hieros Gamos Index, a global legal site with great links to legal and non-legal sites.
• http://www.ilrg.com	Internet Legal Resource Guide, a meta-index of more than 4,000 Internet legal sites.
• http://www.lawoffice.com	Site providing basic information regarding legal issues and a searchable directory of legal professionals.
• http://www.law.indiana.edu/law/v-lib/lawindex.html	World Wide Web Virtual Law Library, arranged by subject with links to numerous legal sites.
• http://www.lawcrawler.com	Legal search engine offering numerous links to law-related sources and sites.
• http://www.law.cornell.edu	Excellent starting place for legal issues, many tools, and links to sites.
• http://www.catalaw.com	Catalog of law resources; easy to use.

2. *Best Sites for Locating Cases*

• http://www.supremecourt.us	United States Supreme Court site allowing searching by party name, citation, or docket number and providing schedules of arguments, the Court's calendar, and Court rules.
• http://www.vcilp.org/Fed-Ct/fedcourt.html	United States federal courts home page and gateway to federal cases.
• http://www.findlaw.com/casecode/supreme.html	Site offering searches of United States Supreme Court cases by citation, party name, or keyword.
• http://supct.law.cornell.edu/supct	Site offering access to United States Supreme Court cases since 1990 and other important historical Court decisions.
• http://www.ll.georgetown.edu/Fed-Ct/	Site providing map of federal circuits for "point and click" access to federal court opinions and related federal sites.
• http://www.ll.georgetown.edu/lr/lg/justice.html	Site offering linking to United States Supreme Court and lower federal court cases as well as home pages for lower federal courts.
• http://www.law.emory.edu/FEDCTS	Map of United States allowing immediate linking to federal court decisions since 1994.
• http://www.fjc.gov	Federal Judicial Center home page offering directory of offices, phone numbers, and links to federal courts.

3. *Best Sites for Locating Statutes*

• http://guide.lp.findlaw.com/casecode	Site offering direct linking to the Constitution, the United States Code, and statutes from all states.
• http://guide.lp.findlaw.com/casecode/uscodes	Site offering searching of United States Code by citation, keyword, or popular name.
• http://www.ll.georgetown.edu/lr/lg/state.html	Site offering direct linking to statutes from all states.
• http://www.law.upenn.edu/library/	Drafts of uniform laws and model acts.
• http://www.law.cornell.edu/ucc/ucc.table.html	Uniform Commercial Code.
• http://www.nccusl.org	Web site of National Conference of Commissioners on Uniform State Laws.

4. *Best Sites for Government Materials*

In many instances, you can "guess" at Web site addresses for government agencies. For example, the Web site of the Internal Revenue Service is http://www.irs.gov, and the Web site of the Federal Trade Commission is http://www.ftc.gov. Following are some useful sites for locating federal and state government materials:

- http://thomas.loc.gov — THOMAS, offering United States legislative information, bills, voting records, public laws, and other legislative information. (See Figure 12-4.)
- http://www.access.gpo.gov/nara/cfr/index.html — Providing direct links to the Code of Federal Regulations, *Federal Register*, public laws, *United States Government Manual, Weekly Compilation of Presidential Documents*, and other government materials.
- http://www.fedworld.com — Guide to federal government resources and reports.
- http://www.senate.gov — Home page of United States Senate.
- http://www.house.gov — Home page of United States House of Representatives.
- http://www.whitehouse.gov — Home page of White House.
- http://www.state.gov — Home page of Department of State.

5. *Best Sites for Locating Forms*

- http://www.lectlaw.com/form.html — Forms for litigation, business, real estate, wills, trusts, corporations, and other areas.
- http://findlaw.com — FindLaw site; select "Forms."
- http://www.washlaw.edu — Select "Legal Forms."
- http://www.uscourtforms.com — More than 40,000 legal forms, including forms for state and federal courts.

Figure 12-4
Home Page for THOMAS

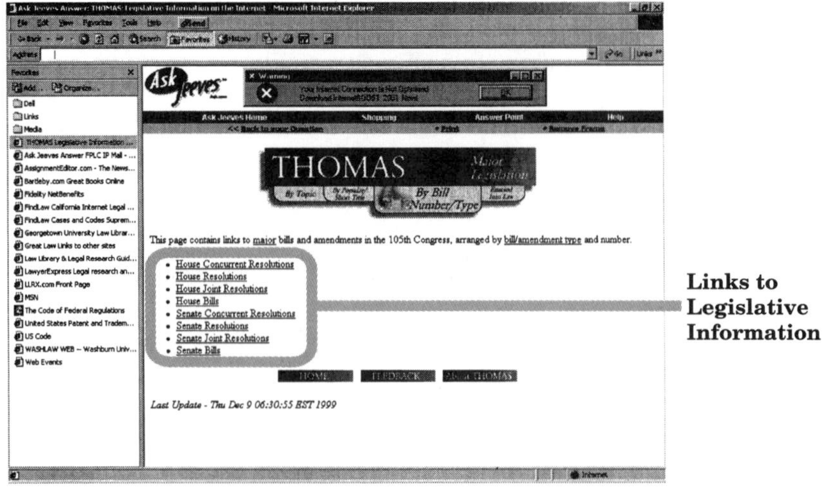

6. *Paralegal Sites*

• http://www.paralegals.org	Site of the National Federation of Paralegal Associations, with networking and career opportunities, professional development information, and links to numerous other law-related sites.
• http://www.nala.org	Site of the National Association of Legal Assistants, with information about the paralegal profession and links to numerous law-related sites.
• http://hg.org/assistants-assoc.html	Listing of national and state paralegal associations.

7. *Best Specialty Sites*

Following are some sites for specialized legal topics:

Americans with Disabilities Act Site

• www.adabbs.hr.state.ks.us/dc	Information and links relating to the Americans with Disabilities Act.

Attorneys and Ethics Sites

• http://www.abanet.org/home.html	Web site of American Bar Association.
• www.martindalehubbell.com	Lawyer locator offered by Martindale-Hubbell.
• http://www.lawoffice.com	Searchable directory of more than one million lawyers and law firms.
• http://www.legalethics.com	Comprehensive site providing ethics information and links to other ethics-related sources.
• http://www.law.cornell.edu/ethics	Legal ethics by state.

Corporate, Business, and Securities Sites

• http://www.sec.gov	Web site of the Securities and Exchange Commission, offering full text of filings made by public companies.
• http://www.freedgar.com	Easy to use site offering searching of filings made with the Securities and Exchange Commission.
• http://securities.stanford.edu	Securities law and information.
• http://www.companylink.com	Company news, contacts, and information for more than 65,000 companies.
• http://www.hoovers.com	Profiles of more than 12,000 public companies.

• http://www.bigbook.com	Providing company information.
• http://smallbiz.findlaw.com/tools/tools.stm	Practical business tools including model business documents.
• http://www.law.cornell.edu/topics/corporations.html	Numerous corporate links, including the text of laws and regulations and recent cases.

Environmental Sites

• http://www.epa.gov	Web site of the Environmental Protection Agency.
• http://www.law.indiana.edu/law/v-lib/envlaw.html	Index of environmental law materials.
• http://www.law.cornell.edu/topics/environmental.html	Links to statutes, regulations, federal and state agencies, and recent cases.

Intellectual Property Sites

• http://www.uspto.gov	Official site of the United States Patent and Trademark Office, offering the text of statutes relating to patents and trademarks, forms, general overviews of trademark and patent procedure and law, and a fully searchable database allowing one to search for registered trademarks and patents.
• http://www.loc.gov	Web site of the Copyright Office, offering detailed information on copyright law and links to other resources related to copyright law.
• http://www.ipmall.fplc.edu	Web site of Franklin Pierce Law Center, providing in-depth coverage of intellectual property law and numerous links to other sites and documents.

International Sites

• http://www.un.org	Web site of the United Nations, offering treaties and resolutions.
• http://www.wipo.org	Web site of World Intellectual Property Organization, offering text of various treaties.

Labor and Employment Sites

• http://www.dol.gov	Site of United States Department of Labor.
• http://www.osha.gov	Comprehensive site of Occupational Safety and Health Administration.
• http://www.law.cornell.edu/topics/employment_discrimination.html	Links to employment discrimination cases and statutes.

Legal Research and Writing Sites

- www.ll.georgetown.edu/lr/rs/leglwrite.html — Providing links to sites describing how to conduct legal research and how to improve legal writing.
- www.ualr.edu/~cmbarger/ — Site providing research, writing, and advocacy resources.
- http://cctc2/comment.edu/grammar — Site providing guidance and quizzes on grammar.
- http://www.nara.gov/fedreg/dldhome.html — Office of the Federal Register's guide to legal writing.
- http://www.bartleby.com/index.html — Providing links to many sources, including *The Elements of Style*, the classic guide to good writing.
- http://legalnet.law.stetson.edu/courses/lrw/writing_tips.htm — Stetson Law School legal writing tips.
- http://www.virtualchase.com — Site providing numerous articles regarding legal and factual research on the Internet.

Reference Materials Sites

- http://aallnet.org — Site of American Association of Law Libraries.
- http://www.bartleby.com — Featuring dictionaries, *Bartlett's Familiar Quotations*, and a wide variety of reference materials.
- http://www.courttv.com/glossary.html — Glossary of legal terms.
- http://www.lawoffice.com/pathfind/orans/orans.asp — *Oran's Dictionary of the Law*, searchable by word or phrase.

Tax Sites

- http://www.irs.gov — Site of Internal Revenue Service providing information, forms, and links to other resources.
- http://www.taxprophet.com — Valuable information and links to other tax sites.
- http://www.hsetax.com — Links to tax-related sites and comprehensive information.

8. *Best Non-Legal Sites*

While it is helpful to have a repertory of law-related sites at your fingertips, you also need to be familiar with some basic information sites, so you can determine the weather in the city where tomorrow's deposition will be taken, directions to the client's office, or the last price at which the client's stock was sold. Following are some basic information and reference sites.

• http://starlingtech.com/quotes	Offering quotes (for speeches).
• http://www.tollfree.att.net/tf/html	For looking up toll-free 800 numbers.
• http://www.usps.gov or http://www.zip2.com	Providing zip codes in the United States.
• http://www.refdesk.com/Facts.html	Offering encyclopedia or thesaurus information.
• http://www.mapquest.com	For obtaining a map and directions to a location.
• http://www.hilink.com.au.times	Offering local time around the world.
• http://www.intellicast.com	For obtaining weather in a given city.
• http://www.superpages.com	Nationwide yellow pages for finding businesses in the United States and Canada.
• http://www.cnn.com	Providing links to current news, weather, and stories.
• http://www.usatoday.com	Providing the text of *USA Today*.
• http://www.nationalgeographic.com	Home page of National Geographic Society, offering maps.
• http://nyse.com	Providing stock quotes for companies listed on the New York Stock Exchange; offering a ticker symbol "look up."
• http://www.nasdaq.com	Providing stock quotes for companies listed on the NASDAQ Exchange; offering a ticker symbol "look up."

9. *Where to Start When All Else Fails*

• http://www.ask.com	The site of "Ask," allowing one to type in natural language questions, such as "where can I find a recipe for fudge" or "where can I find currency calculations"; an excellent starting place for nearly any type of question.
• www.yahoo.com	Allows search queries and organizes Web sites by category and displays a link to the related category.
• http://www.google.com	Easy-to-use search engine, allowing simple search strategies.

Other general-purpose search engines include the following:

- http://www.altavista.digital.com
- http://www.excite.com

- http://www.hotbot.com
- http://www.infoseek.com
- http://www.lycos.com
- http://www.metacrawler.com
- http://www.snap.com

G. Cautionary Notes on Internet Legal Research

Many researchers confuse locating information on the Internet with researching. Retrieving a case is not the same as analyzing it. Locating a statute or a case is just the beginning of a research task. Cases that interpret the statute must be analyzed; treatises and restatements should be reviewed; and periodicals, looseleaf services, and other materials should be consulted.

Moreover, much of the material that appears on the Internet is anonymous. Thus, you do not know the credibility or reputation of the author. Just as you would not take medical advice from a stranger on the corner, you should not take legal "advice" from strangers on the Internet corner. Most experts prefer to be paid for their work authoring texts and then to receive royalties based on sales of the material. Those who post materials on the Internet may well be reliable experts. Then again, they may not be; there is no way to know for sure.

There are obviously tremendously valuable research materials on the Internet, particularly the *United States Code,* the *Code of Federal Regulations*, state statutes, and federal and state court cases. Note that all of these materials share one thing in common: They are all materials in the public domain. The well-known legal publishers, such as West and LEXIS, have not posted their valuable databases on the Internet, and you should not expect that these materials will be made available for free.

Finally, always consider that even the most reputable-seeming sites can be subject to abuse. The CIA's and Department of Justice's sites have both been hacked. Thus, at any given moment, the materials you review on the Internet may be false.

As long as you remember these cautionary notes, the Internet remains a valuable and efficient tool for beginning your research project. It can never be a substitute for a full, in-depth analysis of legal materials, such as those you find in a law library or through the well-known and reliable computer research services, such as LEXIS or Westlaw.

H. Citation Form

As discussed in Chapter 8, the *Bluebook* requires the use and citation of traditional printed sources, unless the information is not available in such traditional print form or the traditional print source is obscure or hard to find and citation to the Internet source will substantially improve the reader's ability to locate the information. Rule 18 of the *Bluebook* contains numerous rules for citing to the Internet, some of which are quite complicated. Following are some examples. Additional examples are found in Chapter 8.

- Case accessed in print form but available on the Internet

  Allen v. Dorsey, 520 U.S. 118 (2001), *available at* http://www2.law.cornell.edu/cgi-bin/foliocgi.exe/520 + US + 118.html.

- Statute accessed solely through the Internet

  18 U.S.C. § 1201 (1996), Cornell Legal Info. Inst., http://www.lawcornell.edu/uscode/18/1201.html.

- Journal article found exclusively on the Internet

  Jason Newbold, *Cyberspace Law Issues*, 3 N. Va. Tech. J. 16, ¶ 8 (Nov. 8, 2000), *at* http://www.findlaw.com/articles/1109-019-45.html.

Net Tips

Some advantages of using the Internet:

- Access to Internet sources is available 24 hours a day, from anywhere in the world.
- The Internet provides free access to legal materials.
- E-mail, chat rooms, and newsgroup postings allow you to ask colleagues for assistance and information.
- The Internet provides access to many private materials. For example, some paralegals have posted their case briefs on the Internet and invited others to print and use them. Similarly, law firms often publish memoranda on selected legal topics.
- The Internet provides direct access to invaluable legal materials including cases, statutes, and regulations.
- Office space for library books and binders is expensive. The Web stores incredible amounts of information at no cost.

Some drawbacks to using the Internet:

- Many unpublished cases find their way onto the Internet. On the Internet, with its vast virtual space, no one edits out the "dog" cases. Some courts prohibit citations to unpublished decisions. Thus, exercise care and look carefully for the words "published" or "unpublished" at the beginning of a case.
- The Internet is transient. Sites appear, then vanish with no explanation.
- The Internet is anonymous. The "experts" providing advice via e-mail or chat rooms are unknown and unproved.
- Accessing the law is far different from understanding and analyzing it.

Writing Strategies

Be careful not to fall into the trap of thinking that everything on the Internet is in the public domain and can be used without permission. Thus, avoid excessive quoting from Internet sources unless attribution is given or permission is received. In many instances, you can directly e-mail the author of an article or piece and ask for permission to reproduce the material. Consider the credibility of the source before relying on it in your writings.

Be cautious in using terms of art when discussing materials found on the Internet. Provide definitions for terms such as "browser" or "server" and use jargon sparingly so as not to confuse or intimidate readers.

When setting up Internet citations, ensure that the often long string of numbers and letters in the URL break at a natural point at the end of a typed line. Proofread carefully to ensure readers can locate the material you cite. It is easy to transpose numbers and letters in long URL strings.

Assignment for Chapter 12

1. Access "THOMAS" at http://thomas.loc.gov. Select *Public Laws by Law Number* for the *93rd-107th Congress.* To what does PL 106-152 relate?
2. Return to the home page for THOMAS. On the left column, access *Library of Congress Web Link* for *Legislative* and then select *Members.* Select *U.S. Senate* and then *Directory of U.S. Senators by Name* for the 106th Congress. Select *Thomas Daschle.* Where was Senator Daschle born?
3. Return to the home page for THOMAS. On the left column, select *Historical Documents* and then select *Constitution of the United States.* Review Article VII. How many states were required to ratify the Constitution for it to be sufficient as the Constitution?
4. Access "FindLaw" at http://www.findlaw.com. Select *Legal Subjects* and then *Intellectual Property.* Select *Journals, Newsletters and Articles* and then select *FAQ about Intellectual Property Law.* What is an orphan drug?
5. Return to the home page for FindLaw and select *Legal Subjects* and then *Intellectual Property.* Select *Government Agencies* and then *USPTO*, then *Trademarks*, and then *Check Trademark Status.* What is registered trademark No. 1,266,789?
6. Return to the home page for FindLaw and select *Legal Subjects* and then *Intellectual Property* and then *Government Agencies.* Select *U.S. Copyright Office* and then *Copyright Basics.* Are architectural works protectable under copyright law?
7. Access http://www.ll.georgetown.edu. Under *Law Related Web Sites*, select *Federal*, then *Judicial Branch*, then *Decisions of the Supreme Court* (from FindLaw). In the search box for *Party Name Search*, enter "Gore" and retrieve the decision *Bush v. Gore*. What is the docket number of the case?
8. Access http://www.ll.georgetown.edu. Under *Law Related Web Sites*, select *Federal*, then *Judicial Branch*, then *Decisions of the Supreme Court* (from FindLaw). In the search box for *Citation Search*, enter 425 U.S. 457. What is the plaintiff's name?
9. Return to http://www.ll.georgetown.edu. Access *State, local and territorial*, and then select *California*, and then *California Codes*. Display the contents for the *Business and Professions Code.* To what does Section 336 relate?
10. Return to http://www.ll.georgetown.edu. Select *Legal Topics A-Z*, and then select *Disability Law*. Select *Department of Housing and Human Services*, then *Agency*. What is the budget for the Secretary/Department of Housing and Human Services?
11. Return to http://www.ll.georgetown.edu. Select *Federal*, then *Executive Branch*, and then *GPO Access*. Is the *Federal Register* available online?
12. Return to http://www.ll.georgetown.edu. Select *Legislative Branch* and then select *U.S. Code.* In the right column, access the form permitting you to look up specific sections. In the search

box, type in 17 U.S.C. Section 106. To what does this section relate?

13. Return to http://www.ll.georgetown.edu. Select *Legislative Branch* and then select *U.S. Code*. In the right column, access the form permitting you to look up statutes by *Table of Popular Names*. What is the citation for the Bald Eagle Protection Act?
14. Access the site http://www.washlaw.edu. Select *Bar Associations* and then *ABA*. Select *About*. How many members does the ABA have?
15. Return to http://www.washlaw.edu. Select *Legal Forms*. Select *ILRG's Forms Archive*. Select *Leases and Tenancy*. To what does Paragraph 2 of the "Agreement to Lease (Residential)" relate?
16. Acess http://www.supremecourtus.gov. Select *Court Rules* and then *Rules of the Supreme Court*. Review Rule 33. What is the required color for a Petition for Rehearing? What is the page limit for such a Petition?

Chapter
13

Overview of the Research Process

Chapter Overview

Among the most difficult tasks in performing legal research are beginning and ending the project. It is easy to become so overwhelmed at the task ahead of you that you become paralyzed at the thought of how and where to commence your legal research. Part of the difficulty lies with the tremendous mass of legal publications: millions of cases, volumes of codes, and so many secondary authorities, including encyclopedias, periodicals, treatises, attorneys general opinions, looseleaf services and other sources, that a researcher does not know where to turn first. LEXIS, Westlaw, and the Internet add another layer of complexity to the research process.

Similarly, once you have begun delving into these authorities, you cannot decide when to stop. It seems there is always one more case to read or source to check. This chapter will offer some practical guidelines on beginning your research task and knowing when to end it.

A. How to Begin

1. *Introduction*

There are few inflexible rules in legal research. It is not nearly so precise as mathematics, which provides step-by-step logical guidelines to enable you to systematically reach a solution to a problem. In legal research you are asked to provide an answer to a legal question. To reach that answer, there are a number of strategies available to you. While the sheer number of authorities available to consult offers great flexibility, they can also produce great uncertainty. Where do I begin? How do I begin? These are often the questions that so intimidate legal researchers that they are unable to begin the task itself. Moreover, researching is rarely a straight line but often involves backtracking and revisiting sources, requiring patience and flexibility.

While this chapter will offer you some guidelines and strategies on getting started, the best approach, as always, is the one that works best for you. If everyone you know prefers to consult an annotated code first but you like to become comfortable with a topic by reviewing an encyclopedia before you start, then that is the best approach.

You should view legal research as a process. While the answer to a question is the destination you are traveling toward, there are many roads you can follow to reach that destination. Which road you choose to take is not important. In fact, while the number of sources you can examine may be staggering, this in itself is one of the benefits of our system of legal publishing. If you cannot locate a case or statute using one research technique, there are many alternatives available to help you find those authorities.

In fact, there are really only two "rules" that you must follow when you perform legal research: First, if the book you are reviewing has a supplement or pocket part, you *must* check it; and, second, you *must* Shepardize or KeyCite all primary authorities. As long as you always perform these two tasks, you have tremendous freedom in accomplishing your goal of solving the research problem presented to you.

2. *Thinking Things Through*

While it is tempting to run to the library and start grabbing volumes of books as soon as you are given a research task, the time you spend thinking about a project before you begin is time well spent.

It may be helpful to write the issue on a piece of paper. This will help you "frame" the issue and in and of itself may impose some structure on the project and suggest certain approaches to follow. After you write out the issue, develop a list of descriptive words and phrases. Because almost all legal authorities are accessed by alphabetically arranged indexes and the descriptive word approach is usually the most efficient method of using an index, jot down the words that initially occur to you in examining the issue. These will be the words you will use in examining the indexes.

After you have selected the most obvious words, facts, and phrases, expand your list by thinking of related words, such as synonyms and antonyms. If you cannot think of any such related words right away, consult a dictionary or thesaurus. Consider the following questions, which will help you develop a list of descriptive words or phrases:

Who is involved?
What is the issue being considered?
Where did the activity take place?
When did the activity take place?
Why did the issue develop?
How did the problem arise?

The former Lawyers Co-op recommended that researchers use the "TAPP Rule" in determining which words to insert into an index:

T Consider the Thing involved in the problem
A Consider the Act committed or the cause of Action (or defense) a party would assert
P Consider the Persons involved in a problem
P Consider the Place involved

By focusing on these four areas, you may be able to determine words you can insert into a descriptive word index so you can be directed to relevant authorities.

Once you have prepared your list of descriptive words and phrases, continue to expand your list by adding legal concepts. You must now consider whether the issue relates to criminal law or civil law. Which jurisdiction's authorities should you examine? In other words, is the issue one of Minnesota law enabling you to limit your research strictly to Minnesota authorities or is the issue one of federal law? If the issue is one of federal law, narrow the focus again by considering which district or circuit is involved. If your question relates to a lawsuit filed for violation of the United States Trademark Act and the lawsuit was filed in the United States District Court for the Northern District of Texas, you should initially consult other district court cases from the Northern District of Texas. Because Texas is in the Fifth Circuit, you should look for other cases from the Fifth Circuit. Similarly, when performing research related to a specific state, restrict your search to authorities from that state. Expand your search to other states only if your state lacks authorities. Remember that your jurisdiction need not follow or adopt the viewpoint of another jurisdiction. While authority from outside your jurisdiction may be persuasive, it is never binding.

Once you have identified the issue as being civil or criminal and state or federal and have identified the particular jurisdiction (for example, specific state or district and circuit), you need to consider the legal issues involved in the case. Ask yourself what the plaintiff would allege in a lawsuit based upon this issue. Would the plaintiff's action be for breach of contract? Personal injuries arising out of a car accident? Trespass to his property? Improper search of her house by police officers?

Once you have considered the plaintiff's "gripes," put yourself in the place of the defendant and ask how the defendant would best defeat the plaintiff. What defenses would a defendant assert? Would the defendant allege that there was no agreement or, if there was an agreement, he fully performed its terms? That the plaintiff's failure to wear a seat belt rather than the defendant's conduct caused the injuries suffered by the plaintiff in the automobile accident? That the plaintiff invited the defendant to come onto the plaintiff's property? That the police were acting pursuant to a proper search warrant?

After you look at the issue from the perspective of both parties, consider what remedies the plaintiff is seeking. Is the plaintiff asking for money damages for a breach of contract or injuries sustained in an accident or does the plaintiff want to compel the defendant to repair damage caused to his property by the trespass? If you are unsure as to the theories on which the plaintiff would claim relief, what defenses the defendant would assert, or what remedies the parties desire, consult West's list of more than 400 topics of the law (see Figure 5-2). Use this as a "menu" and pick and choose the words and topics that fit your problem.

Examining these issues will not only help develop a list of descriptive words and phrases that you can look up in the indexes you will be using, it will help ensure that you have the "big picture" focus, which is critical in the legal profession. After all, it is deadly to think that because you have examined an issue from the plaintiff's perspective, you are finished. The plaintiff may, in fact, have a cause of action enabling her to recover substantial money damages. Nevertheless, the defendant may have a perfect defense, which would completely defeat the plaintiff's action. If you examine questions only from one party's side, you will be sure to miss critical issues.

To develop your list of descriptive words, facts, and phrases, use any approach that works best for you. Perhaps rough notes jotted down on a legal pad are sufficient. You may prefer to use index cards or a word processor. It is not the technique you use that matters at this juncture—far more important is the thinking process and analytical skill you will develop by examining these legal issues in a precise fashion.

Figure 13-1 provides an approach that you may wish to follow to help develop the working outline described herein, that is, the road map you use in reaching your destination. This outline will also help you develop words to use in formulating a search using LEXIS or Westlaw. Feel free to copy and use this outline for each project you research.

3. *Tackling the Project*

Once you have formulated the descriptive words, facts, and phrases that you will insert into an index, you need to decide with which sources to start. There are two categories of books you can consider: primary authorities (cases, constitutions, statutes, and administrative regulations) and secondary authorities (everything else).

Some research questions will immediately suggest or even dictate the source to consult. For example, if the question is what the statute of limitation is for an action by a patient against a doctor for professional negligence, how many days a defendant has to answer a complaint, or the number of people required to witness a will, the answer will undoubtedly be found in a statute. In such cases, you should proceed directly to an annotated code, look up your descriptive words in the index, read the statute to which you are referred, and examine the library references and annotations following the statute to review how courts have interpreted the statute.

It is altogether likely, however, that you will not know which source to consult initially. In such instances, consider the following strategy.

a. Familiarization

When you are unsure where or how to start a research project, invest an hour or so in becoming familiar with the general area of law involved

Figure 13-1
Research Project

Name: ____________

Client Name: ____________ Case Name: ____________ Assigning Attorney or Supervisor: ____________

Client/Billing No.: ____________ Date Given: ____________

Date Due: ____________

ISSUE/QUESTION/TASK ____________

Law Category	Jurisdiction	Descriptive Words/Facts	Synonyms	Antonyms	Plaintiff's Action	Defenses	Remedies
Civil ____ Criminal ____ Administrative ____ International ____ Municipal ____ Other ____	State ____ Federal ____ District ____ Circuit ____						Money Damages ____ Compensatory ____ Punitive ____ Other ____ Equitable Relief ____ Injunction ____ Other ____

(contracts, property, wills). The best place to "get your feet wet" is an encyclopedia, which will offer you introductory information on an area of the law. If you live in one of the more populous states that publishes its own encyclopedia, start with this. If your state does not have a local encyclopedia, familiarize yourself with the topic by reviewing C.J.S. or Am. Jur. 2d.

If you read C.J.S., a West publication, and you locate a particularly relevant section, make a note of the topic name and key number (**Partnership** 14, **Negligence** 121, **Contracts** 42) as this will unlock the door to other authorities.

If, on the other hand, you are reviewing Am. Jur. 2d, look for relevant annotations in A.L.R., which can provide extremely useful information to you.

Consider also using specialized treatises for your issue. For example, if the question involves corporations or bankruptcy, browse those sections of the law library to see if a treatise exists for that topic. Treatises provide excellent analyses of legal topics as well as references to supporting case law.

b. Consult Primary Sources

After you have begun to feel comfortable with the subject matter, consult the primary authorities: constitutions, statutes, and cases.

(1) Constitutions

If your issue is a federal one, it may be governed by the United States Constitution. Both U.S.C.A. and U.S.C.S. contain the text of the United States Constitution as well as annotations referring you to cases interpreting constitutional provisions. If your issue is not federal but may involve your state constitution, consult your state's annotated code, which will contain the state constitution as well as annotations to cases construing provisions of your constitution.

(2) Statutes

Always examine an annotated code because under the American common law theory of stare decisis, it is not merely the language of a statute or law that controls, but the interpretation of that language by a court.

For federal statutes, consult U.S.C.A. (West's publication) or U.S.C.S. (the LEXIS publication), insert your descriptive words into the indexes to U.S.C.A. or U.S.C.S., and read the statutes to which you are referred. After you read applicable statutes, review the library references and cases to determine how the statute is interpreted by courts.

For state statutes, examine your state's annotated code, insert the relevant descriptive words into the index to the code and review the statute to which you are referred, followed by an examination of the library references and cases construing the state statute. Once you have a reference or citation to a specific statute, consider consulting the Table of Statutes construed in an encyclopedia or treatise, which will direct you to a discussion of treatment and interpretation of the specific statute in which you are interested.

Always check pocket parts or supplements to the statutes to determine if the statute has been amended or repealed and to find cases more current than those in the hardbound volume.

(3) Cases

If a review of the annotations for a constitutional or state statutory provision has not yielded any cases on point, use digests, which function as case finders.

Many experts believe that finding "one good case" solves many research problems. If you can find one good case, you can use its topics and key numbers to locate other cases in the Amerian Digest System (if the case is published in a West reporter) and you can Shepardize or KeyCite the case to find other authorities that mention or discuss your case, thereby leading you to a host of other relevant sources. Note that the advice involves finding one *good* case, not one *perfect* case, because there likely is no such thing as the perfect case for a legal issue.

(a) Federal Issues

For a global approach, use the decennial digest system. For a more focused approach, concentrate on West's federal practice digests (*Modern Federal Practice Digest*, *West's Federal Practice Digest 2d*, *West's Federal Practice Digest 3d*, *West's Federal Practice Digest 4th*). Use the Descriptive Word Index for any of the digests. Insert your descriptive words, facts, or phrases and allow the Index to provide you with a topic name and key number (**Venue** 42, **Larceny** 106, **Zoning and Planning** 123). Look up these topic names and key numbers in the appropriate digest and out will spill the cases you need. Focus on the particular state, district, or circuit you need. All of the West's digests organize the cases according to state or district and circuit, so you may easily locate cases on point.

(b) State Issues

If the issue is governed by state law and you wish to find cases from a particular state, the best case finders are digests. West has published a digest for every state but Delaware, Nevada, and Utah (these states use a regional digest such as the *Atlantic Digest* or *Pacific Digest*). Use the Descriptive Word Index available for each set and look up the words, facts, and phrases listed on your research outline. You will be provided with a topic name and a key number such as **Wills** 56. Insert this topic name and key number into your state digest, and you will be provided with other cases from your state dealing with this same issue.

Figure 13-2 provides a chart showing the sets to review when conducting legal research using primary authorities (in any area other than administrative law, in which case you should consult C.F.R.'s Index and any looseleaf services published for that specific topic).

c. Consult Secondary Sources

After you have reviewed the pertinent primary authorities (constitutions, statutes, and cases), consult the secondary authorities to fill in the gaps. Many secondary authorities will refer you to cases, thus ensuring that you find all of the case law relating to your topic. The most commonly consulted secondary authorities are A.L.R. annotations, encyclopedias, periodicals, Restatements, texts and treatises, and law dictionaries.

There are several secondary sources, and you should examine the list of secondary authorities shown in Figure 13-3 and ask yourself if your issue would be addressed by the particular authority in question. If so, review the authority. You need not examine every secondary authority for every issue you research. It is possible that a review of a treatise and an A.L.R. annotation may provide you with such useful information as well as sufficient references to cases that you need not examine other secondary authorities.

d. Miscellaneous Research Guides

In addition to the primary and secondary authorities discussed above, there are a few other sources that you may wish to consult when performing research. Consider using *Shepard's Citations* or KeyCite not only to let you know whether the authorities you rely upon are still good law, but to lead you to other sources. *Shepard's* and KeyCite will refer you to law review articles, opinions of the attorneys general, and annotations that mention your case, statute, or constitutional provision. It is possible that these authorities have so thoroughly examined an issue that for you to conduct additional research would be "reinventing the wheel."

Figure 13-2
Chart of Primary Authorities

I. *Constitutions*

Federal: Consult U.S.C.A. or U.S.C.S.
State: Consult your state's annotated code

II. *Statutes*

Federal: Consult U.S.C.A. or U.S.C.S.
State: Consult your state's annotated code

III. *Cases*

Federal: Consult digests (American Digest System or Federal Practice Digests)
State: Consult your state's digest or a regional digest

Figure 13-3
Chart of Secondary Authorities

Secondary Authority	*Coverage*	*To Use*
Encyclopedias		
C.J.S.	All U.S. law	Consult alphabetically arranged index
Am. Jur. 2d	All U.S. law	Consult alphabetically arranged index
State-specific sets	Law of one state	Consult alphabetically arranged index
A.L.R. Annotations		
A.L.R. Fed.	Federal issues	Consult Index to A.L.R.
A.L.R., A.L.R.2d, 3d, 4th, & 5th	State & common law topics	Consult Index to A.L.R.
Texts and Treatises	Law related to one topic	Consult alphabetically arranged index or table of contents
Legal Periodicals	Various topics	Consult *Index to Legal Periodicals* or *Current Law Index*
Restatements	Various topics	Consult alphabetically arranged index to each Restatement
Attorneys General Opinions		
U.S.A.G. Opinions	Federal topics	Consult alphabetically arranged index
State A.G. Opinions	State topics	Consult alphabetically arranged index
Dictionaries	Legal words and phrases	Look up alphabetically arranged words or phrases
Martindale-Hubbell Law Digest	International and state law	Consult list of states and countries arranged alphabetically
Form Books	Various topics	Consult alphabetically arranged index
Uniform Laws	Various topics	Consult *Uniform Laws Annotated, Master Edition* and *Directory of Uniform Acts and Codes*
Looseleaf Services	Various topics	Consult alphabetically arranged index
Jury Instructions	Federal or state	Consult alphabetically arranged index

Do not forget to use common sense. If the question can be easily answered by an individual or organization, call or write. Thus, if your question relates to zoning in your county, contact your county supervisor or the county zoning officer. If your question relates to the current minimum wage, contact a local employment agency. Many basic questions can be answered by Internet legal research techniques.

Browse the library for useful materials. For example, if your issue deals with bankruptcy, locate the section of the law library containing books related to this topic. Scan the shelves for helpful sources. When you come to a dead end, ask your law librarian for assistance.

Use the Research Game Plan shown in Figure 13-4 to ensure you have consulted all applicable sets of books. Fill out the plan as you perform your research to verify that your research has been thorough and has focused on both primary and secondary authorities. Identify the particular source you consult and then rate its helpfulness or value to you on a scale of 0-10, with 10 being the highest. If you later have only a vague recollection of a source that provided valuable information, the Research Game Plan may jog your memory. It also serves as a reminder to check all pocket parts and to Shepardize or KeyCite all primary sources.

e. Strategies for Effective Research

Following are eight hints to ensure your research is sufficiently thorough:

(i) Always examine the statutes. Use an annotated code because it will refer you to cases.

(ii) Use encyclopedias (C.J.S., Am. Jur. 2d, or a local set for your state) to obtain introductory information about the issue you are researching.

(iii) If you cannot locate cases through an annotated code (because the issue is not dealt with by statutes), use digests: The decennial digests can be used for a global approach; the federal practice digests can be used for federal cases; and state and regional digests can be used to locate cases from a particular state or region.

(iv) If there is a well-known treatise or text on this topic, examine it because it will provide excellent analysis as well as references to cases.

(v) For a complete overview of a topic, consult A.L.R. (or A.L.R. Fed. for federal issues).

(vi) For discussions of new or controversial issues or a thorough examination of an issue, find legal periodicals through the *Index to Legal Periodicals* or *Current Law Index*.

(vii) If a looseleaf service is devoted to the topic you are researching, examine it; it will provide an exhaustive treatment of the topic.

(viii) Use *Shepard's Citations* or KeyCite to locate other cases, legal periodical articles, attorneys general opinions, and A.L.R. annotations.

Figure 13-4
Research Game Plan

Source	*Specific Source & Section Consulted*	*Date Consulted*	*Rating*
Encyclopedia	______	______	______
Constitutions	______	______	______
Codes/Statutes	______	______	______
Annotations following statutes	______	______	______
Digests (topic ____, Key Number ____)	______	______	______
A.L.R. Annotations	______	______	______
Texts/Treatises	______	______	______
Legal Periodicals	______	______	______
Restatements	______	______	______
Attorneys General Opinions	______	______	______
Dictionaries	______	______	______
Martindale-Hubbell	______	______	______
Form Books	______	______	______
Uniform Laws	______	______	______
Looseleaf Services	______	______	______
Jury Instructions	______	______	______
Experts Consulted	______	______	______
Law Librarian Assistance	______	______	______
Computer-Assisted Legal Research	______	______	______
Internet	______	______	______
All Pocket Parts and Supplements Checked	______	______	______
All Primary Sources Shepardized or KeyCited	______	______	______

B. Working with the Authorities

1. *Note-Taking*

As you begin to read the primary and secondary authorities, you need to develop some focused plan for taking notes. Ultimately, the results of your research must be communicated to someone either by way of a letter to a client, an internal office memorandum, or a brief submitted to a court, and the notes you take will form the basis for your written project. There is nothing more frustrating than beginning to write your project, having a vague recollection that some source provided a perfect analysis or quote, and then being unable to find a reference to it in your notes. Equally frustrating is having to go back to the law library or go online at additional expense to a client to obtain complete citations because your notes do not reflect the date of a case or the page of a quotation.

These time-consuming tasks can be avoided by effective note-taking during the research process. This way you do not have to waste time later by retracing your steps to locate information you should have obtained earlier. Effective note-taking requires some practice and is often developed through trial and error. Once you neglect to include the page of a quotation in your notes, thus necessitating another trip to the law library, you will not make the same mistake twice.

Notes that can be used to help you write your project are more than scribbling on a legal pad. If you simply jot down phrases, parts of cases, and isolated sentences on pages in a pad, you will find they are a muddle when you later try to use these notes to construct a written project, with information relating to one issue being hopelessly intertwined with information relating to entirely separate issues.

a. Organizing Your Notes

You should develop a system for taking and organizing notes during your research efforts so you can effectively use these notes to write your project. One of the best approaches is to use a looseleaf notebook that is divided into separate sections through the use of tabs or dividers. You can devote each section to a particular issue. For example, you could use the first section to reflect information relating to the standard of care of physicians, the second section to record information relating to conduct constituting a breach of that standard, the third section to contain notes relating to defenses the doctor could assert, and the fourth section to relate to damages for injuries caused by the physician's breach of his duty of care, or malpractice. Consider leaving at least one section untitled for a while because you will invariably discover issues during the course of your research that you had not planned on.

As you research you may discover that each of these major issues comprises sub-issues. Either insert new tabs or dividers so you can compile information relating to these newly discovered sub-issues, or assign a number or letter to each sub-issue and reflect that in the margin next to any notes relating to it.

If you find that some authorities or cases discuss more than one issue, take notes in one section and in the other(s) simply insert a reminder to review the authority, such as the following: "For discussion of damages in malpractice action, see *Jones v. Smith*, 421 N.E.2d 609, 614 (Ind. 1989), Tab I." Alternatively, you can photocopy the case and "cut and paste" it by placing certain portions of it in your Tab I section and other portions in your notes for Tab III. An advantage of using a looseleaf notebook is that you can shuffle sections of your argument around. If you decide Section II should be discussed after Section IV, it is easy to switch the pages in your notebook.

Some students prefer to use looseleaf sheets (rather than a binder or spiral notebook), label each sheet with a topic name (Duty of Care, Breach of Duty, Damages), and then record information relating to these topics on the appropriate pages. Often students will use different colors of looseleaf paper for different issues so that white sheets relate to the issue of Duty of Care, pink sheets relate to Breach of Duty, and blue sheets reflect notes relating to Damages for such breach.

Other individuals find index cards useful and label each card with a topic name (Duty of Care, Breach of Duty, Damages) and devote a separate card to each case, law review article, A.L.R. annotation, or other authority, briefly summarizing the case, article, or annotation. Some individuals prefer using different colored index cards for different issues. This system allows immediate recognition and retrieval of the sections you later desire to review.

The advantage to any of these techniques is obvious: When your research is completed, it is already partly organized and prepared for the writing stage. All of your information relating to Duty of Care, Breach of Duty, or Damages is in one place rather than hopelessly scattered among numerous pages.

Another advantage of keeping notes related to separate issues in separate sections is that you can take your separate sheets of paper or index cards and shuffle them around so that you can physically organize the results of your research and determine the order in which you will discuss the cases relating to damages or some other topic. For this reason, try to keep your notes about any one case, law review article, annotation, or other authority to one page or one index card. The purpose of taking notes is to record only the critical portions of a case, not to write out the entire case in longhand.

You can always photocopy the case itself so you will have it to refer to when writing your project, but for note-taking purposes, be brief and keep notes to one page or one index card per authority. If you are photocopying cases, invest a bit of time and always maintain them in alphabetical order. Then, when you need to refer to them when writing your project, you will be able to locate the case you need easily. Many individuals prefer to photocopy almost all cases they intend to rely upon (and, in fact, some attorneys insist that finished research projects be accompanied by copies of all cases cited therein).

If you photocopy cases, you will invariably mark or highlight the significant portions of the case so when you review it later you can readily locate its relevant sections. Once again, consider imposing some order on this process by using different color pens or highlighters to reflect different issues so that the portions of the case dealing with a physician's standard of care are highlighted with yellow while the portions of the case relating to damages are highlighted in pink. When you later review the case, you will then be able to quickly locate the portions you need. Do not be afraid to record your own thoughts and reactions on your copies of cases. An interjection such as "perfect" or "oops" may later jog your memory as to the value of a case you read days earlier. You should consider rating the cases on a scale of 1 to 10 so you will have an easier time of weeding out weaker authorities.

A product of use to students is "LEXIS-NEXIS Office for Legal Education," which integrates the ability to conduct online searching in the LEXIS-NEXIS databases with a feature to store and organize information. This product was developed expressly for students, who are continually presented with new information, class notes, and research information. LEXIS-NEXIS Office allows you to store all of that information in one place and then retrieve and search it later.

Any kind of text can be stored in your "infobase," including cases you have downloaded from LEXIS, class notes, or other materials. You can insert notes wherever you like, just as you would attach sticky notes to a text you read. You can highlight portions of text. Finally, you can search the entire text of your infobase, much like you search for words or phrases on LEXIS-NEXIS, thereby allowing you to locate immediately your notes and information on "jurisdiction" or "venue."

This electronic version of note-taking may appeal to many individuals. Similarly, many students take laptop computers to law libraries and "take notes" on the laptop as they research. No one method of note-taking is superior to another. The method that works best for you is the best method. For those students who are decidedly "low tech" or "technologically challenged," do not despair: If the majority of judges in the country do not need computers to do their work, it is likely you can succeed as they do and as legal professionals have done for hundreds of years—with pen and paper.

b. Contents of Notes

If your notes are to be of any assistance to you in constructing your written project, they will need to be more than random words or isolated phrases. The best approach for taking notes on cases is to brief the cases. You will recall from Chapter 4 that briefing a case is, in fact, described as taking notes on a case. Thus, any sheet or index card relating to a case should be a brief of the case and should include the following elements:

- complete citation
- brief overview of facts
- procedural history
- issue(s)
- reasoning
- holding

It is not necessary that your sheet of paper or index card be perfect. It should contain only the most important and relevant information. You can "fill in the gaps" when writing your project by referring to your photocopy of the case itself. The sheet of paper or index card is only for reference purposes. Do not expect to be able to put your project together by simply assembling your sheets of paper or organizing your index cards and turning them over to a word processor or secretary. Your notes provide only the framework for your project. They are not the project itself.

For taking notes on other authorities such as law review articles or A.L.R. annotations, simply summarize the most relevant points. While these authorities may be quite lengthy and often exceed 20 pages, they are secondary authorities, and thus you should not rely too much on them. Such authorities serve as great backups to the cases you rely upon and, because your project will not solely depend upon these authorities, you should be able to record the information you need on one or two pages or index cards. Often, in fact, these authorities are used to introduce you to an area of the law or provide an overview of a topic. While they may be of invaluable help in educating you on a topic, you may decide not to cite these authorities at all in your project, preferring instead to rely upon the primary authorities to which they referred you.

c. Complete Notes

Your notes will be of little help to you if you are constantly returning to the library to obtain additional information. Your goal upon completion of the research phase of your project is to return to your office to write the results of your research, having everything you need in your notes. If you need to return to the library during the writing phase to get a parallel cite or the name of the author of a law review article, your note-taking was ineffective.

It is a great temptation when researching simply to jot down part of a citation and then start taking notes, figuring you will obtain the complete cite later. Resist this temptation and always include all of the information you will need for citation purposes in your notes. Follow *Bluebook* form. This will save time later.

For cases, record the complete name of the case, parallel citations, and date. If your notes contain a quote from the case, indicate the page of the case on which the quote appeared so you can later include this pinpoint in your citation.

When taking notes, clearly identify whether your notes reflect a quote or are merely paraphrasing the judge's or author's statements. It is nearly impossible to remember days after you performed the research whether a statement in your notes that "physicians are liable for the harm to their patients proximately caused by their negligent or intentional wrongful acts" is a quotation or your own summary of a case unless your notes remind you. Any system is sufficient so long as it works for you. You may use quotation marks only for direct quotes and then any material not in quotes is a paraphrase; you may label each statement in your notes with a "q" or a "p"; or you may elect to use a different color pen to show a quotation.

It is wise to record the page even a paraphrase occurs on because you may wish later to review the original language in the case or you may wish, as a courtesy to the reader, to include in your citation a reference to specific pages, whether or not the statement is a direct quote. Including pinpoints for paraphrasing is expected professional courtesy. Similarly, if your quotation appeared in headnote 6 of a case or you are relying primarily on headnote 6 of a case, indicate this in your notes as **[6]**. When you later Shepardize or KeyCite, you will be able to focus on the treatment of this portion of the case by later authorities and will not waste time reading later cases relating to headnote 12 when you were not relying on that portion of the case.

Your notes should reflect whether you have checked the pocket part or supplement to the authority and whether any information was found therein as this may need to be included in your citation. Similarly, notes relating to primary authorities should record that they have been Shepardized or KeyCited and are still "good law." You can simply include a "box" on each page or index card and complete it as follows:

PP/Supp x
Info in main vol. yes or p.p./supp. no
Shep. x on 2/6 . Problems/concerns **None** .

2. *Staying Focused*

One of the most difficult tasks in performing legal research is staying focused on a specific issue or question. Students commonly report that as they are in the process of researching an issue such as negligence and reading a pertinent case, they come across a reference to what appears to be a promising law review article. Without completing the reading of the case, they then grab the law review article, which refers to two other cases. These new cases are then pulled from the shelves, and they also refer to other promising authorities. At the end of a full morning of research, the student is surrounded by a pile of books, none of which has been thoroughly analyzed and some of which, when later re-read, are a mystery as to their relevance because they discuss topics completely unrelated to the original issue of negligence.

This hopscotch approach to research will invariably lead you away from your answer rather than toward it. The reason it occurs so frequently is that it is incredibly tempting to interrupt your analysis of an issue with the thought that the "perfect" authority is the next one, or that if you do not grab the authority now you will forget about it later.

Train yourself to stay focused on each specific issue. If you are researching a problem, for example, whether a physician is liable for injuries sustained by a patient during surgery when the patient consented to the risks of surgery and violated the doctor's orders prior to surgery, devote yourself to one topic at a time. Decide that the first morning you will only research the general duty of care required of a doctor. If you come across cases or references that relate to the consent issue or the issue of damages, jot these down in the sections of your notebook corresponding to those topics so you can review them later, but do not interrupt your research on the assigned issue.

After you are thoroughly satisfied that you understand a physician's general duties, assign yourself the issue of whether the patient's consent was valid; that is, whether it is wrong for a doctor to obtain, in effect, a release prior to surgery for acts that occur during surgery, and whether the patient had any choice but to sign a written consent without which the doctor would not perform the surgery. If, during the course of research related to these consent issues, you come across other references to the physician's duty of care or damages recoverable in malpractice actions, write them down for future reference, but do not allow yourself to be sidetracked from the consent issue on which you are working. With any luck, when it is time to research your last issue, the question of damages, you will already have a list of promising cases and other authorities to review, thus eliminating the need for you to start at the beginning with encyclopedias, codes, or digests.

The hopscotch effect also occurs during Shepardizing or KeyCiting. For example, in the middle of Shepardizing one case, you may find a reference to a later case that explains your case. Avoid the temptation to leave your Shepardizing and obtain that case. Once again, jot down the reference and then look it up after you have completed your review of all of the volumes of *Shepard's*. If you interrupt your Shepardizing to read a case, you may forget where you are in the Shepardizing process. Thus, when you return to the task, you may assume you completed Shepardizing the original case when in reality you only examined some rather than all of the requisite volumes of *Shepard's*. The exception to this is in computer-assisted Shepardizing or KeyCiting, or Shepardizing using CD-ROM, which allow you to quickly flip back and forth between *Shepard's* or KeyCite and the authorities that mention or discuss your case.

C. When to Stop

One of the most difficult tasks in legal research is knowing when to stop. No one will come up to you in the law library, tap you on the shoulder, and inform you that time is up and your task is complete. Moreover, it seems as if some issues can be researched endlessly. If you read a landmark case, it may refer to five other cases, which you may also decide to read. When it is time to Shepardize or KeyCite these six cases, you may discover that each of the six cases has been mentioned or discussed in ten other cases (as well as numerous law review articles, opinions of attorneys general, and A.L.R. annotations). You now have 60 other cases that could be examined, each of which refers to other authorities and each, when Shepardized or KeyCited, is in turn discussed by other cases and authorities. This process could continue indefinitely and is a bit like a funnel that gets wider and wider. Eventually, you need to call a halt to your research.

1. *Practical Considerations*

Sometimes there is a practical reason for stopping your research. It is possible that the client's claim is for $40,000. You cannot possibly afford to expend $20,000 in legal research and then present the client with a bill after the trial that charges the client $20,000 for legal research and $10,000 for other costs and attorneys' fees, leaving the client with a mere $10,000 recovery. Thus, in many cases, economics will dictate how thorough your research will be. When the client's budget dictates the amount of research that can be performed, you will have to be as efficient and streamlined as possible. Keep track of your hours as you go along and after a few hours report back to your supervisor on your progress and estimate how much longer you think will be required. Before you commence the project, discuss the budget with your supervisor and agree on a strategy and a time to meet and discuss your efforts. When you are given the project, your supervisor may expressly tell you that you should allot five to six hours for research and might even suggest a specific statute or case as a beginning point.

This balance between the duty to research adequately and the economic realities of a case is a delicate one. It is the attorney's task to resolve this issue and give you proper guidance. If you do not receive any instruction, take the initiative and state that for time-management purposes, you would like to inquire as to the date the project is due (this in and of itself may give you a clue as to how thorough the project is to be) and a range of time the attorney estimates for the research.

Research as efficiently as possible. If your research efforts produce a number of potentially relevant cases, all of which look promising but the reading of which would be impractical and time-consuming, adopt a strategy that will produce the best results in the least amount of time. For example, read newer cases before you move on to older cases, read cases from higher courts before those from lower courts, and read cases from your forum jurisdiction before those from a foreign jurisdiction.

If you find that the project is far more complex than you and your supervisor originally anticipated and that the authorities are unclear or conflicting, stop your research and go back to your supervisor, explain your progress thus far and why the issue is more complex than anticipated, and ask for direction. Your supervisor would much prefer to find out after six hours of research that you are having difficulty rather than after 30 hours, which cannot be billed to the client.

Do not be embarrassed to ask for direction or acknowledge that you are having difficulties. If the answer to a question was so easy, everyone would already know it and there would be no need to research it.

Attorneys are always interested in economic efficiency, and if you present your question in a manner that shows you are aware of the economics of a law practice, you will be commended rather than criticized. For example, instead of telling your supervisor, "I can't find any authorities on this, so I'm quitting," state "I haven't yet been able to find any authorities on point. If I can't turn up some leads in the next hour, let's meet and discuss our next step." Alternatively, you can report, "I've spent the six hours you suggested and because the circuit courts are in conflict on this issue, I believe I need two to three more hours. Will the client approve this additional time?"

2. *Complex Projects*

If the project is complex, you may find yourself in the "funnel position," that is, the situation in which there is an ever-expanding list of authorities that could be reviewed. Knowing when to stop researching this type of project is difficult. It is hard to know if you have gotten the "right answer." Seldom, if ever, is there one perfect case or authority that is directly responsive to your research task. It is far more likely that you find numerous cases that are somewhat responsive and that you must patch together to arrive at an answer.

One clue that your research is complete is that you keep bumping into the same authorities. For example, assume that in the course of reading a 1982 case entitled *Jones v. Smith* you make note of a 1970 case referred to therein called *ABC v. XYZ*. When you later read *ABC*, it discusses the same principle discussed in *Jones*. When you Shepardize or KeyCite *ABC*, you are referred to *Jones* and a 1985 case entitled *Henderson v. Powell*. A reading of *Henderson* reveals the same general discussion you read in the earlier cases. When you Shepardize *Henderson*, you are referred to a 1990 case called *O'Connell v. Rowe*. A reading of *O'Connell* discloses a discussion of the previous cases, *Jones* and *Henderson*.

These references to the same authorities are a signal that the principle originally set forth in *ABC* has been continually repeated by later cases. If nothing significant or new is added by the line of cases decided after your "best" case, and Shepardizing or KeyCiting reveals that the cases you rely on are still valid, stop researching. This circular procedure is a hint that your research is complete. You may want to "flesh out" your research by reviewing a law review article or other secondary authority, but if these confirm the results of your earlier research, you will know you have been sufficiently thorough.

Often beginning researchers lack the confidence to stop researching and are convinced there is one perfect case that they will find if they can only devote enough time to the effort. This is a fallacy. Seldom, if ever, is a perfect case sitting on the shelves—for the reason that no two cases are exactly alike. You will find cases that are similar to yours, and you will be able to argue that because the cases are similar the reasoning in the reported cases should apply to your particular problem. It is highly unlikely, if not impossible, however, to find an identical case, so do not waste your time looking for one. Once you have cases "on point" (similar legal issues as your case, similar facts as your case, from the highest courts in your jurisdiction, and that are still valid) this is sufficient.

Another sign of lack of confidence in beginning researchers is their unshaken conviction that they cannot be right and there must be some case hidden in the library that will render meaningless their efforts. If you have examined the statutes (and, if applicable, constitutional provisions) from your jurisdiction as well as the cases interpreting the statutes and have updated the statutes by checking the pocket parts and Shepardizing or KeyCiting the statutes and cases, and the authorities are in agreement, your research is concluded. It is only when you neglect to review the cases interpreting a statute or fail to update by checking pocket parts and Shepardizing or KeyCiting that your research is an unexploded mine field.

After you gain confidence in your research skills through practice, you will be able to trust your instincts and say, "I'm finished," rather than thinking, "I can't possibly have found the right answer even though 22 cases all say the same thing so I'll continue to look for something to prove me wrong."

3. *Quick Questions*

Often your research task is specific and well-defined. You may be asked to check how many days a defendant has to provide answers to interrogatories propounded by a plaintiff or what the statute of limitations is to sue for breach of contract in your state.

Such specific questions are easily answered by examining your state's annotated code. Review the statute and the cases construing it. Update and Shepardize or KeyCite the authorities to determine they are still valid. Generally, this approach will be sufficient to answer questions that are straightforward.

4. *Established Issues*

If your research task relates to an established area of the law, such as the elements of a cause of action for breach of contract, a landlord's duty to provide habitable premises to a tenant, or the damages recoverable in fraud actions, you may find a multitude of authorities. Some of the authorities may be decades old, and there may be numerous cases, periodical articles, A.L.R. annotations, and discussions in texts and treatises. These authorities, however, may reflect remarkable unanimity. That is, researching an issue related to an established area of law usually results in numerous authorities in agreement.

Determining when to stop researching will be relatively easy because the authorities will begin referring to each other over and over again. Once you update and Shepardize or KeyCite to ensure that the primary authorities are still valid, your task is complete.

Conversely, research in newly emerging areas of law can be frustrating because there will often be substantial conflict among courts as judges grapple with a difficult issue and try to establish rules of law. Thus, research relating to the liability of an Internet service provider for defamatory statements made on a Web site or research relating to contracts for hiring a surrogate parent will be fraught with conflict. Often periodical articles or A.L.R. annotations will be most helpful because they will offer an overview of new topics and attempt to explain and reconcile conflicts. Update a law review article with *Shepard's Law Review Citations* and update A.L.R. annotations through the use of pocket parts. Remember computer-assisted legal research, which has the ability to locate hundreds of documents if you carefully formulate the search query.

Research for these newly developing legal topics is difficult because often you cannot find one single right answer. If this is the case, you simply need to follow the standard research techniques and realize that your conclusion may well be that the authorities are uncertain and conflicting.

5. *Issues of First Impression*

Often the most difficult research task is the one that yields no results whatsoever. Thus, after hours of research, you may not have found any authorities. There are two conclusions to draw from this occurrence: "There are no authorities relating to this issue" or "I must be doing something wrong because I can't locate any authorities." Beginning researchers will always draw the second conclusion and refuse to stop researching even though they are retracing their steps over and over again.

It is possible that an issue is one of "first impression," that is, one not yet considered in your jurisdiction. Unfortunately, there is no foolproof way to determine this. There is no list produced by the legislature or courts of "topics not yet considered." There are, however, two techniques you can use to assure yourself that it is not your research strategy that has resulted in a total lack of authorities.

First, select a populous and varied jurisdiction such as California or New York, which has a rich body of law. Use the same research techniques, sets of books (annotated codes, digests), and descriptive words that you used in your home jurisdiction. If you obtain results, you will know that your strategies, choice of books, and descriptive words were sound and that the lack of authorities in your jurisdiction is the result of an issue of first impression, not misguided research efforts.

Second, computer-assisted legal research, with its ability to search for thousands of documents that contain specific terms, will help verify your research techniques. If your search query is "blood and product and infect! and HIV or AIDS /50 bank" and after you have selected the database for all Utah statutes and cases you obtain no references whatsoever, you should feel more confident that Utah has simply not yet considered this issue. To achieve a final comfort level, contact the service representatives for LEXIS or Westlaw and ask for assistance in formulating a search.

6. *How Many Authorities Are Enough?*

Beginning researchers usually want to know how many cases or authorities should be cited in a brief or project. There is no answer to this question. As a general rule, however, you will need fewer authorities to support a well-established principle and more authorities to discuss an emerging area of law or one in conflict.

Is one citation enough? It is possible that a single citation may suffice to answer a quick question. Thus, the question of how many days a defendant has to answer interrogatories propounded in a federal court action can be responded to as follows: A party served with interrogatories has 30 days after the date of service to answer or object to the interrogatories. Fed. R. Civ. P. 33(a). A further review of the Federal Rules of Civil Procedure, however, discloses that the answering party has three extra days to respond if served by mail and that if the last day is a Saturday, Sunday, or holiday, the party has until the next business day. Fed. R. Civ. P. 6(a), (e). More complex questions, such as whether a landlord may turn off the heat of a tenant who has not paid rent, may require careful reading of several statutes, cases, and other authorities.

Remember the weight of authorities: Primary authorities (cases, constitutions, and statutes) must be followed by a court. Secondary authorities (encyclopedias, periodical articles, annotations, and so forth) are persuasive only. Thus, you should always aim to have at least one primary authority to support each of your arguments. Do not make the mistake of assuming, however, that if there are 12 cases from your jurisdiction, all of which state that punitive damages are recoverable in fraud actions, you should discuss and cite all 12. Courts are impatient with string citing or repetitive arguments. Exercise discretion and select the most articulate case or the one most similar to your case. Consider selecting the landmark case in this area and then one recent case from your highest court. See Figure 13-5.

Cite secondary authorities if they provide a concise analysis of a topic or if the author is a well-respected and renowned authority in that legal field. Consider combining primary authorities with a secondary authority to support your argument. Do not, however, believe that legal research is like a recipe and that if you always cite two cases and a law review article your argument will win. Different topics require different levels of analysis, and you will need to exercise your own discretion to determine how many authorities are enough.

Technology Tips

http://www.ualr.edu/~cmbarger/Research.htm	This site includes numerous links to sites to enable you to conduct legal research.
http://comp.uark.edu/~ksampson/research2.html	This "legal research library" includes good links to state and federal sources as well as a research outline.

Figure 13-5
A Blueprint for Research

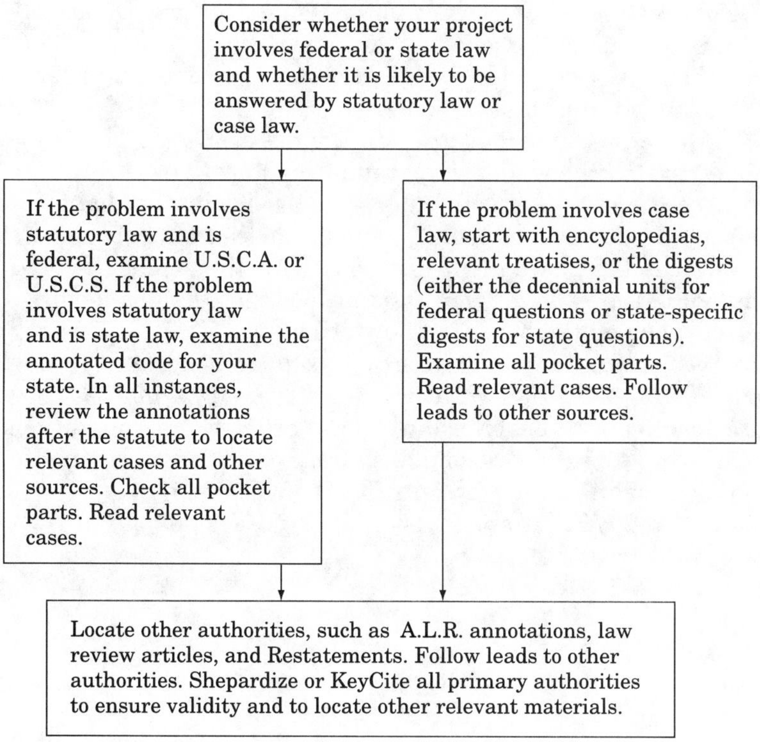

Consider whether your project involves federal or state law and whether it is likely to be answered by statutory law or case law.

↓

If the problem involves statutory law and is federal, examine U.S.C.A. or U.S.C.S. If the problem involves statutory law and is state law, examine the annotated code for your state. In all instances, review the annotations after the statute to locate relevant cases and other sources. Check all pocket parts. Read relevant cases.

If the problem involves case law, start with encyclopedias, relevant treatises, or the digests (either the decennial units for federal questions or state-specific digests for state questions). Examine all pocket parts. Read relevant cases. Follow leads to other sources.

↓

Locate other authorities, such as A.L.R. annotations, law review articles, and Restatements. Follow leads to other authorities. Shepardize or KeyCite all primary authorities to ensure validity and to locate other relevant materials.

Ten Tips for Effective Research

1. ***Be prepared.*** The time you spend thinking about a project before you begin is time well spent. Give yourself a few minutes to plan your research strategies.
2. ***Be flexible.*** If the books you need aren't on the shelf or if your efforts are not yielding results, switch to another set of books.
3. ***Be thorough.*** Check all pocket parts and supplements to be sure you have the most recent materials. Shepardize or KeyCite all primary authorities to make sure the law is still "good." Take complete notes. Be scrupulous in transcribing citations to avoid backtracking. Consider a variety of research methods (print sources, CALR, and the Internet) to achieve the best results.
4. ***Be patient.*** Research can be a difficult process. Expect some roadblocks.
5. ***Be organized.*** Tackle one topic or issue at a time. Do not allow yourself to get sidetracked on a minor issue or diverted in another direction. Address each research issue with a laser, not a buckshot, approach.
6. ***Be efficient.*** Gather together all the materials you need so you don't waste time wandering around the library.
7. ***Be creative.*** If all of your colleagues are beginning their research in one set of books, begin in another to avoid the crowd as well as the crowd mentality. Try contacting agencies and individuals and asking for assistance rather than depending exclusively on the books in the stacks.
8. ***Be wary.*** Make sure you approach your problem from all angles. Play devil's advocate. What will the adversary argue?
9. ***Be resourceful.*** Look for law review articles and annotations on your legal topic. If someone has already written a thorough analysis of an issue, why reinvent the wheel?
10. ***Be calm.*** If you get stuck, ask a librarian for help. That's what they're there for.

Writing Strategies

As you prepare to write, invest time in "brainstorming." On a piece of paper, jot down anything that comes to mind relating to the project. You can later omit any ideas or topics that are not useful. The mere process of starting to write something will get your creative juices flowing and some ideas that you originally believe are far-fetched may later develop into a creative line of reasoning.

If you initially think of more than one way to express a thought, write down both expressions. Later you can decide which to omit or perhaps you will find a way to combine both ideas.

If an argument occurs to you during the research process, write it down as clearly and completely as possible. You may later be able to "lift" these notes intact and place them verbatim into the written project. That is, the more complete your note-taking is, the easier it will be for you to write the project. In some instances, your notes will almost be the equivalent of a first draft. If your "note-taking" consists merely of photocopying cases and passages of writings, however, you will need to devote far more time to the initial draft as much work needs to be done to develop what is in those cases and writings into a reasoned and concise project.

Legal Writing

Chapter 14

Back to Basics

A. The Mechanics of Writing
B. Grammar, Spelling, and Punctuation

Chapter Overview

The goal of legal writing is to communicate. The style of the communication may simply be informative, for example, to inform the reader of certain facts or events, or it may be persuasive, for example, to persuade the reader to adopt a certain point of view. No matter what style or form legal writing takes, its mechanics (grammar, spelling, and punctuation) must be correct. Failure to use good grammar results in cloudy and incomprehensible writing. Incorrect spelling casts doubt on your skill and credibility. Improper punctuation results in an unclear project.

This chapter will review these basics of writing so your final product will effectively communicate to its intended audience, whether it is a client, an adverse party, or a court.

A. The Mechanics of Writing

Even if your research is flawless and you have found primary authorities "on point," these will do you no good unless you can communicate your results to a reader. Flaws in the communication process, such as improper spelling, awkward word usage and sentence construction, and errors in punctuation distract your reader from the import of your project, making the reader doubt your abilities and reflect on your carelessness.

Some legal professionals have strong writing backgrounds and are comfortable with grammar, spelling, and punctuation. Others have more scientific or technology-oriented backgrounds and are unused to writing. Even those individuals who have done a great deal of writing in college or on the job may be unfamiliar with the strictures of legal writing. For example, typical undergraduate writing is marked by more flexible punctuation. Punctuation in legal writing is considerably more rigid because a misplaced or omitted comma can change the meaning of a statement. There is vigorous debate among grammarians regarding some punctuation marks and usages. Select a well-known text such as *Chicago Manual of Style* and use it to support your position, if necessary.

After years of communicating primarily by telephone, many people in the business fields are now communicating more in writing. Thanks to e-mail and electronic chat rooms, people are writing more now than ever before. Unfortunately, communicating via computer is often so informal that careless errors are perpetuated. Thus, while many of us may be writing more, we're also writing worse, with less attention to spelling, punctuation, and proofing. Do not be seduced into thinking that because e-mail to your supervisor or colleagues is easy and informal, it can be incorrect. The way you communicate communicates a message about you. Invest the time and effort in producing a clear and well-written document or message every time you write and no matter what the means of communication. A final word of caution about e-mail: Most law firms and businesses have strict policies about the use of e-mail for business purposes only. Moreover, the security of e-mail is open to question. Many employers monitor e-mail use. Therefore, do not use e-mail for anything other than business reasons and do not say anything you wouldn't want your boss to read.

While there are many guides to grammar, perhaps the best known and easiest to understand is *The Elements of Style* by William Strunk, Jr., and E.B. White. First introduced in 1919, *The Elements of Style* sets forth in clear and concise fashion principles of usage and composition with illustrative examples. Some writing instructors recommend a cover to cover re-reading of "the little book" each year to refresh one's understanding of the fundamentals of English style. Additionally, most dictionaries include sections on grammar, spelling, and punctuation together with useful examples. Finally, any bookstore's reference section will include numerous books on writing and style. Invest in a few reference tools and keep them near you when you write.

Don't let the rules of grammar and its incomprehensible terms (such as "pluperfect" or "subjunctive") intimidate you. You do not need to know all of the parts of speech to be a good writer, just as you do not need to know all of the parts of a microwave oven to be a good cook.

This chapter will discuss the rules most commonly misunderstood or violated by legal writers.

B. Grammar, Spelling, and Punctuation

1. *Grammar Do's and Don't's*

Rules of grammar are used so that we can communicate clearly. Following are some of the most common grammatical errors made by beginning and even experienced writers.

a. Subject-Verb Agreement

A verb must agree in number with the subject of a sentence. That is, if the subject of a sentence is singular, the verb must also be singular. Similarly, if the subject of a sentence is plural, the verb must also be plural. Most problems in subject-verb agreement occur when a subject is used that has more than one word, when the subject is a collective noun, or when several words or a prepositional phrase intervene between the subject and the verb.

(1) Multiple Word Subjects

Examples

Incorrect	*Correct*
Compound Subject: The judge and jury was unpersuaded by Smith's testimony.	The judge and jury were unpersuaded by Smith's testimony.

Because the subject of the sentence in the preceding example consists of two words connected by "and," it is plural, and thus a plural verb (were) is needed.

If the subject is composed of singular words connected by "or" or "nor," use a singular verb.

Incorrect	*Correct*
Neither the defendant nor his counsel were prepared.	Neither the defendant nor his counsel was prepared.

If the subject is composed of a singular and a plural word, the verb should agree with the noun or pronoun nearer to the verb, as in "The judge and the *jurors have* gone home."

Often confusion regarding subject and verb agreement arises when a word that ends in -one or -body, such as "someone" or "everybody," or a word such as "each," "either," "neither," or "no one" is used. These words are considered singular, and a singular verb must be used. Moreover, a singular pronoun (he, she, it) must be used with these words.

While it is common to use plural pronouns in speaking or informal writing, legal writing is more formal and one must be scrupulous in using singular pronouns with such words.

Incorrect	*Correct*
Does everyone have their tickets to the movie?	Does *everyone* have *his* ticket to the movie?

Incorrect	*Correct*
Each of these incidents involve a consumer who mistakenly purchased one product when they intended to purchase another.	*Each* of these incidents *involves* a *consumer* who mistakenly purchased one product when *he* intended to purchase another.
Somebody forgot to file their papers.	*Somebody* forgot to file *his* papers.
When your child loses their confidence	When your child loses *his* or *her* confidence . . . . (or When your child loses confidence . . . .

While the correct examples above show proper usage, you may wish to avoid the words "his" or "he" if they strike you as sexist. As discussed later in this chapter, there are several ways to remedy sexist language. In the first example, you could rewrite the sentence as follows: "Does everyone have *a* ticket to the movie?"

(2) Collective Nouns

Collective nouns (nouns that stand for a group of people or items) such as committee, crowd, court, and jury are usually singular. Watch for the word "the" before a noun because it is often a signal that the word to follow is singular.

Incorrect	*Correct*
The jury have adjourned to deliberate the defendant's guilt.	The *jury has* adjourned to deliberate the defendant's guilt.
The court are discussing the plaintiff's right to a speedy trial.	The *court is* discussing the plaintiff's right to a speedy trial.

If you wish to discuss the individuals composing the unit, for the sake of clarity use the following form:

	Correct
	The *jurors have* adjourned to deliberate the defendant's guilt.
	The *members* of the court *are* discussing the plaintiff's right to a speedy trial.

(3) Intervening Words

Subject-verb agreement problems often occur when several words or a phrase intervenes between a subject and a verb.

Incorrect	*Correct*
The remainder of the goods to be distributed are in storage.	The *remainder* of the goods to be distributed *is* in storage.
The purpose of the will left by the decedents are to provide for their children.	The *purpose* of the will left by the decedents *is* to provide for their children.

In the preceding examples, the subjects are "remainder" and "purpose." Both of these words are singular and therefore they require the singular verb "is." Focus on the subject of the sentence and ignore intervening words.

(4) Prepositional Phrases

Prepositional phrases that intervene between a subject and a verb often confuse writers who may be tempted to match the verb with the noun in the prepositional phrase rather than with the subject of the sentence.

Incorrect	*Correct*
One of the best teachers are available.	*One* of the best teachers *is* available.
The deposition, along with many exhibits, show the defendant was speeding.	The *deposition,* along with many exhibits, *shows* the defendant was speeding.

In summary, always carefully scrutinize your writing to identify the subject. Once you have located the subject, classify it as singular or plural and then select the appropriate verb form, ignoring any intervening words or extraneous words.

b. Sentence Fragments

Sentence fragments, or incomplete sentences, are caused by a failure to include a subject and a verb in each sentence. Often a sentence fragment occurs because the writer has assumed that a dependent clause, that is, one that cannot stand on its own, is a sentence by itself. Sentence fragments can often be avoided by correcting the punctuation or by making the dependent clause into a complete sentence.

Incorrect	*Correct*
I gained two valuable lessons. First, the importance of being bilingual. Second, the need to understand a different culture.	I gained two valuable lessons: first, the importance of being bilingual and, second, the need to understand a different culture. *or* *Correct* I gained two important lessons. The first lesson was the importance of being bilingual and the second was the need to understand a different culture.

c. Run-on Sentences

In many ways, a run-on sentence is the opposite of a sentence fragment. A run-on sentence combines two sentences into one. Run-on sentences can usually be corrected by inserting the proper punctuation or by dividing the run-on into two separate sentences.

Incorrect	*Correct*
The members of the jury were deadlocked, they could not reach a verdict.	The members of the jury were deadlocked; they could not reach a verdict. *or* The members of the jury were deadlocked. They could not reach a verdict.

d. Modifiers

The incorrect placement of a modifier (a word that limits or qualifies another word or group of words) causes ambiguity. Place modifiers next to or as close as possible to the words they modify. For example, the sentence "Ginny agreed only to lend her sister money" is capable of two interpretations. Does it mean that Ginny agreed to lend her sister money and no other item? Or does it mean Ginny will lend her sister money and will not lend money to anyone else? It may be necessary to add words to a sentence with a modifier in order to achieve clarity. Either of the following two sentences will reduce ambiguity:

Ginny agreed to lend her sister only money and nothing else.
Ginny agreed to lend money only to her sister and not to anyone else.

Modifiers such as "apparently," "ultimately," "frequently," "immediately," "eventually," "finally," and "only" are notorious causes of ambiguity. Exercise caution in using these words.

The typical modifiers are adverbs and adjectives. Once again, try to place these modifiers adjacent to the words they modify.

Incorrect	*Correct*
. . . former female attorney	. . . female former attorney

e. Split Infinitives

A split infinitive is caused by the insertion of an adverb between an infinitive such as "to innocently ask" or "to forcefully demand." It is easy to remedy a split infinitive: Simply place the adverb after the infinitive so the phrase is "to ask innocently" or "to demand forcefully." Avoid splitting infinitives unless your goal is to stress the adverb. While it is fairly common to see split infinitives in nonlegal writing, including newspaper articles, and while most grammarians accept split infinitives, legal writing is more traditional and formal than other writing and care should be taken to avoid split infinitives, which can produce awkward looking and sounding projects. Moreover, readers such as judges tend to be perfectionists. Thus, in the interest of erring on the side of caution, comply with the "old" writing rules (don't split an infinitive; don't end a sentence with a preposition; don't start a sentence with a conjunction such as "and" or "but") whenever possible.

Awkward	*Better*
The attorney asked me *to thoroughly review* the pleadings.	The attorney asked me *to review* the pleadings thoroughly.

Do not insert "not" or "never" in an infinitive because the result is awkward and incorrect.

Incorrect	*Correct*
She agreed to not examine the witness.	She agreed not to examine the witness.

f. Dangling Participles

A participle is an adjective created from a verb such as the word "running" in the phrase "the man running down the street." A participial phrase is one that has no express subject. Because it has no express subject, it must correctly refer to the subject of the sentence. The phrases that cause confusion or convey an unintended meaning are those in which the implied subject in the participial phrase does not match up with the express subject in the independent clause that follows it.

For example, the sentence "Being violent, the attorney refused to be alone with the defendant" is confusing because it indicates that the attorney rather than the defendant was violent. Similarly, a sentence such as "Entering the darkened room, his eyes slowly adjusted to the dimness" is incorrect because it lacks an identification of the subject and implies that the eyes entered the room. If a participial phrase is not immediately followed by its subject, it is said to "dangle."

Other dangling participles often result in unintended humor. For example, the following statement was published in *The Westhampton Beach* (N.Y.) *Hampton Chronicle News*: "Boasting a voracious appetite and stocked with both male and female sex organs capable of producing 1,000 offspring per year, officials at the U.S. Department of Agriculture are warning Long Islanders to report any sightings of the oversized escargot immediately."

To remedy a dangling participle, either add a subject to the participial phrase or re-word the sentence and eliminate the dependent participial phrase, as follows:

> Because the defendant was violent, the attorney refused to be alone with him.
>
> *or*
>
> The attorney refused to be alone with the violent defendant.

Incorrect	*Correct*
Entering the darkened room, his eyes slowly adjusted to the dimness.	As he entered the darkened room, his eyes slowly adjusted to the dimness.
Having reviewed the transcript, a few comments occur to me.	Having reviewed the transcript, I have a few comments.

g. Pronouns

(1) Personal Pronouns

Personal pronouns (I/me, he/him, she/her, we/us, they/them) change forms depending on whether they function as the subject of a sentence or the object of the sentence. When the pronoun functions as or replaces the subject of a sentence, use "I," "he," "she," "we," or "they."

Incorrect	*Correct*
It was me who prepared the document.	It was I who prepared the document.

Incorrect	*Correct*
James and her drafted the appellate brief.	James and she drafted the appellate brief.
Either him or me will do the cite-checking.	Either he or I will do the cite-checking.
Us on the jury voted to convict the defendant.	We on the jury voted to convict the defendant.
It was them who informed the police.	It was they who informed the police.

When the pronoun functions as or replaces the object of a sentence, use “me,” “him,” “her,” “us,” or “them.”

Incorrect	*Correct*
You must give John and I clearer instructions.	You must give John and *me* clearer instructions.
We urge you to release Susan and he from their employment contracts.	We urge you to release Susan and *him* from their employment contracts.
She has provided the committee and we with the budget analysis.	She has provided the committee and *us* with the budget analysis.
The prisoner was released into the custody of Janet and they.	The prisoner was released into the custody of Janet and *them*.
Between you and I, the defendant is liable.	Between you and *me*, the defendant is liable.

As an aid to determining which form of pronoun to use, omit the noun and the word “and” accompanying the pronoun and this will provide a clue as to which pronoun to use. For example, in the sentence “you must give John and *I/me* clear instructions,” omit “John and” so the sentence reads “You must give __________ clear instructions.” This reading makes it clear the correct pronoun is “me.”

(2) Reflexive Pronouns

The reflexive pronouns are the “self” pronouns such as “myself,” “yourself,” “himself,” “herself,” “ourselves,” “yourselves,” and “themselves.” Reflexive pronouns usually reflect back on a subject as in “She injured herself.” Do not substitute a “self” pronoun for a personal pronoun (I/me, he/him).

Incorrect	*Correct*
Susan and myself attended the trial.	Susan and I attended the trial.
The accident was witnessed by Mrs. Hendrix and myself.	The accident was witnessed by Mrs. Hendrix and me.

(3) Relative Pronouns

The relative pronouns are "who," "whom," "this," "it," "that," "such," and "which." To decide whether to use "who" or "whom," you need to determine if the relative pronoun is the subject of the sentence. If so, use "who." If the relative pronoun is the object of a sentence, clause, or prepositional phrase, use "whom."

Incorrect	*Correct*
The man whom is being arraigned is 22 years old.	The man who is being arraigned is 22 years old.
This is the woman who I mentioned earlier.	This is the woman whom I mentioned earlier.
To who am I speaking?	To whom am I speaking?

It may be easier to remember that "who" takes the place of the words "he" or "she" while "whom" stands for "him" or "her."

Examples

Who is testifying tomorrow? (*He* or *she* is testifying tomorrow.)

Whom did you depose today? (You did depose *him* or *her.*)

Use "who" to refer to humans (as in "the paralegal who was hired"). Use "that" or "which" to refer to non-humans, places, or objects (as in "the deposition that was taken" or "the argument that was made").

"That" is used in a restrictive clause (a clause that is essential to the meaning of a sentence) while "which" is used in a non-restrictive clause (a clause that merely adds an idea to a sentence that would be complete without the clause). For example, in the sentence "The corporation that was formed in Delaware has no assets," the word "that" tells us which particular corporation has no assets (namely, the one formed in Delaware, not the one formed in Iowa). On the other hand, review the sentence "The corporation, which was formed in Delaware, has no assets." In this sentence you are given a fact about one corporation. The phrase "which was formed in Delaware," provides additional information about the corporation but is not essential to the meaning of the sentence. Many writers have difficulty determining whether to start a clause with "that" or "which." Remember these hints:

- If you can drop the clause and still retain the meaning of the sentence, use "which." If you can't, use "that."
- A clause beginning with "which" is surrounded by commas.
- A clause beginning with "that" is not.
- "That" introduces essential information; "which" does not.

Examples

- My car, which was brand new, was damaged in the collision. (You can drop the "which" clause and the sentence still makes sense. Use "which.")
- The car that was damaged in the collision was my car. (Elimination of the "that" clause causes the sentence to lose meaning. Use "that.")

Writers often substitute pronouns for names in a manner that creates ambiguity. For example, in the sentence "The document Ellen drafted for Teresa was given to her for review," it is unclear whether the "her" refers to Ellen or Teresa. Clarifying such an ambiguous statement usually requires rewriting the sentence. Thus, "The document Ellen drafted for Teresa was given to Ellen for her review" makes it clear which individual received the document for review.

Similarly, the sentence "Don likes these cookies more than me" creates confusion. Because the word "cookies" is used as the object of the verb, the sentence means that Don likes the cookies more than he likes me. To reduce confusion, rewrite such sentences. Thus, "Don likes these cookies more than I do" makes it clear Don likes the cookies more than I like them.

Use "it" to refer to collective nouns such as jury, court, committee, or association unless you are referring to the members of the group. Also use "it" or "its" to refer to non-human entities or institutions such as corporations.

Incorrect	*Correct*
The corporation held their annual meeting in May	The *corporation* held *its* meeting in May.
The court issued their opinion.	The *court* issued *its* opinion.

(4) Gender-Linked Pronouns

Avoid the use of gender-linked pronouns. For example, the sentence "A nurse should always keep her thermometer handy" is objectionable because it implies that nurses are always female. Similarly, the sentence "A judge must give his instructions to the jury" is likewise objectionable because it presupposes the judge is male.

There are several techniques you can use to avoid offending readers. One technique is to change the singular nouns to plural. This in turn will necessitate a change in the singular pronoun "he" or "she" to a neutral plural pronoun such as "they" or "their." Thus, the first example would read "Nurses should always keep their thermometers handy," and the second example would read "Judges must give their instructions to the jury."

A second technique is to rewrite the sentence to avoid using any pronouns. The first sentence would then read "A nurse should always keep a thermometer handy" and the second sentence could be rewritten as "A judge must always give instructions to the jury."

Another alternative is to use the noun "one." Using this technique, the first example would be rewritten as "One should always keep one's thermometer handy" and the second example would be "One must always give one's instructions to the jury." As you can see, however, the use of "one" often results in a vague sentence that is stuffy in tone.

Another alternative in some situations is to use the pronoun "you." Thus, rather than saying "The applicant must provide his or her address," say, "You must provide your address."

There are some instances in which none of these techniques will work for you. In those cases you could use "he or she" throughout the document. This, however, can result in a clumsy document if used continually. Avoid the use of "he/she." This construction creates an awkward appearance because slashes are seldom used in legal writing. Their use is noticeable and distracting to a reader. The combination "s/he" is even more noticeable and distracting.

If you are drafting a document, you may use "he" throughout and at the end include a statement that the use of a masculine gender is deemed to include the feminine. Avoid alternating between "he" and "she" in a single document, especially in a single paragraph. This attempt to be fair and gender-neutral is misguided and disruptive to the flow of a project.

When addressing a letter to an individual whose gender is unknown, for example, a letter to the Secretary of State of Utah, address it to "Dear Sir or Madam." While "madam" is an archaic form of address, it is correct in such a situation. Similarly, when you are responding to a letter written by an individual whose name is ambiguous, such as Terry L. Smith, consider calling and asking how the letter should be addressed. Rest assured, you will not be the first person confused by such a name. If contacting the person is not possible or practical, you could address the letter "Dear Terry" or "Dear Terry Smith."

In sum, correct gender-linked pronouns to avoid offending readers *if* you can do so without causing an awkward and distracting document. For example, the use of specially crafted words such as "personholes" (rather than "manholes") is jarring to a reader. Thus, it is still acceptable to use "he" or "him," if changing the pronouns or rewriting the sentence would result in clumsy and distracting writing.

2. *Spelling*

Many persons readily acknowledge they are poor spellers by proclaiming, "I've never been a good speller" as if this is some justification for a writing problem that negatively affects a project and the reader's view of its author. If you know that spelling is your weak spot, you need to work harder on this area rather than shrug it off with excuses. Keep several dictionaries handy—one in your office, one at home, and a pocket one in your briefcase. You may want to go to a professional bookstore that stocks legal books or to the bookstore at a law school to purchase a legal dictionary. A legal dictionary will include words used in legal settings such as "rescission" as well as Latin terms and phrases commonly used. Don't be afraid to write in your dictionary. Circle or highlight words you have reviewed. Chances are you will need to look up the word several times before you memorize the correct spelling. Similarly, you may wish to keep an index card handy with your top ten list of commonly misspelled words. Refer to it often. Over time, you will learn the words on the list.

Using a dictionary is not a sign of weakness. It is a signal that you are striving for professionalism in your work product. When you look up a word such as "canceled" in the dictionary, you may notice that you are given the alternate spelling "canceled" and then "cancelled." Usually the entry given first is the preferred spelling and you should use this form of the word. Similarly, use the commonly accepted spelling of a word rather than some foreign or exotic variety. For example, use "organization" and "behavior" rather than "organisation" and "behaviour," which are British spellings of those words.

One of the wonderful features of many word processor systems is their ability to check the spelling of words. Be sure to use this feature to help you catch spelling errors but do not rely on it exclusively. In fact, many experts believe spelling checkers encourage complacency. While the spelling checker will let you know if you misspelled "restaurant," it cannot check word usage. Thus, if you used the word "principle" rather than "principal" the spelling checker will not inform you so long as "principle" is spelled correctly. When I asked whether one should rely solely on a spell checker, one expert replied, "I'm a frayed knot."

Be thorough in your review of your finished project and read through the last draft for spelling errors. You should also keep a list of your own common spelling errors handy and refer to it. If you find it difficult to review your own work, ask a co-worker or friend to read through your project for spelling errors.

One of the most distressing results of misspelling is the effect produced in the mind of a reader. If your aim in writing is to inform or persuade your reader and the reader is confronted with spelling errors, any value your product may have may well be overshadowed by the misspellings. Readers of legal documents, such as employers, clients, attorneys, and judges, tend to be highly critical and perfectionistic. When confronted with spelling errors they may react by assuming that if you cannot be trusted to spell properly, you cannot be trusted to have found the correct answer to a legal problem. Thus, spelling errors cast doubt on more than your ability to spell by causing readers to question the correctness of your conclusions. At best, spelling errors make readers believe you are careless. At worst, they may question your intelligence.

Following are some words commonly misspelled in legal or business writing:

Correct

absence
accommodate
acknowledgment
admissible
affidavit
allege
bankruptcy
basically
boundary
breach
brief
calendar
cancellation
causal
cease
challenge
circuit
collateral
column
commitment
complaint
concede
condemn
conscious
controversy
counsellor
deductible
defendant
definite

Correct

dependent
descendant
desperately
dilemma
dissatisfied
environment
exercise
exonerate
feasible
foresee
fulfill
goodwill
grateful
grievous
harass
immediately
inasmuch as
indict
irrelevant
judgment (preferred)
labeled
license
lien
lightning
marshaled
minuscule
mortgage
occasionally

Correct

occurred
offense
permissible
perseverance
persistent
possess
practically
preceding
predecessor
privilege
proceed
publicly
rarefied
receive
recommend
relevant
renowned
rescind
rescission
seize
separate
sheriff
sincerely
succeed
supersede
statutes
transferred
warrant

Following are some tips to becoming a better speller:

- Learn some rules. Many spelling rules are easy to remember and have few exceptions, such as "place *i* before *e*, except after *c*, or except when it sounds like *a*, as in neighbor and weigh."
- Use a dictionary. Always consult a dictionary to check spelling and mark and highlight troublesome words. Some dictionaries contain no definitions; they only list spelled words. These dictionaries are useful and portable.
- Don't over rely on a spell checker. Studies show that papers written with the help of a spell checker are only marginally better than those that are not.
- Use mnemonic devices to help you remember words, such as "the princi*pal* of your school is your *pal*."
- Pronounce your words carefully. It will be difficult to remember the correct spelling of February if you pronounce it as *Febuary*.

- Write your misspellings several times. If you catch yourself writing "privelege" rather than "privilege," write it ten times to train yourself.
- Proofread carefully. In many instances, a misspelled word will not look "right " to you and you can then correct the error.

3. Punctuation

a. Introduction

When you speak, you use pauses and changes in voice inflection as well as gestures to signal meaning to the listener. In writing, these signals are given through the use of punctuation. Punctuation makes writing more understandable to a reader. For example, a period instructs the reader that a complete thought or sentence is concluded. Without periods, all of a writing would be one incomprehensible sentence. Similarly, quotation marks signal to a reader that the exact words of another are being used.

This portion of the chapter will discuss commas, apostrophes, colons, semicolons, quotations, parentheses, and the less frequently used marks in legal writing such as dashes and exclamation points.

There is some variation in punctuation. Given the same paragraph, two writers may punctuate slightly differently from each other. Nevertheless, the basic rules of punctuation have remained relatively unchanged since about the mid-1880s. While the newer, more modern approach to punctuation, referred to as "open" punctuation, uses fewer punctuation marks than the older approach (for example, many modern writers no longer use the serial comma discussed below), legal writing, like business writing, tends to be somewhat formal. Therefore, just as recommended in the section in this chapter on grammar, when in doubt, err on the side of caution and use the more conventional approach to punctuation rather than some unusual approach.

b. Commas

A comma indicates a brief pause and is considered the most troublesome of punctuation marks due to its numerous uses. Use a comma:

(i) After the salutation of an informal letter and after the closing of any letter:

Dear Aunt Kay,	Sincerely,
Dear James,	Very truly yours,

(ii) To set off digits in numbers, dates, and addresses:

> There are 4,182 pages in the transcript. (Note, however, that *Bluebook* Rule 6.2(a) states to use a comma only where numbers contain five or more digits and would therefore write this number as "4182.")

The plaintiff filed her complaint on June 9, 1997, the day she was fired from her job.
The defendant resides at 2202 Oak Brook Terrace, Evanston, Illinois 07816.

(iii) To set off an introductory word, phrase, or clause:

According to the plaintiff's testimony, the car was traveling west on Burgener Street at the time of the accident.
Nevertheless, the defendant failed to comply with the terms of his agreement.
First, the defendant entered Mrs. Smith's dwelling place.
Although she was quite elderly, she made an effective witness.

(iv) To set off interruptive or non-essential words or phrases:

While looking for her pen, however, she found the missing checkbook.
The defendant, over the strenuous objection of his counsel, insisted on testifying.

(v) To set off appositives (a word or group of words inserted immediately after another word that explains the previous word):

William Emery, the noted attorney, consulted on the case.

(vi) Before a conjunction such as "and," "but," "or," "nor," "for," or "yet" introducing an independent clause, namely, one that can function as a complete sentence. You may omit the comma if the clause is short (five words or less) or when the last part of your sentence is a subordinate or dependent clause, that is, when it does not make sense by itself:

The plaintiff intended to amend the complaint, but the statute of limitations had expired.
The defendant's answer had been amended several times, and the judge expressed impatience with the many amendments.
The attorney argued but the jury convicted.

(vii) To set off items in a series. Although the final comma in a series is optional in most writing, in legal writing you must place a comma after each item in the list and before the conjunction. For example, examine the sentence, "I leave my property equally to Susan, Bill, Louise, and Tom." Each individual would receive one-fourth of the estate. Note that the omission of the last comma would cause a completely different result, for example, "I leave my property equally to Susan, Bill, Louise and Tom." The omission of the comma after "Louise" arguably indicates the property is to be divided equally into thirds: one-third to Susan, one-third to Bill, and one-third to Louise and Tom together, rather than in equal fourths to each individual. Because the omission of the last comma in a series (the serial comma) can cause ambiguity, always include it. To determine how many commas to use, some writers count the number of items in the list or the series and then use one less comma than the number.

(viii) Before and after quotations:
"I need the pen," Bob said.
Lee replied, "I agree."

c. Apostrophes

Use an apostrophe:

(i) to show possession or ownership: If a word is singular, always add "'s" to show possession even if the word ends in "s," "k," or "z."

Singular:	The plaintiff's evidence
	John's legal pad
	Xerox's marketing plan
	The court's docket
	Arkansas's election
Plural:	The defendants' witnesses
	The girls' coats
	Shareholders' objections
	The judges' conferences

Some plural nouns (men, children, women, mice) do not end in "s." Form the possessive just as you would for singular nouns.

men's shoes
children's shouts
women's voices
mice's cages

To form the possessive of a proper noun that ends in a sibilant ("s," "x," or "z"), add an apostrophe and an "s."

Examples:

Texas's statehood
Mr. Jones's hat (but Mr. and Mrs. Joneses' children)
Mrs. Higgins's testimony

Some authorities suggest that the possessive of a multi-syllable personal name should be formed by adding an apostrophe only (as in "Jefferson Davis' papers" or "Mrs. Higgins' testimony") but most authorities, including *The Chicago Manual of Style* (14th ed. 1993), prefer the rule given above. You will find that there is much disagreement on this rule, with great emotion on both sides. The newer approach seems to be that both "Marcus' boat" and "Marcus's boat" are acceptable.

If a one-syllable word ends in "s," form the possessive by adding an apostrophe and an "s," as follows:

James's answer
Charles's book

If a word ends in "ss," just add an apostrophe, as in "my boss' plan."

To merely pluralize names that end in "s," "es" at the end, as in "the Joneses" or "the Collinses."

Do not use an apostrophe to show possession for personal pronouns such as "his," "hers," "ours," "yours," or "its."

Incorrect	*Correct*
The corporation had it's tax returns audited.	The corporation had its tax returns audited.

(ii) to show plurals of numbers and letters:

The audit showed all 9's.
How many exhibit A's are there?
Dot your i's.

(iii) to indicate omission of letters, as in contractions:

can't (cannot)
hadn't (had not)
it's (it is)
don't (do not)

One of the most common errors students and beginning writers make is misusing "it's." "It's" is a contraction for "it is" (or "it has"). The apostrophe is used to indicate that the letter "i" has been omitted. To form the possessive of it, use "its." Only use "it's" when you mean to say "it is" or "it has," not when you mean to indicate possession.

Example: *It's* a learned court that has the wisdom to reverse *its* decisions.

d. Colons

Use a colon:

(i) after the salutation of a formal letter:

Dear Mr. Smith:
Dear Sir or Madam:

(ii) to introduce a list; use a colon especially after expressions such as "as follows" or "the following":

The defendant asserted the following three defenses: laches, acquiescence, and unclean hands.

(iii) to indicate that something will follow:

We have instituted a new policy: Goods may not be returned without a sales receipt.

(iv) to introduce a formal or long quotation:

The court stated in unequivocal terms: "Liability is founded on this act of gross negligence."

(Note that this quotation could also be introduced by a comma.)

Capitalize the first word after a colon if the material following the colon can stand on its own as a sentence. Conversely, do not capitalize the first word after a colon if the material cannot stand on its own as a sentence.

e. Semicolons

Use a semicolon:

(i) to connect two independent but related clauses:

That was his final summation; it was strong and forceful.

(Note that these two ideas could also be expressed as complete sentences separated by periods.)

(ii) to connect two independent clauses joined by a transitional word or conjunction such as *therefore*, *however*, or *nevertheless*:

> The defendant was not credible; therefore, the jury voted to convict her.
> The attorney argued persuasively; however, the judge overruled her.

(iii) to separate items in a list containing commas:

> Standing trial for embezzlement were Connie Rivers of Portland, Oregon; Samuel Salter of Seattle, Washington; and Susan Stone of Butte, Montana.

(iv) to separate items in a list introduced by a colon:

> The elements to be proved in an action for breach of contract are as follows: the existence of a contract; the unjustified breach of the contract by one party; and damage caused by the breach to the non-breaching party.
>
> (Note that these items can also be separated by commas.)

f. Quotation Marks

Use quotation marks:

(i) to indicate the exact words of a speaker:

> Patrick Henry said, "Give me liberty or give me death."
> "Show me," I said.

(ii) to explain or draw emphasis to a word:

> The writer misspelled the word "defendant" in the brief.

Use quotation marks only for quotes of 49 words or fewer. For quotes of 50 words or more, block indent the quote and use single spacing. The indentation of these longer quotes itself indicates a quotation.

Always place commas and periods inside quotation marks. Place colons and semicolons outside quotation marks. When a quotation includes another quotation, single quotation marks (') are used:

> "It was the jury foreman," announced Betty, "who said, 'The defendant is guilty.' "

g. Parentheses

Use parentheses:

(i) to set off interruptions or explanations:

> His primary argument was *res ipsa loquitur* (a Latin phrase meaning "the thing speaks for itself").

(ii) to direct the reader to other information:

> The plaintiff has failed to allege justifiable reliance in the fraud cause of action (Compl. ¶ 14).

(iii) to introduce abbreviations:

> The plaintiff, Southwest Avionics Industries ("SAI"), alleged seven causes of action.

If what is included in the parenthetical is a complete sentence, place a period inside the parenthetical. Otherwise, the period is placed outside the ending parenthesis.

h. Dashes

Dashes create drama and draw a reader's attention to a page. In general, however, they are considered too informal for legal writing, and, in most instances, other punctuation marks, such as commas, parentheses, or a colon would be more appropriate. A dash is made by two hyphens. Use a dash:

(i) to indicate a break or interruption:

> The defendant—not his brother—testified.

(ii) to substitute for "to" in dates or numbers:

> He practiced law from 1980–1990.
> You should read pages 80–94 of the case.

i. Exclamation Marks

Exclamation marks are used to emphasize an idea. They are rarely, if ever, used in legal writing other than when they appear as part of a direct quotation.

j. Hyphens

Use a hyphen:

(i) to divide words between syllables at the end of a line of text. Avoid hyphenating proper names. Use a dictionary if you are unsure where to divide the word. The use of word processors with their automatic ability to space words evenly eliminates much of the need for hyphens in dividing words.

(ii) between the parts of a compound adjective when it modifies the next word:

would-be informant
employment-related injury
high-tech espionage

(iii) after certain prefixes:

(a) prefixes preceding proper nouns

anti-American
pro-Israeli

(b) prefixes ending with a vowel when the root word begins with a vowel (other than "re," generally)

anti-intellectual
co-op
de-emphasize

(iv) to form compounds:

ten-year lease
ex-president
on-the-job training

k. Slashes or Virgules

The diagonal slash or virgule causes ambiguity and should be avoided. It means "or," *not* "and," when used between two words. Thus, the sentence "The judge/jury agreed to acquit" means that the judge agreed to acquit or the jury agreed to acquit, *not* that the judge *and* jury agreed to acquit.

Dictum

- In choosing "a" or "an," consider the sound rather than the spelling of the following word. Use "a" before all consonant sounds. Use "an" before all vowel sounds except long "u" and before silent "h."

a uniform	an heiress
a house	an IPO
a unit	an eight-day vacation

- Commonly used abbreviations:

B.C.	A.D.
a.m.	p.m.
PST	EDT
Ph.D.	J.D.

- Only one word ends in "sede": supersede

  Only three words end in "ceed": exceed, proceed, and succeed

  All other words with the "seed" sound end in "cede": precede, concede, intercede

Technology Tips

Numerous Web site addresses for guidance on writing and grammar are provided at the end of Chapter 15. One additional site of interest is GrammarLady, located at http://www.grammarlady.com, a site devoted to grammar and usage. The GrammarLady sends a free newsletter via e-mail to interested subscribers and will respond to grammar and writing questions.

Assignment for Chapter 14

GRAMMAR

Select the Correct Word.

1. The bank has filed it's/its annual report.
2. The exhibits were given to John and me/myself.
3. For whom/who was the transcript prepared?
4. Al and her/she testified yesterday.
5. None of the witnesses has their/his-her own counsel.
6. The hosptial committee had rescheduled their/its board meeting.
7. Who's/Whose witness failed to appear?
8. The jury has/have retired to deliberate.
9. Nearly all of the briefs submitted to the court include/ includes exhibits.
10. The paralegal instructed him and I/me to return tomorrow.

SPELLING

Select the Correct Spelling.

1.	Occurrence	Occurence
2.	Occassion	Occasion
3.	Rescission	Resission
4.	License	Lisense
5.	Acknowledgement	Acknowledgment
6.	Sincerely	Sincerly
7.	Renown	Reknown
8.	Harrassment	Harassment
9.	Environment	Enviroment
10.	Supercede	Supersede

PUNCTUATION

Correctly Punctuate the Following Sentences.

1. The elements of fraud are a misrepresentation that causes justifiable reliance, actual reliance and resulting damage.
2. Although the witness was prepared she failed to sway the jury.
3. The courts opinion was long and complex.
4. The expert witness Dr. Hogarth failed to appear at the trial.
5. The jury appeared confused by the first plaintiffs testimony.
6. The following elements must be shown for a patent to be granted, novelty, nonobviousness and usefulness.

7. The plaintiff alleged two causes of action. First, breach of contract. Second, that fraud had occurred.
8. The four plaintiffs attorneys were well dressed they were articulate as well.
9. The judge admonished the defendant however the defendants poor behavior continued.
10. She was an effective witness. Because she was credible.

Chapter 15

Strategies for Effective Writing

Chapter Overview

Once you have mastered the mechanics of writing you must focus on making your writing effective. This chapter will present techniques to achieve the five hallmarks of effective legal writing: precision, clarity, readability, brevity, and order.

A. Introduction

The cornerstone of the legal profession is communication — communication with a client, adverse party, or judge. In most cases the communication will be in written form. Even in those instances in which you communicate orally, you will often follow up with a written letter or memo to a file. Because paralegals do not generally appear in court, they often spend even more time than some attorneys in preparing written documents. Thus, effective legal writing is critical to success as a paralegal.

B. The Plain English Movement

One of the recurring criticisms of legal writing is that it is rendered incomprehensible to the average reader by its use of jargon, redundancies, and archaic words and phrases. The use of words and phrases such as "whereas," "aforesaid," and "notwithstanding anything in the foregoing to the contrary" confuses and angers readers. A Yale law school professor once remarked there were two things wrong with the way attorneys write: content and style.

The increased activism of consumers frustrated with the impossibility of understanding an insurance policy, mortgage, or agreement for the purchase of an appliance, led to the requirement in many states that certain documents be written in "plain English." The Federal Trade Commission requires that agreements for the sale of a franchise be written in plain English. Similarly, the Securities and Exchange Commission ("SEC") has issued a "Plain English Handbook" to assist attorneys in creating clear disclosure documents for the SEC. The Commonwealth of Pennsylvania forbids the use of Latin or double negatives in consumer contracts.

Similarly, in 1998, President Clinton initiated his Presidential Memo on Plain Language, which requires all federal agencies to write clearly to their customers. The Plain Language initiative rests on three principles:

- Writing should be reader-oriented, clearly showing the author is writing to the customers of the agencies, not to other government employees;
- Writing should use natural expressions, using commonly known and used words; and
- Documents should be visually appealing.

A government Web site at http://www.plainlanguage.gov/main.htm offers writing tips, writing resources, and numerous samples of documents and letters written in plain language. Although the House of Representatives attempted to follow the plain language principles when it released its simplified rules in 1999, unfortunately, the rules were nearly 100 pages long, demonstrating that writing in a plain style is much easier said than done.

The trend toward plain language has also gained acceptance in legal writing. Law students and beginning writers are now encouraged to avoid "legalese" whenever possible and to write in plain English to enhance readability and comprehension of writings.

The plain English movement rightfully shifts the focus away from you as the author to the reader as the recipient. If you have produced what you believe is a beautifully crafted letter and yet the client doesn't understand it, you have failed. A writer is responsible for ambiguity in a document.

Writing in plain English so your reader understands you is not an easy task. Many legal concepts are very complex, and translating them into plain English is difficult. Similarly, some use of "legalese" such as Latin phrases may be unavoidable in certain instances. Falling into the habit of using archaic phrases such as "the instant case at bar" when you really mean "this case" is easy and you must make a conscious effort to avoid confusing jargon. See Figure 15-1.

Figure 15-1
SEC Guidelines for Plain English

Following is a brief summary of the SEC's guidelines for writing in plain English:

- Use short sentences.
- Use definite, concrete, everyday language.
- Use the active voice rather than the passive voice.
- Use tables and lists to present complex information.
- Avoid legal and financial jargon and highly technical business terms.
- Avoid multiple negatives.
- Avoid weak verbs, abstract terms, and superfluous words.
- Enhance readability through attractive design and layout.

C. Prewriting

Many experts agree that the time you invest in a project before you begin writing can be the most valuable time you spend on the project. Two threshold questions are of particular importance in helping you shape your writing so it is effective and understood on the first reading. Always ask yourself "What is the purpose of this writing?" and "Who will be reading this writing?"

1. Purpose

There can be several reasons for writing something. It is possible that your purpose is to relay information such as notifying a client that his deposition has been scheduled for next month. Another purpose may be to obtain information such as asking a client to explain an answer given to an interrogatory question posed by an adverse party. You may be explaining something to a reader, such as in a letter discussing the results of a settlement meeting. Finally, you may be aiming to convince a reader in a trial or appellate brief when your objective is to convince the court to adopt your argument.

If, before you begin any project, you ask yourself, "What is the purpose of this document?" you will set the stage for the tone of the document. After all, there is no point in using persuasive language when your sole mission is to notify a client that a will is ready to be executed. Conversely, you do not want to adopt a neutral and purely informative style if a client's last chance to succeed is your appellate brief. By reminding yourself of the purpose of your writing, you will be able to shape the appropriate tone and style of the project.

2. *Audience*

In addition to considering the purpose of a document, focus on the intended reader. Who will be reading the project — a client, a supervising attorney, adverse counsel, or a judge?

If the writing is prepared for a client, try to obtain a thumbnail sketch of the individual. Some clients may be novices in the legal world and even a term such as "interrogatory," which is commonplace to you, may be puzzling to a newcomer to litigation. Conversely, a client may be a sophisticated real estate broker and a complex discussion of prepayment penalty clauses in mortgage notes may be easily understood. In general, use a straightforward style for laypersons. Clients will not be impressed by your command of Latin phrases but will be frustrated by their use. Clients expect to be informed, not mystified, by legal writing. Immediately following the reaction of frustration is one of anger: anger that they had to pay you once to write the letter and then a second time to have you explain the letter. The goal of your writing is to communicate, not impress.

The highly respected and renowned financier, Warren E. Buffett, explains that when writing Berkshire Hathaway's annual report, he pretends he's talking to his sisters. Though highly intelligent, they are not accounting or financial experts. Mr. Buffett believes that he will be successful if they understand his writing. Similarly, United States Supreme Court Justice Stephen Breyer says that he tries to write his legal opinions so that they are understandable to high school students.

One of the most difficult tasks can be writing for a supervisor. Often the supervisor has not really thought through the way the project should be structured and as a result your approach will not meet the supervisor's expectations. Sometimes the supervisor may have access to certain facts and information you do not have, and your writing may be criticized for being incomplete. You may find that you adopt one writing style for one supervisor and an entirely different style for another. As you get to know the people you work with, you will be able to understand their writing techniques and be better able to meet their expectations. Obtain samples of documents written by your supervisors so you can get an idea of their styles and approaches. One of the most frustrating tasks is writing for individuals who are so committed to their style of writing they are never satisfied with anyone else's approach. They will endlessly revise a document, making insignificant small-scale revisions, such as changing all the "glad's" to "happy's." If you find you can never make such an individual satisfied with your work, try a direct approach and ask outright what the individual likes and dislikes in a writing.

If the letter is to adverse counsel, adopt a neutral and objective style. Avoid language that is confrontational or condescending. While letters to other legal professionals may include certain terms of art ("The Lanham Act," "The ADA," *ex parte*) that need no further explanation, avoid a tone that implies you are giving a lesson on the law. Not only are combative or condescending letters generally unproductive, you never know when they may be made part of a record in a court proceeding. You do not want a letter written in anger to come back to haunt you.

Writing for judges presupposes a level of expertise, and you need not give definitions or long-winded explanations for commonly known terms or phrases. Nevertheless, keep in mind that most judges rely heavily on law clerks to read briefs and then give an initial opinion to the judge. Thus, you need to make a strong and forceful argument because the judge may only scan the brief and rely on a law clerk's review. Moreover, judges are usually overwhelmed with heavy case loads and will not appreciate an overly long document that resorts to jargon and legalese. They will be much happier if you make the points you need to make as forcefully, persuasively, and briefly as possible, and then move on. As an inducement to legal writers to adopt more concise writing styles, more and more courts, including all of the courts of appeal and the United States Supreme Court, are establishing page limits for documents submitted. Thus, it is imperative to be brief.

By asking yourself, "Who is my reader?" you will automatically tailor the document so it is understood by the reader. The critical question is not whether *you* love your project but whether the reader will immediately be informed or persuaded, that is, whether your writing achieves its purpose.

D. Precision

The most important characteristic of legal writing is precision. Clients will rely on the information and opinions given to them by legal professionals. Judges, administrators, and others will assume the information provided to them is correct. Therefore, being right is fundamental to effective legal writing. No judge will render a decision in a client's favor by saying, "The legal conclusions you have reached are faulty and incorrect but the brief is so well-written that I will rule in your favor."

Be accurate with regard not only to the "big" issues, such as legal conclusions and arguments, but also as to the "small" elements of a writing, such as names, dates, and dollar amounts. An error in the client's name or address may attract more attention than anything else in the project. Just as spelling errors cast doubt on your ability, so do accuracy errors have a disproportionately negative impact on the reader. The legal profession has become more adversarial in recent years, and even clients (sometimes, especially clients) are quick to point out an error. Similarly, many of your writings are sent to an adverse party who will be more than happy to call attention to a mistake you have made. Thus, because your audience is highly critical, you must be as accurate and precise as possible.

One cause of imprecise writing is an overreliance on forms. Drafting a contract requires more than merely locating another contract in your office and then changing the names and addresses. If this is your approach to drafting, you will no doubt find yourself explaining to a client engaging in accounting services why his or her agreement refers to restaurants and bars. Using forms as a starting point or guide is perfectly acceptable. Just avoid relying exclusively on forms. When you have used a form originally drafted for another client, proofread carefully to ensure the language is appropriate for this new client's needs. Use the "find and replace" feature in word processing programs to ensure the consistent use of terms.

1. Word Choice

The selection of an improper word or the use of vague words causes imprecision in your writing. Similarly, the use of qualifying language or words can cause unintended meanings. For example, no employee would be comforted by hearing "Your department is not in any immediate danger of being downsized." The use of the qualifier "immediate" implies that a danger exists; it simply is not immediate. Select the most descriptive and specific word possible. Descriptive words lend strength and vitality to your writing. Moreover, the selection of an incorrect word can be fatal in legal writing. A document that states "The Buyer may deposit the purchase price into the escrow account prior to May 15" means something entirely different from "The Buyer shall deposit the purchase price into the escrow account prior to May 15." The second statement clearly imposes an obligation on the Buyer while the first statement does not.

The use of "will" or "may" for "shall" causes ambiguity and inaccuracy. One writing professor has estimated that more than 1,000 published cases debate the meaning of "shall." Use "may" for optional action, "will" for future action ("I will appear in court on Thursday"), and "shall" or "must" for obligatory action. Many plain English guidelines recommend the use of "must" rather than "shall" on the basis that "shall" is an obsolete word.

Following is a list of words that are commonly misused in legal writing. Just as you use a dictionary to avoid spelling errors, use a dictionary or thesaurus to help you select the precise word you need.

affect/effect

Affect means "to influence" as in "I was greatly affected by the victim's story."

Effect means "to cause or bring about" (as a verb) or "result" (as a noun) as in "He effected a resolution of the case" or "One of the effects of the judgment was impairment of his credit rating."

If you have difficulty remembering the difference between these words, do not use either of them. Use their synonyms (influence, or produce, or result).

among/between

Among is used to refer to *more than two objects or persons*, as in "The agreement was entered into by and among Smith, Jones, and Andersen."

Between is used to refer to *two objects or persons*, as in "The settlement was negotiated between Peterson and Powell."

and/or

Many experts criticize the use of *and/or*, which can be confusing and ambiguous. Avoid using *and/or*. Use either "and" or "or."

Unclear You must provide a reference and/or a resume.

Preferred You must provide a reference, or resume, or both.

apprise/appraise

Apprise means "to notify or inform," as in "I will continue to apprise you of further developments in this case."

Appraise means to "estimate value," as in "He appraised the value of the property at $100,000."

beside/besides

Beside means "at the side of," as in "Please sit beside me." *Besides* means "in addition to," as in "Besides leaving Angela his property, Grandfather gave her his jewelry."

compose/comprise

Compose means "to make up," as in "The contract is composed of three sections." *Comprise* means "to include or contain or consist of," as in "Tina's collection comprises rare porcelains." Do not use "of" after *comprise.*

disinterested/uninterested

Disinterested means "neutral" and "impartial," as in "Judges must be disinterested in the proceedings they decide."

Uninterested means "not interested or bored," as in "The jurors appeared uninterested in the masses of statistical evidence presented."

ensure/insure

Ensure means "to make definite," as in "We must ensure the tenant pays all rent due." *Insure* means "to protect against loss," as in "We must insure our valuables for at least $10,000."

fact

A *fact* is something that has occurred or is known to be true. Writers often characterize something as a fact when it is merely an allegation or contention. Use the word "fact" only when you are describing an event or something proven. For example, it is a fact that a defendant has blue eyes. It is not a fact that the defendant murdered a victim until the jury or court says so.

guilty/liable

The word *guilty* refers to criminal wrongdoing. *Liable* refers to responsibility for a civil wrong. Thus, it is correct to say that "defendant Smith is guilty of robbery while defendant Jones is liable for damages in the amount of $50,000 for breach of contract."

libel/liable

Libel is a form of defamation, as in "The magazine libeled our client by stating he was a crook."

Liable means responsible for some civil wrong, as in "She is liable for all the harm proximately caused by her negligence."

memoranda/memorandum

Memoranda refers to several documents (plural) while a *memorandum* is a single document.

oral/verbal

Oral means something spoken, as in "The plaintiff's oral testimony at trial confirmed her earlier deposition testimony."

Verbal means a communication in words and could refer to a written or a spoken communication.

ordinance/ordnance

An *ordinance* is an act or resolution enacted by a local jurisdiction, as in "Buffalo recently enacted an ordinance prohibiting smoking in public places."

Ordnance is military weaponry, as in "The troops came under heavy ordnance fire."

overrule/reverse

A court *overrules* prior decisions in its jurisdiction. Thus, "The 1954 case *Brown v. Board of Education* overruled the 1896 case *Plessy v. Ferguson.*" A court *reverses* the very case before it on appeal as in "The defendant in *Edwards v. Anderson* appealed the decision rendered against him; the court agreed with the defendant's reasoning and reversed the lower court's holding."

prescribe/proscribe

Prescribe means to order, as in "The physician prescribed complete bedrest for the patient."

Proscribe means to prohibit or forbid, as in "Massachusetts laws proscribe littering."

principal/principle

Principal is the supervisor at a school or a dominant item, as in "The principal objective to be gained is the prisoner's freedom." Another meaning of "principal" is a sum of money on which interest is paid, as in "The promissory note required repayment of the principal amount of the debt as well as interest."

Principle is a fundamental rule, as in "The principles of physics are complex."

respectfully/respectively

Respectfully means "with respect" and is a commonly used closing in a document, as in "Respectfully submitted, Andrew Kenney."

Respectively means in a certain order, as in "The attorneys took their respective positions in the courtroom and the trial commenced."

since/because

Since refers to the passage of time, as in "It has been six years since she rented the house." The word "since" should not be used as a substitute for *because*. Saying "She moved out of the house since it leaked" is ambiguous.

2. *Vague Words*

To lend forcefulness to your writing, use concrete and descriptive words. Avoid vague words such as "matter," "development," "circumstances," "system," "situation," "problem," and "process," which provide little, if any, information to the reader. Thus, a sentence beginning "Regarding this matter . . ." offers no guidance to the reader as to what "this matter" might be. A much better approach is to write "Regarding your lease . . .".

Similarly, avoid using words such as "above," "whereas," or "herein." For example, if in an agreement you state on page 18, "As described above . . ." the reader does not know where in the previous 17 pages you discussed the issue. Be specific. State, "as described in paragraph 4(b) . . .".

The words "it" and "this" are often used in an indefinite and confusing manner. Consider the following: "The court ruled the defendant should be granted probation. This enables the defendant to participate in a work release program." The word "this" could refer either to the court's ruling or the defendant's probation. When using "it" or "this," you should, if necessary, repeat the word that "it" or "this" refers to. Thus, the prior statement would read, "The court ruled the defendant should be granted probation. Probation will enable the defendant to participate in a work release program."

Similarly, avoid "made-up" words. While you may have heard of, used, and even written "dialogued," "Borked," "liaising," "mentee," or "strategize," these "words" are not generally found in most dictionaries because they are not yet recognized words in English. Our conversation and writing are often influenced by business and technology terms. Thus, a number of terms, such as "cutting edge," "synergy," and "empower" are overused. Do not say "We need to *interface* to resolve the litigation" when you mean "meet." Do not use "impact" as a verb, as in "His actions will *impact* our ability to obtain a loan." Use "influence" or "affect" instead. While English is an evolving language, do not use a word before it has evolved into an entry in a dictionary.

3. *Word Connotation*

Many words have more than one meaning. When you select a word, consider its connotation, or suggested meaning. There is a great difference, for example, in referring to an item as "cheap" rather than "affordable." The word "cheap" connotes shoddy or low quality while "affordable" conveys either a neutral or desirable meaning. Consider the effect of telling someone he or she is "stubborn" rather than "determined," or "blunt" rather than "candid." Certain words carry hostile undertones and will immediately make the reader defensive or angry.

Use care when selecting words to ensure they have the connotations you intend. If correspondence to an adverse party suggests there is a "discrepancy" in damage figures, rather than simply asking for a clarification of the figures, you can be sure of an immediate, and probably angry, response.

E. Clarity

The second feature of effective legal writing is clarity—that is, ensuring that your project is easily understood by the reader. Your writing style should be invisible. It is bad writing that is noticeable. Because legal writings are read not for pleasure but for function, readers expect you to make your point clearly and quickly. The three primary legal writing flaws that obscure clarity are elegant variation, the overuse of negatives, and improper word order.

1. *Elegant Variation*

Elegant variation refers to the practice of substituting one term for another in a document to avoid repetition of a term. Writers are often loath to repeat a term, in the belief that repetition of a term is boring or unsophisticated. Unfortunately, selecting alternate terms creates the impression that something entirely different is intended. Consider the following sentence: Four of the defendant's witnesses were women, while all of the plaintiff's witnesses were ladies. In an attempt not to repeat the word "women," the writer conveys something entirely different about the plaintiff's group of witnesses

Elegant variation is deadly in legal writing. For example, if you are drafting a document that continually refers to an individual as a "landlord" and then suddenly you refer to this individual as the "lessor," the reader may believe that the "landlord" is not the same individual as the "lessor." You should therefore be cautious about varying words and terms you have used. While you may believe that selecting alternative terms shows your extensive vocabulary and lends interest to the document, you unwittingly may be creating the impression that there is a reason that different terms have been selected and that there is a legal distinction to be drawn based upon this variation. Use the "find and replace" feature of your word processing program to ensure terms are used consistently.

2. *Negatives*

The overuse of negatives can be confusing to a reader. While statutes are often set forth in negative fashion by describing what is prohibited, using more than two negative words in a sentence usually forces the reader to stop and think through what you have said. The phrase "not unlikely" should be converted to "likely" or "probable." Anytime the reader is interrupted from reading the project, your message is weakened. As a writer, your task is to ensure that a reader proceeds smoothly through the document without needing to puzzle over phrases. For example, the statement "No individual shall be prohibited from refusing to submit to a breathalyzer examination" is confusing. It requires a reader to consider three negative words: "no," "prohibited," and "refusing."

In drafting projects, keep in mind that there are many more negative words than the obvious ones: "no," "none," or "never." Many words function in a negative fashion, such as "refuse," "preclude," "deny," "except," and the like. While it is impossible to purge your writing of all negative terms, you should carefully scrutinize your writing to ensure that you have not used too many negative words that obscure your meaning.

The other disadvantage of using negative words is that they are not as forceful as affirmative expressions. For example, it is more effective to say "the plaintiff was late for her deposition" than "the plaintiff failed to timely appear for her deposition." To give strength and vitality to your writing, use affirmative and positive terms.

3. *Word Order*

The most common sentence structure in the English language is the placement of the subject first, the verb second, and the object third. Thus, the sentence "The defendant attacked the victim" is phrased in this standard order. While the thought can certainly be expressed in another way, such as "The victim was attacked by the defendant," readers typically anticipate that sentences will follow the expected pattern of subject, verb, and object. Although you may not want to structure every single sentence in a project in the same fashion, excessive variation from the expected sentence structure will cause confusion and lack of clarity. Just as you should avoid exotic spellings of words because they draw attention to your writing rather than to your message, avoid exotic sentence structure. For example, an article written in a national newspaper about the 1991 Tailhook Convention began, "The Navy Thursday asked the Pentagon's inspector general to investigate the 1991 Tailhook incident . . . ." This oddly structured sentence catches the reader's attention in a distracting way.

Vary from the anticipated sentence structure of subject, verb, object only when you want to draw attention to a thought. Thus, if you have a point you want to emphasize, vary the way it is structured. Keep this technique in mind if you need to "bury" a weak portion of an argument: Phrase it in the manner commonly anticipated because this will draw the least amount of attention to it.

One of the other benefits of using "normal" sentence structure is that you will be compelled to phrase your thoughts in the active voice. When you vary from the anticipated order of sentences, the result is often conversion to the passive voice, which creates a weakened point (see Section F.1).

F. Readability

Because the subject matter discussed in most legal writing is complex, and often rather boring, you need to make your product as readable as possible. Clients will be unfamiliar with legal topics. Judges and other legal professionals will be too busy to struggle through a complex and pompous document. Remember that the more complicated a topic is, the more important is the need for readability. To enhance readability:

1. *Prefer the Active Voice*

The active voice focuses attention on the subject of the sentence that performs or causes certain action. The active voice is consistent with standard sentence structure of subject, verb, and object.

The passive voice focuses attention on the object of action by placing it first and relegating the subject (actor) of the sentence to an inferior position.

Active Voice	*Passive Voice*
The court held the defendant violated the statute.	The holding of the court was that the defendant violated the statute.
The defendant's attorney argued for acquittal.	An argument for acquittal was made by the defendant's attorney.
The doctor testified that the patient consented to the operation.	Testimony was given by the doctor that the patient consented to the operation.

The active voice is stronger and more forceful than the passive voice. Readers do not have to search through the sentence looking for the actor or subject. Another advantage of using the active voice is that it usually results in shorter sentences.

There are situations, however, in which the passive voice may be preferable. For example, assume your law office represents a defendant accused of fraud. Instead of stating "The defendant deposited checks in his bank account," you could write "Checks were deposited in the defendant's bank account." This use of the passive voice shifts the focus away from the defendant. The reader is informed of what occurred but not who did it. Consider using the passive voice in the discussion of weaker parts of your argument to deflect attention from them. Conversely, be sure to structure the strongest parts of your writing in the active voice because it lends strength and vitality to your writing. A classic example of passive voice is seen in the recent statement of a politician accused of wrongdoing who stated, "Mistakes were made" rather than "I made mistakes."

2. *Use Lists*

Another way to enhance readability is to use lists when discussing complex matters. Lists not only enable readers to comprehend information quickly, they create visual impact and interest because they are usually numbered and set apart from the rest of the text. When setting forth items such as the elements of a cause of action or the components of a definition, use a list.

Lists can be structured in several ways, but to increase interest:

- Set the list off from the rest of your narrative by spaces above and below your list;
- Indent your list;
- Identify the items in your list with numbers, letters, or "bullets" (•); and
- Punctuate correctly by putting a semicolon after each item (except the last item) and include "or" or "and" before the last item.

Not all lists need to be indented. If the list is short, you may separate each item from the other by a comma and include the list as part of your narrative text.

The grammatical structure of all of the items in any list must be identical or parallel. Thus, if the first word in a list is a verb, all of the following items must also be verbs. Similarly, if the first word in the first item ends in "ing," all subsequent items must also begin with words ending in "ing."

Incorrect

The elements of a cause of action for breach of contract are as follows:

- an agreement
- a breach of that agreement by one party
- the act of the breaching party must have caused damage.

Correct

The elements of a cause of action for breach of contract are as follows:

- an agreement;
- a breach of that agreement by one party; and
- damage caused by the act of the breaching party.

Lack of parallel structure is often seen in resumes in which job applicants will describe their experience as follows: "Drafted documents. Prepared pleadings. Assisting in trial preparation." The last item should be "assist<u>ed</u>" to retain parallel structure.

Similarly, lack of parallel structure can be seen within a sentence; for example, "It is more important to write the brief than arguing it." Revise as follows: "It is more important to write the brief than argue it."

3. *Avoid Nominalizations*

A nominalization occurs when you take an adjective, verb, or adverb and turn it into a noun. While the nominalization itself is technically correct, overuse of nominalizations drains your writing of forcefulness and makes it read as if written by a bureaucrat.

	Nominalizations
The defendant argued.	The defendant made the argument.
The witness concluded.	The witness drew a conclusion.
The contract was enforced.	Enforcement of the contract was accomplished.
We considered our options.	Consideration was given to our options.
We applied for an extension.	An application for an extension was made.

As you can see, nominalizations not only take strong action words such as verbs and convert them into dull nouns, they also tend to make your writing overlong.

Avoid overusing nominalizations by proofreading carefully. Generally if you use active voice, you will greatly reduce nominalizations. While not all nominalizations can be avoided, their repeated use will render your writing unimaginative.

4. *Avoid Legal Jargon*

The use of "legalese" frustrates readers and results in stodgy writing. Legalese or jargon includes not only archaic and stuffy words and phrases such as "accord," "aforesaid," "whereas," "opine," and "hereinafter referred to," but words and phrases that are unfamiliar to a reader,such as Latin phrases or legal terms (*res judicata*, laches, collateral estoppel). The Texas State Bar has recognized this problem and holds an annual contest of "legaldegook" for atrocious legal writing. A recent "Wooliness Award" was presented for the following:

> For purposes of paragraph (3), an organization described in paragraph (2) shall be deemed to include an organization described in Section 501(C)(4), (5) or (6) which would be described in Paragraph (2) if it were an organization described in Section 501(c)(3).

Try to avoid using legal jargon. Often archaic or jargon-filled phrases can either be omitted entirely or replaced with more familiar terms. For example, an agreement may begin as follows:

> THIS AGREEMENT is made and entered into this fourth day of May 2001, by and between ABC, Inc. (hereinafter referred to as "Landlord") and Susan Andrews (hereinafter referred to as "Tenant") regarding the premises and covenants hereinafter set forth.

You may easily change the sentence as follows:

> THIS AGREEMENT is entered into May 4, 2001 between ABC, Inc. ("Landlord") and Susan Andrews ("Tenant") regarding the following facts.

The omission or replacement of archaic words and phrases with familiar ones not only enhances readability but also results in a more concise writing.

You may not be able to omit all of the legalese you would like, particularly when drafting wills, deeds, contracts, and other legal documents that have more rigid structures. These documents are often drafted in accordance with standard forms and conventions of many years ago. In any case, simply try to eliminate as much of the jargon as possible. For example, the phrases "enclosed please find" or "enclosed herewith is" are often used in letters enclosing other documents. While there is nothing grammatically wrong with these expressions, they are examples of legalese. If something is enclosed, won't the reader find it? Simply use the phrase "enclosed is" followed by a description of the item enclosed.

If you are using legal terms or Latin phrases, be sure to give a brief definition for your reader. A client may be completely bewildered by a letter informing him or her that "the doctrine of laches precludes your claim." Rewrite as follows:

> The doctrine of laches, that is, an unreasonable and prejudicial delay in bringing an action, precludes your claim.

While the insertion of a definition or explanatory phrase produces a longer document, the effect of enhanced readability is well worth the extra words.

Even if a document is prepared for another legal professional who will be familiar with the Latin phrase or legal term, add the definition because it often serves as a smooth transition for any reader. Readers experienced with the terms will not be offended by your inclusion of a definition and will readily be able to skip over it. Other less experienced readers, such as a law clerk or a client receiving a copy of the writing, will be greatly assisted by the "translation" you provide.

5. Keep Subjects and Verbs in Proximity

Because the two most critical parts of a sentence are the subject and the verb, readers typically look for these first to make sense of a sentence. Legal writing is known for creating huge gaps between the subject of a sentence and the verb. When too many words intervene between the subject and the verb, readers no longer remember what the sentence is about by the time they locate the verb. They are then forced to reread the sentence and hunt for the subject.

While you need not immediately follow every subject in every sentence with a verb, avoid large gaps between these two parts of a sentence. Statutes are especially notorious for separating subjects and verbs by long word strings.

Example

> Any *person*, including an organization, institution or other entity, that presents or causes to be presented to an officer, employee or agent of this office, or any department thereof, or any state agency, a claim, as defined in subsection 2(g) of this paragraph, that the person knows or has reason to know was not provided as claimed, *is guilty* of a class 1 misdemeanor.

In this sentence, there is a gap of 55 words between the subject (person) and the verb (is guilty). To eliminate these huge gaps, rewrite the sentence, moving the verb closer to the subject.

Example

Any *person*, including an organization, institution or other entity, *is guilty* of a Class 1 misdemeanor by presenting or causing to be presented to an officer, employee, or agent of this office, or any department thereof, or any state agency, a claim, as defined in Section 2(g) of this paragraph, that the person knows or has reason to know was not provided as claimed.

Alternatively, you can make the words intervening between the subject and verb into their own sentence.

Example

The *partnership*, an entity organized and existing under Missouri law and formed after the passage of the Missouri General Partnership Act, *is composed of* Smith, Jones, and Kimball.

Rewrite as:

The *partnership is composed of* Smith, Jones, and Kimball. It is an entity organized and existing under Missouri law and was formed after the passage of the Missouri General Partnership Act.

6. *Use Forceful Words*

Because legal writing is formal, writers often tend to adopt an emotionless, pallid tone in their writing. While your writing should not read like a romance novel, the use of vivid and forceful words will not only keep your readers interested but will aid in converting them to your viewpoint.

Emphasis cannot be obtained by merely underlining or italicizing words or phrases or by adding a modifier such as "very" or "hardly." You need to select a word vivid enough to carry the meaning you desire. Use a thesaurus or dictionary to help you select words that are vivid and forceful.

Weak	*Forceful*
The defendant *stated* he knew where the witness was *located*.	The defendant *boasted* he knew where the witness was *secreted*.
Smith *misrepresented* the condition of the premises.	Smith *lied* about the condition of the premises.
very sad	sorrowful
not allowed	forbidden, prohibited
disagree with	contradict
raining hard	pouring
acknowledge guilt	confess
could not believe	incredulous
withdraw a statement	recant

Conversely, do not take a concrete word, which is strong in and of itself, and dilute it such as converting "improbable" to "somewhat unlikely" or "rapid" to "pretty fast." In fact, some words stand on their own and are not susceptible to degree such as "unique," which means the only one of its kind. Something cannot be "quite unique" or "very unique."

7. *Repeat Strong Words and Phrases*

While you want to avoid redundancy in legal writing, there are certain situations in which repetition can add emphasis to your writing. The repetition of a key word or phrase creates interest and adds drama to writing.

Example

The defendant misled the plaintiff. He misled her by promising the premises were quiet. He misled her by promising the premises were habitable. He misled her by promising the premises were safe.

Each repetition of the words "misled" and "promise" builds on the previous reference. When you use this technique, be sure to structure the sentence so you end with the strongest element.

Example

She was a diligent worker. She was a loyal friend. She was a loving mother.

8. *Vary the Length of Sentences*

Short sentences are easier to comprehend than long, complex sentences. Nevertheless, you do not want a project filled with sentences of approximately the same length. Such a writing would be tedious to read.

Just as you may need to vary the pattern of your sentences from the standard sentence order (subject-verb-object) to add interest, vary the length of your sentences to enhance readability. For example, a short sentence such as "She refused" is concise and powerful. Generally, sentences that exceed three lines are too long for most readers.

Nevertheless, you do not want a writing filled only with short sentences. Such a project would have a choppy and abrupt tone and would read like a telegram. For example, note the clipped tone of the following sentences.

The landlord sent her the rent statement. She refused to pay. He evicted her. She countersued. He asked for a jury. The jury agreed with her version.

The following version has a much smoother and more readable quality:

The landlord sent her the rent statement. She refused to pay and he evicted her. She countersued. Even though he asked for a jury, the jury agreed with her version.

G. Brevity

The length of a project does not necessarily translate into quality. Some of the most compelling and well-known writings are the briefest. For example, the Lord's Prayer has only 66 words. The Gettysburg Address has 286 words. Yet just one federal statute relating to hospital and medical expenses paid under Medicare has more than 700 words. One of the most dramatic yet brief statements about a person is that engraved on Machiavelli's tomb: "There are not enough words to say his eulogy."

While almost all writers agree in principle that brevity is an admirable goal in legal writing, brevity is not easily accomplished. One of the reasons brevity is difficult to achieve is that the legal research that is the basis for your project represents time and effort. After going to the library, researching, writing, re-writing, Shepardizing or KeyCiting, revising, proofreading, and editing, writers are loath to abandon the words that evidence their hard work. Like pets and children, we quickly find fault with those belonging to others and defend and love our own. For example, one of the entries in the annual Texas State Bar "legaldegook" contest was a sentence written by a lawyer that began "Accordingly, in the interest of brevity," and continued for more than 60 words.

Another contributing factor to the length of legal documents is that the topics discussed are often complex, requiring thoughtful analysis. Finally, over-review of a writing causes increased length. Each paralegal or attorney who works on a project will feel a need to improve a writing, generally by adding to it, changing "now" to "at the present time" or "if" to "in the event that." Thus, being brief is difficult.

While judges complain about lawyers' inability to write succinct briefs, some writing experts suggest that judges themselves contribute to the mass of legal publication by writing longer opinions with more footnotes. One solution proposed by one writing scholar is that judges impose page limits on themselves similar to those imposed on attorneys.

You must be merciless. Your reader's time is at a premium and you cannot afford to frustrate the reader by redundancy and long-winded phrases. Moreover, if the reader continually encounters a rehash of previous material and never encounters new material, he or she may simply abandon the project and never read some of your later, more persuasive arguments.

To achieve brevity:

1. Omit Needless Words

There are numerous phrases in English that we use simply by habit. Many of these can be eliminated or reduced to a more concise word or phrase.

Long-Winded Phrases	*Substitutions*
Due to the fact that	Because
As a result of	Consequently, therefore
In addition to	Additionally
Despite the fact that	Although
At the present time	At present, now, currently
During the time that	While
At such time as	When
With regard to	Regarding, concerning
In the event that	If
As to whether	Whether
In order to	To

Careful writing and revising will help you eliminate extra words. Ask yourself if you absolutely need a phrase and whether there is an effective substitute for it. Many commonly used phrases can be replaced by single words with no loss of meaning. In particular, avoid constructions that include more than one preposition, such as "*in* regard *to*." Use "regarding."

2. *Avoid "Throat-Clearing" Introductions*

"Throat-clearing" refers to introductions that are mere preludes for the main topic that is to follow. Writers often feel compelled to warm up the audience by preparing them for the main idea rather than simply presenting the idea.

Throat-Clearing Phrases	*Substitutions*
In this regard it is important to remember that . . .	Remember
The next issue to be considered is . . .	[none—state the issue]
Attention should also be called to the fact that . . .	[none—state the fact]
It is interesting to note that . . .	Note

Other overused introductory words are "clearly" and "obviously." Writers often add "clearly" before introducing a topic, believing that this word will lend persuasive force. To paraphrase a famous jurist, adding the word "clearly" to a sentence won't make it clear; and if the sentence is clear, you don't need the word "clearly."

The word "obviously" should be avoided for the same reason as "clearly." Moreover, "obviously" carries a hostile meaning. By introducing a sentence or topic with the word "obviously" you signal to readers that you believe they lack the capacity to discern the meaning of the sentence on their own. When you introduce a thought with "obviously" what you really are saying is "even to a moron such as you it should be obvious . . . ."

3. *Avoid Redundancy*

Those in the legal profession are wedded to redundancy. They cannot resist saying "null and void and of no legal effect." Is all this needed? If something is null, isn't it void? If it is void, can it have legal effect?

The reason legal writing is so prone to redundancy lies in the history of our language. English has its roots in Latin and French as well as in the language of the Celts and Anglo-Saxons. Often word pairings were used to ensure that readers would understand phrases no matter what their background or station in life. Thus, the French word "peace" joined with the Latin word "quiet." The French "devise" joined the Latin "bequeath." These redundant doublings have persisted long after their need. Their use today is often the result of pure habit rather than necessity.

If you find yourself using these "stock" redundancies, stop and ask whether one word is sufficient.

Common Redundancies

acknowledge and agree
alter or change or modify
basic fundamentals
cease and desist
close proximity
consented and agreed
covenant, warrant, and represent
current status
due and owing
each and every
force or effect
free and clear
full and complete
give, devise, and bequest
made and entered into
null and void and of no legal effect
past history
previous experience
refuse and fail
release, remise, and discharge
true and correct
unless and until
vitally necessary

4. *Avoid Repetition*

Once you have stated your contention or communicated the information you need to communicate, stop. Many beginning legal writers believe they should make every point three times by

- telling the reader what the writing or project will say;
- saying it; and
- reminding the reader of what was said.

There is no place in legal writing for such needless repetition. If you write to clients, they will be sufficiently interested in your communication to grasp what you are telling them. Supervisors, adverse counsel, and judges are sophisticated enough or busy enough that they do not need an argument repeated three times. In many instances, court rules will dictate the maximum number of pages in briefs submitted to that court. In such cases, you will not have the luxury of being able to repeat your argument. The only exception to the rule of avoiding repetition is that in a long document, readers often appreciate a separate conclusion, which briefly and concisely summarizes your analysis.

H. Order

1. *Outlines*

Just as you would never begin a car trip to a far-off destination without a road map, you should never begin a writing without some idea as to how you intend to approach the project. A project that is poorly organized not only fails to inform or persuade the reader, it may so frustrate the reader that it will not be read.

The best system for organizing a writing is to use an outline. Many writers doubt the benefits of outlining and have resisted using an outline since elementary school. While the most complete outline includes full sentences or topics divided into headings and subheadings, an outline need not be so formal. The looseleaf notebook containing the notes you took while researching or the index cards containing notes of your research results are working outlines. By shuffling the index cards or the pages in your notebook, you are outlining, that is, organizing your approach to your writing.

Similarly, your outline can consist of your thoughts on the project scribbled on scratch paper. It is not the format of the outline that is important; rather it is that the mere existence of any type of outline forces you to consider and organize the structure of your writing. The outline should disclose the basic sections of your project and the order in which they will be addressed.

If the notes taken during research are not helpful in preparing an outline, simply jot down on paper all of the words and phrases you can think of that relate to your project. Keep writing and listing the entries; do not worry about organizing these entries. After you have finished listing every topic you can think of, carefully examine the list and then group related items together. After you have settled on these rough groupings, decide the order in which the groups should be discussed.

Another method of outlining is called "clustering." Place a circle or "nucleus" in the middle of a blank page of paper. Place the key word or topic of your project in the nucleus. Now write a related topic or issue nearby. Encircle it and draw a line back to your nucleus. Continue by either branching out from the nucleus or the new circle. Trust your instincts to select new words and topics. The final product should look like a spider web. Write your project with your web nearby.

When your outline or "cluster" is completed, regardless whether it is a working outline, a formal outline, or your list of topics, you should be able to determine immediately whether you have included all of the items that need to be addressed and whether you are devoting too much time and effort to minor points at the expense of major points.

Some writers prefer to devote substantial effort to outlining. The actual writing stage is then that much easier. In many instances the writer is simply expanding upon the ideas already set forth in the outline, adding citations, and polishing.

2. *Internal Organization*

The way you organize the project can affect the reader's perception of the project. There are four tips to follow in organizing your writing so it achieves your desired objectives.

a. Use Headings

In longer writings, use headings and subheadings to alert the reader to the subject being discussed. It is nearly impossible for a reader to comprehend page after page of narrative containing no breaks or divisions. Similarly, it is very frustrating for readers to suddenly find themselves in the midst of a discussion of contracts when the preceding paragraph related to fraud.

Headings serve as signals to readers to alert them to the topics you are discussing and to show a change in topics. If, for example, your brief states there are four prerequisites to the awarding of an injunction, it will be helpful to the reader for you to label your discussion in four separate parts, each relating to the element to be discussed next.

In persuasive documents such as briefs, try to make your headings as convincing as possible. ("Plaintiff has suffered irreparable harm as a result of Defendant's actions.") In non-persuasive documents, your headings may be neutral and may consist of a mere word or phrase ("Irreparable Harm").

b. Use Effective Paragraphs

Just as you use headings to break up a solid mass of narrative, use paragraphs to break up a discussion into units that are easy to read. Readers will expect that each of your paragraphs relates to a distinct idea and will also expect that the first sentence of your paragraph will "set the stage" for what follows. This first sentence is the topic sentence.

Avoid paragraphs that are too long. How long is too long? Most readers have difficulty with paragraphs that cover more than one-half of a page. Not only does the mind crave a break from a long discussion, so does the eye. Remember the visual effect of your writing and create a project that is pleasing to the eye. Also avoid short paragraphs. The traditional rule is that a paragraph must have more than one sentence. On occasion, however, you may want to use a one- or two-sentence paragraph in legal writing for emphasis and visual impact.

c. Use Effective Transitions

To move smoothly from one sentence, paragraph, or idea to another, use a transition word or phrase. Without transitions, writing would be choppy and telegram-like. Transitions connect what you have said with what will follow. Avoid using the same transition words. Two of the favorite transition words of beginning writers are "however" and "therefore." If you find yourself continually introducing sentences and paragraphs with the same words, examine your project and try to find other transitions to lend variety and interest to your writing.

Commonly used transition words and phrases are as follows:

To introduce a topic
- in general
- initially
- primarily
- to

To show contrast
- although
- conversely
- however
- in contrast
- nevertheless
- on the contrary
- on the other hand
- while
- yet

To show similarity or contrast
- in the same way
- just as
- likewise
- similarly

To show examples
- for example
- for instance
- in fact
- namely
- specifically
- that is
- to illustrate

To show conclusions
- accordingly
- as a result
- because
- consequently
- for this reason
- inasmuch as
- therefore
- thus

To show additions
- additionally
- again
- furthermore
- in addition
- moreover

To summarize
- finally
- in brief
- in conclusion
- in summary
- to conclude
- to summarize

d. Use Position and Voice for Emphasis

In nearly every project, there are stronger points and then points writers wish they did not have to mention. Use the location or placement of information as well as voice to draw your reader's attention to the more compelling parts of your writing and to minimize the impact of "negative" or weak sections of your argument.

The most prominent parts of a writing are its beginning and its ending. Readers tend to start projects with great enthusiasm, lose interest in the middle, and then become attentive again when the end is in sight. Therefore, put your strongest arguments and information at the beginning and ending of your project, your paragraphs, and your sentences.

Bury negative information in the middle of your project, in the middle of your paragraphs, and in the middle of your sentences. These locations will attract the least attention and may even be overlooked. This is another compelling reason for crafting strong topic sentences in each paragraph. These topic sentences, typically placed at the beginning of paragraphs, not only convey the main idea of each paragraph but may be the only parts of a project read by a busy reader. Thus, if the first sentence of each paragraph may be the only portion of your project that is read, put favorable information in these prominent positions.

Negative information that is buried in the middle of a project, the middle of a paragraph, or in the subordinate clause of a sentence will be less likely to be noticed. Be extremely careful when including these unfavorable portions of your writing because a careless spelling error or typo will immediately draw your reader's attention to them.

There are other techniques you can use to "hide" flaws in your argument. Because active voice is much stronger and more forceful than passive voice, use passive voice in discussion of information you believe is negative.

For example, if your client sold a house with known defects to the plaintiff, this fact can be disclosed in the following two ways:

Active Voice	The defendant intentionally sold a house with known defects to the plaintiff.
Passive Voice	The house was sold to the plaintiff.

You can easily see that the plaintiff would prefer the first sentence while the defendant would prefer the second. By using the passive voice you deflect attention away from the actor (the defendant) and onto the object of the action (the sale of the house). Note how the use of the passive voice here eliminates any reference whatsoever to the defendant.

Similarly, the techniques discussed above for making writing vivid, such as selecting descriptive and concrete words and avoiding nominalizations, should not be used in discussions of negative information. Selecting vague words ("situation," "matter") and including nominalizations ("The plaintiff underwent an operation" rather than "The doctor operated on the plaintiff") will de-emphasize negative information.

Finally, use detail in describing facts and issues favorable to you and discuss unfavorable facts and issues in general fashion. For example, consider the following two descriptions of an accident, one from the plaintiff's perspective and one from the defendant's.

Plaintiff's version:

As the plaintiff was safely driving within the legal speed limit, defendant's car careened down the hill and collided with the left front door of the plaintiff's car. The plaintiff was pinned behind the steering wheel for three hours. After being forcibly removed from the totally damaged car by the police and firefighters at the scene, the plaintiff was rushed to the hospital by ambulance, where she was treated for her severe and disabling injuries, including a broken pelvis, a concussion, and internal bleeding.

Defendant's version:

The accident occurred as defendant was travelling westward on Adams Avenue. After the collision, the plaintiff remained in her car until she was transported to the hospital, where she received treatment for her injuries.

Note the detail in the plaintiff's version, which paints a vivid picture for the reader. In contrast, the defendant's version glosses over the event by summarizing it in a general fashion. In fact, the defendant's version doesn't even make clear that the defendant was involved in the collision.

I. Drafting Techniques

1. Getting Started

For most writers, the most difficult task is getting started. The research is completed, the deadline is looming, and yet the writer cannot begin.

The best cure for this common disease is to write something. Write anything. Just get started. If the idea of beginning an argument paralyzes you, don't begin there. Start writing the section of the document you are most comfortable with, even if this is not the correct order. If you are familiar with the facts, begin with a statement of facts. If you know how you want to conclude a letter, memo, or brief, begin with the conclusion. The mere act of writing any section of a document will relieve some of your anxiety about being able to write.

Consider telling or speaking about the project to a friend or colleague. This may help you organize your thoughts and give you ideas on how to begin writing.

Set a goal for yourself. Tell yourself that the statement of facts must be completed by noon. Challenge yourself to complete a task within an hour. These techniques may help you get started.

2. *Finishing on Time*

You will often be given deadlines for finishing projects. Similarly, documents prepared for courts may need to be filed by a specified date. If you have a deadline date, you may find it helpful to work backward from this date and establish a schedule for yourself. Set a date by which all of the research will be done, another date for completing the first draft, another for cite-checking, and another for revising.

If you are a habitual last-minute worker, always finding yourself operating in crisis mode, it may help to announce a deadline date to someone. Go public. By telling your supervisor, "The first draft will be on your desk by Wednesday morning," you will commit yourself to meet this self-imposed deadline. If there is no deadline for filing the document with the court, ask your supervisor, "When would you like this completed?" Without some deadline date, the project will languish on your desk and continually be relegated to the back burner while you work on other projects.

Once the deadline is established, allow yourself some time for emergencies. The copier may break down, you may get sick, or someone else's project may have a higher priority. If you don't allow room for these last-minute crises, you may fail to meet the deadline.

Set small goals for yourself. Tell yourself, "I will have the statement of facts done by 11:00 A.M. today." These self-imposed deadlines will help you tackle the project bit by bit and meet the real deadline.

3. *Methods of Writing*

There are three primary methods used for the actual writing process: writing by hand, dictating, and writing on a word processor.

a. Writing by Hand

Some people are most comfortable writing in longhand. While this can be a very effective technique, its primary drawback is that it is extremely time-consuming, especially for a long memo or brief. In fact, some law firms are vehemently opposed to writing in longhand and will insist that a faster method be used. Despite this, projects written in longhand often need less revising than projects dictated or composed on a word processor.

b. Dictating

Dictating is probably the speediest method of drafting. It can take some time, however, to shed self-consciousness when you dictate. Initially, dictating may seem painfully slow. Confidence is rapidly gained, however. Stick with it until you become comfortable.

In the beginning, you may prefer to prepare a mini-outline for your dictating efforts and follow that as you dictate. You may also find that your initial attempts include repetitious sentences and poorly organized paragraphs. With time and practice, however, you will acquire skill at dictating together with a certain mental discipline enabling you rapidly and effectively to organize your thoughts. This skill at verbalizing complex thoughts may translate into ease and confidence in speaking as well. This enhanced competence in oral presentation is one of the hidden benefits of dictating.

One of the drawbacks to dictating lies in its convenience. You may be tempted to dictate as you speak. This can result in long-winded paragraphs and a somewhat informal tone. Moreover, for the ease of the person transcribing your tapes, you should insert punctuation and paragraphing. For example, the transcriber will likely hear the following on the tapes you dictate:

> "Dear Mr. Smith colon Paragraph This letter is written in response to your request for information relating to the duties of landlords with regard to rental premises period Paragraph You have informed us that comma according to the lease you signed on June 4 comma 1999 comma . . . ."

Similarly, you may need to spell certain words to ensure the transcriber types "very" rather than "vary" or "marry" rather than "Mary." With practice, however, dictating can become an extremely effective method of drafting.

c. Using a Word Processor

Many individuals prefer to draft using a word processor. While this method may be very speedy, and allows much flexibility in changing the placement of sections, individuals tend to spend excessive time revising as they go along. Revising is a task better left until the end of a project. Your project need not be perfect with the first draft. Your initial draft should be focused on including the major issues and arguments needed to be addressed. Try to fight the temptation to engage in micro-editing as you draft on a word processor. Allow your first draft to flow smoothly and then devote effort to revision later.

J. Electronic Communications

New forms of communication, namely, electronic communications, have arisen in the past several years, changing the way people communicate at the workplace. While many of them are great timesavers, others are traps for the unwary. Consider the following when using any of the newer forms of electronic communcations.

1. *Phones and Voice Mail*

Although conference calls and voice mail can both reduce the time you spend on communications, there are a couple of guidelines that will assist you:

- When setting up a conference call, treat it as a meeting and be prompt in dialing in to the conference number.
- Make sure that introductions are made for all participants and that all participants can hear each other.
- Always ask for permission before placing someone on a speakerphone.
- Always disclose that another is listening with you if you are on a speakerphone.
- Do not leave overly long or rambling voice mail messages.
- Clearly and slowly state your name and phone number in voice mail messages. Repeat at the end of your message for those unfamiliar with you so they do not have to replay the message to obtain your name and number.
- Avoid using voice mail to "dodge" callers and to evade bad news.
- Avoid disclosing confidential information over a car phone or cell phone. Messages may be easily intercepted.
- Check your office policy to see if cell phones can be used for business while you are driving. After a large law firm was sued in 2001 for an accident caused by one of its attorneys who was driving while using the cell phone for firm business, many firms now prohibit such use.

2. *Communication by Facsimile*

Communicating by facsimile is so commonplace that many firms use "real" correspondence only for more critical matters, such as advice and status reports. Check your firm or office policy as to documents sent by facsimile. Most facsimile cover sheets will include a confidentiality notice indicating that if someone receives the communication in error, he or she should return it to the sender. Such notices are used to maintain attorney-client confidentiality and privilege. Consider sending voluminous materials by mail because even the best facsimile machines produce a copy that is less readable than an original. Always double-check the facsimile number before pressing "send." Once the document is sent, it cannot be recalled.

3. *E-mail*

E-mail is becoming an increasingly common method of communication, both within the workplace and to clients. E-mail creates an air of informality and the ease with which a message can be composed and sent causes countless errors. We have all heard stories of people who, much to their chagrin, have mistakenly replied to an entire "list" rather than solely to the sender of a message. Many firms and offices have policies as to the types of communications that can be sent via e-mail and will include confidentiality notices at the conclusion of each e-mail message. Follow these guidelines:

- Spell-check all e-mail and proof for accuracy. If necessary, print a hard copy of the message, proof it, correct it, and then send it. It is far better to be overly cautious than to be perceived as sloppy.
- Because e-mail is generally "dashed off" without a great deal of thought, it often results in brusque and abrupt communications. The reader will not be able to see your expression, gauge your body language, or hear any intonation. Thus, attempts at sarcasm and humor may be misperceived. Consider receiving a communication saying, "I resent your message." You may be tempted to respond in a curt or hostile fashion before you realize the reader meant to say, "I re-sent your message."
- Never pass along inappropriate e-mail at your workplace. Politely inform the sender that you do not care to receive such information.
- Do not assume e-mail is confidential. Many employers monitor e-mail communications.

Technology Tips

http://www.sec.gov	The Web site of the Securities and Exchange Commission offers excellent guidance on writing in "plain English," with numerous samples, explanations, and tips.
http://www.plainlanguage.gov	This is the Web site of the Plain Language Action Network, a government group working to improve communications by the federal government. Numerous samples and tips are given for writing user-friendly documents, and various links to other useful resources are provided.
http://www.nara.gov/fedreg/dldhome.htm	The Web site of the National Archives and Records Administration offers materials on drafting legal documents.
http://www.ll.georgetown.edu/lr/rs/leglwrite.html	Georgetown University Law Center's site offers excellent links to numerous useful writing sources.
http://www.ualr.edu/~cmbarger/RESOURCES.HMT	This Web site of a law school professor offers links to references and a varity of resources for legal writers, including tips on grammar, style, and composition.
http://cctc2.commnet.edu/grammar	This site offers helpful and specific guides to grammar and writing.
http://www.quintcareers.com/writing	This site offers a collection of writing essentials.
http://www.bartleby.com/index/html	This site offers direct linking to numerous writing resources, including dictionaries, thesauri, *Bartlett's Familiar Quotations*, and Strunk and White's classic book, *The Elements of Style*.
http://www.grammarlady.com	This site offers useful advice and information on grammar and writing. The Grammar Lady will send a free newsletter to subscribers via e-mail. Each issue includes tips on grammar and word usage.

Assignment for Chapter 15

PRECISION

Select the Correct Word in the Following Sentences.

1. You must ensure/insure that no one overhears your confidential calls.
2. She is liable/libel for all the damage she caused.
3. The agreement was entered into between/among Sue Harris, Liz Gray, and Evan Stone.
4. Beside/Besides the plaintiff, the defendants also attended the conference.
5. The principal/principle announced in the case will bind the lower courts.
6. What was the effect/affect of the mother's testimony?
7. She was found liable for/guilty of trademark infringement.
8. The 1998 case reversed/overruled the holding in the 1976 case.
9. We agreed to the terms of the agreement in our oral/verbal telephone call.
10. I need you to prepare a memorandum/memoranda on the issue of damages.

CLARITY

Rephrase Each of the Following to Produce a Clearer Sentence.

1. Benefits will be granted to all senior citizens on May 1. Additional benefits will be granted to the elderly on July 1.
2. It is critical that you not be uninformed about the defenses asserted.
3. You are not precluded from denying the allegations of the complaint.
4. A party cannot refuse or fail to respond to interrogatories.
5. The plaintiff's car was involved in the collision. The motor vehicle was towed to an impound lot.
6. If you do not initiate litigation by March 15, you cannot bring a claim thereafter.
7. There is evidence that indicates that the doctors did not provide inadequate care to their patient.
8. Mr. Farr informed Mr. Peters that his claim was barred by the statute of limitations.
9. On Monday, the priest counseled the defendant. He then went skiing at Vail.
10. You cannot deny that you failed to adhere to the terms of the contract.

READABILITY

Rewrite the Following Sentences to Make Them More Readable by Using the Active Voice.

1. The investments may be approved by the board of directors.
2. The testimony was reviewed by the jurors.
3. A decision was made by the judge that the statement was hearsay.
4. Ownership of the company's stock will be vested in the shareholders.
5. A decision to seek arbitration was agreed to by all the parties.

Rewrite the Following Sentences to Make Them More Readable by Using Parallel Structure.

1. We invest in the fund's assets in securities to provide you with liquidity, protection of your investment, and to generate revenue.
2. Speaking clearly and written skills are the two components of successful communication.
3. The plaintiff proposed the following settlement: payment of $50,000; returning the property; and revoking the agreement.
4. The settlement conference will be held for the following purposes:

   - Reviewing each party's exhibits
   - Preparing jury instructions
   - Finalization of trial briefs

5. If you want to buy shares, fill out the application, sign the form, and the payments should be made to your broker.

Rewrite the Following Sentences to Make Them More Readable by Eliminating Jargon.

1. Enclosed herewith please find the invoice that was the subject of our earlier telephonic communication.
2. The object of said actions of the said defendants was to engage in the aforementioned fraudulent scheme.
3. After perusing the documents, the jurist opined that they were not admissible.
4. With reference to your instant inquiry regarding the said leasehold interest, my opinion is not changed by any of the matters that have subsequently been communicated by you to me.
5. A cause of action must be initiated by the complainant not later than 100 days after the injury is sustained or caused to be sustained.

BREVITY

Rewrite the Following Sentences to Achieve Brevity by Omitting Needless Words and Redundancies.

1. Rent must be paid on a monthly basis.
2. In the event that you are successful, damages will be awarded and given.
3. The agreement is in compliance with the terms of the parties' agreement.
4. If the state agency finds that an individual has received a payment to which the individual was not entitled, whether or not the payment was due to the individual's fault or misrepresentation, the individual shall be liable to repay to the State the total sum of the payment to which the individual was not entitled.
5. Each and every term of the agreement must be acknowledged and agreed to by the defendants.

Chapter 16

Legal Correspondence

Chapter Overview

While television and movies would have you believe that lawyers spend all day arguing interesting and exciting cases in court, the truth is that much of a lawyer's time is spent writing. Lawyers often rely on paralegals to assist in the writing process and often delegate an entire writing task to paralegals.

This chapter will introduce you to one of the most common forms of legal writings: legal correspondence. Letters are written for several purposes, and thus the style and tone you use will vary according to the purpose of the letter.

As you work and have the opportunity to review the writings of others, start collecting samples of the writings you find most effective. Use these samples to build up your arsenal of writing tools.

A. Letterwriting

1. *Introduction*

Unlike other legal writings, such as contracts, wills, and briefs, there is no rigid list of elements that must be included in a letter. While letters should, of course, contain the basics (date, salutation, body, and closing), you will be able to exercise great creativity in letterwriting based upon the goal you seek to achieve in your letter. The tone you adopt and the order in which you elect to discuss items are at your discretion. To beginning legal writers this flexibility can be intimidating. Without a rigid format to follow, some writers become paralyzed.

Letters can be extremely effective tools. The first letter you send to a client or adversary often establishes the basis for a relationship. If your letter to adverse counsel is hostile and arrogant, you will be responded to in kind, and this will mark the tone of future correspondence. Thus, you need to do some planning and thinking before you write.

The two most important questions to ask yourself before you begin a letter are "Who will be reading this letter?" and "What will this letter say?" The answer to the first question will set the tone for your letter, and the answer to the second question will tell you what type of letter you should write.

a. Who Will Be Reading This Letter?

The tone or style of your letter must be appropriate for the reader. If the letter is directed to an individual who is relatively inexperienced with litigation, you will need to explain the information you present in the most clear and complete fashion possible. If the letter is directed to another legal professional, such as a judge, attorney, or other paralegal, you will know that your discussion of some matters need not be as detailed or elementary as for a layperson.

If you find your letters are becoming stuffy and legalistic in style, there are a few techniques you can use to warm up the tone. One is to use personal pronouns, especially "you." Therefore, rather than saying "tenants have a right to withhold rent if the leased premises are not habitable," try saying "as a tenant you have the right to withhold rent because your premises are no longer habitable." Similarly, contractions such as "can't" and "wouldn't" rather than "cannot" and "would not" tend to make a letter slightly less formal and more personal, although contractions are not commonly used in legal or business writing.

The fact that you will adapt your tone in legal letters to suit different readers is no different from what you already do: A letter written home to your family is written in a style entirely different from a letter responding to a job announcement.

b. What Will This Letter Say?

Before you begin drafting any letter, focus on the central purpose of your letter. Try to distill this to one or two sentences. For example, some purposes may be as follows:

- The client needs to know a deposition has been scheduled for next month.
- The debtor needs to understand that failure to repay the client will result in litigation.
- The adverse counsel needs to be persuaded to dismiss the client from litigation.
- The client needs to be provided advice regarding cutting down trees on a neighbor's property.

These four examples represent the four basic types of legal correspondence: *informative*, *demanding*, *persuasive*, and *opinion* letters. Once you decide what type of letter you need to write, a style will come almost naturally.

Before discussing techniques for writing these four varieties of letters, we will examine the format and elements of legal letters in general.

2. *The Elements of Letters*

While there are different types of letter you will write, there are certain "basics" that are common to all legal correspondence. The components of legal correspondence are similar to those used for general business letters.

a. Letterhead

Law firms, government offices and agencies, and corporations all use special stationery that serves to identify the office by name, address, telephone and facsimile numbers, and other relevant information. This is called letterhead. While usually placed at the top of a page, some businesses and firms place letterhead information in a column running down the left side of the page or at the bottom of the page. Law firms (unless they have a large number of attorneys) usually list the attorneys associated with the firm on the letterhead. Be careful when drafting and setting up a letter that you recognize how much room the letterhead takes up because you need some space between the letterhead and your writing. Use letterhead for all correspondence connected with your employer because it conveys the message to the recipient that the correspondence is "official." Letterhead is used only for the first page of a letter. The remaining pages match the color and quality of the letterhead page but are not imprinted with the letterhead.

b. Date

Every item of correspondence must include a date, written out by month, day, and year (for example, August 12, 2001). The date is usually centered three lines beneath the letterhead, although occasionally it is placed at the left margin. Because dates in legal matters can be critical, be sure the date given is the date the letter is actually mailed, rather than the date of an earlier draft.

c. Special Mailing Notations

If your correspondence will be sent to the recipient by any means other than first class mail, indicate such as follows: "Hand Delivered," or "Registered Mail," or "Via Facsimile." This notation should be placed two lines below the date or above the address. Similarly, any other special notations such as "Attorney-Client Communication—Privileged and Confidential" should appear before the inside address.

d. Inside Address

The addressee's name and address should appear two lines below the date or any special mailing notations. Always follow the addressee's or organization's preferences for spelling, capitalization, and punctuation. Use titles if appropriate, such as Ellen Cochran, M.D., Stanley L. Williams, Esq., or David P. Kimball, Executive Vice President. If you do not know the marital status of a female addressee, use "Ms." unless you are directed otherwise. The form "Mrs. William Trainor" is acceptable only in social letters. Use "Ms. Madelyn G. Trainor." See Figure 16-1 for sample addresses.

e. Reference or Subject Notation

The reference notation indicates the subject matter of the correspondence. The notation may refer to the title of a case, the topic to be discussed in the letter, or a file or claim number. The reference notation gives the reader an immediate snapshot of what is to be discussed and also helps you later if you need to locate a letter you previously wrote. The reference notation (abbreviated as "Re:") is usually placed two lines below the inside address. As a courtesy to your reader, include his or her file or reference number if you know it. If your office uses internal file numbers, indicate those as well, because they often assist in mail-sorting. See Figure 16-2 for sample reference notations.

Figure 16-1
Sample Addresses

Ms. Donna A. Higgins
4529 Grandview Avenue
San Diego, CA 92110

Mr. Allan N. Navarro
President
ABC Distributing Company
1429 Burgener Boulevard
Chicago, IL 96104

Janet F. Sanderson, Esq.
Mills, Arnold and Smith
2900 L Street, NW
Washington, D.C. 20006

Director of Human Resources
Smith Management Company
2800 Arlington Avenue
Irving, TX 75247-3159

Figure 16-2
Sample Reference Notations

Re: *Calvin v. Temple Motors, Inc.*
Civil Action No. 92-696-VMA

Re: Estate of Boyer
Our File: 9204\91-646
Your File: CN-9220

Re: Punitive Damages in Fraud Actions

f. Salutation

The salutation, or greeting, usually appears two lines beneath the reference notation. Unless you are acquainted with the addressee, err on the side of formality and address the letter to Mr. Brown or Ms. Taylor, for example. Once again, unless you have been directed otherwise, address letters to females as "Ms." Letters to an unknown recipient such as the attorney general of a state should be directed to "Dear Sir or Madam:" Follow the salutation with a colon in business letters and with a comma in personal letters. See Figure 16-3 for sample salutations.

g. Body

The body of the letter begins two lines below the salutation. The body is the critical part of your correspondence because it conveys your message. The first sentence and paragraph should set the stage for the rest of your letter by indicating the purpose of the letter.

Business letters and legal correspondence are usually single-spaced and then double-spaced between paragraphs. The second and following pages will not be on letterhead but will match the color and quality of the first letterhead page and will usually contain information such as the following (a "header") in the upper left-hand corner of each page:

Mr. Elliot Anthony
Page Two
December 14, 2001

h. Closing and Signature

Most letters close with statements such as the following:

Please do not hesitate to call me if you have any questions.
Thank you in advance for your cooperation and courtesy.
If you have any questions or comments you may reach me at the number given above.

The complimentary closing is usually "Very truly yours," "Sincerely," "Best regards," "Yours truly," or something similar, followed by a comma. "Very truly yours" is generally regarded as more formal and is used less fre-

Figure 16-3
Sample Salutations

Dear Mr. Smith:
Dear Ms. Anderson:
Dear Sir or Madam:

quently than "Sincerely." If the letter is addressed to a judge, senator, or representative, the complimentary closing is typically "Respectfully." Capitalize the first letter in the complimentary closing and place it two lines below the body of the letter.

Avoid informal or unusual closings such as "Affectionately," or "Successfully yours." Do not merge your complimentary closing with the last line of your letter. These merged closings were fashionable hundreds of years ago but have a stilted and archaic look. An example of a merged closing is as follows:

Thanking you for your attention, I remain,
Yours very truly,

Suzanne Forrest

For letters that you will sign, be sure to indicate your title underneath your signature so the reader will know your position in the firm. Allow four lines between the complimentary close and your typed name. Some individuals prefer to use blue ink for their signatures, so readers can easily tell the document is an original rather than a copy.

Very truly yours,

Matthew K. Lyons
Legal Assistant

Sincerely,

Paula L. Wagner
Senior Paralegal

Best regards,

Elizabeth A. Murphy
Legal Assistant to Kenneth Trainor

i. Copies and Enclosures

Copies of the letter you write may be sent to others. For example, the client will routinely be provided with copies of letters you write to adverse counsel because this is a way of keeping the client informed of the progress of a case. To indicate the recipients of copies use "cc:" followed by the names of those who will be receiving copies. While "cc" stands for "carbon copies," which have universally been replaced by photocopies, the signal "cc:" remains in use.

There may be instances in which you do not want the reader of your letter to know who received a copy of it. In such cases, simply sign your letter, mail it, and then mark the copies that will go to the unidentified individual (here, Theresa Stone) that will be placed in the file: "bcc: Theresa Stone." This is a reference to "blind carbon copy."

If you are enclosing something in a letter, indicate this by the abbreviation "Encl." or "Encls." for more than one enclosure. "Enc." or "Encs." are also used. Some writers list or identify the items enclosed. See Figure 16-4 for sample notations for copies and enclosures. Avoid archaic expressions such as "enclosed herewith please find." A simple "enclosed is" is sufficient.

The last notation in a letter is a reference indicating who wrote the letter and who typed or prepared it. If the author is Maria M. Adkins and the secretary who types it is Gregory L. Huntington, the reference "MMA/glh" would appear at the left margin beneath any references regarding copies sent to others and enclosures. The use of "mma:glh" is also common.

j. Format Considerations

Letters are written on standard 8½″ × 11″ paper and are usually single-spaced and then double-spaced between component parts (for example, between the date and inside address, between the inside address and reference notation, between the reference notation and salutation) and between paragraphs.

Some letters show no indentations for paragraphs because new paragraphs are clearly indicated by the double-spacing between paragraphs. This style is referred to as "block form" or "left justified." In block form, all elements of the letter, including the date and complimentary closing, begin at the left margin.

Other firms and authors prefer to indent five spaces for new paragraphs even though they are set apart by double-spacing. This style is called "modified block form." Here the date, complimentary closing, writer's identification, and signature are all centered or placed just to the right of center.

When the right-hand margin is even and every line ends at the right at the same space, this is referred to as "right justification." Such letters present a very crisp appearance. One drawback to right justified margins is that the spacing in some words will be cramped while others may be

Figure 16-4
Sample Notations for Copies and Enclosures

cc: Susan M. Everett
Thomas L. Cruz

Encl.

cc w/encl.: Stephen S. Neal

slightly spread out. Reading studies have documented that word-processed right-justified documents are more difficult to read because the added spaces eliminate distinctive word spatial characteristics, which aid comprehension and ease of reading. To a reader, the use of right justification is often distracting. Continuing improvements in word processors are eliminating these spacing problems. Neverthless, some writers prefer a "ragged edge" at the right margin, believing it has less of a "computer" look and more of a "personally typed" look. Many word processing programs now offer letter templates for business letters in which spacing and common closings are already included, allowing you to "fill in the blanks" of the form. Spacing is pre-set as well.

Never allow a page to begin or end with one line by itself or one heading by itself. Referred to as "widows and orphans," these single lines or headings present an unprofessional appearance. Use 12-point or 10-point typeface for readability. Twelve-point type is preferred. Use a common typeface such as Times New Roman or Courier.

3. *Types of Letters*

a. General Correspondence

General correspondence letters may include letters requesting information or responding to requests for information, cover letters that accompany some document or other enclosure, confirmation letters that confirm some agreement or arrangement reached with another party, or status or report letters providing a report to a client or insurance company of the progress of a case. Except for status letters, these letters are often brief and may be only one or two paragraphs in length.

These letters should contain the components of all letters (date, inside address, reference notation). They also should conform to the elements of good legal writing set forth in Chapter 15, namely, precision, clarity, readability, brevity, and order. If you misspell the client's name or send the letter to the wrong address, this will attract far more attention than the content of the letter.

If you are unsure whether a letter should be sent to confirm some matter or clarify some detail, err on the side of caution and write the letter. This will keep the file complete and help establish the progress of the case if you aren't there to explain it. Always send a confirming letter to opposing counsel to confirm dates, amounts, or any other matter. If adverse counsel has offered to settle the case for $20,000, immediately confirm this in writing and then notify the supervising attorney, who will likely conduct negotiations or give you instructions regarding such negotiations. If adverse counsel has granted you an extension to answer interrogatories or produce documents, immediately confirm this in writing so no dispute can later arise as to the dates. See Figure 16-5 for several sample general correspondence letters, including confirmation, cover, and status letters.

Figure 16-5
Sample General Correspondence Letters

A. Sample Confirmation Letter

LAW OFFICES
OF
MICHELLE L. MONACO
2300 BIRCH DRIVE
PHOENIX, ARIZONA 60234
(609) 788-4000

November 8, 2000

Stephen L. James, Esq.
6200 Tenth Street
Phoenix, AZ 60244

Re: *Brownell v. Kaplan*

Dear Mr. James:

This letter will confirm that you have granted us an extension to respond to the plaintiff's complaint in the above-referenced action until December 6, 2000. As I explained, the additional time is needed due to my client's hospitalization. Thank you for your courtesy and cooperation.

Please feel free to call me if you have any comments or questions.

Sincerely,

Michelle L. Monaco

cc: Sharon J. Kaplan
MLM/pmr

Figure 16-5 (*Continued*)

B. Sample Cover Letters

SMITH, CHURCH, AND UPSHAW
1414 SOUTH ADAMS STREET
SUITE 1000
BOSTON, MASSACHUSETTS
(214) 649-1200

January 14, 2001

Ms. Ann B. Milstead
2001 Elysian Fields Avenue
New Orleans, LA 70015

Re: *Sanderson v. Milstead*

Dear Ann:

I am enclosing a copy of the transcript of the deposition of the plaintiff in the above-referenced action. Please review this carefully and call me with any comments you may have. As you know, we are particularly interested in the plaintiff's version of the events in the two hours preceding the accident. Any inconsistencies that you may find in the plaintiff's testimony would be extremely helpful. We look forward to hearing from you.

Very truly yours,

William B. Church

Encl.
WBC/swa

Figure 16-5

B. Sample Cover Letters (Continued)

LAW OFFICES OF THOMAS N. MILLER
1600 ELM STREET
SUITE 202
PORTLAND, OREGON 60102
(402) 657-1990

February 6, 2001

Mr. and Mrs. James E. Bailey
2002 Artesia Boulevard
Portland, OR 60435

Re: Execution of Wills

Dear Mr. and Mrs. Bailey:

I enjoyed meeting you last week and discussing the preparation of your wills. I have prepared the first drafts of the wills. They are enclosed for your review. After you have examined the wills, please call me with any changes or corrections you have. I will then revise them according to your instructions and schedule a date for you to come to my office to sign the wills.

Please feel free to call me if you have any questions or comments.

Sincerely,

Thomas N. Miller

Encls.
TNM:scg

Figure 16-5

B. Sample Cover Letters (Continued)

LAW OFFICES
OF
TAYLOR AND GILBEY
4305 WILLETT STREET
KANSAS CITY, MISSOURI 45609
(421) 678-1299

September 14, 2000

Cynthia A. Chan, Esq.
5000 Missouri Avenue
Kansas City, MO 45609

Re: *Anders v. Patterson*
Your File: CV 1895

Dear Ms. Chan:

In reviewing my correspondence to you of yesterday, I observed that I neglected to include a copy of Exhibit A, which should have been enclosed with the letter. I am enclosing Exhibit A with this letter and apologize for any inconvenience this may have caused you.

Please feel free to call me if you have any questions or comments.

Sincerely,

Francis K. Taylor

Encl.
FKT:wlm

Figure 16-5 (*Continued*)

C. Sample Status Letter

FENTON, HOGUE AND HOGUE
1200 B STREET, SUITE 1900
LOS ANGELES, CALIFORNIA 90234
(405) 765-1400

July 16, 2001

Dale L. Curtis, M.D.
3200 Montana Avenue
Los Angeles, CA 90256

Re: Fontana v. Curtis, et al.
Our File: 94081

Dear Dr. Curtis:

This letter will provide you with a brief status report on the progress of the above-referenced action. As you know, we have provided interrogatories, or written questions, to the plaintiff, which he is required to answer under oath and return to us within thirty (30) days. After we have had an opportunity to review the plaintiff's answers, we will be in a better position to evaluate which documents we should request and which individuals and witnesses should be deposed so we may obtain their testimony regarding the acts of professional negligence alleged against you.

The Superior Court has recently notified us that a settlement conference has been scheduled on the matter for Wednesday, August 12, 2001, at 2:00 p.m. in Room 2404 of the Los Angeles County Courthouse, located at 1212 Wilshire Boulevard in Los Angeles. You are required to attend that conference, at which time the judge assigned to the case will explore the possibilities of settlement. The plaintiff will also attend and will be expected to make a reasonable demand for settlement. If we are unable to settle the case at that time, a trial date will be assigned. We expect that the trial will occur after the first of the year.

As soon as we receive the plaintiff's answers to the interrogatories, we will provide you with a copy for your review and comment. Please contact us if you have any questions.

Very truly yours,

Linda J. Fenton

LJF:sfk

b. Demand Letters

Demand letters set forth a client's demands. The most common type of demand letter is a collection letter, which outlines the basis for a debt due to a client and sets forth a demand that it be paid. Other demand letters, however, demand that certain action be taken, such as a demand that a landlord repair a leaking roof or a demand that one company cease using a trademark similar to one owned by another company. Your tone should be firm and business-like, not strident or nasty. To eliminate any disputes whether the letter was received, send the letter by some verifiable type of delivery, such as registered mail. The only portion of a demand letter that will differ from a general correspondence letter is the content of the body. Include these elements:

- *Introduction of your firm.* Identify your firm and specify your role. A simple sentence stating "This firm represents James K. Matthews regarding the automobile accident that occurred on January 8, 2001" is sufficient.
- *Recitation of facts.* You must include the facts upon which the client's claim is based. Because your aim is to motivate the reader to pay your client or take some action, phrase the factual statement as persuasively as possible.
- *Demand.* Set forth as clearly as possible your client's demand. If this is a collection letter, specify the exact amount due. If you are demanding that the reader take some specific action, such as repairing a leaking roof, say so. If there are several components to your demand, you may wish to set them forth in a list.
- *Consequence of non-compliance.* Because your aim in a demand letter is to persuade the reader to pay your client or take some action, you should include a statement telling the reader of the consequence of not complying with the demand letter. These consequences may include the institution of litigation, the cessation of work on a project, or some other adverse action. While most readers will be offended by heavy-handed threats, there is nothing wrong in clearly and concisely explaining to a reader what will occur if the client's demands are not met.
- *Date of compliance.* You must set forth in explicit terms the deadline for compliance. Do not say "You must pay the sum of $10,000 immediately." When is immediately? Two days? Ten days? Three weeks? Set forth an express date so the reader will know exactly when compliance is expected.

Follow these guidelines in drafting demand letters:

(i) *Know the facts.* Be sure you have all of the relevant facts. It is not enough to have most of the facts. If the client has informed you that a debtor has breached a contract, determine if the contract is written or oral. If written, you need to obtain a copy of it and review it. A mistake in reciting the facts will immediately call forth a response by the recipient pointing out your error, and any momentum you may have had, along with your credibility, will be lost. To be sure your recitation of the facts is correct, send a copy of your demand letter in draft to your client asking that your client review the letter and approve it before it is sent to the other party. If it later turns out that the facts recited in the letter are incorrect, you have protected yourself from your supervisor's or client's wrath by having obtained the client's approval.

(ii) *Know the law.* You cannot send a letter demanding money for breach of contract if enforcement of the contract is barred by the statute of limitations or some other law. You must perform some minimum amount of research to ensure that the client's claim is valid and enforceable. Similarly, review the code of ethics for your state. It is unethical to correspond with a person who is represented by counsel. Therefore, once you know an individual has retained counsel, all correspondence must be directed to counsel. Most codes of ethics set forth other rules you should be familiar with, such as that it is unethical to threaten criminal prosecution if a demand is not met.

Many states have consumer protection or debt collection statutes, and demands for payment of debts must comply with the requirements of these statutes. Be sure to research any such requirements in your state because failure to follow the statutory requirements may invalidate the demand.

(iii) *Don't argue the case.* A demand letter should set forth the facts underlying the demand, state the demand, and outline the consequences of non-compliance. You need not, and should not, present all the evidence you would need to prevail at a trial of this matter. The debtor will undoubtedly know some of the facts relating to the claim, and you need not provide copies of every item of correspondence and the names of every witness who supports your client's version of the matter. If the problem cannot be resolved by direct negotiation, you will have ample opportunity to argue the case at trial. Don't tip your hand at this juncture. While a few legal authorities may be cited in some instances, routine collection letters rarely include legal analysis.

(iv) *Do what you say.* If you have told the recipient of the letter legal action will be instituted by December 10 unless the amount of $10,000 is paid to the client, you must be prepared to do so. Nothing jeopardizes credibility more than empty threats. If December 10 comes and goes and you issue another demand letter setting forth another deadline date, the reader will know you do not mean what you say and will understand there is no reason to comply with the renewed demand.

This issue of doing what you say is often a matter of communicating with the client. If the client has no intention of suing or is aware the reader may have certain counterclaims, the letter can be structured appropriately. For example, rather than stating a deadline date, the letter could leave the issue open and state any of the following:

- We look forward to receiving your prompt response to this demand.

- Please contact us to discuss this matter further.
- Unless we receive a satisfactory response from you by December 10, we will take all appropriate legal action.
- We invite your response to this claim and hope this matter can be resolved amicably.

Note, however, that if you write, "We look forward to a counterproposal from you," you have made a serious concession and have invited the recipient to play "let's make a deal." See Figure 16-6 for a sample demand letter.

c. Opinion Letters

Letters offering legal advice or opinions can only be signed by attorneys. Nevertheless, you may find that you are given the task of researching the law and writing the letter. Thus, while the letter is reviewed, approved, and signed by an attorney, you may be the author. While these opinion letters are usually requested by clients seeking advice on a particular matter, on occasion they may be requested by a third party, such as an accountant who requires a legal opinion as to a client's progress in litigation before the accountant can prepare financial statements.

In addition to the standard components of a letter (date, reference line, and so forth), there are eight key elements to an opinion letter. Opinion letters share many elements in common with legal memoranda, although their analysis of legal authorities is more simplified, and they are written to a client rather than to another legal professional.

(1) Date

While all letters include dates, the date of an opinion letter is especially important because the opinion will relate to the status of the law on that date. Changes in the law after that date may well affect the correctness of the opinion.

(2) Introductory Language

It may be a good idea to remind the client why he or she is receiving an opinion letter. An opinion letter may take several hours to research and prepare and may well be costly. Reminding a client that he or she specifically requested the opinion may protect you from a client's refusal to pay the bill on the ground that this work was never requested. Consider the following introductions:

- We enjoyed meeting you last week. As you requested, we have researched whether a landlord is liable for injuries sustained by a tenant . . . .
- Per our telephone conversation of March 10, 2001, we have reviewed the issue . . . .
- At your request . . .
- You have asked for our opinion whether . . .
- According to your instructions of July 18, 2001 . . .

Figure 16-6
Sample Demand Letter

DOUGLAS, FRANK, KELLY AND MORGAN
5600 K STREET, SUITE 2500
ALBANY, NEW YORK 12004
(612) 567-8999

August 9, 2001

Mr. Peter M. Todd
Todd Contracting Co.
1255 Stanley Avenue
Albany, NY 12966

Re: *Harris Engineering, Inc.*

Dear Mr. Todd:

This firm represents Harris Engineering Co. ("Harris") regarding its legal affairs. As you know, on January 4, 2001, Todd Contracting Co. ("Todd") entered into a written contract with Harris. This contract required Harris to provide engineering services for Todd for the construction of Nathan Public Park in Albany, and Todd was to pay the sum of $24,550 to Harris for those services. That contract was signed by you on behalf of Todd.

Our client has informed us that it has provided all engineering services required by the contract. Those services were critical to the improvements performed at Nathan Public Park and no objections were made by any individual at Todd regarding these services. Our client has further informed us that while it received one payment from Todd in the amount of $15,550 on March 1, 2001, no further payments have been made to it, despite numerous requests therefor.

This letter is a formal demand that the sum of $9,000 be paid to Harris on or before August 19, 2001. Our client has asked us to inform you that if this sum is not paid as directed, it will institute litigation against Todd for the remaining balance of $9,000 due to it as well as interest and attorneys fees as provided in the written contract which you signed.

Please contact us within the time provided to confirm your compliance with the terms of this letter and to avoid litigation being filed against Todd.

Sincerely,

Anthony P. Kelly

APK:tmb

This introductory language not only protects you from a client's faulty memory, it also sets forth the scope of the letter by stating the issue that is addressed by the letter.

(3) Review of Facts

An opinion letter should always set forth the facts upon which it is based. Facts are usually given in a narrative (sentence-by-sentence) form rather than in an outline or list form. Including the facts gives the client the opportunity to correct you if any of the facts are wrong. Even a minor factual change such as a change in a date or dollar amount can cause an opinion to be incorrect. Thus, include the facts so the reader understands that the accuracy of the opinion depends upon these facts and that changes in the facts may cause changes in the legal conclusions reached. Consider introducing the facts as follows:

- You have informed us you entered into a written lease on August 18, 2001 . . .
- As we understand them, the facts are as follows: On June 24, 2001, while traveling west on Ash Street . . .

(4) Conclusions

The essence of an opinion letter is the advice given to the client. Clients are particularly eager to get to the "bottom line," and many writers immediately give their opinion or conclusion after a recitation of the facts, and then follow the conclusion with an explanation. This is an effective technique if the opinion you give is one the client wants to hear. If, on the other hand, you will be giving the client bad news, such as informing him or her that a lawsuit cannot be initiated because the statute of limitations has expired, you may want to lead the reader to this unfavorable news gradually. By explaining the law first you will be preparing the reader for the unfavorable outcome so by the time you actually give the bad news, the reader understands exactly why the outcome is unfavorable. Consider introducing the conclusion as follows:

- Based upon the facts you have provided us and the applicable law in this state, it is our opinion that you may initiate an action for wrongful death against Timothy Allen.
- We have concluded that you may bring an action for wrongful death against Timothy Allen. Our conclusion is based upon the facts set forth above and our analysis of the law in this state.

You may have observed that many opinion letters use "we" and "our" rather than "I" and "my." For example, an opinion is often introduced as follows: "It is our opinion" or "Based on the foregoing, our advice is . . . ." This use of "we/I" is a matter of preference by attorneys. Some attorneys believe it is cowardly to hide behind the royal "we" and insist on using the first person "I/me" as in "It is therefore my opinion . . . ." Other attorneys believe the opinion is actually issued by the firm itself rather than by any one particular attorney and thus the "we/our" form is appropriate. You must learn the preference and policy of your supervisor and firm to determine which form to use. If you are working for a sole practitioner, however, "we/our" is never correct.

(5) Explanation of Conclusion

This portion of the letter explains and summarizes the law upon which your conclusions are based. Because most opinion letters are received by laypersons who may not be familiar with the law, avoid detailed discussions of statutes and cases. It is sufficient to summarize the legal authorities in a general fashion.

Should you include citations to cases and statutes? Generally, avoid giving citations unless your reader is sufficiently sophisticated to understand the citations. Similarly, do not merely set out the text of a statute or case; rather, explain what the case or statute means. Refer to the legal authorities as follows:

- Applicable case law provides . . .
- We have researched the pertinent statute that governs this issue. It provides . . .
- The legal authorities in this state are in agreement that . . .

Use headings and subheadings if this portion of the letter is long and you can divide your explanation into easily understood separate sections.

(6) Recommendation

After you have explained the law that governs the conclusion you have reached, provide a recommendation to the client. Be sure that your recommendation is not unduly optimistic. Never inform a client that he or she will recover a substantial amount of money or that he or she "cannot lose" because you will seldom be able to deliver as promised. Phrase your advice as a probability rather than a certainty. Thus, say "a court would likely hold that" rather than "your claim is undoubtedly valid." Do not include any language that could be viewed by a client as a guarantee of success. Similarly, if you need to give the client bad news, try to soften your approach by saying, "Success is extremely unlikely" or "The chances of a favorable outcome are remote at best," rather than a blunt "Taking your case would be a waste of time and money." Be sure, however, that you clearly deliver the bad news. Don't soften your approach so much that you haven't accurately conveyed your meaning. Readers often perceive what they want to, and there is no room for ambiguity in delivering unfavorable news to a client. If you must give bad news, try to find an alternative avenue for the client, as follows:

> Because the statute of limitations has expired, you will not be able to bring an action against your neighbor for trespass. We would suggest, however, that you attempt to directly negotiate with your neighbor. If this approach is unsuccessful, contact the company that issued your homeowners insurance because it may offer coverage for the damage to your property.

Use wording such as "we regret" or "unfortunately" when delivering bad news.

(7) Instructions

The last portion of an opinion letter should be a clear direction to the client to contact the office or take some other action. Consider the following:

> Because the statutes governing this matter require that a claim be submitted to the city within 100 days of the wrongful act, please contact us immediately and provide us with your instructions. Failure to file the claim by May 10, 2001, will bar any action against the city.

(8) Protection Clauses

On occasion, you may not have all of the information you need to provide a complete opinion. For example, the client may have informed you that he is a tenant under a written lease and yet has not provided the lease to your office for your review. In such cases, protect yourself by explaining that you lack certain information, and that the opinion may change depending upon the information you receive. Similarly, if certiorari has been granted for the authorities you rely on, explain this to the reader so if the cases you rely on are reversed or limited, the client will have been forewarned. Finally, think ahead and consider what defenses or arguments the other party may assert. Prepare your client to meet these arguments.

Consider the following examples:

- This opinion is based upon the facts you have provided us. Once we have had an opportunity to review the addendum to the lease entered into between you and your landlord, we will be better able to provide you with our opinion and analysis. Assuming the addendum does not materially alter the original lease, however, it is our opinion . . .
- The landmark case in this area of the law is *Wolfson v. Dana Point, Ltd.*, 929 P.2d 817 (Cal. 2001). That case is presently being reheard by the California Supreme Court. An adverse opinion by the court could affect the conclusions in this letter. We

will continue to monitor this case before the court and notify you once the court has issued its decision.

- While your employer may argue his business is not subject to the provisions of the Family Medical Leave Act, we believe such an argument is without merit because . . .

B. Conclusion

Always write your letter with its intended audience in mind and clearly understand your goals in sending the letter. This will help you achieve the correct style and tone.

After you have finished the letter, re-read it, putting yourself in the recipient's place. This will allow you to focus on whether the letter conveys the information it needs to, whether it will be readily understood by the reader, and whether the tone is appropriate.

Because you have the opportunity to review correspondence from others, keep copies of those that you feel are well written and adopt the techniques you believe make the letters effective. Notice the way others order their paragraphs or conclude their letters. Learn from others.

Assignment for Chapter 16

You have been given the following fact situation by the senior partner in your law firm, John F. Breyer. He has asked that you prepare an opinion letter to be written to the client regarding this fact situation. The letter should be prepared for his signature.

The firm represents Mrs. Sinatra, the heir and widow of Frank Sinatra, who died approximately three years ago. Mrs. Sinatra, a resident of New York, recently viewed a television advertisement using images from Frank Sinatra's famous film, *From Here to Eternity*, which were digitally inserted into a nationwide commercial promoting the sale of athletic gear by a well-known company. Similarly, Mr. Sinatra's voice was recently used in a one-minute segment as part of a six-hour television documentary about famous war films. The estate has not authorized either use and would like to know if such uses can be prohibited.

The controlling statute in your state provides as follows:

(a) Any person who uses a deceased personality's name, voice, signature, photograph, or likeness, in any matter, on or in products, merchandise, or goods, or for the purposes of advertising or selling or soliciting purchases of products, goods, or services, without prior consent from the persons specified in subsection (c) shall be liable for any damages sustained by the persons injured as a result thereof. In addition, the person who violated this section shall be liable to the injured party in an amount equal to the greater of $750 or the actual damages suffered by the injured party as a result of the unauthorized use and any profits from the unauthorized use that are attributable to the use. Punitive damages may also be awarded.

(b) For purposes of this statute, a play, book, magazine, radio or television program, or musical composition, work of political or newsworthy value, or an advertisement for any of these works shall not be considered a product, article of merchandise, good, or service if it is fictional or nonfictional entertainment.

(c) The rights recognized under this section are freely transferable by contract or by means of trust or testamentary documents and may be exercisable by the heir, trustee, or transferee of the deceased personality.

(d) No action shall be brought under this section by reason of any use of a deceased personality's name, voice, signature, photograph, or likeness occurring after the expiration of 70 years after the death of the deceased personality.

(e) A "deceased personality" means any natural person whose name, voice, or likenesss has commercial value at the time of his or her death.

(f) A "photograph" includes any photographic reproduction, still or moving, such that the deceased personality is readily identifiable.

There are no cases interpreting this newly enacted statute, N.Y. Civil Practice Law and Rule § 7.04-225.

Chapter 17

Legal Memoranda

Chapter Overview

An office or legal memorandum is a well-known document in legal writing. It calls for you to research an area of law thoroughly and set forth your findings, both positive and negative, in a specific format.

It is only by being completely knowledgeable about the strengths and weaknesses of a case that the law firm can make a fully informed decision whether and how best to

- represent the client
- prepare pleadings and motions
- settle the case
- proceed to trial
- appeal an adverse decision

Thus, office memoranda or "memos" are used to guide those representing the client in every aspect of a case — from the initial decision whether to accept a case to a final appeal. If the law firm knows in advance the weaknesses of a case, it can adopt certain strategies to overcome these weaknesses and prepare the client for a possible negative outcome. If the memo shows the weaknesses are fatal, the memo saves the client time and money that would be expended in a trial and assists in making a decision to settle the case. A well-written memo can form the basis for motions to be made later in the case or even a trial or appellate brief. Thus, skillful research and careful analysis at this early stage of a case will contribute to the successful management of a case throughout its progress in your office.

Paralegals frequently prepare legal memoranda, and your employer will expect you to be familiar with the purpose, style, and format of an office memorandum. Preparing and writing a memorandum is often a challenging and satisfying task because it calls for you to integrate both your research and writing skills and to present them in such a way that a reader has a complete and objective "snapshot" of the case, including both its strengths and weaknesses.

A. Introduction

An office memorandum is a research document designed to provide information about a case or matter. You will be asked to research a question, and your answer will be provided in the form of a written memorandum. It is an internal document, meaning it is prepared for use within a law firm, corporation, or agency. While a copy of the memo may be provided to a client, it is generally protected by the "work product" privilege and thus is not discoverable by an adverse party.

Because the office memo is not usually discoverable and will only be read by those representing the client (and possibly the client as well), its distinguishing feature is its objectivity. It should set forth not only the strong points of a case but the weak points as well.

Focus on the following three guidelines for effective memoranda writing:

1. *Be Objective*

The most difficult part of writing a memo is remaining neutral and objective. Once we hear the words "our client" we immediately tend to ally ourselves with the client's position and ignore the negative aspects of a case while focusing only on the positive. Thus, phrases such as "I believe" or "I feel" have no place in a memorandum. You should be informing the reader of the findings of the authorities you have located, not interjecting your opinions and judgments.

If you are not objective in pointing out weaknesses and flaws in the client's case, you do the client a disservice. It is much better (and far less costly) to determine early in the representation that the other party has a complete defense to your client's action than to find this out at trial.

Force yourself to play devil's advocate. Approach the project as your adversary might and closely examine the cases that appear unfavorable to your position. Your adversary will certainly do so, and you should be as prepared as possible to overcome weaknesses in your case.

2. *Be Specific*

If you are asked to determine whether a tenant may sublease rented property when the lease fails to address such an issue, focus on this specific question. You need not address the issue as if you were writing a text on the history of landlord-tenant problems from the feudal period to the present. If, during the course of your research, you come across other issues that you believe may be relevant, simply note them and include them in a section at the end of the memo entitled "Additional Research" or "Recommendations."

3. *Be Complete*

The supervisor who assigned you the task wants a finished project, not a sheaf of notes or series of photocopied cases. Anyone can locate cases and photocopy them. Your task is to read and analyze these cases, apply them to the facts of the client's case, and present this as a finished professional research memorandum. Put yourself in your supervisor's place and consider what you would need to know to understand fully the client's case. Assume the supervisor expects a final, polished product that will need no additional work.

B. Format of Memoranda

Unlike documents filed in court, there is no one rigid format for an internal office memorandum. Some law firms have developed their own formats, and you may wish to ask to review memos previously prepared because these will serve as a guide for you. If you cannot locate a previous memo, use the format suggested below, which is a very common and standard format.

There are usually seven components to an office memorandum, each of which should be set forth as a heading and capitalized and centered or in some other way set off from the narrative portion of the memo. In large part, the elements of a memorandum are similar to those of a case brief, discussed in Chapter 4. See Figure 17-1.

1. *Heading*

The heading identifies the document, the person for whom the memo is prepared, the person who prepared the memo, his or her position, the subject matter of the memo, and the date it is prepared. The subject matter of the memo (found in the "Re:" line) should include a brief statement of the topic of the memo as well as a file name and number. Thus, a topic description such as "Injunctive relief" will help facilitate indexing and later location of the memo. See Figure 17-2.

Figure 17-1
Elements of a Typical Memorandum

MEMORANDUM

To:

From:

Re:

Date:

- -

ISSUES

1.
2.

BRIEF ANSWERS

1.
2.

STATEMENT OF FACTS

ANALYSIS

1.
2.

CONCLUSION

2. *Issue(s) or Question(s) Presented*

This section of the memo sets forth the issues that will be addressed by the memo. In some memos, only one issue will be discussed. Other memos may address several issues or questions. If your memo will discuss more than one issue, number each one. Do not number a single issue. Drafting the issues can be very difficult. In fact, you may not be able to formulate the issues until you are almost finished researching the law to be discussed in the memo.

The issues are normally set forth in a question format. They are usually one sentence, although they may include subparts. Be careful that a one-sentence issue is not so long as to be confusing. The issues should be phrased so that they relate to the particular fact the problem presented. For example, questions such as "What is a sublease?" or "What are a landlord's duties?" or "What is burglary?" are far too broad. Better questions would be as follows:

- Under Massachusetts law, may a tenant sublease rented property when a written lease fails to address this issue?
- Under Illinois law, does a landlord have a duty to disclose to tenants information about crimes that have occurred on the premises?
- In New Jersey, has a burglary occurred when an intruder enters a residence through an unlocked and open door?

Some writers prefer the issues or questions to start with the word "whether," as in "whether a tenant may sublease rented property when a written lease fails to address this topic" or "whether a battery occurred when parties involved in a fistfight consented and agreed to fight." Because questions that begin with the word "whether" result in incomplete

Figure 17-2
Sample Heading for Memo

MEMORANDUM

To: Michael T. Gregory, Esq.

From: David H. Hendrix, Legal Assistant

Re: *Smith v. Jones*
Our Ref.: 94061
Sublease of Rented Property

Date: July 15, 2001

sentences, many attorneys disfavor this form. Whichever format you choose, be consistent, and use the same format for all questions.

The questions presented should be phrased in a neutral manner so that an answer is not suggested by the question itself.

3. *Brief Answer(s)*

This section of the memo sets forth brief answers to the issues you presented together with the reasons therefor. It is insufficient to merely repeat the question in a declarative sentence. For example, statements such as "Subleases are common arrangements" or "A landlord has duties to tenants" are hardly helpful to a reader.

Much better answers would be as follows: "A tenant may sublease property rented from another unless there is an unequivocal written lease provision forbidding subleasing" or "Inherent in a landlord's duty to provide habitable premises is a duty to inform tenants of crimes that have occurred at the leased premises." Avoid answers that merely respond "yes," "no," or "maybe." Your answers should incorporate the reason for your conclusions.

Keep your answers brief — no more than one or two sentences. Do not include citations in the brief answers. This section of the memo is only a quick preview of what will be discussed in greater detail later in the body of the memo.

Maintain symmetry in your brief answers. If you have set forth three issues, you must have three answers, each of which corresponds in order and number to the questions previously asked. See Figure 17-3 for sample issues and brief answers.

Figure 17-3
Sample Issues and Brief Answers

Issues

1. Under New Jersey law, may a written contract be rescinded due to one party's fraud?
2. Under New Jersey law, can a failure to comply with the terms of a consent agreement entered in court be the basis for contempt?

Brief Answers

1. Yes. A contract may be rescinded if one party procured the contract through fraud and the other party was misled thereby.
2. Yes. Failure to obey any order of a court, even one based upon the consent of the parties, is contempt of court.

4. *Statement of Facts*

The statement of facts may precede the issues or follow the brief answers. Either approach is acceptable. Many readers prefer the facts to be given first so they can make sense of the questions the memo will address.

The statement of facts will be based upon what you know about the case, what your supervisor and client have told you, and your review of the file. In brief, you are telling the client's "story." The factual statement is to be neutral and objective. Therefore, you will need to include even unfavorable facts. Do not allow your opinions about the case to color your presentation of facts. For example, the statement "He endured four years of employment by Smith" includes an opinion or judgment. State "He was employed by Smith for four years."

Do not include argument in your memo or conclusions that are not supported by the file. If you are unsure whether a statement or event is true, refer to it as an "alleged" statement or event. If there is a dispute as to the facts, include both versions. It is perfectly acceptable to state, "While the tenant alleges she provided notice to the landlord of the leaky roof, the landlord disputes this."

While only relevant facts should be included, the factual statement should be thorough. Do not omit the facts on the assumption that "surely the attorney who gave me this project knows the facts." It is possible a new paralegal or attorney may be assigned to the case and your memo may be the first source consulted to become familiar with the case. Therefore, the Statement of Facts should be self-contained and not require reference to other sources, such as pleadings or correspondence. To eliminate unnecessary facts, reread your Statement of Facts after you have completed your first draft of the memo. If the Statement of Facts includes facts that are not later mentioned in the Analysis or Discussion section, those facts can probably be omitted.

The best presentation of a factual statement is narrative, that is, sentence after sentence, paragraph after paragraph, written in the third person. Presentations of facts in outline form, for example, in separate bullets or numbered sentences, appear choppy and rigid. Use the past tense to present your facts unless facts are developing as you prepare the memo. Finally, while other approaches are acceptable, the most typical approach is to present a statement of facts in chronological development. In other words, relate the facts in the order in which they occurred.

At this point, you probably realize that a legal memorandum is unlike any document you have yet prepared. The presentation of questions, followed by answers, followed by facts, is indeed unusual. Remember, however, that your final project will include these critical elements within the first page or two, allowing your reader to review only a portion of the memo and yet comprehend a total view of the project. These three elements provide a snapshot of the essence of the client's situation. The critical questions in the case are enumerated, answers to these questions are provided, and an overview of the facts is given. Simply by reading these first three sections, the reader will know the strengths and weaknesses of the client's position.

5. Applicable Statutes

Many memos include a section describing or setting forth any applicable statutory provisions that will be discussed in the memo. This section is optional and need not be included. If you include applicable statutes, you may either paraphrase the statutes or quote from them. If the statute is short, set it out in full. If the statute is long, set forth the pertinent parts and consider attaching a copy to the completed memo. Provide citations to any statutes in *Bluebook* form.

6. Analysis or Discussion

The heart of the memorandum is the analysis, or discussion, section. This portion of the memo provides an in-depth analysis of the issues presented. Cases, statutes, and other authorities will be presented and discussed. Citations should appear in the body of the memorandum, not as footnotes. See Chapter 18 for additional information on footnotes. Citations should be prepared according to *Bluebook* form unless local or other form is used. Keep in mind the critical distinction between primary and secondary sources: Primary sources are mandatory and binding authorities, which must be followed, while secondary authorities are persuasive at best. Thus, rely on secondary authorities only when there are no relevant primary authorities.

It is not enough to merely locate authorities and summarize them. Almost anyone can read a case and then restate its holding. You will be expected to do more: to analyze the authorities and discuss how and why they relate to your particular problem. This requires you to interweave and compare the facts of your case with the authorities you rely upon. If the client's particular situation can be distinguished from the situation in the case law, say so. Explain *why* cases apply and why they do not. Be sure to give some of the facts of the cases you rely on so readers can see how and why they apply to your issue. One warning sign that you are merely providing case summaries rather than analysis is that each paragraph in your memo discusses a single case. If you find this happening, restructure the memo to ensure the cases you rely upon are being analyzed and compared with the client's fact situation rather than merely being summarized. Do not mention a case unless you discuss it at least briefly by explaining how and why it applies to the client's issue.

This section of the memo will require all your effort to remain objective. Thoroughly discuss not only the authorities that support the client's position, but also those that do not. If you find weaknesses in a client's case, continue researching to determine if there are ways to surmount them. If new issues are disclosed by your research, discuss them.

If a direct quotation is particularly apt, use it. Be careful, however, to ensure that your analysis consists of more than a series of quotations. It is easy to read cases and then retype what the judge has stated. Use quotations but make sure you explain their relevance to your research problem.

Retain symmetry in your memo. If you have identified three issues and provided three brief answers, divide your discussion into three parts, each of which corresponds in number and order to the issues you formulated. Each section should be labeled with a descriptive heading. Brief headings, such as "Elements of Contract," "Fraud," and "Damages," are acceptable and clearly alert the reader as to the topic to be addressed. If desired, you may repeat your issues as headings, although this will add to the length of your brief. Use subheadings if these would be helpful to a reader.

Be sure your discussion is readable. If every paragraph starts with a phrase such as "In *Smith v. Jones* . . . the court held . . . ," your finished project will have a choppy, stodgy style and appearance. The most important part of the memorandum is not a dull recitation of facts and holdings of several cases, it is your analysis of the impact these cases and other authorities will have on the client's particular situation.

Most effective discussions contain the following three elements:

- A discussion of the relevant authorities;
- An analysis and comparison of these authorities to the client's issues and facts;
- A conclusion as to the effect and impact of the authorities as they relate to the client's problem.

In many instances, while writing style and techniques should vary to enhance readability, the analysis can be reduced to the following basic format for each separate issue:

> According to . . . [citations], the law is . . . [explain and discuss]. In the present case, . . . [compare with authorities]. Therefore, . . . [conclude] . . . .

In discussing and analyzing authorities, many writers follow what is referred to as the "IRAC" method. "IRAC" is an acronym for *I*ssue, *R*ule, *A*nalysis or *A*pplication, and *C*onclusion. Many writers, whether writing memos, letters, or briefs for courts, use the IRAC approach in discussing a legal problem.

First, the *i*ssue being considered is presented. Introduce the question or topic you will be analyzing. In a memo, the issue is set forth in the form of a question, such as "Does the Uniform Partnership Act govern a partnership that has no partnership agreement?" In a discussion section, the issue is often set forth in the following form: "The key issue is whether the Uniform Partnership Act governs a partnership that has no written agreement." This serves to frame the discussion that will follow.

Next, provide the *r*ule or legal authority that you rely upon to respond to the issue. The authority can be a case, a statute, or some other primary or secondary authority or authorities. If you rely on a case, give sufficient facts from the case that the reader will understand why and how it governs your case. If your rule is a statute, set forth the applicable provisions. Several authorities may be used. In fact, you should have at least one primary authority for every conclusion you reach. Complex matters will require more authorities, including secondary authorities.

The most critical part of an IRAC discussion is the *a*nalysis or *a*pplication of the rule to your case. Explain why the rule you have set forth does or does not apply to your particular case. Do more than merely summarize a case or statute. Summarizing should have taken place when you set forth the rule. Analyzing requires you to compare and contrast the facts of your case to those in the case you rely upon or to review a statute and show the reader why your client's situation falls within (or without) the activity described by the statute. Apply the reasoning of the case or other legal authorities to your case.

Finally, after a thorough analysis, present the reader with a *c*onclusion based upon your analysis of the rule. If the rule has been set forth clearly and the analysis is complete, the reader will likely be able to draw a conclusion even in advance of your stating it. Nevertheless, presenting a conclusion wraps up your analysis and serves as reinforcement of prior discussion as well as a signal that discussion of a particular topic is complete and that a new topic will likely be presented next, once again using the IRAC method. Readers need closure on one issue before tackling the next. Many beginning researchers are reluctant to draw a conclusion. They simply summarize applicable cases and then move on to the next topic. You will need to synthesize the authorities you discuss by comparing and contrasting them to each other and then applying them to the client's particular case to reach a conclusion. For example, after discussing the authorities relating to sexual harassment in the workplace, you could conclude by saying, "Because the authorities are in agreement that the conduct an employee complains of must be severe to constitute harassment, it is highly unlikely that a court would find a single passing remark such as the one made to our client to be actionable." See Figure 17-4 for an example of an IRAC discussion.

Following the IRAC approach to discussing problems helps ensure that you conduct a thorough analysis of an issue and is a commonly accepted writing approach both for law students and legal practitioners.

Figure 17-4
Sample IRAC Discussion

Issue	The central issue in this case is whether a single remark made in a workplace environment (namely, "Hey babe—looking good") constitutes sexual harassment.
Rule	The cases interpreting the Civil Rights Act of 1964 are in agreement that while a single utterance can constitute harassment, the remark must be so severe and outrageous that it creates an intolerable and hostile work environment.
Application	[Discuss cases and give citations.] In the present case, the remark, while offensive and inappropriate, is not "severe" and "outrageous" as those terms are used in the cases governing this issue.
Conclusion	Thus, the remark is unlikely to rise to the level of sexual harassment.

7. *Conclusion*

The conclusion should be brief and should be a highlight of the conclusions you reached earlier in the discussion or analysis section of the memo. In many ways, the conclusion will resemble your brief answers, although it tends to provide more information than the brief answers do. Do not include citations in your conclusion. Simply sum up your analysis.

If you cannot draw a conclusion because the authorities are in conflict, say so. It is not your function to predict the client's chances, but rather to report and analyze the authorities.

It is possible that during the course of your research you determine that certain information is needed or that a certain course of action should be followed, such as locating witnesses or propounding interrogatories to the adverse party. You may include these recommendations as part of your conclusion, or you may prefer to create a new section titled "Recommendations." Similarly, if certain issues have not been discussed, identify those excluded issues. In some instances, tables, photographs, or copies of cases or statutes will be attached to the memorandum in a separate appendix. If your memo is unusually long, you may wish to add a table of contents to help the reader. See Appendix A for a sample memorandum.

C. A Blueprint for Preparing a Memorandum

Although legal professionals will invariably adopt individual approaches in preparing a legal memorandum, there are several steps you can follow to ensure you provide a thoughtful, complete, and objective analysis of a client's case. The process usually begins with an assignment from your supervising attorney. The assignment may be written but will usually be given to you orally. Take careful notes, ask when the memo is due, and whether it will be sent to the client. Do not be reluctant to go back to the attorney if you later discover you need additional facts or information. Take the following steps:

1. Consider whether the issue is governed by federal law or state law. Next, consider whether it is a matter more likely to be covered by statutory law or case law.
2. Draft a preliminary issue statement based on the information you have. For example, your initial issue might be written, "Under California law, are non-competition agreements entered into by employees valid?"
3. Develop a research plan. If the matter is likely to be covered by statutory law, review the applicable statutes and then examine the case annotations following the text of the statutes. If the matter is likely to be covered by case law, consider starting with an encyclopedia or reviewing digests to find cases. If you are unfamiliar with the topic of law, initially consult a treatise or ency-

clopedia to "get your feet wet." Prepare a list of key words or search terms using the indexes to the statutes, encyclopedias, treatises, digests, and other authorities. For example, terms might include "employment," "employer-employee," "non-competition," and "competition."

4. Conduct research, paying attention to leads to other sources, such as law reviews, A.L.R. annotations, and Restatements. Take careful notes as you read the authorities you locate.
5. Shepardize or KeyCite the primary authorities to ensure they are still valid and to direct you to other authorities on point.
6. Brief the cases you locate if this is helpful to you.
7. Organize your notes, using index cards, notebooks, sheets of paper, or computer files. Use these to construct a working outline.
8. Begin writing. If you have difficulty getting started, begin with the section that is easiest to write. In many instances, this will be the Statement of Facts. Proceed to other sections, always checking to make sure your writing is balanced and objective. Consider using the IRAC method in the discussion section to ensure you are analyzing cases rather than merely summarizing them.
9. Revise the memo. Check for content. Make sure each conclusion you have drawn is supported by legal authority. Review to ensure that the cases you discuss include sufficient facts that the reader will immediately be able to discern why they do or do not apply to the client's situation.
10. Edit the memo to eliminate unnecessary material and clarify ambiguous portions. Proofread to omit spelling and typographical errors. Do a final check of citation form. Present the finished product to the assigning attorney, along with copies of cases and other authorities. Place a copy in the client's file, keep a "chron copy" (a copy placed in a chronological file you maintain showing your work throughout the year), and place a copy in the firm's memo bank, if applicable. See Figure 17-5.

Figure 17-5
Examples of Elements in Legal Memo

	Poor	*Better*
Issue	Does the client have a cause of action?	Under the Civil Rights Act of 1964, does harassment occur when a single remark is made in the workplace—namely, "hey, babe—looking good"?
Brief Answer	No	Because courts consistently require that conduct be severe in order to constitute harassment, the single remark made in this case is highly unlikely to rise to the level of sexual harassment.
Facts	Our client, Grace Parks, was subject to intolerable conduct in the workplace when a co-worker leered at her and teased, "hey, babe—looking good" when Grace entered a conference room full of employees. Grace was thoroughly humiliated by this remark.	Our client, Grace Parks, is an employee of ABC Inc. Two months ago, when Ms. Parks entered a conference room, a male co-worker stated to her, in front of others, "hey, babe—looking good." Ms. Parks would like to know if this remark constitutes sexual harassment.
Discussion	A poor discussion will: • Merely summarize cases • Fail to include facts from cases • Rely upon non-similar cases, such as those involving physical conduct and touching rather than verbal utterances • Lack objectivity and examine only cases in which harassment is found and ignore cases unfavorable to the client • Finish with mere summaries of cases and fail to draw conclusions as to whether harassment is likely to be found	A better discussion will: • Provide text of governing statute • Discuss and analyze cases with similar fact problems, focusing on cases involving verbal remarks rather than those involving physical conduct and touching • Discuss cases holding that a single remark can constitute harassment and compare and contrast these to client's case in order to reach a conclusion • Use the IRAC method to analyze cases
Conclusion	A poor conclusion will: • Be overlong • Include citations • Include topics not previously discussed in the body of the memorandum	A better conclusion will: • Quickly summarize the major points of the memorandum

Tips for Memo-Writing

- Do not use first person pronouns. Avoid statements such as "The next case I found . . ." or "I believe . . ."
- Use complete *Bluebook* citation form so that if the memo becomes the basis for a document submitted to court, you will not have to return to the law library to track down cites.
- Some law firms maintain files or "banks" of previously prepared memos. Before beginning a new project, check the memo bank to see if a memo on your topic has previously been prepared. If no memo bank exists, offer to establish one. Similarly, check with your fellow legal assistants to see if anyone else in your office has prepared a memo on a similar topic.
- Some attorneys prefer that all cases cited in the memo be photocopied and attached to the memo for ready reference. Check to see if the individual assigning the memo prefers this practice.
- Gather all documents and materials before you begin to write.
- After you Shepardize or KeyCite, provide your supervisor with copies of cases that negatively affect any cases cited in the memo so thay can be reviewed.
- Save memos you have prepared and others you come across in your own mini-memo bank. You may be surprised how often you will need to retrieve previously prepared memos to verify certain legal issues or to use as a starting point for a new project.

Legal Memorandum Assignment for Chapter 17

Our client, Sally Turner, lives next door to Andy Larkin, the owner of two large German shepherds. The dogs have barked loudly at Sally, routinely growl at her, and prowl the edge of Andy's yard. Sally has shouted at the dogs to be quiet.

Last month, when Sally was unloading groceries in front of her house, the dogs escaped from Andy's yard and attacked her. Sally believes the gate to Andy's yard was unlatched, allowing the dogs to escape. Sally was badly injured and was taken to the hospital, where she received more than 30 stitches. Sally may require plastic surgery in the future. Another neighbor, Randall Price, told Sally last week that the dogs had attacked him several months ago. Sally would like to know if Andy Larkin is liable for his dogs' actions.

Please prepare a memorandum for me regarding this issue. The memorandum should be no more than six pages in length, double-spaced. Use *Bluebook* citation form. Our state has no cases or statutes regarding this issue. Therefore, you should not restrict your research to the law of any one jurisdiction.

Chapter 18

Legal Briefs

Chapter Overview

This chapter will introduce you to documents submitted to court. These documents, commonly referred to as "briefs," differ from letters and memoranda in their purpose and audience. While letters and memoranda are intended primarily to inform and explain, briefs are intended to persuade judges. The writing techniques used for briefs are therefore different because each element of a brief must be crafted with its objective in mind: to persuade a court to rule in your client's favor.

A. Introduction

Briefs are formal written legal arguments submitted to a court. Briefs attempt to persuade a court to rule in favor of a party. On occasion, such a brief is referred to as a "Memorandum of Law" or "Memorandum of Points and Authorities." Be careful not to confuse these with the internal office memoranda previously discussed. Similarly, be careful not to confuse the briefs discussed in this chapter with the case briefs or case summaries discussed in Chapter 4.

The fact that the document submitted to a court is referred to as a "brief" does not necessarily mean the document is concise. A common joke is that only a lawyer would call a 50-page document a brief!

Briefs are submitted in pending actions and may relate to a variety of issues, including the following:

- a motion requesting a preliminary injunction
- a motion to dismiss a case
- a motion to change venue
- a motion to exclude evidence
- a motion to compel a party to answer interrogatories
- a motion for a new trial
- an appeal of a judgment

There are several types of briefs. Most are submitted to trial courts to persuade the judge to rule a certain way. After a trial is concluded, the losing party may appeal the judgment and will submit a brief, called an "appellate brief," to the reviewing or appeals court. Finally, briefs may be submitted to administrative agencies or other government units.

If an office memorandum has been prepared in a case, it may be a good starting point for a brief because it will contain an analysis and discussion of the authorities pertinent to the case. While the memo then may serve as a source of cases and other authorities, the manner in which these were discussed in the memo and the manner in which these will be discussed in a brief vary greatly. The style of writing used in a memo is informative because your function as a memo writer is to explain the law. The style of writing used in a brief is persuasive because your function as a brief writer is to persuade the court.

B. Tips on Writing Briefs

1. *Be Persuasive*

In some ways, you may find it easier to prepare a brief than a memo. Most writers find it difficult to maintain the neutral and objective tone required in a memo. It is often easier and more natural to advocate the client's position.

Aim at being persuasive throughout every portion of the brief. Even the Table of Contents and headings provide an opportunity for you to persuade the court. Consider the following two headings:

PUNITIVE DAMAGES

DEFENDANT'S FRAUD ENTITLES
PLAINTIFF TO PUNITIVE DAMAGES

While both headings inform the reader that the next topic will deal with punitive damages, the second one is considerably more forceful. Many writers include a "reason" in their point headings throughout their briefs. This is an extremely effective technique for drafting point headings. Consider the following point heading:

THE TRIAL COURT SHOULD AWARD PUNITIVE DAMAGES BECAUSE DEFENDANT'S CONDUCT WAS INTENTIONAL, WILLFUL, AND RECKLESS

Each point heading should have all capital letters, be centered, and assigned a Roman numeral placed directly above the point heading. Use parallel structure so if a reader reads only the point headings in a brief, the headings provide a clearly written outline of the argument. Maintain consistency in your headings. Headings are usually one sentence. Maintain this approach and do not switch to only phrases. Do not include citations in your headings.

If your headings appear as elements in a Table of Contents, you have another opportunity to reach the reader. The Table of Contents will be the first part of the brief to be viewed. Use this opening as your first attempt to convince the reader to rule in favor of the client.

To achieve a persuasive tone, remember the techniques discussed in Chapter 15:

- Use active voice;
- Use parallel structure;
- Use strong, forceful, and descriptive words;
- Use sentence structure to achieve strength, placing the strongest part of the sentence in the dominant clause;
- Use placement to achieve attention, placing the strongest parts of your argument in the beginning and ending of the brief;
- Use repetition, but sparingly, for drama and emphasis;
- Use positive statements rather than negative statements.

After you have completed the brief, review it carefully to eliminate words such as "clearly" and "obviously," which are overused, ineffective, and often insulting words inexperienced writers believe will persuade a reader. Similarly, omit vague and equivocal expressions such as "it would seem that" or "apparently," which have no place in a document aimed at persuading a reader.

While accuracy, brevity, and clarity are always required in legal writing, these characteristics are mandated by the United States Supreme Court, which has stated, "The failure of a petitioner to present with accuracy, brevity, and clarity whatever is essential to ready and adequate understanding of the points requiring consideration is sufficient reason for the Court to deny a petition." Sup. Ct. R. 14(4). In May 2000, the *National Law Journal* reported that the Kentucky Supreme Court suspended an attorney for 60 days for submitting a "virtually incomprehensible" brief.

2. *Be Honest*

While you need not present the adversary's argument, you have an ethical duty to be honest and bring to the court's attention anything that would assist the court in reaching a decision. If, in the course of your research, you discover cases that do not support your position, mention these in a straightforward fashion and then show the reader why they do not apply to your situation.

Act on the assumption that your adversary will discover these cases and that if you introduce these problem areas first, you will decrease the impact of the adversary's "smoking gun." Moreover, the integrity shown by an honest and direct discussion of these issues will carry over to the rest of your argument. Assertions you make in other sections of the brief will then be likely to be believed and trusted by the reader.

Discussing these authorities does not mean you need to highlight them and make the adversary's case for him or her. Use placement in the brief to assist you and "bury" the most troublesome parts of your argument in the middle of the discussion. Use passive voice to minimize the impact of these weak spots.

3. *Know the Rules*

Most courts issue rules relating to briefs filed before them. Some of these rules relate to the size, color, and quality of the paper used, while others relate to citation form, length of the document, and the elements required in a brief. Many courts establish maximum page limits and require that briefs exceeding certain page limits include tables of contents and authorities. For example, the First Circuit Court of Appeals now requires a copy of all briefs submitted to be on a 3.5-inch disk as well as in hard-copy form. Similarly, a newly revised federal rule has reduced the page allowance for principal briefs from 50 pages to 30 pages. Fed. R. App. P. 32. Make sure you have obtained a copy of the court rules and have thoroughly read them before you prepare your brief because failure to follow the rules may be fatal. Many courts have posted their rules on the Internet. The rules of the United States Supreme Court can be found at the Court's Web site at http://www.supremecourtus.gov. Each state's judicial Web site is given in Table T.1 of the *Bluebook*. Additionally, your law firm may have a copy of the rules in its law library. If not, contact the court clerk and order a copy of the rules. Always check the date the rules were issued and verify that the rules are still current.

C. Trial Court Briefs

1. *Introduction*

Briefs submitted to trial courts are aimed at persuading the judge to rule in a certain way. These briefs may be accompanied by other documents, such as deposition transcripts, declarations, or exhibits. They may be written in support of a certain position or in response or opposition to an argument. On occasion, they are written in response to a judge's request for legal argument on a certain issue.

In some jurisdictions this brief is referred to as a Memorandum of Law or Memorandum of Points and Authorities. While some jurisdictions have rules relating to the format, citation form, or length of these trial court briefs, these rules tend to be far less formal than the rules for appellate briefs.

As in all legal writing, remember your audience. The judge who will read the brief will be busy and will become frustrated with a lengthy and repetitious document. The other reader, opposing counsel, will have a hostile attitude toward your brief and will scrutinize the brief looking for errors and flaws in everything from citation form to Shepardizing and KeyCiting to the conclusions you draw from your research. While it is a futile effort to believe you can persuade opposing counsel, aim at presenting a brief that at least cannot be attacked by opposing counsel. A sample trial brief is found at Appendix B.

2. *Elements of a Trial Brief*

The elements of a brief submitted to a trial court will vary to some degree from jurisdiction to jurisdiction. The following elements are found in most briefs, but you should be sure to review your local court rules to determine if there is a required format.

a. Caption

Because the brief submitted to the court is a pleading, it must display the "caption" of the case. The caption identifies the pertinent information about the case: the court, the parties, the docket number, and the title of the document, such as "Defendant's Memorandum of Law in Support of Motion to Change Venue." Table T.8 of the *Bluebook* provides instructions for abbreviations and capitalization in court documents.

b. Introductory Statement

The party submitting the brief typically begins with a brief introductory statement such as the following: "Defendant Vincent T. Parker respectfully submits the following Memorandum of Law in Support of His Motion to Change Venue."

c. Statement of Facts

To save the judge the bother of reviewing all of the pleadings submitted in a case to determine what the case is about, the brief should include a statement of facts. While these facts must be accurate, you should strive to present these facts in a manner most favorable to the client. Use active voice and descriptive words to emphasize facts supporting your position. Use passive voice and placement of unfavorable facts in less noticeable positions to minimize facts that are troublesome. For example, consider the following two ways of describing a defendant's experience with the law:

- Defendant's version: The record discloses some prior convictions.
- Plaintiff's version: The Defendant has a long history of serious criminal conduct and victimization of innocent parties, including three separate convictions involving violence to women and two additional convictions for assault with a deadly weapon, specifically, a ten-inch jagged-edge hunting knife.

Most facts are presented in chronological order, though you may depart from this order and discuss facts by topic if you wish to emphasize certain facts. Present the facts in the third person and in past tense unless they are still unfolding as you write the brief. Be careful not to jump the gun and argue your case. This section of the brief should be devoted solely to facts, for example, events that have occurred, not legal theories and analysis. Personalize your client by referring to him or her by name (Ms. LaPointe) rather than role (Plaintiff). Although most writers present their statement of facts in a narrative, some courts require numbered paragraphs, each of which includes a reference to supporting materials and documents.

Do not overlook the importance of the statement of facts. Because most judges have a thorough understanding of the law, they may begin forming impressions and drawing conclusions even as they read the facts. Moreover, at this stage of the brief, the reader is still enthusiastic and fresh. Do more than merely recite the facts in a dull fashion. Use the statement of facts to win over your reader.

d. Argument

The argument section of a brief is the heart of the brief. This section contains the analysis of the legal authorities that support the client's position and demonstrates why and how those authorities support the position advocated.

Divide your argument into sections, giving each section a heading and a Roman numeral and centering the heading on the page. The headings should be as persuasive as possible. You may need subheadings. These can consist of short phrases or even single words. Subheadings are usually preceded by capital letters (A, B, and C). Citations should appear in the body of your brief. While footnotes are popular with some writers, they are distracting to most readers.

The use of footnotes in legal documents engenders vigorous debate. Footnotes are commonly seen in law review articles and in legal treatises; however, they are seen far less frequently in published cases. There are two schools of thought on the use of footnotes in legal memos and court briefs. Some experts believe that the placement of a footnote number at the end of a sentence jars curious readers who are then compelled to glance at the bottom of the page, leaving the narrative discussion in the body of the text. These experts believe that if the point of a logical argument is to carry the reader through seamlessly from the first sentence to the last, footnotes detract from this objective. Conversely, if some readers are so disciplined that they ignore the footnote notations and continue reading the narrative text, of what use are the footnotes? Despite these criticisms, footnotes continue to be used. Recently, in fact, some writing experts have advocated more extensive use of footnotes on the basis that citations and extraneous comments clutter arguments and are better placed at the bottom of a page. In fact, some judges in California are experimenting with writing citation-free opinions, placing all citations and extraneous comments in footnotes in an effort to create more readable opinions. Other judges have reached the opposite conclusion, believing that if something is important enough to be discussed, it should be discussed in the body of the text; if a point is not important enough to be in the body of the text, it probably doesn't merit any discussion whatsoever. Check your firm or office policy or practice, but in any event avoid footnotes that "wrap" from one page to the next, or even beyond. Some readers will leave the narrative discussion, review the footnote that meanders on for several pages and then simply resume reading where they are, rather than returning to the page on which the footnote began. Endnotes are seen in other disciplines but seldom, if ever, in legal documents.

As you discuss cases and other authorities, emphasize the extent to which favorable cases are similar to the client's case. In the interests of credibility, point out unfavorable authorities and then distinguish them from the client's position by showing why and how they are different and thus inapplicable. Discuss cases in the past tense because references to "this case states" or "the plaintiff argues" will be interpreted as references to your brief itself rather than precedents. Avoid referring to the court by the name of a case. For example, assume you are discussing the case *Horn v. Wagner*, 382 U.S. 116 (1988). In discussing this case, do not say, "The *Horn* Court held . . . ." While this error is common, it is nonetheless improper. The only way a court is referred to is by its title ("the United States Supreme Court") or by the name of its chief or presiding judge or justice ("the Rehnquist Court").

Review your arsenal of writing tips and organize your argument so it flows logically. Consider which techniques make for a strong and persuasive document and give care to techniques that allow you to minimize cases unfavorable to the client's position. Be definite. Avoid expressions such as "it seems" or "it is likely," which immediately convey the message to the reader that the writer is not sure of the position taken.

Avoid any use of the first person. Do not say "we argue" or "it is my contention." Instead use expressions such as "Defendant will show" or "Plaintiff has contended." This keeps the focus on the parties, not on you as the writer.

Be sure you have done more than merely summarize a series of cases. Analyze and apply the cases and other authorities to the client's case so the reader can readily see why these cases mandate the result you advocate. Remember to use the IRAC approach (discussed in Chapter 17) to ensure you thoroughly analyze and discuss each issue. It is perfectly acceptable to rely upon cases in which a different result was reached than the one you desire. Simply say, "Although the Court denied injunctive relief in *Gray v. Smith*, 508 U.S. 110, 112 (1995), that denial was directly related to the plaintiff's failure to take prompt action. In the present case, however, ... Thus, the decision reached in *Gray* is not applicable to this case."

While the aim of your document is to persuade, you need not denigrate the adversary's position. A logical and well-reasoned argument will command respect. A hostile and sarcastic diatribe will destroy your credibility and render your brief suspect.

e. Conclusion

The conclusion should be a very brief recap of the highlights of the argument. Because it is a summary, no citations should be included. The last sentence of the conclusion should remind the reader of the relief requested, such as the following: "For the foregoing reasons, Defendant Vincent T. Parker respectfully requests the Court grant his Motion for Change of Venue."

Many writers use this request for relief as their entire conclusion. While this is easy for the writer because it eliminates the difficult task of condensing a complex argument into a readable summary, do not forgo this last opportunity to persuade, especially because a reader often picks up interest at the end of a project and will thus pay special attention to the conclusion. The conclusion should be no more than half a page. Any conclusion longer than this will likely be ignored.

f. Signature and Date

The brief is typically "closed" much like a letter. The favored closing is as follows:

Respectfully submitted,

Dated: ______________ ____________________________

Sandra Taylor Jones
Jones and White
Attorneys for Defendant
Vincent T. Parker

Jones and White
162 C Street, Suite 1725
Chicago, Illinois 97205
Bar No. 764110

g. Certificate of Service

For all pleadings filed in court you must verify that all parties have received copies. A Certificate of Service is placed at the conclusion of a pleading and states that a copy of the pleading has been served on all parties. The method of service, such as hand delivery or first class mail, and the date of service must be specified.

h. Exhibits

It is possible you may have attached exhibits to the brief for review by the court. These may consist of correspondence, transcripts of deposition testimony, answers to interrogatories, affidavits, or other documents. Each exhibit should be fully described in the brief itself and then should be appended after the end of the brief and clearly labeled. Do not insert exhibits into the middle of your argument because they will disrupt the flow of your narrative and detract from the persuasive nature of your brief. Use tabs to make it easier for the judge to locate your exhibits. If there are several exhibits, prepare a table of exhibits.

Remember these three techniques for effective brief writing:

(i) Be scrupulously accurate in your statement of the facts of the case. Include unfavorable facts and resist the temptation to overemphasize facts in your favor.
(ii) Focus on your best arguments. If some arguments are "long shots," do not include them. Inclusion of weak or ludicrous arguments causes readers to question the writer's credibility.
(iii) Analyze the cases you rely on rather than merely summarizing them. Describe the cases relied upon, giving sufficient facts so the reader will see how and why these cases are similar (or dissimilar) to your case. Give the holding and reasoning from the cited cases. Then compare and contrast the cases you rely on with the facts of your case. Convince by applying the holding and reasoning from the cited authorities to your case.

See Appendix B for a sample brief for a court.

D. Appellate Briefs

1. Introduction

After a trial court decision or other final ruling, the losing party may appeal the decision. While the trial court judge who rules on a motion supported by a memorandum of law may be familiar with the case and the facts presented in a trial brief and may, in fact, have been assigned to a case from its filing, appellate judges will have no such familiarity with cases before them. You will thus have to be as articulate and persuasive as possible to convince the appellate court to rule in your client's favor. An appellate brief is a formal document filed with a reviewing court. The appellate brief seeks reversal, affirmance, or some modification of a lower court's action. A sample appellate brief is found in Appendix C.

2. *Steps in the Appeal Process*

After a judgment is entered in a case, the losing party, usually called the appellant but sometimes called the petitioner, initiates an appeal by filing a notice of appeal. This serves to notify the adverse party, called the appellee or occasionally the respondent, that an appeal has been instituted. This notice of appeal must be timely. In federal court, the notice of appeal must be filed within 30 days (or 60 days if the United States is a party) after the final judgment is entered. Most state courts have similarly limited time periods for filing the notice of appeal. Failure to timely file the notice of appeal is fatal, and usually no relief can be granted from the untimely filing of the notice. The notice of appeal is usually filed not in the appellate court but with the trial court.

A filing fee is required when the notice of appeal is filed. The appellant then must order the transcript (or selected portions of it) from the court reporter who transcribed the trial proceeding because it is this record of the proceedings upon which the appeal is based. The trial court record also includes all pleadings filed in the case together with all exhibits entered at the trial.

Rules governing appeal briefs are usually more stringent than rules for any other documents submitted to courts. Moreover, these rules are rigidly adhered to, and a brief that is too long or lacks the proper color cover sheet will be rejected. Briefs submitted to appellate courts may be required to be printed rather than merely typewritten or word-processed. Know the rules.

The appellant sets forth his or her grounds for the appeal in a document called the appellant's brief or opening brief. The appellee will then prepare and file his or her response brief. The appellee's brief must usually be filed within a specified time period (often 30 days) after the appellant's brief. Some courts allow the appellant to submit a brief in reply or rebuttal to certain issues raised by the appellee's brief. This is uncommon, however, and in most cases the appellate court will determine the appeal solely on the basis of the appellant's brief, the appellee's brief, and the record from below. No testimony is received.

The clerk of the appellate court will then schedule oral argument. Each side typically has only a half-hour to present the oral argument. The appellate judges usually sit as a panel of three and may ask questions of the parties. Parties should not make the mistake of believing they will save a persuasive issue for oral argument and omit it from the brief. Briefs should contain *all* of the arguments to be presented to the appellate court because a party may be interrupted by questions from the judges and never have the opportunity to present a certain issue during oral argument.

After oral argument, the appellate court will take the case under advisement or submission and will review the briefs and records, reach a decision, and write the appellate opinion. This may take several months. The parties will then be notified of the decision. If the losing party believes the appellate court has overlooked something, he or she may request a rehearing. Requests for rehearings are usually denied.

The losing party may then proceed to the next higher court, if it exists. In most states, there is an intermediate appellate court, and then the highest state court, usually called the Supreme Court. Adverse decisions of the highest court in a state may be appealed to the United States Supreme Court only if a federal question is at issue. Even then, the United States Supreme Court may deny certiorari and refuse to take the appeal.

In federal cases, after a party loses a trial in the district court, an appeal is taken to the appropriate circuit court of appeals. For most litigants, this is the end of the process because an appeal from the circuit courts of appeal to the United States Supreme Court is dependent upon issuance of the writ of certiorari by the Court. As you will recall from reading Chapter 2, issuance of the writ is discretionary with the Court, and the vast majority of petitions for writs of certiorari are denied. Because appellate work is complicated, some firms specialize solely in appellate practice and prepare appeals for cases tried by other firms.

3. *Standards of Appellate Review*

The appellant is not entitled to a reversal of the trial court decision simply because he or she is unhappy with the outcome. The appellant must show that an error of law occurred at the trial. For purposes of appeal, the appellate court will assume that the facts found at the trial were true (unless these facts are totally unsupported by the record). Thus, if a jury determines a defendant was driving at a speed of 70 miles per hour and this caused an accident injuring a plaintiff, an appellate court cannot substitute its judgment for that of the jury and determine the defendant's rate of speed was 45 miles per hour. It may, however, decide that a prejudicial error of law was committed at the trial and that this affected the jury's verdict. Examples of such errors of law include admission of evidence, such as hearsay, that should have been excluded, errors given in the instructions to the jury, and exclusion of evidence that should have been admitted.

Even if an error of law occurred at the trial, the appellate court will not reverse the lower court decision unless this error was clearly erroneous or prejudicial to the appellant. Many errors can occur in a trial. Harmless errors, however, are not reversible. A prejudicial error is one that likely affected the outcome of the case. Additionally, appellate courts review only those errors that were raised at trial. Otherwise, trial judges would not have the opportunity to correct their own mistakes.

Generally, appellate courts give great weight to the trial court's conduct of a trial because the trial court was in the best position to evaluate the credibility of witnesses and to make "on the spot" determinations. Only if the trial court clearly erred or abused its discretion will its decisions be reversed.

Because of the difficulty in meeting these strict requirements and because of the high costs involved, the vast majority of trial court decisions are not appealed.

4. Amicus Curiae *Briefs*

On occasion, an issue being appealed is of importance not only to the litigants, but also to a wider group of people. The case may involve constitutional issues that will have a substantial impact on a significant number of individuals. In such cases, these individuals, companies, or entities who were not parties to the suit may request that the court allow them to file *amicus curiae* ("friend of the court") briefs. Appellate courts have discretion to accept or reject such requests, though they will permit *amicus curiae* briefs if it is believed such briefs would be of assistance to the court.

5. *Elements of an Appellate Brief*

Many of the elements of an appellate brief are the same as the elements of a memorandum of law or trial brief. In some instances, portions of an earlier memorandum or trial brief may be used for the appellate brief. (See Figure 18-1 for a comparison of the elements of trial court briefs and appellate court briefs.)

Following are the elements typically found in an appellate brief, although, as always, you should carefully review the rules of the appellate court to which you are submitting the brief to determine whether there are required rules as to format or elements for the brief.

Figure 18-1
Elements of Trial Court Briefs and Appellate Court Briefs

Trial Court Briefs	Appellate Court Briefs
Caption	Cover Sheet
Introductory Statement	Identification of Parties
	Table of Contents
	Table of Authorities
	Jurisdictional Statement
	Constitutional and Statutory Provisions
	Questions Presented
Statement of Facts	Statement of the Case
	Summary of the Argument
Argument	Argument
Conclusion	Conclusion
Signature	Signature
Certificate of Service	Certificate of Service
Exhibits	Appendix

a. Cover Sheet

The cover sheet or title page identifies the following information about the case:

- the specific appellate court hearing the appeal
- the names of the appellant and appellee
- the docket number of the appeal
- the lower court that handled the trial or prior appeal
- the title of the document, such as "Appellant's Brief"
- the attorneys representing the party submitting the brief

Some courts require the party instituting the appeal to be identified first in the caption. This often results in a reversal of the plaintiff's and defendant's names. For example, if the original case was *Davids v. Stephenson* and Stephenson appealed the trial court's decision, some courts require that Stephenson's name be listed first. Due to the confusion caused by this rule, most courts retain the original listing of the parties, no matter who appeals.

Many courts require that the cover sheet be a certain color. For example, the United States Supreme Court requires that the appellant's cover color be light blue, the appellee's cover color be light red, and an amicus curiae brief (in support of the petitioner) cover color be light green. This assists the justices reading the briefs because they can identify at a glance whose brief they are reading.

b. Identification of Parties

Unless all of the parties are identified on the cover sheet, a list of all parties to the lower court proceeding usually must be given, including parent companies and wholly owned subsidiaries. This allows justices to review for conflicts and disqualify themselves from cases involving parties they know or with whom they have financial involvement.

c. Table of Contents

A Table of Contents or Index must be included. While the primary purpose of a Table of Contents is to identify for the reader the location of each element in the brief, a secondary purpose is to serve as an outline of a party's contentions. Many software programs will automatically generate a table of contents.

The Table of Contents should include all of the headings and subheadings contained in the brief. These should be phrased as persuasively as possible. Thus, a heading such as "The best evidence of likelihood of confusion of trademarks is evidence of actual confusion" is considerably stronger than the neutral heading "likelihood of confusion." Headings are usually presented in uppercase letters. Subheadings appear with initial letters capitalized and are usually underlined.

Judges reviewing the Table of Contents will be able to comprehend quickly the scope of your argument. If you organize your brief effectively and phrase your headings persuasively, you are able to make a favorable impression on the judges reviewing the brief even before the argument is begun.

d. Table of Authorities

An appellate brief must include a list of every primary and secondary authority referred to in the brief together with an indication of the page(s) on which it appears. Complete citations in *Bluebook* form must be given (unless court rules provide otherwise).

Authorities should be grouped together so that all cases are listed together, then all constitutional provisions, followed by statutes, followed by secondary authorities. Within each group, arrangement is alphabetical (or numerical, for statutes).

The Table of Authorities allows readers to identify quickly the location in a brief of a discussion of a certain case or statute. It may be helpful for a reader to compare the appellant's discussion of *Smith v. Jones* with the appellee's discussion of this same case. The Table of Contents and Table of Authorities cannot be prepared until the brief is in final form because it is only then that you will know on which page a certain topic or case is mentioned.

Paralegals often play a major role in preparing the Table of Contents and Table of Authorities. The task requires painstaking care to ensure you have carefully noted each time a case is discussed and the exact location of each authority or heading. Moreover, because this task cannot be completed until the brief is completed with no insertions or deletions to cause changes in pagination, it is often a pressure-filled task done at the eleventh hour.

Many software programs will automatically generate a table of authorities from your document. The program "reads" your document, locates the cites, sorts them, alphabetizes them, and then notes where the cites appear in your writing. They also correct some common citation errors. Because the programs extract citations from your document, case citations will undoubtedly appear in both "stand alone" and "textual sentence" format, meaning that, depending on your usage and placement of citations, the word "Technology" may appear as "Tech." in one case name and as "Technology" in another. Thus, you will need to do some revising to ensure consistency in appearance.

The *Bluebook* includes no guidance on preparing a table of authorities. Many authors prefer to write out case names in full rather than using abbreviations such as "Sur." or "Hosp." in the table of authorities, although citations in a table are clearly in stand-alone format. The preference toward using full case names is based upon the fact that the table will be one of the first pages reviewed by a reader, and the presentation of full case names is polished and complete.

If your word processor does not automatically prepare the table of authorities, use index cards to list each case and then shuffle them until they are in alphabetical order. Be sure to note if a case is discussed on more than one page. Carefully review the footnotes because they may also include citations you will need to include in the Table of Authorities. While most word processors will automatically compile a table of contents and a table of authorities, you should always double-check for accuracy. See Appendix D.

e. Jurisdictional Statement

The appellate brief should include a concise statement of the grounds upon which the court's jurisdiction rests, including a reference to the pertinent authority. This jurisdictional statement simply tells the appellate court which statute allows the appeal.

A sample jurisdictional statement would read:

> This Court of Appeals for the Eighth Circuit has jurisdiction to hear this appeal pursuant to 15 U.S.C. § 1071(b) (1998).

f. Constitutional and Statutory Provisions

If the case involves constitutional provisions, statutes, ordinances, or regulations, they must be set forth in full together with their citation in *Bluebook* form. If the provisions involved are especially lengthy, you can set forth their pertinent parts. Alternatively, their citation alone will be sufficient so long as they are set forth verbatim in an appendix to the brief.

g. Questions Presented

Many courts require the parties to present the issues to be addressed in the brief in question format. Some writers prefer true question format while others rely on the "whether" format. These questions are somewhat similar to the questions presented in an office memorandum but should be drafted in such a persuasive manner that the desired answer is obvious. An example would be as follows:

> Whether the trial court erred in excluding evidence showing the Plaintiff provoked the disagreement between the parties.

This question includes sufficient facts so the reader understands the issue you intend to address. It suggests an affirmative answer and is written persuasively from a defendant's point of view. The plaintiff's version of such an issue might read thus:

> Whether the trial court properly excluded hearsay evidence relating to Plaintiff's alleged involvement in the incident in which Defendant battered her.

While questions in an office memorandum are immediately followed by brief answers, there is no answer section in an appellate brief.

h. Statement of the Case

Next to the argument itself, the Statement of the Case is the most important part of the brief. This Statement of the Case or Statement of Facts includes neither argument nor allegations. The only facts to be included are those that have already been proven at trial. Thus, each fact you state must be followed by a reference to the location in the record or clerk's transcript where such fact was established, as follows:

> Defendant Smith was found to be driving at a speed of 70 miles per hour at the time the accident occurred. (R. at 74.)

While you are restricted solely to facts established at trial, you should still strive to present these in a persuasive manner.

In many ways, the statement of the case for an appellate brief will parallel the statement of facts for a brief submitted to a trial court. You must be honest and straightforward. Establish credibility by being accurate and including all facts, even those unfavorable to the client's position. Remember the techniques of passive voice and placement to de-emphasize unfavorable facts.

The facts are best set forth in a narrative rather than outline form because a narrative is more readable. Present your facts in chronological order in the past tense. Use descriptive words, verbs, and adjectives to describe favorable fact scenarios. Use parallel structure and careful repetition for drama and impact.

Because the justices reading the brief will be unfamiliar with the case, introduce the statement of the case by including background information or procedural history of the case. Some courts require this procedural history to be provided in a separate section. An appropriate statement of procedural history is as follows:

> This is an appeal from a final judgment entered October 12, 2000 by the United States District Court for the District of New Jersey. (R. at 79.) A jury found Defendant and Appellant ABC, Inc. ("ABC") to have defrauded its customers in the resale of certain automobiles. (R. at 70.) ABC filed a timely notice of appeal on October 20, 2000. (R. at 80.)

Do not include argument or legal conclusions in your statement of facts. Thus, do not state that the defendant "battered" the plaintiff (unless such a conclusion is supported by the record below). You can, however, recite the facts that the defendant "pushed and shoved" the plaintiff, which will lead the reader to the logical conclusion that a battery occurred.

i. Summary of the Argument

A concise summary of the argument is often included. This is a preview or condensation of the argument to follow. This is the first section of the brief that allows advocacy, and you should take advantage of this opportunity to persuade the reader to rule in favor of the client.

Because justices are so busy, they may only have time to skim quickly the entire argument. This summary of the argument, then, may be the best opportunity to win the reader over. Avoid citations in this summary and keep it brief—no more than one page if possible. A mere recitation of the point headings is not sufficient. Present the summary in a narrative fashion.

j. Argument

Like the argument in a brief submitted to a trial court, the argument in an appellate brief is the heart of the document. This section analyzes the authorities and convinces the reviewing justices to rule in favor of the client.

Divide the brief into separate sections with each section receiving its own point heading. These point headings should correspond to the questions or issues you set forth earlier. Work at making your point headings persuasive and relevant to your case. If possible, discuss topics in the order in which they were presented in the statement of the case. Compare the following point headings drafted for a plaintiff:

A BATTERY IS AN INTENTIONAL AND UNPERMITTED TOUCHING OF ANOTHER.

DEFENDANT SMITH BATTERED EVELYN WOODALL BY REPEATEDLY PUSHING HER AND SHOVING HER TO THE GROUND.

The second point heading is far more likely to grab the reader's attention and persuade the reader that Smith is a horrible fellow. This impression is conveyed as follows:

- By the use of a label, the reader is reminded that Smith is the defendant, that is, "the bad guy";
- The plaintiff is personalized by the use of her name and a reminder of her gender;
- Smith's acts are described in vivid detail.

Written from Smith's perspective, the point heading may read as follows:

BECAUSE PLAINTIFF PROVOKED THE MUTUAL DISAGREEMENT, DAMAGES FOR BATTERY WERE IMPROPERLY AWARDED.

This point heading focuses on the plaintiff's actions rather than the defendant's and provides the critical fact to the reader that the plaintiff provoked the incident. Moreover, the vivid description of the fight is now minimized to a mere "mutual disagreement." Remember to ensure your point headings have parallel structure so that, read in sequence, they provide an outline of the argument.

Use subheadings within your point headings if needed. While the point headings should consist of one persuasive sentence, subheadings are typically mere phrases consisting of just a word or short phrase such as "provocation" or "punitive damages."

Through analysis and discussion of legal authorities, the body of the argument will demonstrate to the reviewing court the errors of law made by the lower court. Do more than merely summarize cases you have located. Compare and contrast the authorities with your particular fact situation so the reader can readily see why the authorities are controlling. Use the IRAC method and discuss the Issue involved and the Rule that applies; Analyze and Apply this rule and then provide a Conclusion. Always analogize and compare the facts in the cases you cite to the facts before the court.

Because your argument will be more credible and respected if you discuss unfavorable precedents and because the adversary will undoubtedly raise them, acknowledge these problem areas. Do so, however, only after you have set forth the strongest part of your argument and have, perhaps, already gotten the reader "on your side." Discuss why these precedents are not applicable. Explain that the fact pattern in the unfavorable case is so different from the fact pattern in the case being appealed that it cannot serve as precedent; or you may argue that public policy or public interest favors the result for which you argue. If the unfavorable case is older, you can challenge it as antiquated or outmoded. Of course, expect your adversary to characterize it as the landmark or seminal case on the subject. If there are no legal authorities to support your position, argue that public policy and the interests of society compel a change in the law.

k. Conclusion

The conclusion of an appellate brief often does not summarize the argument section. This summary has already been given before the argument. Instead, the conclusion may merely specify the relief sought, such as requesting that the court affirm or reverse the lower court's decision.

l. Signature

The name of the attorney representing the party is set forth after the conclusion together with an address and telephone number and an identification of the party on whose behalf the brief is submitted.

m. Certificate of Service

All documents filed with a court must also be served on all other parties in the action. This certificate demonstrates to the court that the brief has been provided to all parties and specifies the date and manner of such service, such as hand delivery or first class mail.

n. Appendix

Appellate briefs often include an appendix. This may consist of portions of the transcript, pleadings from the lower court action, or exhibits entered as evidence in the trial. When you refer to these materials in your argument, set forth the relevant portions in the argument and then refer the reader to the appendix, where the entire document can be found. Do not interrupt the flow of your narrative with pages of testimony, maps, or graphs. Your aim is to present a logical, persuasive argument. Insertions of extraneous materials disrupt the argument and distract the reader. Make it easy for the justice by using exhibit tags, including a table of contents for the appended materials, and highlighting relevant material. See Appendix C for a sample appellate brief.

E. Ten Pointers for Effective Brief Writing

Whether you are submitting a brief to a trial court or to an appellate court, remember the following ten tips:

1. Know the rules of the court to which the brief will be submitted.
2. Do more than summarize cases. By following the IRAC method, show the reader how and why the cases and other authorities apply to the client's situation.
3. Write from the client's perspective. Omit any references to yourself as the writer, such as "we believe" or "we argue." The brief is not a forum for your personal opinion but a logical and persuasive argument. Use the third person.
4. Avoid a rote or routine method of writing. If each paragraph discusses one case and ends with a citation to that case, the brief will have a rigid appearance and tone. Variety in the method of analysis of the cases will enhance readability.
5. Avoid string-citing unless there is a definite need to do so. Select the best case supporting a contention and use that case.
6. Avoid sarcasm, humor, or irony. While these techniques may provide drama in oral argument, they are often misinterpreted in written documents. Maintain a respectful tone toward the court.
7. Avoid the overuse of quotations. It is often the case that a judge has said something so articulately and eloquently that you prefer to use a direct quote. Used sparingly, quotations give force and impact to your writing. Overuse of quotations, however, dilutes their strength. Anyone can retype language found in a case. Do more: Analyze why this language applies to the case at hand.

8. Keep the focus on your argument. If you spend too much time refuting the opponent's position you will shift the focus of the brief from the client's point of view to that of the opponent. Fully argue the client's position before you respond to the opposition.
9. Do not distort or overstate your position. If any portion of the brief is not supported by valid authority, the entire brief is undermined.
10. Use prominent placement to emphasize the strongest arguments. Bury weaker portions of the argument in the middle of the brief, the middle of paragraphs, and the subordinate clauses of sentences.

Appellate Brief Errata

1. The highest number of *amicus curiae* briefs filed for one United States Supreme Court case is 490. Eighty-five percent of all United States Supreme Court cases include at least one amicus brief, often filed by organizations such as the ACLU or AFL-CIO.
2. The United States Supreme Court accepted its first brief in CD-ROM form in 1997. Such CD-ROMs allow direct access to court transcripts, records, and other documents through hyperlinking, making review easier for many justices.
3. The private company that printed most briefs for the United States Supreme Court ended its hot-metal printing process and went digital in mid-2000. Printing a brief using the hot-metal process generally took three weeks, while digital printing enables reproduction of a brief in three days.
4. Supreme Court rules recognize brief writers' tendency to try to squeeze additional wording into a brief by using a small typeface. The rules provide that "increasing the amount of text by using condensed or thinner typefaces, or by reducing the space between letters, is strictly prohibited." Sup. Ct. R. 33.

Court Brief Exercise for Chapter 18

From: Susan Dunn, Partner
To: Legal Assistant

Our client, Gibson Technology, Inc. ("Gibson"), is a large corporation engaged in computer consulting work. Gibson was recently sued in federal court for sexual harassment by one of its former employees, Nick Ellison. The facts, as disclosed by discovery in this matter, are as follows. Prior to leaving Gibson, Mr. Ellison had been employed by Gibson for two years. During that time he received exemplary performance ratings and was granted steady increases and bonuses. Mr. Ellison was assigned to a work group of ten men, whom he had informed that he was homosexual. The group occasionally engaged in joking and banter. Some of the jokes told were sexually suggestive. Mr. Ellison acknowledged during his deposition that he also told at least two sexually suggestive jokes to the work group. Approximately six months ago, Tom Barnes, Mr. Ellison's supervisor, sent Mr. Ellison an e-mail communication titled "Ten Reasons a Beer Is Better than a Homosexual." At one meeting, Mr. Barnes put his arm around Mr. Ellison and said, "That's a cute outfit you're wearing, Nick."

Mr. Ellison followed Gibson's sexual harassment policy and filed a complaint with the company's human resources department about Mr. Barnes's conduct. The company investigated the incidents, determined that there was no previous or other complaints that had been made against Mr. Barnes, counseled Mr. Barnes, sent him to a seminar on workplace sensitivity, and concluded the matter.

Furious that Mr. Barnes was not fired, Mr. Ellison quit his employment with Gibson and filed the complaint against Gibson in federal court.

We intend to move for summary judgment on behalf of Gibson. Please prepare a brief in support of a motion for summary judgment that will persuade the United States District Court for the Anywhere District that no sexual harassment occurred.

Court rules dictate that the brief not exceed ten typewritten and double-spaced pages and that *Bluebook* citation form be followed.

Assignment for Chapter 18

You have been asked to prepare the table of authorities for an appellate brief to be filed in the United States District Court. There are no special rules for citation form. You should use the rules set forth in the current edition of the *Bluebook.* Do not worry about the page numbers. The following citations will appear in the brief.

Jacobsen v. Jefferson Technology Company, 104 F.3d 154 (Ninth Circuit 1999)
Andrews v. Western Group Life Insurance Co., 512 U.S. 324, 333 S. Ct. 109 (1993)
18 U.S.C. § 1092
Peters v. Taylor, 514 U.S. 889 (1994)
42 U.S.C. § 442
California Civil Code Section 422
Patterson v. Naylor, 13 F. Supp. 3d 189 (S. Dist. N.Y. 2000)
Bailey v. Flatley, 339 S. Ct. 102, 516 U.S. 122 (1996)
State v. Kennedy, 799 P. 2d 119 (Cal. App. 1998)
California Code of Civil Procedure § 432
42 U.S.C. § 443
In re Towson, 18 F.3d 990 (2d Cir. 1995)
Hendrix v. Delane, 301 Wash. 2d 119, 790 P. 2d 114 (1994)

Chapter 19

Postwriting Steps

Chapter Overview

Paralegals not only engage in the drafting of documents for themselves, but also they are often asked to review and revise the writing of others or perform proofreading for others. While these tasks are typically accomplished at the end of a writing project, their importance cannot be overlooked. It is at this stage of the writing process that unclear passages should be revised, redundant phrases should be omitted, and spelling and grammatical errors should be corrected. Even a typographical error will impair the professionalism of your project.

This chapter focuses on reviewing and revising your writings, proofreading, and polishing the finished product so its appearance enhances readability.

A. Reviewing and Revising: Stage One

When you have the first draft of your project in hand, the difficult tasks of reviewing and revising begin. Your initial review should be to ensure that the writing accurately conveys all the information needed. At this stage, focus on content. Try to review the project from the perspective of the intended reader and ask if the reader will understand the writing.

Always keep the purpose of the project in mind. If the project is a brief, its purpose is to persuade. If the project is a memorandum, its purpose is to inform. Ask yourself if the writing meets these goals. Consider whether the tone is appropriate for the reader and whether the project is either too formal or too informal.

Review to ensure the writing flows smoothly and that its organization assists the reader's comprehension. Move paragraphs and sections to other locations if you believe they would be better placed elsewhere.

Be careful not to engage in micro-revision during the writing process itself. Agonizing over the choice of each word and continually striking out or rephrasing sentences may be a waste of time and energy because you may eventually omit a section you spent considerable time revising during the first effort.

Do not interpret this advice to mean that no revisions should be done during the writing stage. It is both necessary and helpful to revise throughout the process of writing. Do not, however, write your initial draft expecting that the first typed version will be suitable for submission to court. You may even wish to insert reminders to yourself in the initial draft such as "work on this" or "revise" to remind you that further work needs to be done for a certain section. When writing, if you cannot decide between two ways of expressing an idea, initially include them both. When you read through your completed first draft, you can then decide which version to retain.

Try to allow at least a few hours (and, if possible, overnight or longer) to pass between the completion of your first draft and your initial review. It is extremely difficult to review effectively a project with which you are too familiar. If you can come to the review "cold," you will be better able to detect flaws and gaps in the writing.

Focus 100 percent on the review. Ask someone to hold your calls and find a quiet space where you can concentrate on your task. If you attempt to review a project and are interrupted by phone calls and meetings, you will be unable to devote the effort you need to make a critical evaluation of the project and may unintentionally skip over sections.

You may find it helpful to close the door to your office or the library and read aloud. This will enable you to hear repetition or awkward phrasing or to realize something is missing from the project. Make sure each draft of a project includes a date. Often, several versions of a project will accumulate in a file. Because some drafts will vary only slightly from each other, sorting out the current version can be nearly impossible unless each draft is identified by date, and perhaps even time, for example, "DRAFT 12/16/01 10:30 a.m."

If you have collaborated on the project with another writer, be especially alert to ensure your headings, numberings, and presentations of lists are consistent.

If you are aiming to improve your writing skills in general, focus on one or two problem areas (such as overly long sentences or overuse of nominalizations), work on correcting these, and then move on to other weak spots.

B. Reviewing and Revising: Stage Two

The first review and revision of your project should alert you to major problems in content and organization. Use the second review to focus on four specific areas.

1. *Sentence Length*

Go through your second draft and place a red slash mark at the end of each sentence. Observe if a pattern of overly long sentences emerges. If most sentences are several lines in length, you need to trim your writing. Use sentences of varying length to create interest. Various software programs assist by informing you of average sentence length in a project.

2. *Needless Words and Phrases*

Read through the project looking for unnecessary words. It is easy to become attached to your product. Writers often have difficulty omitting words and phrases because they are reluctant to omit anything after hours of research and hours of writing. Be merciless. Most writers are far better at adding words than at deleting them. Watch carefully for modifiers such as "clearly," "obviously," or "naturally." These should be omitted for two reasons: They add nothing to a sentence, and they often create a patronizing tone.

3. *Legalese*

Keep alert to the use of jargon and legalese, including the overuse of archaic words and phrases and the overuse of nominalizations such as "discussion" or "exploration" instead of strong words like "discuss" or "explore."

4. *Passive Voice*

The overuse of passive voice will result in a distant and weak project. The active voice, coupled with the selection of forceful words, will lend strength and vigor to your writing.

C. Proofreading

The third and final review of your writing should focus on technical errors such as grammatical errors, spelling mistakes, and typos. The more familiar you are with a project, the more difficult this task becomes. Your mind will automatically supply the word you intended, and you will not be able to see errors. Do not rely exclusively on the spelling and grammar checker programs of your word processor. A spelling checker will not inform you to use "from" rather than "form" because both words are properly spelled. Do not proofread on a computer screen. Print a copy of the document and work from that. Reading a hard copy is easier on your eyes. Moreover, it is presented in the way it will be to the ultimate reader, allowing you to see it as it will be seen by its audience. Consider photocopying the document in an increased size, for example, to 120 percent of its original size, to allow you to read the document easily and make notes in the margin.

While there are a few techniques you can use to assist you in proofreading, the best tip is to allow as much time as possible, preferably two to three days, to elapse before you begin this final step in writing. This will allow you to come to the project with a fresh approach and will counterbalance the familiarity that hampers a careful scrutiny of your writing. Energy levels are often higher in the morning, so try to schedule your proofreading as the first thing you do in the day.

Do not underestimate the difficulty of proofreading and editing. All major publishers require that writings be edited by professional editors and proofreaders for the very reason that authors are notoriously unlikely to catch their own errors.

Because a normal reading of your project will naturally focus on content and you will read groups of words and phrases rather than isolated words, you need to force yourself to slow down and focus on each word. Try the following techniques:

(i) Place a ruler under each line as you read the document. This will prevent you from jumping ahead to the next sentence or thought and force you to focus on each word.

(ii) Read the project backwards, from the last page to the first page and from right to left. While this technique is excellent for finding typos and spelling errors, it will not help you pick up a missed word or ensure that you have used a word such as "united" rather than "untied."

(iii) Read the document aloud with a partner who has a copy of the document. Each of you will then focus on isolated words, and the listener, in particular, will concentrate on the mechanics of the project rather than the content. Additionally, if your partner stumbles over certain sections, you will know these need to be fixed.

(iv) Read sections of the project out of order. Read Section V first, then the Conclusion, then Section III, then the Statement of Facts, and so on. You will not be able to focus on the flow of ideas, and your concentration will then be aimed at the mechanics of spelling, grammar, and typos.

(v) Devote extra attention to the parts of the project that were prepared last. More errors occur when you and the word processor are tired.

If you find yourself getting tired or losing concentration, stop and take a quick break. Get up and walk around the office. Get some juice or a fresh cup of coffee and then return to the task. Because you are not reading for content, but for mechanics, these interruptions will do no harm.

You can also ask someone else to proof the project for you. Having someone else review the project can be extremely helpful because this newcomer will have no familiarity with the writing. He or she will be able to review the writing with a fresh approach and no preconceived ideas or expectations. If you only want the reader to review for mechanical errors, say so, or you may receive a project with substantial corrections and suggestions. It is an intrusion on someone else's time to review your work; therefore, if you have asked for help, you should give the reviewer the courtesy of considering his or her comments or suggestions without becoming defensive. If you have difficulty accepting comments and criticism from others about your writing, do not ask for help. It is a waste of the other person's time if you are not able to keep an open mind about accepting suggestions.

Be alert to the dangers of overreliance on word processor spell checking programs. While these programs can be of great assistance and even offer suggestions for word choice, they do not recognize contextual misspellings. Thus, if you mistakenly referred to the complaint as "compliant," the spelling program will not alert you because the word "compliant" is correctly spelled. Although spell checking programs help speed up the editing and proofing process, they also encourage complacency. There is no substitute for human proofreading, as witnessed by the fact that a review of some recently published court decisions disclosed 23 cases referring to "Santa Clause" and 817 cases referring to the "trail court."

Similarly, the use of templates and forms prepared for an earlier transaction increases the risk of importing incorrect terms into later documents. Thus, a document prepared for a tenant needs to be scrupulously checked when it is later used for a subtenant. Make sure that defined terms are used consistently. For example, if an agreement uses the term "Franchisor," check to make sure the term is defined in the agreement, that it is always capitalized, and that it is consistently spelled and used. Use the "find and replace" feature in your word processing program to check for consistent presentation and use.

D. Proofreading Projects by Others

If you are asked to review someone else's work, obtain clear instructions so you know if you should review for content or review only for mechanics such as typos, spelling mistakes, and grammatical errors. Reviewing for mechanical errors in someone else's writing is fairly easy. If you are not familiar with the content, the errors will fairly leap off the page at you (just as they will for the ultimate reader, such as the client or the judge).

If you are asked to review for content, be judicious. All writers are sensitive about their product and overcriticizing may result in the writer believing you have a grudge and then discounting everything you suggest.

Recognize that each writer has a unique style. Just because a thought is not expressed in the exact way you would express it does not mean it is inaccurate or vague. Limit your corrections to meaningful items. It is unproductive to change "glad" to "happy" or "concerning" to "regarding." Your credibility as an effective reviewer will be jeopardized if you engage in such meaningless changes.

Comments such as "weak," "poor," or "expand" placed beside a paragraph are nearly useless. Specifically explain to the writer why the section is weak and make a suggestion for improving it. Harsh comments such as "What are you thinking of?" or "ridiculous!" will cause the writer to avoid seeking your help and to become a passive writer. Try phrasing suggestions diplomatically, such as "have you considered . . . ?" or "let's discuss some alternatives . . . ." These approaches focus on the two of you as colleagues committed to producing a quality product rather than on the writer's perceived inadequacies.

In some instances, a letter to a client or a memo may bear the notation "dictated but not read," which means that the author dictated the project to someone else but has not reviewed it for errors. Avoid such a notation. The message it conveys to a reader is either "I'm too busy for you" or "don't blame me if there are errors in this document."

E. Proofreaders' Marks

While there is some variety in the marks writers use to show errors, most legal writers employ the standard marks, called proofreaders' marks, used by professional editors. Many attorneys learned these marks while writing articles for law reviews. Their use in law firms and among legal professionals is common.

Most dictionaries will provide descriptions and illustrations of proofreaders' marks. These marks are designed to show clerical staff where and how to make corrections in your project. Be sure all of your working drafts are double-spaced so you will have sufficient room to note corrections. The most commonly used proofreaders' marks are shown in Figure 19-1.

F. Polishing Your Writing

Even if your project is well written, clear, and readable, it should be presented in such a manner that it creates a favorable impression on the reader. One of the reasons many appellate courts insist that a brief submitted must be printed rather than merely typed is that printed briefs are easier to read and present a uniform appearance.

Many factors play a part in making a project readable, including quality of paper, typeface, margins, and headings. If your goal in writing is to communicate, you must avoid producing a document so messy in appearance that it frustrates a reader or one that is simply not read because of its physical appearance.

Visually appealing documents are easier to understand. Replace blocks of text with headings, tables, lists, and more white space. Make sure the layout of your project is uncrowded.

1. Paper

Use the highest-quality paper possible. Some courts require that the paper used for documents submitted be of a certain quality. The United States Supreme Court, for example, requires all 8½ by 11 documents to be produced on unglazed opaque white paper. Sup. Ct. R. 33.2(a).

Select a paper of sufficient weight so that page two of a document doesn't show through to page one. While some law firms use cream or ivory colored paper, most use white. White is the more traditional color and many readers find it easiest to read because black type provides a greater contrast on white paper than on cream colored paper.

2. Typeface

Use ordinary Roman type for most of your writing. Italics (or underscoring) must be used for case names, book titles, law review article titles and other publications, citation signals, and foreign words and phrases. Italics (or underscoring) may be used to emphasize certain words or phrases. Use boldface (letters that are struck two or three times for extra darkness and contrast or through the use of the boldface tab (the "B") on your word processor) only for headings or special purposes, such as emphasizing a deadline date in a letter to a client.

Figure 19-1
Commonly Used Proofreaders' Marks

Mark	*Explanation*	*Example*
≡	Capital letters	president bush
/	Lowercase letters	the eleventh Juror
~	Boldface	April 16, 2001
⁀	Close up space	in as much
¶	Begin new paragraph	¶ The plaintiff
ℓ	Delete	The hearing was was
stet	Let original text stand	Many courts ~~have~~ concluded
∧	Insert item	The plaintiff and his attorney argued
#	Add space	the court.The defendant
∾	Transpose	compliant
[	Move left	any jury
]	Move right	any jury
∧	Insert comma	the Plaintiff John Brownell argued
∨	Insert apostrophe	its a fact that
⊙	Insert period	the court The jury also requested
○ or (sp)	Spell out	Jan. 10, 2001

Word processors can easily create italics. Some writers prefer italics to underscoring because it creates an elegant look. Other writers believe underscoring draws more attention to a word or phrase.

As to type of font, many experts prefer a "serif" style, which is one that adds small decorative strokes to the edges of letters. Serif styles are generally viewed as enhancing readability because they draw the eye from one word to the next. Old-fashioned typewriters always used a serif style. Well-known serif styles include Garamond, Times New Roman, and Century Schoolbook. This text is presented in a serif style. "San serif" styles (those without extra brushstrokes) such as Arial might be acceptable and dramatic for headings. In any case, do not select a font style that is so different as to be distracting to a reader. Do not use all capital letters, except for short headings, because they are difficult to read.

3. *Type Size*

Word processors can provide you with numerous choices for type size. Type size is measured in "points," such as 10-point type or 12-point type, with the larger the number showing larger print. Some courts require documents to be printed in a certain size type. Similarly, some statutes require certain information, such as language disclaiming a warranty, to be of a specified type size. If there are no rules you must follow with regard to type size, select either 10-point or 12-point type, both of which are easily read. Rules of the United States Supreme Court dictate that the text of documents submitted to the Court be typeset in "Roman 11-point or larger type." Sup. Ct. R. 33.1(b). Many readers prefer 12-point type due to its ease of readability.

On occasion a client may insist that certain information be included in a contract, invoice, or other form. In order to fit all of the information or terms in the document, you may need to use a much smaller type size, such as 6-point or 8-point. Alternatively, many photocopy machines will reduce an image. These reductions, however, impair readability.

4. *Length of Document*

If court rules require that a document not exceed a specified page limit, you will need to be able to calculate and estimate the length of a project. The average typewritten or printed page, measuring 8½ × 11 inches, double-spaced, contains 250 words. If you are handwriting a document, count the words on any one sheet of your handwritten draft. Multiply this by the number of pages in your draft and divide this figure by 250. This will provide a rough estimate of how many typed pages your handwritten draft will produce. Some courts exclude certain sections, such as tables of contents and tables of authorities, from the page limits. Always check your court rules.

If your project exceeds a maximum length requirement, you have several alternatives:

- Revise the project, omitting extraneous material.
- Alter your margins so that more words fit on each page.
- Use a smaller point type size to include more text on each page.

While these last two techniques will allow you to squeeze extra material into the document, some court rules mandate margin size and type size. The rules of the United States Supreme Court flatly state, "Increasing the amount of text by using condensed or thinner typefaces, or by reducing the space between letters, is strictly prohibited." Sup. Ct. R. 33.1(b).

The other disadvantage of squeezing material into a document is that it creates a more cramped appearance, and few, if any, readers will be fooled by artificial techniques adopted to meet length requirements. Pages filled with text from the upper left corner to the lower right corner cause eyestrain and frustration. Using adequate white space will cause headings and quotations to be more easily noticed. While the technique of leaving ample white space on a page, including adequate or generous margins, may seem like an artificial device, reading studies have demonstrated that it results in a more readable project.

Another formatting device that contributes to a pleasing appearance is the use of right justified margins. A right justified margin is one in which all of the words end at the exact same location at the right side on the page. This type of margin creates a clean and crisp-looking document. The only disadvantage is that to ensure the margin is even at the right side, uneven spacing between letters and words may occur. This ragged spacing can reduce ease of reading. Carefully proofread any document with right justified margins to make sure the spacing is acceptable. If it is not, use a ragged right edge.

5. *Headings*

Headings not only provide the reader with an idea as to what will follow, but also create visual drama on a page. Main headings should be in all capital letters, centered, and single-spaced. Each should be given a Roman numeral. Some writers use boldface print to make sure the headings stand out. Subheadings that occur with a main heading should use capital letters only for the first letter in each major word, such as nouns, verbs, adjectives, and adverbs. Do not capitalize the first letter in articles and prepositions, such as "in," "of," or "the," but be sure to capitalize "is," "its," "be," and other short verbs, nouns, and adverbs. Label each subheading with a capital letter and underline or use boldface for emphasis. All headings should be separated from the remainder of the narrative by double-spacing above and below. If the heading is a complete sentence, follow it with a period.

The structure and labeling of headings and subheadings should be as follows:

I.
    A.
    B.
        1.
        2.
        3.
            a.
            b.
            c.
    C.
II.
    A.
    B.
    C.
        1.
            a.
            b.
            c.
                (i)
                (ii)
        2.
    D.
III.

Do not use an "I" or an "A" unless a "II" or a "B" follows. On your final proofreading effort, scan through your project examining only the lettering and numbers of the headings to make sure you haven't skipped over or repeated a letter or number.

6. *Quotations and Lists*

Quotations and lists can serve to provide relief from a long narrative. Select quotations with care and be careful not to overquote. Follow *Bluebook* rules and keep quotes of 49 or fewer words in text. Indent quotes of 50 words or more.

Lists also create interest and are an effective tool for presenting information. Overuse of lists, however, can make your project have an outline-look to its appearance. Be consistent in presentation of lists. Don't use bullets in some lists and dashes to introduce others. Review lists to make sure the presentation of the material is in parallel structure.

G. The Final Review

Just before your writing is sent to the reader, check these four items:

(i) "*Widows and orphans.*" A "widow" or "orphan" is a heading or isolated line occurring at the bottom of a page or an isolated line occurring at the top of a page. Omit that awkward placement. It is distracting to the reader and results in an unprofessional-looking project.
(ii) *Hyphenated Words.* Do not hyphenate a word between one page and the next. Most software programs automatically correct this error.
(iii) *Numbering.* Quickly scan the project to make sure the page numbering is correct. If the document has a table of contents, review it to make sure all references to pages are correct. If footnotes are used, check their accuracy.
(iv) *Exhibits.* Make sure all exhibits or attachments to the project are included and are properly marked.

H. Conclusion

While the foregoing comments relating to paper quality, type size, and white space may seem inconsequential, remember that if your objective is to inform or persuade your reader, any device that keeps the reader's interest is significant. View these techniques as weapons in your arsenal of writing tools. Your goal is to produce a writing that is accurate and readable. Errors and typos impair the accuracy of a writing and an unpresentable project impairs the readability of a writing. If you discover errors, don't be afraid to send the document back for correction. Better that you are viewed as a perfectionist than as someone uninterested in quality.

Strive for excellence. Make every project something you and your fellow legal professionals will be proud to sign.

Common Writing Errors

Watch for the following common errors:

- Repeated words at the end of one line and the beginning of another.
- Errors in figures, dates, monetary amounts, and names.
- Substitutions of letters in small words, such as a change of "now" to "not" or "of" to "or."
- Transpositions of letters such that "complaint" becomes "compliant" and "trial" becomes "trail."
- Misspellings of compound words such as "every one" rather than "everyone" or "can not" for "cannot."

Assignment for Chapter 19

CAREFULLY PROOFREAD THE FOLLOWING PASSAGE AND MAKE THE NECESSARY CORRECTIONS.

Our client, Peterson Consulting Co. (PCC) is a high-tech company which was formed in the state of Delaware in August 20, 2995. Its principles are Jack Petersen and Holly Ford. PCC is engaged in the business of telecommuncations. PSC recently contacted us with regard to the following matter. In conducting routine monitoring of its employees email communications, Peterson noticed that several of its employee's have exchanged vulgar and sexually explicit jokes via e-mail which target one specific employee, Ann Hawthorne ("Hawthorn"). The company believes it has a right to monitor their employee communications since the employee handbook clearly states "Their in a right to monitor the company's electronic communications." PSC is cconcerned that the communications constitute a from of sexual harrasment forbidden by federal statues. More over, the company is concerted that the affect of these communications in to decreases business productivity. Peterson was sued last year for allowing a hostile work enviroment and a judgement was rended against them in the amount of $150,00. Plus attorney fees. In view of the recent lawsuit, PCC has asked us to research the following tow questions: do they have the right to monitor employee communications, is the employee manual an enforceable contract, and whether they can require that e-mail be used only for business purposs.

Please prepare a written memoranda for my by Monday morning a.m.

Appendix

A

Sample Legal Memorandum

MEMORANDUM

TO: Anne C. Simmons, Esq.

FROM: Peter R. Reynolds, Legal Assistant

RE: Moe v. CTN Insurance Co.
Our File No. I-9013

DATE: September 20, 2001

ISSUE

Are computer databases relating to insurance claims discoverable under the Federal Rules of Civil Procedure although they have previously been produced in paper form?

BRIEF ANSWER

Yes. Computer databases are discoverable so long as they are not protectable under the principles of either attorney-client privilege or the work product doctrine. Because the information requested here has already been produced, there is no compromise of either principle. Moreover, the burden on the plaintiff to read hard copy information when a computer can analyze the information much faster and more efficiently tips the balance toward production.

FACTS

Our client, Dolores Moe ("Moe") paid insurance premiums for several years to CTN Insurance Co. ("CTN") for automobile liability insurance. Moe was involved in an automobile accident on March 14, 2001, and submitted an insurance claim to CTN. CTN denied insurance coverage to Moe on the basis that the policy did not cover the automobile accident in which she was involved. We filed a lawsuit against CTN on July 20, 2001, for breach of contract and requested damages for CTN's bad faith in denying coverage to Moe, its policyholder.

To demonstrate CTN's bad faith in denying coverage, Moe needs to review CTN's records regarding how often it denies coverage to its policyholders. In a Request for Production of Documents, we requested that CTN provide copies of any documents pertaining to its denial of coverage to its policyholders. In response, CTN produced more than 3,000 pages of material. These records are so voluminous as to be nearly impossible to read and review. Through interrogatories directed to CTN we discovered that the pertinent records are also maintained by CTN in a computer database, which would be far easier to read than the paper records. CTN has refused to produce the computer database, arguing that hard copies of the information have already been provided.

ANALYSIS

General Discovery Principles. Generally, items are discoverable if they are relevant to either a claim made or a defense asserted by a party. Fed. R. Civ. P. 26(b)(1). In the present case, it will be important to the plaintiff's case (which alleges that her insurance provider denied coverage to her in bad faith) to determine the defendant's policies relating to denying and granting coverage to its insureds. The number of times and circumstances under which the defendant denies coverage to policyholders will be relevant in determining whether the defendant denied coverage to Moe in bad faith. Thus, under Fed. R. Civ. P. 26(b)(1), CTN's records relating to denial of insurance coverage are relevant and therefore discoverable.

Moreover, the discovery rules are liberally interpreted to favor production. As stated in *Chronicle Publishing Co. v. Superior Court,* 600 P.2d 109, 114 (Cal. 1960), "the statutes must be construed liberally in favor of disclosure unless the request is clearly improper by virtue of well-established cause for denial." Only strong public policies weigh against disclosure. *Id.* at 129.

Typically, the only relevant materials that are not discoverable are those subject to privilege or those that are the work product of a party's attorney. *Hickman v. Taylor*, 329 U.S. 495 (1947). In the present case, neither defense has been asserted and, in fact, the materials requested have been produced. Therefore, the only question remaining is whether electronic versions of previously produced written records are discoverable.

Discovery of Electronic Materials and Databases. The Federal Rules of Civil Procedure define "documents" to include "writings, drawings, graphs, photographs, phonorecords, *and other data compilations* from which information can be obtained translated, if necessary, by the responding through detection devices into reasonably usuable form . . . ." Fed. R. Civ. P. 34 (emphasis added). Thus, the materials requested by Moe, namely, insurance records in computer database form, are "writings" as defined by the Federal Rules of Civil Procedure and are discoverable.

In *Fautek v. Montgomery Ward & Co.*, 96 F.R.D. 141 (N.D. Ill. 1982), the plaintiff sought employment records in computer-readable form for specific years relevant to her employment discrimination claim. The defendant asserted that the database was prepared for litigation purposes and was therefore not subject to discovery because it was protectable work product of the defendant's attorney. When it was determined that the defendant had computerized its personnel records in a computer system and that relevant and discoverable information existed on the computer database, the court ordered production of the database.

The Burden of Production. In some instances, parties have resisted discovery on the basis that production of the database would be unduly burdensome. In several cases, the party opposing production has been unable to demonstrate a calculable burden, generally because reproduction of the database can be readily accomplished by inserting a disk into the computer and entering a few computer commands. For example, in *Davies v. Superior Court*, 682 P.2d 349 (Cal. 1984), the California Supreme Court held that information contained in a computerized database was discoverable because it was readily available in that the information had already been compiled in another format.

More importantly, in *National Union Electric Corp. v. Matsushita Electric Industrial Co.*, 494 F. Supp. 1257 (E.D. Pa. 1980), the court balanced the time and expense necessary for a party to analyze 1,000 pages of data *previously produced* against the burden the producing party, the plaintiff, would incur to re-create a database of that same hard copy information. The defendant argued that it could not properly analyze the 1,000 pages of data unless it was presented in computer-readable form. The plaintiff responded that the defendant could create its own computer database by inputting the information already produced by the plaintiff. The court held that the production of a party's data in a form that is directly readable by the adverse party's computer is the preferred alternative. Recognizing that "we now live in an era when much of the data which our society desires to retain is stored on computer disks," *id.* at 1262-63, the court noted that "to interpret the Federal Rules . . . in a manner which would preclude the production of material such as is requested here, would eventually defeat their purpose." *Id.* Thus, strong public policy favors the production of records in a form that can be readily analyzed by a party.

In some instances, however, courts have ordered requesting parties to pay for costs incurred in making databases available. Such orders are pursuant to Fed. R. Civ. P. 26(c)(2), which provides that courts may order that discovery be had on specified terms and conditions. This rule enables the courts to order a party seeking discovery to pay costs incurred in obtaining discoverable materials. Thus, in *Timke Co. v. United States*, 659 F. Supp. 239 (C.I.T. 1987), the United States Court of International Trade ruled that in light of the cost and burden a producing party would incur (specifically, 7,500 keypunch hours at a cost of $200,000), the requesting party was ordered to pay for the cost of copying the tapes. Further, in *Timke*, although the party resisting discovery asserted that the material was subject to work product protection, the court ruled that the work product doctrine was not applicable because the information had already been produced in hard copy format. Similarly, in the present case, the information Moe has requested has previously been produced and therefore cannot be withheld under the work product doctrine although it is possible a court order could order Moe to pay for the costs of production.

In *Donaldson v. Pillsbury Co.*, 554 F.2d 825 (8th Cir. 1977), the plaintiff alleged she needed statistical information to prove her claim of a pattern and practice of racial and sexual discrimination. The defendant responded that the statistical information sought could be imputed from records it had previously produced. The court held that the information was discoverable in computer-readable form, noting, "[d]ata in computer-readable form is more easily subjected to analysis, and two district courts have upheld motions for productions of such documents, in the face of claims that similar information had been provided in readout form." *Id.* at 832. Thus, the material requested by Moe should be discoverable because it will be far easier to read and analyze in computer-readable form, even though it has previously been produced.

CONCLUSION

It the present case, analysis of the documents produced in hard-copy form would be difficult and time-consuming. Analysis by computer would be easier and more efficient. Because the computer database requested includes only materials that have been previously produced in hard-copy form, there is no concern that the material is subject to either the attorney-client privilege or the work product doctrine. Thus, the database should discoverable, although Moe might be ordered to pay the costs involved in the production of the electronic records.

Appendix

B

Sample Brief for Court

STATE OF NEW YORK

IN AND FOR ERIE COUNTY

The People of the State of New York

Plaintiff,

vs. Indictment No. 93-14057

Michael Timothy Stevens

Defendant.

MEMORANDUM OF LAW IN SUPPORT OF MOTION TO SUPPRESS

Defendant Michael Timothy Stevens ("Defendant" or "Stevens") respectfully submits the following Memorandum of Law in support of his motion to suppress certain evidence unlawfully obtained by the Police Department of Erie County, New York.

STATEMENT OF FACTS

On October 7, 1999, at approximately 10:00 P.M., two members of the Erie County Police Department were summoned to the scene of Leroy and Holden Avenues, where a shooting had allegedly occurred. Officers James and Richards proceeded to the intersection of Leroy and Holden Avenues where they observed Stevens walking along the sidewalk of Holden Avenue. With their guns drawn, the officers approached Stevens.

Stevens was then instructed by the officers to face the wall of a nearby warehouse and, while Officer James braced Stevens against the wall, Officer Richards investigated the area and found a rifle lying approximately 100 yards from the scene. Stevens was then frisked and handcuffed with his hands placed behind his back.

According to Officer James, at this point the officers considered Stevens "in custody," meaning that Stevens was not free to leave. Stevens was then locked in the backseat of the patrol car, where Officer James was seated next to him. At this time, Stevens had not been read his Miranda rights.

Officer Richards proceeded to drive the patrol car back to the police station. During the drive, which took approximately ten to fifteen minutes, Officer James asked Stevens if Stevens wished to "talk" about the shooting that had occurred earlier. Stevens replied that he had no involvement in, or knowledge of, any shooting incident in the vicinity. He also stated that he did not own a rifle and had no idea whose rifle had been found near the scene.

Officer James then informed Stevens that it would be in Stevens' "best interest" if Stevens cooperated with the police and told them everything he knew about the shooting incident. Officer James threatened to conduct an investigation of Stevens' hands at the police station to determine whether Stevens had recently fired a weapon. Officer James also stated that fingerprints would be taken from the rifle and these would undoubtedly show that Stevens had touched the weapon.

After these statements were made by Officer James, Stevens acknowledged involvement in the shooting. It was only *after* this confession that Officer James "Mirandized" Stevens. When Stevens and the officers reached the police station, Stevens was left in a small interrogation room for approximately 35 minutes. Stevens was unattended, although various officers proceeded to walk in and out of the room. After approximately 35 minutes, Officer James entered the interrogation room, re-read Stevens his Miranda rights and took a formal written statement from Stevens.

THE MIRANDA WARNING WAS NECESSARY BEFORE THE FIRST CONFESSION WAS TAKEN AND IN ITS ABSENCE, STEVENS' ORAL STATEMENTS MUST BE SUPPRESSED

The right of a suspect to receive the warnings enumerated by the United States Supreme Court in *Miranda v. Arizona*, 384 U.S. 436 (1966), hinges upon whether an individual being questioned is in custody. This jurisdiction adheres to the "reasonable person" test to determine whether an individual is "in custody." "The test for determining whether a defendant is in custody is whether a reasonable man, innocent of any crime, could have thought he was in custody had he been in defendant's position." *People v. Baird*, 155 A.D.2d 918, 919, 547 N.Y.S.2d 740, 741 (1989).

In this case, there can be no doubt that Stevens was in custody at the time he made his oral statements to Officer James. Stevens had been braced against a wall, handcuffed, and placed in a locked patrol car next to a police officer. He was considered by the arresting officer, Officer James, to be in custody. Accordingly, Stevens was "in custody" for the purpose of determining whether he should have received his Miranda warnings. No reasonable person could have thought otherwise.

Stevens gave his oral statement to Officer James only after Officer James asked if Stevens wished to "talk." Stevens initially denied involvement in any shooting incident. Officer James then proceeded to issue a series of overt threats designed to ensure that Stevens confess any involvement in the shooting incident. Stevens' oral statements to Officer James were the direct result of the threats made to Stevens while he was in custody and before he had been afforded the rights safeguarded to him by *Miranda*. Accordingly, the oral statements made by Stevens in the patrol car are inadmissible.

In *People v. Rivera*, 57 N.Y.2d 453, 454, 443 N.E.2d 439, 440, 457 N.Y.S.2d 191, 191 (1982), the court held that "when a criminal suspect is subjected to custodial interrogation by police without being apprised of his right against self-incrimination, any pertinent communication, whether made by statement or conduct, in response to the interrogation, is inadmissible at trial." In determining whether a communication is made "in response to interrogation," the test is whether the defendant's statement is spontaneous rather than the "result of inducement, provocation, encouragement or acquiescence, no matter how subtly employed." *People v. Newport*, 149 A.D.2d 954, 956, 540 N.Y.S.2d 87, 88 (1989) (quoting *People v. Maerling*, 46 N.Y.2d 289, 308, 385 N.E.2d 1250, 1258, 413 N.Y.S.2d 316, 324 (1978)).

In this case, it cannot be said that Stevens' statement was anything other than one that occurred as a result of inducement or encouragement. It was only after Officer James informed Stevens that various scientific tests would be conducted on Stevens and on the rifle that Stevens began communicating with Officer James.

STEVENS' SUBSEQUENT ORAL STATEMENT MUST ALSO BE SUPPRESSED

In this jurisdiction, a clear test exists to determine whether a statement made after an unwarned statement is admissible when the first statement is made in violation of a defendant's Miranda rights.

In *People v. Tanner*, 30 N.Y.2d 102, 331 N.Y.S.2d 1 (1972), the court noted that if a defendant made one unwarned statement, the defendant would feel obligated to maintain that statement even after Miranda warnings were given.

> A man who makes admissions under duress or in violation of this constitutional right to warning and advice may feel so committed by what he has then said that he believes it futile to assert his rights after he has been later advised of them before new questioning begins. This state of mind may have an effect on the waiver leading to the later admissions; or on the voluntary nature of those admissions.

Id. at 105, 331 N.Y.S.2d at 3. This is commonly referred to as the "cat-out-of-the-bag" theory.

In *People v. Chapple*, 38 N.Y.2d 112, 378 N.Y.S.2d 682 (1975), the "cat-out-of-the-bag" theory was expanded and the court noted that unless there was a definite and pronounced break in the interrogation, the defendant would be returned to the status of one who was not under the influence of questioning.

In this case, the central questions then are whether there was such a pronounced break between Stevens' first unwarned statement in the police car and the second warned one and whether Stevens felt so constrained by the first statement that he felt compelled to maintain it in his second statement at the police station.

With regard to whether there was a definite and pronounced break in the interrogation, it should be noted that while there was a thirty- (30) to forty- (40) minute period between Stevens' two statements, at all times Stevens remained in police custody and he continued to be interrogated by the same individual, Officer James. In *People v. Graves*, 158 A.D.2d 916, 551 N.Y.S.2d 81 (1990), the court found that an unwarned statement made by a defendant in a police car tainted a subsequent warned statement made at a police station some time later. The court specifically noted that the second statement must be suppressed as the product of one continuous interrogation. Moreover, in *People v. DeGelleke*, 144 A.D.2d 978, 534 N.Y.S.2d 51 (1988), a two-and-one-half hour interval between an on-scene unwarned statement and a later Mirandized statement did not constitute a pronounced break in questioning. The court noted the extent of the statements made by the defendant to the police as well as the continuous custody of the defendant.

It is not the length of time but rather the circumstances of the interrogation that are critical. For example, in *People v. Robertson*, 133 A.D.2d 355, 519 N.Y.S.2d 256 (1987), the court held that a time lapse of one to two hours was insufficient to constitute a pronounced break between interrogations. Similarly, in *People v. Johnson*, 79 A.D.2d 617, 433 N.Y.S.2d 477 (1980), a four-hour break between an unwarned statement and a later warned statement was held not to constitute a definite or pronounced break. Significantly, in both *Robertson* and *Johnson*, the officer who took the second statement either took the first statement or was present while the first statement was made. In fact, in *Johnson*, the court specifically noted that a "two hour hiatus between statements was inadequate to dispel the taint of the improper initial interrogation, particularly as the offending officer was present at and assisted with the second questioning." *Id.* at 619, 433 N.Y.S.2d at 478-79.

Perhaps the most compelling rationale for suppressing the second statement is offered by *People v. Bethea*, 67 A.D. 364, 366, 502 N.Y.S.2d 713, 714 (1986), in which the court noted that the constitutional protection against self-incrimination would have little deterrent "if the police know that they can, as part of a continuous chain of events, question a suspect in custody without warning, provided only they thereafter question him or her again after warnings have been given."

In the present case, a mere break of thirty (30) to forty (40) minutes can hardly constitute a "definite" or "pronounced" break when Stevens remained in custody the entire time and was questioned on both occasions by Officer James. In such circumstances Stevens was undoubtedly constrained by the nature and extent of the first unwarned statements to repeat them even after he had received his Miranda warnings. It is precisely this constraint anticipated by the court in *Tanner* that expanded the "cat-out-of-the-bag" theory.

CONCLUSION

While in police custody, without having received any Miranda warnings and after being threatened by Officer James, Stevens let the "cat out of the bag." Approximately half an hour later, while he was still in police custody and was being re-questioned by Officer James, who read Stevens his Miranda rights, Stevens repeated his earlier statements. There is no doubt but that the first statement made by Stevens must be suppressed inasmuch as it is the direct product of an unwarned police interrogation. The only issue to be determined is whether Stevens' subsequent statement to Officer James is admissible. Due to the continuous nature of the interrogation, the involvement of Officer James in the initial interrogation in the police car as well as the continued interrogation at the police station, and the fact that Stevens, who had let the "cat out of the bag" in the police car, felt constrained to adhere to his earlier statement, the second statement must also be suppressed.

For the foregoing reasons, this Court is respectfully urged to grant this Motion to Suppress.

Dated: ____________________ Respectfully submitted,

Franklin and Trainor
2453 Eleventh Avenue
Buffalo, New York

Attorneys for Defendant

Appendix

C

Sample Appellate Brief

The attached appellate brief (a Petition for a Writ of *Certiorari*) was submitted to the United States Supreme Court and was successful in securing the relief requested.

No. 93-1577

IN THE
Supreme Court of the United States
OCTOBER TERM, 1994

QUALITEX COMPANY,
Petitioner,
v.
JACOBSON PRODUCTS CO., INC.,
Respondent.

On Writ of Certiorari to the United States Court of Appeals for the Ninth Circuit

---

BRIEF OF AMICUS CURIAE INTELLECTUAL PROPERTY OWNERS IN SUPPORT OF THE PETITIONERS

GARO A. PARTOYAN
GEORGE R. POWERS
NEIL A. SMITH
ROGER S. SMITH
HERBERT C. WAMSLEY *
INTELLECTUAL PROPERTY OWNERS
1255 Twenty-Third Street, N.W.
Suite 850
Washington, D.C. 20037
(202) 466-2396
Attorneys for Amicus Curiae

November 8, 1994

* Counsel of Record

WILSON - EPES PRINTING CO., INC. - 789-0096 - WASHINGTON, D.C. 20001

TABLE OF CONTENTS

ii

TABLE OF AUTHORITIES

CASES Page

STATUTES

OTHER

IN THE
Supreme Court of the United States
OCTOBER TERM, 1994

No. 93-1577

QUALITEX COMPANY,
Petitioner,
v.
JACOBSON PRODUCTS CO., INC.,
Respondent.

On Writ of Certiorari to the United States Court of Appeals for the Ninth Circuit

---

BRIEF OF AMICUS CURIAE INTELLECTUAL PROPERTY OWNERS IN SUPPORT OF THE PETITIONERS

INTEREST OF THE AMICUS CURIAE

Intellectual Property Owners ("IPO") files this amicus curiae brief in support of petitioner Qualitex Company on the writ of certiorari to review the ruling of the United States Court of Appeals for the Ninth Circuit.

IPO was founded in 1972 by a group of individuals who were concerned about the lack of understanding of intellectual property rights in the United States. Members now include nearly one hundred large and medium size companies and some smaller businesses and independent inventors who own patents, trademarks, copyrights and other intellectual property rights. Members of IPO's Board of Directors are listed in the addendum to this brief. IPO is a nonprofit association exempt from federal income tax under Internal Revenue Code § 501(c)(6).

Trademarks are symbols of product and service quality and indicators of source. Trademarks enable IPO's members to invest in advertising that builds commercial reputation and public confidence in product and service quality.

Members of IPO register thousands of trademarks each year with the United States Patent and Trademark Office, and enforce their registered marks in the federal courts to prevent infringement, counterfeiting, and piracy. Federal registration is important in helping assure adequate legal protection for marks that IPO's members use on new and existing products and services. It is in the interest of IPO's members for the Court to rule that the Lanham Act does not prohibit the registration of color alone as a trademark.

SUMMARY OF ARGUMENT

The question accepted for review must be answered by recourse to the language in the Lanham Act. Color is capable of distinguishing a product from the products of others, and color comes within the definition of "trademark" in the Lanham Act. None of the exceptions to registrability of marks listed in the Lanham Act have any relevance to Qualitex's mark, so the mark should have been found registrable in accordance with the plain meaning of the words of the act.

The ruling by the Court of Appeals conflicts with the policy underlying the Lanham Act of protecting against unfair competition. The Lanham Act requirements for protecting registered and unregistered marks are similar.

Registration of color alone advances the Lanham Act's objective of encouraging registration of as many of the

3

marks in use as practicable. Firms search registered marks to determine potential conflicts before adopting a new mark. The benefits provided by the Lanham Act to trademark owners who register their marks should be available to owners of color marks to the same extent as to owners of other kinds of marks.

ARGUMENT

I. THE PLAIN MEANING OF THE STATUTORY LANGUAGE IN THE LANHAM ACT PERMITS THE REGISTRATION OF COLOR ALONE AS A TRADEMARK

The question accepted for review—whether the Lanham Act prohibits the registration of color as a trademark—must be answered by relying on the language in the act.

Section 2(f) of the Lanham Act is the principal section that is relevant to the question of whether the act prohibits the registration of color alone as a trademark. This section, which relates specifically to marks that have become distinctive of the applicant's goods (marks that have acquired secondary meaning), reads as follows:

> Except as expressly excluded in paragraphs (a), (b), (c), (d), and (e)(3) of this section, nothing herein shall prevent the registration of a mark used by the applicant which has become distinctive of the applicant's goods in commerce. . . .[1]

Since none of the exclusions referenced in this section relate to color, it is clear that the Lanham Act does not prohibit the registration of color alone as a trademark.

The foregoing conclusion is supported by the Court of Appeals opinion, which states:

> Registration of mere color is not explicitly barred by the Lanham Act, which provides that "[n]o trade-

---

[1] 15 U.S.C. § 1052(f) (Lanham Act, § 2(f)). The preamble to Section 2 of the act also indicates that marks must be registered unless one of the exceptions in the act applies: "No trademark . . . shall be refused registration . . . unless . . . ."

> mark by which the goods of the applicant may be distinguished from the goods of others shall be refused registration," 15 U.S.C. § 1052, unless one of the specific exceptions to registrability set forth in 15 U.S.C. § 1052 applies. Color is not listed as an exception.[2]

A related question is whether the Lanham Act not only does not prohibit the registration, but in fact contemplates the registration of color alone when the color has met all of the other requirements of the act for registration. It is submitted that registration of color alone clearly is contemplated by the act. If a color has acquired secondary meaning and none of the exceptions of Section 2(f) are applicable, then a fair reading of the language of the Lanham Act taken along with legislative history supports the view that registration of the color alone is to be permitted under the act.

The term trademark is defined in Section 45 of the act as including "any word, symbol, or device, or any combination thereof . . . to identify or distinguish his or her goods . . . ." Although color is not specifically listed in the definition, it is submitted that the listed terms "symbol" and "device" include color. In 1988, Congress confirmed this interpretation of the definition, in its Senate committee report on the Lanham Act amendments of that year, stating:

> The revised definition intentionally retains
>
> . . .
>
> (iv) the words "*symbol or device*" so as not to preclude the registration of *colors*, shapes, sounds or configurations where they function as trademarks.[3]

---

[2] Pet. App. 5a. IPO will use the citation form "Pet. App." and a page number to refer to the appendix to Qualitex's petition for writ of certiorari.

[3] S. Rep. No. 100-515, 100th Cong., 2d Sess. 44 (1988) (emphasis added).

5

The North American Free Trade Agreement (NAFTA) and its 1993 implementing legislation [4] provide further support for the proposition that color is included within the Lanham Act's definition of trademark. More particularly, Article 1708(1) of the NAFTA agreement provides:

> For purposes of this Agreement, a *trademark consists of any sign*, or any combination of signs, capable of distinguishing the goods and services of one person from those of another, *including* personal names, designs, letters, numerals, *colors*, figurative elements, or the shape of goods or of their packaging. . .[5]

Although "colors" was included in the NAFTA definition of trademark, Congress did not find it necessary in 1993 to amend the Lanham Act definition of trademark in order to implement Article 1708(1). This undoubtedly was because Congress intended in 1993, as in 1988, that "color" be included within the meaning of the terms "symbol" and "device."

Since it is clear that "color" is reasonably included within the definition of a trademark under the Lanham Act, a color should be registrable on the same basis as words, logos, and other forms of marks. Courts should not unilaterally decide to refuse registration based on non-statutory considerations when all statutory criteria for registration have been met and such registration is contemplated by the Lanham Act.[6]

---

[4] Pub. L. No. 103-182, 103rd Cong., 1st Sess. (1993).

[5] North American Free Trade Agreement, 32 I.L.M. 605 (signed December 17, 1992) (emphasis added).

[6] Not all rules of trademark law are statutory. It is well-established by court decisions that functional features may not be protected or registered as trademarks, even though the Lanham Act does not explicitly prohibit registration of functional features. However, unlike registration of color, there is nothing that would lead to a conclusion that registration of functional features is contemplated by the act.

It is therefore submitted that (1) the Lanham Act does not prohibit the registration of color alone as a trademark and (2) the Lanham Act clearly contemplates the registration of color alone as a trademark.

II. THE RULING BY THE COURT OF APPEALS CONFLICTS WITH THE POLICY UNDERLYING THE LANHAM ACT OF PROTECTING AGAINST UNFAIR COMPETITION

The Court of Appeals affirmed the District Court's finding of trade dress infringement under Section 43(a)[7] of the Lanham Act, finding that: (1) the trade dress is nonfunctional, (2) the trade dress has acquired secondary meaning, and (3) there is a likelihood of confusion between the products.[8]

Although trade dress differs from a trademark by relating to the total impression created by the use of the package, and not just to the trademark itself, the factors considered in determining trade dress infringement are similar to those considered in determining trademark infringement.[9] If it is found that the facts support a finding that (1) the color itself is nonfunctional, (2) the color itself has acquired secondary meaning, and (3) there is a likelihood of confusion between products based solely on the use of the same color or confusingly similar colors,[10] then the color itself is performing as a trademark. To

---

[7] 15 U.S.C. § 1125(a).

[8] Pet. App. 14a.

[9] *Cf.* Two Pesos Inc. v. Taco Cabana Inc., 120 L.Ed.2d 615, 618 (1992) ("[T]he general principles qualifying a mark for registration under § 2 of the Lanham Act are for the most part applicable in determining whether an unregistered mark is entitled to protection under § 43(a).").

[10] Nonfunctionality, secondary meaning, and likelihood of confusion, mistake, or deception are requirements for registering and enforcing a color mark. *E.g.*, In re Owens-Corning Fiberglas Corp., 774 F.2d 1116 (Fed. Cir. 1985).

deny full recognition of trademark status under the Lanham Act to color marks meeting the foregoing criteria would be inconsistent with the trademark law policy of preventing unfair competition and the deceptive and misleading use of marks.

Color is a universal language that is capable of identifying and distinguishing between competing products and providing useful information to customers.[11] Where a color has acquired secondary meaning and is nonfunctional, there can be no reason to deny exclusive rights and registration to the party who originated the mark. Such a result would promote confusion and deception in the marketplace by permitting others to adopt and use with impunity the same or confusingly similar colors (as long as the overall impressions of the products do not give rise to trade dress infringement).[12]

New entrants in a market are not deterred by a prior user's registration of color alone as a trademark. Only colors for which no competitive need exists are nonfunctional and therefore possibly registrable, and new entrants can choose from many colors that are not confusingly similar.[13]

---

[11] Qualitex presented evidence that many purchasers of dry cleaning press pads do not speak or read English well. Pet. App. 13a.

[12] The Eighth Circuit Court of Appeals in *Master Distributors* concluded:

> A per se rule prohibiting the protection of color alone would essentially render a valid color trademark registration ineffective and unenforceable. This would be extremely confusing and inconsistent. Although the aquamarine blue color of MDI's Blue Max tape is not registered, we think it would be equally confusing and inconsistent to rule that registered color marks may be protected, while common law color marks may not.

Master Distributors, Inc. v. Pako Corp., 986 F.2d 219, 224 (8th Cir. 1992).

[13] The District Court in *Qualitex,* for example, found that in the industry in question the range of tones of suitable colors was in the hundreds, if not thousands.

The task of determining likelihood of confusion among shades of color is not inherently more difficult than the task of determining likelihood of confusion among words. Registrability of color does not mean registration of large numbers of color marks. The standards for secondary meaning [14] and nonfunctionality [15] are difficult to meet.

III. THE RULING BY THE COURT OF APPEALS CONFLICTS WITH THE POLICY UNDERLYING THE LANHAM ACT OF ENCOURAGING REGISTRATION OF MARKS IN ORDER TO ENABLE COMPETITORS TO KNOW OF RIGHTS IN MARKS

Registration of color alone advances the Lanham Act's objective of registering as many of the marks in use as practicable so that competitors will be able to avoid conflicts by searching a relatively complete Principal Register,[16] and Supplemental Register,[17] and will be able to learn of rights from the Federal registration symbol "®".[18]

The Lanham Act encourages registration by providing various benefits for trademark owners who register their marks.[19] These benefits should be available to owners of

---

14 Trademark Manual of Examining Procedure, 2d ed. 1993, U.S. Patent and Trademark Office, § 1202.04(e) ("The applicant must submit evidence that the proposed color mark has become distinctive of the applicant's goods in commerce. The burden of proof in such a case is substantial.").

15 E.g., Inwood Laboratories, Inc. v. Ives Laboratories, 456 U.S. 844,853 (1982) (color of capsules functional); Brunswick Corp. v. British Seagull Ltd., —— F.3d ——, 32 USPQ 2d 1120, 1124 (Fed. Cir. 1994) (color black for outboard marine engines functional).

16 15 U.S.C. §§ 1052 and 1072 (Lanham Act, §§ 2 and 22).

17 15 U.S.C. §§ 1091, 1093 and 1094 (Lanham Act, §§ 23, 25, and 26).

18 *See generally* J. E. Hawes, Trademark Registration Practice § 2.03 (1994).

19 *E.g.*, 15 U.S.C. § 1072 (Lanham Act, § 22) (registration as constructive notice of claim of ownership); 15 U.S.C. § 1065 (Lanham Act, § 15) (incontestability of right to use registered mark under certain conditions).

nonfunctional color marks that have acquired secondary meaning to the same extent that benefits of registration are available to owners of other kinds of marks.

CONCLUSION

IPO urges the Court to reverse the ruling by the Court of Appeals for the Ninth Circuit that color per se cannot be registered as a trademark under the Lanham Act.

Respectfully submitted,

GARO A. PARTOYAN
GEORGE R. POWERS
NEIL A. SMITH
ROGER S. SMITH
HERBERT C. WAMSLEY *
INTELLECTUAL PROPERTY OWNERS
1255 Twenty-Third Street, N.W.
Suite 850
Washington, D.C. 20037
(202) 466-2396
Attorneys for Amicus Curiae

November 8, 1994

* Counsel of Record

1a

ADDENDUM

MEMBERS OF BOARD OF DIRECTORS OF INTELLECTUAL PROPERTY OWNERS

Robert L. Andersen
FMC Corporation
Philadelphia, PA

Joseph H. Ballway, Jr.
Amoco Corporation
Chicago, IL

Norman L. Balmer
Union Carbide Corporation
Danbury, CT

Erwin F. Berrier, Jr.
General Electric Company
Fairfield, CT

W. Dexter Brooks
Coca-Cola Company
Atlanta, GA

James L. Fergason
Optical Shields, Inc.
Menlo Park, CA

Michael W. Glynn
Ciba
Hawthorne, NY

Gary L. Griswold
3M
St. Paul, MN

Robert P. Hayter
United Technologies Corp.
Farmington, CT

Edward P. Heller, III
Seagate Technology, Inc.
Scotts Valley, CA

Wayne C. Jaeschke
Henkel Corporation
Plymouth Meeting, PA

John J. Klocko, III
E.I. DuPont de Nemours & Co.
Wilmington, DE

Paul J. Koivuniemi
Synergen, Inc.
Boulder, CO

William E. Lambert, III
Rohm & Haas Company
Philadelphia, PA

Edward T. Lentz
SmithKline Beecham Corporation
King of Prussia, PA

William F. Marsh
Air Products & Chem., Inc.
Allentown, PA

John P. McDonnell
AT&T
Berkeley Heights, NJ

Alexander McKillop
Mobil Oil Corporation
Fairfax, VA

Garo A. Partoyan
Mars, Incorporated
McLean, VA

2a

Ralph D. Pinto
University of Virginia
Charlottesville, VA

Jacobus C. Rasser
Procter & Gamble
Cincinnati, OH

Peter C. Richardson
Pfizer, Inc.
New York, NY

Allen W. Richmond
Phillips Petroleum Company
Bartlesville, OK

Melvin J. Scolnick
Pitney Bowes Inc.
Stamford, CT

Roger S. Smith
IBM Corporation
Thornwood, NY

Howard C. Stanley
Monsanto
St Louis, MO

Herbert C. Wamsley
Intellectual Property Owners
Washington, DC

Richard G. Waterman
The Dow Chemical Co.
Midland, MI

Ogden H. Webster
Eastman Kodak Company
Rochester, NY

John K. Williamson
Westinghouse Electric Corp.
Pittsburgh, PA

Richard C. Witte
Cincinnati, OH

Appendix D

Sample Table of Authorities

The following Table of Authorities is from an actual brief filed with the United States Supreme Court and offers guidance on compiling a table that refers to numerous sources.

TABLE OF AUTHORITIES

CASES **Page**

CASES **Page**

STATUTES AND REGULATIONS

STATUTES AND REGULATIONS **Page**

OTHER

Glossary

A.L.R.: *See American Law Reports.*

ALWD citation system: A system introduced in 2000 by the Association of Legal Writing Directors ("ALWD") to provide an easier, more readily understood citation format.

Adjudication: An administrative proceeding before an administrative law judge.

Administrative agencies: A governmental body that enacts rules and regulations on a specific topic and settles disputes relating thereto, for example, the FCC, FDA, or NLRB.

Administrative law: The law relating to administrative agencies.

Administrative law judge: An individual who presides over an administrative adjudication.

Advance sheets: Temporary softcover books that include cases prior to their publication in hardbound volumes.

Am. Jur. 2d: A general or national encyclopedia published by the former Lawyers Co-op covering all United States law.

American Digest System: West's comprehensive set of digests designed to help researchers find cases.

American Law Reports: Sets of books publishing appellate court decisions together with comprehensive essays or annotations relating to the legal issues raised by those cases.

Amicus curiae: Literally, "friend of the court"; a brief submitted to a court by one who is not a party to the action or proceeding.

Annotated: Literally, "with notes"; generally, a reference to one-sentence descriptions of cases that follow statutes in codes such as U.S.C.A. or a state code.

Annotated code: A set of statutes organized by subject matter that contains material accompanying the statutes, chiefly references to cases.

Annotated law reports: *See American Law Reports.*

Annotation: A one-sentence description of a case; an article or monograph about a legal topic published in A.L.R.

Appeal: Review by one court of a lower court's decision.

Appellant: A party who initiates an appeal; sometimes called a petitioner.

Appellate brief: A document presented to a reviewing court to obtain affirmance, reversal, or some alteration of a lower court's ruling.

Appellee: A party who responds to an appeal; sometimes called a respondent.

Attorneys general opinions: Opinions by executive officials on various legal topics; opinions by the U.S. Attorney General or individual state attorneys general.

Auto-Cite: A computer service provided by *Shepard's* showing the appellate history of a case, used primarily to confirm that the authority in question is still good law.

Bicameral: A two-chamber legislature.

Bill: A proposed law.

Bill of Rights: The first ten amendments to the Constitution.

Binding authority: Legal authority that must be followed by a court.

Block form: Style of letter writing in which all the elements, including the date and the closing, begin at the left-hand margin.

Block quotation: A quotation from another source of 50 words or more, indented (typically ten spaces) left and right, that appears without opening and closing quotation marks.

Bluebook: The best-known and used guide for citation form; subtitled *A Uniform System of Citation,* now in its 17th edition.

Boolean searching: A method of conducting research online using symbols and characters rather than plain English.

Brief: A summary of a case; or a written argument presented to a court.

Browser: Software that helps access and review information on the Internet and translates HTML-encoded files into text and images that one can read and view; Netscape and Microsoft Explorer are examples of browsers.

CALR: *See* computer-assisted legal research.

CCH Congressional Index: Sets of books used to compile legislative histories.

CD-ROM: Literally, "compact disk, read-only memory"; a hard disk containing thousands of pages of information.

C.J.S.: West's general or national encyclopedia covering all United States law.

Case of first impression: An issue not yet decided by a jurisdiction.

"Case on point" approach: System used by a researcher following West Group's headnotes and Key Numbers to locate other similar cases by inserting a topic name and Key Number into the various units of the Decennial Digest System.

Certificate of Service: A verification that a document or pleading has been "served on" or presented to a party.

Certification: The process by which a court of appeals refers a question to the United States Supreme Court and asks for instructions and direction.

Certiorari: Writ of *certiorari;* the most widely used means to gain review of a case by the United States Supreme Court; issuance of the writ (meaning a decision to review a case) is discretionary with the Court.

Cert worthy: A case for which *certiorari* has been granted.

Chamber opinion: An opinion written by a United States Supreme Court justice in his or her capacity as the justice assigned to a particular circuit rather than in the capacity of writing for the majority of the Court.

Charter: The governing document for a municipality.

Chat room: A location in cyberspace fostering real-time communications among several people.

CheckCite: A software program providing automatic validation of all cases cited in a document.

Checks and balances: The system whereby each division of the United

States government is to exercise its own powers and function separately from the others.

Chief Justice: The presiding justice of the United States Supreme Court.

"Chron" copy: A copy of a legal document placed in a chronological file for law office purposes.

Circuit: A geographical area in which courts are located; the United States is divided into 12 numbered circuits, each with its own court of appeals.

Citators: Sets of books published by Shepard's or Westlaw's KeyCite that direct one to other materials discussing or treating legal authorities.

Cite-checking: The process of verifying that citations in a document are accurate and in compliance with rules for citation form and then verifying that the authorities are still "good law."

CiteFinder: A search engine that uses the databases in the CD-ROM to generate a statistically ranked list of relevant authorities.

CiteRite II: A citation checking software program that checks citations for proper form using *Bluebook* rules or the *California Style Manual*.

Civil law: A body of law depending more on legislative enactments than case law, often seen in non-English-speaking countries.

Code: A compilation of statutes or regulations arranged by subject or topic.

Code of Federal Regulations: The codification of administrative rules and regulations, by subject, into 50 titles.

Codification: The process of organizing laws or regulations by subject matter rather than chronologically.

Committee report: Document reflecting decisions reached by legislative committees considering proposed legislation.

Committee transcript: Report of proceedings before committees considering proposed legislation.

Common law: The body of law that develops and derives through judicial decisions rather than from legislative enactments, usually seen in English-speaking countries.

Complimentary close: The ending of a letter, such as "Sincerely."

Computer-assisted legal research: The process of conducting legal research through computer rather than conventional print sources.

Concurrent jurisdiction: The sharing of jurisdiction over a case by federal or state court so that a litigant can select which forum in which to bring the action.

Concurring opinion: Opinion written by a member of the majority who agrees with the result reached in a case but disagrees with the reasoning of the majority.

Congress: The lawmaking body of the federal government, composed of the Senate and the House of Representatives.

Congressional Information Service: Sets of books used to compile legislative histories.

Congressional Record: A publication that publishes the remarks of the speakers debating a bill prepared for each day Congress is in session as well as other remarks and speeches made on the floor of the House or Senate.

"Congressional Universe": Source provided by CIS on the Internet offering more than 25 years of congressional information, including bills, hearing transcripts, committee reports, and the *Congressional Record*.

Constitution: The document that sets forth the fundamental law for a nation or state.

Constitutional courts: Courts such as the United States Supreme Court that exist under the United States Constitution and whose judges are protected as to tenure and salary reductions.

Convention: A type of treaty, usually relating to a single topic.

Court reports: Sets of books that publish cases.

Courts of Appeal: Intermediate appellate courts; in the federal system, these are sometimes called circuit courts.

Courts of first resort: Trial courts.

"Current Awareness Commentary": A section of the monthly issue of U.S.C.S. *Advance* that includes summaries of pending legislation.

Current Law Index: Separately published index designed to direct researchers to periodicals, such as articles in law reviews.

Cyberspace: The electronic or computer world in which vast amounts of information are available; sometimes used as a synonym for the Internet.

Dead-tree publishing: The publication of materials in conventional print form.

Decision: Technically, the final action taken by a court in a court case; generally, the term "decision" is used synonymously with "opinion," "judgment," or "case."

Demand letter: A letter setting forth a client's demands or requirements.

Depository library: A library designated by the United States government to receive selected government materials and publications.

Descriptive word approach: A method of locating legal materials by inserting words describing a problem or issue into an index that then directs the reader to relevant information.

Dictionary (legal): An alphabetical arrangement of words and phrases providing the meaning or definition of those words and phrases.

Dictum: Technically, "obiter dictum"; a remark in a case said for purposes of illustration or analogy; dictum is persuasive only.

Digests: Books or indexes that arrange one-sentence summaries or "digests" of cases by subject.

Directory: A list of lawyers.

Dissenting opinion: An opinion written by a judge in the minority who disagrees with the results reached by the majority of a court.

District courts: The 94 trial courts in our federal system.

Diversity jurisdiction: A basis upon which federal courts take cases, due to the different or diverse citizenship of the parties in the case.

Docket number: A number assigned to a case by a court to track its progress through the court system.

Domain name: The name that identifies an Internet site, such as "www.ibm.com." Domain names have two parts: the "generic top-level domain," which is the last part of the domain name, such as "com," or "gov," and which usually refers to the type of provider of the information; and the "secondary domain," which is more specific and is to the right of "www," such as "ibm" in the above example.

Download: Transferring files or information from the Internet to your personal computer.

E-mail: Electronic mail or messages sent through the computer rather than in physical form (which is often called "snail mail").

Ellipsis: Three periods separated by spaces and set off by a space before the first and after the last period, used to indicate omission of a word or words.

Enabling statute: A statute that creates an administrative agency such as the FDA or FCC.

En banc opinion: Literally, "in the bench"; an opinion in which all judges in an appellate court participate.

Encyclopedias: Sets of books that alphabetically arrange topics related to legal issues; treatment of legal issues is somewhat elementary; the best known general sets are C.J.S. and Am. Jur. 2d; some state-specific sets exist.

Enrollment: A process wherein a bill that has been passed by both the

House and the Senate is then printed by the Government Printing Office, following which the bill is certified as correct and signed by the Speaker of the House and by the vice president.
Exclusive jurisdiction: The basis upon which a court's ability to hear a case is exclusive to the federal court, such as a bankruptcy case, and which cannot be heard by another court.
Executive agreement: An agreement entered into with a foreign nation by a president acting without Senate approval.
Executive branch: The branch of the United States government that enforces laws.
Executive order: Regulations issued by a president to direct government agencies.
Extract: A *Shepard's* tool that automatically extracts all citations in a legal document and Shepardizes them.
Extranet: An internal company or law firm intranet that provides access to select outsiders on a case-by-case basis.

FAQ: "Frequently asked questions," often included on Web sites and that respond to the most commonly asked questions about the site or about the information provided by the site.
FTP: File Transfer Protocol, a common method of moving files or communicating between two Internet sites.
FULL: A feature of "Shepard's for Research," a software program provided by LEXIS that lists every authority that mentions a case.
Federalism: Sharing of powers by the federal and state governments.
Federal question jurisdiction: The power of a federal court to hear a case based upon the fact the case arises under the United States Constitution or a United States law or treaty.
Federal Register: A pamphlet published every weekday relating to administrative law and publishing agency rules and regulations.
Federal Reporter: West's unofficial publication containing cases from the federal courts of appeal.
Federal Supplement: West's unofficial publication containing cases from the federal district courts.
Form books: Sets of books including forms for use in the legal profession; may be general or related solely to one area of law.
Freestyle: *See* Natural language.

GPO Access: Online source offering free direct links through its *Manual* to information about government agencies, their addresses, appointees, staff members, and functions, as well as direct links to the Federal Register, C.F.S., congressional, and executive materials.

HTML: Hypertext Markup Language, a standard language of computer code.
HTTP: Hypertext Transfer Protocol, a common method of moving files or communicating between two Internet sites.
Header: Information found on the second and any following pages of letters in the upper left-hand corner listing the addressee, page, and date.
Headnotes: Short paragraphs prepared by editors, given before a case begins to serve as an index to the points of law discussed in a case.
History references: References provided by Shepard's relating to the subsequent history of a primary authority.
Home page: The first or main page sent when accessing a person's or business's Web site.
Hornbook: A one-volume treatise devoted to one area of the law, such as contracts, torts, or real property.
Hyperlink: A method of instantaneous transport to another destination; hyperlinks are often underscored or appear in different color on the computer screen; by clicking the col-

ored line, you will be immediately transferred to that particular site or page.

IRAC: An acronym for "*I*ssue," "*R*ule," "*A*pplication" or "*A*nalysis," and "*C*onclusion"; a method used to analyze authorities and legal issues in a memo or brief.
Id.: A signal used in citation form to direct a reader to an immediately preceding citation.
Index: An alphabetical arrangement of words and terms designed to direct researchers to relevant cases, statutes, or legal information; usually contained in the last volume of a set of books or in separate volumes after the last volume.
Index to Legal Periodicals: Separately published index designed to direct researchers to periodicals such as articles in law reviews.
Infra: A signal used in books or citation form meaning "below" directing a reader to a later (though not immediately following) citation.
International Court of Justice: A court under the responsibility of the United Nations, created to hear and decide disputes between and among nations; also called the World Court.
International law: The law relating to relations among nations.
Internet: A collection of worldwide inter-connected computer networks originally developed for defense purposes and which are linked together to exchange information; the Internet is not owned by any one person or company.
Internet Service Provider (ISP): A company that provides Internet access, such as America Online or Roadrunner, for a monthly fee.
Intranet: A private network inside a company or law firm that provides access only for internal use to those in the company or firm and not to outsiders; for example, a law firm's intranet could be used only by those in the firm and could not be accessed by any member of the general public.

Judge: Individual who sits on a lower court.
Judiciary: The branch of the government that interprets laws.
Jump cite: *See* Pinpoint cite.
Jurisdiction: The power of a court to act.
Jurisdictional statement: A statement in a brief explaining the grounds upon which the court's jurisdiction to hear the case rests.
Jury instructions: Sets of books containing proposed instructions to be used to charge a jury in a civil or criminal case.
Justice: Individual who sits on an appellate court, especially the United States Supreme Court.

KWIC: A computer program offered by LEXIS that provides subsequent appellate history of a case; used primarily to confirm that authority in question is still good law by showing negative history only. Also a method of displaying a band or window of words around a requested search term or phrase.
KeyCite: A citation service offered through Westlaw providing valuable and automatic information relating to the validity of primary authorities cited in a document.
KeyCite Alert: A software clipping service that automatically notifies a researcher of changes in treatment of a case.
Key Number: West's assignment of a number to a particular topic of law, allowing researchers to retrieve numerous cases dealing with the same point of law.

Law: *See* Statute.
Law review: The periodic publica-

tion by a law school providing scholarly treatment of a legal topic.

Legalese: The overuse of legal terms and foreign words and phrases in legal writing.

Legis: A LEXIS database library for legislative information.

Legislative courts: Specialized courts, such as the United States Tax Court, which do not exist under the Constitution and whose judges are appointed for specific terms.

Legislative history: The documents reflecting the intent and activity of a legislature at the time it enacts a law.

Legislature: The branch of the government that makes law.

Letterhead: Information printed on stationery identifying the correspondent.

LEXIS: The computerized legal research system offered by Reed Elsevier.

"Library References": A feature of U.S.C.S. comparable to that of U.S.C.A. in that it provides cross-references as well as directing the researcher to books, encyclopedias, annotations, and a wide variety of law review articles.

Link: *See* Hyperlink.

Listserv: A system that allows groups of people to e-mail each other and participate in group discussions, usually about a topic of common concern; for example, there may be a listserv comprising law students and when one message is sent by a user, it is automatically sent to all others in the group; sometimes called "newsgroup."

Log in: (n.) the account name used to gain entry to a computer system and which is not secret, as is a password; also called a "user name"; (v.) the method of accessing a computer system.

Looseleaf (or looseleaf service): A set of materials collected in ringed binders due to the need for frequent updating and related to a specific area of law such as labor law or tax; includes both primary and secondary authorities.

Majority opinion: Any judicial opinion written by a member of the majority after a court reaches a decision.

Martindale-Hubbell Law Directory: A comprehensive directory of lawyers in the United States and in foreign countries, which also includes summaries of law for the states and various foreign countries.

Memorandum (legal): A document explaining legal issues involved in a case in a neutral and objective manner.

Memorandum of Law: Document presented to a court to persuade the court to rule in a party's favor; also called Memorandum of Points and Authorities.

Memorandum of Points and Authorities: *See* Memorandum of Law.

Memorandum opinion: An opinion that provides a result but offers little or no reasoning to support that result.

Merged closing: The disfavored combination of a complimentary close with the last sentence of a letter.

Microfiche: Celluloid strips of film used in cataloging or archiving documents.

Microfilm: 16-mm or 35-mm film containing images displayed on screens and often used for efficient storage of voluminous records.

Microform: A type of technology embracing microfilm, microfiche, and ultrafiche, based on photography and that stores material more efficiently than print sources.

Modem: A device that connects to your computer and to a phone line, allowing the computer to communicate with other computers, much the way telephones allow humans to communicate with each other.

Moot: Resolved; cases that have been resolved or settled in some manner are said to be moot.

National Reporter System: A set of unofficial court reporters published by West and including federal and state cases.
Natural language: A "plain English" computer method of conducting legal research offered by LEXIS; also called "Freestyle"; in contrast to using Boolean connectors.
Netiquette: The code of etiquette or conduct for the Internet.
Network: The connecting of two or more computers so that they can communicate with each other and share resources and information.
NEXIS: An online library affiliated with LEXIS offering the full text of almost 700 general news, business, and financial publications.
Nominalization: The conversion of an adjective, verb, or adverb into a noun, for example, the conversion of the verb "decide" into "render a decision."

Obiter dictum: *See* Dictum.
Official: Publication of cases, statutes, or other legal materials as directed by a statute.
On all fours: *See* On point.
Online: The process of being connected to the Internet through electronic communication.
Online catalog: An electronic database used by libraries in place of a conventional card catalog to catalog materials owned by the library.
Online journal: A journal that is published exclusively online, not in print form.
On point: A case that is factually similar and legally relevant and that controls another case; sometimes called a case "on all fours."
Opinion: A court's explanation of the law in a particular case; also called "case" or "decision."
Opinion letter: A letter setting forth advice to a client.
Ordinance: A local law.
Original jurisdiction: The ability of a court to act as a trial court.
Overrule: The overturning of a case by a higher court considering a different case on appeal.

PDF: Portable Document Format, a format that duplicates on a computer screen what a conventional print source looks like.
Parallel cite: Two or more citations to the same case allowing researchers to read a case in two or more sets of reports.
Parallel structure: The requirement that the grammatical structure of all items in a list be identical or parallel.
Password: The secret code used to gain access to a computer system.
Per curiam: An opinion by the whole court.
Periodical: A publication issued on a periodic, such as monthly or quarterly, basis, for example, the *Computer Law Journal.*
Permanent law: A law that remains in effect until it is expressly repealed.
Personal digital assistant (PDA): A handheld computer device such as the Palm Pilot, which provides wireless access for updating and validating through both Shepard's and KeyCite.
Persuasive authority: Legal authorities that the court is not required to follow but might be persuaded to do so; secondary authorities are persuasive.
Pinpoint cite: A reference to the exact page in a source to which a reader is directed; also called a "jump cite" or "spot cite."
Plain English movement: A modern approach to legal writing calling for the use of plain English and an end to stuffy, archaic, and jargon-filled writing.

Plurality opinion: The result reached when separate opinions are written by members of a majority.
Pocket part: A booklet or pamphlet inserted into the back of a hardbound volume to provide more current information than that found in the volume.
Popular name: The practice of calling certain statutes or cases by a popular name.
Popular name approach: A method of locating cases or statutes by looking up their "popular names"; generally the names of the sponsoring legislators, the parties to the case, or a name assigned by the media.
Posting: The entering of information or messages into a network, for example, cases are "posted" to the Web site of the United States Supreme Court and legal professionals "post" messages on a listserv.
Primary authority: Official pronouncements of the law, chiefly cases, constitutions, statutes, administrative regulations, and treaties, all of which are binding authorities.
Private international law: The law relating to which country's law will govern a private contractual transaction or arrangement.
Private law: A law affecting only one person or a small group of persons, giving them some special benefit not afforded to the public at large.
Proclamation: A statement issued by a president having no legal effect.
Proofreading: The process of reviewing a writing to correct errors.
Public domain system: With regard to format- or vendor-neutral citation systems, the citation appears the same whether the reader has accessed the case by conventional print format or by electronic methods, such as CD-ROM, LEXIS, Westlaw, or the Internet.
Public international law: The law relating to the conduct of nations.
Public law: A law affecting the public generally.

Quick Index: An easy-to-use one-volume index published by West that directs the researcher to annotations in A.L.R.3d, A.L.R.4th, and A.L.R.5th. Note that there is also an A.L.R. Federal Quick Index.

Ratio decidendi: The "reason of the decision"; the holding of a case.
Reference notation ("Re"): An indication of the subject matter of a document.
Regulation: A pronouncement by an administrative agency; sometimes called a rule.
Regulatory body: An administrative agency.
Report: Set of books publishing cases, generally official sets.
Reporter: Set of books publishing cases, generally unofficial sets.
Resolutions: *See* Ordinance.
Restatements: Publications of the American Law Institute designed to restate in a clear and simple manner legal doctrine in specific areas, such as contracts, torts, or trusts.
Reverse: The overturning of a lower court decision by a higher court considering that same case on appeal.
Root expander: A device provided by LEXIS in computerized legal research, such as an asterisk or an exclamation point, that substitutes for a character or any number of additional letters at the end of a word, respectively.
Rule: *See* Regulation.
Rule of Four: The decision by four of the nine Supreme Court Justices to grant *certiorari* and take a case.
Rules of Court: Procedural requirements issued by courts and that must be followed by litigants.

Salutation: The greeting in a letter, such as "Dear Ms. Howard."
Sans serif style: Print style without embellishments of extra lines forming letters, such as the Arial font.
Scope note: A brief paragraph outlining the matters treated in a legal

discussion and those to be treated elsewhere.

Search Advisor: A service offered by LEXIS designed for research in a known area of law; ideal source to begin researching an issue because it assists in selecting a topic or jurisdiction by suggesting terms to search.

Search box: A blank box on a computer screen, in which you type or key in the word or terms you are interested in researching.

Search engine: A particular service that helps one locate useful information on the Internet, usually through the use of keywords; common search engines are "Yahoo," "Google," "Lycos," and "AltaVista." A search engine is a Web site that looks for and retrieves other Web sites. Search engines look for words in the millions of Web pages on the Internet and direct you to pages that include the search words or keywords you enter in a search box.

Secondary authorities: Legal authorities that are not primary law and which explain, discuss, and help locate primary authorities; persuasive authority; includes encyclopedias, A.L.R. annotations, law reviews, texts, and treatises.

Selective enforcement: A defense raised whereby a party asserts that he or she has been singled out for prosecution.

Selective publication: The process whereby not all cases are published but rather only those that advance legal theory are published.

Serial Set: Conventional bound pamphlet set of books publishing congressional committee and subcommittee reports.

Series: Newer or more recent editions of cases or other legal materials.

Serif style: A style of print that adds small decorative strokes to the edges of letters, generally viewed as enhancing readability, such as Garamond and Times New Roman fonts.

Server: A computer or software package that provides or serves information to other computers.

Session laws: The chronological arrangement of laws prior to their arrangement in a code.

Shepard's: Sets of books that allow researchers to verify that primary authorities are still "good law."

Shepardize: The process of ensuring that authorities are still "good law."

Short form citation: An abbreviated form of a citation used after a citation has been given in full.

Signal Indicator: A symbol showing on the computer screen that informs the user of the precedential status of a case by indicating through colors or letters the history and treatment of the case.

Slip law: A piece (or pieces) of looseleaf paper containing language of a law; the manner in which laws are first published.

Slip opinion: A court decision available on looseleaf sheets of paper; one not yet available in a published reporter.

Spamming: Sending blanket, unsolicited messages to others, similar to "junk mail."

Spot cite: *See* Pinpoint cite.

Standing: Personal injury or damage sustained by a plaintiff enabling the plaintiff to bring suit.

Stare decisis: The concept whereby courts follow and adhere to previous cases.

Star paging: A technique to convert page numbers in cases published in unofficial sets to page numbers in cases published in official sets.

Statute: An act of a legislature declaring, commanding, or prohibiting something.

String citing: The somewhat disfavored practice of citing more than one authority in support of a proposition.

Supplement: A softcover pamphlet that updates material found in a hardbound volume.

Supra: A signal used in books or citation form meaning "above," directing a reader to a preceding (though not immediately preceding) reference or citation.

"Supreme Court Update": A feature of U.S.C.S. *Advance* that includes summaries of recent United States Supreme Court cases.

Surfing the 'Net: The process of moving or linking from one site to another in the course of reviewing information.

Syllabus: A comprehensive but unofficial summary preceding an opinion of a court, prepared by the court's reporter of decisions or the publisher.

Synopsis: A brief summary of a case prepared by editors to provide a quick overview of the case and given before the case begins.

TAPP: An acronym for "*T*hing, *A*ction, *P*erson, and *P*lace" and referring to a technique used to determine words to insert into an index to locate relevant research materials.

THOMAS: Web site for legislative information provided by the federal government that offers text of proposed and enacted legislation, committee information, calendars for hearings scheduled, and House and Senate Directories.

Table of authorities: List of authorities cited in a brief or document and that must be arranged in a certain order.

Temporary law: A law that has specific language limiting its duration.

Topic approach: A method of locating legal materials by bypassing the general index and going directly to the appropriate title or topic in a source.

Total Client-Service Library: Collectively, the sets of books published by the former Lawyers Co-op and including U.S.C.S., Am. Jur. 2d, A.L.R., *Proof of Facts, Am. Jur. Trials,* and various form books.

Transitions: Words or phrases that connect preceding language with that which follows.

Treatise: A scholarly book (or set of books) devoted to the treatment of a particular legal topic, such as *Treatise on the Law of Contracts.*

Treatment references: References provided by Shepard's relating to the later treatment and discussion of primary authorities by other cases, attorneys general opinions, law review articles, and so forth.

Treaty: An agreement between two or more nations.

URL: Uniform Resource Locator, one's address on the Internet. Most Internet addresses begin with "www" or "http://www." The URL of IBM is "www.ibm.com."

Ultrafiche: An enhanced microfiche holding a great many images.

Unicameral: A one-house legislature.

Uniform law: Model legislation prepared by the National Conference of Commissioners on Uniform State Laws on various legal topics, such as the Uniform Commercial Code, and designed to be adopted by the 50 states.

Uniform Resource Locator: *See* URL.

United States Code: The official publication of all federal laws, arranged by topic.

United States Code Annotated: West's annotated version of the *United States Code,* including all federal statutes arranged by subject.

United States Code Congressional and Administrative News Service: A publication including public laws, legislative history of selected bills, summaries of pending legislation, presidential proclamations and executive orders, various federal regulations, and court rules.

United States Code Service: Annotated set of federal statutes arranged by subject and published by LEXIS Publishing.

United States Government Manual: A manual or handbook providing information about the United States government, particularly the administrative agencies.

United States Law Week: A weekly publication that prints the text of significant public laws.

United States Reports: The official publication containing cases from the United States Supreme Court.

United States Statutes at Large: The set of books containing all federal laws, arranged in chronological order.

Universal symbols: Symbols and characters used in constructing a search on LEXIS or Westlaw; sometimes called root expanders.

Unofficial: Publication of cases or statutes not directed by statute.

Unreported case: A case marked "not for publication," by a court; persuasive authority.

Unwritten law: A reference to the common law tradition of dependence upon cases.

User name: *See* Log in (n).

V ("Versus Law"): A commercial legal research system offering cases via the Internet for a moderate fee.

WWW: World Wide Web, commonly used to refer to the entire collection of resources that can be accessed in cyberspace, through the Internet.

Web: *See* WWW.

Web page: A particular file or "page" included in a Web site.

Web site: A collection of Web pages; for example, IBM's Web site (www.ibm.com) will consist of numerous Web pages, each of which is devoted to a specific topic. A Web site always begins with a "home page," which is the first screen viewed when the Web site is accessed.

Weekly Compilation of Presidential Documents: Publication including materials relating to the executive branch.

WestCheck: A West software program providing automatic validation of all cases cited in a document.

WestFax: A service established by West Group that for a fee will send the full text of cases by facsimile transmission, overnight or by regular mail.

Westlaw: The computerized legal research system offered by West.

WestMate: A software package provided by West that customizes a computer to be capable of doing research under the Westlaw system.

WesTrain: A free software teaching program offered by West that offers lessons on legal research.

Widows and orphans: A heading or isolated word or line occurring at the bottom or top of a page.

Words and Phrases: A multi-volume set of books directing researchers to cases that have construed certain terms.

World Court: The United Nations court, officially named the International Court of Justice, which provides final decisions regarding international disputes.

World Wide Web: *See* WWW.

Written law: A reference to statutes.

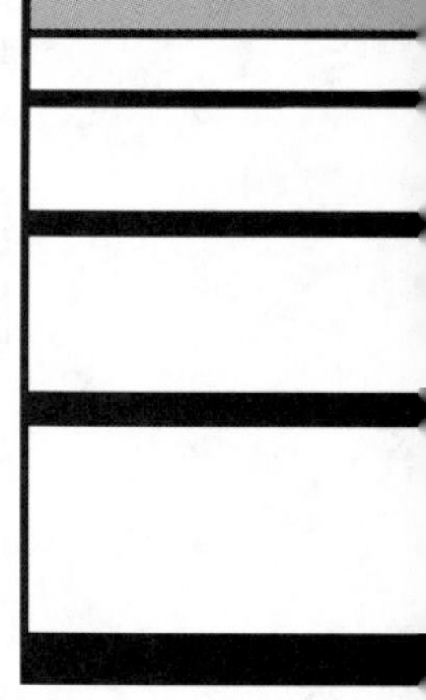

Resources

Legal Publishers

Aspen Law and Business
1185 Avenue of the Americas
New York, NY 10036

Bureau of National Affairs
1231 25th Street, N.W.
Washington, D.C. 20037
(202) 452-4200

The *Bluebook*
The Harvard Law Review Association
Gannett House
1511 Massachusetts Avenue
Cambridge, MA 02138
http://www.legalbluebook.com

Commerce Clearing House Incorporated (CCH)
2700 Lake Cook Road
Riverwoods, IL 60015
(800)-TELL-CCH
http://www.cch.com

Congressional Information Service, Inc.
4520 East-West Highway
Bethesda, MD 20814
(800) 638-8380

Foundation Press, Inc.
11 Penn Plaza, 10th Floor
New York, NY 10001
(212) 760-8700

LEXIS Publishing
9443 Springboro Pike
P.O. Box 933
Dayton, OH 45401
(800) 227-9597
http://www.lexis-nexis.com
http://lexispublishing.com

Martindale-Hubbell
121 Chanlon Road
New Providence, NJ
(908) 464-6800
(800) 526-4902
http://www.martindale.com

Matthew Bender
See information for LEXIS Publishing
http://www.bender.com

The Michie Company
701 E. Water Street
Charlottesville, VA 22902
(804) 972-7600

Pearson Publications Company
9614 Greenville Ave.
Dallas, TX 75243
(972) 661-8800

Shepard's
555 Middle Creek Parkway
Colorado Springs, CO 80921-6000
(800) 899-6000

West Group
610 Opperman Dr.
Eagan, MN 55123
(800) 328-9378
e-mail: editor@westpub.com
WESTLAW Customer Service:
(800) 937-8529
http://www.westgroup.com

William S. Hein & Co.
1285 Main Street
Buffalo, NY 14209
(800) 828-7571

Government Agencies and Offices

Attorney General of the United States
Department of Justice
950 Pennsylvania Avenue, N.W.
Room 4400
Washington, D.C. 20530-0001
(202) 514-2000
www.usdoj.com

Department of Commerce
14th Street between Constitution and Pennsylvania Avenues, N.W.
Washington, D.C. 20230
(202) 482-2000

Commission on Civil Rights
624 Ninth Street, N.W.
Washington, D.C. 20425
(202) 376-8177

Equal Employment Opportunity Commission
1801 L Street, N.W.
Washington, D.C. 20507
(202) 663-4900

Executive Office of the President
1600 Pennsylvania Ave., N.W.
Washington, D.C. 20500
(202) 395-3000

Federal Judicial Center
One Columbus Circle, N.E.
Washington, D.C. 20002
(202) 502-4000

Federal Register
800 N. Capitol Street, N.W.
Suite 700
Washington, D.C. 20001
(202) 523-5240

Government Printing Office
732 North Capitol St., N.W.
Washington, D.C. 20401
(202) 512-1800/0688 (Orders)
(202) 512-0000 (Information)
(202) 512-1800 (Superintendent of Documents)

House of Representatives
Washington, D.C. 20515
(202) 224-3121

Justice Department
950 Pennsylvania Avenue, N.W.
Washington, D.C. 20530-0001
(202) 514-2000

Department of Labor
200 Constitution Avenue, N.W.
Washington, D.C. 20210
(202) 219-5000

Library of Congress
101 Independence Avenue, S.E.
Washington, D.C. 20540
(202) 707-5000

National Archives
700 Pennsylvania Avenue, N.W.
Washington, D.C. 20408
(202) 501-5400

United States Senate
Washington, D.C. 20510
(202) 224-3121

U.S. Supreme Court
U.S. Supreme Court Building
One 1st St., N.E.
Washington, D.C. 20543
(202) 479-3000
Clerk: (202) 479-3011
Opinion Announcements:
(202) 479-3360
Librarian: (202) 479-3037/3175
Public Information Officer:
(202) 479-3211
http://www.supremecourtus.gov

U.S. Courts, Administrative Office
One Columbus Circle, N.E.
Washington, D.C. 20544
(202) 502-2600

White House
1600 Pennsylvania Avenue, N.W.
Washington, D.C. 20500
(202) 456-1414 (Switchboard)
(202) 456-1111 (Comments)

Bibliography for Legal Research and Writing

Bieber's Dictionary of Legal Citations
and
Bieber's Dictionary of Legal Abbreviations
Mary Miles Prince
William S. Hein & Co.
1285 Main St.
Buffalo, NY 14209
(800) 828-7571

Effective Legal Writing by Gertrude Block (4th ed.)
Foundation Press, Inc.
College Department
615 Merrick Avenue
Westbury, NY 11590
(516) 832-6950

Grammar Gremlins
Don K. Ferguson
Glenbridge Publishing Ltd.
(800) 986-4135

Law Books and Serials in Print
R.R. Bowker
121 Chanlon Road
New Providence, NJ 07974
(888) 269-5372

Legal Writing in a Nutshell
Lynn B. Squires and Marjorie Dick Rombauer
West's Nutshell Series (1082)

Plain English for Lawyers
Richard C. Wydick (3d ed. 1994)
Carolina Academic Press
700 Kent Street
Durham, NC 27701
(919) 489-7486

Quote It: Memorable Legal Quotations
Compiled by Eugene C. Gerhard
William S. Hein & Co.
1285 Main St.
Buffalo, NY 14209
(800) 828-7571

Untangling the Law — Strategies for Legal Writers
Kristin R. Woolever (1987)

Index